The Foundations of MODERN FREEMASONRY

The Grand Architects
Political Change and the Scientific Enlightenment, 1714–1740

RIC BERMAN

sussex
ACADEMIC
PRESS
Brighton • Portland • Toronto

Copyright © Ric Berman, 2012.

The right of Ric Berman to be identified as Author of this work has been asserted
in accordance with the Copyright, Designs and Patents Act 1988.

2 4 6 8 10 9 7 5 3 1

First published 2012 in Great Britain by
SUSSEX ACADEMIC PRESS
PO Box 139, Eastbourne BN24 9BP

and in the United States of America by
SUSSEX ACADEMIC PRESS
920 NE 58th Ave   Suite 300
Portland, Oregon 97213-3786

and in Canada by
SUSSEX ACADEMIC PRESS (CANADA)
8000 Bathurst Street, Unit 1, PO Box 30010, Vaughan, Ontario L4J 0C6

All rights reserved. Except for the quotation of short passages for the purposes of criticism
and review, no part of this publication may be reproduced, stored in a retrieval system,
or transmitted, in any form or by any means, electronic, mechanical, photocopying,
recording or otherwise, without the prior permission of the publisher.

British Library Cataloguing in Publication Data
A CIP catalogue record for this book is available from the British Library.

Library of Congress Cataloging-in-Publication Data
Berman, Ric.
 The foundations of modern Freemasonry : the grand architects : political
  change and the scientific enlightenment, 1714–1740 / Ric Berman.
   p. cm.
 Includes bibliographical references and index.
 ISBN 978-1-84519-479-6 (h/b : alk. paper) —
 ISBN 978-1-84519-506-9 (p/b : alk. paper)
  1. Freemasonry. 2. Freemasons—Great Britain—History—18th century.
 I. Title.
 HS418.B47 2012
 366'.109033—dc23
                                                                                         2011040269

Typeset & designed by Sussex Academic Press, Brighton & Eastbourne.
Printed by TJ International, Padstow, Cornwall.
Printed on acid-free paper.

Contents

List of Tables & Illustrations, Preface & Acknowledgements

INTRODUCTION
1

CHAPTER ONE
English Freemasonry before the Formation of Grand Lodge
8

CHAPTER TWO
John Theophilus Desaguliers: *Homo Masonicus*
38

CHAPTER THREE
Grand Lodge: The Inner Workings
64

CHAPTER FOUR
The Professional Nexus
98

CHAPTER FIVE
The Rise of the First Noble Grand Masters
118

CHAPTER SIX
'Through the paths of heavenly science'
165

CONCLUSIONS
190

Appendices, List of Abbreviations, Notes
Electronic Reading & Research
Select Bibliography
Index

List of Tables and Illustrations

Tables
1 Grand Lodge Officers, 1718–30.   69
2 The First Charity Committee.   94
3 The Noble Grand Masters.   105
4 The Royal Society: Freemasons Proposing Freemasons.   108
5 The Society of Antiquaries.   114
6 The Gentlemen's Society of Spalding.   116

Illustrations (plate section after page 88)
1 The Rev. John Theophilus Desaguliers (1683–1744).
2 The Rev. James Anderson.
3 Unknown Senior Warden
4 Anthony Sayer, first Grand Master of Grand Lodge.
5 Martin Folkes (1690–1754).
6 William Stukeley (1687–1765).
7 The Constitutions of the Freemasons, title page.
8 The Book of Constitutions, engraved frontispiece.
9 The inside cover and frontispiece of John Pine's 1725 *Engraved List of Lodges*.
10 Regulations of the Charity Committee.
11 John Montagu, 2nd Duke of Montagu, (1690-1749). Grand Master, 1721.
12 John Montagu, 2nd Duke of Montagu.
13 Philip Wharton, 1st Duke of Wharton (1698–1731). Grand Master, 1722.
14 Charles Lennox, 2nd Duke of Richmond (1701–1750). Grand Master, 1724.
15 Alexander Chocke (16__?–1737).
16 John Pine (1690–1756).
17 Frederick, Prince of Wales (1707–1751).
18 Desaguliers: Depiction of Experimental Equipment.
19 Desaguliers: Examples of Experiments.
20 Henry Hare, 3rd Baron Coleraine (1691–1749). Grand Master, 1728.
21 John Lindsay, 20th Earl of Crawford (1702–1749). Grand Master, 1734.
22 John Campbell, 4th Earl of Loudon (1705–1782). Grand Master, 1736.
23 Robert Raymond, 2nd Lord Raymond (1717–1756). Grand Master, 1739.

Preface and Acknowledgments

Many books have been written on the supposed origins of Freemasonry but relatively few on its intimate connection with the development of the scientific Enlightenment and the political changes that accompanied the Hanoverian accession and its Whig ministries. This work has its foundations in a doctoral thesis based on an analysis of largely unexplored primary material, digital access to which was recently made available by the British Library and other British and US archival sources.[1] However, rather than stand as a purely academic work, the purpose of the book is to make the study of the eighteenth century foundations of modern Freemasonry accessible to both Freemasons and others seeking a broader and deeper understanding of the origins of the Craft as it is today. For those researching the period, there is an attempt to illuminate the interplay between Freemasonry, politics, philosophy and the cultural and economic inflexion point that was the scientific Enlightenment. With this objective, a substantial number of footnotes have been included together with an extended bibliography in order to provide a resource to those who wish to investigate the subject further and explore for themselves relevant primary and secondary sources.

When this book was first developed in concept, an *a priori* expectation was that the primary evidence would lead to a narrow focus on a relatively limited group of 'architects' at the helm of the new Grand Lodge of England that had been instituted in 1717, and to an examination of the personal relationships and networks within a few learned and professional societies. But as analysis progressed and additional source material was evaluated, attention was instead directed to a far more diverse group of Masonic 'movers and shakers' and – crucially – to the identification of a multiplicity of associations and channels through which Freemasonry expanded rapidly from its London hub. Certain of these key Masonic vectors and, in particular, the London and provincial scientific lecture circuits and the London magistracy, have not been explored previously and this book sheds light for the first time on such associations.

A second working assumption had been that the early noble Grand Masters – the first aristocrats to head Grand Lodge – would be revealed as simple figureheads. The assumption proved to be an over-generalisation. In its place, primary source material including correspondence and contemporary press reports suggests that a small number, including Charles Lennox, 2nd Duke of Richmond, were active Masonic proselytisers. It also points to their Freemasonry and that of other senior Masons having served a political purpose.

All illustrations used in this book are copyright © UGLE Library & Museum of Freemasonry, and used with their kind permission.

I would like to express my thanks for their kind assistance to Professors Jeremy Black, Nicholas Goodrich-Clarke, Martin Thomas, Andrew Prescott, Henry French, Bill Gibson and Dr Andrew Pink, and to the staff of the UGLE Library at Great Queen Street, London, in particular, Diane Clements, Director, Martin Cherry, Librarian, and Susan Snell, Archivist.

Introduction

In *The Craft*, John Hamill, then the librarian and curator of the United Grand Lodge of England, argued that prevailing historical methodology which posited 'a direct descent from operative to speculative masonry through a transitional phase' was without substance.[1] Despite nearly three centuries of currency, Hamill suggested that there was no firm evidence to support the established thesis of a gradual shift from the mediaeval working masons' guilds to the more gentlemanly and 'spiritual' form of masonic lodge of the latter part of the eighteenth century. However, as Jan Snoek commented subsequently, although Hamill may have queried the thesis, the absence of an antithesis or alternative hypothesis remained an issue.[2] This may have been the reason why Hamill's (largely accurate) analysis has failed to prevent academic and semi-academic scholars – not to mention Freemasons as a whole – from continuing to cleave to a gradualist approach tracing Freemasonry's origins to a mediaeval past or to 'time immemorial'.

The absence of a robust counter argument to the traditional gradualist theory suggested the need for a detailed examination of the economic, social, political and intellectual background to the establishment of modern English Freemasonry in the early-decades of the eighteenth century, and for the subject to be placed in a broader historical context. It also advanced the corollary that English Freemasonry at each stage in its development would reflect the social make-up of those who populated its ranks and the composition and mindset of those who led its numbers.

The material identified and appraised in the research for this book provides the foundation for a fresh interpretation of – and an alternative hypothesis for – the development in the 1720s of what is commonly regarded as the current form of English Freemasonry. And to the extent that eighteenth-century English Freemasonry established the pattern of Freemasonry within North America, the Indian sub-continent, Europe, and across much of what later became the British Empire, the portrait and explanation that the current volume offers provides a hypothesis that may have implications wider than England alone.

Whereas it should be clear intuitively that any study of Freemasonry cannot be separated from the contemporary context, a number of academic and Masonic historians have considered the interaction to be little more than a tangential or 'fringe' issue.[3] In contrast, the view presented here is that any comprehensive analysis requires an understanding of the interplay between Freemasonry and the relevant economic, intellectual, political and religious milieus. Indeed, these factors are at the core of an historical analysis. The evidence presented suggests that Freemasonry was both a product of its environment and that it exercised a reciprocal influence upon it, particularly in connection with the dissemination of the scientific and philosophical ideas associated with the scientific Enlightenment.

The vectors through which such influence was put into effect included the individuals who controlled and moulded English Freemasonry after the formation of its new Grand Lodge in 1717. These men were the architects of modern Freemasonry – the 'Grand Architects' of the title. They designed and established an organisation that was radically different from that from which it had nominally descended. The new structure reflected the various political, philosophical and other intellectual dynamics that drove the leadership. And on a more mundane level, it also echoed their idiosyncrasies and desire for personal advancement.

On a national scale, Freemasonry developed rapidly over a short two decades from its re-launch in the early 1720s to become, as Peter Clark acknowledged in *British Clubs and Societies*, the most prominent of the many eighteenth-century fraternal organisations.[4] It also had a uniquely large provincial network and grew internationally where it tracked colonial trade routes and military expansion.[5] The movement was replicated elsewhere and complementary and sometimes competing Grand Lodges were established in Ireland, Scotland, France, the Netherlands, Sweden, Germany and Russia, where Freemasonry gained a following among the aristocracy, within the military and among the intellectual and political classes.

Many aspects of Masonry's moral and philosophical tenets, ersatz history and scientific Enlightenment substance had resonance. Within continental Europe in particular, Masonic lodges created a 'public sphere' for intellectual debate that could elsewhere be more circumscribed.[6] Pierre-Yves Beaurepaire has commented cogently on academic research into this 'relational Masonic space' within Europe and noted academic work by Margaret Jacob and others that places 'Masonic lodges . . . at the heart of their studies of eighteenth and nineteenth century sociability'.[7]

Unfortunately, a barrage of factors fundamental to an understanding of eighteenth-century Freemasonry and its development are often ignored or skirted. Such issues include the Protestant succession, Huguenot diaspora, struggle for political and religious power, and economic, financial and intellectual footfall of the scientific Enlightenment. Of course, there have been partial exceptions. Douglas Knoop and G.P. Jones in the 1930s and early 1940s examined Freemasonry through a predominantly economic lens.[8] And more recently David Stevenson, Andrew Prescott and Jessica Harland-Jacobs, among other eminent academics, have explored alternative determinants.

David Stevenson's powerful examination of the origins of Scottish Freemasonry in *The Origins of Freemasonry, Scotland's Century, 1590–1710* set a high academic standard.[9] However, his widely-accepted theory, that

English Freemasonry had its roots in the Master of the King's Works in Scotland – William Schaw's – administrative re-organisation of Scottish operative masonry at the tail end of the sixteenth century, has significant drawbacks. In particular, it failed to give sufficient weight to independent developments in England, ignored the contribution of England's multiplicity of 'Ancient Charges' and largely disregarded economic and social factors south of the border. Indeed, Stevenson himself confirmed subsequently that *The Origins* was not designed to present an analysis of Freemasonry as a whole, but rather to evaluate that of Scottish Freemasonry alone; the somewhat misleading title was a product of his publisher rather than a function of his content and conclusion.[10]

Pre-dating and later running alongside Stevenson's studies, Margaret Jacob's pioneering academic work concentrated principally on European Freemasonry and on the Low Countries especially.[11] Although much of her research is of significance and she sought to explore the origins of Freemasonry in *The Origins of Freemasonry: Facts and Fictions*,[12] her focus has been on continental Europe and her observations are not always relevant or specific to developments in England. David Stevenson has been more critical in his appraisal, perhaps verging on the blunt. He described *The Origins* as 'incoherent' and 'plain inaccurate', and commented that 'Jacob's knowledge of British masonry is limited'.[13]

Andrew Prescott, a leading researcher into Freemasonry, has examined certain economic factors underlying English Freemasonry's development in a series of lectures and articles. He has recognised – correctly – the requirement to 'establish a framework of interpretation',[14] and has pointed to the political, scientific and aesthetic features of Freemasonry. However, Prescott's conclusion, that Freemasonry 'sits most comfortably [within] the history of religion', narrows rather than broadens an historical analysis and is at odds with the notably latitudinarian and sometimes irreligious approach of many at its eighteenth-century core.

Jessica Harland-Jacobs' research into Freemasonry has been connected principally to its cultural role within the context of imperialism. She examined developments from the mid-eighteenth century to the early twentieth rather than Freemasonry's earlier formative period, and her analysis is largely silent on Freemasonry's foundations.

In contrast, this book concentrates on early modern English Freemasonry and its re-engineering over a period of two decades or so from 1720 to 1740. It argues that Freemasonry's development after the Hanoverian succession in 1714 mirrored the impact of economic, political, religious and intellectual forces, and suggests that in the 1720s and early 1730s Freemasonry was part of the process of change and in some ways an integral component. In short, it seeks to expose and understand the inter-relationship between Freemasonry and contemporary English society, and to examine key focal points and catalysts for change.

Given the almost vertiginous growth of Freemasonry in the eighteenth century, two fundamental questions are 'how did it happen?' and 'why?' An analysis of key protagonists within Grand Lodge and of a number of prominent constituent lodges such as the Horn Tavern in Westminster, the Bedford Head in Covent Garden and the Rummer at Charing Cross, reveals a diverse range of interconnected individuals and political, social and professional networks through which influence was exercised. Only a limited number of these relationships have previously been examined.

Unfortunately, there are – perhaps unsurprisingly – relatively sparse contemporary records and correspondence concerning eighteenth-century English Freemasonry. Notwithstanding the publicising of the *Constitutions*, lodge meetings and the eminence of those connected to the organisation and their philanthropic endeavours, Freemasonry was initially a relatively loosely organised and a semi-secret society. The corpus of written lodge records is limited and much is formulaic in style, and there is barely more relevant personal correspondence. As a consequence, many of the personal links and Masonic relationships that are posited and discussed are based on the balance of probability and the accretion of evidence rather than on hard primary proof.

Before outlining the structure of this book, it is important to note what it does not contain. There has been no attempt to provide an analysis of and comparison with Scottish Freemasonry, nor to examine Schaw's Scottish ordinances and administrative changes. In contrast to preceding, parallel and subsequent developments in England, these are areas that are not relatively under-researched but instead have received comprehensive academic attention. For the same reason, continental European Masonry has not been considered other than in a few instances where specific events are directly derivative of or relevant to English Grand Lodge, for example, through the involvement of Desaguliers or Charles Lennox, 2nd Duke of Richmond. As with Scotland, broader developments in continental Europe have been and are researched by many organisations and academics, both Masonic and otherwise. Jan Snoek in particular has provided a comprehensive summary of developments in the field. A detailed examination of Masonic ritual and its spiritual and quasi-religious components has similarly been bypassed, as have other factors explored extensively elsewhere, such as the role of women in Freemasonry, or developments that occurred only later in the eighteenth century, for example, Freemasonry's connection with international trade.

Chapter Outline

The book is divided into six chapters. Apart from the first – which provides an historical perspective – each explores complementary aspects of what should more properly be regarded as a holistic episode.

CHAPTER ONE sets the background context to what emerged as 'Free and Accepted' Masonry in the third decade of the eighteenth century and proposes an alternative, economic and social perspective to English

Freemasonry's mediaeval and post-mediaeval development. It reinforces the arguments against modern Freemasonry forming part of an unbroken evolutionary continuum of ritual and association dating from 'time immemorial'.[15] Instead, economic and socio-political determinants are examined, beginning with the outbreak of plague in the mid-fourteenth century and the shift in the purpose of the guilds from predominantly religious orders to embryonic collective bargaining organisations. The chapter also explores the guilds' subsequent absorption into the social and political structure.

CHAPTER TWO focuses on Desaguliers, arguably the most important individual among those that directed Grand Lodge and reconfigured English Freemasonry. His émigré Huguenot background, Newtonian scientific education and position within the Royal Society are outlined and discussed together with other factors that moulded his character and outlook.

CHAPTER THREE examines George Payne, Charles Delafaye, William Cowper, Nathaniel Blackerby and others who can be regarded as among Desaguliers' principal Masonic colleagues and collaborators. The chapter explores the extensive network of personal and political relationships centred on the London magistracy and especially among senior members of the Middlesex and Westminster benches. It develops the thesis that political involvement in Freemasonry went beyond simple government acquiescence and raises the argument that Freemasonry became associated with the apparatus of state. The reasoning is examined further in chapter five in connection with the role of the aristocracy.

CHAPTER FOUR looks at parallel networks based on the learned and professional societies including the Royal Society, the Spalding Society and the Society of Antiquarians, and comments on the contribution of Martin Folkes and William Stukeley, among others, to the development of the Masonic nexus. The membership of two lodges is explored: that of the Bedford Head in Covent Garden and of the Horn in Westminster.

Folkes' relationships with the Dukes of Montagu and Richmond provide a bridge to CHAPTER FIVE, which evaluates the influence of the first aristocrats to head Grand Lodge and popularise and promote what became 'national' Freemasonry. These were the noble Grand Masters who took the titular or occasionally actual helm of Grand Lodge, Freemasonry's largely self-appointed governing body. The impact of their involvement on Freemasonry's public persona is considered as is the extensive press coverage achieved after 1720. The personal networks of members of the aristocracy and their connections to the military, government, and the patriotic opposition allied to Frederick, Prince of Wales, provide a contemporary background.

Lastly, CHAPTER SIX considers Freemasonry's association with the scientific Enlightenment. The chapter outlines and explores how Desaguliers' Masonic ideology was disseminated through private lectures and public demonstrations alongside the popularisation of Newton's scientific theories, and the attraction of the lodge as a forum for entertainment and education and commercial and personal advancement. It also looks briefly at Freemasonry's role as a political vehicle and how it provided a platform for private debate within Europe.

We conclude that despite sharing nomenclature with the stonemasons' guilds, the Freemasonry of the eighteenth century deployed new ideas connected to the scientific Enlightenment. The evidence suggests that the creation of English Grand Lodge was not another step in an unbroken evolutionary flow as James Anderson pronounced some three hundred years ago[16] and as many subsequent historians have stated, but rather a step change that reflected principally the actions and philosophical and political input of Jean Theophilus Desaguliers and a core group of associates.

Four appendices follow the Conclusion. The first sets out for reference purposes the names of Grand Lodge Officers during the period covered by this book. The second examines the derivation and text of the *Charges* and *Regulations* at the core of the *1723 Constitutions* and its function as a means by which Grand Lodge exercised authority. The third provides a register of Irish, Scottish and other military lodges. And the fourth records the names of probable and possible Masonic members of two of the five professional societies discussed in CHAPTER FOUR: the Royal College of Physicians and the Society of Apothecaries.

If correct, the argument that Desaguliers and others within the upper circles of English Grand Lodge appropriated Freemasonry such that it became a vehicle for the expression and transmission of their ideas and ideals has significant implications not only for the history of Freemasonry but also for any analysis of contemporary culture. The central threads that defined Masonic change in the eighteenth century and connected and attracted Freemasonry's nascent membership included its pro-Hanoverian and pro-establishment stance, the social imprimatur of an elite celebrity aristocratic leadership, a strong association with the Newtonianism and the egalitarian fraternalism on offer. Nevertheless, despite their importance, it can be acknowledged that Desaguliers and his fellow architects' impact on Freemasonry was not indelible. By the late 1730s and 1740s their authority had begun to wane as age and death reduced both their influence and number. Subsequently, as different élites emerged at the helm of English Grand Lodge the movement shifted to reflect the altered political, commercial and social mores of its new masters.

As a direct result of the policies adopted by English Grand Lodge in the mid- and late 1740s, a schism in English Freemasonry occurred that led directly to the founding of the rival 'Ancient' Grand Lodge of England in 1751. The division persisted until 1813, when the original Grand Lodge of England, pejoratively termed the 'Moderns', merged with the newer and rival 'Ancients' to form the United Grand Lodge of England. The Masonic superstructure established by Desaguliers and his circle would remain *in situ*, as would the structural divorce from Freemasonry's mediaeval religious and operative incarnations, but Freemasonry's profile and purpose would later be altered by successive leaders to the point where many of its principal concerns had become substantially divorced from those of its founders.

CHAPTER ONE

English Freemasonry before the Formation of Grand Lodge

The Economic Imperative

Andrew Prescott has commented forcefully in a number of papers and lectures that the search for any single point of origin for English Freemasonry should be regarded as unproductive or an academic dead end.[1] Although his position may technically be correct, it would be wrong to ignore the tectonic shift in the economic and social environment and the consequential financial dynamics that accompanied the Black Death in the mid-fourteenth century. Market dislocation and soaring mortality followed the outbreak of plague in 1348 and widespread labour shortages caused pay rates to accelerate rapidly.[2] Although labour guilds had been in existence for several centuries, principally as quasi-religious orders,[3] many underwent transformation during subsequent decades as a reaction to ordnances and legislation that responded to rising wage rates by seeking to depress labour costs by statute.[4]

Passed in 1349, Edward III's *Ordinance of Labourers* attempted to reduce wages to the levels that had applied in 1346 before the Black Death. The *Statute of Labourers* enacted by Parliament in 1351 reinforced the legislation and imposed wage rates in relation to specific occupations for piecework and on a daily basis. In 1368, legislative enforcement was incorporated by statute into the duties of the Justices of the Peace; and by 1390, Justices were empowered to determine at their discretion what they considered reasonable maximum wage rates for their districts. Other laws and ordnances restricted labour mobility and improved the terms of contracts in favour of employers.[5]

The Parliament that enacted this legislation encompassed principally landowners with a vested interest in ensuring that inexpensive labour was available for their estates. Such landowners, the gentry, and others from their political and social circles, also served as local magistrates and were responsible for law enforcement. The inherent friction between the interests of agricultural capital and labour was clear, and it endured in the wake of successive outbreaks of plague in the 1360s and 1370s. Popular disquiet was catalysed by the imposition of higher taxes through the Poll Tax and culminated in the Peasants' Revolt of 1381.[6] Although the Revolt did not succeed as such, a similar pattern of disruption, disorder and legislative intervention in labour markets was repeated over the next two and a half centuries as successive outbreaks of pneumonic and bubonic plague reoccurred and price inflation took hold.[7]

In an influential work, Henry Phelps Brown and Sheila Hopkins calculated that as a direct function of plague-related labour shortages (and notwithstanding legislation to the contrary), daily nominal cash wages of skilled building workers in southern England rose by two thirds over the second half of the century from 3*d* per day in the mid-1340s to 5*d* per day in the 1390s. During the same period, the wages of unskilled labourers doubled from around 1½ to 3*d* per day.[8] They concluded that real wages for artisans rose by around 45% in the half century to 1390 with those of unskilled workers up to 60% higher.

The position was to change dramatically, and real wages generally declined across most of England during the late fifteenth, sixteenth and seventeenth centuries as prices increased more than six-fold and wages failed to maintain parity. Douglas Knoop and G.P. Jones drew a graphic portrait in *The Mediaeval Mason*.[9] Inflation was caused by an unprecedented expansion of money supply linked to the flow of New World bullion to Europe, large-scale silver production in central Europe[10] and repeated debasement of English coinage.[11] In a labour market still characterised by hostile legislation and with judicial sanction threatening local pay negotiations, stonemasons and other workers experienced earnings volatility on a scale not previously encountered. And it was in this context that the guilds gradually became a more visible part of a process by which craftsmen combined for their mutual economic benefit and protection. The change was reflected in the scope and content of what are now termed the *Old Charges*, which represent the first written evidence of early English Freemasonry. Their contextual development is discussed in Appendix 2.

Skilled artisans from many trades including stonemasons and other construction workers established and operated closed shops designed principally to create or sustain local monopolies.[12] Using the justification of appropriate training and quality control, as well as contract enforcement and other arguments, workers' guilds imposed and operated restrictive employment practices. Membership was controlled by rationing the number of apprenticeships and establishing a minimum period for such apprenticeships. In broad terms, the guilds set or supported prices and protected their members' proprietary skills from counterfeit by outsiders, the un-apprenticed and 'cowans' – those who had not served a regular apprenticeship. They also levied fines for infraction.[13] Although guilds also provided a framework for mutual assistance in periods of unemployment and offered help with rudimentary healthcare, funeral expenses and basic education, these aspects were secondary to their principal functions: influencing prices; protecting their members' rights and privileges; and, most importantly, maintaining their earning capacity.[14] In his *History of British Freemasonry*, Prescott termed this process the 'syndicalist phase' and it is hard not to concur.

Having been admitted to a Masonic guild, a member would progress through three stages from initial acceptance or initiation as an apprentice, usually at the age of 14, through to 'craftsman' or 'journeyman' and, finally, to master mason. Upon initiation into the guild and at each stage of the progression from apprentice to fellowcraft, and from fellowcraft to master mason, the aspiring candidate would swear an oath to keep private the craft's operational methodology, and at each stage he would be entrusted with the working secrets appropriate to his new rank and with a password, a sign and a token. Training would last for at least seven years. The minimum age for completion and being raised to the status of a master mason was 21, the legal age of maturity. The rate of progression would have been a function of tradition, skill and economic conditions: there would have been little point in allowing an apprentice to advance too rapidly if there was insufficient work. There was also a substantial financial advantage for a master mason to control and exploit an indentured labour force during a period of economic growth.

The stonemasons' architectural and engineering skills were fundamental to the creation of the visible symbols of authority and power of both church and state in the construction of abbeys, cathedrals, churches, castles and city walls: what might be regarded as the commanding – religious and political – heights of medieval society. Tangentially, unlike certain other craftsmen and a majority of agricultural labourers, stonemasons had the flexibility to travel to work at different construction sites.[15] It has been argued that such relative autonomy provided the origin of the term 'freemason'. However, there are two alternative and more robust explanations. The first is the derivation from 'freestone' mason: a stone that is fine-grained and 'soft' such that it can be carved or sculpted without shattering or splitting. The second, proposed by Knoop and Jones, is that the word 'free' was derived linguistically from 'noble' or 'superior', that is, a skilled worker able to command a premium above rough masons and journeymen employed in less expert work.[16] In the same vein, the term 'lodge' may have originated in the 'loggia' or temporary shelter created at a construction site for masons working on that project.

Despite the dissolution of the monasteries and the introduction of brickwork, the guilds developed over time to become influential economic units. They gradually became integrated into civic leadership structures, particularly in London and in prominent provincial cities, including Chester and York. In addition to nominating members to the city council, strong social, financial and political connections emerged that tied the guilds closely to the municipal authorities and *vice versa*.[17] Over time, guild membership increasingly became dominated by the more affluent artisans and master builders who, as master masons, employed journeymen and apprentices as construction workers on a piecework basis or on a daily or weekly wage.[18] Such men had a similar social standing to the local civic burghers and other freemen of the city and possessed comparable economic and political interests. Indeed, Heather Swanson, commenting on and extending Maurice Dobb's Marxist economic analysis,[19] argued that the local merchant and artisan oligarchy controlling provincial towns and cities manipulated the guild system in order to advance their own self-interested political and financial purposes.[20] As Dobb noted, the prevailing condition of relatively inefficient and parochial markets encouraged exploitation:

> Monopoly was of the essence of economic life in this epoch . . . since the municipal authority had the right to make regulations as to who should trade and when they should trade, it possessed a considerable power of turning the balance of trade in [its own] favour.[21]

The degree of interdependence between the guilds and the municipalities was cemented further as guilds recognised the value of admitting local dignitaries to their ranks. The benefits were palpable. The local Justices' authority extended to setting wage rates and the local politicians, aldermen, sheriffs and mayors were responsible for the grant of guild charters and commissioning civic building works. Evidence for such a quasi-deterministic interpretation can be found even among traditional Masonic scholars. Referring to 'a very old MS', William Preston – in whose honour the annual Prestonian lectures are named – noted that:

> When the Master and Wardens met in a lodge, if need be, the sheriff of the county, or the mayor of the city, or alderman of the town, in which the congregation is held, should be made fellow and sociate to the Master, in help of him against rebels.[22]

In short, there were clear economic benefits to both sides. Albeit a simplification, the municipalities received fees, taxes and a share of fines for granting the guilds the privilege of operating quasi monopolies, and the guilds gained the remit to control the availability and to a certain extent the price of labour and output. Certainly, members of the local oligarchy were present in and eventually dominated both sides of the table.[23] The inter-relationship endured and only came under sustained economic and political attack from the late seventeenth century when changes to working practices combined with political disquiet at the guilds' innate conservatism and what came to be viewed as their unenlightened opposition to innovation and free trade, led the guilds to be perceived as a limiter on economic progress and restrictive of industrial development.[24]

Despite such changes to their form and function, the stonemasons' guilds, in common with other guilds, retained elements of their traditional ritual, including the passwords and non-verbal signs of recognition. They also preserved their traditional histories and the nominal codes of conduct set out in the *Old Charges*. However, it is likely that over time such features became more important for their outward appearance rather than for any substance as lodges reflected the altered composition and elevated status of their new entrants and adopted attributes that were more social than 'working'.

The admission of 'gentlemen' to the lodge has been advanced by Masonic historians as evidence of the beginnings of a 'spiritual' or 'speculative' interest in Freemasonry, and it is quite possible that certain non-operative Masons such as Elias Ashmole and other antiquaries, may have been motivated, at least in part, by a desire to study the more esoteric aspects of lodge traditions. However, others are likely to have had different motives. Certain gentlemen members of the lodge may have acted principally as local benefactors, attending only rarely and in the same manner as the aristocracy and gentry had acted as patrons to earlier religious orders. However, for many, if not most, it would be a reasonable conjecture that business and political socialising on a local level, accompanied by periodic dining and drinking, would have been the principal rationale.

Gervase Rosser has commented that 'feasting and drinking were in the Middle Ages regarded as [the] defining activities of the guilds'.[25] In support of the point, he quoted in paraphrase a thirteenth-century clerical opponent of the fraternities who claimed, perhaps somewhat ironically, that 'if it were not for the feasting, few or none would come'.[26]

Rosser also noted the ritualistic and charitable aspects of the annual feast and its function in the fifteenth and sixteenth centuries as a means whereby 'links of solidarity and patronage could be forged'.[27] There is little reason to believe that the position was fundamentally different in the seventeenth century. In short, it is likely that many gentlemen and other non-masons entered the lodge for reasons that had little to do with any spiritual characteristics per se. Although Peter Kebbell and others have argued that the 'elite science' of Freemasonry had an intellectual attraction for an 'Enlightened' seventeenth-century audience, this book suggests (and, I hope, substantiates) that such an interest did not develop materially until the 1720s at the earliest, and that it was principally a function of Desaguliers and his colleagues' input during both that and the subsequent decade.[28]

Whatever the proximate reason for their membership, guilds that admitted affluent non-operative masons benefitted from the subscriptions and social and political gravitas that such members brought.[29] As a direct result, it is apparent that a number of lodges, including those in Warrington and York, evolved to comprise a majority of non-operative masons. Surviving lodge membership data suggest that prominent non-working members perpetuated their influence through invitations to friends and successive generations of family to the extent that such lodges became predominantly social and political clubs where dining and networking took precedence.[30]

In a number of books and lectures, Neville Barker-Cryer has reflected on the civic status of Randle Holme III, his father, grandfather and other members of the masonic lodge at Chester in the seventeenth century, such as Thomas Chaloner.[31] In *York Mysteries Revealed*, Barker-Cryer noted, for example, that in the 1660s the lodge at Chester was 'made up largely of the City fathers'.[32] Lewis and Thacker's *History of the County of Chester* made a similar point:

Chaloner was a deputy herald, whose widow married Randle Holme I. Holme and his son, Randle II, both served as churchwardens at St. Mary's, aldermen of the company of Painters, Glaziers, Embroiderers, and Stationers, deputy heralds, and mayors; industrious and accurate, they amassed large collections from the city records, monumental inscriptions, genealogies, and gentlemen's papers.[33]

Barker-Cryer has noted similar social characteristics to lodge membership in York. Interestingly, despite favouring in general a gradualist approach to the development of Freemasonry, his analysis provides considerable support for the social integration argument. Commenting on the membership records for York in 1705, which are among the earliest currently extant, Barker-Cryer noted the presence of the city's first families and that the lodges had the 'support and patronage of significant Yorkshire gentry'. In summary – and importantly – he observed that Freemasonry had created a 'notable niche for itself socially'.[34]

Non-Operative Masonry prior to the Formation of Grand Lodge

Although modern English Freemasonry has been viewed by many Freemasons as the product of a transition over a period of centuries from working or 'operative' masonry to spiritual or speculative 'Free and Accepted Masonry', the evidence suggests otherwise. Relevant primary material comprises newspapers; ecclesiastical records; pamphlets and books; the records of the 'Acception', an inner circle of the London Company of Masons; the *Old Charges*; and State and Parliamentary records. But despite this data, many scholars have relied only on a sparse collection of sixteenth and seventeenth-century sources.[35] Despite the wide availability of relevant information, academic and Masonic attention has for many years focused principally on two extracts from Elias Ashmole's *Memoirs*;[36] Richard Rawlinson's *Preface* to Ashmole's *Antiquities of Berkshire*;[37] Robert Plot's *Natural History of Staffordshire*;[38] Randle Holme's *Academie of Armoury*;[39] and John Aubrey's references to Sir William Dugdale's comments in Aubrey's *Natural History of Wiltshire*.[40]

It is rarely – if ever – mentioned that the above figures were connected: Ashmole, Aubrey and Plot were contemporaries at Oxford and at the Royal Society; and Ashmole, Dugdale, Holme and Plot were colleagues at the College of Arms. In addition, all shared an interest in alchemy and the esoteric and were members of the same antiquarian circles. Lastly, Dugdale and Ashmole were related by marriage: Ashmole became Dugdale's son-in-law.

Richard Rawlinson was of a later generation but is also connected: his most commonly cited Masonic contribution, the *Preface* to the *Antiquities of Berkshire*, was derived virtually in its entirety from previously published versions of Ashmole and Aubrey's books.[41] These were re-published by Edmund Curll in the second decade of the eighteenth century. Rawlinson was at the time a jobbing essayist and wrote the *Preface* at Curll's instigation. The work took place around a decade before Rawlinson became a Freemason. The matter is discussed in more detail below.

Despite what should be regarded as the possible 'contamination' of evidence from what were clearly associated parties, other seventeenth-century sources provide a measure of validation. John Locke's letter of 6 May 1696 to his friend, Thomas Herbert, the 8th Earl of Pembroke, a past President of the Royal Society (1689–90), if genuine, provides another example of an early scholarly interest in Freemasonry. The letter and its attachment were publicised in the *Gentleman's Magazine* in the mid-eighteenth century. However, a number of scholars including Esmond Samuel de Beer, who edited Locke's letters, and, more recently, Andrew Prescott, have stated that they consider the letter and the attached manuscript a probable Victorian fabrication.

The Earl of Pembroke was in 1696 Lord Privy Seal. A moderate and later pro-Hanoverian Tory, he was an antiquary and a patron of the arts and sciences.[42] Locke, referring to a Masonic manuscript purportedly uncovered at the Bodleian earlier that year, wrote to Pembroke in May 1696 commenting that:

> I know not what effect the sight of this old paper may have upon your lordship; but for my own part I cannot deny, that it has so much raised my curiosity, as to induce me to enter myself into the Fraternity, which I am determined to do (if I may be admitted) the next time I go to London, and that will be shortly.[43]

The reference to 'the Fraternity' may be to the 'Acception' of the London Company of Masons.

Perhaps with greater reliability, a previously unidentified but potentially highly significant reference to Freemasonry is contained within the following extract from Charles II's State Papers. Given its importance, the relevant quotation is given in full:

> *April 4, 1682*
> *Secretary Jenkins to Mr. Chetwynd.* I did not think Mr. Palmer's business to be ripe enough to trouble you, but intended to have recourse to you, when a just occasion should present itself, but now there is an incident in that affair of Mr. P.'s that I must acquaint you with.
>
> Last night Mr. Leveson Gower came and desired me to help him to make a full vindication of himself against a calumny that made him a partaker, as he said, in the society of Freemasons. I never heard he was one of them, only Mr. P. intimated that he had many arms in his house. Mr. L. G. hereon charged Mr. P. of having accused him of being of this fraternity and that he

English Freemasonry before the Formation of the Grand Lodge

had told a friend of his (Mr. L. G.) that he had given me advertisement of his so being. I told Mr. L. G. that I had notice by several letters of that brotherhood in Staffordshire but that I had not heard he was one, and this I said very truly, for Mr. P.'s accusation was that he had arms in his house.

Secretary Jenkins to Mr. Palmer. Mr. Leveson Gower desires to have the liberty of the law against you for accusing him as having part in the fraternity of Freemasons. He came to me last night with that complaint and desire, but I, not remembering anything of his being a Freemason in the notices given me, answered that no such charge was come to me and that, if any came, I would take his Majesty's pleasure in it, wherewith he went away seemingly satisfied. I did not mention the charge of having arms in his house, it being his Lord Lieutenant's business to look after that, nor did he complain of any other charge. I desire you therefore to take your measures with Mr. Chetwynd, to whom I have written.[44]

'Mr Leveson Gower' was William Leveson-Gower, Bt. (*c.* 1647–1691), one of the two MPs for Newcastle-under-Lyme, the second son of Sir Thomas Gower and Frances Leveson. He took the name 'Leveson-Gower' in 1668 when he inherited estates at Tretham and Lilleshall from Sir Richard Leveson, who had adopted him as his sole heir. Gower married Lady Jane Granville, the eldest daughter of the Royalist 1st Earl of Bath, and served as a Whig MP virtually uninterrupted from 1675 until his death.[45] His older brother predeceased him and he succeeded to the baronetcy in 1689. The family was an economic and political force in Staffordshire, and later nationally. Members of the Leveson-Gower family were in the eighteenth century connected socially to senior Freemasons and there is evidence to suggest that at least in the nineteenth century they were themselves Masons. George Granville Leveson-Gower, 2nd Duke of Sutherland, owned a copy of the *Egerton Manuscript*,[46] one of the *Old Charges*, and Frances Leveson-Gower, his brother, was initiated into Apollo Lodge, Oxford, in 1819.

'Secretary Jenkins' was the lawyer, diplomat and administrator, Sir Leoline Jenkins (1625–1685). Jenkins was Secretary of State at the Northern Department from April 1680 until his transfer to the Southern Department in February 1681, where he served until his resignation in April 1684. Although foreign affairs of state were split geographically between the two departments, domestic affairs were common to both.

To place the extract in context, the late 1670s and early 1680s were marked by political divisions in England that created the foundations of the Whig and Tory factions in Parliament. The Whigs opposed the hereditary accession of the Catholic Duke of York as monarch, favouring his exclusion. Charles II and the anti-exclusion Tories supported the Duke's succession to the throne as James II. The episode described in the State Papers is potentially significant and provides support for three propositions: first, that membership of the Freemasons could be viewed pejoratively; second, that 'the [Masonic] brotherhood' was active in Staffordshire in the seventeenth century; and third, that Freemasons were monitored by the government, after all, Secretary Jenkins 'had notice by several letters'.

There were various reasons why Freemasonry might have been perceived negatively at that time, and why membership of a lodge might be politically sensitive. An affiliation with any supposedly covert society, no matter how banal, could be viewed as potentially treasonous and certainly suspicious by a nervous establishment; and such suspicion could serve as a justification for possible government action. Indeed, in 1683, following hard on the 1679–1681 Exclusion Bill crisis,[47] the Rye House Plot,[48] an attempt to assassinate Charles and James, provided clear confirmation that not all establishment fears were baseless. In its wake, the Whigs were virtually excluded from government and a number of prominent Whig politicians exiled.

Less damning but nonetheless important, being 'a partaker' in a Masonic lodge in the seventeenth century may also have been shorthand for disreputable behaviour or drunkenness. In Rosser's words, 'even the smallest clubs consumed significant quantities of ale'.[49] Indeed, the practice continued into the following century and internationally:

> We have about 30 or 40 Free Masons they have a fine Supper every Saturday night and often 2 or 3 in the week besides; where such an Expence can be born I am at a Loss to know. One night amongst other Disorders they went to the Guard cut the Capt. down the Head and disarmed the rest carrying the Arms away. When they came to reflect on it on the morrow, to make things up they call'd a Lodge at night and admitted Gough the Capt. a Free Mason, so I suppose the thing dropt.[50]

Hogarth's *Night*, the final print in his series *Four Times of the Day*, with its drunken Master, Thomas de Veil, staggering back from a London lodge meeting, also provides another (albeit later) uncomplimentary image. Viewed through such prisms, Leveson-Gower's alleged patronage of Freemasonry could be seen, at least in some eyes, as both politically damaging and socially unwise.

However, such negative themes are not apparent in other sources. Ashmole, Aubrey and Plot also wrote of Masonic activity in Staffordshire. In each case, their writings underscore simply the presence of gentlemen and non-operative 'Free Masons' within the lodge.[51] Somewhat superficially, this has been used to argue that there was in the seventeenth century a move towards 'spiritual' or 'speculative' masonry. But the presence of gentlemen within a lodge *per se* and their description as 'freemasons' as opposed to 'masons', did not indicate and does not prove the conventional contention that seventeenth-century English Freemasonry was in transition. It is simply evidence of the existence of operative lodges with a leavening of the gentry. This had been the position for some time and is not contentious. Moreover, the use of the word 'spiritual' is also confusing. As Tobias Churton has commented, in seventeenth-century Britain everything had a spiritual dimension.[52]

If contextual language analysis is to be meaningful, it is important to know how the term 'freemason' was understood in the seventeenth and earlier centuries. The word can be dated back to the twelfth century and through to the sixteenth, seventeenth and eighteenth centuries[53] it was used to define a skilled and non-indentured stonemason. Its meaning was extended later to include non-working or honorary members of a masonic guild or lodge. However, it was only in the 1720s and 1730s that it can be recognised as referring principally to 'Free and Accepted' Masons whose use of Masonic tools was allegorical. 'Speculative freemasonry' before this period referred only to the theoretical or mathematical aspects of operative masonry.

'Freemason' and its variants are present in myriad sources. They include Henry VIII's State Papers, for example, those which set out the detailed building accounts for Cardinals' College in Oxford:

> to the master masons, 12*d* a day each; to the wardens, masons, and setters, 3*s* 8*d* a week; and to every other free mason, 3*s* 4*d*.[54]

> a fre mason . . . shall take but 3*d* a day mete and drinke from ester to Michelmas.[55]

Other instances are found across numerous parish records, wills and coroners' rolls, and in contemporary books and pamphlets. In the sixteenth century, examples include books by John Foxe[56] and Raphael Hollinshead,[57] and in the seventeenth century, John Stow's eponymous *Survey of London*,[58] Alexander Brome's comedy *The Cunning Lovers*[59] and Thomas Blount's *Glossographia*, where 'Lapicide (lapicida)' is defined as 'a digger or hewer of stones; a Stone-cutter or Freemason'.[60] There are further examples in Howell's *Londinopolis*, which referred to 'the company of Masons, otherwise call'd Free Masons',[61] and Babington's *Notice to Grand Jurors*,[62] which set out a schedule of current wage rates, including that for 'Free Masons'.

In the press, the *Tatler* wrote the epithet: 'like they had some secret intimation of each other like the Freemasons'.[63] The identical phrase was used a few years later by Richard Steele.[64] Knoop and Jones in their *Early Masonic Pamphlets* pointed to other early references to Freemasonry including the satirical description of the 'Company of Accepted Masons' in *Poor Robin's Intelligence*:

> These are to give notice, that the Modern Green-ribbon'd Caball, together with the Ancient Brotherhood of the Rosy-Cross; the Hermetick Adepti, and the Company of Accepted Masons, intend all to Dine together on the 31st of November next, at the Flying-Bull in Wind-Mill-Crown-Street; having already given order for great store of Black-Swan Pies, Poached Phoenixes Eggs, Haunches of Unicorns.[65]

The phrase 'Mason's Word' appeared in Marvell's *The Rehearsal Transprosed* – 'those that have the Masons Word, secretly discern one another'.⁶⁶ It was also in *A new dictionary of the canting crew* which alluded to the tradition of mutual assistance:

> 'Masons-Word': who ever has it, shall never want, there being a Bank at a certain Lodge in Scotland for their Relief. 'Tis communicated with a strict Oath, and much Ceremony, (too tedious to insert) and if it be sent to any of the Society, he must, (nay will) come immediately, tho' very Busy, or at great Distance.⁶⁷

The definition refers implicitly to the Masonic admission ceremony in Scotland at which the 'Mason Word' was imparted. However, it seems unlikely that the 'Mason Word' was restricted to Scotland or would have been used by Scottish masons alone.⁶⁸

Both individually and as a whole, each reference and quotation either provides evidence for the conventional, long-established association between working masons and their trade secrets or refers to the mutual assistance offered by the guild or lodge to its members. None point to the existence of spiritual Freemasonry as it developed in the eighteenth and nineteenth centuries.⁶⁹ Indeed, the first recorded use of the term 'speculative' Freemasonry was not until the latter part of the eighteenth century in a letter written by Dr Thomas Manningham, Sir Richard Manningham's son and a former Deputy Grand Master, on 12 July 1767 to a 'Bro. Sauer' at The Hague:

> in antient time the Dignity of Knighthood flourish'd amongst Free Masons; whose Lodges heretofore consisted of Operative, not Speculative Masons.⁷⁰

The word 'freemason' was used widely prior to the 1720s and does not represent evidence for the existence of 'spiritual' or 'speculative' Freemasonry. Any stirring of semi-scholarly interest in the 'mysteries' of the Craft in the seventeenth century was quite distinct from what became 'speculative' Freemasonry in the eighteenth and nineteenth century. The works of Randle Holme (1627–1700) and Thomas Tryon (1634–1703) underline the point.

RANDLE HOLME III AND THOMAS TRYON

Randle Holme III's *Academie of Armory* invited its readers to enquire into the arts and sciences and offered to assist them:

> Now for the better understanding . . . I shall in two examples, set forth all their words of Art, used about them: by which any Gentleman may be able to discourse [with] a Freemason, or other workman, in his own terms.⁷¹

English Freemasonry before the Formation of the Grand Lodge 19

Holme's objectives were explicit, to provide a guide to

> the instruments used in all trades and sciences, together with their terms of art: also the etymologies, definitions, and historical observations on the same, explicated and explained according to our modern language: very usefel [sic] for all gentlemen . . . and all such as desire any knowledge in arts and sciences'.[72]

There was no allegorical content and the books were not particularly popular. Although the first two volumes were printed in 1688 at Holme's own expense, demand was insufficient to warrant publication of the third and fourth, and these were not published until over two centuries later by the bibliophile Roxburghe Club.[73] One reason was that Holme's bland and pedestrian literary style had almost no merit:

> The *Pedestall*, that is the Foot or Bottom of a Pillar, whither it be round or Square.
> The *Pillar*, is the Body or middle part between the Head and Foot, be it round or Square.
> The *Capitall*, is the Top of the Pillar, or Head, on which the round Ball stands.
> The *Chapiter*, is the Ball or any other kind of work that is made to adorne the Capitall, is a Chapiter of such and such a thing.
> There are other terms used for the severall Mouldings about Pillars, Columns, and Pillasters; which I shall in *numb*. 66 67 at the end of this Plate shew and further describe unto you.[74]

The Holme family had been integrated into Chester's civic establishment for several generations. Holme's father and grandfather had been Aldermen and Mayors of the city[75] and had served as Justices of the Peace and Deputy Heralds for Lancashire.[76] Holme's father had also been Clerk to the Stationers' Company and family influence may have smoothed his son's appointment as Steward to the Company in 1656 and election as an Alderman in 1659.[77] Like his father, Holme was a Royalist,[78] a loyalty rewarded with a sinecure in 1664 that exempted him from arrest but precluded his serving as Mayor,[79] the probable reason he did not follow his father and grandfather into office.[80]

In an early section of the *Academie*, Holme defined what he meant by a guild and set out how the organisation was structured:

> A *Fraternity*, or *Society*, or *Brotherhood*, or *Company*: are such in a Corporation, that are of one and the same trade, or occupation, who being joyned together by oath and covenant, do follow such orders and rules, as are made, or to be made for the good order, rule, and support, of such and every of their occupations. These several Fraternities are generally governed by one or two Masters, and two Wardens, but most Companies

with us by two Aldermen, and two Stewards, the later, being to receive and pay what concerns them.[81]

Given the strong links between the guilds and the civic establishment in Chester, it is unsurprising that Holme, like his father before him, was a Freemason:

> I Cannot but Honor the Fellowship of the *Masons* because of its Antiquity; and the more, as being a Member of that Society, called *Freemasons*: In being conversant amongst them I have observed the use of these several Tools following, some whereof I have seen born in coats Armour.[82]

Although the *Academie* sets out a detailed description of 'Masonic Tools' and their operative uses, it provides no evidence of speculative or spiritual Freemasonry in Chester, nor any suggestion of the allegorical use of the working tools outside of heraldry and religion. Holme's 'Masonic Tools' is indistinguishable from the preceding and following sections of the book which cover 'Husbandry Instruments' and 'Slaters' Tools'. Historians who have argued otherwise are mistaken.[83]

The number of gentlemen Freemasons in the Chester guild suggests that it had become by the mid to late seventeenth century a mixed and largely non-operative, social and dining club. In Lewis and Thacker's words, the lodge provided a forum for 'well-off employers, notably in the building trades' and for the gentry.[84] Indeed, the social aspect of Freemasonry became so popular in Chester that by the early eighteenth century there were three lodges, more than any other provincial city.[85] Alfred Ingham's observation that Chester's lodge membership was of a high social standing comprising country gentlemen, the urban élite and officers from the city garrison, is confirmed by Grand Lodge membership lists for the 1720s.[86]

Chester's civic authorities were from the late 1660s increasingly interventionist in guild affairs, settling differences, ensuring an adequate enrolment of apprentices and judging demarcation disputes. Similar issues arose elsewhere in the country as a function of post civil war expansion in the construction industry and other trades. Interestingly, Chester ruled against the formation of new guilds on several occasions including, in around 1691, a petition from six master stonemasons seeking a new charter. They were instead placed into the Carpenters' Company. That they had left and had no wish to re-join the original company reinforces the suggestion that the lodge had by then developed into something rather different from an operative guild managing local employment issues. It also highlights the corporation's influence over guild regulation and underlines the political dimensions of civic control.[87]

Thomas Tryon's *Letters* 'written both at the Request of divers Friends and Country-men at home, as well as of some Strangers from abroad' were slightly more readable than Holme's *Academie* and had moderately more success as a publishing venture.[88] However, they fulfilled a similar purpose:

'necessary and practical Truths cannot be too often taught and repeated, till they are well understood, learned and distinguished'. His work comprised a series of basic texts leavened with faux philosophy from *The Sense of Hearing* and *The Nature of Smells*, to *Bricks and various sorts of Earths*, and was not aimed at a readership seeking a better understanding of the theoretical mathematics and geometry of masonry so much as an introductory guide to 'how things work'. The now little-known Tryon was a successful merchant and a (less successful) animal rights campaigner: 'it is not said that the Lord made all Creatures for Man to Eat . . . [but] for his own Glory'.[89] Although his early writings on Pythagoras indicate an interest in the esoteric,[90] it is hard to extend the argument further. Like Holme, 'necessary and practical Truths' were at the core of his writings.

ELIAS ASHMOLE

One of the most frequently cited examples of non-operative or 'speculative' seventeenth-century Freemasonry is that of the antiquary and founder of Oxford's Ashmolean, Elias Ashmole (1617–1692). Ashmole's autobiographical *Memoirs* document two often mentioned Masonic events: his initiation in Warrington on 16 October 1646 and his attendance at a lodge meeting at Masons' Hall in London on 11 March 1682.

His diary entries have been interpreted by historians as providing firm confirmation that gentlemen who, using William Stukeley's words, were 'interested in the mysteries of the Ancients',[91] were members of operative lodges in the mid-seventeenth century. This standard interpretation was exemplified by Robert Gould's comment that 'it is obvious that symbolical masonry must have existed in Lancashire for some time before the admission of Ashmole and Mainwaring'.[92] However, an alternative analysis of text and context suggests that Ashmole's interest in Freemasonry was more probably motivated by social factors rather than a purely alchemical or antiquarian interest.[93]

In his entry for 16 October 1646, Ashmole recorded that he:

> was made a Freemason at Warrington in Lancashire with Coll. Henry Mainwaring of Kerthingham in Cheshire, the names of those that were then at the Lodge, Mr Richard Penkett Warden, Mr James Collier, Mr Richard Sankey, Henry Littler, John Ellam, Richard Ellam, and Hugh Brewer.[94]

That of 10 March 1682 stated that:

> About 5 Hor. post merid. I received a Summons to appear at a Lodge to be held the next Day at Masons Hall in London.[95]

And the entry for 11 March set out the events that followed:

Accordingly I went, and about Noon were admitted into the Fellowship of Freemasons,[96]
Sir William Wilson, Knight, Capt. Richard Borthwick, Mr William Woodman, Mr William Grey, Mr Samuel Taylour, and Mr William Wise.
I was the Senior Fellow among them (it being 35 Years since I was admitted) . . .
We all dined at the Half-Moon-Tavern in Cheapside, at a Noble Dinner prepared at the Charge of the new accepted Masons.[97]

Ashmole's *Memoirs* comprise brief notes that suggest material prepared for an unwritten biography. The entry for 16 October 1646 is significant only because it is the first contemporary record of the admittance of a non-operative Freemason in England, although those persons noted present by Ashmole would obviously have already been admitted as Masons. The details of this first recorded initiation are non-existent but may have involved elements of traditional guild ritual, that is, an enjoinment to secrecy, reading the *Charge* and the disclosure of an identifying pass grip and password – a sign and token.

W.H. Rylands' analysis of those present confirmed that the lodge consisted substantially of non-working masons.[98] Writing in the *Masonic Magazine*, Rylands established the evidence and set out the conclusion that few or none of those attending the lodge were working stonemasons. Tobias Churton has also analysed the members present and concluded that the lodge was 'largely made up of landed gentry from Cheshire and from that county's border with south Lancashire'. He noted the 'repeated connection between gentleman landowners and the monastic and confraternal system'[99] and although the commercial connections were unexplored, Churton's analysis tends to confirm that the predominant aspect of lodge membership may have been social. His view is supported by Peter Kebbell's observation that Ashmole had a strong social connection with Henry Mainwaring, who was a relative of Peter Mainwaring, Ashmole's father-in-law.[100]

Looking at seventeenth-century Freemasonry more widely, Yasha Bereseiner in an article for *MQ Magazine* queried why there was no mention of Freemasonry in Ashmole's memoirs other than on the above two occasions.[101] His analysis – that seventeenth-century 'Freemasonry was not an organisation of consequence' and that Ashmole 'may well have found nothing of consequence' – has an element of possibility but may be at odds with the activities of the 'Acception': the exclusive inner lodge within the larger setting of the operative Masons' Company.

Ashmole's summons to attend a lodge at the London Masons' Company in 1682 and his short note describing the meeting supports the view that the invitation was to the Acception:

. . . about Noon were admitted into the Fellowship of Freemasons, Sir William Wilson, Knight, Capt. Richard Borthwick, Mr William Woodman, Mr William Grey, Mr Samuel Taylour, and Mr William Wise . . .

present beside myself . . . [were]
Mr Thomas Wise, Master of the Masons Company this present Year; Mr Thomas Shorthose, Mr Thomas Shadbolt, – Waindsfford, Esq.; Mr Nicholas Young, Mr John Shorthose, Mr William Hamon, Mr John Thompson, and Mr William Stanton.

Eight of the nine named in the second paragraph were already members of the Masons' Company, as were Sir William Wilson (1641–1710) and William Woodman.[102] Three of the initiates – William Grey, Samuel Taylour and William Wise, the son of the Master – were similarly members of the Company. This suggests not that the Acception was a 'speculative' lodge open to non-operative men, such as Ashmole, but rather an inner circle of élite senior working masons who could also be regarded as 'gentlemen'.

Thomas Wise, the Master of the Masons' Company, was an eminent stonemason who had, among other projects, worked with Sir Christopher Wren on the construction of Chelsea Hospital.[103] He was supported at the meeting by his two Wardens, John Shorthose and William Stanton, an indication that the meeting had formal sanction. Indeed, Andrew Prescott noted that the names of members of the Masons' Company who had been admitted to the Acception were recorded publicly on panels in the Company's livery hall and that the Acception paraded under its own banner.[104]

Sir William Wilson's admittance into the select inner circle of the Acception was the probable catalyst for Ashmole's attendance. Wilson was a stonemason of some stature. He had married into the local Staffordshire gentry and been knighted in 1681, possibly because of Jane Pudsey, his then future wife's connections rather than through any political affiliation.[105] They had met when Wilson was commissioned to sculpt a memorial to her late husband. Pudsey may have been unwilling to marry her social inferior and a knighthood provided the required social elevation. Interestingly, there is a short note relating to William Wilson in the records of the *Wren Society* that refers to this entry in Ashmole's *Memoirs*. It confirms that: 'the Fellows last recited [were] nearly all Masons employed by Sir Christopher Wren'.[106]

Wilson worked principally in the Midlands, in Lichfield and Sutton Coldfield in particular, and in 1669 had sculpted the statue of Charles II erected at Lichfield cathedral.[107] Ashmole had been born in Lichfield, studied there as a cathedral chorister and retained a solid connection with the city: he was a benefactor of the cathedral, presenting new service books in 1662; and had sought election (albeit unsuccessfully) as a parliamentary candidate.[108] Although it is impossible to determine with certainty, Ashmole's summons to the Acception implies that his Freemasonry was known to those involved, most particularly to Wilson and others within the Staffordshire gentry. However, beyond his relationship with Wilson, with Lichfield and its cathedral, Ashmole's public standing and wealth may have been another contributory factor in his invitation to attend.

Ashmole's Royalist loyalties had been rewarded after the Restoration. In 1660, he had been appointed Comptroller of the Excise and in 1668,

Accountant General. Both were well remunerated positions which offered considerable scope for patronage. (Ashmole had previously been associated with the Excise as Commissioner at Lichfield (1644) and as Commissioner at Worcester (1644–1646). His patron, James Pagitt, a relation through his mother, was Baron of the Exchequer.) Ashmole had also been appointed Windsor Herald at the College of Arms in 1660, a role he held until his resignation in 1675.[109] And alongside Sir Robert Moray, another (albeit Scottish) Freemason, who had been initiated in May 1641, five years prior to Ashmole,[110] Ashmole had status as one of the original Fellows of the Royal Society of London.[111] Finally, and perhaps not coincidentally, Ashmole was the founder and chief benefactor of Oxford's Ashmolean Museum, established in 1682, the year that he was invited to attend the Acception.

In short, the most probable function of the Acception was that of an élite inner grouping of the Masons' Company, each member of which had attained sufficient social and financial stature to be deemed a 'gentleman'. Rather than gathering for what has been interpreted as spiritual or 'speculative' purposes, the Acception's own records suggest that their social and dining arrangements comprised a central element of the meetings.

Matthew Scanlan has argued against this viewpoint and, in a reference to an earlier meeting of the Acception in 1638 recorded in the Renter Warden's Accounts of the Company of Masons, noted that five masons were 'taken into the Accepcon', each paying a fee of ten shillings:[112]

> Pd wch the accompt layd out wch was more than he received of them wch were taken into the Accepcon whereof Xs is to be paid by Mr Nicholas Stone, Mr Edmund Kinsman, Mr John Smith, Mr William Millis, Mr John Colles.[113]

However, the size of fee is a strong indication that membership of the Acception was not open to the average mason: 10 shillings amounted to around four weeks' wages at a time when an average stone mason might earn 4*d*–6*d* per day.[114]

Nicholas Stone (1586–1647) is an important figure in the extract. He was appointed Master Mason at Windsor Castle in 1626 and as the King's Master Mason in 1632, in which year and the following year he was elected Master of the London Company of Masons. He had previously served twice as Warden.[115] Stone was regarded by his contemporaries as one of the most eminent sculptors and architect/builders in London. But notwithstanding his operative eminence, he was only 'taken into the Accepcon' in 1638, by which date he had become relatively affluent via commissions for clients and patrons that included the Countess of Middlesex,[116] Viscount Dorchester,[117] the Goldsmiths Company,[118] the Earl of Danby[119] and Sir Christopher Hatton.[120]

Knoop and Jones provide additional support for a social dimension to the Acception.[121] They observed that the surviving Masons' Company accounts mention the Acception throughout the seventeenth century and, significantly, the records and statements detail the sums spent on the Acception dinners and list the balances owed by members. A number of entries also set down the names of those admitted members. One such record for 1649–50 listed six new members, of whom four were members of the Company. The two non-members paid an acceptance fee of 40*s*, double that of working members of the Company. The differential suggests that such non-working masons may have been invited to join as a form of subsidy, a common practice among many guilds. The description resonates with Ashmole's own record of the March 1682 lodge meeting and his observation that dinner was 'prepared at the Charge of the new accepted Masons'. The clear inference is that there was an inner social élite rather than a speculative or operative lodge meeting, and that the new members financed the evening.

Tangentially, the argument that the existence of the Acception points to a 'speculative' inner circle within the Company of Masons is also contradicted by an analysis of the later Grand Lodge membership rolls. Very few members of the Acception joined Desaguliers' Free and Accepted Masonry: Woodman became a member of the lodge meeting at the Horn, Westminster (he appears in both the 1723 and 1725 lists);[122] and Stanton a member of the lodge at the Queen's Arms in Newgate Street.[123] A William Woodman, possibly the same person, was also later a member of the Carpenters' Company; the *Minute Book of Courts and Committees* described him as 'William Woodman Citizen and Mason made Free'.[124] Although a Thomas Wise was a member of the King's Arms in New Bond Street in the 1730 list of members, the fifty-year gap would suggest on balance that this was not same person as the Master of the Masons Company in 1682.

JOHN AUBREY AND WILLIAM DUGDALE

John Aubrey (1626–1697), a colleague of Ashmole both at the Royal Society and at Oxford, referred to Freemasonry in his *Natural History of Wiltshire* and his comments have been cited often as evidence of Masonry's transition. Aubrey wrote the work in the ten years to 1685. He was unable to procure finance for publication and the book remained in manuscript form until 1690 when the Royal Society ordered a copy to be made at their expense in order that Fellows would not have to travel to Oxford to consult it.[125] The duplicate was finished in 1691 and is held in the Royal Society's archives (Misc. MS. 92). Aubrey's additions and amendments to the text were written to the left of each page of the original, which pages had previously been left blank. The version of Aubrey's manuscript held at the Bodleian and quoted varies slightly in text and spelling as compared to the version held at the Royal Society, although the content is virtually the same.

Aubrey was a somewhat dysfunctional peripatetic scholar whose family wealth had been dissipated in a series of fruitless personal lawsuits over a period of some twenty years.[126] A keen amateur scientist, antiquarian and natural historian, he was elected to the Royal Society in 1663 where he took an active part, presenting several papers.[127] In his first reference to Freemasonry, Aubrey recorded his conversation with the antiquary and scholar, Sir William Dugdale (1605–1686):

> Sir William Dugdale told me, many years since, that about Henry the Third's time the Pope gave a bull or patents to a company of Italian Freemasons to travel up and down over all Europe to build churches. From those are derived the fraternity of adopted Masons. They are known to one another by certain signs and watch-words: it continues to this day. They have several lodges in several counties for their reception, and when any of them fall into decay the brotherhood is to relieve him, &c. The manner of their adoption is very formal, and with an oath of secrecy.[128]

There is considerable archival material relating to Sir William Dugdale including over a hundred entries referenced in the National Archives' Access to Archives database, the majority linked to his heraldic and antiquarian activities, and around twenty manuscript references at the British Library. Although absence of data is not proof, there are no archival records – nor any other published correspondence or diaries – that offer confirmation that Dugdale was a Freemason, albeit that there is strong evidence that he was on good terms with both the Leveson-Gower family and Elias Ashmole.[129]

Dugdale and Ashmole were both Royalists and each had robust links to Staffordshire: Ashmole had been born in Lichfield and his family lived in the city; Dugdale's connections to the county were via his mother, Elizabeth Swynfen, and his wife, Margery Huntbach.[130] Ashmole and Dugdale had met in the mid-1650s when Ashmole began his research into the Order of the Garter. They shared an interest in heraldry and antiquities and in 1660 Ashmole became a fellow member of the College of Heralds. Dugdale served as Chester Herald at the College from 1644 until 1660. He was subsequently promoted Norroy King of Arms (1660–1677).[131] Probably with Ashmole's support, Dugdale was in 1677 appointed to the most senior role at the College, Garter King of Arms. He was also knighted and gained an increase in salary from £40 to £100 per annum.[132] Ashmole and Dugdale also enjoyed a strong personal relationship. The two travelled together on several industrious fact-finding heraldic expeditions across provincial England[133] and Ashmole stayed frequently at Blyth Hall, Dugdale's country house.[134] Marriage cemented the connection. After the death of Ashmole's third wife on 1 April 1668, Ashmole married Elizabeth Dugdale (1632–1701), one of Dugdale's nine daughters, on 3 November of the same year.[135]

Aubrey and the Wren Controversy

Aubrey made a second reference to Freemasonry that was wholly distinct from his reported conversation with Dugdale. In an addendum to his original manuscript, he referred to the initiation of Christopher Wren:

1691. Memorandum, this day (May the eighteenth being Monday after Rogation Sunday) is a great Convention at St. Paul's church of the Fraternity of the Accepted Free Masons where Sr Christopher Wren is to be adopted a Brother: and Sr Henry Goodric[136] . . . of ye Tower and divers others – There have been kings that have been of this Sodalitie.

The entry has been the cause of some Masonic controversy. Gould and subsequent scholars have argued against its validity as an accurate record of events; others have argued in its favour.[137] However, despite the alleged significance of the event – the initiation of Wren into Freemasonry – it is notable that there is no reference to any 'Convention' at St. Paul's nor to Christopher Wren or Henry Goodricke) being adopted into Freemasonry in any newspaper published in 1691 or 1692 held within the *Burney* collection. The National Archives' Access to Archives database, *ECCO* and *EEBO*[138] are similarly silent on any connection with Freemasonry for the whole of the decade 1690–1700. In short, there is no third party evidence of any 'great Convention at St. Paul's church' whether of 'the Fraternity of the Accepted Free Masons' or otherwise.

Gould and others have also stated the improbability of early eighteenth-century Masonic luminaries such as Desaguliers, James Anderson, George Payne and Martin Folkes being unaware of Wren having been made a Freemason in 1691. They have argued that had it been the case, it would have been be reasonable to presume that it would have been worthy of note in the *1723 Constitutions*. In fact, although the *1723 Constitutions* contains a list of 'gentlemen Freemasons', Wren's name is omitted and he is described only as 'the King's Architect'. Indeed, with one possible exception, Wren is not identified as a 'Free and Accepted' Mason in any book or document – Masonic or otherwise – until the publication of Anderson's *1738 Constitutions*.[139] The exception is a reference in the *Post Boy* on 2 March 1723, around a week after Wren's death. The text was reprinted in the *British Journal* on 9 March the following week but not in any other newspaper:

This evening the Corpse of that Worthy FREE MASON Sir Christopher Wren, Knight, is to be interred under the Dome of St. Paul's Cathedral.[140]

This was the third time Wren's death had been mentioned by the *Post Boy*. Wren had not been described as a Freemason in either of the paper's earlier obituaries nor in any of the many others published at the same time. At issue is the significance of Wren's description. On one level, the *Post Boy's* use of 'Freemason' was an obvious depiction of Wren in a conventional sense as a skilled architect and stonemason. Contemporary records hold numerous examples of the term being used as such during the decade. A good example is a local petition supporting a Richard Hardwick of Shepton Mallet who had been indicted for working as a 'freemason' when qualified only as a 'rough mason'.[141] In this sense, to have declared that Wren had been a freemason would have been to state the obvious.

However, the term could also have been used to connect Wren, albeit obliquely, with the recently re-launched 'Society of Free and Accepted Masons'. A cynic might have observed that it was not coincidental that the announcement of Wren's burial arrangement beneath the dome of St. Paul's Cathedral and his ostensible connection with the new Free and Accepted Masonry occurred at precisely the time the *1723 Constitutions* was published and prominent classified advertisements for its sale were placed in the *Post Boy* and other newspapers. The first advertisement for the *Constitutions* appeared in the *Post Boy* on 26 February 1723. Wren's death 'on Monday last' was recorded on the same day and on the same page. His obituary noted that 'he was deservedly one of the greatest Architects in Europe; and was lately elected Vice President of the Corporation of Clergymen's sons'. No mention was made of any connection to Freemasonry until a week later.

In reality, Wren's Masonic status is tangential. He was clearly the principal architect and geometrician of his generation and had he been made a Freemason within the Acception or otherwise, what is of more significance is that it was not deemed worthy of mention in the three decades prior to his death nor in the vast majority of published obituaries: fifteen of sixteen. His standing as a 'speculative' Freemason in Anderson's *1738 Constitutions*[142] may have been an inaccuracy, embroidery of his operative role or – more probably – an intentional blurring of the line between pre-and post 1720s Freemasonry in order to emphasise the purported antiquity of the Craft. However, if Wren *had* been admitted to the Acception, there is an explanation for the absence of publicity that would be consistent with the events that followed.

Were Wren and Goodricke to have been members of the Acception, Desaguliers, Anderson and their contemporaries may have wished to gloss over the subject. An involvement with the Acception and the London Company of Masons would have undermined the *bona fides* of the newly reinvented form of English Freemasonry. A public and formal recognition of the precedence of the Acception could have led to a question as to whether the Company of Masons had jurisdiction over Grand Lodge and 'Free and Accepted' Masonry. Rather than potentially undermine the authority and diminish the attraction of Grand Lodge, it may have been considered more appropriate broadly to ignore the Company of Masons.

The argument is persuasive and reinforced by a reference in Michael Leapman's *Inigo: The Troubled Life of Inigo Jones*. Leapman noted that Nicholas Stone wrote that Inigo Jones 'was Grand Master of the Freemasons from 1607 until 1618 and again from 1636 until his death in 1652', and that 'the relevant document is believed to have been destroyed in 1720.'[143] The *1738 Constitutions* make the same point: 'several very valuable Manuscripts . . . one writ by Mr Nicholas Stone . . . were too hastily burnt'. Had such a document existed and been destroyed in 1720, its destruction would provide strong anecdotal evidence of a desire to draw a line between 'Free and Accepted Masonry' and its relatively recent past.

> To fill up this Page, it is thought not amifs to infert here a Paragraph from an old Record of *Mafons*, viz. The Company of Mafons, *being otherwife termed* FREE MASONS; *of auncient Staunding and good Reckonning, by means of affable and kind Meetings diverfe Tymes, and as a loving Brotherhood fhould ufe to doe, did frequent this* mutual Affembly *in the Tyme of* King HENRY V. *the 12th Year of his moft gracious* Reign. And the faid Record defcribing a *Coat of Arms*, much the fame with *That* of the LONDON COMPANY of *Freemen* Mafons, it is generally believ'd that the faid *Company* is defcended of the ancient *Fraternity*; and that in former Times no Man was made *Free* of that *Company* until he was inftall'd in fome *Lodge* of *Free* and *Accepted Mafons*, as a neceffary Qualification. But that laudable Practice feems to have been long in Diffuetude. The Brethren in foreign Parts have alfo difcover'd that feveral noble and ancient *Societies* and *Orders* of Men have derived their *Charges* and *Regulations* from the *Free Mafons*, (which are now the moft ancient *Order* upon Earth) and perhaps were originally all Members too of the. faid ancient and worfhipful *Fraternity*. But this will more fully appear in due time.

The construction is supported by there being only a single reference to the Company of Masons in the *1723 Constitutions* (reproduced above), and that almost by way of an aside.[144]

Other than acting as a 'space filler', we don't know if there was any ulterior reason for the inclusion of this paragraph in the *Constitutions*. Perhaps the answer lies in the observation that 'no Man was made Free of that Company until he was installed in some Lodge of Free and Accepted Masons, as a necessary Qualification': the words validate the new Freemasonry and provide additional historical legitimacy. The Acception ceased to exist after the formal incorporation of the London Company in 1677 and the status of the Company itself declined thereafter following the demise of its monopoly under Charles II and the restrictions placed on City livery companies more generally by James II.[145] Although there is an element of elegance in Prescott's comment that 'it is tempting to assume that . . . the formation of a Grand Lodge of Free and Accepted Masons was in effect a revival of the Acception',[146] the evidence does not support the parallel and the dissimilarities between the two organisations undermine the argument that one was as a natural extension of the other.

ROBERT PLOT

Masonic historians have used Robert Plot's seventeenth-century accounts of Freemasonry in the same cause as Wren's alleged initiation: to substantiate the argument in favour of a gradual transition from the medieval working guild to the modern lodge.[147] Plot (1640–1696) graduated from Oxford University and later taught there as Professor of Chemistry, appointed in 1683. He was the first Keeper of the Ashmolean, serving from 1683 until 1690, approved and supervised by Ashmole.[148]

Plot was elected FRS in 1677 and became the Society's second secretary. He edited the *Philosophical Transactions* from 1682 until 1684 and was a Council member in 1680, 1682–3, 1687–88, 1692 and 1694.[149] Following the publication of the *Natural History of Oxfordshire*,[150] he completed the *Natural History of Staffordshire* in 1686, and it was in the latter book that his references to Freemasonry appear. Plot's connections to Ashmole and

Dugdale went beyond academia and the Royal Society to include alchemy, antiquarianism and chivalry: Plot was appointed Registrar of the Court of Chivalry in 1687, Historiographer Royal in 1688 and Mowbray Herald Extraordinary in 1694, where he worked under Dugdale.[151]

Although there is no evidence that Plot was a Freemason, his access to at least one copy of the *Old Charges* and his appraisal of the 'York legend' suggests that he was knowledgeable and prepared to be critical.[152] His description of Freemasonry over several paragraphs (two of which are summarised below) added considerably to the detail set out by Aubrey and Ashmole:

> To these add the Customs relating to the County, whereof they have one, of admitting Men into the Society of Freemasons, that in the moorlands . . . seems to be of greater request, than anywhere else, though I find the Custom spread more or less over the Nation; for here I found persons of the most eminent quality, that did not disdain to be of this Fellowship. Nor indeed need they, were of it that Antiquity and honour, that is pretended in a large parchment volume they have amongst them, containing the History and Rules of the craft of masonry . . .

> Into which Society when any are admitted, they call a meeting (or Lodg as they term it in some place) which must consist of at least 5 or 6 of the Ancients of the Order, whom the candidats present with gloves and so likewise to their wives ad entertain with a collation according to the Custom of the place. This ended, they proceed to the admission of them, which chiefly consists in the communication of certain secret signs, whereby they are known to one another over the Nation, by which means they have maintenance whither ever they travel: for if any man appear though altogether unknown that can shew any of these signs to a Fellow of the Society, whom they call an accepted mason, he is obliged presently to come to him . . . to know his pleasure and assist him.[153]

Plot's comments allow a deduction that Freemasonry in the Midlands by 'persons of . . . quality' was not uncommon; that the *Old Charges* – 'large parchment volumes' – were in regular use; and that ritual and benevolence were relatively widespread, at least in Staffordshire. Although Gould and other commentators have queried the extent to which any reliance can be placed on Plot's account,[154] apparently confirmatory evidence appeared thirty years later in an article in the Whiggish *Post Man and the Historical Account* quoting *inter alia* from an 'Assembly . . . held in 1663'.[155]

Following a précis of the *Old Charges*, the *Post Man* printed three pieces on Freemasonry in late July and August 1722.[156] The last was titled *The Conclusion of the History of the Society of Freemasons*; it was followed by a second section – the *Apprentices' Charge*. The series of articles were published at around the time that the *1723 Constitutions* were released, and they should probably be viewed in that context.

The following passage is particularly significant in that it reflects and supports many of Plot's observations:

Additional Orders and Constitutions made and agreed upon at a General Assembly held at _____, the 8th Day of December, 1663
  i. That no Person, of what Degree soever, be accepted a Free Mason, unless he shall have a Lodge of five Free Masons at the least, whereof one must be a Master or Warden of that Limit or Division where such Lodge shall be kept, and another to be a Workman of the Trade of Free Masonry.
  ii. That no Person hereafter shall be accepted a Freemason, but such as are able Body, honest Parentage, good Reputation, and Observers of the Laws of the Land.
  iii. That no Person hereafter, which shall be accepted a Free Mason, shall be admitted into any Lodge or Assembly, until he hath brought a Certificate of the Time and Place of his Acception from the Lodge that accepted him.

The first point, that at least one of the Freemasons at an 'acceptance' must be 'a Workman of the Trade of Freemasonry', was a record of a practice current through to the second and third decades of the eighteenth century. It was maintained even within the Horn, the most influential and least operative of the four lodges that later founded the Grand Lodge of England, where the gentlemanly stonemason, William Woodman, was among the members.

The second point provided a summary of the *Charges*, which were set out in full in the article; and those that followed, four through seven, were similarly uncontentious. There was however one exception:

That for the future the said Society, Company and Fraternity of Freemasons shall be regulated and governed by one Master and as many Wardens as the sad Company shall think fit to chuse at every yearly General Assembly.

The words 'for the future' suggest that this was a contemporary insertion. Although there was no national organisation for Freemasons in the seventeenth century, it was a probable objective of its eighteenth-century architects that Grand Lodge be established 'for the future' as Freemasonry's governing body. Similarly, the statement permitting the selection of 'as many Wardens as the said Company shall think fit to chuse' provides a justification for extending patronage: it would have helped to have been able to refer to a precedent that indicated that the position had been such since at least the prior century. The remaining *Additional Orders* and the *Apprentices' Charge* are otherwise broadly in line with earlier versions of the *Old Charges*.

The *Post Man*'s three articles were designed to achieve historical legitimacy for the new Freemasonry, an argument supported by the content and tone of later press comment, and it is useful to speculate how the articles came to appear and how their placement may have been arranged. A little can be inferred from the background to the paper's establishment and its pro-

Whig bias. The *Post Man* had been spun out of Richard Baldwin's Whig *Post Boy*. The *Post Man*'s editor and principal writer had been John (Jean Lespinasse) de Fonvive, a Huguenot émigré. He was one of the best known and most popular and successful newspapermen of the period, reputed to earn some £600 per year from the *Post Man* alone:[157]

> as his News is early and good, so his style is excellent. . . . his remarks witness he knows how to soar to a pitch of fineness when he pleases . . . In a word, The Post-Man . . . out-flies The Post-Master, Post-Boy, Daily Courant . . . Fonvive is the glory and mirror of News-Writers.[158]

Fonvive was naturalised in 1702.[159] He had settled in London after the Revocation of the Edict of Nantes and became an integral part of the Huguenot community: elected a church elder at Hungerford Market, he later became a trustee of the Huguenot Hospital, *La Providence*, and well known as a philanthropist.[160] Fonvive was also close to the Whig political establishment who were eager to adopt him more formally. He was offered the position of editor of the official *London Gazette*, a role equivalent to head of the government's propaganda machine, but ultimately rejected the position: it paid insufficiently compared with his newspaper publishing and, perhaps, carried less prestige. As the Whiggist John Dunton (1659–1732) noted, 'Fonvive is so wise and knowing that a man would think Nature had made all the rest of mankind in jest'[161] and '[although] the *Postboy* is best for the English and Spanish news, the *Daily Courant* is the best critic, the *English Post* is the best collector, the *London Gazette* has the best authority . . . the *Postman* is the best for everything'.[162]

Fonvive's editorials gave him a platform as a representative for the Huguenot community. Itamar Raban noted that he frequently 'commented on the Huguenots' continuing loyalty to the "legal" king of France, the criteria for citizenship in society, and the proper relations between ruler and citizen'.[163] Fonvive's perspective was important politically – and not simply from a Whig standpoint. His views and the way in which he expressed them had influence within the Huguenot community, and his ideas and comments raised issues that were integral to the newly established Society of Free and Accepted Masons and to its *Charges* and *Regulations*. Although Fonvive had retired from an active editorial role by 1721, the *Post Man* could still be regarded as a natural outlet for the placement of such an article.

There is no record of Fonvive being linked directly to Freemasonry. However, Fonvive and Desaguliers would have known each other. Both were prominent in the Huguenot community and each shared a connection to the French church at Hungerford Market where Fonvive had been elected an 'elder'. The church was one of four that had formed an operational union in the 1690s and been staffed by a small pool of clergy that included Desaguliers' father.[164]

Richard Rawlinson

Freemasonry and its philosophical and moral ideals were outlined at some length in Rawlinson's *Preface* to the 1719 and later editions of Ashmole's *Antiquities of Berkshire*. Rawlinson (1690–1755), was an Oxford-educated antiquary, scholar and Nonjuring cleric.[165] Although closely associated with Freemasonry – not least through his collection of Masonic miscellanea now part of the Rawlinson Manuscripts collection at the Bodleian,[166] he became a Freemason only a decade or so later in or around 1727 after his studies and travel in continental Europe. Rawlinson visited France, the Low Countries, Italy, Sicily and Malta. He studied at Utrecht (1719), Leiden (1719) and Padua (1722), and returned to Britain in 1726.

Initiated into Freemasonry in 1726 or 1727, Rawlinson embraced the Craft and by the 1730s was Master of the lodge meeting at the Oxford Arms in Ludgate Street, Warden of a second, and a member of two more, respectively, the Rose Tavern in Cheapside, Three Kings in Spitalfields and St. Paul's Head in Ludgate Street.[167] He was committed and connected and it was not coincidental that he was appointed a Grand Steward in 1734.

Rawlinson's *ODNB* entry notes his editorship of several books, including Aubrey's *Natural History and Antiquities of Surrey* and Ashmole's *Memoirs* in editions published by Edmund Curll (16__?–1743).[168] Curll, a controversial bookseller, was aware of the commercial value of topicality and notoriety.[169] Rawlinson's *Preface* was written just as interest in the subject was beginning to develop in London but was unoriginal and mirrored Aubrey's quote from Dugdale:

> Kings themselves have not disdain'd to enter themselves into this Society, the original Foundation of which is said to be as high as the reign of King Henry III, when the Pope granted a Bull Patent, or Diploma, to a particular Company of Italian Masons and architects to travel all over Europe.[170]

And Rawlinson's observations on mutual assistance were taken from the same Curll-derived source:

> Certain Signales and watch Words known to them alone . . . when any of the fall into Decay, the Brotherhood is to relieve him'.

Rawlinson was elected to the Society of Antiquaries in 1727, proposed by fellow Freemason William Jones of the Queen's Head lodge in Hollis Street. He became an avid collector of Masonic miscellanea only in his later years and any contribution to Masonic research as early as 1719 would have been improbable. Although Rawlinson had latent Jacobite sympathies and Nonjurist beliefs that led eventually to a breach with colleagues at the Royal Society and Society of Antiquaries, his Masonic life was unimpaired. Indeed, until the late 1730s, it represented a practical example of Masonic latitudinarianism:

to oblige them to that Religion in which all Men agree, leaving their particular Opinions to themselves . . . to be Good men and True, or Men of Honor and Honesty, by whatever Denomination or Persuasion they may be distinguished.[171]

THE ANCIENT LODGE AT YORK

As with Chester Freemasonry, the records of the 'Ancient Lodge at York' – also known as the Grand Lodge at York – point to a membership that included a high proportion of gentlemen and a leadership closely linked to the city's corporation and political élite.[172] Yorkshire Freemasonry was based on a long and relatively unbroken tradition reaching back several centuries. Had Desaguliers and his colleagues' actions in and control of English Grand Lodge been trivial in impact and un-related to their political, military and professional connections, the 'Grand Lodge' at York could have been a valid contender for Masonic leadership in England. But notwithstanding its longevity and the political weight of York and Yorkshire county politics, there were several probable reasons why York lacked the motivation, resonance and national influence of the London-based Grand Lodge of England.

Perhaps crucially, Yorkshire Masonry was largely disassociated from the scientific Enlightenment epitomised by Desaguliers, Folkes, Martin Clare and others, and the public and private influence and authority that such an intellectual association was able to exert. Yorkshire Masonry was led principally by provincial politicians and local worthies, some Catholic, whose Tory politics was generally anti-Walpole and although not always overtly anti-Hanoverian had only a limited and negative influence on the national stage. In contrast, English Grand Lodge benefited from the presence of senior aristocrats at its titular head who were close to the government and the Crown.

York's distance from the Court and the principal seats of political power may also have reduced its political weight, most particularly since its leaders did not hold national office. As Schwartz commented, 'nobody aspiring to national influence could stay away from [London] for too long'.[173] Another factor was that Yorkshire's leaders were bound to the past in terms of their view of Freemasonry as a social club. In contrast, Desaguliers, Folkes, Payne, Cowper and others at Grand Lodge in London, had the vision to perceive it as a vehicle for the transmission of new ideas, and the discipline and determination to pursue their objectives. Finally, below the aristocratic figureheads, Grand Lodge in London and senior lodges such as the Horn, Westminster, and the Rummer at Charing Cross were populated by officials with political influence and government connections.

A list of Past Grand Masters of York was set out in a letter in 1778 from the then Grand Secretary of York to the Lodge of Antiquity in London:

> In compliance with your request to be satisfied of the existence of a Grand Lodge at York previous to the establishment of that at London, I have

inspected an Original Minute Book of this Grand Lodge beginning at 1705 and ending in 1734 from which I have extracted the names of the Grand Masters during that period as follows . . . [174]

One of the most prominent of York's early eighteenth-century 'Grand Masters'[175] was Robert Benson (1676–1731), GMY 1707. Benson provides an elegant illustration of the lack of effective influence after the Hanoverian succession. Benson's principal links to aristocratic society were through his stepfather, Sir Henry Belasyse,[176] and through his marriage to the eldest daughter of Heneage Finch (1649–1719), who had been made Baron Guernsey by Queen Anne and was later created 1st Earl of Aylseford. Benson was Tory MP for Thetford (1702), and later York (1705–13), and appointed to the Treasury under Robert Harley (1661–1724). He was promoted to Chancellor of the Exchequer (1711–13), and made a Privy Councillor when Harley became Earl of Oxford. Created Baron Bingley in 1713, Benson was disliked by many of his fellow peers, lost office after the Hanoverian succession, and was subsequently out of favour as an opponent to Walpole's ministry.[177] He returned to office only briefly in 1730 having spoken in favour of the Treaty of Seville[178] and was appointed Treasurer to the Household, a sinecure by Royal Warrant and paying c. £1,200 per annum.

Benson was succeeded by Sir William Robinson (1655–1736), GMY 1708–10, a prosperous local silk merchant. Two members of his family had served as MPs twice in the seventeenth century and twice in the sixteenth. In keeping with his position as a local dignitary, Robinson was appointed High Sheriff of Yorkshire in 1689. His baronetcy, which had lapsed at the death of his uncle, Sir Thomas Robinson, was revived in 1690. Robinson was appointed Lord Mayor in 1700, and sat uncontested as Tory MP for Northallerton (1689–95) and for the City of York (1698–1722). Between 1705 and 1713, his fellow MP was Robert Benson.[179] Robinson married the wealthy Mary Aislabie of Studley Park; his brother-in-law, John Aislabie, was Tory MP for Ripon and, in 1718, Chancellor of the Exchequer.

Robinson's successor was Sir Walter Hawksworth, GMY 1711–12, Tory MP for York in 1714 and High Sheriff in 1721, who was succeeded by Sir George Tempest of Tong Hall, GMY, 1713, then Charles Fairfax, GMY 1714–19, a Jacobite sympathiser. While President of the lodge at York, Fairfax was one of several leading Catholics summoned by the Mayor and city aldermen and asked to make a declaration of loyalty in favour of the Hanoverian succession and to give up their horses and any arms in their household. Others summoned included Benson and at least eight other Catholic families connected to York Freemasonry.[180] Fairfax refused the request. He was fined, imprisoned and released only in November 1715 after the Jacobites' unconditional surrender. Pointedly, his political allegiance met with local Masonic approval and he remained GMY for a further four years.

Fairfax was replaced by Hawksworth, who was reappointed from 1720 until 1723 and succeeded in 1724 by Charles Bathurst, a landowner and Tory MP for Richmond. Bathurst, also GMY 1726–28, was appointed High

Sheriff of Yorkshire in 1727. Edward Thompson, GMY 1729–32, a merchant and a Commissioner of Land Revenue for Ireland, served as a Tory MP for York from 1722–42.[181]

The contrast with the politically well connected, affluent and influential pro-Hanoverian Whig aristocrats who provided the nominal leadership at the summit of the Grand Lodge of England, and their coterie of supporters from the Royal Society, the judiciary, the military and the upper ranks of the London professions, is apparent. As with Chester, York Freemasonry principally represents an example of local fraternal networking allied to dining clubs. Functionally, Yorkshire Masonry failed to break new ground and there was an absence of any overt philosophical agenda. A press report in the *Leeds Mercury* for 16 January 1721, quoted by Barker-Cryer, which described a Masonic meeting in Pontefract, underlines the point:

> the Lodge consisting of about thirty persons in Number walk'd to several of their Brothers' Houses, having on white Gloves and Aprons, Music before them etc . . . Afterwards returning to the Gallery of the Lodge Room, they drank . . . loyal Healths. Money was thrown to the Crowd by Handfuls and the Night concluded with Illuminations.[182]

In this sense, the Ancient Lodge at York stood in contrast to the emergent Grand Lodge of England and to the new London-based Free and Accepted Masonry whose reputation and ritual was developed in a fundamentally different direction under the aegis of its new management team. Indeed, the Grand Lodge at York acknowledges the fact directly on its website, in which it details its development from 1705:

> the new organization in the South . . . under the denomination of The Grand Lodge of England . . . on account of its situation, being encouraged by some of the principal nobility, soon acquired consequence and reputation; while [York] . . . seemed gradually to decline.

LATE SEVENTEENTH CENTURY LONDON FREEMASONRY

Explaining and excusing the virtual absence of speculative Masonic lodges in London in the late seventeenth and early eighteenth centuries, James Anderson noted that 'in the South the Lodges were more and more disused . . . and the annual Assembly . . . not duly attended'.[183] However, Anderson qualified his comment slightly: although 'particular lodges were not so frequent and mostly occasional in the South', the exception were those located 'in or near the Places where great Works were carried on'.[184]

That London Freemasonry had become moribund appears to be substantiated by the absence of any meaningful documentary evidence to the contrary. However, despite Anderson's assertion, there is no independent evidence that there were any material exceptions. In particular, there are no contemporary records that suggest that a speculative London lodge, ostensibly established by the Whig banker and politician Sir Robert Clayton (1629–1707), existed at St. Thomas's Hospital 'to advise the Governours about the best Design of rebuilding that Hospital'. Clayton was president of St. Thomas's Hospital and responsible for its reconstruction. Thomas Cartwright (1635–1703), the architect, was employed by Clayton for that purpose. Nor is there evidence that other 'speculative' (as opposed to working) lodges operated 'in Piccadilly over against St. James's Church, one near Westminster Abby, another near Covent-Garden, one in Holborn, one on Tower-Hill', or elsewhere.[185] In the same vein, despite Andersen's statement, there is a similar absence of evidence that 'the king [William of Orange] was privately made a Free Mason', or that he 'approved' of the choice of Wren as 'Grand Master'.

In itself, this would not normally be a substantial issue. Anderson's 'history' and record of Masonic events was embroidered for a purpose. Unfortunately, a number of scholars have taken Anderson's comments at face value. Jacob, for example, has declared that 'even the official histories of speculative Freemasonry acknowledge that the earliest known lodge in London, of a totally speculative variety, was headed in the 1690s by . . . Clayton'. The comment was made in support of her argument that 'the transformation of operative Masonry into speculative may have been one of the by-products of the Whig exclusionists search for artisan allies after 1679'. The analysis is over complex and more probable arguments exist for the development of speculative Freemasonry.[186]

We have seen how the economic and social changes that followed the outbreak of plague in 1348 led to the transformation of the guilds from quasi-religious orders to embryonic collective bargaining organisations, and how the guilds thereafter evolved to become more socially based organisations that were gradually absorbed into provincial social and civic structures. There is no need for historians to argue about whether operative and non-operative Freemasonry co-existed before the formation of the Grand Lodge of England. They did, albeit to a limited extent and effect and within the relatively uncomplicated context of provincial networking, politicking and socialising. And although some antiquaries may have been attracted to Freemasonry by its medieval *Old Charges* and oral ritual, this did not create a 'speculative' form of Freemasonry. In brief, there was no unique thread that joined pre-mediaeval and mediaeval Freemasonry to what was to develop in the eighteenth century. And if there was no 'continuum' underlying Masonic development, then there is a need to analyse the determinants and catalysts that caused English Freemasonry to develop so radically and so significantly in the 1720s.

CHAPTER TWO

John Theophilus Desaguliers: Homo Masonicus

The central argument is that John Theophilus Desaguliers (1683–1744), jointly with colleagues within the orbit of Grand Lodge, altered English Freemasonry fundamentally to produce an entity that reflected and reinforced the philosophical, intellectual and economic transformation then under way in eighteenth-century England. The organisation and its ethos were promoted actively by members of the Whig aristocracy and their efforts were rewarded with extensive press coverage. Principally as a function of this powerful imprimatur, together with its attractive fraternalism, embroidered faux history and its credentials as a partial derivative of the scientific Enlightenment, Freemasonry became fashionable. By the mid- and late 1720s, its membership included aristocrats, politicians, soldiers, lawyers, physicians and other professionals, affluent merchants and tradesmen, and a substantial portion of London's scientific and antiquary communities.

The number of lodges within the jurisdiction of Grand Lodge increased almost vertiginously from the founding four in 1717 to over 60 in 1725 and to more than 100 in 1730. Although certain lodges failed to survive for more than a few years, by the late 1730s, the Grand Lodge of England had extended its reach from the eastern seaboard of the Americas to India – from Boston and Savannah to Bengal. And by the end of the century, the number of lodges that acknowledged London's authority had expanded to around 500, a figure exclusive of derivative and competing Masonic lodges formed under the jurisdiction of Irish, Scottish, French, German, Dutch, Swedish, and other national governing bodies established in the wake of the Grand Lodge of England.

No analysis of eighteenth-century English Freemasonry should be divorced from the contemporary macro environment of economic, political, religious and social change. But to the extent that Freemasonry's transformation can be viewed as having been influenced substantially by Desaguliers, it is constructive to explore those factors that moulded him. A first step is to chart the background and provide a structure to Desaguliers' influence as one of the pivotal figures in the 1720s and early 1730s, a short but key period in eighteenth-century English Freemasonry. His influence was both a function of his rank – he was elected the third Grand Master of Grand Lodge in 1719 and appointed Deputy Grand Master in 1722, 1723 and 1725

– and of his wider activities, including his Mastership or membership of several influential lodges including the Horn, Bear and Harrow, and the 'French' lodge – Solomon's Temple.

Examination proceeds from Desaguliers' flight from persecution in France and childhood in London among the émigré Huguenot community with its self-preserving support for the Hanoverian *status quo*, belief in education and promotion of latitudinarian religious tolerance. His Oxford education, introduction to Newtonian science and subsequent return to London are explored, as is his fellowship of the Royal Society, subsequent work as its Demonstrator and Curator and, perhaps most importantly, his position as one of Newton's most effective proselytisers and acolytes.

Desaguliers financed himself and his family via public scientific lectures and through scientific commissions from wealthy patrons, particularly James Brydges, Duke of Chandos. Both spoke to his financial insecurity and at the same time opened avenues for Masonic proselytising, embraced by Desaguliers as a means by which both his and the Huguenot community's philosophical, religious, political and social objectives could be advanced.

Displacement and Poverty: An Insecure Childhood

they make it a point of Religion to destroy Protestants, over whom that Church pretends to have a sovereign and absolute Dominion; . . . thousands of French Protestants now in England confirm the Truth [and] are fled from thence to avoid the . . . insupportable violence.[1]

Desaguliers was born on 12 March 1683 at Aytré, a village near La Rochelle. The date was recorded in a family bible in which his father, Jean Desaguliers ('Jean Desaguliers'), and Desaguliers successively recorded domestic family events. The bible, quoted by Rev. David Agnew in *French Protestant Exiles*, and by other sources, appears no longer to be extant.

Jean Desaguliers had served as Aytré's Pasteur but was forced to flee France in late 1682: a sermon preached to his congregation had been reported to the Catholic authorities as unlawful. The last entry in Aytré's church register that refers to him was recorded on 24 August 1682. Having left France, Jean Desaguliers journeyed to London where on 8 November 1682, he was ordained a deacon in the Church of England at Fulham Palace. The ordination was undertaken by Henry Compton (1631–1713), the politically connected Bishop of London, the youngest son of the 2nd Earl of Northampton. Compton both then and later played a prominent role in uniting Protestant dissenters with the established church.[2]

Jean Desaguliers remained in London only briefly and in December, the Bishop of Winchester, George Morley (1598–1684), granted him a licence to serve on Guernsey.[3] Although there appears to be no record of Jean Desaguliers having obtained a living on the island, there exists a note of his presence on 16 May 1683 at Guernsey's Ecclesiastical Court at a session devoted to the abjuration of priests.[4] Huguenots had been escaping to the Channel Islands for many years and St. Peter Port, Guernsey's capital, housed Huguenot families who had settled as early as the mid-sixteenth century. However, for most Huguenots, as for Jean Desaguliers and later his family, the town would represent only a relatively temporary home before they moved on. With its French-speaking Protestant merchants and solid trade routes, the island offered an effective escape route to England, the Low Countries and the New World.

Jean Desaguliers' wife, Marguerite Thomas la Chapelle, left France with her baby son to join her husband in Guernsey between 1683 and 1684.[5] This was the period of the Dragonnades: the intimidatory billeting of mounted Dragoons on Huguenot families instigated by Louis XIV some years earlier that caused outrage in England and across Protestant Europe. The date is earlier than many scholars have appreciated and pre-dated the Revocation of the Edict of Nantes.[6] The family remained on the island in probable penury for several years until leaving for the mainland and London. A return to France was not feasible. Despite the privation and risks, including that of execution if caught, the Revocation had triggered a Huguenot exodus with an estimated 200,000 fleeing France.[7] The contemporary press and literature illustrated the religious, physical and financial imperatives that drove them, from forced conversion – 'que l'on a trainé par force au catéchisme',[8] to penury or death – 'being accused, with some neighbours of his of having had [Divine Service] in his country house; he was condemned to be hanged and his house demolished, and his woods destroyed'.[9]

Already ordained in the Church of England, Jean Desaguliers obtained an appointment in 1692 as one of five deacons practicing at the French Anglican church in Swallow Street.[10] The conformist French churches of Hungerford Market, Soho Square, Jewin Street and St. James' and Swallow Street had two years earlier agreed to cooperate and pool their ministers, paying them from a common fund. And as a result, Jean Desaguliers served concurrently at La Patente church in Soho and at Le Carré in Berwick Street.[11]

The ministers and deacons at the four churches received only a nominal stipend, pay being supplemented by the congregation in return for their services at baptisms and marriages. Without this, poverty knocked. Unfortunately work was limited, and Jean Desaguliers officiated on only three occasions at La Patente and a mere once at Le Carré.[12] Supplementary work was also scant at Swallow Street and although Jean Desaguliers officiated at a baptism on 12 September 1692[13] and succeeded Jérémie Majou as Lecteur in April 1693,[14] he was engaged less than twice a year in the four years to 1696: on seven occasions out of some thirty-seven marriages and baptisms in total, the last being 7 June 1696.[15]

With such a meagre level of activity, the four churches were able to provide little more than a subsistence wage. Indeed, the Swallow Street church regularly had to find additional funds to supplement the income of their minsters. The church register records one occasion on which the four ministers were given £10 in compensation for the absence of regular pay: 'de trouver quelque rafraîchissement qu'il est juste de donner à Messieurs les Pasteurs de cette Eglise qui n'ont rien receu depuis plus de six mois'.[16]

As a child, Desaguliers is likely to have felt such financial insecurity acutely and been aware of the widespread poverty among others in the Huguenot community. Around 50,000 refugees had fled to England in the years immediately after the Revocation, of which some 30–40,000 had settled in London, representing around 6% of the population and a higher proportion of the labour force. Notwithstanding that London had been devastated by plague two decades earlier, the Huguenot influx placed considerable downward pressure on labour rates and many refugees found it difficult to obtain reasonably paid work. The consequential strain on the churches and their relatively sparse funds, and the full extent and nature of Huguenot poverty, was set out clearly in church records and in the press: 'the Lamentations, and Sighs of the Refugees throughout all Europe, has in a great Measure made us sensible of their sufferings'.[17]

In the years that followed the Glorious Revolution, the English establishment sought to ensure that Huguenot refugees received tangible financial support.[18] It was expressed through general parish collections across the country, with over £90,000 donated nationally from collection plates and through contributions from the Crown, the aristocracy and parliament, with £39,000 being donated from the Civil List among other large individual donations.[19] To place such numbers in perspective, Phyllis Deane and W.A. Cole suggested that average annual income in 1688 was less than £10 per person, aggregate government expenditure was around £3 million, and national expenditure on the Poor Rate was around £600,000 as a whole.[20]

Parish collections and parliamentary support were insufficient to provide effective universal support to the thousands of refugees entering England and many émigrés turned to their local communities and to the numerous charity committees and special collections established by their churches.[21] As a frontline deacon, Jean Desaguliers, perhaps with his young son alongside him, would have taken an active part in the process of gathering charitable funding and the weekly allocation and distribution of grants and pensions within the *quartier* to which he would have been assigned. Indeed, poverty appears to have been an enduring issue for Jean Desaguliers and his family. The accounts of the Royal Bounty Fund, published periodically from 1705, record 'Sara Desaiguillers' receiving £9 0s 0d in 1705 and £10 0s 0d in 1707; and Marguerite Ferrier, the daughter of Henry Ferrier and 'Marguerite Desaiguilliers', a 'minister's widow', receiving £6 6s 6d in 1705, £2 9s 0d in 1707 and 17s in 1722.

Despite their relative deprivation, the rise in the number of Huguenots settling in Leicester Fields and Soho in the decade after the Revocation was matched by an increase in the number of competing places of worship. By 1700, fourteen new French churches had been consecrated: seven conformist churches, including the popular *Des Grecs* in Hog Lane, and seven non-conformist. Perhaps because of this the attractions of the church in

Swallow Street declined and the area was marked as 'a part of the town where Dissenters are very little in fashion'.[22]

Swallow Street had faced severe financial difficulties as early as 1696 when 'la Compagnie considérant que cette Eglise déchoit sensiblement tous les jours', and whether the church 'est chargée de debtes considérables dont elle paye un gros interest'.[23] Although the Minute books record nothing after September 1696, the prospect of further financial degeneration and years of low earnings probably encouraged or obliged Jean Desaguliers to leave Swallow Street to establish his 'French School' in Islington. Indeed, the church at Swallow Street did decline further and in 1709 the building was acquired by a congregation of Presbyterians. Coincidentally, their minister was the Rev. James Anderson.[24]

The move to Islington would have represented more than a geographic shift across London. London's Huguenots were divided into conformist and non-conformist communities centred on the Anglican Savoy and French Protestant Threadneedle Street churches, respectively. Although anglicised ritual might not have had an immediate or obvious appeal to Huguenot émigrés, the West End churches that used it had the arguable advantage of being better connected to the establishment through Henry Compton and other prominent members of the aristocracy who provided funding, including Atholl, Derby, Devonshire, Newcastle, Ormonde, Ossory and Stafford.[25] However, despite differences in ritual and occasional clerical schisms, both communities shared a common anxiety and a profound sense of political and religious insecurity. Huguenot churches both east and west made overt protestations of allegiance to the Crown. Given the tensions with France and their relative insularity, these are likely to have been both genuine and born of insecurity. The English government's 'Eminent Zeal for the Protestant Religion, and the tender Compassion and Charity . . . shewn to multitudes of French Refugiez, of all Ranks and Degrees, who have been forced to fly hither for . . . Protection and Relief', was neither perfect nor permanent.[26] Moreover, the 'astonishing Barbarity [with which] the formerly Flourishing Churches of France have been ruined and destroyed' such that 'many . . . miserable Innocents [had to] run to find Sanctuary' remained a constant threat and a present danger.[27]

The negotiations preceding the Treaty of Utrecht in 1713 had aroused some hope among the Huguenot émigrés that the Protestant powers might exert influence on Louis XIV to roll back Huguenot religious persecution, even if recognition of their faith was not a probable option. Henri de Mirmand, the leading Swiss Huguenot, acted as their advocate. But Mirmand was unsuccessful, writing to London's French churches on 2 June 1713 to advise of his failure and recommend patience, but to no avail.[28] Matters deteriorated and eighteen months later in 1715, the Huguenot community – and the newly installed George I and his Whig ministry – came under threat with what de Ruvigny, Lord Galway, termed 'de l'invasion d'un prétendant papist': the Jacobite Rising.

Both the Hanoverian and the Huguenot establishment took the Jacobite threat seriously. In a letter to the West Street Church, Lord Galway asked apprehensively 'combien il y auroit de gens de votre église capables de prendre les armes en cas de nécessité?'. And with the government concerned about the possibility of papist spies, London's French churches were instructed to monitor and report on any non-Huguenot members admitted to their congregation.[29]

Religious and political insecurity was a constant theme within the Huguenot community in London and elsewhere. Notwithstanding the Jacobite setback in 1715, four years later, the Pretender and his supporters found a new ally in Count Giulio Alberoni, a cardinal, favourite of and leading minister to Philip V of Spain. This and other potential threats wove fear into the Huguenot psyche and underpinned a self-interested loyalty to the Hanoverian Crown and its successive Whig governments. The position would remain unvarying over the next three decades. Indeed, Robin Gwynn, referring to the Jacobite rising of 1745, noted that the City of London's leading citizens in a demonstration of fidelity to the Crown offered upwards of 2,000 men to fight the Jacobite threat. He recorded that a majority of the names were Huguenot: 'in all some three-fifths of those who promised men had foreign names, and they promised about twice as many men as the English manufacturers signing the same declaration'.[30]

Oxford University, John Keill, and a Newtonian Education

In common with other émigré influxes over the centuries, the Huguenots were motivated and entrepreneurial. Hard work and a drive to succeed and to influence were key attributes instilled in their children. Desaguliers was no exception: studying with his father, assisting him at his French School and, after his father's death in 1699,[31] continuing his education at Bishop Vesey's school in Sutton Coldfield.[32]

An obviously intelligent student, Desaguliers was admitted in 1705 to Christ Church as a servitor scholar to read divinity and experimental natural philosophy. The largest college in Oxford, Christ Church was High Church Anglican, the college chapel also serving as cathedral for the diocese. Audrey Carpenter has argued that Desaguliers probably benefited from the patronage of John Wilkins, a trustee of Bishop Vesey's school, whose son also attended Christ Church as a gentleman scholar. The difference in their respective social and financial position was substantial. Samuel Johnson, a servitor scholar in 1728, purportedly commented: 'the difference ... is this, we are men of wit and no fortune and they are men of fortune and no wit'.[33]

Desaguliers studied under John Keill (1671–1721), a 34 year-old Episcopalian from Presbyterian Scotland and, like Desaguliers, something of an Oxford outsider.[34] Keill had read mathematics and natural philosophy at Edinburgh under David Gregory (1661–1708), an early Newtonian, and Keill had followed Gregory to Balliol when the latter took the Savilian Chair of Astronomy in 1691.[35] Incorporated MA in 1694, Keill was subsequently appointed lecturer in experimental philosophy at Hart Hall where he taught one of the earliest courses on Newton's natural philosophy[36] and developed an innovative method of presenting and demonstrating Newton's theories using practical experiments and scientific apparatus, rather than pure mathematics. In his *Preface* to *A Course of Experimental Philosophy* (London, 1734), Desaguliers commented that Keill was 'the first who . . . taught Natural Philosophy by Experiments in a mathematical manner: for he laid down very simple Propositions which he prov'd by Experiments, and from those he deduc'd others more compound, which he still confirm'd by Experiments'.[37]

Despite his intellectual brilliance, Keill was unable to obtain academic preferment at Oxford. Although he had deputised for Sir Thomas Millington (1628–1704),[38] the Sedleian Professor of Natural Philosophy, and had published his Newtonian lecture course, been elected FRS and become a regular contributor to the Society's *Philosophical Transactions*, Keill lacked connections and failed in his attempt to succeed Millington.[39] And four years later in 1708, Keill was again overlooked, on this occasion for the Savilian chair following Gregory's death. The effect on Desaguliers of his mentor's lack of preferment is not known but perhaps presented him with a poignant example of academic insecurity.

Frustrated at his lack of progress, Keill sought alternative positions away from Oxford. He eventually received assistance from Robert Harley, whose career culminated in his elevation as Earl of Oxford and Mortimer and appointment as Lord Treasurer. With Harley's help, Keill was made treasurer of a government fund to support German Palatine refugees. And after Keill's return from North America at the beginning of 1711, rather than return to academia, he took up appointment as a government decipherer or code breaker, again through Harley's offices.[40]

Nevertheless, following the death of John Caswell, Gregory's successor, and with Newton's intercession, Keill was elected to the Savilian chair in 1712. Newton's support for Keill at Oxford, the Royal Society and in the wider academic world (he was awarded a further doctorate in 1713 by public act), mirrored the assistance he proffered to other acolytes. And Newton's support was requited: Keill's research papers and lectures, and his growing academic standing, provided a muscular buttress to support Newton's own academic reputation.

While Keill shepherded refugees from the German Palatine to the colonies in New England, Desaguliers substituted for him as a lecturer at Hart Hall. There Desaguliers emulated and enhanced Keill's methodology, using experiments rather than mathematics to demonstrate the validity of Newton's scientific principles. He taught a natural philosophy that was based on observation and calculation. The course and approach was one that augmented Protestant teaching. Importantly, there was no perceived or real contradiction or threat to the Anglican Church from the scientific Enlightenment.

London, Again

Desaguliers obtained his BA in 1709 and was made a deacon the following year ordained, like his father, by Bishop Compton at Fulham Palace. He received his MA in 1712 and in 1713, following his marriage to Joanna Pudsey, returned to London. The marriage ceremony was held at St Paul's, Shadwell – the 'Church of the Sea Captains' – an Anglican church originally built in around 1657 and rebuilt in a grander style in 1669. Desaguliers retained a connection with Oxford and returned periodically to lecture; he was awarded his doctorate in 1719, which he incorporated LLD at Cambridge in 1726.

Little is known of his wife other than that she was born in Kidlington, Oxfordshire, to a middle ranking family.[41] Of greater significance is that she was not a Huguenot. To marry outside of the Huguenot community was relatively uncommon until much later in the eighteenth century and the marriage may conceivably be seen as an early indication of Desaguliers' aspiration to assimilate into English society and perhaps to achieve a measure of social advancement.[42]

Desaguliers initially took lodgings in the City in Plough Yard off Fetter Lane. This was close to the Royal Society's rooms which were a few steps away in Crane Court. His address was recorded in the register of the local church, St. Andrew's, Holborn, where his son was baptised on 14 March 1715.[43] Later that year, Desaguliers moved to Channel Row in Westminster, a narrow lane running parallel to the Thames from the back of Richmond Terrace to Bridge Street. The Westminster Rate Book indicates that Desaguliers paid a Poor Rate of just over £30 per annum from 1715 to 1735, when the rate was reduced to c. £25.[44] His name remained in the Rate Book until 1741, the year that the house was demolished with others to clear a route for the approach to the newly constructed Westminster Bridge. A Poor Rate of £30 suggests that Desaguliers had one of the larger properties in Channel Row, a supposition supported by the scale of his lectures. Indeed, his lecture room was recorded as being '30 foot long, 18 wide and 15 high'.[45]

Perhaps not coincidentally, Channel Row was also the location of the Rummer & Grapes, John Strype's 'Rhenish Wine House of good resort' and host to an exclusive Masonic lodge.[46] Moreover, it was hard by New Palace Yard, the location of many of those who later became Desaguliers' key Masonic colleagues and allies in Grand Lodge and home to the Horn tavern, to which the lodge at the Rummer later transferred.

Desaguliers supported his wife, their four sons and three daughters,[47] and his mother and mother-in-law,[48] through a combination of enterprises. These included his work at the Royal Society, private commissions and his lectures on mechanical and experimental philosophy to paying audiences at Channel Row and elsewhere. Desaguliers' lectures were fashionable and achieved some financial success. Science was emerging into popular culture and interest in Newton's theories had spread beyond the confines of Oxbridge, the Royal Society and aristocratic cliques, to embrace coffee houses and taverns.[49]

In this approach Desaguliers followed others. His predecessors included John Harris (1666–1719), who had lectured on mathematics at the Marine Coffee House in Birchin Lane in 1702 and 1703 and had published his *Lexicon technicum* in 1704;[50] Francis Hauksbee (1660–1713), lauded by Harris as one of six 'ingenious and industrious artificers';[51] and the brilliant but controversial and theologically unorthodox William Whiston (1667–1752), expelled from Cambridge University and his Lucasian professorship in 1710 for anti-trinitarian religious heterodoxy.[52]

Hauksbee's election as FRS in December 1703 at the first meeting of the Royal Society's Council under Newton's presidency is an example of Newton's support for an acolyte whose advancement was a function of his utility. Newton exploited Hauksbee, whose research and discoveries populated the *Philosophical Transactions*. He presided over Hauksbee's weekly experiments at the Society and took credit for his research into light, magnetism and optics. Hauksbee was unhappy with the arrangement and his later self-published RS papers – Francis Hauksbee, *Physico-Mechanical Experiments on Various Subjects* (London, 1709) – were dedicated to Lord Sommers, a former President of the Royal Society and a member of the Privy Council, rather than to Newton.[53]

Unlike those of his predecessors, Desaguliers' experiments were designed to entertain as well as inform and, intentionally and astutely, were a vehicle for his showmanship:

> a great many Persons get a considerable Knowledge of Natural Philosophy by Way of Amusement; and some are so well pleas'd with what they learn that Way, as to be induc'd to study Mathematicks, by which they at last become eminent Philosophers.[54]

Scientific demonstrations and scientific entertainment developed in tandem.[55] As had been the case with Hauksbee, Newton's first demonstrator, Desaguliers' experiments and demonstrations were given weekly at the Royal Society.[56] But Desaguliers also offered them to a wider public audience where the effects of electricity, the physical properties of gases, the gravitational pull of the moon and the orbits of the planets, were demonstrated and explained with a mixture of novel devices. These included Desaguliers' new planetarium, reported in an advertisement in the *Daily Post* of 9 December 1732 as 'a new Machine, contrived and made by himself'.[57] Indeed, as Sir John Plumb noted, albeit of a slightly later period, theatricality had become integral to the lecture circuit:

> Public demonstrations of the powers of electricity became exceedingly popular and profitable. To see brandy ignited by a spark shooting from a man's finger became one of the wonders of the age.[58]

Jeffrey Wigelsworth commented on the high financial returns to be made from popular demonstrations of Newtonian science, characterising it as an exceptional opportunity 'to make money in early eighteenth century London'. He also noted the disputes and squabbles that arose as a result.[59] Indeed, even before he had succeeded Hauksbee as Newton's principal demonstrator, Desaguliers had been presenting his lectures and displays on a regular basis in London's coffee houses.[60] His enthusiasm and showmanship ensured an attentive and appreciative audience.[61] The press was also harnessed and could be effusive:

> That so much Dexterity was necessary to make the experiments . . . that even Monsieur Mariotte who had such a Genius for Experiments and had been so successful on many other Subjects, yet even He miscarried when he undertook to separate the Rays of Light.[62]

Among the many Newtonian demonstrators and lecturers that emerged to create a public lecture circuit in London and the provincial cities, Desaguliers was pre-eminent.[63] Science and commerce had become integral to each other's success: no more 'vain hypotheses' but 'experiments judiciously and accurately made'.[64] Desaguliers recognised that personal and commercial success lay in the application of natural philosophy to engineering and to the solution of practical commercial problems.[65] Experiments and demonstrations under the auspices of the Royal Society and otherwise were part of a process of the commercialisation of science. As Larry Stewart noted, for active natural philosophers such as Desaguliers, the world of mechanics was full of opportunities to develop the essentially economic principles of work and force.[66]

The aristocrats, gentlemen and affluent artisans and tradesmen who subscribed to Desaguliers' works and attended his popular and fashionable lecture courses had utilitarian concerns.[67] In Stephen Pumfrey's words, natural philosophy was 'infiltrated by the values of trade, the market place and the *monied interest*'.[68] Science had become less theoretical and more empirical, and was recognised by many as being potentially of considerable commercial use.[69] Construction, farming, mining and navigation were among a range of areas that benefited from the implementation of Newtonian scientific ideas and the practical machines it spawned. As productivity advanced, not only entrepreneurs but the economy benefited.

A widespread perspective among historians of science is that the eighteenth century was relatively devoid of new scientific theories and inventions as compared to those preceding and following. This analysis fails to recognise the application of scientific innovation that underpinned commercial and military expansionism. A movement in which Desaguliers was at the core:

> Natural Philosophy is that Science which gives the Reasons and Causes of the Effects and Changes which naturally happens in Bodies . . . We ought to call into question all such things as have an appearance of falsehood, that by a new Examen we may be led to the Truth.[70]

Having returned to London from Oxford, Desaguliers was introduced, most probably by Keill, to Isaac Newton, who dominated the Royal Society as President from his election in 1703 and who would utilise and exploit Desaguliers much as he had Hauksbee. Keill also introduced Desaguliers to the Duke of Chandos, one of England's wealthiest men and a fellow member of the Society's Council. The result was a substantial boost to Desaguliers' career. Newton's sponsorship and Desaguliers' subsequent election as FRS reinforced and provided a firm foundation for his scientific credibility; and in Chandos, Desaguliers secured a wealthy, high profile, connected and entrepreneurial patron.

The Royal Society's intellectual imprimatur, Chandos' commercial validation and, later, the Masonic platform of Grand Lodge, gave Desaguliers a network of contacts and relationships which he used effectively, something seen clearly in the godparents he provided for his children. The roll of those willing to fulfil the responsibility tracked Desaguliers' social, scientific and Masonic standing over the next decade. And his children's baptisms, which took place at St. Andrew's, Holborn, and St. Margaret's, Westminster, once again demonstrated a desire for social assimilation and advancement: both churches were High Church Anglican.[71]

Desaguliers' first two children were born in 1715 and 1718 and had lowly godparents: his brother and sister-in-law; Mary Hauksbee, whose widowed mother had permitted Desaguliers to use her address to advertise and to host his early lectures;[72] and local neighbours. Their modest status was in stark contrast to that of the godparents of his next four children, born between 1719 and 1724 when Desaguliers was at his Masonic apogee. This second group included the influential and aristocratic Henry Brydges, Marquis of Carnarvon,[73] second and surviving son of the Duke of Chandos, Desaguliers' principal sponsor; and Cassandra, the Duchess of Chandos, the Duke's second wife, who was wealthy in her own right. Thomas Parker, 1st Earl of Macclesfield, a keen mathematician and later Lord High Chancellor;[74] Archibald Campbell, Earl of Islay and 3rd Duke of Argyll, later Privy Seal, an influential Scottish politician and a government adviser and intermediary on Scottish affairs;[75] and Theodosia, 10th Baroness Clifton, the daughter of Viscount Clarendon, who was married to John Bligh, Earl of Darnley,[76] also consented to act as godparents, as did Countess de la Lippe, whose husband, the Count, was a member of the Horn,[77] and the Duchess of Richmond, the wife of the 2nd Duke and future Grand Master.[78] The roll also included two influential non-aristocrats: Sir Isaac Newton himself, who was godfather to Desaguliers' second son; and Lady Hewet, the wife of Sir Thomas Hewet,[79] Surveyor General to George I and retained in that role by George II.

The Earls of Macclesfield and Islay were godfathers to Thomas Desaguliers (1721–80). Thomas joined the Royal Regiment of Artillery as a cadet in 1740, fought at Fontenoy, and returned to England in 1748, promoted Captain. He subsequently became Chief Firemaster at Woolwich where he was responsible for improving English gunnery, a position he held until his death. Success led to promotion as Colonel Commandant, Major

General (1772) and Lieutenant General (1777). He was also elected FRS in 1763.[80] It is possible that his initial military preferment was linked in part to his connection through his father to the Duke of Montagu, Grand Master of Grand Lodge in 1721. Montagu, a stalwart Freemason discussed in chapter five, was appointed head of the Ordnance at Woolwich in 1740 with overall responsibility for developing the Royal Artillery.

By the time Desaguliers' seventh child was baptised in 1727, his status had passed its zenith. Albeit that they had political influence, Desaguliers' final collection of godparents was non-aristocratic and linked to the second tier of Grand Lodge. This latter group included William Cowper, the past Grand Secretary and Deputy Grand Master of Grand Lodge, Clerk of the Parliaments, Chairman of the Westminster magistrates' bench and a nephew of Lord Cowper, the former Lord Chancellor; and Alexander Chocke, another Westminster justice and senior civil servant who succeeded Cowper as Deputy Grand Master. The others comprised Chocke's wife and the wife of Francis Sorrel, another senior civil servant, Westminster justice and former Grand Warden.[81]

An Appliance of Science

Desaguliers' self-promotion and Newtonian proselytising was expressed in prolific authorship, particularly after he was elected FRS, with a torrent of publications alongside his lectures and the experiments and demonstrations he gave at the Royal Society and elsewhere. In 1711, while still at Oxford, Desaguliers translated Ozanam's six-part *Treatise of Fortification*.[82] The book was dedicated to the Hon. John Richmond Webb (1667–1724), a popular military hero of the War of Spanish Succession.[83] And the following year he translated Ozanam's *Treatise of Gnomonicks or Dialling*.[84] However, once established in London, Desaguliers' work rate increased. His first major publication was a translation in 1715 of Nicolas Gauger's *Treatise on the Construction of Chimneys*,[85] dedicated to the Earl of Cholmondeley, Treasurer to the Royal Household.[86] The book was published by John Senex, who would later become a fellow Freemason and one of Desaguliers' principal publishing collaborators.

It was unlikely to have been a coincidence that George Cholmondeley, the Earl's younger brother, was proposed for election to the Royal Society by Desaguliers the same year and was so elected in June. His election as FRS would have reflected positively on Desaguliers and been welcomed by the Earl, one of Desaguliers' patrons. The association was also politically advantageous. George Cholmondeley was a staunchly pro-Huguenot Whig aristocrat with strong political connections. His father-in-law was the Governor of Sas van Ghent, van Ruytenburgh, and his mother-in-law the daughter of the officer commanding the army of the States General. Cholmondeley was himself Colonel of the 1st Troop of Horse Guards and between 1725 and 1733, served as Lord Lieutenant for Cheshire. And given his association with and patronage of Roger Comberbach, Cholmondeley was also connected to Freemasonry in Chester.[87]

Comberbach was an active Chester Freemason, later appointed Provincial Senior Grand Warden under Col. Francis Columbine, Master of the Sun Inn and Provincial Grand Master. Comberbach obtained a number of significant posts through Cholmondeley's influence, including Controller of the Chester Customs and Clerk of the Crown for Cheshire and Flintshire. He was also appointed a Justice of the Peace and later Recorder of North Wales. Other Chester Freemasons prominent within Grand Lodge included William Cowper, the Grand Secretary, whose successful visit to the city was recorded in *Grand Lodge Minutes*, and George Payne, twice Grand Master and one of Desaguliers' close friends and allies.[88]

Desaguliers' translation of the *Treatise on Chimneys* reinforced his scientific status and self-confident reputation:

> The usefulness of the Book has induced me to give it to the World in English . . . I have omitted whatever I thought superfluous in the Author, to make way for some Observations of my own . . . He has considered only the improvement of wood fires, but I have shown how Turf or Coal may be burnt.[89]

And a recommendation and advertisement placed near the head of the book underlines his financial opportunism:

> ### ADVERTISEMENT.
>
> THE best Workmen that I know for curing the smoaking Chimneys, and performing what is directed in this Book, most effectually, and at the most reasonable Rates, are *Henry Hathwel*, Bricklayer; living over against the *George Inn* in *Hedge-Lane*, near *Leicester-fields*; and *William Uream*, who may also be heard of there: Having try'd them several times with good Success.

The publication brought Desaguliers' self promoted skills to the attention of a broader audience and with John Rowley (c. 1668–1728), George I's 'Master of Mechanics',[90] the 'ingenious' Desaguliers was later commanded to 'remedy the defective atmosphere' of the Houses of Parliament:[91]

> Ordered, That Mr. Disaguliers do view the Chimney in this House, and consider how the same may be made more useful; and report what is proper to be done therein to the Lords Committees, appointed to review

the Repairs of The Parliament-office; whose Lordships are hereby empowered to receive the said Report on Friday next.[92]

Completed in around 1723, the work was reported to have 'succeeded in a tolerable degree'.[93] Desaguliers had been employed for the same purpose by his principal patron, the Duke of Chandos, at his mansion, Cannons, and Chandos' recommendation may have assisted Desaguliers to obtain the parliamentary commission alongside the better-known Rowley.[94] However, it was probably William Cowper, Clerk to the Parliaments and a fellow member of the lodge at the Horn tavern, who was likely to have been more instrumental in Desaguliers being granted the appointment.

A year after having published simultaneously in English and French his *Leçons physico-mechaniques*,[95] Desaguliers translated Marriotte's *Treatise of Hydrostaticks*, again printed by Senex and dedicated to Chandos.[96] The *Preface* gave Desaguliers another canvas for self-acclaim and he used it, stating that Marriotte had given him 'the Liberty of changing, or leaving out what I should think fit'. Moreover, despite the book being largely as in the original, Desaguliers wrote that 'if I had undertaken to have altered anything, it should have been with the Advice of the whole [French] Academy',[97] an organisation which then benefited from an arguably exaggerated reputation for the practical application of new scientific techniques.[98]

Desaguliers compiled his several lecture courses into a number of books including *Lectures of Experimental Philosophy*;[99] *A System of Experimental Philosophy*;[100] and *An Experimental Course of Astronomy*,[101] and used the works to enlarge upon and explain the principles of mechanics, hydrostatics and optics. His translation of an *Introduction to Sir Isaac Newton's Philosophy*[102] was a particular success with a print run of seven editions, and his growing reputation assisted by assiduous image-management and self-promotion led to commissions in ventures ranging from brewing to mining.[103]

Desaguliers' proposers for his Fellowship of the Royal Society in July 1714 included the two most prominent members of the Council: Isaac Newton and Hans Sloane (1660–1753). Sloane was Secretary from 1693–1713 and Vice President in 1713. He became President after Newton's death in 1727. At Newton's instigation, the Society's entrance and annual fees were waived 'in consideration of his great usefulness to the Royal Society as Curator and Operator of Experiments he be excused from paying his Admission money, signing the usual bond and Obligation and paying the weekly contributions'.[104]

Although many Fellows were affluent and aristocratic, Desaguliers was far from unique in being 'excused from paying his Admission money'. Other useful or connected FRS of modest means were similarly exempted from the annual fees of some £2 12s.[105] Indeed, the joining fee for the anatomist William Cheselden (1688–1752), one of Sloane's close colleagues, was waived at the same Council meeting that approved Desaguliers' election.[106] However, Desaguliers' concurrent appointments as Curator and Operator were exceptional. The positions provided Desaguliers with a base level of income and as a *quid pro quo* ensured that Newton's reputation would continue to be burnished. Retrospectively, Desaguliers' selection by Newton can be considered inspired given that he became one of Newton's most successful and effective proselytisers.[107] During his thirty years at the Royal Society and in addition to his weekly demonstrations and experiments, Desaguliers published around sixty papers and compilations of lectures, most of which provided a Newtonian exegesis.

As Curator and Demonstrator, Desaguliers received relatively modest fees based largely on piece work amounting to around £30–40 a year,[108] equivalent to a figure of perhaps *c.* £6–12,000 today.[109] His income was supplemented by periodic grants: a Minute from the Council on 3 July 1718 recorded that 'Mr Desaguliers be allowed five pounds on account of the Experiment he shew'd before the Society on the fifth of December', which may have been provided to cover the cost of his equipment.[110]

Stephen Mason has suggested that Desaguliers' experimental demonstrations at meetings of the Royal Society were provided with increasing reluctance over time, with his motivation linked to monetary rewards from the Copley bequest that had been established in 1709 to encourage new experimental studies.[111] However, although it would be correct to state that Desaguliers was able to earn significantly greater fees from his public lectures, the Royal Society's imprimatur and his designation as 'FRS' underpinned his external earnings capability.

Desaguliers' income from the Society was clearly inadequate to support his family and finance his escalating level of Masonic and commercial interests, including expensive new patent applications, such as that for a steam powered drying machine, granted in 1720 to Desaguliers, Daniel Niblet and William Vream,[112] and a stream of publications. Moreover, in order to continue with his popular demonstrations, Desaguliers was obliged to commission bespoke scientific equipment. These factors drove Desaguliers to lecture widely, demonstrating Newton's *mechanicks, hydrostaticks and opticks* across the London and the provinces. He also took up private commissions from Chandos and other patrons to improve their estates and consult on commercial projects.

Desaguliers' mounting reputation among the aristocracy, embryonic industrialists and the professional classes, and his ability to network, brought him projects from many sources, including an invitation to advise Edinburgh council on its water supply. The commission followed an introduction to John Campbell, Edinburgh's Provost, at a dinner hosted by Chandos at Cannons in July 1721. At the time, Desaguliers was engaged in designing and installing a piped water system at the estate.[113] However, within a few weeks, he was on his way to advise on improving the flow of water in Edinburgh's three-mile Comiston aqueduct.[114] Desaguliers' scientific expertise was authentic and capable of solving practical engineering problems; early examples of success date from 1711 and his cooperation with Henry Beighton (1687–1764) to improve steam engine design.[115]

In later years, Desaguliers' scientific approval became something of a formal imprimatur: a letter from Edward Trelawney to Joshua Howell of Trebursye, Cornwall confirming Desaguliers' good opinion of Howell's cousin led directly to the latter's appointment as a schoolmaster 'as soon as possible' as one verifiably qualified to teach mathematics.[116] Desaguliers' explanations of natural phenomena were also circulated in the provinces, and both the Yorkshire and Shropshire archives contain contemporary notes of his lectures.[117] Even Parliament sought his services, requesting that Desaguliers 'examine and prove the dimensions and contents of the standard coal bushel' used as a benchmark by the Exchequer.[118] In this task, Desaguliers was bracketed with two eminent scientists: Edmund Halley, the Astronomer Royal, and James Hodgson, Master of the Royal Mathematical School at Christ's Hospital.

Desaguliers' approach to problem solving hinged on a combination of theoretical analysis and hands-on experimentation, and he benefited from a reputation as one who could explain, entertain and readily demonstrate Newton's largely impenetrable theories. The scientific and practical problems he tackled ranged across the engineering spectrum from major hydraulic projects, to assessing the relative utility of different wheel sizes against different obstacles and inclines,[119] to measuring the relative muscular strength of William Joy, a Kentish strongman.[120]

This combination of skilled scientific entertainer, FRS and Newton's leading protégé, virtually ensured that he would be brought to the attention of the Court to show his experiments before George I:

> His Majesty and the Royal Family continue in perfect heath at Hampton Court; where, among others, the ingenious Mr. Desaguliers, FRS, has the Honour to divert them with several curious Performances upon the Globes, and other Philosophical Experiments; for which Purpose, he has a Lodging allow'd him in one of the Pavilions of the Garden.[121]

George I's command of English was rudimentary but Desaguliers would have been willing to offer his lectures in a combination of languages: the *Evening Post* of 16 April 1717 confirmed that they were available in French, Latin or English as 'the Gentlemen present shall desire'. The 'ingenious Mr. Desaguliers' was a Court success and rewarded with the living of Bridgham in Norfolk worth £70 per annum. And in 1727, following Desaguliers' demonstrations to George II and the Royal Family earlier that year, Bridgham was replaced with the higher yielding Little Warley in Essex.

Desaguliers was also appointed chaplain to Frederick, Prince of Wales, a position of which he was particularly proud and which he publicised extensively notwithstanding the role was probably unsalaried and that other clerics enjoyed the same title.[122] Desaguliers was also made chaplain to the 12th Regiment of Dragoons (the Prince of Wales's) in 1738.[123] It is interesting to speculate whether these latter positions were linked to the Whiggish patriotic opposition that centred on the Prince of Wales. The Grand Lodge of

England had a presence in both pro- and anti-Walpole Whig camps. William O'Brien, the 4th Earl of Inchiquin, and Thomas Coke, Lord Lovel, Grand Masters in 1727 and 1731, respectively, could both be characterised as Walpole's men, whereas others such as the Marquis of Carnarvon, later 2nd Duke of Chandos, were firmly in the patriotic opposition. The issue is discussed below in chapter 5.

Desaguliers lectured both in London and in the provinces, where taverns and societies hosted practical demonstrations that showcased the improvements that had been made to steam and water technology. As Simon Schaffer noted, 'the aim of demonstration was to make a specific doctrinal interpretation of these devices' performance seem inevitable and authoritative'.[124] Desaguliers' combination of entertainment and experimental philosophy provided an effective means by which the practical commercial application of the underlying scientific theories might be established. His apparatus and machines might not necessarily have proved a proposition with rigor, but they illustrated it successfully and to a practical purpose, and they engaged the audience. Larry Stewart has documented the link between Desaguliers and other lecturers' popularisation of Newton's natural philosophy and the process of industrial development. And it is evident that Desaguliers' association with Chandos spanned a spectrum of commercial applications from steam pumps and water drainage from mines, to improvements to land irrigation.[125]

Desaguliers' objective was expressed succinctly: that there should be no difference between the 'Notions of Theory and Practice'.[126] His work on steam engines, hydraulics and other projects, demonstrated that there was only the narrowest of gaps between his position as a natural scientist and that of a consulting or practical engineer. Desaguliers' lectures and papers given before the Royal Society reinforce the point. Implicitly if not explicitly, his lectures advertised his skills and his availability for private commissions and consultancy services.[127] The commercial value of his work, including his debunking of scientific myths such as that of perpetual motion,[128] was understood by his audience and by potential financiers. The new technologies he outlined and explained provided what was seen as a firm basis for financial speculation and investment.

Entrepreneurs were to be found on both sides of the lectern in the early eighteenth century.[129] One such commercially minded lecturer was Thomas Watts (16__?–1742), another Freemason, with whom Desaguliers gave a joint lecture course in 1719 at Richard Steele's 'Censorium' at the York Buildings near the Strand. Interestingly, Steele had recognised as early as 1712 the entertainment value and profitability of scientific lectures: 'all works of Invention, all the Sciences, as well as mechanick Arts will have their turn in entertaining this Society'.[130] Like Desaguliers, Watts was also funded by Chandos for whom he probably provided insider stock market intelligence. Ruth Wallis in her *ODNB* biography of Watts suggested that he acted as Chandos' agent in the takeover of the Sun Fire insurance company. There is certainly no doubt that Watts was closely involved with Sun Fire: he became its secretary from 1727 until 1734, when he appointed his brother to succeed him; and was its cashier from 1734 until his retirement in 1741. Watts' penchant for nepotism was also reflected in his Freemasonry: a member of the lodge that met at the Ship behind the Royal Exchange, he married Susannah Gascoyne, the sister of another member, and employed at Sun Fire Susannah's brothers, John and Crisp, the latter later Lord Mayor.

The Duke of Chandos had appointed Desaguliers as his chaplain in 1714 and having taken priestly orders two years later from the Bishop of Ely, Desaguliers was made Rector of St. Lawrence's church in Stanmore and subsequently presented with the living of the Parish of Whitchurch. With little time for his church duties, Desaguliers delegated the majority of his parish work to curates. This freed Desaguliers to concentrate on his commercial, scientific and Masonic projects, but led to an ongoing dispute with Chandos over the efficacy or otherwise with which his role was fulfilled. Chandos's letter to Desaguliers of 20 March 1739 is illustrative:

> Sir, I find by the Church Wardens that ever since the 6th day of Nov'r there has been no settled Minister to officiate in the Parish in so much that the Inhabitants & Officers of it have been forced to go a begging to other Ministers to bury their dead; This is a very shameful neglect of what I have more than once complained to you of. Your saying that you have appointed a Curate and made him a handsome allowance is no excuse; it is your duty to see he does his, and if he neglects it, rather than let the Parish suffer to do it yourself.[131]

Chandos was at the vanguard of the burgeoning scientific Enlightenment and curious about new developments, noting in his diary that he had viewed 'an anatomical dissection after a public execution, saw the circulation of blood in a cat, and talked with the Archbishop of Canterbury about the plantations and the new discoveries that might be made'.[132] Like others, he was eager to profit from new scientific inventions and theories in his financial and commercial speculations. Desaguliers was employed accordingly:

> I desire you will let me know what Strength is usually allowed for the Boyler of the Fire Engine, which it is to force water up to the height of about 140 Feet at a Mile & an half or two Miles Distance.[133]

Indeed, Chandos could be insistent:

> you will inform me, whether you have yet spoken to Mr Niblet about the Copper Pipe of 7 Inches Bore and 200 Yards in length which I design to lay in the Garden at Cannons . . . you will discourse with him about it and agree upon the Price at the easiest rate you can.[134]

The correspondence between Chandos and Desaguliers suggests that Desaguliers was engaged principally as a scientific advisor and only a distant second in a religious role. There is no evidence that Chandos was enamoured of the supposed glamour of association with a senior Freemason and, unlike his son, no evidence that Chandos became a Freemason himself. For Chandos, Desaguliers' value lay chiefly in the utilitarian aspects of his scientific knowledge.[135]

Despite his fees from the Royal Society, modest awards from the Copley bequest[136] and sinecures, chaplaincies, lectures and business ventures, Desaguliers suffered from financial insecurity throughout his life. Probably both real and imagined, his insecurity was compounded by an apparent inability to manage his financial affairs and his sense of impecunity was a permanent presence in his mind. There are many instances. On 15 January 1729, for example, Desaguliers wrote a poignant letter to Dr John Scheuchzer at the Royal Society, one of Sloane's protégés, Sloane being ill, regarding the non-payment of his fees:

> I must beg of you to be my advocate to Sir Hans to desire him . . . to be so good as to settle my last year's salary in the next council . . . This would be [of] great service to me at present, because I am entirely out of money, and have pressing occasion for it.[137]

As Larry Stewart has commented, Desaguliers continually pressed Sloane for payment of his fees.[138] Similar concerns remained even in the 1740s. On 13 December 1743, Desaguliers wrote from his lodgings at the Bedford Coffee House to Martin Folkes, then President of the Royal Society, requesting that the Society purchase the second book of his latest two-volume publication, and offering the incentive of acquiring the first volume free of charge.[139]

Stewart has also noted correspondence between Chandos and Desaguliers regarding Desaguliers' failure to account for money allocated to the local parish school.[140] The Duke's letter dated 14 June 1739 stated that:

> I am sorry to write you upon the occasion I do, but as it is a matter that has been represented to me by the Church Wardens & Overseers of the Parish of Whitechurch I cannot forbear it. They tell me that of the 20£ a year I paid for Rent for the Freeschool Fields, there is 5£ a year of it which you have not accounted for three years & a half past, by which means they have not been able to put out any boy apprentice for this last year & half, tho' there have been sev'l ready for it, & even the Masters of the two boys who were bound out the two preceeding years have not been able to get the money agreed to be given with them, but are every now & then levying & dunning the vestry for it. This is really an abuse which I cannot suffer, & as the principle care of this Charity rests upon me, I am obliged to see that it is not any ways diverted from answering the Intention of the Founder. I must therefore desire you will forthwith pay the money due to the respective Masters of the two Boys, or give them such Security for it as shall satisfy them so as to discharge the Charity from any demand of theirs on that

Head, & likewise that you'l have the rem'r of the money ready to pay to the Master of the Boy now going to be bound out Apprentice.[141]

There is no record of any reply from Desaguliers. However, although Stewart has suggested that this was the last recorded letter between the two, this is incorrect. There were at least two subsequent letters from Chandos to Desaguliers dated 25 October 1740, referring *inter alia* to a gift of Newton's works to an Oxford College, and 28 August 1741, declining an unspecified request.[142] Given the continuing correspondence, it may be more reasonable to interpret the incident as evidence of Desaguliers' inability to grasp the intricacies of financial management rather of the misappropriation of funds.

Scientifically, Desaguliers continued to be well regarded and his lectures well attended. In his later years, he was recognised by the Royal Society as a scientist in his own right and awarded the Copley Medal on three occasions, in 1734, 1736 and 1741.[143] Nonetheless, his skills as a demonstrator continued to be respected and utilised: 'yesterday the Prince of Modena was elected a fellow of the Royal Society, and Dr Desaguliers showed his highness several experiments'.[144]

Desaguliers' services as a firework impresario similarly remained in demand. He had honed his skills at Cannons where he 'play'd off a very handsome Firework at Night to conclude the rejoining [of the proclamation of George II as king'.[145] And Desaguliers was employed by the Mayor and Corporation of Bristol as late as 1738 'to entertain their Royal Highnesses' on the visit of the Prince and Princess of Wales to the city.[146] He passed his expertise to his son, Thomas, by then an artillery officer, who later created the firework display that accompanied Handel's *Music for the Royal Fireworks*, performed in 1749. Ironically, Thomas Desaguliers' fireworks caused part of the temporary pavilion that had been erected for the event to catch fire. Nonetheless, the general view of the press was that the fireworks 'were mighty fine and gave more than a general satisfaction'.[147]

In a letter dated 6 March 1741, the Prussian Ambassador commented that he attended Desaguliers' lectures twice a week and that 'we pay him generously [and] he in return spares no pain to entertain us and to discover to us all the hidden springs of nature'.[148] The same letter described Desaguliers' planetarium and the theatricality of the presentation, and observed that Desaguliers' machine, constructed by 'Mr Graham, the most able and celebrated watchmaker', had cost 'more than one thousand pounds sterling'. Even if the figure was somewhat exaggerated, it emphasises that Desaguliers had substantial financial outgoings and his lecture successes came at a price. However, science was only one of several key threads in Desaguliers' life. A connected and perhaps equally important interest was Freemasonry.

Matters Masonic

Desaguliers' introduction to London Freemasonry, most probably by George

Payne, is discussed in chapter three. Desaguliers clearly found the milieu attractive and became a member of several lodges. Although his principal lodge was the Rummer & Grapes in Channel Row, which later transferred to the Horn tavern in New Palace Yard, he also joined the Duke of Montagu's lodge and the University lodge, both of which met at the Bear and Harrow, and the French Lodge at the Dolphin in Tower Street, which later met at the Swan in Long Acre, Covent Garden.

As one of the most senior members of the newly formed Grand Lodge, Desaguliers was a pivotal figure in English Freemasonry. From his vantage point in Grand Lodge, he co-directed and promoted what became a uniquely prominent organisation, supportive of the establishment and its Hanoverian centre. Desaguliers' status within Grand Lodge and as a member and Master of a number of aristocratic constituent lodges gave him influence in areas that were fundamental to Masonic development. He was active in re-working Masonic ritual; had co-authorship and oversight of the *Charges* and *Regulations*; developed a federal structure; oversaw the introduction of lectures at lodge meetings; revived the 'ancient toasts' at lodge dinners; and promoted the concept of Masonic 'benevolence'. All received considerable press publicity. In short, together with a core group of similarly minded colleagues within Grand Lodge and its circle, Desaguliers created a structure that combined latitudinarian religious tolerance with support for the parliamentary establishment, sociability and entertainment, and the quest for and disbursement of knowledge. These were ideas and concepts that can be considered rightly to be at the core of the English Enlightenment.[149]

Understandably, given the insecurities of his Huguenot upbringing, Desaguliers made personal use of Freemasonry as a vehicle to promote and support his own social advance and financial well-being. His actions were in parallel to his networking at the Royal Society and elsewhere, and mirrored a pattern of self-promotion that found expression in his publications, lectures and engineering undertakings. Desaguliers worked his connections and relationships across the spectrum. Indeed, he even used the installation of a patent fireplace at the Royal Society's Crane Court buildings as an endorsement of the efficacy of his invention. This and other examples feature prominently in classified advertisements placed to advertise his services.

Through the Eyes of Others

Despite his relatively eminent Masonic status and scientific position, Desaguliers was probably regarded with some ambivalence by those outside his immediate circle. Although a prominent and popular scientist, Desaguliers could also be perceived as a jobbing engineer and a mere servant of the Royal Society. Moreover, despite his success and popularity as speaker who had lectured in London, The Hague and Paris, he was also foreign and a Huguenot. This uncertainty of perception among those of the establishment who knew him and elsewhere was encapsulated by Hogarth

(1697–1764) with his mildly ironic mocking of Desaguliers' sermonising and lecturing in the *Sleeping Congregation*, published in 1736, with its obvious Masonic imagery and overtones.[150]

In this etching, Hogarth depicted Desaguliers as a short-sighted minister whose boring sermon has gone on for far too long and driven the majority of the congregation to sleep. But Hogarth's satire was moderate and witty; it was far removed from the incisive moralising of the *Rake's Progress* engraved the previous year, or the incisive and bloody bite of an Alexander Pope. Although the various and precise meanings that are attributed to Hogarth's imagery are often disputed, there can be little doubt that the main aspect of the picture is humorous.[151] Indeed, a principal aspect of his life that Desaguliers was known *not* to favour was that of his clerical duties.[152]

The tongue-in-cheek depiction of Desaguliers is in a similar vein to Hogarth's representation of him in *The Indian Emperor, or The Conquest of Mexico* (*c.* 1732) where Desaguliers is shown with his back to the audience acting as a prompter to the child actors on stage. Hogarth's picture is of a children's production of Dryden's *The Indian Emperor* at John Conduitt's house in Hanover Square. Conduitt and his wife appear as portraits above their guests and Roubillac's bust of Newton, whom Conduitt succeeded as Master of the Mint, is resplendent on the mantelpiece. Three royal children are on stage: William, Duke of Cumberland, and Mary and Louisa, his sisters, together with Catherine, Conduitt's daughter. Mary, the Duchess of Delorraine, is in the small audience. On her left is the Duchess of Richmond. Her husband the Duke is shown leaning on the back of her chair. Behind him, Thomas Fermor, the Earl of Pomfret, speaks with Thomas Hill, Richmond's confidant and friend, then Secretary to the Board of Trade; the Duke of Montagu is also part of this group. Conduitt, Montagu, Richmond, Hill, Delorraine and Desaguliers were, of course, all senior Freemasons.[153] And although the portrayal of Desaguliers in *The Mystery of Masonry Brought to Light by the Gormogons*, completed in 1724, and probably before Hogarth became a Freemason,[154] may have been modestly off-putting, Hogarth's later characterisations were more entertaining than offensive, and were unlikely to have had any materially negative impact on Desaguliers himself.

Hogarth was himself recorded in the 1729 Grand Lodge lists as a member of the small lodge meeting at the Hand and Apple Tree,[155] one of the four 'founding lodges', and subsequently of the more prestigious Bear & Harrow lodge in Butcher Row.[156] He was appointed a Grand Steward in 1734, nominated by Thomas Slaughter.[157] Sir James Thornhill, Hogarth's father-in-law (after 23 March 1729) and early mentor, was Master of the lodge at the Swan, Greenwich. Thornhill had been appointed Senior Grand Warden of Grand Lodge in December 1728.[158] With such relatively substantial Masonic connections, Hogarth's occasional representation of Freemasons and Freemasonry danced the line between irony, satire and ridicule, possibly with an eye on future commissions from affluent and eminent Masonic clients such as Conduitt, David Garrick and Martin Folkes, all of whom became patrons.

Hogarth's pre-eminent Masonic works were *Night*, the last painting in his *Four Times of the Day*, completed in 1736 and later reproduced as a series of engravings, and *The Mystery of Masonry Brought to Light by the Gormogons*. These and other allusions to Freemasonry, such as in *The Four Stages of Cruelty* (1751), have been examined in depth elsewhere.[159] Hogarth's comments on his Masonic contemporaries such as Colley Cibber (1671–1757), Barton Booth (1681–1733) and Robert Wilks (*c.* 1665–1732) (*A Just View of the British Stage*, 1724); and John Heidegger (1659–1749) (*Masquerades and Operas*, 1724), have also been analysed in detail in a number of publications and articles.[160]

It is possible to portray Hogarth's later view of Desaguliers and, by extension, Freemasonry, as a minor part of a more negative reaction to Freemasonry that began to develop in the later 1730s. In part, this echoed political and religious disquiet in continental Europe. In 1736, Frederick I of Sweden prohibited Freemasons from meeting under penalty of death. Masonic assemblies were abolished in France the following year, and the Inquisition closed the English lodge meeting in Rome. In 1738, Pope Clement XII's Papal Bull against Freemasonry was published and Charles VI also issued an edict prohibiting Masonry in the Austrian Netherlands. Poland followed, in 1739, when Augustus III (1696–1763) proscribed Masonic meetings. This had wider impact since Augustus III was also the Elector of Saxony, Frederick Augustus II and Grand Duke of Lithuania. And in 1740, Philip V of Spain (1683–1746) issued a decree against Freemasonry, with those deemed Masons condemned to the galleys.[161] But notwithstanding Marie Mulvey-Roberts' probably accurate assessment of a 'Masonic malaise' between the 1730s and 1760s,[162] the position in England was less extreme and the relatively modest negativity was tinged with satire. As Horace Walpole, himself a Freemason, noted ironically in his letter of 4 May 1743 to Sir Horace Mann:

> the Freemasons are in so low repute now in England, that one has scarce heard the proceedings at Vienna against them mentioned. I believe nothing but a persecution could bring them into vogue here again.[163]

Desaguliers' influence on Freemasonry was marked for over two decades by the ripples originating from the philosophical and moral re-engineering that he with colleagues had instigated in the early 1720s. However, by the late 1730s and 1740s, his authority and influence had waned. Indeed, there is evidence that the erstwhile 'grave' Desaguliers became more manipulated than manipulator in his later years. The apparently spontaneous initiation of Robert Webber in 1734 at a house party at the Duke of Montagu's estate at Thames Ditton was an act Desaguliers might once have regarded as quite inappropriate. The event was reported in a letter to the Duke of Richmond by Broughton, his secretary:

dissection. Newton provided a philosophical and scientific framework for religious tolerance and the natural hierarchy of a constitutional monarch and parliamentary élite atop a stable and prosperous country. Desaguliers expressed such concepts succinctly in *The Newtonian System of the World*[170] and was clear that Divine providence coexisted with natural law. As Pope noted ironically, 'safe in the hand of one disposing Pow'r . . . one truth is clear, whatever is, is right'.[171]

The Hanoverian succession, religious tolerance, property rights and constitutional government were central to both Whig prosperity and Huguenot protection, and it is unsurprising that under Desaguliers and his colleagues' influence, English Freemasonry became a component of a pro-establishment intellectual and moral structure that promoted latitudinarianism. Margaret Jacob has termed this the 'mentality of official masonry' – a 'taste for science . . . craving for order and stability . . . worldly mysticism [and] rituals, passwords and mythology, [and a] religious devotion to higher powers, be they the Grand Architect, the king or the Grand Master'.[172] And although perhaps over-simplistic, the description would have resonated with Desaguliers and other Huguenots as he and they sought to assimilate into and find a niche within English society.

Desaguliers has no known epitaph but a phrase from John Gay epitomises his self-reliance and determination to succeed despite, indeed, perhaps because of, his origins: 'there is no dependence that can be sure, but a dependence upon one's self'.[173]

CHAPTER THREE

Grand Lodge:
The Inner Workings

Despite evidence to the contrary, The Rev. James Anderson (c. 1679–1739) is regarded by many as having been pivotal to the development of modern Freemasonry. But Anderson was not the fulcrum on which Grand Lodge and Freemasonry turned. In addition to Desaguliers, the more central players within Grand Lodge and London Freemasonry included George Payne, Martin Folkes and William Cowper, alongside the lesser known Alexander Chocke, Nathaniel Blackerby, John Beale,[1] George Carpenter and Charles Delafaye. All were linked via several over-lapping political, social and professional networks to which Anderson was at best only loosely connected: the Middlesex and Westminster magistrates' benches, the Royal Society and other learned and professional associations, and the government and civil service. Within each ran the thread of pro-Hanoverian politics: a belief in the rights and power of the establishment.

Rather than Anderson, Desaguliers, Payne and Folkes provided the three interlinked foundations for a range of Masonic alliances which were the principal vectors for change and influence over the next two decades. Within this chapter is explored the connection between the Middlesex and Westminster magistrates benches, many of whose members were senior Freemasons and at the helm of the Craft's organisational transformation. The following chapters extend the analysis to other networks based on the learned and professional societies, and to the aristocracy, whose social prominence, political power and court position influenced Freemasonry's political and public persona. Key associations are tracked in relation to specific individuals and with respect to four prominent lodges: the Horn at Westminster; the Rummer at Charing Cross; the Bedford Head, Covent Garden; and the King's Arms in the Strand.

From the early 1720s, Grand Lodge began to regulate and control Freemasonry and to connect it to the Hanoverian and Whig political establishment. In the first instance, influence was exerted via the introduction of the *1723 Constitutions* and, in particular, the new *Regulations* and *Charges.*

JAMES ANDERSON AND THE AUTHORSHIP OF THE 1723 *Constitutions*

David Stephenson's analysis of Anderson and his influence on eighteenth-century English Freemasonry is based in part on Anderson's own account of events set out in the *1738 Constitutions*. In the absence of other records, the *1738 Constitutions* has provided the principal source of information on the creation of Grand Lodge, the selection of the early Grand Masters and the adoption of the new *Charges* and *Regulations*. Stephenson argued that Anderson's fundamental importance lay in his authorship of the first two editions of the *Constitutions*, the provision of a Masonic history emphasising the Craft's antiquity and, *inter alia*, his record of Grand Lodge's early history. His views are shared by other Masonic historians who have emphasised Anderson's strong relationship with Desaguliers, both of whom were members of the Horn and the French lodge, 'Solomon's Temple'.[2] There is a broad acceptance that Anderson through his authorship of the *1723* and *1738 Constitutions*, laid the principal foundations of the new Freemasonry; indeed, Stephenson has stated that Anderson's work 'set the standards of British Freemasonry for nearly a century'.

However, an important component of Anderson's *Constitutions* can be regarded as more self-serving than objective, and his record of at least certain events at Grand Lodge may have been as patchily inaccurate as his lengthy faux Masonic history. Anderson's account of his professed role as a Grand Warden in 1723, a position to which he stated *he* was appointed by Wharton, rather than William Hawkins, is illustrative.[3] The issue was evaluated critically by William John Songhurst in his editorial notes to the QCA transcription of *Grand Lodge Minutes*:

> In regard to the words added by Anderson in the List of Grand Officers at the end of Minute Book 1, I need only point out that in the list preserved by the Lodge of Antiquity, there is no mention of his Wardenship, and that it is not until the 3 December 1731 (Book 2) that we find him actually described in the Minutes as "formerly Grand Warden".[4]

Songhurst commented that he had no doubt that the text describing Anderson's replacement of Hawkins – 'who demitted, as always out of town' – had been altered to exaggerate, perhaps falsify, Anderson's own position, and that the relevant words had been inserted by Anderson himself.[5]

In the *1738 Constitutions*, Anderson wrote that the *Old Charges* had been found 'wanting' and Grand Lodge – for which we might substitute Desaguliers and his inner cohort – 'finding fault with all the copies of the Gothic Constitutions order'd Brother James Anderson A.M. to digest the same in a new and better method'. However, the *1723 Constitutions* did not provide an updated or modernised version of the *Old Charges*. It did far more, setting the parameters for a new operating structure and establishing the foundations of what would rapidly become a national organisation. The details are discussed in appendix two, which sets out in brief a comparative analysis of the *Regulations* and *Charges*.

Under the aegis of Desaguliers and his colleagues, Grand Lodge provided the impetus for the inclusion of scientific lectures and entertainments at lodge meetings. These were complemented by a loose ritual based on historic precedent, and dining, toasting and singing designed to emphasise and maintain fraternal bonding. The assertion that Desaguliers had been attracted to Freemasonry by its 'ethos of education and religious tolerance', as David Harrison argued in the *Genesis of Freemasonry*, is disingenuous. These concepts were not inherited from some sylvan past but were rather the central components of the newly introduced form of eighteenth-century Freemasonry.

Stephenson and other historians have sought to underline Anderson's key Masonic role by attributing to him sole authorship of the *1723 Constitutions*. It can be accepted that the faux history was probably 'compiled and digested' by Anderson. But although the largest section in terms of pages, this component of the *Constitutions* is of secondary importance. In common with similar historical passages in the *Old Charges*, Anderson's artificial history was designed to set a literary context for Freemasonry. By positioning it as an ancient institution, the narrative afforded the Craft legitimacy, lent it an antiquarian status and gave it an aura and attraction that a more recently formed organisation would have found difficult to attain. The subsequent dismissive categorisation of the first Grand Lodge of England as the 'Moderns', and the adoption in 1751 of the title 'Ancients' by a rival London Grand Lodge, reinforces the point. As in previous centuries, Freemasonry's perceived longevity offered an element of protection in a society that remained heavily tradition-based. Few would have taken Anderson's history as a literal and truthful record of events. It was then and can now be viewed as falling within a tradition of legend and literary hyperbole.

Leaving Anderson's 'history' to one side, the more significant constitutional features of the book were the *Charges* and *Regulations*. The *Charges* occupy seven pages, from 49–56, and the *Regulations*, compiled by Payne, fourteen pages, from 58–72. They represented 21 out of 100 pages of the *1723 Constitutions* and an even smaller proportion of the *1738 Constitutions* with its much extended history and 244 pages. In contrast to the laboured literary style of Anderson's history, the unambiguous content of the *Charges* and *Regulations* suggest that these sections were either cowritten by Desaguliers with Payne, or substantially edited by Desaguliers. Indeed, they may have been written solely by him, although there is no direct evidence for this.

The *1723 Constitutions* was dedicated by Desaguliers to the Duke of Montagu, Desaguliers writing that *he* was dedicating the *Constitutions* to the immediate past Grand Master: '*I* humbly dedicate', and not that this was a dedication by or on behalf of any others. Although it can and has been argued that this was simply convention, it is interesting to note that within the dedication Desaguliers refers to the 'author' having 'accurately . . . compared and made everything agreeable to History and Chronology'. In this context, the absence of any explicit reference to the *Charges* and *Regulations* is significant and by implication these sections were not of Anderson's design or authorship. It has also been argued that the content of the *Charges* stood uneasily with Anderson's Presbyterian Calvinist beliefs.[6] However, this can be regarded as unproven and perhaps of limited significance, particularly if Anderson is regarded as a 'hired pen', a role suggested by Andrew Prescott.[7]

It is significant that Anderson is identified as 'the author of this book' almost as an afterthought and only on page 74 of the *1723 Constitutions* in the middle of the second page of the *Approbations*. In his *AQC Transactions* paper, Prescott contrasted Anderson's lack of status with the prominence on the frontispiece of Senex and Hooke, who co-financed the publication of the *1723 Constitutions*. Senex, who was a friend of and publisher to Desaguliers and others at the Royal Society, was rewarded later the same year with promotion to Grand Warden.[8] Had Anderson fulfilled a substantive rather than subservient role, it would have been conventional for him to have received recognition with his name on the first page or an acknowledgement or reference in the *Introduction*.

Anderson's subsequent role within Grand Lodge is similarly inconsistent with the status that would have been granted to the sole author of the *Constitutions*. According to Anderson's own record, on 29 September 1721, he was instructed by 'His Grace and Grand Lodge' to 'digest the Gothic Constitutions'. A committee was appointed to examine the manuscript and on 22 March 1722, after some amendments, the book was approved. The *Approbation* states that Anderson submitted his draft for 'perusal and corrections' by the past and current Deputy Grand Masters, that is, Beale and Desaguliers, 'and of other learned brethren', and once approved it was presented to Montagu for formal endorsement. However, the list of those described as having approved the book is simply a record of the officers and Masters of the constituent lodges falling within the orbit of Grand Lodge. Indeed, Anderson's name also appears in the list, described as 'the Master of lodge number XVII'. John Beale was also likely to have taken a relatively junior role to Desaguliers in any extended correction of the draft *Constitutions*. Although a senior Freemason and Master of the lodge that met at the Crown & Anchor near St. Clements Church, he was also an active and eminent physician and male mid-wife; he also sat as a magistrate.

Had Anderson acted as sole or principal author of what was arguably the most significant contemporary Masonic publication, it would have been reasonable for him to have attended Grand Lodge with some frequency and indulged in the prestige his position would have warranted. As it was, although Anderson attended Grand Lodge on 24 June 1723, the *Minutes* suggest that he did not attend again for over seven years until the quarterly meeting held on 28 August 1730. Indeed, Anderson attended Grand Lodge on a regular basis only after 1730, when he was recorded present on thirteen occasions between 1731 and 1738.

In determining authorship of the *Constitutions*, it is useful to consider whether there was any rationale for Anderson to have been so chosen or hired, and why he accepted the task. Although we cannot know for certain, there may have been several relevant factors. First, there may have been a financial motivation: Anderson is believed to have lost money in the collapse of the South Sea Company in 1720[9] and he was unlikely to have made a satisfactory living from his Swallow Street congregation, a church that had failed to provide a meaningful income to the Desaguliers family and which was described as being 'much out of repair'.[10] Second, being a Minister he was literate, familiar with history and had published a number of sermons.[11] Third, he was a Freemason.[12] In short, Anderson offered Grand Lodge and its publishers a biddable combination of financial motivation, broadly relevant knowledge and a familiarity with publishing. Such an analysis may help to shed light on Anderson's unhappiness at the later pirating of the *1723 Constitutions* and his suggestion in 1735 that a revised edition be issued, designed in part to render redundant any pirated versions which would not have paid Anderson a royalty. It would also explain the inconsistencies between the 1723 and 1738 versions of the *Constitutions*.

Having made a complaint to Grand Lodge on 24 February 1735 that the *1723 Constitutions* had been much plagiarised and advised Grand Lodge that there were only few copies of the original remaining, Anderson was asked to organise the printing of a new edition containing a list of all Grand Officers and Stewards. The updated version was published three years later in 1738 and, in contrast to the 1723 edition, the style and format (and the manner of the Dedication) suggests that Anderson worked alone. Although Grand Lodge had requested a straightforward re-print, the *1738 Constitutions* differed substantially from its predecessor. In particular, it set out the *Regulations* in a manner that confused the text with notes and amendments and prevented a clear understanding as to which rules remained in force. The complicated format suggests an absence of input from any third party into either presentation or editing.

THE INFLUENCE OF OTHERS

The *1723 Constitutions* contain virtually no mention of the events that immediately preceded and followed the formation of Grand Lodge in 1717. The absence of press coverage and lack of personal correspondence limits independent verification of Anderson's 1738 account and our knowledge of the episode more generally. The difficulty is compounded by the absence of *Grand Lodge Minutes* prior to 24 June 1723 when William Cowper was appointed Grand Secretary. Nonetheless, we can presuppose that in the first few years after Grand Lodge was established, today's monolithic organisation with its rigid set of rules and practices had yet to emerge. Instead, a small group of individuals taking their first steps shaped both Grand Lodge and Freemasonry during what was a relatively short but nonetheless profound formative process.

The new 'Free and Accepted Masonry' combined revised ritual with a novel structure based on a Grand Lodge. It developed not as a product of any set of regulations or precedents imposed by any predecessor body or external third party but as a direct function of the input of the figures controlling the organisation. Although its jurisdiction was limited initially to lodges within the area of the Bills of Mortality, principally the cities of London and Westminster and the adjacent areas of Lambeth, Southwark, Bermondsey and districts to the immediate east and north of the City, it was extended rapidly over the next decade to cover much of England and Wales.

Table 1 Grand Lodge Officers, 1720–30

Name	Grand Offices	Networks	Lodge
George Payne	GM 1718 & 1720, GW 1724, DGM 1735	JP, CS	Horn
John Beale	DGM 1721	JP, FRS	Crown & Anchor
J.T. Desaguliers	GM 1719, DGM 1722–3 & 1725	FRS, Hug.	Horn
Martin Folkes	DGM 1724	FRS, Sq.	Bedford Head
William Cowper	DGM 1726, GS 1723–7	JP, CS	Horn
Alexander Chocke	DGM 1727, GW 1726	JP, CS, Sq.	Horn
Nathaniel Blackerby	DGM 1728–9, GW 1727, GTr 1731	JP, CS	Horn
Thomas Batson	DGM 1730–4, GW 1729		Horn
Josias Villeneau	GW 1721	Hug.	Goose & Gridiron
Thomas Morris	GW 1718–19, 1721	Hug.	Goose & Gridiron
Joshua Timson	GW 1722		Not known
William Hawkins	GW 1722		Not known
Francis Sorrel	GW 1723–24	JP, CS, Hug.	Horn
John Senex	GW 1723	FRS, Hug.	Fleece
Col. Daniel Houghton	GW 1725	JP, Sq.	Rummer
Sir Thomas Prendergast	GW 1725		Horn
William Burdon	GW 1726	JP, Sq.	Horn
Joseph Highmore	GW 1727	JP, CS	Swan
Sir James Thornhill	GW 1728	JP, FRS	Swan
Martin O'Connor	GW 1728		Red Lyon
Col. George Carpenter	GW 1729	JP, FRS	Horn

Notes:
CS = Civil Servant; holder of a salaried government office
FRS = Fellow of the Royal Society
Hug. = Huguenot
JP = Justice of the Peace for Westminster and/or Middlesex
Sq. = 'Squire' to a Knight of the Bath at the installation of the Order

The preceding table details the Officers of Grand Lodge who stood behind the often-passive aristocrats at its titular helm. Of the more important (shown in bold), only one, Sir Thomas Prendergast,[13] who acted as Senior Grand Warden of the Grand Lodge of Ireland the same year, was likely to have been appointed at the behest of his patron, Charles Lennox, 2nd Duke of Richmond, rather than at the suggestion of Desaguliers, Payne, Cowper, Blackerby, Chocke or Folkes, in their capacity as Deputy Grand Masters.

George Payne – A Known Unknown

It was no coincidence that many of those chosen to sit as magistrates were or later became Freemasons, nor that many senior figures from the Westminster and Middlesex benches were at the helm of Freemasonry's organisational transformation during 1720–1740. A pro-Hanoverian and Whiggist political philosophy, and a commonality of social status, united many from both organisations.

The probable starting point for the connection between the Craft and the bench was George Payne (1685?–1757), one of Desaguliers' closest Masonic collaborators. Payne has attracted limited academic or Masonic interest and only minimal information regarding his personal and professional life has been unearthed. From a Masonic perspective he was – uniquely – both the second and fourth Grand Master of Grand Lodge, in 1718 and 1720, respectively. He was subsequently appointed Senior Grand Warden in 1724 and Deputy Grand Master in 1735. Away from Grand Lodge, Payne was noted in the *1723 Constitutions* as the Master of lodge number IV and, in 1749, became Master of the influential and aristocratic King's Arms Lodge in the Strand – now the Old King's Arms, No. 28. However, these facts only illuminate the surface of a Masonic career that was as active and arguably as important as that of Desaguliers – and one which lasted some ten years longer.

Payne's commitment to Freemasonry was evident throughout his Masonic life and not only in his willingness to compile the *General Regulations* in 1720 and activities within Grand Lodge, documented in *Grand Lodge Minutes* from the 1720s through to the 1750s. The records indicate more. They suggest that Payne was regarded highly by his colleagues throughout his Masonic career, perhaps to an even greater extent than Desaguliers. Successive examples include his appointment to 'inspect' *Philo-Musicae et Architecture Societas-Apollini* in 1725; his selection to the Charity Committee in June 1727; acting as Grand Master in 1735 in Viscount Weymouth's absence; and his appointments to the committees advising on the Calcutta lodge in 1741 and that tasked with revising Freemasonry's *Constitutions* in 1754.

Philo-Musicae – the 'society of true lovers of music and architecture' – comprised a number of well-known Freemasons who established the irregular custom of initiating and raising their members into Freemasonry.

Payne's visit to the society in September 1725 was followed by a cease and desist letter from Richmond, then Grand Master. The society's Minutes for 16 December 1725 record the receipt of Richmond's letter and noted that he 'erroneously insists and assumes to himself a Pretended Authority to call our Right Worshipful and Highly Esteemed Society to account for making Masons irregularly'.

The society largely ignored Richmond's letter, and Grand Lodge reciprocally took the matter no further.[14] Grand Lodge's failure to act was almost certainly a function of *Philo-Musicae*'s well-connected membership. The society's members included William Jones, the mathematician, a friend to both Martin Folkes and the Duke of Richmond, who had initiated him on 22 December the previous year. At the time, Richmond was Master of the Queen's Head in Hollis Street, which lodge had several members who were part of *Philo-Musicae*, including Charles Cotton and Papillon Ball.

Another indication of Payne's stature was his joining the King's Arms lodge on 5 May 1747 with the recorded 'unanimous consent' of its members. The absence of any blackballs was unusual given the lodge's reputation for disputed admissions. Payne joined the King's Arms within a month of the temporary erasure of the Horn – a result of its failure for over two years to attend the Quarterly Communications of Grand Lodge. Interestingly, the Horn's subsequent reinstatement was later described as being due largely to Payne's influence.

John Entick's comment regarding 'the fervency and zeal of GM Payne' also appears apposite[15] and is substantiated by press reports of Payne's performance at Grand Lodge in the 1740s and 1750s, including those in the *London Evening Post* of 24 February 1741 and the *General Evening Post* of 22 March 1743. However, despite his Masonic eminence, Payne had a relatively low public profile and in contrast to Desaguliers does not appear to have been an active self-promoter. Perhaps as a consequence, his life has largely been unrecorded. With the exception of Albert Calvert's brief piece in *Notes & Queries* in *AQC Transactions* 1917 and two other short references in *AQC Transactions* 1912 and 1918, no biographies have been produced by Quatuor Coronati. The *ODNB* is silent and other sources, such as Albert G. Mackey's *Encyclopaedia of Freemasonry*, have sparse or incomplete data. Overall, the absence of information has led to Payne being regarded as subordinate to Desaguliers and as an inferior adjunct to James Anderson, whose reputation has as a consequence been artificially elevated. However, an analysis of material in the Cheshire and Chester archives, press reports, government and Parliamentary papers, and Payne's professional and social networks, suggests that such an interpretation would be incorrect.

Payne was born in Chester, the son of Samuel Payne and Frances Kendrick.[16] His mother had two unmarried sisters, Mary and Elizabeth, in relation to whose respective estates he later acted as executor.[17] The family's assets at that time included 'barns, stables, yards, meadows and pasture', and appear relatively substantial.[18] The supposition is partly supported by

Payne's younger brother, Thomas (1689–1744), being admitted to Christ Church, albeit as a servitor scholar. Thomas graduated BA and subsequently took a position as Chaplain at New College.[19] He later became Canon of Windsor, a Chaplain to the King and a Prebendary of Wells.[20]

There is no evidence that George Payne attended Oxford or any other university. This may have been a consequence of his family's earlier indebtedness and of the legal action taken against his father in 1703–4 for debt and damages.[21] However, it is known that Payne moved from Chester to London in or before 1711,[22] at which time he was employed as a clerk in the Leather Office in St. Martin's Lane,[23] a position possibly obtained through family connections.

Payne's name and office address were published in classified advertisements as one of several locations where Desaguliers' 'catalogue of experiments' was available for purchase and information on his lectures could be obtained: 'one Guinea at the time of Subscription, and one Guinea . . . the third night after the Course is begun'.[24] The date – 1713 – suggests the probability that Desaguliers and Payne had been introduced before Desaguliers moved to London rather than through their common membership of the lodge at the Rummer and Grapes in Channel Row. Indeed, given that Desaguliers had previously lived in Holborn after coming down from Oxford, with lodgings close to the Royal Society's rooms at Crane Court, it may not have been coincidental that he later moved to a house in Channel Row. After all, Payne's rooms at New Palace Yard were only a few steps away.[25]

Payne was employed in various divisions of the Taxes Office and enjoyed steady promotion over a period of forty years, principally via seniority.[26] In 1713, he was recorded as one of two assistants to the Acomptant General earning £50 per annum.[27] By 1716, he had been promoted to become the senior of the two principal clerks working at the Taxes Office at an annual salary of £60. And two years later he had been promoted again, to First Clerk and Assistant, working directly with Francis Sorrel whose immediate subordinate he would remain for the next twenty-five years. Payne's salary was then noted by John Chamberlain in his *Magnae Britanniae* at £80 per annum,[28] although other sources indicate he may have earned less.[29] Over time, Payne collected additional jobs and sinecures, including that of 'carrying Treasury warrants for taking Receivers General's securities to the King's Remembrancer's Office'.[30] The *Treasury Papers* hold four references to him in the 1730s and 1740s and note that he succeeded Sorrel as Secretary to the Tax Commissioners in 1743, a position with an annual salary of £90.[31] The British Library's *Burney* collection of eighteenth-century newspapers includes around forty other references published between 1721 and his death in 1757 that mark his official work at the Taxes Office, Lottery Office and as a Commissioner of the Peace on the Westminster bench.[32]

The press also recorded his other paid appointments, including that of a commissioner for the construction of the Westminster Bridge, with which many other Freemasons were involved,[33] as a manager for the Westminster

Bridge lottery,[34] and in 1743 as a Lottery Commissioner,[35] to which position he was reappointed in subsequent years.[36] By the late 1740s, Payne was of sufficient social standing to be mentioned in the gossip columns in connection with the marriage of two of his nieces: Frances, to the Hon. George Compton in 1748;[37] and, the following year, Catherine, to the Very Rev. Lord Francis Seymour, fifth son of the 8th Duke of Somerset. Payne was by now regarded as a member of the gentry and described as such in a list of those polling in Westminster.[38] Within Grand Lodge, he had been accorded the title of 'esquire' since 1725.[39]

The circumstances of Payne's appointment to the magistracy are not known but could have been connected to the recommendation of Charles Delafaye, a well connected government official and fellow member of the Horn. Payne was first listed as a Westminster Justice in 1715,[40] which suggests that his political loyalties were beyond doubt. He remained on the bench for some thirty-five years: the Westminster Sessions Papers, Justices' Working Documents, note him sitting in 1750.[41]

Payne was one of many Justices of the Peace among the ranks of Grand Officers and senior Freemasons. The number comprised around a third of the members of the Horn and included William Cowper, Clerk of the Parliaments; Alexander Chocke, a fellow civil servant at the Exchequer; and Francis Sorrel, Payne's superior at the Taxes Office. It was also unlikely to have been a coincidence that all were neighbours at New Palace Yard.

Mackechnie-Jarvis has commented that Desaguliers was probably introduced to George Payne by his brother, Thomas Payne, when they were both at Christ Church College, Oxford.[42] This has the ring of probability: the academic community at Christ Church was relatively small, and both men were servitor scholars and later ordained. Although there is no evidence other than circumstantial, it is possible, perhaps even probable, that either George or Thomas Payne introduced Desaguliers to Freemasonry. Given their upbringing in Chester, both were likely to have been a member of or at least familiar with Freemasonry. The more probable of the two was George Payne.[43] Payne's earlier entry to Freemasonry could provide an explanation for his Masonic seniority at the Horn and the rationale for him having been selected as Grand Master before Desaguliers. It would also illuminate why he was appointed Richmond's Deputy at the Horn and acted as Master in his absence.

It is interesting to speculate why Payne and Desaguliers collaborated on the reformation of Freemasonry. Having been introduced to Freemasonry, perhaps Desaguliers saw in Payne both a potential colleague and – as someone who already held positions at the Horn and within government service – a catalyst for his own advancement. And perhaps Payne saw in Desaguliers an effective public speaker and potential collaborator, willing and able to act as a driver and public face of change. Regardless, they collaborated at Grand Lodge for over twenty-five years: preparing and introducing the new *Charges* and *Regulations* of the *1723 Constitutions*; networking to bring their associates into the Craft and, more particularly, Grand Lodge;[44]

and, with others, regulating and controlling the development of English Freemasonry over the next two decades.

Although perhaps as a function of his self-promotion and networking, Desaguliers became the more visibly influential of the two, Payne and Desaguliers were equally senior within Grand Lodge, and Payne's return as Grand Master in 1720 can perhaps be explained by the need for a senior, trusted and competent colleague to hold the Chair while awaiting an answer from the Duke of Montagu as to whether he would become the Society's first noble Grand Master. But in addition to Payne's reciprocated support for Desaguliers within Grand Lodge, his main contribution to the development of Freemasonry appears to lie in his networks and relationships within Westminster, which were complementary to those of Desaguliers and Martin Folkes within the learned and professional societies and among the Whig aristocracy.

One of Payne's most important connections may have been with William Cowper, later Chairman of the Westminster and Middlesex bench. Cowper was Clerk of the Parliaments, heading the administration of the House of Lords and House of Commons. A member of the Horn, Cowper was also a fellow resident of New Palace Yard.[45] He was appointed Grand Secretary in 1723 and, subsequently, Deputy Grand Master.

Given the intimacy of the government and judicial circles in which Payne and Cowper moved it is probable that Francis Sorrel, Nathaniel Blackerby, Alexander Chocke and other civil servants and JPs who shared similar political and philosophical views, were introduced to Freemasonry – directly or indirectly – by Payne and Cowper. Others so introduced may have included Charles Delafaye, Charles and Thomas Medlicott, Capt. Edward Ridley, Leonard Streate – also written as 'Street' or 'Streete', and Col. George Carpenter. All became members of the Horn; indeed, around twenty members of the lodge sat as London magistrates.[46]

Payne died on 23 February 1757. He had no descendants and the bequests and legacies in his will were principally to his brother's children. His death generated a few brief obituaries in the press, which referred uniformly to his years of service at the Taxes Office.[47] Payne's will was proved in London on 9 March 1757. His wife, Anne, was the sole executor and the principal beneficiary. £2,000 was distributed to the children and grandchildren of 'my late beloved brother, Rev. Thomas Payne'. His nephew, also Rev. Thomas Payne, received £200, as did his nieces, Francis, Countess of Northampton, Catherine, Lady Frances Seymour, and Sarah Way (the wife of Lewis Way). A fourth niece, Mary Payne, a spinster, was given £500. The loans that had been made by George Payne to a second nephew, the Rev. Joseph Payne, were forgiven, and Payne's grand nieces, Joseph Payne's daughters, were each willed £100. Amelia Payne, who had lived with George and Anne, received £500. Legacies of £10 each were left to the Earl & Countess of Northampton; Lord & Lady Frances Seymour; Lewis and Sarah Way; Rev. Joseph Payne & his wife; Hugh Watson of the Temple, his attorney; and James and Edward Batson (his wife's nephews). With respect to the final legacy, it was probably not coincidental that Thomas Batson, a barrister (described as a councillor-at-law) and Payne's brother-in-law, and another member of the Horn, was appointed Junior Grand Warden in 1730 and became an active and influential Deputy Grand Master from 1730 until 1732.

Unlike Desaguliers, the absence of a substantial public persona suggests that Payne had a relatively self-effacing rather than self-promoting character. However, the prominence of government officials and members of the Westminster and Middlesex magistrates' bench among Freemasonry's ranks suggests that he was nonetheless an effective networker.

THE WESTMINSTER AND MIDDLESEX BENCH: A NEW CONNECTION

The sheer number of JPs appointed to the benches of the Liberty of Westminster and County of Middlesex who were – or later became – Freemasons has been overlooked by historians and has remained unexplored. However, given the quantity and seniority of many of those magistrates so far identified as Freemasons, it is reasonable to argue that the nexus may have been as important to the development of Freemasonry as that centred on the Royal Society and other professional learned societies. This was particularly likely to have been the position during the early years of English Grand Lodge, and among its more senior but non-aristocratic Grand Officers.

The absence of lodge membership records earlier than 1723 – and the partial nature of membership data thereafter – precludes any definitive analysis of the inter-relationship between the Middlesex and Westminster benches and Grand Lodge and London Freemasonry. A second complication arises in the variations in the spelling of the names of many of those involved. Nonetheless, there is certainty that many senior magistrates including William Cowper, Nathaniel Blackerby, Leonard Streate, Charles Delafaye, George Carpenter, Alexander Chocke and Thomas de Veil, were at the same time influential and senior Freemasons and, given the publicity that attended Freemasonry at the time, it would be a reasonable conjecture to suggest that they set a positive public example both to their judicial colleagues and more widely.

The influence and power of the magistracy was significant. In Munsche's words, the Justice of the Peace 'occupied a pivotal position in eighteenth century England'.[48] The role incorporated not only 'the preservation of the king's peace and justice'; the magistracy also determined the legal seriousness of offences brought before the bench and therefore the appropriate type of punishment. Magistrates were likewise responsible for tax assessment, licensing and the administration of the poor laws. The London magistracy was regarded properly as a principal line of defence against the London mob and the Grand Jury at the Middlesex Quarter Sessions pronounced on allegations of all offenses, including treason.[49]

Given the explicit political remodelling of the bench that followed the Hanoverian succession, it is probable that the presence of so many Freemasons on the Westminster and Middlesex benches would have required at a minimum the acquiescence of the Whig government and, more probably, its approval. In this context and in others, publicly averred magisterial support for the Craft provided a powerful judicial imprimatur.

There are several instances where English Freemasonry received official and unofficial endorsement. Prominent and obvious examples are the raising of the Duke of Lorraine and the initiation of the Duke of Newcastle at Houghton Hall in 1731, and the well publicised initiation of other senior Whig Parliamentarians, including Walpole. But in some ways it is the minor examples that are of greater interest. A number of Walpole's most prolific press apologists were Freemasons, including James Pitt, a member of Folkes' Bedford Head lodge in Southampton Street, whose phraseology and philosophy had a close commonality with the new Masonic liturgy:

> every created Being must fall infinitely short of the Perfection of an infinite Being; for whatever is Created must be Finite, and limited in all its Powers; and therefore necessarily subject to, or capable of Error and Irregularity.[50]

Another was Raphael Courteville, a member of the lodge at the George at Charing Cross. Whereas Pitt wrote for the *London Journal* and later the *Daily Gazetteer*, Courteville wrote for the *Daily Courant* and later edited the *Daily Gazetteer*. Other prominent pro-government Freemasons and press apologists included Lord Hervey, Horatio Walpole and Theobald Cibber.[51]

The encouragement and acceptance of Freemasonry by the Whig government was a direct product of Grand Lodge's overtly pro-Hanoverian stance and the positive social and political functions that it fulfilled. The establishment characteristics of those on the bench, particularly figures such as William Cowper, Charles Delafaye and Thomas De Veil, reinforced the relationship, as did the broader social arc from which the magistracy was beginning to be selected.

Norma Landau has emphasised the blatantly political nature of appointments to the magistracy and its personification of the 'might of party' in the seventeenth and eighteenth centuries.[52] The changes made to the composition of the bench from 1714 onward were substantive and reflected the ascendancy of the Whigs and their political schematic at a national level. Albeit that central government's influence over provincial local government remained relatively circumscribed when compared to that of London,[53] Landau has demonstrated that successive Hanoverian Lord Chancellors sought to appoint dependable political allies and remove potential opposition Tories and Jacobite sympathisers. This was above all the case in the ultra politically sensitive areas of Westminster and Middlesex, where the bench was configured to be explicitly supportive of the Hanoverian regime and its political, religious and economic objectives. In Landau's words: 'fidelity to the Hanoverian [government was] a touchstone for fitness'.[54]

Reinforcing this analysis but not mentioned by Landau or others, it is notable that the first three Hanoverian Lord Chancellors all had family connections with Freemasonry. The three Lord Chancellors were William Cowper, 1st Earl Cowper, Lord Chancellor from 1714–1718; Thomas Parker, 1st Earl of Macclesfield, who succeeded in 1718 and remained in post until 1725; and Peter King, 1st Baron King of Ockham, who sat from 1725–1733.

Earl Cowper's nephews included William Cowper, the pivotal Grand Secretary of Grand Lodge and later Deputy Grand Master, and his brother, the Rev. John Cowper, a fellow member of the Horn. The Earl of Macclesfield's son, George Parker (1697–1764), the 2nd Earl, was a Freemason – a member of the lodge at the Swan in Chichester, as was his tutor and close friend to both father and son, William Jones, a member of the Queen's Head in Hollis Street. Peter King's son, John (1706–40), 2nd Baron Ockham, was appointed a Grand Steward in 1731 and was recorded as a member of the Lodge of Antiquity in 1736.[55]

CHARLES DELAFAYE, LOYALTY PERSONIFIED

Hail Masonry! Thou Craft divine!
Glory of Earth! From Heav'n reveal'd;
Which dost with Jewels precious shine,
From all but Masons Eyes conceal'd.[56]

Freemasonry's association with the government and its supporters on the Westminster and Middlesex benches may have been typified by men such as Cowper, Blackerby and Chocke, but it reached an apogee in Charles Delafaye (1677–1762).[57] Delafaye, a member of Richmond's Horn Tavern, is best known as the author of the *Fellow Craft's Song* and other Masonic verse.[58] However, his influence was far more significant than such a relatively trivial contribution would suggest. Delafaye's presence reinforced Freemasonry's pro-Hanoverian public profile and provided confirmation to the government that Freemasonry could and should be regarded as a politically steadfast and dependable organisation.

A Huguenot émigré, Delafaye graduated from Oxford in 1696 and joined the diplomatic service. He was appointed secretary to Sir Joseph Williamson, the English ambassador to the United Provinces, and following Williamson's return to London obtained employment in the Southern Department. Delafaye's career under successive Secretaries of State began as a clerk under James Vernon, Secretary for the South, whose son, also James, would similarly become a Freemason.[59] In December 1706 Delafaye was promoted to Chief Clerk and worked under Sunderland until June 1710 and thereafter Dartmouth until August 1713. From 1702 to 1727, he also wrote for the *London Gazette* and between 1707 and 1710 assisted Richard Steel during the latter's editorship of the paper.⁶⁰ They remained close friends. Delafaye left the Southern Department in 1713, taking up appointment as private secretary to Lord Shrewsbury when the latter was made Lord Lieutenant of Ireland. Shrewsbury subsequently arranged for him to become Secretary to the Justices in Ireland in 1715. When Sunderland returned to London in April 1717 as Under Secretary at the Northern Department, Delafaye accompanied him.⁶¹

Delafaye's political reliability had such renown within the government that he was provided with a seat in the Irish House of Commons in order to add weight to the pro-government faction. He remained one of the members for Belturbet, County Cavan, until 1727.

Delafaye was appointed a Justice of the Peace for Westminster in or around 1714–15, a position he held for approximately twenty years.⁶² The nature of his judicial decisions and notably loyal approach were such that it cannot have been coincidental that many of the cases he adjudicated were overtly politically linked.⁶³ One of his first published court cases – in 1717 – concerned the committal of a Jacobite sympathiser 'for publicly affirming in St. James's Park that the Pretender was the only rightful and lawful King'.⁶⁴ Press coverage of his decisions and judicial examinations continued until at least 1736 when press reports record that he investigated a printer suspected of 'printing the libels dispersed in Westminster Hall'.⁶⁵

After serving under Sunderland between April 1717 and March 1718, Delafaye worked as Under Secretary to Stanhope until February 1721 and thereafter Townshend, providing an exceptional degree of permanency and stability at the Northern Department. In April 1724, he transferred to the Southern Department to work for the Duke of Newcastle, a role he retained until stepping down in July 1734.⁶⁶ Despite his retirement as Under Secretary of State for the Southern Department, Delafaye retained the position of Deputy Secretary of State for Scotland until his resignation in 1739. The appointment would have kept him close to the centre of any potential Jacobite threat.⁶⁷ Indeed, his political usefulness was such that he preserved an informal connection with government business until at least the 1750s.⁶⁸

Furbank and Owens have commented on Daniel Defoe's espionage-related letters to Delafaye⁶⁹ that were originally uncovered by William Lee.⁷⁰ Regardless of whether the content was true, fabricated or both, it is an indication of the regard in which Delafaye was held by the British government and by Lord Harley that he was trusted with such communications. A multitude of other examples of Delafaye's activities and of his diplomatic and political correspondence has been noted by historians including Patrick McNally;⁷¹ Geoffrey Holmes;⁷² Philip Haffenden, who wrote that 'he was the main channel through much of the pressure directed at Newcastle passed';⁷³ James Downie;⁷⁴ A.C. Wood;⁷⁵ David Hayton;⁷⁶ Jeremy Black;⁷⁷ and others.⁷⁸ Paul Fritz's comment that 'Charles Delafaye was one of the most highly trusted members of the English Government, especially in all matters involving Jacobites',⁷⁹ was correct, and it is important to recognise

Delafaye's central position as Under Secretary and the reliance placed upon him in collating domestic espionage and collecting foreign intelligence.

Delafaye was rewarded generously by the government and granted sinecures as a Gentleman Sewer to His Majesty (1717)[80] and Clerk of the Signet under the Lord Privy Seal (1728).[81] In May of the same year, he was awarded an honorary doctorate of law from Cambridge University. This would have been a particular tribute in that it was conferred by the King personally and Delafaye was granted the honour alongside a barrage of eminent peers and politicians including the Dukes of Dorset, Grafton, Ancaster, Newcastle and Manchester, and Sir Robert Walpole himself.[82] He was elected FRS in November 1725, proposed by Sir Francis Nicholson (1655–1728), previously Governor of the South Carolina colony,[83] with whom Delafaye had corresponded professionally.[84] One of his last government appointments in 1750 was conferred by the Lords of the Treasury, who assigned him the sinecure of Wine Taster at Dublin.[85]

Delafaye's Masonic verses reveal an almost religious attachment to Freemasonry – 'thou Craft divine' . . . Sweet Fellowship, from Envy free',[86] and a close affiliation with the science it embodied, a subject Delafaye referred to as his 'Inclination to Mechanicks'.[87] However, although Delafaye may be regarded as one of the best examples of a pro-establishment Freemason and Justice of the Peace, and someone for whom Freemasonry was an integral part of his life, there were many others. Over sixty magistrates died or retired from the bench in the four years to 1727, with other sizeable groups excluded for political reasons.[88] Consequently, the Westminster and Middlesex benches were populated by a large number of new entrants.[89]

Although the hand written records of London magistrates held at the London Metropolitan Archives are somewhat hard to decipher, contemporary newspaper reports permit the analysis of four relatively large sets of appointees to the bench. The appointments were those of April 1719, June 1721, August 1724 and November 1727.[90]

WILLIAM COWPER AND THE 1719 INTAKE

The 1719 intake of 41 commissioners of the peace included four later eminent Grand Officers: James Hamilton, Lord Paisley, subsequently Grand Master of Grand Lodge; William Cowper, later Grand Secretary and Deputy Grand Master; Nathaniel Blackerby, later Grand Treasurer and Deputy Grand Master; and the Hon. George Carpenter, later Grand Warden. If a further eight 'probables' are added, it can be noted that c. 30% of the 1719 appointees to the bench were or later became Freemasons.

William Cowper (16__?–1740), was one of the most influential of the 1719 intake. The eldest surviving son of the Hon. Spencer Cowper (1669–1728), Chancellor of the Duchy of Lancaster, Attorney General to the Prince of Wales and Chief Justice of Chester, Cowper had been Clerk of the

Parliaments for almost four years when appointed to the bench.[91] The role and function of Clerk incorporated responsibility for the administration of both House of Lords and Commons, the employment of Parliamentary staff, entering into contracts on behalf of Parliament and the acquisition and management of its assets. The Clerk also served as the chief accounting officer, exercised formal authority in respect of the judicial functions of the House and provided advice on procedural matters to the Speaker and Members. The position had been held formerly by his uncle, Sir William Cowper, a lawyer and Whig MP for Hertford Borough. Cowper acquired the reversionary interest in 1715 and remained Clerk until his death. His place was inherited first by Ashley Cowper, his brother, then by his son.[92]

Although the office commanded only a relatively low base salary of £40 per annum, Cowper's earnings were supplemented by the substantial fees he received for the provision of ancillary parliamentary services. For example, in 1717–18, he collected £279 for 'delivering to the Chancery and Rolls Chapel several Acts of Parliament' and a similar quantum in relation to private members' bills.[93] With responsibility for the allocation of a range of appointments and sinecures within the Palace of Westminster and in accordance with custom, Cowper would have received appropriate reward from those selected.[94] This was likely to have been substantial: two appointments in 1736 and 1737 had salaries of £400 and £300, respectively.[95]

Cowper occupied successively senior positions within the London magistracy. He was chosen as chair of the City of Westminster bench in 1723,[96] a post held until he stepped down in December 1727;[97] and was appointed Chairman of the Middlesex County bench in 1729 and again in 1730.[98] A few months later, Cowper was appointed Patentee to the Commission of Bankrupts, a position described by the press as 'very valuable'.[99] He was re-elected chair of the Middlesex bench in 1733[100] and the same year appointed one of several commissioners charged with a review of the Courts of Justice to 'enquire into their fees'.

Cowper's loyalty to the government was beyond doubt. His *Charge* to the Grand Jury of Middlesex delivered on 9 January 1723 provides a particularly apposite example of a loyal Hanoverian address:

> It ought always to be a Matter of particular Distinction . . . that Justices would be vigilant to detect and produce to Punishment all those who . . . attempt the Subversion of the Great basis upon which stands all that is or can be dear to England and Protestants . . . It is . . . for our Religion, our Liberty and our Property.[101]

The address delivered on 30 June 1727 to the newly invested George II and reported verbatim in the *London Gazette* the following day was similarly clear: 'to preserve our current constitution in Church and State'. The *Charge* Cowper gave to his fellow magistrates three years later was analogous:

The Magistrate ... is trusted to uphold the Honour, the Dignity, and the Majesty of the State; to see that Order is observed; that equal Right be done according to known and approved Law; ... and ever to bear in Mind the high Nature, and vast importance of this Trust; and whoever assumes ... such Powers upon any other Principle, is, and should be treated as, a Subverter of Peace, Order, and good Government, of the world, and an Enemy to human Society.[102]

The parallels with Payne's Masonic *Charges* are evident. Not only was a Mason 'a peaceable Subject to the Civil Powers ... never to be concerned in Plots and Conspiracies against the Peace and Welfare of the Nation', but each Freemason was obliged to agree specifically:

to be a good man and true, and strictly to obey the moral law ... to be a peaceable subject, and cheerfully to conform to the laws of the country in which [he] reside[d] ... not to be concerned in plots and conspiracies against government [and] patiently ... submit to the decisions of the supreme legislature [and] ... the civil magistrate.

Cowper was central to Freemasonry's development both as a senior member of the Horn and as the first Grand Secretary, holding the office from 1723 until 1727, creating what became a central position. He succeeded Desaguliers as Deputy Grand Master in 1726.

Although Cowper earned and inherited sufficient funds to become a small-scale philanthropist, donating £100 towards a new town hall in Hertford where he had a country home, towards the end of his life he was financially distressed. His reverse stemmed from lengthy and costly family litigation.[103] On the 1st Earl's death in 1723, Cowper's father entered a claim on his brother's estate which led to a long and complex dispute in Chancery involving both the late Earl's will and that of wife, who died shortly after him. The claim was pursued by Cowper after his father's death. The case was ruinously expensive and although it eventually settled in 1739, Cowper was sued for unpaid debts in the late 1730s and forced to sell assets, including prized property in Lincoln's Inn Fields.[104]

NATHANIEL BLACKERBY

Nathaniel Blackerby (16__?–1742), another 1719 appointee to the bench, worked at the Exchequer as Clerk of the Patent. Tangentially, Alexander Chocke, also later a Deputy Grand Master and a fellow JP, was Clerk of the Registers in the same department.[105] In early 1722, Blackerby was concurrently appointed Treasurer to the Commission for Building Fifty Churches. The position had significant financial responsibility. An indication of the quantum of money processed by the Commission is set out in papers held at Lambeth Palace Library. They provide details of both receipt and expenditure warrants and among other things the payments and reimbursement of fees and expenses received by Blackerby himself.[106] These were substantial, including a gratuity of £50 on 28 June 1725 and the reimbursement of extensive personal expenses of £83 8s 10d on 25 August 1727, £134 18s 0d on 29 March 1728, £75 10s 6d on 6 February 1731, £31 6s 4d on 7 April 1733 and £62 3s 9d on 2 May 1740.[107] They were among the smaller sums: in January 1729, the receipt of £1,000 'to be distributed by him among the Workmen employed in building the said Churches' was noted by the press.[108] The Lambeth Palace archives reveal the work involved, the multiple accounts and records generated, and the dissatisfaction of Blackerby and his staff with their pay.[109]

As Treasurer to the Commission, Blackerby worked closely with Nicholas Hawksmoor (1662–1736), the Principal Surveyor, with the pair responsible jointly for signing completion certificates for the works undertaken.[110] Perhaps not coincidentally, Hawksmoor was also a Freemason as was his assistant, John James, the Second Surveyor, who had been a colleague of Hawksmoor for some time.[111] John James was a member of the lodge at the Swan in East Street, Greenwich, of which Sir James Thornhill was WM. The Swan was close to Greenwich Hospital where James had been the Assistant Clerk of Works and Hawksmoor the Deputy Surveyor and his superior. Another member of the Swan was Alexander Chocke.

Blackerby and Hawksmoor's relationship functioned on both a professional and personal level. Their tour of England together in the early 1730s included a visit to Blenheim on which Hawksmoor had worked with Edward Strong Jr., yet another member of the Swan. It also incorporated Castle Howard, on which Hawksmoor had worked with Sir John Vanbrugh. Blackerby married Hawksmoor's daughter, Elizabeth, in 1735 and when Hawksmoor died in March the following year, Blackerby wrote his obituary. He and Elizabeth inherited the estate.[112]

In 1726, in addition to his positions at the Treasury and the Commission, Blackerby was appointed Housekeeper in Ordinary at Westminster Palace, a position in the gift of William Cowper.[113] Interestingly, he was once again unhappy with the level of salary and petitioned for a fresh grant.[114]

Like Cowper, Chocke, Delafaye, Payne and Desaguliers, Blackerby was also a member of the Horn Tavern lodge. He was subsequently invited to become a member of Grand Lodge, serving as Grand Warden in 1727 and Deputy Grand Master in each of the following two years. Like Delafaye, Blackerby actively proselytised Freemasonry and in 1729, and again in 1730, wrote the prologue and epilogue for plays performed at the Theatre Royal, Drury Lane in front of a largely Masonic audience:

> The Grand Master, Wardens, and most of the gentlemen present, took tickets to appear in white gloves at the Theatre Royal in Drury Lane . . . where the Play of Henry IV, Part II was enacted for their Entertainment.[115]

While Deputy Grand Master, Blackerby was appointed Grand Treasurer of the Charity Bank, holding the position until his resignation in 1738. His departure was triggered by a request from Grand Lodge that the Treasurer post security for monies held on behalf of the Bank. Although there was no accusation or evidence of financial impropriety and 'several of the Brethren ... acquainted [Grand] Lodge that they had not the least intention of offering any Indignity ... to the Treasurer', Blackerby regarded the demand as a slur. In response, he commented that:

> he could not be insensible of the Indignity offered him in the above Resolutions & the ill treatment he had met in the Debate & that he resented the same in the highest manner.[116]

The *Minutes* continue:

> [He] then resigned his Office of Treasurer & promised to send the next morning to the GS a Draught [sic] on the Bank for the Balance in his hands.

Grand Lodge's anxiety for the security of its increasingly sizeable charitable funds was, perhaps, understandable. Their apprehension may have been instigated or heightened by Blackerby's involvement with the Charitable Corporation which had collapsed in 1731 following embezzlement by John Thomason, an employee, and George Robinson, a stockbroker.[117]

Nevertheless, Blackerby's concern for his reputation was understandable given that he held positions in several prominent charities and government sponsored organisations. In common with other prominent Freemasons, including Henry Herbert, the 9th Earl of Pembroke, Payne, Desaguliers and Charles Labelye (1705–81), one of Desaguliers' several protégés, Blackerby was closely involved with the re-building of Westminster Bridge as Treasurer to the commission overseeing the project.[118] Blackerby was also a trustee for the new colony of Georgia, another semi-Masonic project.[119]

With regard to the Middlesex and Westminster magistracy, following Cowper's resignation as chair of the Westminster bench in 1727, Blackerby was nominated as his successor. However, 'after a Letter ... intimating his Desire of being excused the chair', Leonard Streate, another of the 1719 intake and again a member of the Horn, was 'unanimously chose'.[120] Streate had last chaired the Westminster bench in 1725.[121] He was at the time Steward of the Borough Court, Southwark, and a barrister in the Middle Temple.[122] In 1725, he had been appointed one of the commissioners nominated to enforce the bankruptcy laws and was later made a deputy commissioner in the Alienation Office.[123] Streate had been elected chair of the Middlesex bench before – in 1722 – but had stood down and been replaced by Cowper the following year. This may have been linked to his marriage.[124] The East Sussex and Hertfordshire archives contain the record of a 1723 marriage settlement with Gratiana, one of Sir Charles Cox's several daughters.[125] Cox was Whig MP for Southwark where he owned a brewery and had extensive property interests. Maintaining the Masonic link, he was also a leading member of the lodge at the Bedford Head.

Although there are relatively few press reports of judicial cases heard by Streate,[126] his obituary, published in 1729, referred to him as 'an excellent Magistrate, using no mean Artifices to draw Business, never making Justice a Trade'.[127] The LMA holds records of his judicial activities between 1721 and 1726 at each of the Middlesex, Westminster and City of London Sessions.[128] Streate's proposed re-appointment as chair of the Westminster bench in 1727 was heavily publicised with articles in the *London Evening Post*, *Evening Journal*, *Daily Journal*, *British Journal* and other newspapers in late November and December 1727. However, on 30 December 1727, a note in the *Daily Journal* indicated that Streate had unexpectedly declined the position. The paper gave no explanation and Streate continued to serve as a magistrate, albeit less actively than as before. Poor health may have been the cause of his demurring; he died just over 12 months later.[129]

In contrast to Streate, Blackerby's judicial activities were reported extensively by the press, with several hundred items appearing over the course of his career on the bench. The LMA contains around 200 records.[130] Newspaper articles date from 1721 and suggest that he was a rigorous jurist.[131] In this he continued in his father's steps: *The Justice of the Peace – a Companion*, published by Blackerby and widely promoted by him in the classified ads, was compiled by his father, Samuel, a barrister at Gray's Inn.[132]

In 1738, shortly after his appointment as a Deputy Lord Lieutenant for Middlesex,[133] Blackerby finally agreed to become chair of the Westminster bench.[134] His speech to the Westminster Justices that year followed the passage of the controversial Gin Act of 1736 and other legislation against 'spiritous liquors'. It was similar in tone to Cowper's earlier *Charges* and like Cowper, Blackerby reminded his audience that duty, liberty and property were fundamental important to good society:

> the Cause you are engaged in, is the Cause of your God, your King and your Country . . . consider the Duty you owe as Subjects to your King, under whose mild Government, and wise Administration, every Man enjoys the Fruits of his Labour, his Liberty, his Property.[135]

His passion for order and respect for property rights were matched by other colleagues on the bench. The Hon. Colonel George Carpenter (*c*. 1694–1749), later 2nd Baron Carpenter of Killaghy and MP for Morpeth from 1717 until 1727, was another (probable re-appointee) who featured in the 1719 intake. Carpenter sat as a magistrate for some 30 years.[136] Perhaps best known for his introduction of a Parliamentary Private Bill to alter his marriage settlement,[137] he was appointed Grand Warden in 1729 and was a member of three London lodges: the Horn in Westminster; the Bedford Head; and lodge no. 63, subsequently St. George's and Corner Stone Lodge No. 5.

Carpenter's appointment to the bench was in keeping with his family's pro-Hanoverian Whig politics and strong Protestant beliefs. His father, also George (1657–1732), had been nominated by Stanhope as Ambassador to Vienna but, following the 1715 uprising, was instead appointed to command British forces in northern England against the Jacobites. Made commander-in-chief in Scotland in 1716, he was elected MP for Whitchurch (1715–22) and for Westminster (1722–27).

Carpenter continued in the family's military tradition, and his Lieutenant Colonelcy of the 1st Foot Guards was followed with a Lieutenant Colonelcy in the 1st Life Guards, the regiment of which the Duke of Montagu was Colonel from 1715 until 1721. Like his father, Carpenter also served as a churchwarden at St. George's, Hanover Square,[138] where a number of other Freemasons were parishioners. They included Sir Cecil Wray, also a fellow churchwarden, who was later Master of the King's Arms lodge and Deputy Grand Master.

Alongside Blackerby, Carpenter was a member of the Council of the Georgia Society. Overall, Freemasons funded around a tenth of the cost of establishing the colony, mainly through lodge collections, the balance coming from Parliament. Thomas Batson, then Deputy Grand Master, a fellow Georgia commissioner, steered the fund raising process through Grand Lodge:

> Then the Deputy Grand Master opened to the Lodge the Affairs of Planting the new Colony of Georgia in America . . . and informed the Grand Lodge that the Trustees had to Nathaniel Blackerby Esq. and to himself Commissions under their Common Seal to collect the Charity of this Society towards establishing the Trustees to send distressed Brethren to Georgia where they may be comfortably provided for.
> Proposed: that it be strenuously recommended by Masters and Wardens of regular lodges to make a generous collection among all their members for that purpose.
> Which being seconded by Br Rogers Holland Esq. (one of the said Trustees) who opened the Nature of the Settlement), and by Sir William Keith Bt., who was many years Governor of Pennsylvania, by Dr Desaguliers, Lord Southwell, Br. Blackerby and many other worthy brethren, it was recommended accordingly.[139]

The contributions to co-finance Georgia represented the first occasion on which Freemasons as a group supported a non-Masonic charity. Notwithstanding its nominal purpose as a home for deserving debtors, the colony was principally an attempt to establish a secure buffer area between the Spanish in Florida and the valuable Carolina colonies. The venture was championed by Major General James Oglethorpe. Although not appearing on any Grand Lodge list of Freemasons, Oglethorpe co-founded the first Masonic lodge at Savannah in February 1734 within a year of first settlement.[140] Several others who sailed with Oglethorpe were or later became prominent Georgia Freemasons. Many also held high office in the colony, most notably Noble Jones, the first man to be initiated a Freemason on Georgia soil, who became its constable, Indian agent, member of the Council and the owner of a large estate to the south of Savannah. He was later made Chief Justice, Commander of the Militia and Treasurer of the Colony. His son also held office as Speaker of Georgia's Commons – both before and after independence – and was one of Georgia's delegates to the Continental Congress.

In addition to Carpenter, others in the 1719 intake included Robert Viner (or Vyner), a member of the lodge meeting at the Rummer, Charing Cross; Thomas Moor, a Grand Steward in 1731; Thomas Cook, a Warden at the King's Head in Seven Dials; Alexander Strahan, another member of the Rummer; and John Collins, a member of the Baptist's Head lodge in Chancery Lane.[141] Further 'possibles' include Raphael Dubois (a Rev. Mr Dubois was a member of the Horn); William Booth (a 'Mr. Booth' was a member of the Masons' Arms in Fulham); and William Lloyd, a member of the influential lodge at the Nag's Head and Star in Carmarthenshire.

Given the relatively aristocratic and affluent membership of the Rummer, 'Robert Viner' was probably Robert Vyner of Swakeley near Ickenham in Middlesex. Thomas Vyner, his father, had held extensive property assets in Uxbridge and Ickenham and these were later inherited by his son.[142] The Berkshire Record Office has details of a bond of £10,000 held by Vyner in 1720 to secure repayment of £5,250 from a John Lansdell of the Tower of London.[143] Vyner was only moderately active as a magistrate and the Middlesex Sessions, Justices' Working Documents contain only ten instances of him sitting between 1724 and 1730.

The June 1721 Intake

Around a third of the thirty-seven Justices of the Peace appointed in June 1721[144] subsequently appeared in Grand Lodge's lists of members, many having senior positions in their lodges, including two with Grand Rank:

Sir George Markham	Warden, Sun, Southside, St. Paul's
Grantham Andrews	Member, Old Devil, Temple Bar
Alexander Chocke	DGM, 1727; Grand Warden, 1726; Warden, Horn; Member, Swan, Greenwich
Christian Cole	Member, Red Lyon, Richmond; and/or Master, Vine Tavern, Holborn
Samuel Edwards	Warden, Horn
Richard Gifford	Warden, Castle Tavern, St. Giles
John Hedges	Member, Bedford Head, Covent Garden
Samuel Horsey	Member, Horn
John Rotheram	Warden, Anchor, Duchy Lane, the Strand
Joseph Rouse	Member, Bear & Harrow, Butcher Row

Francis Sorrel	Grand Warden (1723 & 1724), Horn
Henry Turner	Member, Vine Tavern, Holborn
George Watkins,[145]	Member, Rummer, Charing Cross

At least two of the newly appointed magistrates can probably be linked directly to George Payne: Francis Sorrel, his immediate superior, and Alexander Chocke at the Exchequer. Payne is likely to have introduced both to Freemasonry, as he did Edward Wilson, another colleague at the Taxes Office.

Francis Sorrel (16__?–1743) was a second or third-generation Huguenot émigré. The name was relatively common in Huguenot circles: Jacques Sorel, Marie Sorel, Jean Sorel, Magdelaine Sorel, Anne Sorel and Marie Sorel, all feature in Minet's *Register of Baptisms of the Church of the Artillery, Spitalfields, 1691–1786*; and an Elizabeth Sorelle (also written as 'Sorrel') is recorded in Minet's *Register of La Patente, Soho*. Like Desaguliers, Francis Sorrel assimilated into Anglicanism, being appointed a Gentleman of the Vestry at the new church of St. John the Evangelist in Horseferry Road in Westminster.[146] He was made a Grand Warden in 1723 and was active through to the late 1720s. However, the *Grand Lodge Minutes* of 28 August 1730 suggest that by the end of the decade he was often away from London and was unable to attend meetings of the Grand Charity to which committee he had been appointed in 1725. Payne took up most of his workload.

Alexander Chocke (16__?–1737), a Warden at the Horn, was a reappointee to the bench. He held the position of Clerk of the Debentures at the Exchequer, a lucrative role yielding some £300–£400 annually. The post was in the gift of the Earl of Halifax, Auditor of the Exchequer. Chocke had been promoted from Clerk of the Registers in the same department and had served in the civil service since the turn of the century: his obituary in the *Daily Gazetteer* on 24 January 1737 recorded 'near forty years' of service.[147] He featured in Parliamentary committees and in Treasury correspondence throughout the 1720s and 1730s, and his correspondence and announcements appeared regularly in the *Official Gazette*.

Chocke's activities on the bench in Middlesex and Westminster were reported extensively and suggest he was a solidly loyal Hanoverian jurist. Tangentially, he was one of a small number of JPs – including Blackerby – who were sued by the collectors of the Westminster turnpike seeking compensation over a case found against them. The turnpike collectors alleged false jurisdiction but, perhaps inevitably, lost their case against the bench. Notwithstanding, similar legal actions posed a frequent issue for the more vigorous magistrates and explain why many preferred relative inactivity.

Chocke was a member of three lodges: the Horn in Westminster, close to his home at New Palace Yard; the Swan at Greenwich, where – among others – Thornhill and Highmore were also members; and with Blackerby, the Castle in Highgate. Within Grand Lodge Chocke was of the inner circle. He was recorded as having 'waited on Dalkeith' at the time the latter was appointed Grand Master, and notably provided the thanks of Grand Lodge to Dalkeith for his 'consents'.[148]

Chocke was made Grand Warden in 1726 under Lord Inchiquin, with William Cowper as Deputy Grand Master; and the following year became Deputy Grand Master under Lord Coleraine, with Blackerby and Highmore as his Wardens. He was a notably frequent attendee as a past Grand Officer and an active supporter of Desaguliers and Payne.[149]

In 1726, with William Burdon, his fellow Grand Warden and another magistrate,[150] Chocke acted as one of two squires to Sir William Morgan at the latter's investiture as a Knight of the Bath in June 1725.[151] The invitation to attend the investiture was in all probability at the instigation of Earl Halifax, Morgan's brother-in-law and Chocke's patron at the Exchequer. A significant number of those invested and attending were Freemasons, including the Duke of Montagu, who was appointed Grand Master of the Order, the Duke of Richmond, the Earl of Delorraine and the Earl of Inchiquin. Other Freemasons attending included Martin Folkes and Thomas Hill, squires to the Duke of Richmond; Col. Francis Columbine, a squire to Lord Malpas; Robert Barry, attending on Lord Inchiquin; John James on Viscount Tyrconnel; and Col. Daniel Houghton as a squire to the Earl of Suffolk.

Perhaps not coincidentally given Montagu's position as Grand Master of the Order, Joseph Highmore (1692–1780), a Member of the Swan at Greenwich and a Grand Warden in 1727, was selected to paint the Knights of the Bath in their regalia. Highmore was a lawyer turned society painter who sought to emulate the artistic success of his uncle, Thomas Highmore, who had been Serjeant-Painter to the King. Sir James Thornhill, Grand Warden in 1728, had been apprenticed to Thomas Highmore and Thornhill, the Master of the Swan, succeeded him as Serjeant-Painter in 1720. The circular connection was maintained by Joseph Highmore, who worked with Thornhill at the Royal Naval Hospital and attended his St. Martin's Lane Art Academy alongside Hogarth. All three later donated paintings to Thomas Coram's Foundling Hospital, a popular and high profile charity among Freemasons, with Highmore's *Hagar and Ishmael* given a prominent position in the Court Room.

Portraiture and art more generally, played a largely positive role as a means of enhancing the status of Freemasonry's central figures and of Freemasonry itself. Despite occasional sniping, Freemasons and Freemasonry were on balance also depicted positively in the press, at least through to the mid-1730s. Indeed, there were relatively few negative reports even in the Tory press: *Fog's Weekly Journal* and *Mist's Weekly Journal* generally ignored the Masons and carried only a small number of reports in the decade to 1731, few of which were pejorative. One exception was the coverage given to the Gormogons, an organisation probably created by the Duke of Wharton following his departure from Grand Lodge.

The social and professional characteristics of other JPs from the 1721 intake provide confirmation of the conservative and pro-establishment nature of many Freemasons sitting on the bench: Sir George Markham, the

1   The Rev. John Theophilus Desaguliers (1683–1744)

The portrait was painted in 1901 by T.R. Beaufort Hinkes from a 1725 mezzotint Peter Pelham (c. 1695–1751). Pelham's work was based on a contemporary painting of Desaguliers by Hans Hysing (1678–1753).

2   The Rev. James Anderson

This is a detail from William Hogarth's 'The Mystery of Masonry brought to Light by the Gormogons', engraved c. 1730. Many scholars now consider other supposed likenesses not to be of Anderson.

3   Unknown Senior Warden

The sitter was originally thought to have been Sir James Thornhill. The artist is unknown and the portrait painted c. 1730.

4 Anthony Sayer, first Grand Master of Grand Lodge

The portrait was painted in 1885 by T.R. Beaufort Hinkes from a work by Joseph Highmore, c. 1730.

5 Martin Folkes (1690–1754)

The engraving by William Hogarth in 1742 may have marked Folkes' appointment as President of the Royal Society the prior year.

6 William Stukeley (1687–1765)

The mezzotint is by John Smith after Sir Godfrey Kneller, 1721.

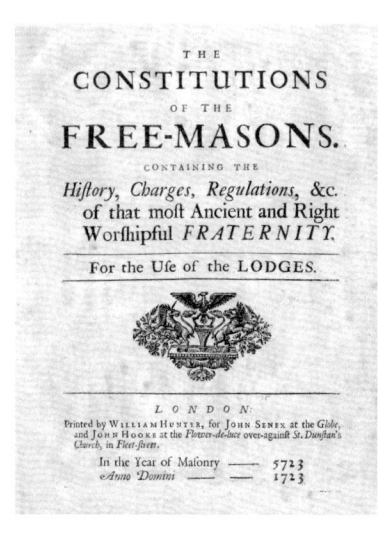

7   The Constitutions of the Freemasons, title page

The first edition of the Constitutions was published in 1723 by John Senex and John Hooke.

8   The Book of Constitutions, engraved frontispiece

The engraving is from the edition by Alfred Benjamin Cole (c. 1697–1783) in 1731.

9   The inside cover and frontispiece of John Pine's 1725 Engraved List of Lodges

THE COMMITTEE, to whom it was refered to consider of Proper Methods to regulate the Generall Charity, after, severall Meetings for that Purpose, came to the following resolutions, which they Submit to the Judgment of the Grand Lodge as conducive to the End proposed by the Reference.

I THAT it is the Opinion of the Committee, that the Contributions from the Severall Lodges be paid Quarterly and Voluntary.

II THAT No Brother be recommended by any Lodge, as an Object of this Charity, but who was a Member of Some regular Lodge, which shall Contribute to the same Charity on or before the 21st Day of November 1724, when the Generall Charity was first proposed in the Grand Lodge.

III THAT No Brother, who has been Admitted a Member of any such Lodge since that time, or shall hereafter be so Admitted, be recommended till three Years after such Admission: And as to the Methods or rules to be Observed by the Grand Lodge in relieving such Brethren who shall be Qualified as aforesaid; whom they shall think fitt, upon Application to themselves, to relieve; Viz. Those concerning the Circumstances of the Persons to be relieved; the sums to be paid; the times or terms of payment; the Continuance, Suspending or taking off such Allowance, with the reasons thereof, whether arising from the Circumstances of the Assisted Brother being better'd, or from his behaviour in any respect rendring him unfitt to have it Continued; and in Generall all other circumstances Attending the regular and Ordinary distribution of the Charity, where the Grand Lodge think fitt to put any One upon it: the Committee are of Opinion They are most decently and securely left to the Wisdom care and Discretion of the Grand Lodge, to do therein from time to time as cases shall happen, in a Manner most Agreeable to the Exigencies of them; Which as the Committee cannot foresee with any Certainty, so they are unable to Lay down any fixed proposalls concerning them; But as it may fall out that a Brother who is in all respects qualified for relief and in need of it, may by the pressure of his Circumstances be forced to Apply perhaps a Good while before a Quarterly Communication may be had, or the Grand Lodge Assembled, for a present relief or subsistance till he can make his Case known to the Grand Lodge for their further favour: the Committee took that Case into their particular Consideration and as to that are humbly of Opinion.

IV THAT three pounds, and no more, may be given to any particular distressed Brother who shall be recommended by any Lodge as an Object of this Charity, without the Consent of the Grand Lodge.

10   Regulations of the Charity Committee

The work was engraved by John Pine in 1730.

11 John Montagu, 2nd Duke of Montagu, (1690–1749). Grand Master, 1721

The mezzotint is by John Faber jr. (1695–1756), after Sir Godfrey Kneller (1646–1723). The date is unknown.

12 John Montagu, 2nd Duke of Montagu

The portrait is attributed to Johannes van Eiest; date unknown.

13 Philip Wharton, 1st Duke of Wharton (1698–1731). Grand Master, 1722

The artist is unknown, but possibly John Simon; c. 1722.

14 Charles Lennox, 2nd Duke of Richmond (1701–1750). Grand Master, 1724

The portrait is by Jonathan Richardson (1665–1745), c. 1724.

15 Alexander Chocke (16??–1737)

Chocke is depicted in the robes of a Squire to a Knight of the Bath. The mezzotint is by John Faber jr. (1695–1756), after Joseph Highmore (1692–1780), c. 1725–6.

16 John Pine (1690–1756)

The mezzotint is by William Hogarth, c. 1740.

17 Frederick, Prince of Wales (1707–1751)

The portrait is by Charles Philips (1798–1747), 1731.

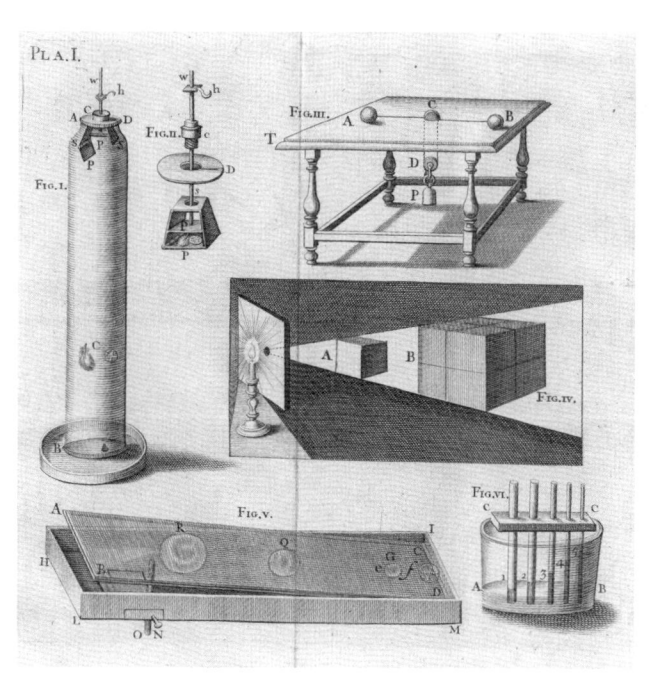

18 Depiction of Experimental Equipment

The plate is from volume 1 of the 1763 edition of Desaguliers' 'Experimental Philosophy'.

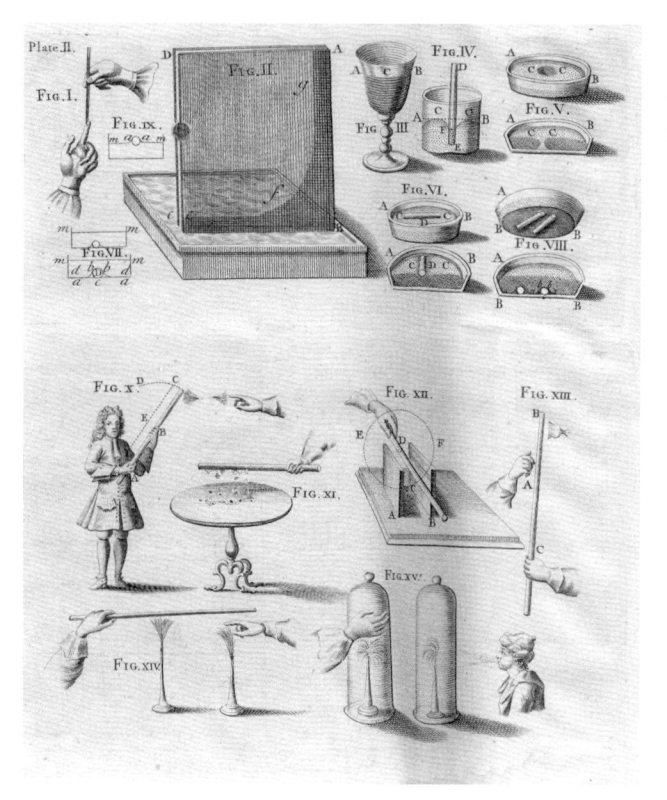

19 Examples of Experiments

The plate is from volume 1 of the 1763 edition of Desaguliers' 'Experimental Philosophy'.

20 Henry Hare, 3rd Baron Coleraine (1693–1749). Grand Master, 1728

The etching was published in 1807 by J. Scott.

21 John Lindsay, 20th Earl of Crawford (1702–1749). Grand Master, 1734

The portrait is taken from AQC, vol. 19, published London, 1906.

22 John Campbell, 4th Earl of Loudon (1705–1782). Grand Master, 1736

Both artist and date are unknown.

23 Robert Raymond, 2nd Lord Raymond (1717–1756). Grand Master, 1739

The mezzotint is by George Vertue; date unknown.

Warden at the Sun by St. Paul's, was a barrister and a member of the Middle Temple;[152] Grantham Andrews was the younger son of the affluent Sir Jonathan Andrews of Kempton Park;[153] and Christian Cole was a diplomat and former Secretary Resident in Venice who later worked for the controversial York Buildings Company.[154] Others included Samuel Edwards, a Deputy Teller at the Exchequer and MP for Great Wenlock in Shropshire,[155] later awarded the sinecure of Constable to the Tower of London in 1725. John Hedges was another MP, representing St. Michael in Cornwall. He was appointed envoy to Sardinia in 1726[156] and in 1728 became Treasurer to his friend the Prince of Wales, a position regarded as exceptionally valuable and 'computed worth £4,000 per annum'.[157]

Colonel Samuel Horsey had been a trustee and provisional governor of the South Carolina colony;[158] he was made Governor of South Carolina in 1738.[159] Horsey had previously served as a director of the York Buildings Company.[160] Colonel George Watkins, a member of the aristocratic Rummer lodge, had been a Major in Sir Robert Rich's Regiment of Foot.[161] Rich was a prominent member of the Horn. Watkins was later appointed Governor of South Sea Castle, Henry VIII's fort at the mouth of the Solent.[162]

Joseph Haynes, a member of the Ship without Temple Bar, was yet another probable JP. Although not listed among the 1719 or 1721 intake, a 'Joseph Hayne' appeared in the General Orders of the Court, Middlesex Sessions, on 7 December 1722. Haynes was one of several magistrates including Streate, Cowper, Blackerby, Sorrel and Delafaye, appointed to inquire into the collection of the municipal rates and the 'great Sumes of money on pretence of cleaning the Streets' by the Burgesses within the Liberty of Westminster.[163] 'Gwin Vaughan', another magistrate on the same list, was probably not William Vaughan, a member of the Rummer in Queen Street, off Cheapside, who was appointed a Grand Warden in 1739.

The August 1724 Intake

Among the 54 appointees to the Westminster bench listed on 25 August 1724 were 14 probable Freemasons, or just over a quarter. They included the Hon. Col. Daniel Houghton, then a company commander in the 1st Foot Guards who was in 1725 appointed a Grand Warden and a member of the Grand Lodge Charity Committee.[164]

The August 1724 Masonic intake as a whole comprised:

Col. Daniel Houghton	GW, 1725; Master, Rummer, Charing Cross
Joseph Gascoigne	Warden, Rummer, Henrietta Street and/or Member, Ship, Royal Exchange
Robert Jackson	Member, King's Arms, St. Paul's; and/or Member, One Tun, Noble Street; and/or Member, St. Paul's Head, Ludgate Street

William Jones	Warden, Queens Head, Hollis Street
John Nichol	Member, Crown, Royal Exchange
Francis Reynolds	Member, Rummer, Charing Cross
Col. Edward Ridley	Member, Horn Tavern[165]
John Smith	Member, Queen's Head, Knaves Acre and/or Member, Vine, Holborn; or Castle & Leg, Holborn
Bowater Vernon	Member, Bedford Head, Covent Garden

Other 'possible' Freemasons include:

Edward Harrison	Black Posts, Great Wild Street
Thomas Jackson	Nag's Head, Princes Street, and/or King's Arms, St. Paul's
Ralph Radcliff	Ship without Temple Bar
John Kirby	Black Posts, Great Wild Street
Simon Mitchel	Horn, Westminster

Not within the above list, a Stephen Hall was separately recorded as a magistrate in 1723.[166] This was probably the Dr Stephen Hall who sat as Worshipful Master of the Ship in Bartholomew Lane and was Master of the Globe at Moorgate. Hall deputised as Grand Warden for Sir Thomas Prendergast in 1726.[167]

The November 1727 Intake

The 22 November 1727 intake represented one of the largest groups of new appointees.[168] Headed by Charles Lennox, 2nd Duke of Richmond, who had been appointed Grand Master in 1725, the list contained around 130 names. Clearly identifiable and probable Freemasons comprise a smaller percentage of the total number relative to previous years but nonetheless represent a relatively large quantum. They were:

Sir William Billers	Rummer, Charing Cross
Sir George Cook	Rummer, Charing Cross
James Cook	Rummer, Charing Cross, and/or Swan Tavern, Fish Street Hill
John Cress	Warden, Coach & Horses, Maddox Street
Ambrose Dickens	Vine Tavern, Holborn
Charles Hayes	Rummer, Charing Cross
John Hicks	Mitre, Reading
Samuel Lambert	Green Lettice, Brownlow Street, and/or Swan Tavern, Fish Street Hill, and/or King's Head, Pall Mall
William Lock	Queens Arms, Newgate Street

Richard Makdowal[169]	King's Arms, St. Paul's
Thomas Medlicott	Horn, Westminster
James Naish	Steward, lodge unknown
Henry Norris	Cheshire Cheese, Arundel Street
John Oakley[170]	Bedford Head, Covent Garden
Andrew Osborn	Swan on Fish Street Hill
Col. Thomas Paget[171]	Horn, Westminster
Richard Parsons[172]	Kings Arms, New Bond Street
John Savage	Goat at the Foot of the Haymarket
Samuel Savill	Cock & Bottle, Little Britain
Barwell Smith	Red Lyon, Richmond
John Smith	Griffin, Newgate Street, and/or other lodges
William Thompson	Mitre Tavern, Covent Garden
Henry Vincent	Bedford Head, Covent Garden Street Hill and/or Three Tuns & Bull's Head

The two names that head the list again demonstrate the political and social characteristics of those made magistrates. Sir William Billers (1689–1745), was portrayed by Nicholas Rogers as a member of the 'big bourgeoisie of Hanoverian London'.[173] He was a stalwart of the Haberdashers' company, a City Sheriff in 1721, an Alderman in 1722; and elected Lord Mayor in 1734.[174] Billers also commanded the Honourable Artillery Company, the oldest regiment in the British army and rightly considered a bulwark against the London mob, and the 'Blue regiment of Train'd-Bands', one of six such regiments in the London militia under the jurisdiction of the Lord Mayor. A Privy Councillor, Billers' robust judicial approach is detailed in around 700 press reports of court cases from 1727 until his death in 1745.

Sir George Cook held a substantial estate at Uxbridge and owned a town house at Lincoln Inn Fields. He held office as Chief Prothonotary of the Common Pleas, the chief administrator of the Civil Division of the Court of Common Pleas.[175] Cook subsequently stood (albeit unsuccessfully) as a knight of the shire for the county of Middlesex. It is notable however that he was recommended for the position by the Duke of Newcastle.[176]

Others within the 1727 intake include Charles Hayes (1676–1760), the mathematician and barrister and a member of Gray's Inn. He is known for having written the *Treatise of Fluxions, An Introduction to Mathematical Philosophy*, published in 1704 and one of the first books to explain Newton's calculus. Hayes was additionally a member of the Court of Assistants for the Royal African Company. A traveller and geographer, he became Deputy Governor of the Company in 1733 and remained in that position until the dissolution of the company in 1752. The Royal African Company was involved in the slave trade until 1731 when it diversified to trade ivory and gold.

Thomas Medlicott, another appointee, was a member of the Commission for Building Fifty Churches and a Commissioner of the Revenue in Ireland, appointed 31 May 1716. He was elected Knight of the Shire for Milborne Port in Somerset in the first parliament of George II.

The absence of complete biographical data precludes an analysis of more than a limited number of other magistrates identified as a Freemasons. However, among those who were, a few, such as Henry Norris (c. 1671–1762) should be singled out. Norris was the author of the eponymous 'Justicing Notebook'.[177] Norris's 'Notebook' was published in 1991, edited by Ruth Paley, and her comments provide a striking indication of his political and personal motivations:

> Norris [like his father and grandfather] became a merchant; in addition to his Hackney property, he also held lands in Southwark and the City. We know little of his character and personal life, although his justicing activities certainly suggest a man of somewhat harsh and authoritarian views. He was a fervent supporter of the Whig government of the day: so much so that in 1731 he (along with Samuel Tyssen) was chosen to sit as a member of the notoriously packed jury that convicted Richard Francklin, publisher of the opposition journal, the *Craftsman* . . . Becoming an active justice clearly gave Norris much power in the community [and] resolved all doubts about his social status. His conduct as a justice (which was, by contemporary standards, impeccable) enhanced his claim to gentry status still further, and one suspects that his reputation for integrity was just as important a part of his legacy to his descendants as his house and fortune. When in 1739 a list of 'Chief Gentlemen of the Parish' was drawn up, Henry Norris's name topped the list.[178]

In all, Paley identified six 'exceptionally active' fellow magistrates in Middlesex among Norris's contemporaries on the bench. The six – of some 78 magistrates recorded as working in 1732 – were responsible for just under half of the approximately 2,000 recognizances returned to the general and quarter sessions that year, an average of around 165 each. To put this figure into perspective, the majority of Justices, that is, over 70%, each returned less than 25 cases.

The 'active' magistrates singled out by Paley were [Richard] Gifford;[179] [Valentine] Hilder;[180] [Richard] Manley;[181] [Colonel John] Mercer;[182] [Clifford William] Philips; and [Thomas] Robe.[183] Three of the six were Freemasons and were zealous in their loyalty to the government and to the maintenance of property rights. Richard Gifford was Warden of the Castle Tavern, St. Giles; Manley a member of the Bedford Head in Covent Garden; and William Philips a Member and later Warden of the Rose & Crown in King Street, Westminster. Although the absence of complete membership data means that we cannot be certain of their Masonic status, there is currently no evidence to suggest that Hilder, Mercer or Robe were also Freemasons. However, there are other prominent examples.

Sir Thomas de Veil (1684–1746) is notable as the subject of Hogarth's

Night, the final print in the series *Four Times of the Day*.[184] He was appointed to the Middlesex and Westminster bench in 1729 and was one of the first magistrates to sit at Bow Street, which opened in 1739. Contemporary press reports record that he frequently sat alongside Blackerby and prosecuted many of the cases that followed passage of the Gin Act in 1736, the principal theme explored by Hogarth in *Night*. De Veil was also the author of a magistrates' handbook, published in 1747 but previously circulated in manuscript form.[185] Philip Sugen in his *ODNB* entry for de Veil commented that his fervour was such 'that the government turned to de Veil whenever it needed a magistrate's services'.[186] His favours were reciprocated and the government rewarded him accordingly: 'for his extraordinary services in trying etc. at the Old Bailey, felons from Middlesex, Westminster and London – £100 by Mr Lowther'.[187] De Veil also acquired government grants,[188] appointment as Inspector General of exports and imports at a salary of £500 per annum.[189] He later became a colonel in the Westminster militia and was invested a knight in 1744.

Martin Clare (16__?–1751), 'one of his Majesty's Justices of the Peace, and the Master of the Academy in [Soho] Square'[190] was also a member of the Middlesex bench virtually until his death.[191] One of the most influential members of the King's Arms lodge, Clare was appointed a Grand Steward in 1734, Junior Grand Warden in 1735 and Deputy Grand Master in 1741. A review of *Grand Lodge Minutes* and of those of the King's Arms lodge support the view that he was one of the more influential Freemasons in the mid- and late 1730s. He and the King's Arms lodge are discussed below.

It would be unjustifiable to claim that the relationship between Freemasonry and the Middlesex and Westminster benches was interdependent or that there was any government or Masonic conspiracy to crowd the bench with Freemasons. However, it is reasonable to conclude that many London Freemasons represented precisely the type of men that the Whig government would have favoured on the bench as active defenders of the Hanoverian establishment's status quo. Cowper and Delafaye are pre-eminent examples.

The aggregate number of Freemasons sitting on the Middlesex and Westminster bench has not been established and given the partial records available and that many names were spelled in different forms, the data may never be clarified in full. Nevertheless, the presence of such a high proportion of key figures from the magistrates' bench in conjunction with an analysis of contemporary Justices' Working Papers that indicates that many sat together as colleagues both on the bench and on judicial committees, suggests that the influence of the network should not be underestimated. Indeed, given their position in terms of Masonic rank and role, senior members of the London magistracy can be argued to have held a quasi-dominant sway over Grand Lodge from shortly after its inception through to the mid- and late 1730s. It can also be suggested that the pro-establishment and pro-Hanoverian political characteristics of English Freemasonry – and of Grand Lodge in particular – were fundamental to its success: demonstrating to the government that Freemasons were reliable partners in the promotion of the Hanoverian succession and the safeguarding of its Whig administration.

The Bench and the General Bank of Charity

The significance of senior members of the magistracy to the operation of Grand Lodge is reinforced in part by an analysis of the composition of the committee that governed the seminal General Bank of Charity. Having put down the foundations for a new federal structure and begun the process of standardising ritual, a further means by which Grand Lodge projected and maintained its administrative authority and public profile was via philanthropy and through the distribution of Masonic patronage: what might be termed impolitely as 'cash and honours'.

The idea of a Charity Bank was proposed formally by Earl Dalkeith in November 1724 following a petition from Anthony Sayer, whether at his own instigation or otherwise. A committee was chosen by the Duke of Richmond at the next quarterly meeting of Grand Lodge in March 1725 in order to investigate and report. The key figures at the meeting which took place at the Bell Tavern in Westminster were Richmond as Grand Master, Martin Folkes, his Deputy, and Francis Sorrel and George Payne, the Grand Wardens. The composition of those selected for the committee reflect in microcosm the combination of aristocrats, professionals and others who respectively headed and were senior members of London Freemasonry.

Table 2 The First Charity Committee

The Committee	Lodge	Rank	JP
Duke of Montagu	Horn	GM	Yes
Earl Dalkeith	Rummer	GM	Possible – not known
Lord Paisley	Horn	GM	Yes
J.T. Desaguliers	Horn	GM, DGM	No
William Cowper	Horn	DGM, GS	Yes
Sir Thomas Prendergast	Horn	GW	Possible – not known
Brook Taylor[192]	Bedford Head	Warden	No
Col. Daniel Houghton	Rummer	Master	Yes
Major Alexander Harding[193]	Horn	Master	Yes
Thomas Edwards[194]	Horn/Crown	Master	Possible – not known
Giles Taylor[195]	Bell	Master	Yes
William Petty[196]	Swan	Master	No
William Richardson[197]	Dolphin	Master	Possible – not known

Montagu, Dalkeith and Paisley, as Whig aristocrats and past and prospective Grand Masters, endowed the committee with aristocratic credentials and the prospect of financial credibility. Each had been and continued to be associated with Desaguliers and Folkes through the Royal Society, in addition to their shared antiquarian interests. They were also all members of the Horn. Although not a member of the Society of Antiquaries, Dalkeith was prominent in the Spalding Society where Desaguliers was a corresponding member and had lectured. *Grand Lodge Minutes* suggest that he had a particularly close and seemingly compliant Masonic relationship with Desaguliers, discussed below in chapter five. All three had worked closely with Desaguliers and Folkes during the period that the new Masonic ritual and governance structures had been developed. In short, they were reliable. The fourth – and fringe member of the aristocracy on the committee – was Sir Thomas Prendergast (*bap.* 1702, *d.* 1760): a young lawyer recently admitted to the Inner Temple and a cousin through marriage to the Duke of Richmond, the then Grand Master. Letters from Prendergast to Richmond suggest that he had pressurised the Duke to provide him with patronage, and this was initially Masonic.[198]

The non-aristocratic section of the committee comprised a number of those within Folkes, Desaguliers and Payne's immediate spheres of influence. Brook Taylor, the mathematician and physicist, was a colleague of both Folkes and Desaguliers at the Royal Society, and had served on the committee tasked with adjudicating between Newton and Leibnitz.[199] Taylor had worked with Desaguliers at the Royal Society and was also close to Keill, Desaguliers' mentor at Oxford.[200] In addition, he was one of several FRS who were members of Folkes' Bedford Head lodge in Covent Garden.

Cowper and Houghton were linked to Payne. All three sat on the Westminster bench. Houghton was also a member of Dalkeith's lodge at the Rummer at Charing Cross and Master in 1723. Cowper was a member of the Horn. Daniel Houghton and Sir Thomas Prendergast had been appointed Grand Wardens by Paisley. Both had previously worked with Desaguliers when the latter was Paisley's Deputy Grand Master. Houghton was at the time an officer in the 1st Foot Guards, appointed its second Major in 1724.[201] There he would have served alongside George Carpenter who commanded another company in the same regiment. Harding, another army officer, was attached to a sister regiment: Sir Charles Hotham's Regiment of Foot.[202]

The remaining members of the committee were Masters of their respective lodges: Giles Taylor, the long-standing Master of the Bell in Westminster; Thomas Edwards of the Horn and Crown, Acton; and William Petty and William Richardson, Masters of the Swan and Dolphin, respectively. Taylor and Richardson were also members of the Society of Antiquaries. At least three were also Governors of the Bridewell Royal Hospital under the supervision of the Mayor and Aldermen of the City of London. The committee's quorum was agreed at seven, perhaps allowing for the non-attendance of its aristocratic members; Cowper was appointed to the Chair.

Although formal Minutes can never give a complete picture of past events, early *Grand Lodge Minutes* provide a strong flavour. The Charity Committee reported in November 1725 and outlined its proposals regarding accountability, control and fund distribution. The Committee made three propositions: first, a voluntary quarterly contribution would be made by each constituent lodge; second, each charity distribution would be determined by a Grand Lodge standing committee and limited to members of 'regular' lodges, that is, only to those coming under the authority of Grand Lodge; and third, disbursements would be made only to members of at least five years' standing, with payments of up to £3 each to be sanctioned by a standing committee without the approval of Grand Lodge.

Bureaucratically and politically, the key to administrative control would be the composition of its standing committee. It was suggested that membership should comprise the Grand Master, his Deputy, the two Grand Wardens and three other members of Grand Lodge nominated by the Grand Master. A Treasurer would also be appointed and regular accounts produced. An inner cabal of Payne, Folkes and Sorrel were nominated members, with Blackerby proposed as Treasurer. The apparent intention was to cement further the influence of Grand Lodge and, in particular, that of its inner core. That the composition of the committee was contentious was made clear in *Grand Lodge Minutes* of 21 April 1730 when Desaguliers 'seconded the Deputy Grand Master in recommending the General Charity and made some proposals for the better regulation thereof':

> several Disputes arising thereupon, particularly concerning the Establishment of the Committee: Bro Cowper moved that the Original Report of the Committee might be read and . . . after several debates it was resolved that the Committee of Charity should stand as at first agreed.[203]

Although accepted, the proposed composition proved impractical. Blackerby subsequently admitted that the absence of committee members meant that a 'quorum can seldom be had for half a year and . . . the timely relief of distressed brethren is thereby greatly obstructed'.[204] Desaguliers agreed. Grand Lodge subsequently approved a new motion whereby twelve Masters of lodges contributing to the Charity would be co-opted quarterly according to lodge seniority, 'every Master of a Lodge to take the said Office in his turn for one quarter', and that the required quorum be reduced to five, to include one Grand Officer.

Over time, alongside the Grand Feasts and the regulation of subordinate lodges, the collection, administration and distribution of Masonic charity came to dominate the activities of Grand Lodge. Beneficiaries included several past Grand Officers – Sayer, Morrice and Timson – among a range of petitioners, successful and otherwise. Perhaps much as intended, charity became a principal component of the influence Grand Lodge sought to wield:

> Many people are in great Hopes that this mysterious Society that is honoured with several persons of high Rank as Members thereof having

made a very laudable beginning will soon vie with those Societies that are at present the most famous for Charitable Deeds.[205]

The letter from William Reid, Grand Secretary, to Edward Entwistle of Bolton Le Moors in Lancashire, provides primary evidence of the importance of philanthropy within and to Grand Lodge.

> I received your request and showed it to the Deputy Grand Master [Thomas Batson] who told me that he will never excuse any lodge after this from payment of the two Guineas to the Charity Box But however says that he will not press hard until you are in better circumstances for there is likely to be an order of the Grand Lodge that every new lodge shall pay five Guineas.[206]

The role of the Charity Committee grew further after May 1733, following Grand Lodge's decision to delegate to the Committee a matter of non-charity related business for their determination:

> A dispute arising between the Master, Wardens and some of the Brethren of the Lodge held at the Coach and Horses in Maddox Street . . . was referred (nemine contradicente) to the next Committee for disposal of the General Charity.[207]

And in December of that year, since 'Business usually brought before a Quarterly Communication is increased to so great a Degree that it is almost impossible to go through with it in One Night', it was proposed formally that 'all such Business which cannot conveniently be dispatched by the Quarterly Communication shall be referred to the Committee of Charity'.[208] With this act, the power of the Committee was sealed in its favour. Unfortunately, no Minutes of its subsequent meetings are extant.

POWER AND PATRONAGE

From the early 1720s, Masonic patronage was distributed to favoured members of the aristocracy, those within the inner circle of the London magistracy and to close colleagues of Desaguliers, Payne and Folkes. The pattern suggests that Grand Lodge was controlled by a core of interconnected individuals, an argument supported by *Grand Lodge Minutes* and reflected in the new *Regulations* and *Charges* and federal governance structure. The pivotal relationships within Freemasonry's inner cohort were based on shared intellectual, political and philosophical interests, and embraced a powerful pro-Hanoverian and Whig attachment.

CHAPTER FOUR

The Professional Nexus

Although in Peter Kebbell's words, 'London was awash' with clubs and societies,[1] many were informal and short-lived.[2] Moreover, with a few exceptions, in comparison with the more established professional and learned societies membership was fluid and often sparse. The examination of any interconnections between Freemasonry and other (particularly London-based) societies has therefore been focused towards organisations such as the Royal Society, the Royal College of Physicians, the Society of Apothecaries and the Society of Antiquaries, whose longevity and membership records allow for a meaningful analysis.

Even a cursory glance at the underlying data would suggest that the learned and professional societies had formidable interrelationships with Freemasonry. Individually and collectively their members established a range of professional and social connections that – intentionally or otherwise – captured many of society's commanding heights. The ties were appreciated at the time. As James Bramston commented ironically:

> Next Lodge I'll be Freemason, nothing less,
> Unless I happen to be FRS.[3]

As with all organisations, a small number of members were more prominent and influential than their peers. Among this group was arguably one of Desaguliers closest collaborators: Martin Folkes.

Martin Folkes and the Lodge at the Bedford Head

Unlike Desaguliers, a Huguenot and a servant of the Royal Society paid on a piece-work basis who, as Stephen Pumfrey noted, could be rebuked by the Council for any real or imagined disregard of his duties, Martin Folkes (1690–1754), was a privately wealthy and clubbable intellectual.[4] The well-connected eldest son of an eminent Gray's Inn bencher – also named Martin, a former Solicitor General and later Attorney General to Queen Catherine – Folkes was educated privately before being admitted to Clare College in Cambridge. His father's death, when Folkes was fifteen, brought an inheritance, estimated by Stukeley at around £3,000, which permitted Folkes the luxury of leisured study and, in October 1714, marriage to Lucretia Bradshawe, an actress.[5]

Folkes' intellectual abilities, particularly in philosophy and mathematics, resulted in his election as FRS in July 1714: 'the progress he made . . . after he left the University, in all parts of Learning, & particularly Mathematical & Philosophical, distinguish'd him'.[6] His renowned sociability would not have hindered his selection for the Society's Council to which he was elected in 1716 and again from 1718 until 1726. In January 1723 Folkes was made a Vice President under Newton, with whom he developed a close relationship and in whose place he presided when Newton was unable to attend Council meetings.[7] Although James Jurin (1684–1750) believed that Newton had 'singled [him] out to fill the chair',[8] Folkes lost the battle to succeed Newton in 1727 to his fellow Vice President, Hans Sloane, the former Secretary, in a contentious election that led to a temporary rift between the two men. Reconciled, Folkes was reappointed to the Council in 1729 and 1730, and became one of Sloane's Vice Presidents in 1732, succeeding him on his retirement.

The club-like atmosphere of the Royal Society and of other professional and scholarly bodies such as the Spalding Society and the Society of Antiquaries, to which he was elected in 1720 and where he was President from 1750 until 1754, provided a perfect milieu for the intellectual and amiable Folkes. There is good anecdotal and written evidence that Folkes encouraged his colleagues to join him in the Craft, and several became members of his lodges at the Bedford Head in Covent Garden[9] and the Maid's Head in Norwich, near Folkes' Norfolk estate.[10] More particularly, when Folkes' close friend the Duke of Richmond became Grand Master in June 1724, Folkes was selected as his Deputy Grand Master, succeeding Desaguliers in the post and continuing his work. Just over a year later, Folkes was nominated to serve on the politically important and highly visible committee for managing the Bank of Charity.

Partly because of his European travels and antiquarian studies, Folkes' attendance at Grand Lodge in the 1730s was sparse and he was present only on 14 May 1731 and 2 March 1732.[11] He attended with similar infrequency in the 1740s: on 22 April 1740, at the installation of the Rt. Hon. John, Earl of Kintore as Grand Master; on 19 March 1741, at the installation of the Earl of Morton; and on 23 March 1741, at the naming of the Rt. Hon. John, Lord Ward, Baron of Birmingham as the next Grand Master. On the last of these occasions Folkes was described in the Minutes as 'PRS', President of the Royal Society, a position to which he had been elected unanimously that year. He was elected to the French Academy of Science the following year.

Although perhaps not a frequent attendee at Grand Lodge, Folkes was an effective Masonic proselytiser and actively worked his social and scientific relationships. Archival data suggests that he had a relatively wide nexus:

1725. Thursday, 11th March. When we were at dinner the Duke of Richmond and Mr. Foulkes [came in] . . . The Duke of Richmond was very merry and good company; Mr. Foulkes just mentioned my having found out shorthand, but nothing more was said on it then. I came to the Society in the coach with the Duke of Richmond, Mr. Foulkes, and Mr. Sloan and we talked about Masonry and Shorthand.[12]

1725. Tuesday, 6th April . . . to Paul's Church Yard, where Mr. Leycester and I went, Mr. Graham, Foulkes, Sloan, Glover, Montagu . . . There was a Lodge of Freemasons in the room over us, where Mr. Foulkes, who is Deputy Grand Master, was till he came to us.[13]

Charles Richmond, in his edited *Life and Letters* of his forebear, described the 2nd Duke as 'Martin [Folkes]'s greatest friend'.[14] The Duke's affection for and positive view of Folkes were expressed clearly: 'one of my most intimate friends . . . a gentleman of very good family, and one of the leading Savants of this kingdom'.[15]

In another example – a letter of introduction – the Duke wrote that:

this letter will be attended with one agreeable circumstance . . . of introducing one of the most learned and at the same time most agreeable men in Europe to you, besides this he is one of the most intimate and dearest friends I have in the world, which I am vain enough to hope will not lessen him in your Excellency's esteem. His name is Mr. Folkes: he is a member of our Royal Society and has been a great while our Vice-President, he was an intimate acquaintance of the great Sir Isaac Newton, for whose memory, as every man of learning must, he has the utmost veneration.[16]

The Duke's personal correspondence also underlines their friendship:

Nothing but your goodness can excuse my laziness . . .
To *Chanter vos Louanges*, Dear Foulks, is a very easy thing . . .
The Duke of Montagu and all our friends here are very well.
I received two letters from you from Holland and Venice . . . and I would beg you would continue writing to me now and then;[17]
and for your absence, I do assure you, can never in the least diminish the sincere love and value, I ever had, have, & ever shall have for you.[18]

Folkes reciprocated, and the 'most faithful and affectionate friend[ship]' extended to their respective families:

You'l give the Duchess of Richmond leave to bring Miss Folkes with her, if you allow her to dine at Claremount herself on Sunday. I shall have nobody else with me to trouble you with;[19] and

Mrs Folkes had been a distinguished actress . . . she was one of the greatest and most promising geniuses of her time, and that Martin took her off the stage for her exemplary and prudent conduct. She was handsome as well.[20]

Folkes was integral to Freemasonry's development in the 1720s and supportive of Desaguliers, Payne and the inner core within Grand Lodge.[21] Their relationship dated from 1714 when both were elected to the Royal Society and their mining of friends and colleagues offers a parallel to the networking activities of Cowper, Blackerby and Payne with respect to the Middlesex and Westminster magistracy. Jointly with Richmond, Folkes promoted the Craft actively at the Royal Society, proposing at least eleven Freemasons as FRS. It is also significant that there were ten FRS who were members of the Bedford Head out of some 40 members, including John Arbuthnot, the physician, mathematician and author, whose own circle extended from Alexander Pope to Philip Dormer Stanhope, 4th Earl of Chesterfield.[22]

The Bedford Head mixed Fellows of the Royal Society with other establishment figures, such as the Hon. Mr. Cornwallis, Sir Thomas Jones and Sir Charles Cox, MP for Southwark and, in 1717, Sheriff of Surrey. Its members also included a relatively high percentage of Huguenot financiers and merchants – Messrs. Cantillon,[23] Varenne, Desbrostes and Botelcy, and the banker and magistrate, Sir Thomas Jones (16__?–1731).

Although he inherited the title in 1722,[24] the Hon. Mr Cornwallis was most probably Charles Cornwallis (1700–62), 5th Baron Cornwallis, later the 1st Earl, whose wife, Elizabeth Townshend, was the daughter of Charles, 2nd Viscount Townshend, the Whig Secretary of State for the Northern Department (1721–1730).[25] Cornwallis's brother-in-law, also Charles, was MP for Yarmouth and a member of the lodges at the Devil Tavern at Temple Bar and the Fleece in Fleet Street. He was sponsored in the Lords in 1723 by Cornwallis with the title Lord Lyn.[26] Charles Townshend was a Lord of the Bedchamber from 1723 until 1727 and was appointed Master of the Jewel House from 1730 until 1739. He served as Lord Lieutenant of Norfolk from 1730 until 1738, when he succeeded his father as 3rd Viscount.[27]

Sir Thomas Jones (16__?–1731) had been appointed a Justice of the Peace for Middlesex and Westminster in September 1722.[28] There were three appointees on that occasion, the second being Sir Henry Bateman, a fellow Freemason and a member of the Rummer Tavern at Charing Cross. Jones, a barrister at Lincoln's Inn, lived in Boswell Court, fifty yards east of Southampton Row and a short walk to the Bedford Head.[29] He became Chairman of the bench in 1724[30] and was rewarded with appointment as Register of the County of Middlesex, 'a position worth £1,000 per annum ... in the gift of ... the Master of the Rolls'.[31] A Welshman by birth, Jones was the first treasurer and secretary of the Society of Antient Britons, London's first Welsh expatriates' club. His loyal address to George I on its behalf resulted in a knighthood in 1715.

Charles Cox MP (1660–1729), a brewer with substantial property holdings in Southwark, combined commercial proficiency and political intelligence with philanthropy and an interest in experimental science – among other things he had financed John Harris' mathematical lectures at the Marine Coffee House in Birchin Lane.[32] Philanthropically, he had been involved in supporting the Palatine émigrés travelling from London to the

American Colonies, where the government wanted them to act as a buffer between the French to the north and the British to the south, and to Ireland, to bolster the Protestant position in that country.[33] Of the 13,000 or more refugees that arrived in London, around 6,500 were billeted at Blackheath and in the naval ropeyard at Deptford. Cox sheltered around 1,400 others in his warehouses at his own expense. His political, legal and commercial interests in Southwark and their mutual Freemasonry connect him to Leonard Streate, later his son-in-law.[34]

A relatively large group of taverns and coffee houses in Covent Garden hosted Masonic lodge meetings. Their number included the Two Black Posts and Lebeck's Head, both in Maiden Lane; the Mitre and the Globe in Globe Lane; the Cross Keys in Henrietta Street; the Apple Tree in Charles Street; and the Bedford Arms in the piazza. Bury's Coffee House and the Theatre Coffee House, both in Bridges Street; the Shakespeare's Head to the north east of the piazza; and its neighbour, the Bedford Coffee House, where Desaguliers lodged after leaving Channel Row, were among others.

One of the best known was the Bedford Head in Southampton Street, at the southern edge of Covent Garden. The tavern had a reputation as a 'luxurious refractory' and was celebrated for its food and gaming.[35] In his 1733 imitation of Horace's second satire, Alexander Pope's Oldfield, an infamous glutton who exhausted a fortune of £1,500 a year in the 'simple luxury of good eating' declared 'let me extol a Cat, on oysters fed, I'll have a party at the Bedford-head'.[36] And in a later poem Pope enquired 'when sharp with hunger, scorn you to be fed, except on pea-chicks at the Bedford-head?'[37] Horace Walpole also mentioned the tavern, telling a story of eight gentlemen who having enjoyed a spree in Covent Garden 'retired to a great supper prepared for them at the Bedford Head'.[38]

Its culinary reputation, if borne out by fact, would have commended the tavern to Folkes, whose interest in dining was renowned and captured effectively in Hogarth's 1741 portrait. However, perhaps belying its hedonistic reputation, the tavern was also a location for scientific lectures given by Desaguliers and James Stirling (1692–1770), among others.[39]

THE BEDFORD HEAD LODGE AND THE ROYAL SOCIETY

The membership of the Bedford Head lodge included many influential figures from the Royal Society. Among these were Brook Taylor (1685–1731), the barrister and mathematician, who had been elected FRS in 1712 and was a member of the Royal Society's Council from 1714 to 1717 and again in 1721, 1723 and 1725. He was Secretary from 1714–1718. Taylor had been proposed FRS in 1712 by John Keill, and subsequently worked with both Hauksbee and Desaguliers. His scientific loyalties were recognised by Newton and Taylor was accordingly appointed to the committee tasked with 'adjudicating' between Newton and Leibnitz over the invention of calculus.

Thomas Pellet (1671–1744), also elected FRS in 1712, was another Council member of the Royal Society (1713, 1715–16, 1719, 1724 and 1726). He had been proposed FRS by William Jones. Elected FRCP in 1716, Pellet was later President of the Royal College from 1735–9. He co-edited with Folkes Newton's *The Chronology of Ancient Kingdoms* published in 1728.

John Machin (1686–1751), had been elected FRS in 1710 and was Professor of Astronomy at Gresham College from 1713 until 1751. He was Secretary of the Royal Society from 1718–1747, a Council member from 1717–1730 and a Vice President from 1741. Like Taylor, Machin was appointed to the committee to adjudicate between Newton and Leibnitz and, again like Taylor, was also a governor of the Royal Bridewell Hospital.

John Arbuthnot (1667–1735), elected FRS in 1704, was a classic eighteenth-century polymath: a renowned mathematician, physician (FRCP) and author. He was a Council member of the Royal Society in 1706, from 1708 until 14, and again in 1716, 1726 and 1727.

Other FRS included William Rutty (1687–1730), elected FRS in 1720, and a FRCP and barrister. He had been proposed FRS by Pellet and Stukeley, and became the Royal Society's second Secretary in 1727. James Vernon (1677–1756), had been elected FRS in 1702 and was a Commissioner for Excise and Clerk of the Council. A magistrate, he also sat as MP for Cricklade between 1708 and 1710. He was the son of James Vernon, formerly the Secretary of State for the Southern Department. Hewer E. Hewer (1692–1728), a gentleman and an antiquarian, had been elected FRS in 1723, proposed by Folkes. Born Hewer Edgeley, he took his godfather's name upon inheriting his fortune. His godfather was William Hewer, Samuel Pepys' assistant.

The Hon. John Trevor (1692–1753), was elected FRS in 1728, proposed by William Rutty. Trevor was a barrister (later KC and Judge) and a JP. He inherited his father's title, becoming 2nd Lord Trevor. Robert Gray (16__?–1731), was also elected FRS in 1728. He was proposed by three fellow Freemasons: George Parker, 2nd Earl of Macclesfield; William Jones; and John Georges, a member of the King's Arms at St. Paul's, of which lodge he was later Senior Warden. 'Mr Holloway' in the Bedford Head membership list is likely to have been Benjamin Holloway (1691–1759), elected FRS in 1723.

Other notable members of the lodge include 'Mr Herbert', most probably Henry Herbert, later the 9th Earl of Pembroke (he inherited in 1733), described as such in the *Weekly Journal or British Gazetteer* on 15 July 1727. The 9th Earl was a friend and correspondent of the Duke of Richmond, and assisted the Duke with the rebuilding of his London home – Richmond House – in Whitehall. He was elected FRS in 1743.

The Royal Society and the Horn Tavern

Although the Bedford Head had a higher proportion of FRSs as members, the absolute number of members of the Bedford Head who were Fellows of the Royal Society was second to the Horn Tavern, where Desaguliers was a member alongside a multitude of aristocrats and members of the gentry that included the Dukes of Richmond and Montagu. That many were also friends with Martin Folkes is suggested by their active scientific and social correspondence. At least thirteen members of the Horn were FRSs in the 1720s. Given that the lodge did not submit any membership returns to Grand Lodge in 1730, it is possible that the number may later have been higher.[40]

In addition to Desaguliers, Richmond and Montagu, members of the Horn who were FRS include the Hon. George Carpenter, proposed in 1729 by Desaguliers, Folkes and Sloane; Charles Du Bois (1656–1740), a botanist and cashier-general of the East India Company; Jean Erdman, Baron Dieskau (1701–67), a French soldier and diplomat;[41] Charles Du Fay (1698–1739), a member of the French Royal Academy of Science who had been proposed by Richmond, Folkes and Sloane; Nathan Hickman (1695–1746), the physician, who was elected FRS in 1725; Sir Richard Manningham (1690–1759), the physician and male midwife, proposed by Sloane in 1720; James Hamilton, Lord Paisley (1686–1744), proposed by Sloane in 1715 and later a member of the Society's Council; Charles Douglas, 3rd Duke of Queensberry (1698–1778), elected in 1722 and *inter alia* Lord of the Bedchamber to George I (1720–7), Vice-Admiral of Scotland (1722–1729), Privy Councillor (1726–8) and Gentleman of the Bedchamber to Frederick, Prince of Wales (1733–51);[42] Charles Delafaye; and George Stanley (?–1734), a merchant, proposed by Folkes in 1719 and married to Hans Sloane's daughter, Sarah.

Although hard primary evidence is lacking, it is both conceivable and probable that Desaguliers and Folkes were instrumental in encouraging a succession of aristocrats to join Freemasonry. It is unlikely to have been a coincidence that four of the first five noble Grand Masters were FRS and were friends of Folkes: Montagu, appointed in 1721 (elected FRS in 1718); Dalkeith, appointed 1723 (elected FRS in 1724); Richmond, appointed 1724 (elected FRS in 1724);[43] and Paisley, appointed in 1725 (elected FRS in 1715).

A large number of later Grand Masters through to the late 1730s maintained the same connection with the Royal Society. The group included Baron Coleraine, proposed FRS by Desaguliers; Lords Lovell and Raymond; and the Earls of Strathmore, Crawford, Loudoun and Darnley. Anecdotally, a number of later Grand Masters were also Fellows including Sholto Douglas, Lord Aberdour, later 15th Earl of Morton, Grand Master in 1757, elected FRS in 1754; and Washington Shirley, 5th Earl Ferrers, Grand Master in 1762, elected FRS in 1761.

Freemasonry's ranks both within and without Grand Lodge were populated by FRSs. The flow went in both directions, with Fellows becoming Freemasons and Freemasons being invited to join the Royal Society.

Table 3 The Noble Grand Masters

Grand Masters	Birth/Death	Installed GM	Elected FRS
John Montagu, 2nd Duke of Montagu	1690–1749	GM 1721	FRS 1718
Philip Wharton, 1st Duke of Wharton	1698–1731	GM 1722	
Francis Scott, 5th Earl of Dalkeith[44]*	1695–1751	GM 1723	FRS 1724
Charles Lennox, 2nd Duke of Richmond	1701–1750	GM 1724/5	FRS 1724
James Hamilton, Lord Paisley[45]	1686–1744	GM 1726	FRS 1715
William O'Brien, 4th Earl of Inchiquin	1694–1777	GM 1727	
Henry Hare, 3rd Baron Coleraine	1693–1749	GM 1728	FRS 1730
James King, 4th Baron Kingston[46]	1693–1761	GM 1729	
Thomas Howard, 8th Duke of Norfolk	1683–1732	GM 1730	
Thomas Coke, Lord Lovell[47]	1697–1759	GM 1731	FRS 1735
Anthony Browne, 7th Viscount Montagu	1686–1767	GM 1732	
James Strathmore, 7th Earl of Strathmore	1702–1735	GM 1733	FRS 1732
John Lindsay, 20th Earl of Crawford*	1702–1749	GM 1734	FRS 1732
Thomas, 2nd Viscount Weymouth	1710–1750	GM 1735	
John Campbell, 4th Earl of Loudoun*	1705–1782	GM 1736	FRS 1738
Edward Bligh, 2nd Earl of Darnley	1715–1747	GM 1737	FRS 1738
Henry Brydges, Marquis of Carnarvon[48]	1708–1771	GM 1738	
Robert Raymond, 2nd Lord Raymond	1717–1756	GM 1739	FRS 1740
John Keith, 3rd Earl of Kintore[49]	1699–1758	GM 1740	
James Douglas, 14th Earl of Morton[50]*	1702–1768	GM 1741	FRS 1733

Note: * = Scottish Representative Peer

Although the evidence is anecdotal rather than incontrovertible, Desaguliers, Folkes, and others within the Royal Society, appear to have used the prospect of being proposed for election as FRS as an incentive or a reward for suitable non aristocratic Masonic and other acolytes. In addition to John Beale, Deputy Grand Master in 1721 and elected FRS the same year, several other early Grand Officers and Fellows of the Royal Society appear to fall within this category. They include John Senex (1678–1740), Desaguliers' long standing Masonic and scientific publisher, elected FRS in 1728; the Hon. George Carpenter, elected FRS in 1729, proposed by Desaguliers, Folkes and Sloane; and Sir James Thornhill (1675–1755), who was appointed Serjeant Painter to the King, knighted in 1720 and elected FRS in 1723, proposed by William Jones and Brook Taylor. Similarly, Dr George Douglas (____?–1737), a Grand Steward in 1731, was elected FRS in 1733, proposed by Sloane and others; and William Graeme (1700–45), the physician and later Deputy Grand Master, was elected FRS in 1730, proposed by Folkes and others. Martin Clare, another later Deputy Grand Master, was elected FRS in 1735, co-proposed by Desaguliers, Manningham, Chambers, Stuart, among others.

Many influential Freemasons held senior office at the Royal Society. George Parker, 2nd Earl of Macclesfield, served on the Council in 1723 and 1724 and succeeded Folkes as President from 1752 until 1764.[51] Like

Desaguliers and his fellow Freemason, Lord Chesterfield, Parker was a vocal proponent of the adoption of the Gregorian calendar, something Desaguliers had long-advocated. The change was finally agreed by Parliament in 1752.[52] Parker held the sinecure of Teller of the Exchequer from 1719 until 1764 and in such capacity would have known Chocke and Blackerby. A relationship perhaps cemented further on the bench. He was also MP for Wallingford from 1722 until 1727. He succeeded his father as Earl of Macclesfield in 1732. If the same George Parker who was a member of the Swan in Chichester, he would probably have been initiated by the Duke of Richmond.

John Machin and William Rutty have already been mentioned as members of the Council and as successive Secretaries to the Royal Society. Machin was a Council member from 1717–30, Secretary from 1718–47 and Vice President from 1741. Rutty was joint Secretary from 1727–30 and a Council member from 1727–29. Brook Taylor preceded Machin as Secretary, serving from 1714 until 1718; he was a member of the Council between 1714 and 1717, and again in 1721, 1723 and 1725.

Other Masonic office holders at the Royal Society included John Browne (16__?–1735), the chemist, elected FRS in 1721 and a Council member in 1723 and 1725, proposed by Folkes and fellow physician James Jurin; and James Douglas (1675–1742), the physician, proposed by Sloane and elected to the Council in 1714–15, 1717–18, 1720, 1724, 1726–8. William Jones was a member of the Council in 1717–18 and again in 1721, 1723, 1725–26, 1728 and 1730, and Vice President in 1749; as was Sir George Markham (1666–1736), the barrister, proposed by Sloane in 1708 and elected to the Council in 1719.

William Sloane (d. 1767),[53] Hans Sloane's nephew, was also a Council member. He had been proposed FRS by his uncle and William Stukeley, and was elected to the Council in 1725 and 1729. And Alexander Stuart (1673–1742), the eminent physician and physiologist, was proposed by Sloane in 1714 and elected a member of the Council in 1726 and 1730. Stuart received the Royal Society's Copley Medal in 1740 and was physician to Westminster Hospital from 1719 until 733, and thereafter to St. George's Hospital (from 1733 until 1736). He was also the physician to the Queen.

In short, Freemasons occupied the key positions of Secretary or Joint Secretary of the Royal Society from 1714–1747, held the office of President from 1741–1768, and had a substantial presence on the Council and in the Vice Presidency without a gap throughout the period 1714–1770. The only senior Fellows of the Royal Society not acknowledged as Freemasons and who served as President were Newton and Sloane. Although Newton was in his declining years in the 1720s, Sloane was ascendant and his view of Freemasonry was positive: he is known to have owned copies of the *Old Charges* and to have been comfortable discussing Freemasonry. In addition, his much-loved and supported nephew, William, was an active Freemason – a member of the lodge meeting at the Dolphin in Tower Street. Although it has been argued that Sloane himself was a Freemason, there is currently no evidence to support the statement.

The strong Masonic connections descended from the Council through to the more junior ranks of the Royal Society and included less well-known but still influential members. Indeed, by the late 1720s and throughout the 1730s, FRSs featured prominently within both London and provincial Freemasonry. J.R. Clarke in a forensic analysis identified twenty-four FRS who appeared in the 1723 Grand Lodge lists which, as noted, were less than two thirds complete, and another sixteen FRS who later became Freemasons.[54] He identified a further twenty-seven FRSs in the 1725 lists, comprising sixteen who were FRS at the time and an additional eleven who were elected subsequently.

As a function of his methodology, Clarke 'disallowed' those FRSs whose later Masonic membership was not recorded by their lodges. He estimated that by 1730 there were around 35 Fellows who were Freemasons out of a total of some 250, or *c.* 15%, down from *c.* 20% some five years earlier. However, not all lodges provided a list of members each year, including the Horn in 1730, and the actual number and percentage may well have been greater than Clarke allows. Indeed, if the thirteen members of the Horn known to be FRS are added to Clarke's total, the figure rises to *c.* 20%, and the probable proportion is likely to have been even higher, perhaps at around 30–40%.[55] A significant reason is that certain lodges are believed to have recorded in the lists submitted to Grand Lodge only those members present on the evening of 'census', rather than the notional aggregate membership as such. Supporting the contention, Peter Clark, in his detailed study of English clubs and societies, estimated that up to 45% of FRSs were Freemasons.[56] Of those based in London, the proportion can be estimated to be around half, or approximately 100 of the 200 or so relevant Fellows.

Trevor Stewart described the importance of the Royal Society to Freemasonry in his Prestonian Lecture, reprinted in *AQC Transactions* in 2004.[57] The degree of overlapping membership between the two organisations suggests not only shared scientific interests but also hints at a spectrum of personal relationships and mutual patronage. In Appendix III, Stewart detailed thirty-nine FRS proposed for election by Freemasons during the period 1711–54. Although perhaps not exhaustive, the list underlines the relatively large number of Freemasons who joined the Royal Society. Stewart also commented that between 1723 and 1730, Fellows of the Royal Society were members of at least 29 different lodges.

A summary list of the proposers and co-proposers is detailed below. Not included in the list are those Freemasons proposed for election by Sloane in his capacity as Vice President and thereafter as President of the Royal Society, the instigation of which may have been a request by Desaguliers, Folkes or other Masonic Fellows of the Royal Society.

WILLIAM JONES AND WILLIAM STUKELEY

Other than Martin Folkes, the two most prominent figures in *Table 4* are

Table 4 The Royal Society: Freemasons Proposing Freemasons

Proposer	Frequency	Period	Principal Lodge(s)
Martin Folkes	11	1719–42	Bedford Head, Maid's Head
William Jones	9	1711–40	Queen's Head
William Stukeley	7	1718–52	Fountain
John Machin	7	1730–41	Bedford Head
Thomas Pellet	6	1733–40	Bedford Head
J.T. Desaguliers	4	1728–35	Horn, University, Bear & Harrow
William Rutty	3	1728	Bedford Head
Alexander Stuart	2	1730–42	Rummer
Ephraim Chambers	1	1735	Richmond
George Douglas	1	1729	St. Paul's Head
John Georges	1	1728	King's Arms
Thomas Hill	1	1742	Queen's Head
Charles Lennox	1	1729	Horn
John Lock	1	1752	Dick's Coffee House
Richard Manningham	1	1735	Horn
John Martin	1	1728	Golden Lion
John Montagu	1	1742	Bear & Harrow
Frank Nicholls	1	1749	King's Head
Richard Rawlinson	1	1754	Three Kings
William Sloane	1	1729	Dolphin
Charles Stanhope	1	1742	Bear & Harrow
Brook Taylor	1	1723	Bedford Head

William Jones (1675–1749) and William Stukeley (1687–1765). Born in Wales, Jones, a brilliant mathematician, had the good fortune to become tutor to Philip Yorke, 1st Earl of Hardwicke, who later became Lord Chancellor. Yorke introduced Jones to Thomas Parker, the 1st Earl of Macclesfield, and Jones became tutor to his son the Hon. George Parker, later the 2nd Earl. Jones developed a long standing friendship with both father and son and among other gifts George Parker later rewarded Jones with the sinecure of Deputy Teller to the Exchequer.

Jones had lodged with fellow mathematician John Harris in the early 1700s when he had first arrived in London and both embraced and expounded on Newton's theories. Proposed by Edmund Halley, Jones was elected FRS in 1711 and can be linked to a number of prominent FRS, including Brook Taylor. With his pro-Newton credentials it was unsurprising that Jones the following year accepted appointment to Newton's committee investigating the invention of calculus.

Jones became a Mason around 1724 and was a member of the Queen's Head in Hollis Street. He had a wide circle of friends at the Royal Society and proposed or co-proposed around thirty for Fellowship. It is unlikely to have been a coincidence that many of them were or later became Freemasons. These included James Cavendish (FRS 1719); Ephraim Chambers (FRS 1729); Robert Gray (FRS 1728); John Hope, 2nd Earl of Hopetoun (FRS

1728); his tutee, George Parker (FRS 1722); Thomas Pellet (FRS 1712); Richard Rawlinson (FRS 1714); and Sir James Thornhill (FRS 1723).[58] However, Jones's circle extended beyond that of the Royal Society. He was also an active member of Folkes' antiquarian circle and of his 'Infidel Club', an organisation later derided by Stukeley in his *Memoirs* – notwithstanding an invitation to membership[59] – and vividly described by James Force as group of 'radical deists clustered around Martin Folkes'.[60]

Although he had read medicine at Cambridge, William Stukeley also studied natural philosophy and had 'a passionate Love for Antiquitys'.[61] Stukeley later wrote that his 'curiosity' concerning Freemasonry was linked to his interest in 'the mysteries of the ancients', what he may have regarded as the perceived antiquity of Freemasonry and its 'pristine' theology and ritual.[62] However, his attachment to Masonry may also have been a function of a desire to emulate and associate with Montagu and other aristocrats at the Royal Society:

> Providence brought me to an intimacy with the Duke of Montagu, who tho' no scholar himself, had a fine genius and entertain'd the greatest opinion of me in the world.[63]

Stukeley was made FRS in 1718. Among those he later proposed or co-proposed for Fellowship of the Society were William Beckett (FRS 1718), a member of the Three Tuns in Newgate Street; John Beale (FRS 1721); William Rutty (FRS 1720); and William Sloane (FRS 1722). Stukeley was himself proposed by Halley and supported by Isaac Newton. His diary entries suggest that he was on good personal terms with Newton, albeit that the inequality of the relationship is clear:

> 30 June. Went with Sir Isaac Newton to see the Coinage in the Tower. He set his hand in my Album;
> 25 Nov. I din'd with Sir Isaac Newton where we audited the RS Accounts;
> 13 Feb. Sir Isaac Newton presented me with the new edition of his optics. We discoursed about muscular motion.[64]

Stukeley was elected a member of the Council in 1719, 1720 and again in 1725. His interest in antiquarianism led to him co-founding and becoming the first secretary of the Society of Antiquaries in 1718, a role he held for nine years. He was elected FRCP two years later and subsequently gave the Goulstonian lecture at the College.[65]

Each of the Royal Society, Society of Antiquaries and the Royal College of Physicians offered avenues for Masonic proselytising and provided a reservoir of new initiates to be tapped. The process was assisted by the visibility of Montagu, Richmond and other aristocratic Freemasons who were – or later became – senior members of each organisation, and by the ease of crossover of members from one organisation to another. Stukeley's Society of Antiquaries, for example, met at the Mitre Tavern in the Strand. Held on a Thursday, the meeting was arranged to start 'after the Royal Society had broke up' at a time designed specifically to accommodate the attendance of the many FRS who were also antiquaries.[66]

Stukeley recorded in his diary that he 'was made a Freemason at the Salutation Tav., Tavistock Street, with Mr. Collins, Capt. Rowe, who made the famous diving Engine'.[67] He also noted his attendance at George Payne's Grand Feast in June 1721 when Montagu was chosen as Grand Master.[68] Stukeley became Master of his own Lodge later the same year. He recorded on the 27 December that he and others had 'met at the Fountain Ta[vern] Strand & by consent of Grand M[aste]r present, Dr. Beal, constituted a new Lodge there, where I was chose M[aste]r.'[69] Stukeley was present at other lodge meetings, writing on 14 January the following year of 'a qu'ly meeting where Bro. Topping repeated 30 incoherent words either forwards or backwards or by stops after once hearing them'. His interest in Masonry endured. Stukeley's entries nearly five years later in June 1726 documented his journey to Grantham where he 'set up a lodge of freemasons, which lasted all the time I lived there'.[70] Anecdotally, while in Grantham, Stukeley dabbled in local politics, supporting the Whig cause and being rewarded with an invitation to dine with Walpole.[71]

In a letter to Samuel Gale (1682–1754), a fellow antiquary and a co-founder of the restored Society of Antiquaries, written from Grantham on 6 February 1726, Stukeley mentioned again that he had established 'a small but well-disciplined Lodge of Masons' in the town.[72] Samuel Gale and his brother, Roger, are not among those considered to have been Freemasons. However, in addition to Folkes' correspondence, a letter from James Anderson dated 26 February 1731 and signed 'your affectionate Brother' also referred to Masonic issues:

> The inclosed is from Counsellor Edwards, of Lincoln's Inne, the worthy warden of Horn Lodge, of which the Duke of Richmond is master. It is to get the bearer, (who is also a mason true), made a sound excise-man by your benign influence with your brother the commissioner. I am well informed of his moral character that it is very good.[73]

Taken together – and despite his absence from any extant membership records – the letters suggest the probability that Gale was a Freemason. If not, they underline at a minimum that Freemasonry enjoyed a widespread currency and interest.

Both Gale brothers fit the pattern of many Freemasons of the time: politically sound and well-connected, with an avid interest in science or antiquities, or both. Samuel Gale was Comptroller of Customs and a member of the Spalding Society. His brother, Roger (1672–1744), was a FRS, elected in 1717, and a member of both the Society of Antiquaries and the Spalding Society. He sat as MP for Northallerton from 1705 until 1713; was appointed Commissioner of Stamp Duties in 1714 and 1715; and held office as a Commissioner of the Excise from 1715 until 1735. Within the Royal

Society he served as Treasurer from 1728 until 1736; he was a Vice President from 1728 and a Council member in 1718, 1720, 1722, 1724 and 1726 until 1730. Tangentially, Stukeley later became the Gales' brother-in-law, marrying Elizabeth, their only sister, in 1739. It was his second marriage, his first wife, Frances, having died in 1737.

Stukeley's decision to become a Freemason and his multitude of commitments to various learned societies provides an unambiguous example of eighteenth-century networking. Having initially been apprenticed to his father's law firm, Stukeley read medicine and natural philosophy at Cambridge. After graduation and a short stay in London, he moved to Boston in Lincolnshire and practiced as a physician. He also joined the Spalding Society and became friends with Maurice Johnson (1688–1755), another lawyer and the society's founder[74] who characterised its aims succinctly: 'we deal in all arts and sciences, and exclude nothing from our conversation but politics'.[75]

Stukeley subsequently returned to London. His interest in natural philosophy and in antiquarianism led to introductions to Hans Sloane, Samuel and Roger Gale, and to 'my good friend' Martin Folkes,[76] all of whom became members of the Spalding Society.

In common with Stukeley, Sir Richard Manningham (1690–1759), a fellow Freemason and member of the Horn, was also a member of the Royal Society, the Royal College of Physicians and the Spalding Society. Manningham had read law at Cambridge and later took up medicine. He was elected FRS in 1720 and made FRCP the same year.[77]

Manningham became an eminent obstetrician or man mid-wife, with the Princess of Wales among his patients. He was knighted in 1721 and was an avid exponent of practical philanthropy, establishing a lying-in hospital next door to his house in St. James's, the precursor of the dedicated maternity unit and one of the first of its kind in Britain.[78] Manningham was also one of several doctors who investigated Mary Toft – 'the Rabbit Woman of Godalming' – who alleged she had given birth to a litter of rabbits. The claim was exposed by Manningham and others as a hoax but not before he and the medical profession as a whole had been lampooned by Hogarth in his engraving *Cunicularii, or the Wise Men of Godliman in Consultation* (1726). Manningham was also the butt of negative comment from Alexander Pope and William Pulteney in *Much Ado about Nothing: or, A Plain Refutation of all that has been Written or Said concerning the Rabbit-Woman of Godalming*, published in 1727.

OTHER LEARNED SOCIETIES

By the late 1720s, the Masonic lodges had become popular meeting places and served as crossing points for contacts and relationships across a range of social and professional networks. Peter Clark has noted that Masonic membership was spread far more broadly both numerically and socially than any other early eighteenth-century club, and that London's Freemasons included many who shared membership with a variety of learned and professional organisations.[79] Over time such networks became self-reinforcing and common interests, friendship and patronage led to shared lodge membership and *vice versa*. Other albeit later examples of similar clubs or societies would include Lord Sandwich's Egyptian Society, founded in 1741, among whose members were Montagu, Richmond, Stukeley and Folkes,[80] and the Society of Dilettanti, established formally in 1734, about which Horace Walpole commented that although the nominal rationale for membership was that its members had visited Italy on the Grand Tour, the real reason was to get drunk.[81]

Freemasonry had adherents in many of the learned societies and shared interests provided a powerful common nexus. Four of such societies were the Royal College of Physicians, the Society of Apothecaries, the Society of Antiquaries and the Spalding Society.

The Royal College of Physicians

Freemasonry's social credibility and its intellectual attraction for physicians would not have been hampered by the examples set by Thomas Pellet (of the Bedford Head lodge), William Rutty (Bedford Head), William Stukeley (Salutation and Fountain taverns) and Sir Richard Manningham (Horn), all of whom were eminent physicians and prominent Freemasons, nor by the well publicised Masonic activities of the Dukes of Montagu and Richmond, both of whom were Fellows of the College. Cross-referencing the College's fellowship records compiled by William Munk in 1861 with membership data from Grand Lodge suggests that of the 130 Fellows whose fellowship commenced within the period 1690–1740 and a further 80 Fellows whose commencement date was not recorded but who have an 'end date' of between 1725 and 1780, around 60 or just under one third can be identified as possible, probable or actual Freemasons.[82] The proportion of London-based FRCPs who were Freemasons may well have been higher, perhaps up to half. There are two reasons for the supposition: first, only two thirds or so of lodges reported the names of their members; and second, a sizeable fraction of FRCPs lived in the provinces. Of course, the number of Freemasons would have been a smaller percentage of the total number of FRCPs.

Identifiable FRCPs appear to have been members of around thirty different lodges. Among the more popular were the Crown behind the Royal Exchange; the Swan in Ludgate Street; the Ship behind the Royal Exchange; and the Griffin in Newgate Street. Known FRCPs sat as Master or Warden in at least eleven lodges and two served as Master of two lodges simultaneously: Thomas Hodgson, the Master of the Anchor & Baptist's Head and the Sun, Fleet Street; and Stephen Hall, the Master of the Ship in Bartholomew's Lane and the Globe Tavern, Moorgate. A more comprehensive breakdown is given in appendix 3.

The Society of Apothecaries

The Society of Apothecaries' unpublished membership records suggest that by the 1730s, Freemasonry had become embedded within the organisation to the extent that some 102 probable and possible Freemasons can be identified in Grand Lodge lists from the 540 members of the Society admitted between 1700 and 1730: just under a fifth of members.[83] Extending the data range to members admitted between 1700 and 1740, alters the percentage of probable and possible Masons to around 120 out of just over 700 members, or a sixth of the membership. As with the Royal College of Physicians, since not all apothecaries lived in London and not all lodges reported their membership, the actual percentage of London-based members would probably have been higher. Nonetheless, it should be emphasised with respect to both the Royal College of Physicians and the Society of Apothecaries that misspelling of names, absence or abbreviation of forenames, common names and the absence of robust corroboratory evidence, makes absolute identification uncertain.

Certain lodges appear to have been particularly popular. These include the Bell Tavern in Westminster; the Crown behind the Royal Exchange; the Vine Tavern and the Queen's Head, both in Holborn; the St. Paul's Head in Ludgate Street; the Ship behind the Royal Exchange; the King's Arms at St. Paul's; and the Griffin in Newgate Street, where apothecaries were represented both as Master and Warden. In aggregate, some sixteen apothecaries were recorded as Masters or Wardens of twelve separate lodges, and identified 'possible' and 'probable' apothecaries were members of a total of around 40 different lodges. Appendix 3 contains a more detailed list.

The Society of Antiquaries

Antiquarian interest in Masonic ritual and its actual or pretended origins may have acted as a spur to membership, and the Society of Antiquaries and the Spalding Gentlemen's Society included many members who were prominent Freemasons. Within the Antiquaries, Stukeley, the founding Secretary, was joined by three Grand Masters: Lord Coleraine, who was also a vice president, and the Duke of Montagu and Duke of Richmond. William Cowper, Grand Secretary and later Deputy Grand Master, was also a member, as was William Richardson, Master of the lodge at the Dolphin in Tower Street and of other lodges. So was John Johnson, Master of the lodge at the King's Head in Ivy Lane. In all, around 40 antiquaries can be identified as actual, probable or possible Freemasons, representing just over 16% of the total membership. As above, given the many variations in name spelling, the figure is not precise and may be either an over- or underestimate.

The following table sets out probable/possible Masonic members of the Society of Antiquaries and their respective lodge memberships. The scale of

114 *The Foundations of Modern Freemasonry*

overlap with other learned and professional societies, and with other social networks is self evident.

Table 5 The Society of Antiquaries

Name	Rank	Lodge(s)
James Anderson	GW	Horn, Westminster
John Anstis[84]		University Lodge
William Beckett		The Swan Ludgate Street; and/or
		Three Tuns, Newgate Street
Peregrine Bertie[85]		Rainbow Coffee House, York Buildings
John Booth		The Greyhound, Fleet Street; and
		The Blue Posts, Devereaux Court
John Bridges	Grand Steward	Bear & Harrow, Butcher's Row; and
		The Castle, Highgate
Thomas Bryan		The Ship Without Temple Bar
William Busby	Grand Steward	The Rose Tavern w'out Temple Bar
Thomas Clark		Cardigan, Charing Cross; and
		Queen's Head, Bath
John Cole	Master	Vine Tavern, Holborn; and/or
		Red Lion, Richmond
Robert Cornwall		Wool Pack, Warwick; and
		King's Arms, Strand (possible)
William Cowper	GS, DGM	Horn, Westminster
John Creek		King's Head, Pall Mall
William Dawson		Crown & Anchor, St. Clement's Church
Francis Drake	JGW, GM (York)	Grand Lodge at York
Thomas Edwards	Warden	Horn, Westminster
Martin Folkes	DGM	Bedford Head, Covent Garden; &
		Maid's Head, Norwich
Alexander Geekie	Master	Cardigan, Charing Cross
Alexander Gordon		Queen's Head, Great Queen Street
Henry Hare	GM	Swan, Tottenham High Cross
John Hare		King Henry's Head, Seven Dials
Charles Hayes[86]		Rummer, Charing Cross
Richard Hollings		The Rose Tavern without Temple Bar
Daniel Houghton[87]	GW, Warden	Rummer, Charing Cross
John Johnson[88]	Master	King's Head, Ivy Lane; and/or
		King Henry's Head, Seven Dials
		Coach & Horses, Maddox Street
		Red Lion, Tottenham Court Road
		Swan Tavern, Fish Street Hill
Charles Lennox	GM	Horn, Westminster
John Montagu	GM	Bear & Harrow, Butcher's Row
John Nichols		Crown, behind the Royal Exchange
John Palmer		King's Arms, St. Paul's; and/or
		Green Lettuce, Brownlow Street
Edmund Prideaux	Master	Maid's Head, Norwich
William Primate		Swan, Tottenham High Cross
Benjamin Radcliffe		The Ship Without Temple Bar

Richard Rawlinson	Warden	Rose, Cheapside; and/or
		Three Kings, Spitalfields;
		St. Paul's Head, Ludgate Street;
		King's Arms, Ludgate Hill
Richard Richardson[89]	Warden	Dick's Coffee House, Strand; and
		King's Arms, Ludgate Hill
William Richardson	Master	Dolphin, Tower Street; and/or
		Swan, East Street, Greenwich;
		Bull's Head, Southwark;
		Ship behind the Royal Exchange
Christopher Robinson	Master	The Ship, Fish Street Hill; and/or
		St. Paul's Head, Ludgate Street;
		King's Arms, Careton Street
George Shelvocke[90]		Horn, Westminster
Alexander Stuart		Rummer, Charing Cross
William Stukeley	Master	Fountain, Strand
Sir James Thornhill	GW, DGM	Swan, East Street, Greenwich
Samuel Tuffnall	Warden	Bell, Westminster; and/or
		Crown, Acton
John Ward[91]		Anchor & Crown, Short Gardens
John Woodward[92]		Crown behind the Exchange

THE SPALDING SOCIETY

Maurice Johnson founded the Gentleman's Society of Spalding in 1710. It was one of the earliest provincial societies for antiquaries and its lectures and discussions were later expanded to include the liberal sciences and education more generally. Its membership was divided principally between those who were local and Lincolnshire-based; those living elsewhere, mainly in London; and honorary members, often from London, to whom membership was granted in return for corresponding with the society or providing lectures.

Over the thirty-year period from its founding to 1740 the Spalding Society had around 250 members, of which just under a fifth were probably Freemasons. The proportion of members based in London appears to have been around half, although variant name spellings and duplication prevent the percentage being determined with any real accuracy.[93]

Table 6 (overleaf) sets out probable and possible Masonic members of the Spalding Society and their respective lodges. London-based members included Henry Hare, Lord Coleraine; Francis Scott, Earl Dalkeith; and Desaguliers, Folkes, Manningham and Stukeley.

116 *The Foundations of Modern Freemasonry*

Table 6 The Gentlemen's Society of Spalding

Name	Masonic Rank	Lodge(s)
John Anstis		University, Butcher's Row
Peregrine Bertie		Rainbow Coffee House, York Buildings
George Churchill[94]		Rummer, Charing Cross
Richard Collins[95]		Blue Boar, Fleet Street
J.T. Desaguliers	GM, DGM	Horn, Westminster
William Dodd		Horn, Westminster
George Edwards[96]	Warden	Horn, Westminster
Richard Ellis[97]		The Ship behind the Royal Exchange
Martin Folkes	DGM	Bedford Head, Covent Garden; and Maid's Head, Norwich
John Francis		Maid's Head, Norwich
Alexander Gordon		Queen's Head, Great Queen Street
John Grano[98]		Swan, East Street, Greenwich
John Green[99]		Half Moon, Strand
William Green		Cheshire Cheese, Arundel Street
Henry Hare	GM	Swan, Tottenham High Cross
John Jackson	Warden	Horn & Feathers, Wood Street
John Johnson	Master	King's Head, Ivy Lane (and cf. above)
John King[100]	Master	Rummer, Henrietta St., possibly also Antiquity and/or Red Lion, Richmond; King's Head in Fleet Street
Jacques Leblon[101]		Crown & Sceptre, St. Martin's Lane
John Lodge		The Ship, Bartholomew's Lane and/or The Globe, Moorgate
John Lynwood[102]		The Ship without Temple Bar
Richard Manningham		Horn, Westminster
George Markham		Sun, south of St. Paul's
Thomas Mills, Jr.		Not known
John Mitchell		Ship on Fish Street Hill
Michael Mitchell[103]		Horn, Westminster
John Morton[104]		White Bear, King's Street, Golden Sq.
John Perry[105]		Bear & Harrow, Butcher's Row
John Roberts[106]		Mount Coffee House, Grosvenor St.
Francis Scott	GM	Rummer, Charing Cross
George Shelvocke		Horn, Westminster
Edmund Stevens[107]	Master	Mitre, Covent Garden
Alexander Stuart		Rummer, Charing Cross
William Stukeley	Master	Fountain, Strand
John Tatham[108]		Queen's Head, Knave's Acre
John Taylor	Warden	Coach & Horses, Maddox Street
John Thomas[109]		Devil within Temple Bar
Charles Townshend		Devil, Temple Bar
Robert Vyner		Rummer, Charing Cross
John Ward		Anchor & Crown, Short Gardens
James Weeks[110]		Bear & Harrow, Butcher's Row
Adam Williamson[111]		Horn, Westminster
John Wilson[112]		Horn, Westminster

The range of Masonic connections within the learned and professional societies was considerable. The influence of key figures, including Martin Folkes, William Stukeley and Richard Manningham, can be identified and were at the core of the sets of overlapping personal and professional associations. Those based on the Royal Society have been analysed elsewhere and discussed here only briefly. Those in other clubs and other societies offer an opportunity for further research. Nonetheless, the scope of networks suggests that Freemasonry benefited from a unique and formidable nexus. This was enhanced – perhaps partly underwritten – by the presence of fashionable and newsworthy aristocrats, particularly at the level of the noble Grand Masters at the head of Grand Lodge. Their influence is discussed in the following chapter.

CHAPTER FIVE

The Rise of the First Noble Grand Masters

The first wave of aristocrats to take the chair at Grand Lodge transformed English Freemasonry. Their titular leadership and well-publicised presence at lodge meetings, processions, musical extravaganzas and elsewhere acted as a spur to the expansion of Freemasonry into the professional societies, the military and other élite and aspirational groups in London and the provinces. With the support and encouragement of the Duke of Montagu and, in particular, that of the Duke of Richmond, a succession of relatively prominent young Whig aristocrats was persuaded to join Freemasonry and accept the position of Grand Master at the head of the new Grand Lodge. The move catapulted Freemasonry into London's political and social consciousness and created what quickly became a fashionable club whose aspiring members could consider, probably correctly, that they were on the inside of one of the sets that mattered.

The presence of such celebrity and gossip-worthy aristocrats generated extensive press coverage and sustained a rapidly burgeoning public interest in Freemasonry. Large-scale press reporting was activated by the decision of John, 2nd Duke of Montagu, an iconic Whig aristocrat, to head Grand Lodge. Under his leadership and that of all but one of his immediate successors, the organisation was characterised by pro-Whig politics and a strong affiliation with the Hanoverian court. Montagu was followed as Grand Master by the Duke of Wharton and the Earl of Dalkeith. Wharton's inconvenient neo-Jacobite political sympathies and mercurial and rebellious nature were at odds with those of Montagu, Desaguliers, Payne and their pro-Hanoverian colleagues, and their reaction and the effective expulsion of Wharton from Grand Lodge and Freemasonry underscores the otherwise pro-government nature of the Craft, and of Grand Lodge in particular. In contrast, Wharton's successor, the Earl of Dalkeith, was malleable and loyally Whiggish in his politics.

Freemasonry's fourth aristocratic Grand Master, Charles Lennox, the 2nd Duke of Richmond, firmly set a pro-Hanoverian seal on early eighteenth-century Freemasonry. A popular and gregarious man, Richmond was politically and socially connected to the Duke of Newcastle and Sir Robert Walpole, and to the mainstream of the Whig aristocracy. Like Montagu, he also had a strong attachment to the learned and professional societies, particularly the Royal Society, and was close friends with Martin Folkes. His extensive Masonic cooperation with Desaguliers, together with his political influence in France and the Low Countries, were later significant factors in the development of Freemasonry as a diplomatic tool.

Richmond's successors, from James Hamilton, Lord Paisley, to Thomas Howard, Duke of Norfolk, and beyond, are considered only briefly. However, although such successor Grand Masters can be regarded correctly as having consolidated further Freemasonry's public profile, they also spoke to the increased politicisation of the organisation and to a narrowing of its focus, a state of affairs that would later lead to a divide in English Freemasonry and to the creation of the rival Ancients Grand Lodge in the early 1750s.

Aristocratic Patronage

We make for Five guineas, the price is but small,
And then Lords and Dukes, you your Brothers may call,
Have gloves, a White Apron, get drunk and that's all.[1]

The *Song on Freemasons* was included in *Love's last shift: or, the mason disappointed*. Despite the irony, the song captured some of the fundamental components of the new Freemasonry and its appeal to many potential members: an association with celebrated members of the aristocracy; apparent exclusivity; and clubbable, genial, fraternal drinking. In contrast, *Long Livers*, a semi-scientific book dedicated to the 'Grand Master, Masters, Wardens and Brethren of the Most Ancient and most Honourable Fraternity of the Free Masons of Great Britain and Ireland', published in 1722, extolled the spirit of scientific research.[2] This was not a paradox. The themes were often complementary and many lodges hosted and encouraged scientific and other lectures as part of the drive for self-improving education that had become a prominent characteristic of contemporary culture. Freemasonry's evolving connection with the scientific Enlightenment and industrialisation is explored in chapter six in connection with the central role played by Desaguliers and his acolytes.

Folkes and Desaguliers used their direct and indirect influence effectively at the Royal Society and elsewhere to encourage a sequence of generally affluent, fashionable and influential aristocrats to join Freemasonry. The process developed momentum and with the exception of Wharton, Freemasonry began a lengthy period of public association with the Whig aristocracy. Successive members of the nobility invited their friends to join and set an example that encouraged others to do so. By the mid-1720s, Freemasonry was marked out by its conspicuous aristocratic and military patronage, implicit political protection and the novelty of an elected leadership, many of whom were prominent intellectuals and eminent professionals.

Freemasonry offered its members an intriguing mix. Its constitution supported the state and legitimised its authority yet at the same time encouraged, if not demanded, religious tolerance and moral integrity. Masonic meetings combined a genial social setting in which to network, a much-vaunted emphasis on toasting, drinking and dining, 'ancient ritual' and an opportunity to benefit from often-advantageous educational lectures. A positive press – a product of Grand Lodge's aristocratic leaders and their 'quarterly communications', feasts, processions and later theatrical and musical spectaculars – was reinforced by an affirmative self-image generated by philanthropy.[3] Freemasonry had been re-designed to sit above political and social censure: admitting only 'good and true Men, free-born, and of mature and discreet Age, no Bondmen, no Women, no immoral or scandalous men, but of good Report'. And in the second and third decades of the eighteenth century it may have succeeded.

Such a development was not spontaneous but dependent on an inner core which was instrumental in designing and transforming the Masonic milieu. The combination of pro-Hanoverian latitudinarianism and scientific Enlightenment philosophy, instruction and entertainment, incorporated the practical religious tolerance and political orientation that the Whigs and Desaguliers and other Huguenots desired, and reflected an approach that had found expression in Desaguliers' own popular scientific lectures and public demonstrations. Freemasonry under the new Grand Lodge of England was a proselytising force. And it was more. Given Desaguliers' influence, it was unlikely to have been a coincidence that the first Masonic Charge mirrored the objectives sought by London's Huguenot community in the years preceding the Treaty of Utrecht when they had attempted – albeit unsuccessfully – to persuade the Protestant powers to press Louis XIV to ease religious persecution.

Anderson's *1738 Constitutions* asserted that Grand Lodge was formed on 24 June 1717. Although the statement cannot be verified, there is no obvious reason for Anderson to have lied over a matter that would have been within the relatively recent experience of many in the relevant lodges. He recorded that the four founding lodges had convened at the Apple Tree, each being known by the name of the tavern at which it met: the Apple Tree in Charles Street, Covent Garden; the Goose & Gridiron in St. Paul's Churchyard; the Crown in Parker's Lane, near Drury Lane; and the Rummer & Grapes in Channel Row, Westminster. Anderson wrote that the lodges resolved to choose a Grand Master from their own number 'until they should have the Honour of a noble brother at their Head'. Given Montagu's acceptance of the role in 1721, Anderson's account may be correct; equally, his record of events may have offered his readers a retrospective rationale and justification for Desaguliers and Folkes having persuaded Montagu to take the position.

The establishment of Grand Lodge, the election of the Duke of Montagu as its first aristocratic Grand Master and the later publication of the *1723 Constitutions*, did more than develop the concept of what it meant to be a 'Free and Accepted Mason'. The combination created an unprecedented level of public and political interest in Grand Lodge and its reinvented Free and Accepted Masonry, and gave rise to an organisational structure that gave impetus to its carriage across London, provincial England and continental Europe.

A Positive Press Personified

Principally as a function of the far-reaching newspaper coverage generated by its aristocratic leadership, Freemasonry's public profile altered fundamentally from the early 1720s. The press became a catalyst for change and the publicity created aspirant interest across London and the provinces, producing the foundations of what became virtually a mass movement among the gentry and the professional classes.

A simple numerical analysis of the number of occasions on which the English press used the term 'Freemason' or 'Free and Accepted Mason' pre- and post-1721 reinforces the argument. Whereas the British Library's *Burney* collection contains only a short handful of press reports alluding to or focused on Freemasonry in the period before 1720, mention of 'The Society of Freemasons', 'Freemasons' and 'Free and Accepted Masons' between 1720 and 1735 is compelling, with close to 1,000 published news items and classified advertisements.

Some of the earliest newspaper reports and articles are worth quoting at length, for example, in 1721, John Applebee (1690–1750), the newspaper publisher, noted that:

> The following Gentlemen were made and created *Free and Accepted Masons*, at a Lodge held at the Cheshire Cheese in Arundel Street by Dr Beal, Deputy to his Grace John Duke of Montague, Grand Master of that Fraternity . . . all which Gentlemen went Home in their white Aprons very well satisfied, and according to the ancient Institution of that noble and advantageous Brotherhood.[4]

A second item on the same day recorded another Masonic titbit:

> We hear that Mr Innys, the Bookseller, and Mr Cousins, the Grocer, both topping Tradesmen in St. Paul's Churchyard, have lately been admitted into the Society of Freemasons, and have accordingly been invested with the Leathern Apron, one of the Ensigns of the Society.[5]

Applebee would have been conscious of his readers' interest in the aristocracy and in their most trivial engagements and activities, and his paper's focus on Freemasonry was probably inspired by the agreement of one of Britain's more prominent and newsworthy aristocrats, the Duke of Montagu, to become the Society's Grand Master.

Montagu was appointed Grand Master in June 1721 at 'a Meeting at

Stationers' Hall of between two and three hundred of the Ancient Fraternity' attended by 'Several Noblemen and Gentlemen'.⁶ He was not alone. *Applebee's Original Weekly Journal* and the *Weekly Journal or British Gazetteer* each recorded another expression of interest less than two months later on 5 August 1721 in connection with an arguably more gossip-worthy aristocrat:

> Last week his Grace the Duke of Wharton was admitted into the Society of Freemasons; the Ceremonies being performed at the King's Arms Tavern in St. Paul's Churchyard, and his Grace came home to his House in the Pall Mall in a white leathern Apron.

Although Freemasonry had its detractors and provoked some opposition from Tory-leaning opposition newspapers, the majority of assaults were either mild or inconsequential. An early and representative example emerged in the *London Journal* on 15 February 1722:

> a treatise is likely soon to appear . . . to prove, that the Gypsies are a Society of much longer standing than that of the Freemasons.

However, a few – including the anonymous *Hudibrastick Poem* – were more pointedly ironic, if not insulting. The *Preface* to the *Poem* set the tone – which was vituperative:

> Having had the Honour, not long since, when I was admitted into the Society of Masons, of Kissing your Posteriors, (an Honour Superior to Kissing the Pope's Toe) . . .
>
> I take it that Court Politicians and free Masons are oftentimes ally'd; for it is possible the one may build Castles in the Air as well as the other.

The *Poem* itself was equally offensive, with overtones of sodomy:

> They have no Trowels, nor yet Lines,
> But still retain their Marks and Signs,
> And Tools they've got which always fit,
> A Lady, Duchess, or a Cit . . .
>
> His Breeches low pulls down, and shows,
> His Arse, this all must here expose,
> Which the new Mason close salutes,
> For none here durst to hold Disputes;
> And when he thus the Bum has slabber'd,
> And put his Sword up his Scabbard,
> A learned Speech is then held forth
> Upon the Breech, and Mason's worth;

And he's Install'd at last compleat,
And let down to his Mason's seat.

On 11 April the following year a substantially incorrect exposé of Masonic catechisms was published in *The Flying Post*. The article was printed in the wake of the *1723 Constitutions* – released barely six weeks earlier – and was designed to appeal to a readership whose interest had been pricked by the concurrent Masonic publicity. Additional exposures appeared in subsequent years, although many were less attacks on Freemasonry as opposed to successive attempts to ride the public interest. Among several examples in 1724 were the anonymously written *Grand Mystery of Freemasons Discovered* and *A Seasonal Apology for Mr Heidegger*, a notorious Huguenot theatre impresario and an unapologetic Freemason. Samuel Briscoe's *Secret History of the Freemasons* was published the same year. The book had over forty pages of parody and achieved such popularity that a second edition was released the following year. In a similar vein, Samuel Prichard's *Masonry Dissected* was published in 1730 with equal success. However, although popular, these and other literary assaults had a relatively modest impact and may even have stimulated interest in Freemasonry. Perhaps as now, many anti Masonic books were bought by Freemasons themselves. Certainly, they failed to prevent or materially disrupted the growth in Masonic membership amongst the establishment. Indeed, the substantial majority of books and newspaper reports were uncritically supportive. The *Weekly Journal or British Gazetteer* of 29 June 1723 embodied the approach:

> On Monday the ancient Society of Free and Accepted Masons met according to annual Custom to elect a new Grand Master. They assembled to the Number of about 600 at Merchant Taylor's Hall, where they unanimously chose the Right Honourable Earl of Dalkeith . . . There was a noble feast . . . and handsome Entertainment.

Although the press may have been droll or even satirical – 'there is not Mystery sufficient in the whole of my Narrative to furnish out one branch of the Occult Science, nor make even so much as a Freemason'[7] – it was also positive. A whimsical report in *The Flying-Post* on 28 December 1728 is representative:

> Last Friday night at a certain tavern, not far from the Royal-Exchange, there was a Lodge of Freemasons for accepting some new members when an unlucky accident happen'd which had like to have discover'd the grand Secret: for one of the Noviciates was so surpriz'd when they pull'd of his hat and perriwig, unbutton'd his collar and sleeves, took out his shoe-buckles, and stripp'd him to his shirt, that he thought they are going to castrate or circumcise him, and fearing to be made either an eunuch or a Jew, he watch'd his opportunity, upon seeing the door of the room half

open, and ran out into the street: But was pursued by his Fraternity, who perswaded him with good words to return back to the Lodge, and comply with the rest of the ceremonies of the Installation.

The publication in the *Post Man* of a full-page riposte to a letter criticising Freemasonry suggests the passion the subject aroused, at least among its adherents, and demonstrates the space afforded by Whig-supporting papers to Masonic promotion and defence. The *Daily Journal* of 13 July 1722 also took up the case:

> We hear that the poor unfortunate Gentleman who sent the Letter to the *Post Man* [*and the Historical Account*] on Tuesday . . . is confined to a Dark Room . . . being Confident he could not only find out the Philosophers Stone, but also the Secret of the Accepted Masons.

Referring to the earlier 'scurrilous' letter and 'by way of Justice to the injur'd Fame of the Society', on 31 July 1722 an anonymous writer assured the *Post Man's* readership of the 'solid merit of the Worthy Society, whose Original is venerably Ancient, their Continuance inevitably Constant, notwithstanding their interposing Circumstances as Men of Labour and Art'. The letter continued, pointing out that 'a most valuable piece of Antiquity: the Original Draught [sic] of the Sacred Foundations on which the Brotherly Fidelity of the said Society so many years ago was first founded, and has been to this Day preserved' It was termed 'a valuable Secret form'd for the good of Mankind, and made Sacred by the most solemn Appeal to Heaven'. Probably not coincidentally, a few days later on August 4, a 'Continuation of the History of the Society of Masons' was published in the *Post Man*; 'The Conclusion of the History' followed on its heels on 9 August. The semi-cosseted status of the organisation may have had everything to do with the excellence of its Whig political connections and the financial and social stature of its new principals: the noble Grand Masters at the helm of Grand Lodge.

JOHN, 2ND DUKE OF MONTAGU (1690–1749)

It was almost certainly a testament to the example set by John, 2nd Duke of Montagu that a significant proportion of the aristocracy was prepared to join Freemasonry and a number willing to provide its titular leadership. Montagu's installation marked a turning point in the Craft's ability to attract new members and in Grand Lodge's authority over the rising number of 'regularly constituted' lodges in London and the provinces. Before 1720, the annual Grand Feast had taken place above a tavern. With Montagu at its head, the event was moved from the Goose and Gridiron to Stationers' Hall in order to accommodate the several hundred who wished to attend. The publication of a standard set of *Regulations* and *Charges* in 1723 and provision of positions at Grand Lodge to which Masonic patronage could be applied were additional building blocks in what developed into a federal infrastructure.

The *1723 Constitutions* recorded that 'several Noblemen and gentlemen of the best rank, with Clergymen and learned scholars of most professions and denominations . . . joined and submitted to take the charges . . . under our present worthy Grand Master, the most noble Prince, John, Duke of Montagu'. This was the crux. Montagu demonstrated that Freemasonry was acceptable morally, intellectually and politically – and that it could be fashionable and fun. The combination provided the justification and rationale for those of 'the best rank' and for 'learned scholars of most professions and denominations' to join him.

The connections between those involved suggest that over the next two decades senior members of Grand Lodge orchestrated and influenced the appointment of successive Grand Masters and Grand Officers. A strategy of encouraging young and, in some cases, probably impressionable members of the aristocracy both to join Freemasonry and to lead it publicly, acted as a catalyst to development and its metamorphosis into a fashionable and cutting-edge organisation.

Montagu's family background and social and political position explain why he was persuaded to become Masonry's first noble Grand Master. Although Montagu's personal papers and correspondence at the Northamptonshire Record Office, the British Library, Cambridge University Library and Boughton House, lack any material mention of Freemasonry, the range of his correspondents indicates a network of personal relationships with many who were or later became Freemasons. In this context, his friendship with the Duke of Richmond was significant, as was that with Philip Stanhope, Lord Chesterfield, and Lord Herbert, later the 9th Earl of Pembroke, both of whom attended his installation.

> Grand Master Payne proposed for his successor our Most Noble Brother John, Duke of Montagu, Master of a Lodge, who being present was forthwith saluted as Grand Master Elect and his health drank in due form.

Montagu was proposed Grand Master on Lady Day, 25 March 1721. An announcement that he had been chosen appeared in the *Post Boy* on 27 June 1721, the *Weekly Journal or Saturday's Post* of 1 July 1721 and in several other newspapers. The *Post Boy* noted that 'Noblemen and Gentlemen' were present at the meeting at Stationers' Hall and that 'the Reverend Dr. Desaguliers made a speech suitable to the occasion'. Montagu had probably been made a Mason earlier, possibly in 1719 or 1720, perhaps by Richmond in conjunction with Desaguliers at the Horn or possibly privately at a lodge formed for the purpose as was later the case with Frederick, Prince of Wales.[8]

Montagu was intelligent, wealthy and well-connected, the only surviving son of Ralph Montagu, the 1st Duke, and Elizabeth Wriothesley, daughter of the 4th Earl of Southampton, Charles II's Lord High Treasurer, and Rachel de Massue, a Huguenot aristocrat. Ralph Montagu had been Ambassador to Louis XIV of France and had witnessed the persecution of the Huguenots at first hand. He was described by John Macky in his *Memoirs of the Secret Services* as 'a great supporter of the French and other Protestants [driven] to England by the tyranny of their princes, [and] an admirer of learning and learned men'.

John Montagu was not dissimilar: pro-Huguenot and with a comparable interest in the sciences. Among the large number of books dedicated to him were John Quincy's medical *Lexicon physico-medicum*; Richard Boulton's *Some thoughts concerning the unusual qualities of the air*, an early discourse on pollution; John Wynter's *Cyclus metasyncriticus: or, an essay on chronical diseases*; and Francis Moore's *Travels into the inland parts of Africa*.

Desaguliers and Folkes would have recognised Montagu as an ideal figurehead for any club or society seeking to elevate its status. With his obvious consent, Montagu was propelled to the position of Grand Master with the probable intention that his wealth, social standing, Court connections and military rank, would act as a beacon to attract others from his circles and elsewhere – and it did. He was regarded, correctly, as one of the richest men in England, with an annual income that may have exceeded £20,000 from property rents alone.[9] The dowry he gave his youngest daughter, Mary, on her marriage to Lord Brudenel, the son of the Earl of Cardigan, was reported to be £25,000.[10] However, perhaps a more powerful indicator of his affluence was his ability personally to finance the colonisation of St. Lucia and St. Vincent in the West Indies following the grant of those territories by the Crown in January 1722.[11] In the event, the exercise proved abortive and was frustrated by French action, compounded by poor preparation. It cost Montagu an estimated £40,000. Perhaps not coincidentally, one of the largest of the seven ships in the flotilla sent to the Caribbean was named *The Charles and Freemason*.[12]

Montagu was prominent socially and his activities and those of his family were described regularly in the metropolitan and provincial press. There were over 280 news items published between 1721 and 1735. They included his loyal address to George I as Lord Lieutenant of Northamptonshire;[13] his position as chief mourner at the funeral of his father-in-law, the Duke of Marlborough, an iconic figure in the Whig pantheon;[14] and his eldest daughter's wedding to William, 2nd Duke of Manchester.[15] However, even a minor excursion by river along the Thames in a 'large flat bottom boat' was considered worthy of mention;[16] and his appointment as Lord Proprietor and Captain General of St. Lucia and St. Vincent was described as far away as Boston, in the colony of Massachusetts.[17]

Like his father, Montagu had a close association with the royal household. Among other roles, he succeeded as Master of the Great Wardrobe, a sinecure that paid over £3,000 a year and held from 1709 until his death; officiated as Lord High Constable at George I's 1714 coronation; and carried the sceptre at George II's coronation in 1727.[18] Montagu also served as Lord Lieutenant of Northamptonshire, where his father had been an MP, and of

Warwickshire, in both cases for life from 1715.[19] He was appointed to the sinecure of Master Forester and Warden of Rockingham the same year.[20]

Montagu also held a number of prominent military positions. These were not only honorific or a consequence of his position as Marlborough's son-in-law following his marriage to Mary Churchill, the youngest daughter of the Duke, in 1705. He politicked actively to be appointed to the right roles. In a reference to his request for the Governorship of the Isle of Wight, Montagu commented that he wanted it badly that he 'then again may be a military Man, that being a Military Post'.[21] In addition, he raised and financed regiments of Horse and Foot and was later Captain and Colonel of His Majesty's Own Troop of Horse Guards, later the 1st Life Guards, the army's premier cavalry regiment. Montagu was subsequently promoted Major General in 1735 and Lieutenant General and Colonel of the 3rd Regiment of Horse in 1739. Most significantly, the following year he was appointed to the influential position of Master-General of the Ordnance, a Cabinet position, with responsibility for the artillery. The role establishes a link with Thomas Desaguliers, Desaguliers' second surviving son, who joined the Royal Artillery as a cadet in January 1740, possibly as a consequence of Montagu's patronage.[22]

MONTAGU, FREEMASONRY AND THE MILITARY

Although the evidence is not definitive, it is a reasonable conjecture that Montagu's publicised Masonic prominence set an example to other military figures within his social set, a factor that may have been instrumental in promoting Freemasonry among the military's higher ranks. Two well known career soldiers and politicians provide compelling examples. Both were members of the Duke of Richmond's Horn lodge at Westminster: Sir Adolphus Oughton (1684–1736), and Sir Robert Rich (1685–1768).

Oughton, later MP for Coventry, had served with Marlborough, and was commissioned Captain and Lieutenant Colonel in the 1st Foot. He returned to England on the accession of George I and was appointed Groom of the Bedchamber to the Prince of Wales. In 1715, his loyalty was rewarded with promotion to Colonel and appointment as the first Major of the Coldstream Guards. He became Lieutenant Colonel of the regiment two years later. His political proximity to the Crown and to Walpole, despite his abstention on the contentious Excise Bill,[23] brought promotion to Brigadier in 1735 and the colonelcy of the 8th Dragoon Guards from 1733 to 1736. Oughton was also close to Frederick, Prince of Wales, and his example may have been one of several factors in the latter's decision to become a Mason.

Like Oughton, Robert Rich, successively MP for Dunwich (from 1715 until 1722), Bere Alston (1724–27), and St. Ives (1727–41) was also a political supporter of Walpole, and gained preferment accordingly. He was appointed Groom of the Bedchamber to the Prince of Wales in 1718, retaining the position when the Prince succeeded as George II. Militarily,

Rich was promoted Colonel and given command in sequence of the 13th Hussars (1722–25); 8th Light Dragoons (1725–31); and the King's Regiment of Carabiniers (1731–33), where he succeeded his fellow Freemason (and member of the Horn), Lord Delorraine.

Rich also commanded the 1st Troop Horse Grenadier Guards (1733–35), senior and junior officers of which regiment were members of the lodge meeting at the Mitre in Reading, the first Masonic lodge known to have been formed in Berkshire. Rich was promoted Brigadier General in 1727, Major General in 1735 and Lieutenant General in 1739. In 1757, he was appointed commander-in-chief of the British Army and Field Marshall.[24]

Interestingly, Rich's formidable military and Masonic connections were continued by his son, James, who commanded the 37th Foot at Minden in 1759. James Rich was active in both English and Scottish Freemasonry. He became Provincial Grand Master of Minorca (English Constitution) in 1752 when stationed on the island, and later joined Canongate Kilwinning lodge in Edinburgh after being posted to Scotland in 1754. He was Grand Master of the Grand Lodge of Scotland from 1769 until 1771 while at the time serving as commander-in-chief of British forces in Scotland.

Notwithstanding what was later an extensive presence, there are relatively few studies of the impact and extent of Freemasonry within the British military. One of the principal secondary sources is Robert Freke Gould's *Military Lodges*, which comprises a substantial data resource.[25] Unfortunately, many more recent papers and books from Masonic historians tend to the superficial and are often based predominantly on secondary data.[26] Peter Clark, in his seminal *British Clubs and Societies*, dealt with the military aspects of Freemasonry in passing: 'for the middle ranks [on leave in London], a large array of military lodges appeared from the 1750s to keep tedium at bay'.[27] Nonetheless, Clark recognised the contribution of Freemasonry within the military, and the importance of colonial Freemasonry in particular, noting that 'many military lodges played a significant role in the colonies by admitting local civilians to the order'.[28]

Among more recent academic work, Jessica Harland-Jacobs' research has focused specifically on the interplay between Freemasonry and colonialism.[29] Based on her doctoral work, *Builders of Empire* is an excellent analysis of this aspect of British imperialism.[30] Nonetheless, the impact of Freemasonry on the military and the manner in which it was used for political and strategic objectives has generally been considered only tangentially, and the origins and impact of the nexus between the military and Freemasonry remains relatively unexplored.

Objectively, there are three key issues that require analysis: the motivation of those officers who joined Freemasonry; the extent to which Masonry became pervasive within the military; and the wider effect, if any. Within this book, the first two questions are touched upon, but only briefly. The start point is an assumption that the principal attraction of Freemasonry to the military in the eighteenth century would have been broadly similar to that which applied in other fields: the success and sanction of senior Masonic figures. Leading aristocrats and military officers who had publicly embraced Freemasonry were role models and set an example to be imitated. The subsequent advance of the Craft within the army was similarly a function of social convention as Freemasonry became part of the mainstream activities of the gentry, the professional classes and the army's regimental structure, which encouraged emulation.

The expansion of Freemasonry within the military – especially the army – had a political and diplomatic dimension that only became more fully apparent in the later eighteenth and nineteenth century.[31] Harland-Jacobs commented correctly that British regimental lodges (and trade) carried Freemasonry across the globe, from the North American colonies and the Caribbean to the Indian sub-continent, Australia, New Zealand and elsewhere. She noted that it was the decision of the Grand Lodge of Ireland to issue 'travelling warrants' that instigated the trend.[32] However, this was only the proximate cause and methodology; it was not at root. Although Harland-Jacobs and others have argued that prior to the grant of travelling warrants, lodges were situated at particular locations, the statement is not accurate. Many lodges were peripatetic, moving from tavern to tavern and from one location to another. The Grand Lodge of Ireland did not add geographic flexibility as a new dimension to Freemasonry; it extended, albeit materially, a process that was already in place.

In the 1720s and thereafter, English Grand Lodge would grant warrants either to an existing lodge seeking to become 'regular', that is, accepting the jurisdiction of Grand Lodge, or to the prospective founders of a new lodge. In each case, the warrant was held by the Master of the lodge and his successors on behalf of lodge members. The *1723 Constitutions* was clear:

> A lodge is a place where Masons assemble and work: hence that assembly, or duly organized Society of Masons, is called a lodge, and every Brother ought to belong to one, and to be subject to its By-Laws and the General Regulations. It is either *particular* or *general*.[33]

Although a lodge may have been known by its location, its authorisation was by means of a warrant granted to individuals. The Grand Lodge of Ireland under Lord Kingston, previously Grand Master of England (in 1728),[34] broadened the interpretation by granting regimental 'travelling' warrants. But the principle remained the same and the warrant was generally granted to the commanding officer or another officer on behalf of the regiment concerned.

The membership lists of the Horn and of other well-connected lodges date the link between Freemasonry and the military to before 1723. However, the presence of Freemasonry within the army more broadly only became widespread once Freemasonry's cachet had been consolidated and reinforced by subsequent Grand Masters such as the Duke of Richmond, Earl of Crawford, Earl of Loudoun and the Duke of Norfolk, and by the decision of other prominent figures (including the Prince of Wales, Lord Calvert, Sir Robert Walpole and the Duke of Newcastle) to join the Craft.[35]

Freemasonry's appeal to a relatively wide audience within London and the provinces had its parallel in the military. And it is a reasonable conjecture that the promotion of active Freemasons to more senior military rank over succeeding decades reinforced their influence and the desire of subordinates to follow their superiors. The closed regimental system provided a fertile environment for Freemasonry to expand and once it had established a presence, its development was largely self-reinforcing.

A number of Grand Masters and senior army officers provided powerful military paradigms. Within the 3,000 or so members' names recorded by Grand Lodge between 1723 and 1735, the army was represented by over 100 ranking officers, including two later Field Marshalls, twenty-three colonels, eight majors and fifty-six captains. The number includes those whose rank was specified in the *Grand Lodge Minutes* or is otherwise known, but excludes the more than sixty Dukes, Earls, Lords, Barons and Baronets who commanded their own regiments or otherwise held field rank and those whose military rank was not recorded. The two Field Marshalls were Viscount Cobham (appointed 1742, and a member of the lodge at the Queen's Head, Bath) and Sir Robert Rich. The position of Field Marshall, the most senior army rank, was only created in 1736. Although there is anecdotal evidence that the iconic Huguenot soldier, Sir John Ligonier, commander-in-chief and Field Marshall from 1757 until 1759, was also a Freemason, there is currently no proof.

Certain soldiers, such as Jeffrey Amherst (1717–97), who was mentored by Ligonier and appointed commander-in-chief in 1778, were especially proactive in promoting Freemasonry.[36] Amherst established and encouraged the formation of field lodges in almost all of the units under his command. Of nineteen regiments that served under him in North America in 1758, thirteen had field lodges of which ten had been warranted by the Grand Lodge of Ireland.[37] With one exception, the remaining six regiments had lodges in place by the end of the decade.[38]

Military lodges not only became a focal point for the regiment:

> the time passes very wearily when the calendar does not furnish us with a loyal excuse for assembling in the evening, we have recourse to a Freemasons Lodge;[39]

but also and for the local community:

> we have about 30 or 40 Freemasons they have a fine Supper every Saturday night and often two or three in the week besides.[40]

Minden Lodge, No. 63, in the 20th Regiment of Foot, given as an example by Harland-Jacobs, demonstrates how a travelling military lodge could have an impact on a succession of communities.[41] Minden's original warrant was issued by the Grand Lodge of Ireland in 1736/7.[42] The lodge's name was adopted after the battle of Minden in 1759.[43] The regiment was posted to Quebec in 1775, returned to Britain in 1783 and was sent back to North America in 1789, where it was based at Halifax in Nova Scotia until 1792. Harland-Jacobs commented that the lodge 'exposed [different] host communities to Freemasonry's practices, charity, and even buildings', and 'military lodges did more than give Freemasonry a fleeting presence in the empire's colonies; they were also responsible for the permanent establishment of the brotherhood.'[44]

In total, the number of military lodges operating under the jurisdiction of the four 'home' Grand Lodges of England ('Moderns' and 'Ancients'), Ireland and Scotland, grew from 13 Irish-warranted regimental lodges in the 1730s, to 70 (58 Irish, 8 Scottish and 4 English lodges) in 1760. A list of eighteenth- and nineteenth-century military lodges is given in appendix 4.

The Sun Inn at Chester provides an important example of provincial military Freemasonry. The Master of the lodge was Francis Columbine, Provincial Grand Master for Cheshire and commanding officer of the 7th Foot, and the list of lodge members in 1725 indicates that at least 10 of the 28 members were military officers.[45] Colonel Herbert Laurence and Captain Hugh Warburton were Senior and Junior Warden, respectively; and Lieutenant Colonel John Lee; Captains Charles Crosby, John Vanberg and Robert Frazier; Lieutenant William Tong; Ensign Charles Gordon; and Cornet-of-Horse Walter Warburton were members. Captain Hugh Warburton succeeded Columbine in 1727. He became Provincial Grand Master of North Wales the same year, appointed by Lord Inchiquin.

Other military-connected lodges followed a similar pattern of an amalgam of senior and junior ranks. At least 5 of the 19 members of the Mitre at Reading were military officers.[46] Three were in the 1st Troop of Horse Grenadier Guards: Major William Godolphin, the senior ranking Major, also a member of the Rummer, Charing Cross; Captain John Nangle, Adjutant; and Captain John Duvernett, a Huguenot and the senior Captain-of-Horse, who was appointed Lieutenant Colonel in 1746. The others were Captain Andrew Corner, an officer in the 7th Hussars, and Captain John Knight, whose regiment is not known.[47] Similarly, 6 of the 21 members of the Wool Pack in Warwick were from the military: Colonel William Townsend; Captains William Tench, Robert Cornwall and Anthony Rankine; Lieutenant Thomas Dunning; and Cornet William Chaworth, representing another cascade of military rank.

The development of regimental Freemasonry was not wholly dependent on the presence of senior Freemasons at the head of the regiment: although the Earl of Loudoun's 30th Foot received a Masonic warrant in 1738 and his Black Watch in 1747, Loudon's 60th Foot did not do so until 1764 and his 3rd Foot only in 1771. Similarly, Earl Crawford's Scots Greys, the 2nd Dragoons, established its first lodge in 1747 and his 25th Foot in 1749, but the Duke of Montagu's 1st and 2nd Battalions, Royal Artillery, did not obtain a Masonic warrant until 1764 and 1767, respectively.

A Politically Convenient Grand Master

Although not political in the recognised sense, Montagu was a safe Whig, loyal to the Hanoverians and to the Crown without necessarily being a man of party.[48] With the exception of Wharton, he and his successor Grand Masters' political loyalties were central to Freemasonry's pro-Hanoverian position. Montagu was rewarded by the Crown accordingly, being appointed a Knight of the Garter in 1718,[49] made Grand Master of the newly formed Order of the Bath (from 1725 until his death) and, in 1736, raised to the Privy Council.

However, despite his wealth, position and intelligence, Montagu's occasionally jocular behaviour was celebrated[50] and pointedly described in negative terms by his mother-in-law, Sarah Churchill:

> All his talents lie in things only natural in boys of fifteen years old, and he is about two and fifty to get people into his garden and wet them with squirts, and to invite people to his country houses, and put things into their beds to make them itch, and twenty such pretty fancies like these.[51]

In common with other aristocratic Grand Masters in Grand Lodge's formative years, Montagu was relatively young, only 31 at his installation, and arguably open to a degree of manipulation. However, he was not as young as a number of those that succeeded him. The unstable Duke of Wharton was 24 when installed as Grand Master; the Earl of Dalkeith, 28; the Duke of Richmond, 23; Viscount Weymouth, 25; and the Earl of Darnley, 22.

Although Desaguliers would have known Montagu through the Royal Society, and both were friendly with Newton, Folkes, and other prominent FRS, Folkes' personal relationship with Montagu and Richmond probably held the key to Montagu agreeing to serve as Grand Master. Stukeley considered Folkes' influence to be considerable. Indeed, Folkes was later described by Stukeley as 'an errant infidel' who had perverted the Duke of Montagu, Duke of Richmond and other nobles, and had done 'an infinite prejudice':[52]

> When I lived in Ormond Street in 1720 he set up an infidel Club at his house on Sunday evenings, where Will Jones, the mathematician,[53] & others of the heathen stamp, assembled . . . From that time he has been propagating the infidel System with great assiduity, & made it even fashionable in the Royal Society, so that when any mention is made of Moses, the deluge, of religion, Scriptures, &c., it is generally received with a loud laugh.[54]

Other factors are also likely to have had an influence on Montagu. His deep-seated Huguenot connections may have set the context for his willingness to work with Desaguliers. Montagu's father, Ralph, the 1ˢᵗ Duke, had maintained a network of relationships with several prominent Huguenots: his circle included the diplomat and soldier, Henri de Massue, Marquis de

Ruvigny (1648–1720), created 1st Earl of Galway in 1697 and appointed Lord Justice in Ireland; and the scholar, scientist and bibliophile, Henri Justel (1620–1693),[55] elected FRS in 1681 and appointed Keeper of the King's Library at St. James's Palace. Others known to have been associated with the 1st Duke included Michael Le Vassor (1646–1718), the historian and clergyman, elected FRS in 1702; and Charles Saint-Evremond (1610–1703), the soldier, essayist and poet.[56] His extensive patronage of Huguenot artisans and artists, particularly at Boughton House, are mentioned extensively in the relevant account books.[57] In addition to these associations, Montagu's grandmother, Rachel de Massue, had been a Huguenot aristocrat; and the Marquis of Ruvigny, Earl of Galway, was Montagu's second cousin. More immediately, Pierre Sylvestre, Montagu's personal tutor and friend with whom he had travelled on his Grand Tour to France and Italy was yet another Huguenot.[58]

The emphasis placed on Freemasonry's 'distinguishing characteristics of . . . Virtue, Honour and Mercy'[59] were also potentially attractive moral principles for Montagu, an argument supported by the recreation of the chivalric Order of the Bath on 18 May 1725, notwithstanding that the Order, like those of the Garter and the Thistle, was also used for political patronage by the Walpole ministry. And Montagu's dalliance with science and matters intellectual played strongly to both Desaguliers and Folkes' strengths. Montagu was admitted a doctor of physic at Cambridge University in 1717 and, at his own request, was elected FRCP the same year. It was not all show: his book subscriptions comprised a large number of eclectic scientific works including John Senex's *New General Atlas*, Henry Pemberton's *View of Sir Isaac Newton's Philosophy* and Engelbert Kaemper's *History of Japan*.

Montagu's installation as Grand Master in 1721 was preceded by a ceremonial public procession to Stationers' Hall. This was the first occasion on which the Freemasons had held a public procession under the leadership of an aristocratic Grand Master, and the first at which the installation took place at a livery hall. The event was designed to attract public interest. Anderson's *1738 Constitutions* recorded his impression of the event:

> Payne, Grand Master, with his Grand Wardens, the former Grand Officers, and the Master and Wardens of 12 Lodges, met the Grand Master Elect in a Grand Lodge at the King's Arms Tavern, St. Paul's Church-yard, in the Morning; and having forthwith recognized their Choice of Brother Montagu they made some new Brothers, particularly the noble Philip, Lord Stanhope, now Earl of Chesterfield; and from thence they marched on Foot to the Hall in proper Clothing and due Form; where they were joyfully received by about 150 true and faithful, all clothed.

Montagu and his retinue, all in Masonic clothing, would have been a focus for attention, a detail that Desaguliers and his colleagues would have anticipated and welcomed. The annual installation procession was in subsequent years even more elaborate. Dalkeith's in 1723 was a spectacle, in Anderson's words, of 'many Brothers duly clothed [and proceeding] in Coaches from the West to the East'. That of Norfolk in 1730 commenced with Lord Kingston, the outgoing Grand Master, attending 'with ceremony' the Duke of Norfolk's London residence in St. James's 'where he was met by a vast Number of Brothers duly clothed'. From St. James's Square they processed to the Merchant Taylor's hall preceded by:

> Brother Johnson to clear the way, six Stewards . . . clothed proper with their Badges and White Rods, two in each Chariot, [and coaches containing] . . . noble and eminent Brethren . . . former Grand Officers . . . former noble Grand Officers . . . the Secretary alone with his Badge and Bag . . . the two Grand Wardens . . . the Deputy Grand Master . . . and in the final coach, Kingston, Grand Master, and Norfolk, Grand Master Elect, clothed only as a Mason.

It is probable that the processions were orchestrated for optimum effect:

> the Stewards halted at Charing Cross until the messenger brought orders to move on slowly.

The spectacle was repeated annually. Crawford's procession in 1734 included:

> trumpets, hautboys, kettle drums and French-horns, to lead the van and play at the gate till all arrive.

And in 1736, that of Loudoun was even more elaborate:

> being in a Chariot richly carved and gilt drawn by six beautiful Grey Horses [with three] Setts of Musick . . . consisting of a pair of kettle drums, four trumpets and four French horns, the others of a pair of kettle drums, two trumpets and two French horns.

Earl Darnley's parade the following year followed a similar pattern and received widespread publicity, including a note in the *London Evening Post* on 28 April 1737:

> about One o'Clock they proceeded in Coaches and Charriots; attended by Kettle-Drums, Trumpets etc. through the City to Fishmongers' Hall; the Procession being clos'd by the Great Officers, and the earl of Darnley in a fine, rich, gilt Charriot, drawn by six Long Tail Grey Horses, with fine Morocco Harness and Green Silk Reins, and several servants in rich Liveries. The Dinner was exceedingly elegant, and the Collection for the Relief of distress'd Brethren very considerable.

The Daily Advertiser of 29 April 1737 referred to 'upwards of a hundred coaches' and noted the cost of his Lordship's pre-installation breakfast at

£200. Press coverage of the event was described across seven different newspapers and – unusually – differed from paper to paper, indicating that several different 'reporters' had attended rather than the material being recycled from a single source, the most common form of reportage.

A number of Montagu's friends from Court and Parliament attended his installation at which 'Brother Payne, the old Grand Master, made the first Procession round the Hall and . . . proclaimed aloud, the most noble Prince and our Brother, John Montagu, Duke of Montagu, Grand Master of Masons! . . . while the Assembly owned the Duke's Authority with due Homage and joyful Congratulations'.[60] Those present included Philip, Duke of Wharton, and Henry Herbert, later 9th Earl of Pembroke, a Lord of the Bedchamber to the Prince of Wales and Montagu's successor in 1721 as Captain and Colonel of the 1st Troop of Horse Guards.[61] Philip Stanhope, later the 4th Earl of Chesterfield, MP for St. Germans, was also in attendance, together with Lord Hinchingbrook, MP for Huntingdon.

Such invitations were continued by Montagu's successor Grand Masters. The intentional result of Montagu's acceptance of the position of Grand Master was that it became correspondingly easy to persuade other aristocrats such as Earl Dalkeith and the Duke of Richmond, Montagu's close friend and Westminster neighbour, to assume the role.[62] Indeed, Wharton may have been so enamoured of the possibilities afforded by the potential standing and influence of the rank of Grand Master that he did not need to be convinced by anyone but grabbed the position directly, a subject discussed below.

The majority of Montagu's successors through to the late 1730s provided Freemasonry with relatively affluent, politically well-connected and generally popular figureheads. However, probably only Montagu and Richmond supplied relatively active leadership. Under Montagu's auspices, Desaguliers orchestrated the formal adoption of the new *Charges* and *Regulations* that cemented the foundations for Freemasonry's central structure; and under Richmond's aegis, the Grand Charity was established and lodges formed on the continent at Paris and The Hague.

Montagu's formal tenure as Grand Master ended somewhat irregularly with an unplanned handover to Wharton, albeit that the event was also marked by Desaguliers' appointment as Wharton's Deputy, something upon which Montagu may have insisted. It is plausible that Desaguliers had expected Montagu to continue as Grand Master for some years. However, Wharton's impromptu seizure of the position may have led to Montagu relinquishing the role and to it then becoming an annual appointment. Regardless, Montagu continued to be associated closely with Freemasonry both within Grand Lodge, at the Bear & Harrow and elsewhere. His relationship with the Craft gave it prominence and afforded protection, and his wealth remained at its disposal in subsequent years.[63]

Philip, Duke of Wharton (1698–1731)

The frontispiece that illustrated the *1723 Constitutions* was designed to impress. It depicted Montagu wearing the robes of the Order of the Garter, presenting the Constitutional scroll and a set of compasses to Wharton dressed in his ducal robes. Each is supported by his respective Deputy Grand Master and Grand Wardens. Wearing white aprons and gloves, John Beale, Josias Villeneau and Thomas Morris, members of the Goose and Gridiron in St. Paul's Churchyard and Bull's Head in Southwark, are to the left. Both were Huguenot émigrés.[64] William Hawkins and Joshua Timson stand next to Desaguliers on the right, dressed in clerical robes. Hawkins was one of several contemporary figures of that name. If, in Anderson's words, he was 'always out of town', he may have been the Deputy Chief Justice of the Brecon circuit in South Wales and a member of the Inner Temple. Timson was one of the few artisan members of Grand Lodge.

Detailed between the two groups is Euclid's 47th Proposition. A colonnade of pillars representing the different architectural orders is shown in perspective framing the transfer of power and authority from Montagu to Wharton, governing Grand Lodge under the kingdom of Heaven. However, this picture of a seamless transfer of power was a fiction.

Wharton was made a Freemason at the age of 22, only a few months after Montagu had been installed as Grand Master. As *Applebee's Original Weekly Journal* noted on 5 August 1721, 'the Ceremonies being performed at the King's Arms Tavern . . . His Grace came Home to his House in the Pall-Mall in a white Leathern Apron'.

Wharton was in many ways an archetypical rebellious youth. However, his mutinous nature and mercurial approach to life lasted into adulthood and were at the opposite spectrum to his father, Thomas, a leading supporter of William of Orange and vociferous opponent of King James II's government. Following William & Mary's accession, his father was made a Privy Councillor and Comptroller of the Household. He was also created Earl of Wharton and Viscount Wichendon (in 1706), and served as Lord Lieutenant of Ireland from 1708 until 1710, Lord Lieutenant of Oxfordshire and Buckinghamshire, and Lord Privy Seal. In 1715, shortly before his death, he was created Marquess of Catherlough, Earl of Rathfarnam and Baron Trim in the Irish Peerage, and Marquess of Wharton and Marquess of Malmesbury in the English.

In the wake of his father's political eminence and influence, Wharton was provided with both a substantial inheritance and exceptional royal and political connections. Wharton's godparents included King William III, the Duke of Shrewsbury and Princess (later Queen) Anne. Wharton succeeded in 1715, shortly after a marriage made against his father's wishes which was widely understood to have been contributory to his father's early death. He inherited six titles in the English and Irish Peerage.

Thomas Wharton had – albeit unsuccessfully – sought to dominate and control his son. After his father's death, Wharton rebelled. Wharton was

Engrav'd by John Pine in Aldersgate street London

accompanied on his 1716 Grand Tour by a Huguenot teacher on a journey designed to satisfy an obligation in his father's will that he visit Geneva to continue his religious education. He abandoned his tutor in Switzerland and travelled instead to Paris. Wharton wrote to and then visited the Old Pretender, James Stuart, at Avignon, presented him with the gift of a horse and was in turn invested with the title of Duke of Northumberland. He also corresponded with the exiled Duke of Mar, John Erskine. Such potentially treasonable behaviour could have been politically disastrous; but it was overlooked, regarded only as a youthful misdemeanour.

Wharton was only 17. However, despite his not having the required age, he was allowed to sit in the Irish Parliament on his return to Britain; he was also sworn a Privy Councillor in September 1717. As a further incentive to good behavior he was created Duke on 28 January 1718.[65] The letters patent announced 'as it is to the honour of subjects who are descended from an illustrious family to imitate the great example of their ancestors, we esteem it no less a glory as a King, after the example of our ancestors, to dignify eminent virtues by similar rewards'.

Wharton took his seat in the House of Lords on his majority on 21 December 1719. He attracted considerable press interest and comment (the *Burney* collection contains around 500 references over the period 1718–24 that report his social and political activities), and he appeared to have matured. His speeches were pro-government to the extent that the Buckinghamshire archives hold an invitation to Wharton to attend a meeting of 'Gentlemen of the Whig interest' at the George Inn at Aylesbury.[66] Indeed, there had probably been a belief within the establishment that a dukedom was a necessary price to ensure the loyalty of the unpredictable but potentially influential Wharton.

Unfortunately, it became clear quite rapidly that Wharton's principal focus was self-interest. His politics were about ambition, power and influence; sometimes principles, but never party. Predictable only in his unpredictability, Wharton rebelled and launched an effective attack on the government over the South Sea Company, condemning it as 'dangerous bait which might decoy unwary people to their ruin'.[67] This may not have been an entirely altruistic analysis on Wharton's part: he was reported to have speculated and lost £120,000. If so, such loss was an effective spur to his eloquence.[68]

An Inconvenience Incarnate

Handsome, intelligent and rich, Wharton was an eccentric and a classic rake. His interests outside of Parliament revolved around whoring, gambling, drinking and mischief making. He was a founder of the first Hell Fire Club and, in 1721, was proscribed for blasphemy by the Lord Chancellor, a charge he denied.

Wharton sought to usurp rather than succeed Montagu and either to commandeer what he may have perceived as a potentially influential organisation, or simply cause a nuisance:

> Philip, Duke of Wharton lately made a Brother, tho' not the Master of a Lodge, being ambitious of the Chair, got a number of others to meet him at Stationers Hall 24 June 1722. And having no Grand officers, they put in the Chair the oldest Master Mason . . . and without the usual decent Ceremonials, the said oldest Mason proclaimed aloud Philip, Duke of Wharton, Grand Master of Masons . . . but his Grace appointed no Deputy nor was the Lodge opened and closed in due Form. Therefore the noble Brothers and all those that would not countenance irregularities disowned

Wharton's Authority, till worthy Brother Montagu heal'd the Breach of Harmony, by summoning the Grand Lodge to meet 17 January 1723 at the King's Arms aforesaid, where the Duke of Wharton promising to be True and Faithful, Deputy Grand Master Beale proclaimed aloud the most noble Prince and our Brother Philip Duke of Wharton, Grand Master of Masons, who appointed Dr Desaguliers the Deputy Grand Master and Joshua Timson and James Anderson Grand Wardens.[69]

Notwithstanding Anderson's probably biased record of these events, evidence that Wharton was accepted as Grand Master in June 1722, reluctantly, temporarily, or otherwise, can be inferred from contemporary reports of the 25 June dinner that marked his installation as Grand Master and at which Desaguliers and other pro-Whig and Montagu-supporting Masons were present. Wharton's installation was reported in the *Compleat Set of St James's Journals* on 28 June 1722 and in near identical terms in other newspapers over the next several days. Tangentially, but of interest, the report carried in the *London Journal* of 30 June 1722 remarked that membership of the Society was some 4,000. If correct, this would be an astonishing achievement and underlines the impact made by Montagu's appointment a year earlier.

At least one account confirmed that Wharton's appointment was regarded as divisive and noted that the musicians played the Jacobite song 'Let the King enjoy his own again' during the evening, presumably with Wharton's encouragement:

Then let us rejoice, With heart and voice,
There doth one Stuart still remain;
And all sing the tune, On the tenth day of June,
That the King shall enjoy his own again

Laurence Smith in his biographical entry on Wharton for the ODNB suggests that Wharton sang the song rather than simply allowed it to be played. Regardless, by condoning, encouraging or participating in what was an overt anti-Hanoverian display, Wharton was making an unacceptable political point in an extremely offensive manner. As Alexander Pope noted retrospectively in his 1734 *Epistle to Cobham*, Wharton was

A fool, with more of wit than half mankind,
Too rash for thought, for action too refined

David Stevenson's paper, 'James Anderson: Man & Mason', noted that the musicians and Wharton – implicitly, if not explicitly – were 'immediately reprimanded by a Person of great Gravity and Science', without doubt, Desaguliers. Thereafter, in Stevenson's words, 'Hanoverian decorum was restored, and . . . toasts were drunk to prosperity under the present Administration, and to Love, Liberty, and Science'.

Anderson represented the Grand Lodge meeting of January 1723 as having healed the schism between the two Masonic factions as 'loyal' Montagu gave way formally to the mercurial Wharton, but this depiction was over-simplistic and is almost certainly incorrect. Although it would be reasonable to view the episode as a relatively petty squabble between two factions – and Anderson had a stake in depicting the events as such – it was also a skirmish in the wider struggle for political influence, with the government and its supporters on one side and opposition Whigs, Tories and independents on the other. The conflict ran across a broad political and social canvas of which Freemasonry was an important if minor part.

Wharton's June 1723 exodus from Grand Lodge can be categorised as a key event that cemented the pro-Hanoverian and pro-Whig nature of the Craft under Desaguliers and his colleagues' influence. It is notable that it occurred within a week of Wharton's defence of Francis Atterbury, the Jacobite Bishop of Rochester, against the charge of treason. In a boorish gesture to the government and the Crown, Wharton accompanied Atterbury for part of his journey into exile and ostentatiously gave him an engraved sword as a gift. And following Atterbury's exile, he appointed the Rev. Moore, Atterbury's secretary and chaplain, as his own.[70]

This was not an image that Desaguliers, Payne, Cowper, Delafaye or Folkes would have wished to project in connection with Freemasonry, nor one with which they and many others wanted to be associated. The flourish with which Desaguliers signed the Minute that recorded Wharton's departure 'without ceremony' from Grand Lodge may provide an indication of the emotions generated at the time.[71]

Wharton had waived his right to name a successor, leaving Grand Lodge to make its own choice, possibly in the conviction that his friends might move his re-election. But Grand Lodge instead chose narrowly in favour of the young Earl of Dalkeith, a course that had probably been foreseen by Desaguliers given that he had almost certainly arranged for Dalkeith to name himself as Dalkeith's Deputy and the loyal Sorrel and Senex as his Wardens. The Minutes, written contemporaneously in 1723 by the new Grand Secretary, William Cowper, detail a last attempt by Wharton to undermine and displace Desaguliers, and underline Desaguliers' successful resistance:

> Brother Robinson producing a written authority from the Earl [Dalkeith] for that purpose, did declare in his Name, That his Worship . . . did appoint Dr. Desaguliers his Deputy, and Brothers Sorrel and Senex Grand Wardens; and also Brother Robinson did in his said Worship's Name and [on] behalf of the whole Fraternity, protest against the above proceedings of the late Grand Master [Wharton] in first putting the question of Approbation, and what followed thereon as unprecedented, unwarrantable and irregular, and tending to introduce into the Society a Breach of Harmony, with the utmost disorder and Confusion.

Such 'irregularity', 'breach of harmony' and 'utmost disorder and confusion' would have been anathema to the orderly Desaguliers, much as 'dullness' was to Alexander Pope. Desaguliers' antipathy to 'jarring Parties' and 'jarring Motions', and his ideal of 'the Almighty Architect's unaltered Laws' and 'Harmony and mutual Love', are set out clearly in his poem 'The Newtonian System of the World'. The same concepts were mirrored in the new Masonic liturgy.[72] The scientific Enlightenment ideal encapsulated Desaguliers' beliefs and represented an ethos that he and colleagues such as Cowper, Delafaye, Folkes, and others within Freemasonry, not only believed in but also wished to project.

Wharton was not content to let matters pass; rather than acquiesce with Dalkeith's choice of Desaguliers, a man with whom Wharton had nothing in common and whom he would have disliked intensely as a result of the reprimand at his installation, Wharton insisted that a vote be held to approve 'the Deputy nominated by the Earl of Dalkeith' – perhaps he could not bear to say Desaguliers' name. Despite Wharton's rank, the motion was declared narrowly in Desaguliers' favour, by forty-three to forty-two. However, Wharton, after 'some of the regular Healths' had been drunk, repeated his objection and queried the accuracy of the count and the veracity of the tellers. He insisted that the vote be held once again and on being voted down once more, angrily departed:

> Then the said late Grand Master and those who withdrew with him on being returned in the Hall and acquainted with the aforesaid Declaration of Brother Robinson . . . went away from the Hall without any Ceremony. After other regular Healths drank, the Lodge adjourned.

Wharton's antipathy and unsuccessful exploits prompted Desaguliers to act. By the time Dalkeith was installed formally, Desaguliers had instigated changes to prevent or at least forestall any future substantive or subversive alterations to the new model Freemasonry. Grand Lodge accepted formally the new *Constitutions* in January 1723, and the appointment of Cowper as Grand Secretary allowed control of the Minutes to pass to a loyal Whig and fellow member of the Horn. An additional resolution was passed in January which confirmed that 'it was not in the power of any body of men to make any Alteration or Innovation in the body of Masonry without the consent first obtained of the Annual Grand Lodge'. And the following June it was agreed that the Grand Master at installation 'shall next nominate and appoint his Deputy Grand Master'. The last amendment was of fundamental importance: in practice, the Deputy Grand Master exercised authority within Grand Lodge in the name of its aristocratic figurehead.

Wharton's brief reign as Grand Master would have been a nightmare for those seeking to establish Freemasonry's political and moral *bona fides*. Alongside the Atterbury Plot, 1722 had been attended by the possibility of another Jacobite rising. The year was marked by heightened security and surveillance across London, and troops were recalled from Ireland and encamped in Hyde Park as a show of force and insurance against any insurrection. With the government legitimately suspicious of any secret gatherings and societies, the embryonic Grand Lodge duly sent a deputation to Lord Townshend to obtain his formal consent for the June meeting. The *London Journal* of 16 June 1722 gave an account of the event:

> A select body of the Society of Freemasons waited on the Rt. Hon. the Lord Viscount Townshend, one of his Principal Secretaries of State, to signify to his Lordship, that being obliged by their Constitutions to hold a General Meeting now at Midsummer, according to ancient custom, they hoped the Administration would take no umbrage at their convention as they were all zealously affected to His Majesty's Person and Government.

It is perhaps suggestive that there is no reference to the meeting in State Papers Domestic. However, given the close relationship between Townshend and Freemasonry, it is possible that the meeting did not take place in any formal sense and that the press statement was designed instead to reflect the Craft's Whiggist credentials to the public: Townshend's eldest son, Charles (1700–64), was a member of the lodge at the Old Devil, Temple Bar, and Whig MP for Great Yarmouth, and Charles Delafaye, Townshend's ultra loyal Under Secretary of State and a central figure in the government's anti-Jacobite spy network, was a leading Freemason and a member of the Horn. Townshend's consent was forthcoming. Given Delafaye's influence and position, it was probably inevitable.

Simultaneously, Wharton honed his anti-Walpole and anti-Hanoverian rhetoric and reputation, continued to defend Atterbury and established later the same year an anti-Walpole journal, *The True Briton*. Uncomfortable with his enforced departure from Grand Lodge, Wharton founded an alternative society in 1724, satirised by Hogarth in his painting *Masonry Brought to Light by the Gormogons*.

The first reference to Wharton's Gormogons appeared in the *Daily Post* on 3 September 1724. It was followed by an anti-Masonic article in the *Plain Dealer* on 14 September and a subsequent note on 12 December in the *British Journal*:

> We hear that a Peer of the first Rank, a noted Member of the Society of Freemasons, hath suffered himself to be degraded as a Member of that Society, and his Leather Apron and Gloves to be burnt, and thereupon enter'd himself a Member of the Society of Gormogons, at the Castle-Tavern in Fleet Street.

It is a gauge of the interest generated by Wharton and Freemasonry that the press took up the affair, and that Hogarth believed the public's curiosity to be sufficient to justify the production of a print. However, apart from Hogarth's print, little more was heard of the Gormogons. A reference appeared in the *Grub Street Journal* on 16 April 1730, where the paper recorded that 'Mr Dennis the famous Poet and Critic' [John Dennis, 1657–1734] 'was admitted a free and accepted Mason . . . having renounc'd the Society of Gormogons of which he had been a member many years'. And classified advertisements for meetings of the Gormogons, usually at the Castle Tavern, Fleet Street, by 'Command of the Volgi', were also published in the *Country Journal or Craftsman* on 11 October 1729, and in the *Daily Journal* on 28 April 1730. However, these were publicity generators, most probably linked to a 'Pantomime Interlude' – the *Harlequin Grand Volgi* – staged at the Theatre Royal, Drury Lane, which featured a 'Mandarin-Gormogon' played by a 'Mr Thurmond'. The pantomime was staged by Colley Cibber, himself a Freemason. Tangentially, Cibber later helped to organise a theatrical benefit evening for John Dennis.

Wharton's attention was quickly captured by other interests. He formed a second society the same year, the Schemers, which met at Lord Hillsborough's London home 'for the advancement of that branch of happiness which the vulgar call whoring':[73]

> Twenty very pretty fellows (the Duke of Wharton being president and chief director) have formed themselves into a committee of gallantry, who call themselves Schemers; and meet regularly three times a week to consult on gallant schemes.[74]

Wharton's financial profligacy obliged him to sell his remaining assets and to compound for his debts in Chancery where his pro-Jacobite politics and dissolute lifestyle afforded limited political, public or judicial support. He departed for the continent in June 1725 and, after a short period in Paris,[75] left for Madrid where he enlisted in the Spanish army and later appeared against the British at Gibraltar. Despite this, Wharton petitioned Grand Lodge in 1728 – by which date the conflict was over – to form a lodge in Madrid. The petition was granted and the lodge established by Charles Labelye, one of Desaguliers' acolytes, who became its first Master.

Given his reduced circumstances, Wharton's continuing interest in Freemasonry is perhaps understandable: its growing reputation was such that it probably offered some influence and prestige, even in Catholic Spain. It was also a useful political tool and linked to Walpole's continental European spy network. Moreover, at that point, Wharton was still a Duke.

The lodge that Wharton co-founded is now known as *La Matritense* and is recorded as Lodge No. 1 on the register of the Grand Orient of Spain, itself founded in 1817. Freemasonry was banned in Spain by General Franco in 1940 and only re-established after his death.

Wharton died a pauper in 1731 at the age of 33 at the monastery at Poblet, Spain. He had been outlawed by resolution of Parliament on the 3 April 1729 for failing to appear to answer the charge of treason. His titles and property were declared forfeit.

The Earl of Dalkeith (1695–1751)

Francis Scott, 5th Earl of Dalkeith and 2nd Duke of Buccleuch, he succeeded to the title in 1724, was 28 when elected Grand Master. The son of Sir James Scott, Earl of Dalkeith,[76] and the grandson of James Scott, the 1st Duke of Monmouth, the eldest illegitimate son of Charles II who had been beheaded by James II, Dalkeith was wealthy, well-connected and, unlike Wharton, an ardent pro-Hanoverian.[77] His loyalty was rewarded: he was sworn a member of the Privy Council and invested a Knight of the Thistle, Scotland's premier chivalric order, in 1725.

Despite maintaining a large London house at Albemarle Street and later Grosvenor Street, Dalkeith was essentially a Scottish peer and lived principally at his estate surrounding the town of Dalkeith, southeast of Edinburgh. He married Lady Jane Douglas, the daughter of the 2nd Duke of Queensberry, on 5 April 1720 in London.

Tangentially, the unusual circumstance surrounding his wedding supports the suggestion that Dalkeith could be uncommonly compliant. In March 1720, a marriage had been announced between Dalkeith and Lady Jane Douglas, the only sister of the Duke of Douglas.[78] Lady Jane was considered beautiful, intelligent and highly eligible; she lived close to Dalkeith at Merchiston Castle near Edinburgh with her widowed mother, Lady Mary Kerr. However, in an extraordinary sequence of events, Lady Kerr was reported to have broken off the engagement within a few days of the marriage being announced and instead arranged for Dalkeith to marry another Scottish aristocrat.[79] The wedding took place less than a month later.[80] The aborted first engagement led to a duel between Dalkeith and the Duke of Douglas on 25 March, fought behind Montagu House in Westminster. Both were wounded.[81] Nonetheless, the quarrel was resolved through the offices of the Duke of Argyll two weeks later.[82] Dalkeith's replacement bride was also called Lady Jane Douglas.[83] Somewhat ironically given what had occurred the previous month, the marriage brought Dalkeith the estates albeit not the titles of the Douglas clan.[84]

Notwithstanding his absence in Scotland, Dalkeith was declared Grand Master in June 1723 at a meeting at which Desaguliers as Deputy Grand Master presided:

> The Ancient Society of Free and Accepted Masons . . . assembled to thye Number of about 600 at Merchant Taylors' Hall where they unanimously chose the Earl of Dalkeith their Grand Master for the year ensuing.[85]

Dalkeith was present at each meeting of Grand Lodge during his year in office: on 25 November 1723, 19 February 1724 and 28 April the same year, at which the Duke of Richmond – his cousin – was appointed his successor. Dalkeith also attended the following meeting on 24 June at which Richmond was installed.

The date and place of Dalkeith's initiation as a Freemason is not known but pre-dated 3 November 1723, when Stukeley recorded his attendance at the Fountain Tavern in the Strand. Dalkeith was recorded in the *1723 Constitutions* as the Master of the Rummer at Charing Cross, lodge number 'XI' in Anderson's list of lodges in the *Constitutions*. It is possible that he may have been initiated at the Rummer in 1722 or earlier.[86]

Dalkeith's conduct while Grand Master suggests that he was influenced strongly by Desaguliers. Indeed, his actions as prospective Grand Master with the appointment of Desaguliers as his Deputy and Francis Sorrel and John Senex as Wardens, both of whom were supporters of Desaguliers, reinforces the assessment. It is also possible, but in no way certain, that Desaguliers promoted Dalkeith's election as FRS in March 1724 as a way of thanking him for his support.

The Lincolnshire archives which hold the Buccleuch family papers contain around twenty references to Dalkeith. Unfortunately, none refer to his Freemasonry or to his activities within Grand Lodge or at the Rummer. There is however extensive correspondence with several who were Freemasons, including the Dukes of Montagu, Richmond and Newcastle, and such correspondence confirms the strong social and political bonds which existed. Richmond was especially close, and took a particular interest in Dalkeith's son, also Francis (1721–1750). Seeking his preferment, Richmond described him in a letter to Newcastle 'as honest of any of us and vastly desirous to be in Parliament . . . it would be a credit to a ministry to bring him in'.[87]

Dalkeith allowed Desaguliers to reassert stability and provided political reassurance after Wharton's short and disruptive tenure. His first act was to reassert the Grand Master's right to appoint his Deputy, a gesture that could be interpreted as greatly reinforcing Desaguliers' authority. His second was to expel 'Brother Huddleston of the King's Head lodge in Ivy Lane' for casting unsubstantiated aspersions on the character of the Deputy Grand Master and to appoint a new and presumably more loyal Master to that lodge.[88] Under Dalkeith's nominal auspices, the *Grand Lodge Minutes* provide evidence of Desaguliers' drive to centralise and control Freemasonry: no new lodge, nor its Master and Wardens, would be recognised unless such a lodge was 'regularly constituted' by Grand Lodge; and 'no Brother belonging to any lodge within the Bills of Mortality [would] be admitted to any lodge as a Visitor unless he be known to . . . that lodge . . . and . . . no Strange Brother, however Skilled in Masonry [would] be admitted without taking the Obligation over again'.[89]

Desaguliers' requirements and impositions were a continuing theme at Grand Lodge. The *Minutes* of 17 March 1731, for example, recorded that: 'Dr. Desaguliers taking Notice of some Irregularities in wearing the Marks of Distinction . . . proposed that none but the Grand Master, his Deputy and Wardens shall wear their jewels in Gold or Gilt pendant to blue Ribbons about their Necks and white Leather Aprons lined with blue Silk; that all those who have served any of the three Grand Offices shall wear the like Aprons lined with blue Silk in all Lodges and assemblies of Masons when they appear clothed; that those Brethren that are Steward shall wear their aprons lined with red Silk and their proper Jewels pendant to red Ribbons ... and not otherwise'.

It is notable and probably not a coincidence that Desaguliers accompanied Dalkeith on each occasion that he attended Grand Lodge after stepping down as Grand Master. The first instance was on November 1724, the first quarterly communication at which past Grand Masters were permitted to attend. It was at this meeting, most probably at Desaguliers' instigation, that Dalkeith recommended the establishment of the Grand Charity.[90] Dalkeith's two visits to the Horn in March and November 1724 – the year that Richmond was Grand Master – were also with Desaguliers at his side.[91]

CHARLES LENNOX, 2ND DUKE OF RICHMOND & LENNOX (1701–1750)

Dalkeith was succeeded as Grand Master by Charles Lennox, 2nd Duke of Richmond. Richmond was 23. He appointed Folkes, one of his closest friends, as Deputy Grand Master, and Francis Sorrel and George Payne as his Grand Wardens. Richmond's patronage of Payne lasted virtually throughout the latter's life. A late example appears in Richmond's correspondence with Newcastle regarding Payne's application for appointment as a Commissioner for the Lottery:

> I have always recommended one Mr George Payne, an old acquaintance of mine in Westminster, for whom as yet I have always succeeded.[92]

William Cowper also retained his position as Grand Secretary. It was unsurprising: Sorrel, Payne and Cowper were all members of the Horn.

Richmond's installation took place at the capacious Merchant Taylor's Hall on 24 June 1724. The occasion was described at length in Anderson's *1738 Constitutions*.[93] The 'persons of distinction', processions, orations, Masonic music and songs at the installation were again designed to make an impact within and without Freemasonry, and to maintain and enhance fraternal bonding within the Craft. They succeeded, and the popularity of the new 'regular' Freemasonry continued to gain momentum both in London and across the provinces.[94]

London's population in the mid- and late 1720s was around 600,000. Of this number, perhaps around 2–3% could be termed members of the elite: the aristocracy, wealthy gentry and successful bankers and merchants, with perhaps a further 10% or so being of the upper middling sort, such as lawyers, physicians, apothecaries, military officers, traders and large-scale shopkeepers etc. In this context, and excluding women and those under the legal majority of 21, Freemasonry's London membership of around 4,000 would have represented perhaps 20% or more of this section of the adult male population.[95]

Richmond, the only son of the 1st Duke, another illegitimate son of Charles II,[96] was born at the family's Goodwood estate on 18 May 1701. He married at The Hague in December 1719. The marriage was reportedly to satisfy a gambling debt incurred by his father and, without his young wife, Richmond left immediately afterwards for the Grand Tour. Despite this, the marriage was remarkably successful. On his return in 1722, Richmond purchased a commission as Captain in the Horse Guards and was elected MP for Chichester, the family seat. Following his father's death the following year Richmond succeeded to his titles and left the House of Commons accordingly.[97]

Like Montagu, a close friend, Richmond was a loyal Whig. He dominated local Sussex politics and became Mayor of Chichester in 1735. Newcastle described him as 'the most solid support of the Whig interest in Chichester' and Richmond himself commented that he had been 'bred up from a child in the Whig principles'.[98] The two became political allies.[99] Timothy McCann noted that with Newcastle's backing, Sussex returned, unopposed, two government supporters to Parliament throughout Richmond's life.[100] Richmond was rewarded accordingly: appointed Aide de Camp to George I in 1724 and reappointed in the same role by George II; and installed a Knight of the Bath in 1725 and a Knight of the Garter in 1726. Sinecures included the position of Lord High Constable of England and a Lord of the Bedchamber (both appointments in 1727), and Master of the Horse from 1735 until 1750. He was raised to the Privy Council in 1735.

Although Richmond had only a brief military career, it was not insignificant and he was, in McCann's words, 'a conscientious officer'.[101] He served as Aide-de-Camp to George I and held the same position under George II. Promoted Brigadier General in 1739, Major General in 1742 and Lieutenant General in 1745, Richmond was made a full General later the same year.[102] His political loyalty and personal connections to Walpole,[103] and his 'staunch defence of the Hanoverian succession',[104] led in 1740 to his selection as a Lord Justice of the Realm.

Richmond also undertook quasi-diplomatic missions in France and the Low Countries, an activity assisted considerably by his French title, inherited in November 1734 on the death of his grandmother. At her death, Richmond succeeded to the Dukedom of Aubigny and travelled to France the following year to claim his inheritance. The title had been granted by Charles VII in recognition of assistance given by John Stewart, Lord Darnley, against the English army in 1421.[105] Darnley had been awarded the title in perpetuity and as his descendant and now duc d'Aubigny, Richmond was a legitimate member of the French nobility.[106]

Desaguliers accompanied Richmond to France and upon their arrival they established a Masonic lodge at Richmond's estate.[107] Following a formal *ex post* request 'to hold a lodge at his castle d'Aubigny', Grand Lodge granted Richmond a warrant the following year. The lodge, number 133, remained on Grand Lodge's lists until 1768.

Although Freemasonry in France has often been associated with

Jacobitism,[108] certain French Freemasons were anglophiles who favoured the 'natural liberties' and philosophical concepts associated with constitutional government, English culture and the Newtonian scientific Enlightenment. Three Parisian lodges, Louis d'Argent, Coustos-Villeroy and Bussy-Aumont, are reported to have used anglicized Masonic ritual and enjoyed scientific and other lectures similar to those given in English lodges. With the election of members and officers and byelaws enacted based on majority vote, a radical concept in France, such lodges may have set a modest challenge to the monarch-centred institutions that characterised Louis XV's reign.[109] Moreover, from a British standpoint, the (albeit small) group of aristocrats and intellectuals attracted to such 'regular' Freemasonry formed a faction that might be exploited for political gain.

Daniel Ligou's 'Structures et Symbolisme Maçonniques' suggested that there was a tension between the constitutional self-government and religious tolerance espoused by Freemasonry and France's absolutist regime and Catholic dogma.[110] However, it would be wrong to assert that this undermined in any material way the political and religious order, a position substantiated by the relatively modest police actions against France's Masonic lodges and by the initial indifference to Pope Clement XII's Papal Bull of 28 April 1738 condemning and prohibiting 'these . . . Francs Massons'.[111] Later that year, Louis XV's ordered Rene Hérault, his chief of police, to investigate possible sedition[112] and Hérault subsequently raided Waldegrave's ambassadorial residence in Paris. However, Freemasonry was generally permitted to continue.[113] Indeed, Jérôme Lalande, the French astronomer, mathematician and later Master of the Lodge of the Nine Muses, commented that lodge Louis d'Argent attracted up to six hundred members in the late 1730s.[114]

Richmond's engagement with Freemasonry in France – and in the Netherlands – was both social and political, and given impetus by his relationship with Newcastle, Secretary of State for the Southern Department from 1724 until 1748, and with Charles Delafaye, Under Secretary of State, the government's chief anti-Jacobite spymaster and a member of Richmond's Horn lodge since at least 1723.[115] Indeed, Richmond was exporting Freemasonry to France even before he succeeded as duc d'Aubigny. In September 1734, the London papers reported that a lodge had been held at the Duchess of Portsmouth's house in Paris where:

> the Duke of Richmond assisted by another English nobleman of distinction there, President Montesquieu, Brigadier Churchill,[116] Ed. Yonge Esq.[117] and Walter Strickland, admitted several persons of distinction into that most ancient and honourable society.[118]

Among those admitted Freemasons that evening were Marquis Brancas,[119] General Skelton[120] and President Montesquieu's son.[121] The English newspapers reporting the event may have been unaware of the paradox: Louise de Kéroualle (1649–1734), the Duchess of Portsmouth and

Richmond's grandmother, had been sent to England in the 1660s with the expectation that she would become a royal mistress and thereby support French interests at Charles II's court. In broad terms she succeeded – she was rewarded accordingly by Louis XIV. Richmond's Masonic activities in Paris some sixty years later were an ironic reversal.

A letter from Thomas Hill to Richmond dated 23 August 1734 discussed the establishment of the Duke's proposed lodge at Aubigny (and provides a good example of the importance of primary source material). Hill, the Duke's former tutor and by then a friend and member of his household, was a frequent correspondent.[122] His observations offer a window on Desaguliers' methodology and motives, and provide evidence of his willingness to use artifice and embroidery 'in order to give his style the greater air of antiquity and consequently make it more venerable' if the 'further propagation of masonry' would result:

> I have communicated to the new, if I am not mistaken, right worshipful . . . Dr J. Theophilus Desaguliers, your Grace's command relating to the brotherhood of Aubigny sur Nere. I need not tell you how pleased he is with the further propagation of masonry . . . When I mentioned the diploma [warrant], he immediately asked me if I had not *Amadis de Gaula*,[123] or some of the other romances. I was something surprised at his question, and began to think, as the house was tiled,[124] our brother had a mind to crack a joke. But it turned out quite otherwise. He only wanted to get a little of the vieux Gaulois[125] in order to give his style the greater air of antiquity and consequently make it more venerable to the new lodge. He went from me fully intent on getting that or some other such book. What the production will be you may expect to see soon.

> Among other [subjects] we had, he asked me if I intended going over to Holland. I told him it was very probable I might, if nothing fell to hinder me. Why, said the Dr., I might care if I go too, and when we return we shall have brethren anew to make a lodge. It will be very pretty to have one of His Majesty's yachts a lodge . . . [126]

It became the custom for Richmond to travel to Aubigny each autumn. In September 1735, the *St. James's Evening Post* reported that Richmond and Desaguliers had formed a lodge at the Hotel Bussy in Rue Bussy, Paris, where:

> His Grace the Duke of Richmond and the Rev Dr Desaguliers . . . authorised by the present Grand Master . . . having called a lodge . . . his Excellency the Earl of Waldegrave, his Majesty's Ambassador to the French King, the Right Hon. the President Montesquieu, the Marquis de Lomaria, Lord Dursley, son of the Earl of Berkley . . . and several other persons, both French and English, were present; and the following noblemen and gentlemen were admitted to the Order: namely, His Grace the Duke of

Kingston, the Hon. Count de St. Florentin, Secretary of State to his most Christian Majesty; the Right Hon. The Lord Chewton, son to the Earl of Waldegrave; Mr Pelham, Mr Armiger, Mr Colton and Mr Clement . . . After which, the new Brethren gave a handsome Entertainment to all the Company.[127]

The 1st Earl Waldegrave (1684–1741), had been a Freemason for at least twelve years as a member of the Horn.[128] A grandson of James II, he was a convert to Anglicanism from Catholicism and having rejected Jacobitism was held in royal favour: appointed a Lord of the Bedchamber in 1723 and again, unsolicited, in 1730 until his death. Waldegrave had been ambassador to Austria from 1728 until 1730.[129] In common with Philip Stanhope, Lord Chesterfield, a friend and the ambassador at The Hague, he was not only a prominent Freemason but also prepared to use his ambassadorial offices to promote the Craft and use it for political and diplomatic gain.

Charles Louis de Secondat (1689–1755), the Baron Montesquieu, held the title of President de le Parlement de Bourdeaux, a hereditary legal office equivalent to a member of the court of appeal. He had been elected a member of the French Academy of Sciences in 1728. Waldegrave and Montesquieu were friends and Montesquieu had accompanied Waldegrave on the greater part of his journey to Vienna in 1728 and had later been introduced to Chesterfield, then at The Hague, who suggested that Montesquieu return with him to London. Montesquieu stayed in London for two years. He was presented at Court and in 1730 elected FRS, proposed by Sloane and the Huguenots George Teissier[130] and Paul de St. Hyacinthe.[131]

Montesquieu's family had been courtiers in France for over a century and had served the Huguenot Henry of Navarre. He was initiated into Freemasonry at the Horn in 1730 although his name is not recorded in the members' lists submitted to Grand Lodge.[132] Montesquieu's progressive political and social views (he was married to a Protestant), his authorship of the satirical *Lettres Persanes* in 1721 and his stance on the separation of powers within government, would have marked him as a potentially useful political ally. The lodge provided a discrete forum (or a private 'public sphere') for conversation free of political and religious censure. Its significance is suggested by the initiation of his son, Jean Baptiste Secondat de Montesquieu, by Richmond and Desaguliers a year earlier at a lodge held at the Duchess of Portsmouth's house in Paris convened in September 1734.[133] Jean Baptiste Secondat was himself elected FRS in 1744 and succeeded to the post of President of the Bordeaux Parliament on his father's death.

A strong personal relationship between Montesquieu and Richmond is revealed by their correspondence held at the Goodwood archives at the West Sussex County Record Office and re-printed in Robert Shackleton, 'Montesquieu's Correspondence', in *French Studies*, XII.4 (1958), 324–45. The two first met during Montesquieu's visit to London and Montesquieu's familiarity with Montagu, Folkes and Desaguliers is evident. Desaguliers is mentioned as 'le docteur Desaguliers, la première colonne de la maçonnerie'; and Montesquieu's fondness for Freemasonry suggested by 'je ne doute pas que sur cette nouvelle tout ce qui reste encore à recevoir en France de gens de mérite ne se fasse maçon.'[134] John Misaubin, the Huguenot physician based in London and an active Freemason, was another topic of conversation.[135]

The most important initiate at the Rue Bussy lodge meeting was Louis Phélypeaux (1705–77), Comte de Saint-Florentin, Marquis (1725) and later duc de La Vrillière (1770), who was in 1735 Secretary of State to Louis XV and a senior adviser and courtier. He was also the Minister with responsibility for the Huguenots in France.

Phélypeaux would have been considered an appropriate man to cultivate and his initiation as a Freemason was unlikely to have been accidental. The choice would have been guided by Waldegrave and, perhaps, approved by Walpole. The concurrent initiation of the Duke of Kingston[136] and of Earl Waldegrave's son, Lord Chewton, may have been designed to flatter Phélypeaux in the same manner as the parallel initiation of the Duke of Newcastle alongside the raising of Francis, Duke of Lorraine, at Houghton Hall four years before.

The Duke of Lorraine's initiation had taken place at The Hague earlier in 1731 under Desaguliers' auspices at a lodge formed specifically for the purpose at the home of Lord Chesterfield, Britain's ambassador to the Low Countries. Desaguliers had been engaged on a course of scientific lectures and Lorraine had attended:

> The learned and renowned Dr Desaguliers is now presenting a complete course of lectures on Mechanical and Experimental Philosophy which has been attended not only by persons of the first rank, but which has also been honoured on several occasions by the presence of the Duke of Lorraine.[137]

Desaguliers acted as Master of the lodge, John Stanhope and John Holtzendorf as Wardens, and Chesterfield and three other brethren attended. The National Archives contain a letter from Holtzendorf to George Timson, Secretary of State, which informed London that Lorraine had attended Desaguliers' lectures and that Lorraine 'professes himself a great admirer and friend of the English Nation'.[138]

Evert Kwaadgras in *Masonry with a Message and a Mission*, an address to the Internet Lodge in Kingston-Upon-Hull on 8 August 2002, suggested that Lorraine's meeting with Chesterfield had been intended to discuss his forthcoming diplomatic visit to London. Certainly, Lorraine's Masonic initiation was probably as much if not more political as fraternal: the 2nd Treaty of Vienna had led to the collapse of the Anglo-French alliance and made Austria an appealing ally.[139] Tangentially, Anderson, in his report of the meeting in the *1738 Constitutions*, noted that a 'Hollandish Brother' also attended Lorraine's initiation. Although Kwaadgras proposed that this was Vincent La Chapelle, it is difficult to imagine a London-based French Huguenot being described as such (unless ironically). La Chapelle (also written 'Chappelle') was a member of the Huguenot-dominated lodge at Prince Eugene's Head Coffee House in St. Alban's Street. As an aside, La Roche, another member of the lodge and a fellow Huguenot, is known to have spied for the government and corresponded directly with Robert Walpole.[140]

La Chapelle had travelled to the Netherlands with Chesterfield. He had been recommended by Richmond as a prospective master chef de cuisine.[141] He remained in the Low Countries in 1732 after Chesterfield returned to England and became head chef to the Prince of Orange, having earlier held the same position with the Count of Montijo, at that time an envoy to England from Spain. He later moved to Paris to become principal chef to Madame Pompadour. Although there is anecdotal evidence to suggest that he acted as a spy for Walpole, there is currently no proof.

On 30 September 1734, with the assistance of Desaguliers and Richmond, La Chapelle founded a permanent Masonic lodge at The Hague.[142] The lodge was warranted by Grand Lodge in 1735.[143] Robert Freke Gould noted a second meeting of the lodge the following year.[144] On this latter occasion the attendees included the politically important Jacob Cornelis Rademacher (1700–48), Treasurer General to the Prince of Orange, noted as 'Grand Master', and his Deputy, Kuenen, the Dutch translator and publisher of the *1723 Constitutions*.[145]

La Chapelle's lodge at The Hague was dominated by Huguenot émigrés and others with Orangist politics. Margaret Jacob has suggested that the lodge's establishment and, by inference, other Dutch lodges, was politically motivated,[146] and it is hard to disagree. The involvement of Richmond and Desaguliers supports the view and the establishment of such lodges could be interpreted as a parallel move to the institution of similar 'regular' lodges in Paris. Although Dutch Freemasons were later 'instructed to cease their assemblies', and between 1735 and 1737 Dutch Freemasonry was declared illegal, the prohibition was largely ineffective and Masonry burgeoned once the magistrates' edict of suppression was repealed. Jacob's comment that 'prominent Masons played central roles in the [subsequent] restoration of the stadholderate' should be noted.[147]

Following his initiation and during his visit to England later in 1731, Lorraine was invited to attend an 'occasional' lodge at Houghton Hall, Walpole's country house in Norfolk. There in the presence of Newcastle, General Churchill, Lord Burlington,[148] William Capell[149] and others, he was raised to become a Master Mason. The ceremony was followed 'in the proper manner' by a banquet, fraternal toasts and song.

Freemasonry's clubbable fraternalism was fundamental to its social success and was assumed with ease by Richmond. He was held in high regard by his contemporaries. Lord Hervey, a friend, considered that 'there never lived a man of more amiable composition . . . thoroughly noble in his way of acting, talking and thinking';[150] and Henry Fielding described him as 'excellent', and as 'one of the worthiest of Magistrates, as well as the best of men'.[151]

Much like Montagu, Richmond's life and celebrity status was the subject of considerable public interest. *Burney* contains over 600 press articles concerning the Duke over the ten-year period from his father's death in May 1723 to June 1733, and more than 2,300 additional entries in subsequent years. Although he ranked well below Montagu in terms of wealth and his projects at Goodwood proved a constant and draining expense, he was an eminent and popular member of the aristocracy and within Sussex, a prominent and politically valuable politician.[152]

The publication in the press of Richmond's social and Masonic diary added to the regard in which Freemasonry had begun to be held and embedded in the public consciousness what were now perceived as its relatively accessible yet exclusive characteristics:

> Last Saturday his Grace the Duke of Richmond, accompanied by the Rt Hon the Lord Dalkeith, Sir Thomas Macworth, Dr Desaguliers and other Gentlemen, went to the lodge at Richmond, and made John Rily of the Middle Temple, Esq., and another Gentleman Freemasons. After Dinner his Grace returned to Town, and being Grand Master of that Society, presided at their quarterly meeting that was held that night.[153]

Among the attendees, Sir Thomas Mackworth (16__?–1745), the 4th baronet, was an MP for Rutland (1694–5, 1701–8 and 1721–7) and Portsmouth (1713–15). The family had substantial estates within Rutland and his father, the 3rd baronet, had similarly sat for Rutland (1679, 1680–1 and 1685–94). Sir Thomas was appointed a knight of the shire in 1721, to the General Court of the Charitable Corporation in 1726 and was later elected Deputy Governor of the Mine Adventure Corporation. He had a strong interest in practical science, evidence for which was expressed *inter alia* in a 'very advantageous Proposal' made before the General Court of the Society of the City of London 'for making and manufacturing Copper, Brass, etc. at Mitcham Taplow and Temple Mills'.[154] Masonically, Mackworth was Warden of the King's Arms lodge at St. Paul's and a member of the Red Lyon, Surrey.[155]

Before becoming Grand Master, Richmond had been Master of his own lodge at the Rummer and Grapes, later the Horn. It is possible that his father, the 1st Duke, had also been a gentleman Freemason. The Minutes of Grand Lodge for 2 March 1732 record that Edward Hall, a member of the Swan in Chichester, appeared before the Grand Lodge with a charity petition declaring that 'he was made a Mason by the late Duke of Richmond six and thirty years ago.'[156]

Unlike the majority of his fellow noble Grand Masters who were principally figureheads for Grand Lodge, Richmond's interest in and commitment to Freemasonry appears to have been more profound. This was articulated not only through the frequency of his attendance at Grand Lodge[157] and at his own lodges in London, Sussex and France, but also in his assiduity in inviting colleagues from the Royal Society, the Society of Antiquaries and elsewhere from within his circles to join him in the Craft. The press recorded a succession of friends and fellow aristocrats who joined the Horn and other lodges with which he was associated and his initiations were a constant feature in press reports throughout the 1720s and 1730s.[158]

Under Richmond's Mastership and probably with Payne and Desaguliers' active assistance, the Horn became a focal point for 'gentlemanly' Freemasonry and a feeder organisation for Grand Lodge. The Horn's membership included a mixture of influential aristocrats, army officers, parliamentarians, diplomats and professional men together with those from the senior ranks of the Middlesex and Westminster bench and civil service. The authority exercised by the lodge was deep-seated and the number and nature of its members set out in the lists submitted to Grand Lodge attest to its numerical and social dominance over the three other founding lodges, and most of those that followed.

The Horn was by far the largest of the original founding lodges with over 70 members. In contrast, the lodge at the Goose and Gridiron in St. Paul's Churchyard had 22 members; the lodge at the Queen's Head in Knave's Acre, formerly the Apple Tree Tavern in Covent Garden, had 21; and the Queen's Head in Holborn, formerly the Crown Ale House in Parkers Lane, had 14. Moreover, unlike the three other founding lodges where not a single member had sufficient social status to be titled 'esquire', the Horn's members comprised *inter alia* thirteen English and continental aristocrats. These included Charles Douglas (1698–1778), 3rd Duke of Queensberry and 2nd Duke of Dover, a Whig peer and Vice Admiral of Scotland; and Lord Waldegrave (1684–1741), later ambassador to France. James Hamilton, Lord Paisley (1661–1734), Grand Master in 1725; and Henry Scott (1676–1730), 1st Earl of Delorraine, the second son of the Duke of Monmouth, Colonel of the 2nd Troop of Horse Guards and of his own Regiment of Foot, were also members. The lodge's parliamentary connections were similarly distinguished. Many of the lodge's aristocratic members were MPs or like Richmond had influence over who would be selected for seats within their jurisdiction. The Horn also had sway within the army: its members included two general officers and ten colonels, in addition to other officers below field rank.

In common with many other aristocrats and, in particular, the Duke of Montagu, Richmond had strong scientific and antiquarian interests. He was elected FRS in 1722 (as Earl March) and again in 1724 (as Duke of Richmond),[159] in both cases proposed by Sloane;[160] and in September 1728, was invited to attend a meeting of the Académie Royale des Sciences in Paris where Desaguliers was a corresponding member. A letter written in 1728 noted the honour:

> I was the other day at the Academie Royale des Sciences at Paris; where I am persuaded there is not much more real learning, but I'll venture to say there is much more dignity kept up there than at our Society, they have given me some hopes of admitting me, when there is a vacancy among the ignorant ones that they call honorary Fellows; which number is fix'd to ten.[161]

Richmond obtained a doctorate in law at Cambridge in 1728 and requested election as a FRCP the same year. His interest in medicine was genuine: he became President of the London Hospital in 1741 and was one of the earliest to practice inoculation in Sussex. He also collected information on the Chichester smallpox epidemic in 1739, from which he had suffered in 1724/5, and observed and reported on the Swiss naturalist, Abraham Trembley's zoological experiments. Trembley (1710–1784), was later appointed by the Duke to tutor his son and to accompany him on the Grand Tour. A recognised and eminent scientist, Trembley was awarded the Royal Society's Copley Medal in 1743. On Folkes' recommendation, Richmond was elected to the Society of Antiquaries in 1736 and was an active supporter. In March 1750, he became its President.

The officers that ran Grand Lodge under Richmond's leadership were particularly close. Desaguliers' tight connection to the five principal Grand Officers was probably a key factor in their agreeing at the next quarterly meeting that 'all who have been or at any time hereafter be Grand Masters of this Society may be present and have a vote at all Quarterly meetings and Grand Meetings.'[162] Grand Lodge also continued to crack down on 'irregularity', resolving that:

> if any Brethren shall meet irregularly and make Masons at any place within ten miles of London the persons present at the making . . . shall not be admitted even as Visitors into any Regular Lodge whatsoever unless they come and make such submission to the Grand Master and Grand Lodge as they shall think fit to impose.[163]

Perhaps unsurprisingly given the extent of his Masonic activities within Grand Lodge and as Master of lodges at the Horn, Aubigny, Chichester and elsewhere, the Duke's wide-ranging personal papers at the West Sussex Record Office and published letters contain multiple references to his Freemasonry, although his correspondence with the Duke of Newcastle is relatively silent on the subject. Examples were published in *A Duke and His Friends*, edited by Earl March, where several of the 'many letters' written to Martin Folkes are reproduced.

March commented that the Duke 'wrote copiously and amusingly to his brother Mason on several occasions'.[164] Desaguliers was mentioned in a number of instances and referred to with a degree of humour. In a letter to Folkes, for example, apologising for his remiss in thanking him for visiting and dated Goodwood, 27 June 1725, Richmond wrote ironically:

> I wish it lay in my power to show you in a more essential way how great a value and friendship I have for you. I have been guilty of such an omission that nobody less than the Deputy Grand Master of Masonry can make up for me.[165]

And in a second example, referring to Robert Webber's initiation at Montagu's riverside house at Thames Ditton in 1734, Desaguliers is again described somewhat satirically as 'some great Mason . . . wanting to initiate Bob Webber'.[166] As noted, the opposite was more probably the case.

Nonetheless, Richmond took his Freemasonry seriously. His smallpox prevented him from serving actively for part of his term in office and it was agreed that he would retire in December 1724, rather than in June of that year. However, the underlying justification for the extension to Richmond's tenure was most probably not his illness; after all, other Grand Masters were away from London and Grand Lodge for even longer periods. The true rationale was more probably the need to agree the controversial issue of an operating structure for the proposed Grand Charity and a desire on the Duke's part to be seen to have done his duty by Grand Lodge.

At Dalkeith's recommendation following a petition from Anthony Sayer, the formation of a Grand Charity had been proposed 'to promote the Charitable Disposition of the Society of Free Masons' and it was resolved that 'a monthly collection be made in each lodge according to the quality and number of the said lodge' and that a Treasurer be appointed.[167] The relevant *Grand Lodge Minutes* set out in detail over four pages the various constraints under which it was proposed the charity should operate – and these were far from uncontentious.[168]

Arguably for the same reason, the incoming Grand Master, Lord Paisley, re-appointed Desaguliers as his own Deputy on 27 December 1725 with the intention that the proposed Grand Charity should be guided to a successful conclusion.[169] Establishing an optimum structure for the Charity Bank and maintaining control of its disbursements was viewed, probably correctly, as of particular significance to the public profile and successful future of Freemasonry.

The Successor Grand Masters

Richmond's immediate successors, James Hamilton, Lord Paisley, (1686–1744); William O'Brian, 4th Earl of Inchiquin, (1700–77); Henry Hare, 3rd Baron Coleraine, (1684–1749); James King, 4th Baron Kingston (1693–1761); and Thomas Howard, 8th Duke of Norfolk (1683–1732), kept Freemasonry in the public domain, albeit that not every Grand Master succeeded in promoting the Craft to the same degree.

Paisley's installation in 1725 was reported extensively by the press.[170] As a published amateur scientist[171] and FRS – he had been elected in 1715 – he lay within Desaguliers and Folkes' circle of contacts at the Royal Society and at the Horn. Unfortunately, Paisley spent much of his time away from London and although Desaguliers, as Deputy Grand Master, took advantage and 'duly visited the Lodges till [Lord Paisley] came to town',[172] Paisley's absence from the capital and the failure of Grand Lodge to convene between February and December 1726 resulted in a much reduced level of press coverage in comparison to prior years. The experience underlined clearly the importance of an aristocratic name in Masonic promotion and Desaguliers' – or any non-aristocrat's – difficulty in doing so alone.

The appointment as Grand Master of one of Britain's leading Catholics, the Duke of Norfolk, Earl Marshal of England, allowed the Craft to emphasize that it was non-denominational and unaffiliated with the Church of England. However, the Duke's wealth and close connection with the Royal Family and leading Whig peers were probably more important and his accession was described extensively in the press.

Norfolk was nominated to succeed Lord Kingston in December 1729 and installed in January the following year. Unfortunately, neither the National Archives nor those at Arundel appear to contain any relevant correspondence.[173] Norfolk had been made a Mason by the Duke of Richmond at the Horn less than twelve months earlier:

> On Thursday night his Grace the Duke of Norfolk, the Rt Hon the Lord Devlin, and several other persons of distinction, are received into the most ancient Society of Free and Accepted Masons at the lodge held at the Horn Tavern in Westminster of which his Grace the Duke of Richmond is Master . . . there were present the Rt Hon the Lord Kingston, Grand Master, with his Grand Officers, the Rt Hon the Earl of Inchiquin, the Lord Paisley, Lord Kinsale, and many other persons of note.[174]

The new Grand Master was a popular choice. Indeed, so many tickets were sold for the Grand Feast that it had to be relocated to the Merchant Taylors' Hall, the Stationers' being 'too small to entertain so numerous'.[175] The Duke's quarterly communications at Grand Lodge were similarly well attended. On 21 April 1730, 75 representatives from 31 lodges were present in person and over £31 raised for the General Charity; and at the 28 August meeting were 86 representatives from 34 lodges. The appointment of Nathaniel Blackerby as Deputy Grand Master and George Carpenter and Thomas Batson as Grand Wardens, once again kept operational control of Grand Lodge within the inner cabal of the Horn of which all three were members. Under Norfolk's auspices, Blackerby ensured that Charity and the Charity Committee continued to be central to lodge activity – and that any Masonic outriders would be pursued:

> The Deputy Grand Master seconded [Desaguliers' resolution] and proposed several Rules to be observed . . . for their Security against all open and secret enemies to the Craft.[176]

> Mr Richard Hutton . . . charged Mr Lily (who keeps the Rainbow Coffee House in York Buildings) with having made it his business to ridicule Masonry . . . notwithstanding . . . the honour of having a lodge constituted at his house and he being also a Mason [and] Mr Lily [was] summoned to appear at the next Quarterly Communication to answer the said charge.[177]

Norfolk's public duties were reported comprehensively[178] as were the most mundane of his private activities.[179] He promoted Freemasonry vigorously with his involvement recorded in around 100 newspaper reports during his term in office. Events that received particular press attention included his attendance at the consecration of new lodges at the Prince William Tavern, Charing Cross,[180] and the Bear and Harrow,[181] the admission of new members[182] and his donations to the Charity Bank.[183]

Charity was by now integral to Freemasonry's public image and was reinforced positively by the many Masons who acted as Governors of Thomas Coram's socially well-connected Foundling Hospital or were attached to analogous institutions or connected to other charitable acts:

> a good number of Free and Accepted Masons have within these few days been discharged out of several prisons for debt by the charity of their brethren collected at several lodges.[184]

Another topic that caught the public's interest and which was reported extensively in December 1730 and into early January 1731 was Norfolk's donation to Grand Lodge of a sword originally made for Gustavus Adolphus, the King of Sweden. Norfolk ordered that the sword be 'richly embellished' with his Arms and that it serve as the Grand Master's Sword of State.[185] He also presented to Grand Lodge a Minute Book:

> a Large Folio Book of the finest writing Paper for the Records of Grand Lodge, most richly bound in Turkey and guilded [sic], and on the Frontispiece in Vellum, the Arms of Norfolk amply displayed with a Latin inscription of his noble Titles.[186]

His year in office near its close, Norfolk suggested from his travels in France that Charles Spencer, 5th Earl of Sunderland (1706–58), or Charles Colyear, 2nd Earl of Portmore (1700–85), should succeed him as Grand Master. However, having been deputed to enquire on Norfolk's behalf, Thomas Batson, Norfolk's Deputy Grand Master, reported that 'My Lord Sunderland excused himself on Account on his being to go abroad' and 'My Lord Portmore had declined accepting the Office'.[187] Instead, Thomas Coke (1697–1759), later Lord Lovel (also written as 'Lovell'), one of the richest men in England with an annual income exceeding £10,000, agreed to succeed.

Coke was probably initiated a Mason in the 1720s and as Grand Master continued and reinforced Freemasonry's association with Walpole's ministry.[188] He was part of Richmond's Masonic set: a newspaper *Letter* dated 24 April 1728 from Portsmouth reported his visit to the city's docks in the company of Richmond, Montagu and Lord Baltimore. All were Richmond's house guests at Goodwood.[189] Tangentially, around two years later, Baltimore was initiated a Freemason by Richmond at Goodwood.[190]

As Thomas Coke, Lovel was elected a knight of the shire for Norfolk in

1722. He actively and loyally supported Walpole[191] and in common with other more overtly political predecessor Grand Masters, such as Lord Inchiquin, he was honoured accordingly: appointed KB when the Order was established in 1725[192] and sworn a Privy Councillor. Government patronage later brought appointment as joint Postmaster General with an annual stipend of £1,000 and control of local patronage throughout the country. Coke was rewarded further in 1729 with a peerage and created Lord Lovel. He was selected Captain of the Band of Gentlemen Pensioners in 1733 and received an Earldom in 1744.[193]

Lovel's appointment and actions as Grand Master were reported almost as extensively as those of Norfolk.[194] He continued to support the Masonically-linked plays and musical evenings that his predecessor, Lord Kingston, had encouraged and which had achieved considerable success in promoting Freemasonry amongst the public:

> We hear the Opera of the Generous Free Mason having given such Universal Satisfaction at Bartholomew Fair, Mr Oates and Mr Fielding are resolved to perform the same at Southwark Fair, in order to give equal satisfaction to that part of the Town.[195]

Lovel's initiation of Walpole, his Norfolk neighbour, and his raising of the Duke of Lorraine to a Master Mason, primarily suggests a willingness to act in accordance with Walpole's bidding although it also underlines the political utility and importance of Freemasonry to the government both domestically and internationally in Europe.[196]

THE POLITICAL DIMENSION

By the mid-1730s, Freemasonry had cemented its links with the aristocracy, the upper reaches of Hanoverian society and a broad section of the government and patriotic opposition. A 1735 press report of the Grand Feast and Crawford's selection of Viscount Weymouth as his successor Grand Master provides an illustration:

> at the Grand Feast of the Free and Accepted Masons held at Mercer's Hall, the Rt. Hon. the Earl of Crawford, late Grand Master, chose the Rt. Hon. Thomas, Lord Viscount Weymouth Grand Master . . . There were present above three hundred brethren among whom were the Dukes of Richmond and Athol; the Marquis Beaumont Earl Kerr; the Earls of Winchelsea and Nottingham, Balcarras and Wemys; Lord Colville and Lord Carpenter; Alexander Brodie Esq., Lord Lyon, King of Arms in Scotland;[197] Sir Cecil Wray, Sir Arthur Aitchison, . . . Sir Robert Lawley . . . and several other persons of distinction . . . a very elegant Entertainment, and everything was conducted with the greatest Unanimity and Decency.[198]

Like Freemasonry more widely in the 1730s, the named aristocrats and politicians were a combination of government loyalists and pro-Hanoverian members of the patriotic opposition to Walpole. The group embraced a quarter of Scotland's sixteen representative peers: the outgoing Grand Master, John Lindsay, 20th Earl of Crawford (1702–49); Lindsay's future father-in-law, James Murray, the 2nd Duke of Atholl (1690–1764); Sir William Kerr, 3rd Marquess of Lothian (1690–1767); and Alexander Lindsay, the 4th Earl of Balcarres, (16__?–1736). Several other Scottish representative peers were also prominent Freemasons, including Henry Scott, 1st Earl Delorraine, who served from 1715–1730; James Douglas, 14th Earl of Morton, from 1730–1738; and Alexander, 2nd Earl of Hume, from 1727–1734.

James Murray and William Kerr had both been invested Knights of the Thistle in 1734. The Thistle, Scotland's premier honour, had been revived by James II in 1687 and was limited to sixteen knights and in the gift of the Crown. Other eminent KTs included Francis Scott, Earl of Dalkeith, KT 1725 and Grand Master 1723; and James Douglas, KT 1738, Grand Master of Scotland from 1739–40 and Grand Master of England in 1740–1741.

John Lindsay, 20th Earl of Crawford, served as a representative peer from 1732 until 1749. He was appointed a Gentleman of the Bedchamber to the Prince of Wales in 1733. A successful soldier, he held a commission in the Foot Guards and in 1735 received permission to serve under Prince Eugene in the Imperial Army. He distinguished himself in battle at Clausen and subsequently took a cavalry command in the Russian army with the rank of General.[199] Lindsay returned to England in 1739 and became Colonel of the newly established 43rd Regiment of Foot, the Black Watch.[200] Although Lindsay's *Memoirs* refer in detail to his military campaigns they are silent on his connection to Freemasonry.

Before acceding to the title, James Murray represented Perthshire as a Whig MP from 1715 until 1724. His accession as Duke resulted from his brother's attainder for supporting the Jacobites. Murray's loyalty to the Hanoverians was rewarded with appointment as Keeper of the Privy Seal in Scotland from 1733 until 1763, in which position he succeeded Lord Islay, Walpole's election manager in the north.[201] His Masonic connections were widely known. Maxtone Graham noted an event at the Duke's seat at Dunkeld, Perthshire, following the birth of a male heir in March 1735:

> The neighbouring Lairds write to the Duke a round robin congratulating him on the "thumping boy". Dunkeld was illuminated, and a Procession of Freemasons celebrated the event "the fraternity in their aprons made a circle about the Bonfire, crosst arms, shook hands, repeated healths, and a Marquess for ever".[202]

Sir William Kerr represented Scotland from 1730 until 1761. At the time of the Grand Feast, Kerr also held the largely ceremonial but politically

The Rise of the First Noble Grand Masters   161

significant position of Lord High Commissioner of the General Assembly of Scotland, the Sovereign's representative to the Church of Scotland. 'Balcarras and Wemys', Alexander Lindsay, the 4th Earl of Balcarres, sat as a Scottish representative peer from 1734 until his death two years later. 'Lord Colville' was John Colville, 6th Lord Colville and Culross (1690–1740), a loyal Scottish peer who had also supported the Hanoverians during the Jacobite uprising.

Although not technically a member of the Scottish aristocracy, Alexander Brodie (1679–1754), 19th chief of clan Brodie, was another Hanoverian loyalist and allied to Archibald Campbell, Earl of Islay. Campbell was one of Walpole's principal channels for Scottish political intelligence and, among other offices, Lord Justice General (1710–1761). As noted, he was also one of Desaguliers' children's godparents. Brodie had been rewarded in 1727 with appointment as Lord Lyon, King of Arms, where he oversaw state ceremonies and was the ultimate authority for Scottish heraldic matters and an officer of the Thistle. The position carried a relatively modest annual salary of £300 but had considerable power.[203] Brodie held the position until his death in 1754. The role of Lord Lyon had previously been described as the 'centre of Jacobite sympathies' in Scotland[204] and Brodie's appointment was designed to forestall any reoccurrence. He sat as a Whig MP for Elginshire from 1720 until 1741 and served as Lord Lieutenant for Murray, appointed 1725.[205]

Among the English aristocracy and gentry represented at the Grand Feast at the Mercers' Hall was Thomas Thynne, 2nd Viscount Weymouth (1710–51), the incoming Grand Master, who had inherited Longleat at the age of four together with titles and estates in Dorset, Wiltshire and Gloucestershire. Following the death of his first wife in 1729, he had married Lady Louisa Carteret in 1733, the daughter of John Carteret, later 2nd Earl Granville. Carteret, a patriotic opponent to Walpole in the Lords, drew Thynne into his political camp. In 1734, they jointly – albeit unsuccessfully – fought the election at Hindon against Henry Fox, Walpole's candidate; and in 1737, both were signatories to a petition to George II in favour of an increase in the Prince's annual allowance to £100,000. Weymouth was subsequently appointed to the sinecures of Keeper of the Mall, Keeper of Hyde Park and Ranger of St. James's Park; all were held from 1739 until his death. The appointments were regarded as a testament to the work he had commissioned at Longleat rather than as a purely political reward.[206]

Several other English aristocrats present had also served as Whig Members of Parliament. Before succeeding as the 2nd Baron Carpenter in 1732, the former Hon. Col. George Carpenter had been a Whig MP for Morpeth (1717–27) and Weobley (1741–7). Daniel Finch, the 8th Earl of Winchilsea and 3rd Earl of Nottingham (1689–1769), had been MP for Rutland between 1710 and 1730, sitting alongside Sir Thomas Mackworth from 1721 until 1727. He served as Comptroller of the Household from 1725 until 1730. Originally one of Walpole's cheerleaders in the House,

Finch aligned himself with Carteret and the patriotic opposition from around 1735–36.[207]

'Sir Arthur Aitchison' was Sir Arthur Acheson, the 5th Baronet (1688–1748). MP for Mullingar (Westmeath) in the Irish Parliament (1727–48), he was appointed High Sheriff of Armagh in 1728.[208] Despite his personal and literary connections with Jonathan Swift, he was not a 'professed Jacobite' but rather part of the Anglo-Irish landed gentry.[209]

Not Parliamentarians but with significant influence within their counties, were Sir Cecil Wray and Sir Robert Lawley. Wray (16__?–1736), formerly a Captain in General Farrington's regiment, had served under his older brother, the 10th Baronet, and had fought in Flanders, Spain and Portugal. Following his brother's death in 1710, he inherited estates and political influence in Lincolnshire, where he was later Sheriff, and Yorkshire. Wray had previously been appointed as Deputy Grand Master of Grand Lodge. He was also Master of the influential Cross Keys lodge, which subsequently moved to the King's Arms in the Strand. The substantial contribution of the lodge to the popularisation and dissemination of the scientific Enlightenment is discussed in the following chapter.

Sir Robert Lawley, 4th Baronet, of Canwell Hall, Staffordshire (17__?–1779), was later appointed High Sheriff of the county (1744). He had succeeded to the title and estates in 1730.[210] His earlier marriage in 1726 to Elizabeth, the daughter of Sir Lambert Blackwell, with its £30,000 dowry, was featured in many newspaper articles.[211] Lawley had political ambitions but failed in 1734 in a bid to become MP for Bridgenorth. A member of Wray's aristocratic Cross Keys lodge, he was appointed a Grand Steward in 1734 and was subsequently Master of the Stewards' Lodge. An avid attendee at Grand Lodge, Lawley held office as Senior Grand Warden from 1736 to 1738. He was later made Deputy Grand Master.

Despite a hiatus in the late 1740s and 1750s, other prominent aristocrats would follow as Grand Officers and Grand Master. By the end of the eighteenth century and throughout the nineteenth, Freemasonry would have the British Crown at its titular head, albeit that the illegitimate descendants of Charles II had been present virtually since its inception: the Duke of Richmond; the Duke of St Albans; and the Earls of Dalkeith, Delorraine and Lichfield. In 1766, Lord Blaney, as Grand Master, would raise the Duke of Gloucester; and the following year, John Salter, Deputy Grand Master, would raise the Duke of Cumberland. In 1787, the then Prince of Wales would be made a Mason by the Duke of Cumberland, his uncle.

It is clear that the early noble Grand Masters selected as titular leaders of English Freemasonry had formidable social and political influence. The presence of senior members of the aristocracy within the Craft received widespread press coverage and public exposure, spurred the expansion of the organisation across the upper and middle strata of London and provincial society, and afforded Freemasonry political protection and influence. With the redoubtable imprimatur bestowed by its aristocratic Whig members, Freemasonry was transformed into a fashionable club that attracted a large and aspiring membership from amongst the gentry, professional classes and the military. The potentially wider political significance of Freemasonry was underlined by its diplomatic use in both a British and European political context, and its extensive later role in colonial expansion.

CHAPTER SIX

'Through the paths of heavenly science'[1]

By the 1730s Freemasonry had developed into a recognized facet of the upper strata of London and provincial society. And although it was far from omnipresent, Freemasonry had become a prominent fixture within Britain's learned societies, the army and government. In the early 1740s, around 180 lodges had been established across England, with outposts in Western Europe, the Caribbean, North America and India.[2] Indeed, Freemasonry was so integral to London life that Hogarth, who later became a Freemason himself, featured Masonic allusions and prominent Masons in some of his more popular engravings, certain in the knowledge that they would be understood by his audience and that they would sell.[3]

The previous chapters argued that the rise of the noble Grand Masters and the network of relationships and imprimatur of the major professional associations and the magistracy, were central to Freemasonry's metropolitan success. They endowed the organisation with the aspirational characteristics, political protection and connections, and burgeoning financial strength that provided the foundations necessary for it to achieve national and, later, international recognition. However, although clearly important, aristocratic, political and judicial imprimatur alone may have been insufficient to sustain its increasing appeal to a broad spectrum of members and potential recruits.

There were, of course, many powerful and complementary dynamics which were of equal, greater or lesser importance; and it would be a statement of the obvious to say that Freemasonry would have been – as it is now – attractive to different people for varied and often contrasting reasons. It is not feasible to comment on or consider every variant in detail. Nonetheless, we should mention some of the more obvious social, intellectual and philosophical drivers. An acknowledged motive was that Freemasonry provided a forum for community, commercial and political association on both a national and international level, an extension of the local networking that craft lodges and guilds had accomplished on a more narrow scale throughout the previous centuries. The inter-denominational religious character of its membership was another factor that encouraged some to join who may have been unwilling or unable to join other societies or clubs. Freemasonry also publicised both its fraternalism and Masonic and non-Masonic philanthropy, not least through its co-funding of the establishment of the colony of Georgia. Its position in popular art and culture; association with Palladian architecture; elevation of ritual to a quasi religious status; and the key role of the Huguenots who represented a disproportionately large and highly active number of those who joined the Craft, both in Britain and in other countries, represent additional factors that should not be discounted. Indeed, Huguenot Freemasons were not only present in London. They also populated the upper ranks of Irish Grand Lodge in Dublin, with George Boyde, originally from Bordeaux, Grand Treasurer from 1732 until 1735; Captain John Arabin, Grand Treasurer in 1736; and Captain John Corneille, JGW in 1735 and SGW the following year.

In addition to these and other factors, the eighteenth-century's fascination with Freemasonry had another essential foundation which was propagated and disseminated by other means. Here we examine and assess how Desaguliers and Martin Clare associated Freemasonry with the scientific Enlightenment and led the metamorphosis of Masonic lodge meetings to include self-improving lectures and topical discussion of the arts and science. Other prominent Freemasons considered include John Ward, a Midlands landowner and politician, and two of Desaguliers more prominent acolytes: Charles Labelye, a leading engineer, and George Gordon, a popular scientific lecturer.

FREEMASONRY, THE 'PUBLIC SPHERE' AND THE SCIENTIFIC ENLIGHTENMENT

Desaguliers combined his public lectures with unconcealed Masonic proselytising, carrying Freemasonry in concept and practice from London to provincial England and extending its intellectual, moral and political radius to continental Europe. He presided over and attended lodges at The Hague and Paris during his visits to the Low Countries on lecture tours in 1729, 1731, 1732 and 1734, and to France in 1732, 1734 and 1735. His scientific lectures were designed to educate, elucidate and entertain an intellectually curious, commercially minded and financially aware audience. The subjects were topical and often commercial: a discussion of recent improvements to the Savery and Newcomen engines, 'of the greatest Use for draining Mines, supplying Towns with Water, and Gentlemen's Houses';[4] an introduction to 'new machines contrived by Dr Desaguliers';[5] and practical applications and explanations of the latest scientific principles. The Duke of Chandos' view – that Desaguliers was 'the best mechanic in Europe'[6] – may not have been accurate, but it was a laudable testament to Desaguliers' effective manipulation and presentation of his public persona.[7]

Nicholas Hans has suggested that Desaguliers may have given over 100 public lectures consisting of some 300 separate experiments.[8] This was a material under-estimate. Desaguliers' '300 experiments' were mentioned in classified advertisements for his lectures as early as 1721. Desaguliers had started lecturing in 1713. He was well established by 1717 and despite severe gout, only stopped shortly before his death in 1744. His lecture courses often ran daily or weekly for months at a time. For example, the lecture course he gave at Channel Row at the end of 1721/early 1722 was advertised consistently from October 1721 – April 1722[9] as were similar lecture courses given in 1722/23 and 1723/24.[10] Even if Desaguliers gave as few as two lectures a week for only six months of each year, an improbably low figure given that lecturing was one of, if not the principal source of his income, he would have given in excess of 1,500 over his working life. And an average audience of only ten or twelve, a number readily accommodated in his '30 foot long, 18 wide and 15 high' lecture room at Channel Row,[11] would suggest that a significant proportion of metropolitan society attended, even if some were present on more than one occasion.

Scientific lectures were fashionable. In Alan Morton's words, they 'rapidly outstripped parallel developments in universities',[12] and they were a powerful draw to the gentry and the mercantile 'middling classes'. They were also prepared to pay. The fee that Desaguliers received for his lectures at Bath in May 1724 was some 3 guineas per head from an audience of thirty to forty attendees.[13] Simon Schaffer's designation of the activity as 'theatre of the upper classes' is an appropriate description but perhaps underemphasises the utilitarian, as opposed to the cultural and entertainment, value of such occasions.[14] Now at peace, Britain prospered. The bourgeoning, increasingly money and trade-centred economy was based on the foundations of acquired and inherited wealth, rather than predominantly inherited wealth alone. Practical natural philosophers such as Desaguliers, described by Larry Stewart as 'arguably the most successful scientific lecturer of the century',[15] who could apply science to resolve commercial problems and develop realistic ideas to generate income for their audiences, were integral to the process of wealth creation and to the burgeoning momentum towards industrialisation.

JOHN WARD

Among a number of provincial and metropolitan figures, John Ward (1704–74), provides an example of a senior Freemason whose Masonic pursuits were likely to have been bound up, at least in part, with political, economic and financial self-interest. Ward held a unique combination of Masonic positions. He was a Grand Steward in 1732, Junior Grand Warden then Senior Grand Warden from 1732 until 1734, Deputy Grand Master from 1735 to 1737[16] and, following his succession to the title of 11th Baron Ward of Birmingham in 1740, selected as Grand Master of Grand Lodge in 1742. Ward was also a founder and the first Master of Staffordshire's earliest recorded lodge, the Bell and Raven in Rotton Row, Wolverhampton, constituted on 28 March 1732[17] where, Gould noted, he had acted as lodge secretary.[18] And he was a prominent member of the Bear and Harrow lodge in London in the 1730s.[19]

Ward's political and commercial activities were intertwined. He inherited estates in Sedgley and Willingworth in Staffordshire, north-west of central Birmingham, to which was added an entailed estate at Dudley, inherited alongside his first title, Lord Ward, on the death of his cousin.[20] In 1727, at the age of 23, Ward was elected a Member of Parliament for Newcastle under Lyme; he sat alongside the Hon. Baptist Leveson-Gower[21] until losing the seat in 1734.[22] Ward's father, William (1677–1720), had also been MP for Staffordshire, from 1710 to 1713 and, again, in 1715 until his death.

In common with many in the upper ranks of Freemasonry, Ward was also a magistrate, appointed in 1729:

> On Monday last, John Ward, Esq., a near relation to the Rt. Hon. The Lord Dudley and Ward, Esq., and Member of Parliament for Newcastle in Staffordshire, took the Oath at Hick's Hall, to qualify himself to act as a justice of the Peace for the said county. He is a gentleman of so general a good Character, and known Honour, that there is no Doubt to be made but that he will execute his office (agreeable to all other Acts of his Life) with the strictest regard to Justice and Impartiality.[23]

His selection was followed in December of the same year with appointment as Sheriff for Northampton,[24] and he was subsequently appointed Lord Warden of Birmingham, Recorder for Worcester and sworn a Privy Counsellor.[25]

Ward was a Country Whig, and later a Patriotic Whig, allied to William Pitt.[26] His political and judicial activities reflected his affluence and self-interest, and he appears to have been relatively unconcerned with the larger affairs of state. The House of Commons Parliamentary Papers mention him once, on 18 May 1733, and only then in connection with his own estates:

> A Complaint being made to the House, That Jonah Persehouse, of Wolverhampton, in the County of Stafford, John Green, William Mason, Daniel Mason, Thomas Mason, William Goston, Samuel Mason and Benjamin Whitehouse, of Sedgeley, in the said County, having sunk a Coal pit adjoining to the Estate of John Ward, Esquire, a member of this House, have entered upon his said Estate, and taken Coals therefrom; in Breach of the Privilege of this House.[27]

Although it was his son from his first marriage, also John, the 2nd Viscount Dudley and Ward, who was the more celebrated industrialist and politician, Ward was aware of the commercial value of his inheritance, which included one of the most significant holdings of coal and iron in the county.[28] He pursued and safeguarded his commercial interests in the Lords, where he was a prominent supporter and promoter of road construction.[29]

Ward may have had many motives for becoming a Freemason, to which he was clearly committed. However, it would have been reasonable for him to connect Freemasonry with his commercial interests.[30] Desaguliers was, after all, one of the foremost exponents of the practical application of science, most particularly in hydraulics and mining. Moreover, among other prominent Freemasons were eminent members of the Royal Society and leading engineers, many of whom had commercial utility.

Although perhaps more tenuous as evidence, his son continued the connection with both politics and Freemasonry. David Brown, in his *ODNB* entry for the 2nd Viscount, recorded that he became 'one of the leading aristocratic entrepreneurs' and deployed 'parliamentary, proprietorial, and masonic influence . . . to secure beneficial legislation to develop his estate'.[31] Enclosure Acts allowed the estates to be consolidated; canals and turnpikes were built that gave access to the Severn and to Birmingham; and coal pits and ironworks were developed using the latest technology. In a review of Raybould's *Economic Emergence of the Black Country*,[32] George Barnsby commented on the Enclosure Acts initiated by the 2nd Viscount. He noted that 'the Commissioners were Midland men sympathetic to the Dudley interests; [their] secretaries . . . were in every case employees of Lord Dudley; [and] the final award of each Act covered a larger area than originally laid down.'[33]

Ward's principal properties were in Himley where, in 1740, he began the construction of a large Palladian mansion whose gardens were later designed by Capability Brown, and at Upper Brook Street in Mayfair, from which he left in procession to Haberdashers' Hall on 27 April 1742 for his installation as Grand Master. Ward was also present with Desaguliers at the Bear in Bath in 1738, during the Prince's visit to the city.[34]

Interestingly, Sir Robert Lawley (17__?–79), the 4th baronet, a member of the Cross Keys lodge in Henrietta Street who followed Ward as a Grand Steward, Senior Grand Warden and Deputy Grand Master, also came from the industrialising Midlands. His estates were at Canwell in Staffordshire on the northern edge of Sutton Coldfield. In contrast to Ward, his father (Sir Thomas Lawley, MP for Wenlock, 1685–9), and son, (also Robert, MP for Warwickshire, 1780–93[35]), Lawley failed in his bid to enter Parliament. Nonetheless, his political loyalty resulted in his being sworn a member of the Privy Council in 1735 and appointment as Sheriff for Staffordshire.

Ward's Masonic activities after 1740 fall largely beyond the scope of this book. However, schisms in Freemasonry were beginning to develop with 'irregularities in the making of Masons . . . and other Indecencies' reported to Grand Lodge on 23 July 1740. The beginnings of dissension and division over the control of ritual, membership and patronage, is identifiable both in *Grand Lodge Minutes* and in the relative apathy of certain later Grand Masters, including Lord Weymouth. Gould's comment that 'the authority of Grand Lodge was in no wise menaced between 1740 and 1749' appears disingenuous given the background to the establishment in 1751 of a rival London Grand Lodge: the Ancients.[36] It is hard not to speculate whether Desaguliers' death in 1744, Folkes' failing heath and the decline and demise of other founding Freemasons and scientists were at the root of these changes.

SCIENCE AND SELF-IMPROVEMENT WITHIN THE LODGE

It was accepted widely in the eighteenth century that knowledge of natural science was fundamental to both intellectual and financial self-improvement. The Masonic message that Desaguliers carried with him was bound up with and part of the intellectual package that was on offer. The scientific Enlightenment sub-text of Masonic ritual and liturgy – and the Masonic sub-text of Desaguliers' lectures – would have been understood by many in his audience and cannot be disregarded when considering Freemasonry's appeal:

> As Men from Brutes distinguished are,
> A Mason other men excels;
> For what's in Knowledge choice and rare
> But in his Breast securely dwells?[37]

Desaguliers used the opportunities provided by his engineering consultancies and natural scientific lectures accordingly. His journey to Edinburgh to offer advice on the Comiston aqueduct was simultaneously an opportunity to attend the Lodge of Edinburgh on the 25 and 28 August 1721. And it is unlikely to have been a coincidence that John Campbell, the Provost responsible for Desaguliers' commission to advise the city, together with other Edinburgh dignitaries,[38] was admitted a member of the lodge during his stay. Similarly, Desaguliers' visits to consult and lecture in Bath, including that on behalf of the Royal Society to report on the eclipse of 9 May 1724, incorporated a visit to a lodge meeting at the Queen's Head, where the Whig politician and Court favourite, John, Lord Hervey (1696–1743),[39] was made a Mason:[40]

> Dr Desaguliers, from Five this afternoon to the Time of the most Eclipse, read a lecture on this occasion . . . the Gentlemen, between 30 and 40, giving him three Guineas each to hear him, and he gave those ingenious and learned gentlemen great satisfaction for their money. This night at the Queen's Head Dr Desaguliers is to admit into the Society of free and accepted Freemasons several fresh members, among them are Lord Cobham, Lord Harvey, Mr Nash and Mr Mee, with many others. The Duke of St. Albans and Lord Salisbury are here and about 10 other Lords English and Irish.[41]

The same pattern was repeated in Desaguliers' visit to Bath in 1737; and the following year in July in a visit to Bristol, where he attended a lodge meeting at the Rummer Tavern, and in October, at the Bear Tavern in Bath. The latter was arranged to coincide with – and benefit from – the Prince and Princess of Wales's excursion to the city:[42]

> The Rt Hon the Earl of Darnley, late Grand Master, John Ward Esq., Deputy Grand Master, Sir Edward Mansel, Bt., Dr Desaguliers, and several

other brethren of the Society of Free and Accepted Masons, held an extraordinary Lodge at the Bear Tavern in Honour of the Day, and in respect to his Royal Highness, who is a brother Mason.[43]

The attendance of Edward Bligh, 2nd Earl of Darnley, at the meeting was unremarkable. Bligh was not only Grand Master but a prominent member of the patriotic opposition linked with the Prince of Wales. The *Daily Journal* on 27 May 1734, for example, reported Darnley 'waiting on their Majesties at Richmond [where he was] met with a gracious Reception'. He was also an active Freemason outside of Grand Lodge and, in 1737, a member of the Gun Tavern lodge in Jermyn Street and, subsequently, the Lodge of Felicity, No. 58.[44] Similarly, one can understand the presence of John Ward, the Deputy Grand Master. However, the presence in Bath of Sir Edward Mansel (1686–1754), was in some ways more noteworthy and invites comment.

The Mansel Baronets of Trimsaran, together with the Mansels of Margam, Glamorganshire, and the Mansels of Muddlescombe, Carmarthenshire, were established members of the South Wales gentry. The *London Evening Post* described the family as 'one of the most honourable and antient . . . since the Normans and foreigners invaded the Rights and Properties of the antient Britains'.[45] Sir Edward Mansel, the 2nd Baronet, had been High Sheriff for Carmarthenshire in 1728 and 1729. Within Wales, he was a member and Master of the first and pre-eminent Welsh lodge, the Nag's Head and Star at Carmarthen, founded in 1726.[46] Nationally, Mansel had been appointed a Grand Steward and Junior Grand Warden in 1733. He was made Senior Grand Warden in 1734 and also appointed Provincial Grand Master for South Wales.[47]

In common with Freemasonry in London, the social composition of Welsh and West Country Freemasonry was relatively elitist; as an aside, five of the members of the Queen's Head lodge in Bath later became mayors of the city.[48] However, its political composition differed, with many Welsh Masons having strong Tory politics. Philip Jenkins has gone further and has argued with respect to Welsh Freemasonry that 'it was virtually impossible to distinguish between Jacobite secret societies and Masonic lodges'.[49] His analysis was based on the characteristics of the Society of Sea Serjeants in South Wales, an organisation that existed from 1722 or so until the 1760s with a membership that partly overlapped that of the two South Wales lodges. Jenkins saw the Sea Serjeants as overtly political and harbouring Jacobites and, significantly, commented that their Jacobite political sympathies were reflected in Welsh Freemasonry. His view has been supported and reiterated by Harland-Jacobs among others.[50]

Jenkins correctly characterised early eighteenth-century Welsh politics as being dominated by fiefdoms controlled, in his words, by a small number of 'magnates': 'Sir John Phillips "ruled" Pembrokeshire and Carmarthenshire; . . . Cardiganshire fell to two gentry families, the Pryses of Glamorgan and the Powells of Nanteos'.[51] However, the domination of local politics and influence over the choice of those elected to sit in parliament was not specific to the Welsh gentry. And although a complex area with attitudes and allegiances shifting over time, it is important to differentiate between the various shades of opposition politics and 'dining room' Jacobitism. Like many in the South Wales gentry, Mansel may have been a Tory, but London and Grand Lodge would not have regarded him as a Jacobite.

There are two other major fault lines running through Jenkins' argument. First, the overlapping membership between Welsh Freemasonry and the Sea Serjeants was far less than complete; and second, that it would be difficult to categorise the Sea Serjeants as a principally political organisation. Indeed, with regard to the second point, there were relatively few Sea Serjeants in the vein of Sir John Phillips, later MP for Carmarthen, who was not only a staunch Tory but capable of being described by Horace Walpole as a notorious Jacobite.[52]

Although there was an element of cross-over between the two membership sets, for example, the Sea Serjeants' included Emanuel Bowen who was Master of the Nag's Head in 1726, and Sir Edward Mansel, also later Master, it was far from comprehensive. Unlike the Sea Serjeants, Welsh Masonry contained both leading gentry and an assortment of others. Within the thirty-three members of the lodge whose names were recorded and reported to Grand Lodge in June 1726 were around twenty 'gentlemen', including three baronets: Sir Edward Mansel, Sir John Price and Sir Seymour Pile. Pile, in particular, would have been an improbable Jacobite: he was commissioned a Lieutenant, then Captain, in the Royal Regiment of Dragoons.[53] Lodge membership also included Thomas Foy, a doctor; Richard Price, an apothecary; John Lewis, a bookseller; John Tindall, a painter; Thomas Bowen and William Samuell, both glovers; David Davis, a brazier; and William Griffiths, a merchant.

The contrast with the Sea Serjeants has been revealed clearly by Francis Jones, Carmarthenshire's county archivist, in his study of its members' portraits.[54] The portraits, executed in 1748 and on display at the Taliaris estate, were catalogued and assessed by Jones. His descriptions underline that the Society of Sea Serjeants was dominated by inter-married and inter-generational members of the same group of Carmarthenshire and Pembrokeshire families. Unlike Welsh Freemasonry, the Sea Serjeants had little room for anyone outside of the core gentry. Membership was also restricted numerically: the Sea Serjeants, 'who met once a year for a week' comprised 'a President, Chaplain, Treasurer or Secretary, 24 Serjeants, and Probationers, from whom they elected to supply the 24 in case of death . . . the Serjeants wore a Star, with a Dolphin on the left side, and the Probationers on the right.'[55] The Society's first President was George Barlow; the second, Richard Gwynne; and on Gwynne's death, the third was Sir John Phillips.

If the Sea Serjeants were, in Jenkins' words, a 'Jacobite secret society' and a political organisation, they were, at the least, unusual. Their annual meeting lasted a week and was often at a seaside town in west Wales. It was extensively publicised, with advertisements in the press. The Sea Serjeants also sponsored race meetings at Haverford West, among other courses.[56] The club was neither secret nor exclusively political:

> On Saturday, the 10th Day of June next will be the Annual Meeting of the Society of Sea Serjeants, at Tenby in the County of Pembroke, when the Brethren are all desired to attend; And on Monday the 19th following, the Contribution Purse of the said Society amounting to about Thirty Pounds, will be run for on Portfield, near Haverford-West in the said County, by any Horse, Mare or Gelding, carrying eleven Stone, the best of three Heats.[57]

It is probable that Jenkins' statement that 'by the 1750s, the Sea Serjeants were a dining club with a Lady Patroness, and Sir John Phillips was anxious to rebut charges that it was a Jacobite group', could have been applied to the Society some two decades earlier.[58] The Sea Serjeants neither led nor participated in any Jacobite or other uprising in Wales. Politically, they – like much of Wales – could be considered conservative, albeit that they were probably not, in Peter Thomas' characterisation, 'torpid'.[59] As Thomas commented, although 'residual sympathy for the former royal house of Stuart manifested itself in *Jacobitism*', the Sea Serjeants may have 'owed more to masculine clubbability and the contemporary fashion for secret societies than [any] political fervour'.[60]

If this were the position, even in part, other apolitical factors can be examined as potential drivers for Freemasonry in South Wales. Edward Oakley (____?–1765), a founder and Warden at the Nag's Head in Carmarthen, and Warden and later Master of the Three Compasses of Silver Street in London, among other lodges, provides a strong possible indicator.

Oakley, an architect, argued that 'proper Lectures in . . . the Sciences' should be available within the lodge. Given his Masonic seniority, it is a credible assumption that such lectures would have been given at lodges with which he was involved, including the Nag's Head. A speech Oakley gave at the Three Compasses on 31 December 1728 urged Freemasons to both study and disseminate knowledge. The text of his speech was incorporated prominently into an edition of the *Constitutions* published in 1731. The text provides a guide to the motives of at least some Freemasons:

> Those of the Brotherhood whose Genius is not adapted to Building, I hope will be industrious to improve in, or at least to love, and encourage some Part of the seven Liberal Sciences . . . it is ncessary for the Improvement of Members of a Lodge, that such Instruments and Books be provided, as be convenient and useful in the exercise, and for the Advancement of this Divine Science of Masonry, and that proper Lectures be constantly read in such of the Sciences, as shall be thought to be most agreeable to the Society, and to the honour and Instruction of the Craft.

Oakley's views are unlikely to have been shared by all Freemasons. His words were designed to offer support to Freemasonry's 'dutiful and obedient' members, and to encourage others to benefit from the 'Intent and Constitution of the Sciences' and focus less on Masonry's 'merry songs [and] loose diversions'. However, in this regard, Oakley can be seen as part of the mainstream. Advertisements for and reports of 'academical' and scientific experiments, lectures and demonstrations, including those given at the Royal Society, populated the classified and news sections of the daily and weekly press, together with printers' notices announcing the publication of corresponding books and treatises. *Burney* holds more than a thousand examples in the decade from 1725.

In his study of eighteenth-century industrialisation in South Wales and perhaps in contradiction to his views on the Sea Serjeants, Jenkins commented that political loyalties in the South West and South Wales were less important than economic self-interest: 'industrialization in this area was to a remarkable degree a Tory monopoly'. He argued that it was largely irrelevant that the key local magnates were Catholics, Jacobites or Nonjurors. What was important was that they had the support of the local professional and commercial classes. He classified the relationship as a function of their 'strong associations with economic progress'.[61] With respect to Freemasonry it is possible to go further. In addition to a general desire to imitate London society, the manner in which the Welsh and South West gentry and professional classes were interested in Freemasonry can also be attributed to its associations with antiquarianism, agricultural improvement and the scientific Enlightenment. As Gwyn Williams' commented: a section of the South Wales gentry 'prepared their lands for the advance of industry . . . abandoned the romantic *Jacobitism* of their forebears and embraced a *Whig* Great Britain [and] . . . commercial imperialism'.[62] He continued: 'the lodges of *Freemasonry* were its breeding-grounds'.[63]

A parallel can be drawn with the industrialising north east of England. Here Sir Walter Calverley (1707–77), (from 1734, Sir Walter Blackett[64]), of Wallington Hall, was for many years a dominant figure in local Freemasonry.[65] Calverley-Blackett was a wealthy and politically active coal and lead mine owner. He was a magistrate, Sheriff of Northumberland, Tory MP from 1734 until 1777 and five times Lord Mayor of Newcastle.[66] His close Masonic colleague, Matthew Ridley (1716–1778), the first Provincial Grand Master of Northumberland, appointed in 1734, was also elected Lord Mayor of Newcastle (in his case on four occasions), and similarly represented the city as MP between 1747 and 1774. Ridley had complementary commercial interests and was later Governor of the Newcastle-upon-Tyne Company of Merchant Adventurers, an organisation which had a local monopoly in cloth, silk and corn trading.[67]

As in South Wales and the West Country, Newcastle and Northumberland Freemasonry comprised an 'abundance of gentlemen'[68] and 'the principal inhabitants of the town and country'.[69] And as in Wales, the Freemasonry of Newcastle and Northumberland was probably less concerned with political opposition than economic self-interest. Indeed, in the rapidly industrialising north of England, scientific lecturers met with such financial success that

Desaguliers reportedly considered travelling to Newcastle himself to gives lectures to 'Gentlemen concerned in Collieries [about] an infallible Method to clear Coal Pits of Damp'.[70]

Nevertheless, there was political opposition to Walpole within Freemasonry, in particular that linked to the patriotic opposition surrounding the Prince of Wales. Frederick had been initiated a Freemason barely twelve months before Darnley, Ward, Mansel and Desaguliers had met at the Bear to celebrate his visit to Bath. The event had taken place at an 'occasional' lodge in Kew in 1737:

> we hear that on Saturday last was held at Kew a Lodge of Freemasons at which Dr Desaguliers presided, when there were admitted several Persons of high Distinction as Brethren of that Order.[71]

The Prince was the first legitimately born member of the royal family to become a Freemason. Grand Lodge was understandably proud of its royal association and the *1738 Constitutions* was dedicated to him as Prince Royal and a fellow Freemason. His Freemasonry may have been aligned to that of others within the patriotic opposition. One such politician was Charles Calvert, Lord Baltimore, who attended the Prince's initiation at the lodge at Kew. Calvert was a friend of the Prince and a Gentleman of his Bedchamber. And as MP for St Germans, he was a vocal supporter of the Prince's faction in Parliament.

TO THE
Moſt *High*, *Puiſſant* and moſt *Illuſtrious* PRINCE

FRIDERICK LEWIS,

Prince *Royal* of GREAT-BRITAIN,
Prince and Stewart of SCOTLAND,

PRINCE of *WALES*,

Electoral Prince of Brunſwick-Luneburg,
Duke of *Cornwall*, *Rothſay*, and *Edinburgh*,
Marquis of the *Iſle of Ely*,
Earl of *Cheſter* and *Flint*, *Eltham* and *Carrick*,
Viſcount *Launceſton*,
Lord of the *Iſles*, *Kyle* and *Cunningham*,
Baron of *Snaudon* and *Renfrew*,
Knight of the moſt noble Order of the Garter,
Fellow of the *Royal* Society,
A *Maſter* MASON, and *Maſter* of a LODGE.

GREAT SIR,

James Anderson recorded that in addition to the Earl of Baltimore, the Hon. Col. James Lumley, brother to the Earl of Scarborough and commander of the company of grenadiers in the 2nd Regiment of Foot Guards, and the Hon. Major Madden were also present at the Prince's installation. Others within the Prince's retinue who were prominent Freemasons included Lord Inchiquin (Grand Master, 1726), Lord Darnley (Grand Master, 1737) and the Marquis of Carnarvon (Grand Master, 1738), each of whom were also appointed Gentlemen of the Bed Chamber to the Prince in 1742, 1744, and 1729, respectively. Perhaps not coincidentally, the initiation of the Hon. William Hawley, the Prince's Gentleman Usher, preceded that of the Prince by only two months.[72]

The initiation of the Prince can be interpreted as an attempt by Grand Lodge to have a foot in each of the pro- and anti-Walpole Whig camps, and a means of securing insurance against any difficulties that might arise on the succession and from the formation of a new, non Walpole-led ministry. However, this may be to read too much into the event. Regardless of any political rationale, Freemasonry benefited substantially from the kudos allied to Frederick having become a 'Brother Mason'.[73]

But there was arguably greater prestige associated with Freemasonry's connection to the scientific Enlightenment, and this transcended national politics. Given the prevailing aspiration for self-improvement and the influence on Freemasonry of Desaguliers and other natural philosophers from the Royal Society and elsewhere, it is unsurprising that lodge meetings included talks and lectures designed to educate, inform and entertain those present. The comment at a lodge in York in 1726 that 'in most lodges in London, and several other parts of this Kingdom, a lecture on some point of geometry or architecture is given at every meeting'[74] may have been an exaggeration. Nonetheless, there is evidence that Masonic lodges offered lectures on a regular basis and on a range of subjects from anatomy, chemistry, education and experimental science, to architecture and the liberal arts.[75]

Despite the content of Martin Clare's *Discourse*, repeated before Grand Lodge on 11 December 1735 at Robert Lawley's request, there does not appear to have been any 'general rule' that obliged lodges to provide lectures. What lectures were presented and by whom would have been dependent on the character of the lodge. And this would have varied lodge by lodge as a function of its leadership, the collective professional contacts of the Master and members, and of the members' individual abilities and willingness to contribute.

Martin Clare and the Old King's Arms Lodge

There are, unfortunately, only a few extant lodge histories and Minutes that date back to the early eighteenth century. However, those that survive provide modest evidence that it was customary for professional members of lodges, such as architects, lawyers and physicians, and members with particular hobbies, such as antiquarians and artists, to share their knowledge and to give lectures. To repeat Oakley's words: 'proper Lectures . . . in such of the Sciences, as shall be thought to be most agreeable to the Society'.

One of the most unambiguous examples of what Martin Clare termed 'good conversation and the consequent improvements' is that of the King's Arms lodge in the Strand, now known commonly as the Old King's Arms or 'OKA'.[76]

The OKA was renowned for its lectures: 'promoting the grand design in a general conversation'.[77] The first extant OKA Minute Book covers 1733 to 1756[78] and records thirty-six lectures in the decade 1733 to 1743. Seven concerned human physiology, some of which included dissections; six were on ethics; five, architecture; and three described 'industrial processes'. Nine lectures examined different scientific inventions, techniques and apparatus, while others explored a variety of topics within art, history and mathematics. They include a talk by Robert West, a portraitist, on 'some evident faults in the Cartoons of Raphael',[79] and another on Andrea Palladio by Isaac Ware (1704–66), the architect and later Secretary of the Board of Works. Ware was also a member of Thornhill's St. Martin's Lane Academy, re-founded by Hogarth in 1735. Ware's lecture was given immediately after his initiation; the Minutes suggest that it was designed to combine entertainment with self-improvement.[80]

In addition to Martin Clare (1690–1751),[81] a renowned educator and mathematician, prominent members of the OKA included William Graeme (1700–1745),[82] a leading surgeon, and fellow physicians Edward Hody (1698–1759)[83] and James Douglas (1675–1742). All were Fellows of the Royal Society and with the exception of Douglas (FRS in 1706) all had been proposed by other Freemasons. Clare was proposed in 1735 by Desaguliers and Manningham, members of the Horn, and Alexander Stuart,[84] a member of the Rummer at Charing Cross. Graeme was proposed in 1730 by Folkes (Bedford Head) and Stuart (Rummer); and Hody in 1733, proposed by Thomas Pellet, also Bedford Head.[85] Another member of the lodge, 'Bro. Hellot', was probably Jean (John) Hellot (1685–1766). Hellot was elected FRS in 1740; his proposers included Richmond and Folkes.[86]

The OKA's *Minutes* indicate significant member-driven interest in 'useful and entertaining conversation'.[87] As Clare noted in his *Discourse*:

> The chief pleasure of society – viz., good conversation and the consequent improvements – are rightly presumed . . . to be the principal motive of our first entering into then propagating the Craft . . . We are intimately related to those great and worthy spirits who have ever made it their business and aim to improve themselves and inform mankind. Let us then copy their example that we may also hope to attain a share in their praise.[88]

Sir Cecil Wray was elected Master of the OKA in 1730.[89] Later the same year he became the first Master of the Saracen's Head lodge in Lincoln.[90] On succeeding his brother as 11th baronet in 1710 he inherited extensive land holdings and political influence in Yorkshire and Lincolnshire. Wray was present at the installation of Lord Lovel as Grand Master in 1731[91] and probably in recognition of his connections was appointed Deputy Grand Master in 1734 by the then Grand Master, Earl Crawford.[92]

Wray agreed to become Master of what was then the lodge meeting at the Cross Keys in Henrietta Street on the basis that Clare would act as his Senior Warden and in his regular absences from London as Master in his stead. This Clare did, and it was Clare, a Huguenot, who encouraged further lectures within the lodge.[93] Clare had a wide and central influence on eighteenth-century education. His Soho Academy had opened in 1717[94] and his textbook, *Youth's Introduction to Trade and Business*, published in 1720, ran to twelve editions through to 1791.[95] He described his approach to education succinctly and with practicality as one where his charges might 'be fitted for business'.

Clare's Soho Academy was considered one of London's most successful boarding schools, and its emphasis on practical learning as well as the social graces, set a pattern for education. The syllabus combined mathematics, geography, French, drawing, dancing and fencing, with weekly lectures on morality, religion and natural and experimental philosophy, 'for the Explication of which, a large apparatus of machines and instruments [was] provided'. During his tenure at the OKA, lectures were given by both members and visitors. Topics during 1733 and 1734 included 'an entertainment on the nature and force of the muscles'; the 'history of automata: the origin of clockwork to the present day'; 'the requisites of an architect'; and an evidently popular talk on 'fermentation'.

The OKA's *Minutes* draw a vivid picture of early eighteenth-century life within the lodge, with its foibles and idiosyncrasies. Whether because of its lectures and lecturers, the scientific eminence and social status of its members, the quality of its dining or otherwise, applications for membership became numerous. And they were often contentious. After a number of eminent prospective new joiners had – embarrassingly – been blackballed, the OKA attempted to create a structure that would allow 'members of ability and consequence . . . being generally acceptable to the lodge' to join with at least a reduced risk of being rejected. It was agreed accordingly that from 4 March 1734, three blackballs would be required for exclusion. In the wake of the changes and at the following meeting on 11 March, Viscount Weymouth, who was appointed Grand Master the following year, and Viscount Murray, the 2nd Duke of Atholl (1690–1764), were admitted to the lodge. Each gave six guineas to 'defray the cost of the evening'.[96] Just over two weeks later on 27 March, Lord Vere Bertie[97] and 'William Todd Esq.'[98] were made members. The evening was financed by Todd. The Minutes note that their food cost £5 and the drink a more modest £3 4*s* 10*d*.[99] The custom of new members paying for dinner and defraying lodge costs was part of a tradition that dated back to the mediaeval guilds.

Membership fees were subsequently increased to five guineas for 'gentlemen' but left at three guineas for 'artisans', albeit that this would still have been a high price for most. The lodge also agreed somewhat inequitably that membership for a 'gentleman' would be granted with the approval of a simple majority, but that a two-thirds majority would be required for an 'artisan'.[100]

With its relatively exclusive membership and strong connections to Grand Lodge, the OKA cannot easily be considered representative of the average lodge. Nonetheless, the OKA's *Minutes* provide an illustration of the broad pattern of an early eighteenth-century lodge meeting, if not of the many variations that existed within individual lodges and across different regions of the country. The lodge would be opened, an extract from the by-laws or constitutions would be read, and any proposed new member or members announced. The main activity of the evening, a lecture or a less formal talk, would be followed by the initiation of the new apprentice(s), or the Masonic 'examination' of one or more lodge officers to demonstrate their command and knowledge of Masonic ritual. After copious Masonic toasts and songs, the lodge would then be closed. Other than at a feast, the evening would usually commence after dinner, perhaps around 6 p.m., and conclude at around 10–11 p.m.[101]

Lectures Elsewhere

Other lodges are known to have had similar lectures to those presented to the OKA. Although only incomplete records are extant, the Steward's Lodge reportedly 'entertained their visitors with a diversity of knowledge, [including] natural philosophy [and] dissertations on the laws and properties of Nature'.[102] Clare's lecture to the Steward's lodge was noted at Grand Lodge on 11 December 1735:

> Sir Robert Lawley,[103] Master of the Steward's Lodge reported that Br. Clare ... had been pleased to entertain the Steward's Lodge on the first visiting Night with an excellent Discourse'.[104]

Lectures were also held at the Lodge of Friendship, No. 4 in the 1729 list that in 1736 met at the Shakespeare's Head in Little Marlborough Street. Clare spoke there in 1737 and eight lectures were given the following year on topics ranging from astronomy to optics. The Minutes record that two lectures were given in each year from 1739 until 1741.[105] Clare also lectured at the Saracen's Head in Lincoln, OKA's sister lodge.[106]

Warrington's Lodge of Lights, lodge number 352 in the 1755 list, some of whose members later formed a Dissenting Academy,[107] is believed to have hosted lectures. And other lodges can be regarded as 'probables'. For example, the Swan and Rummer in Finch Lane, constituted in 1725 and whose surviving first Minute Book is the oldest extant, had as a leading member the Jewish physician Meyer Schomberg (1690–1761), elected FRS in 1726. Schomberg joined in 1730 and in 1734 was appointed a Grand

Steward. In later years, he reputedly commanded fees of around £4,000 per annum from his clients, at least some of whom are likely to have been Freemasons.[108] Regarded as a self-promoter, it is plausible that he would also have been willing to speak and lecture within the lodge.

The lectures at the Nag's Head in South Wales and lodges in northern England have been mentioned above. Continental lodge records also provide evidence, in Margaret Jacob's words, of 'Freemasonry as an educational force, particularly in mathematics'. Jacob commented that even in remote lodges 'as far away as Sluis, in Zeeland in the southern Netherlands, members were instructed [in the] knowledge of geometry'.[109]

Public scientific lecturing did not commence with Desaguliers. Harris, Hauksbee and Whiston had each preceded him and its popularity had roots in the philosophical and scientific Enlightenment of the latter part of the seventeenth century.[110] However, Desaguliers had taken the concept to a new level, given it impetus and allied it with Freemasonry. The obligation on 'new admitted brethren' was underlined in the 'General Heads of Duty' set out in the *Pocket Companion for Freemasons*:

[A Mason] is to be a Lover of the Arts and sciences, and to take all Opportunities of improving himself therein.[111]

Desaguliers' promotion of Newtonian science through a combination of entertainment and practical experimentation was central to its popularity and his success, as was his emphasis on the commercial application of science. Freemasonry, firmly allied to the Newtonian scientific Enlightenment, benefited in its wake. Other Masonic scientists and engineers followed where Desaguliers had led.

Charles Labelye and the Lodge at Madrid

Born in Switzerland, Charles de Labelye (1705–62), a Huguenot, moved to London with his family in or around 1720. He studied with Desaguliers, became his assistant and subsequently his protégé. Labelye is best known as the architect and main engineer for the new bridge at Westminster. He was appointed by the bridge commissioners in 1738 and the development was finally completed in 1750.[112] The Masonic connection with the project has been noted before. The chair of the commission was Henry Herbert, 9th Earl of Pembroke, and Nathaniel Blackerby and George Payne were two of several well known Freemasons who served as commissioners.

Desaguliers initially relied on Labelye for fairly basic scientific work.[113] The description of Richard Newsham's novel fire engine, a 'water engine for quenching and extinguishing fires', was based on measurements and drawings made 'at my Desire, by Mr Charles Labelye, formerly my Disciple and Assistant'.[114] Desaguliers also trusted Labelye in his account of the then novel method used to transport stone from quarries in Bath – possibly the first documented use of railways; and Desaguliers incorporated various pieces by Labelye in his *Course of Experimental Philosophy*.

Probably with Desaguliers' encouragement, Labelye became a Freemason, joining the French lodge, Solomon's Temple, where Desaguliers was a member and later Master. Labelye was also recorded in 1730 as Senior Warden of the White Bear in King Street, Golden Square. In common with Desaguliers and perhaps in emulation, Labelye mixed engineering with Freemasonry and travelled extensively, both with Desaguliers and alone, in connection with a range of engineering, hydraulic and other projects.

During a visit to Spain in 1727, Labelye helped to establish the lodge at Madrid, the first in Spain, and became its first Master. The petition for its constitution was received and acceded to by Grand Lodge in April 1728. And on his return to London that year, Labelye was thanked by Grand Lodge:

> Mr Labelle the present Master of the Lodge held at Madrid in Spain stood up and confirm'd what was some time past delivered in a Letter from the said Lodge to the Grand Master and Grand Lodge in England (concerning their Regularity and submission to us etc.) and acquitted himself in a handsome manner like a Gentleman and a good Mason. Then the Health to the Brethren of the Madrid Lodge was propos'd and drank with three Huzzas.[115]

In March 1729, having again returned to Spain, Labelye, still the Master of the Lodge at Madrid 'stood up and represented, that his Lodge had never been regularly constituted by the Authority of the Grand Master, Deputy Grand Master and Grand Wardens in England and therefore humbly prayed a Deputation for that purpose.'

Grand Lodge accordingly

> Ordered:
> That the Secretary do likewise prepare a Deputation to Impower Charles Labelle Master of the said Lodge to constitute them with such other Instructions as is likewise necessary for that purpose.
>
> Then Br. Labelle's Health was drank, and after he drank the Grand Master's Health, Deputy Grand Master's and Grand Wardens with all the Brethrens present and prosperity to the Craft wheresoever dispersed.[116]

Labelye's extra-London Masonic activities were not limited to Spain. A visit to Exeter in 1732 involved his attendance at the St. John the Baptist lodge at the New Inn in the High Street. The lodge had been relatively recently constituted on 11 July 1732 and Labelye's 'zealous endeavours to promote masonry' were noted.[117] And the following year during his visit to Bath, Labelye was appointed Senior Warden at another newly constituted lodge at the Bear, albeit that he was shortly thereafter obliged to resign due to the pressure of work in London.[118]

GEORGE GORDON AND THE LODGE AT LISBON

George Gordon, another of Desaguliers' students and subsequently a scientific lecturer in his own right, similarly combined his scientific work with Freemasonry. His name appears in advertisements for books 'published by B. Creake', which were listed at the end of Creake's 1731 edition of the *Constitutions*[119] and in his *Curious Collection of the Most Celebrated Songs in Honour of Masonry*.[120] In each case, Gordon's *Compendium of Algebra* was advertised as having 'so plain a Method, that anyone who understands Numbers may learn the solutions of the said Equations without a Master'. In addition to his own works, Gordon also revised and co-authored *The Young Mathematician's Guide*.[121]

Gordon was a member of the Queen's Head in Knaves Acre. His course of 'Universal Mathematicks' was advertised in 1730 in the *Daily Journal* at a price of 1s per night, a substantial discount to the fees commanded by Desaguliers.[122] He also lectured at Windsor Town Hall 'for the entertainment of the Nobility and Gentry'[123] and offered more generally courses of 'Philosophy, Astronomy and Geography'.[124] Gordon was subsequently awarded an honorary Master of Arts degree from Aberdeen, 'his Diploma . . . to be sent to him in a very handsome manner', perhaps indicating that he was born in the city.[125] In common with Desaguliers and Labelye, Gordon was also involved with private hydraulic projects. An example was his employment by Lord Malton at Wentworth Woodhouse in South Yorkshire, 'one of the great Whig political palaces',[126] where he engineered a pump and pipes that raised water some 80 yards in height along a distance of 1,600 yards.[127]

Gordon lectured actively throughout the 1730s with much of his repertoire based on lectures given previously by Desaguliers, including a course on 'Opticks . . . Newton's Theory of Light and Colours'.[128] He had earlier written two works published in the 1720s, including an *Introduction to geography, astronomy, and dialling*, printed and published by John Senex.[129] This ran to several editions and was dedicated to Walpole: 'a good statesman will not disdain those sciences as a Diversion'. Alongside Blackerby and other Freemasons, Gordon may also have been a member of the Charitable Corporation, although the relatively common name precludes certain identification.[130]

Like Labelye, Gordon was involved with constituting a lodge in the Iberian Peninsula. He was asked by Grand Lodge in April 1735 to take a warrant to a lodge in Lisbon following a petition from Portugal that a 'Deputation might be granted . . . for constituting them into a regular lodge'.[131] This may have been the Protestant lodge founded by British merchants and recorded during the Inquisition as the 'Lodge of Heretical Merchants'.[132] His success was reported in the press. The reference to the English fleet is perhaps significant:

> They write from Lisbon, that by Authority of the Right Hon The Earl of Weymouth, the then Grand Master of all Mason Lodges, Mr George

Gordon, Mathematician, has constituted a Lodge of free and accepted Masons in that City; and that a great many Merchants of the factory, and other people of distinction, have been received and regularly made Free Masons; that Lord George Graham,[133] Lord Forrester,[134] and a great many other gentlemen belonging to the English Fleet, being Brethren, were present at constituting the lodge; and 'tis expected that in a short time it will be one of the greatest abroad.[135]

Linked to this and probably as a reward for Masonic services that were – at least in part – of some potential diplomatic value, Gordon was subsequently appointed to the sinecure of Page of the Backstairs to the Princess of Wales.[136] Tangentially, a few years later in 1741, John Coustos, a diamond cutter and dealer and a member of the Huguenot lodge at Prince Eugene's Head Coffee House in St. Alban's Street, founded a second lodge in Portugal.[137] Accused of heresy and espionage by the Portuguese authorities, Coustos was arrested and tortured. Found guilty, he was sentenced to five years in the galleys. However, he was released after only four months after diplomatic pressure from the British government. William Denslow, in his *10,000 Famous Freemasons*, recorded that 'Admiral Matthews was ordered to anchor his fleet in the Tagas for twenty four hours, thus causing [his] release'.[138] However, James Caulfield, in a rather prosaic but more probable investigation, suggested that Coustos's brother, a member of Stanhope's household, induced Stanhope to speak with the Duke of Newcastle and the Duke thereafter interceded on Coustos's behalf through the British Embassy in Lisbon.[139]

On his return to England, Coustos breached the non-disclosure agreement he had reached with the Portuguese and published a book setting out his experience at the hands of the Inquisition, 'embellished with Copper Plates descriptive of the Tortures he endured'.[140] Perhaps not coincidentally, the book was dedicated to the two Secretaries of State, William Stanhope, Earl of Harrington, and Thomas Holles, Duke of Newcastle, who had been petitioned for assistance.[141] Whether in appreciation of Coustos's services or in sympathy for his suffering, publication – in London and Dublin – was funded by subscriptions from the great and the good and ran to several editions. Three theatrical benefit evenings were later held at the New Theatre, Haymarket.[142]

Freemasonry's Wider Connection with the Scientific Enlightenment

Larry Stewart drew a precise portrait of the interplay between Newtonian science, financial speculation, the Royal Society and the coterie of wealthy aristocrats and merchants that provided patronage to Desaguliers and other lecturers, such as the physician and Newtonian mathematician, James Jurin, proposed FRS in 1717 by Folkes, and the apothecary, Peter Shaw (1694–

1763).¹⁴³ The large attendances and the elevated fees that the most celebrated lecturers were able to charge testify both to the social status of the attendees and the perceived commercial value of such lecture courses in experimental philosophy.

Roy Porter's review of science in the provinces in the eighteenth century also cast a light on the contribution of scientific lecturers to the effective dissemination of knowledge across Enlightenment England.¹⁴⁴ His comment that 'science became . . . widely diffused through Georgian society via the . . . entreprencurship of knowledge and the rise of professional . . . popularisers', was accurate; and he noted the new scientific lecturers and the 'experimental performances' of Jurin, Hauksbee, Whiston, Desaguliers and others who lectured widely in the provinces. Porter argued that the attraction of science was bound up with cultural aspiration:

> Knowledge is now become a fashionable thing, and philosophy is the science á la mode: hence, to cultivate this study, is only to be in taste, and politeness is an inseparable consequence.¹⁴⁵

Indeed, the spread of scientific lectures to 'every great town in our island' was recorded at the time by William Stukeley in his diary:

> About the year 1720 . . . Stephen Gray . . . often shewed experiments . . . at the Royal Society . . . Dr Desaguliers continued these . . . By this time courses of philosophical experiments with those of electricity began to be frequent in several places in London, and travelled down into the country to every great town in our island.¹⁴⁶

Paul Elliott and Stephen Daniels in a comprehensive paper claimed that Freemasonry was the 'most widespread form of secular association in eighteenth century England'.¹⁴⁷ Their paper examined cross membership with other societies, particularly the Royal Society and Society of Antiquaries, and noted the influence of natural philosophy on Masonic development. They concluded that Newtonian science was one of several sources of Masonic inspiration and highlighted, in particular, the importance of antiquarianism. However, although it would be accurate to assert that many Freemasons were also antiquaries, it is less certain that antiquarianism was a principal driver behind the development of eighteenth-century Freemasonry. Curiosity may have led Stukeley and other antiquaries into Freemasonry, but antiquarianism did not shape Masonry's ersatz history nor influence its commitment to the Hanoverian status quo, religious latitudinarianism and the scientific Enlightenment.

Although antiquaries such as Folkes and Stukeley may have influenced the later development of some of what became eighteenth-century Freemasonry's 'ancient ritual', it is hard to categorise antiquarianism, in Elliott and Daniels' words, as a 'primary inspiration'. In fact, it is easier to perceive the reverse: that there was a strong Masonic influence on antiquarian studies. Indeed, Elliott and Daniels confirm as much themselves. In a comment on Thomas Wright (1711–86), an 'enthusiastic Mason' and one of the leading landscape gardeners and architects of the 1740s, Elliott and Daniels noted that his lectures and books were 'imbued with his philosophical and Masonic theories'. Moreover, they commented that Wright's surviving architectural and astronomical manuscripts contain 'many Masonic references and drawings'; and that Freemasonry's Enlightenment characteristics and, most particularly, its commitment to self improvement, 'promoted the value of both natural philosophy and antiquarian study'. Elliott and Daniels concluded that the spread of Freemasonry from London to the provinces, and thence to northern continental Europe and the American colonies and Indian sub-continent, may have 'mirrored and helped to shape the complex geography of British scientific culture'. This is more plausible. It is incontestable that Freemasonry and eminent Masonic scientists such as Desaguliers were powerful facilitators of the dissemination of Newtonian natural philosophy.

As the first half of the eighteenth century evolved, scientific lectures, books and apparatus, coffee house philosophy and self-improvement societies, became key characteristics of scientific Enlightenment England, the Dutch Republic and other countries within Europe. Larry Stewart and Paul Wendling have mapped out the particular importance of public demonstrations of natural science.[148] They argued that the relative accessibility of such forums exerted a central influence and narrowed the divide between 'gentlemanly theory' and the practical application of science. Intellectual inclination, occupation, the potential practical application of science and social fashion among the metropolitan and provincial élites, were among the many different motives driving public interest in science. And this was reinforced by the national and local exposure accorded to popular lecturers which had a substantially positive impact and elevated public attention. The role of the experimental natural philosopher was fundamental to the process, and attendance at lectures was exploited extensively for both social and financial advantage.

The public lecture forum provided potentially substantial benefits for both the lectured and the lecturer. And those unable to access the lecture circuit had a tendency to suffer accordingly. Stephen Gray (1666–1736), originally a Kentish dyer, had been Desaguliers' assistant and one of his collaborators from 1716 until 1719. After 1720 he was awarded a Charterhouse pension on Hans Sloane's recommendation and pursued his own independent – and highly effective – research into electricity. Despite not being elected FRS until 1732, the Royal Society used Gray's innovative electrical experiments in 1731 as the principal 'entertainment' for a meeting of the Council at which the Prince of Wales was present. The Society awarded Gray the Copley medal later that year – and the following year – in recognition of his work.[149] However, notwithstanding his intellectual brilliance, Gray failed to benefit more substantially. His lecturing and presenting skills were limited and, in Michael Ben-Chaim's words, he 'failed to acquire a clientele' or to 'draw the attention of the general public to his work'which was overshadowed in the public's eye by the better known Desaguliers and others such as Willem-Jacob s'Gravesande, whose *Physicae Elementa Mathematica* offered a more accessible approach to an understanding of electricity.[150]

Gray's relatively poor public reputation underlines that effectively presented and well-publicised public experiments were instrumental to the dissemination and validation of scientific theories, and that successful showmanship was an effective mechanism for promoting public interest in both the theory and the theoretician.[151] Tony Judt's comment is apposite: 'for many centuries... how well [one] expressed a position corresponded closely to the credibility of [the] argument'.[152] In this analysis, less than first rate scientists and demonstrators such as Gordon, were imbued with influence principally because they were articulate and enjoyed the celebrity of the relatively well known. With Gray, unfortunately, the opposite was the case.

The entertainment and education provided by engineers, physicians and other professional men within the lodge, FRS or otherwise, were a powerful draw to Freemasonry, and the intellectual benefits were enhanced by the attendance in lodge of local and national social and commercial élites who, as in the past, provided an avenue to possible commissions and opportunities. Masonic lodge meetings in coffee houses and taverns continued and reinforced a tradition of coffee house science that dated back to the late seventeenth century. Robert Hooke (1635–1703) had held meetings in the 1670s at Garraway's in Change Alley and Joe's Coffee House in Mitre Court.[153] John Harris's mathematical lectures at the Marine Coffee House in Birchin Lane had begun in 1698 and continued until 1704. And the Grecian Coffee House in Devereux Court was a fashionable venue at the turn of the century for then-opposition Whigs and Fellows of the Royal Society, including Isaac Newton, Hans Sloane and Edmund Halley. Coffee houses provided an informal setting where companionable men might share ideas. Indeed, Harry Armytage noted that Buttons, a literary coffee house in Russell Street, Covent Garden, provided a 'lion-headed post-box' where ideas and comments could be deposited for publication in Addison's *Guardian*.[154] Folkes, a Buttons' habitué, later arranged for the post box to be moved to the Bedford Head.

Bernard Faÿ reviewed the relationship between Freemasonry, the learned societies and scholarly publications.[155] He commented that Freemasonry exerted influence directly and indirectly via scientific lectures, treatises and book publishing, and singled out Masonic involvement with the first French encyclopaedia brought out in 1738.[156] Probably of greater significance but not mentioned by Faÿ, was the Freemasonry's connection to the publication of the first English language encyclopaedia more than a decade earlier.[157] Ephraim Chambers' *Cyclopaedia* included over thirty references to Newton and one to Freemasonry. Margaret Jacob has argued that the book – widely cited on the continent – was an important component in the spread of Newtonian science to a continental European audience.[158] A definition of Freemasonry was included within Chambers' second volume:

Free or Accepted Masons, a very ancient Society, or Body of Men ... They are now very considerable both for Numbers and Character; being found in every country in Europe, and consisting principally of Persons of merit and Consideration. As to Antiquity, they lay claim to a Standing of some thousand years.[159]

Faÿ based much of his argument on the example of Benjamin Franklin (1706–90).[160] Freemasonry had a fundamental influence on many aspects of Franklin's life, including the founding of the American Philosophical Society and his co-authorship of the US Constitution, and it is marginally possible to present Franklin – a uniquely formidable intellectual and entrepreneur – as part of a wider paradigm for the Americas. However, with respect to Europe, Margaret Jacob, writing of the transmission and popularisation of the new Masonic ideology based on Newtonian principles, identified Desaguliers in London and Willem-Jacob s'Gravesande in Leiden as the pre-eminent vectors.[161]

WILLEM-JACOB S'GRAVESANDE (1688–1742)

s'Gravesande was professor of mathematics and astronomy at Leiden and became one of the most influential scientists in continental Europe, not least as editor of the *Journal Littéraire*.[162] His position had been secured in 1717 with Newton's assistance: he had visited England in 1715,[163] lodging with Desaguliers who had been one of his doctoral advisers, was introduced to Newton and Keill, and attended Desaguliers' lectures at the Royal Society. s'Gravesande adopted Newtonianism as a central intellectual tenet and it was perhaps not unrelated that he was proposed and elected FRS later that year.[164]

s'Gravesande corresponded extensively with Keill and Desaguliers following his return to Leiden and subsequently translated, edited and published scientific works by Keill and Newton. In London, Desaguliers reciprocated, translating and arranging the publication (by Senex) of s'Gravesande's own two-volume work on Newton.[165] Perhaps ironically, s'Gravesande's refinements to Desaguliers and Keill's lectures and experiments overshadowed and later supplanted many of the original demonstrations of Newton's theories.

Within continental Europe, s'Gravesande's scientific reputation became such that even Voltaire, whose works deified Newton as 'l'esprit createur',[166] travelled to Leiden to seek s'Gravesande's approval for his *Elémens de la philosophie de Newton*.[167] His influence is hard to underestimate. In Larry Stewart's words, 'Freemasonry [was] the vehicle by which the Newtonianism of Desaguliers and Folkes found its way to the Continent and to the radical circles of Holland'.[168]

Desaguliers' intellectual authority, particularly within his immediate academic and scientific circle, was also considerable. In addition to Labelye and Gordon, his boarders at Channel Row included several other influential scientists. Stephen Demainbray (1710–82), the natural scientist and astronomer, lodged with Desaguliers while studying at Westminster School and, perhaps not coincidentally, Demainbray later studied under s'Gravesande at Leiden.[169] Isaac Greenwood (1702–45), the American mathematician, boarded with Desaguliers from 1725 to 1726.[170] Described as Desaguliers' 'disciple and sometime assistant',[171] Greenwood was subsequently appointed the first Professor of Natural Philosophy at Harvard (from 1728 to 1738), a chair sponsored by Thomas Hollis, a member of the lodge meeting at the Crown behind the Royal Exchange.[172] Philippe Vayringe (1684–1745), instrument maker to the Duke of Lorraine and later Professor of Experimental Philosophy at Lunéville, stayed at Channel Row in 1721.[173] And Stephen Gray lodged with Desaguliers and served as his assistant for over three years from 1716–19. Indeed, Desaguliers later boasted that 'of the dozen experimental lecturers in the world, eight had been those whom he had taught'.[174]

Many are known to have been or to have become Freemasons. Demainbray was a member of Desaguliers' French lodge at the Swan in Long Acre and s'Gravesande, a member of a lodge in the Netherlands.[175] Although it is hard to determine conclusively whether Isaac Greenwood and Philip Vayringe were Freemasons, Hollis's involvement with Greenwood, and the Duke of Lorraine's employment of Vayringe, provides anecdotal evidence that they may have been. Voltaire, who became perhaps the most famous purveyor of Newtonian ideas in continental Europe, was also a Freemason. However, his formal initiation by Benjamin Franklin at Loge des Neuf Soeurs in Paris occurred only shortly before his death in 1778.[176] More consciously than otherwise, Desaguliers' association with such scientists proved an effective means of extending the radius of his influence and expediting the flow of Masonic ideals and those of the Newtonian scientific Enlightenment.

The dissemination of Newton's theories went beyond academic rigour and commercial utility – it also served a political purpose. Desaguliers' espousal of Newtonian theories in Britain but more particularly in continental Europe, in the Low Countries and France, sought to displace Cartesian ideas and, in Desaguliers' words to rout 'this Army of Goths and Vandals in the philosophical World'.[177] Desaguliers' lectures implicitly if not explicitly underlined the superiority of the Newtonian natural order: a mathematically rational world combined with social stability and mercantile success displayed as the product of a constitutional rather than absolutist monarchy. In Desaguliers' phrase, the perfect political form was that 'which does most nearly resemble the Natural Government of our System, according to the Laws settled by the All-wise and Almighty Architect of the Universe'.[178] His view was clear:

> By his example, in their endless Race,
> The Primaries lead their Satellites,
> Who guided, not enslav'd, their Orbits run,

Attend their Chief, but still respect the Sun,
Salute him as they go, and his Dominion own.[179]

The Parliamentary Imprimatur

The gentry and mercantile classes were not alone in the value they placed on an expert's opinion. Parliament also considered Desaguliers' knowledge useful. In addition to his engineering advice on the construction of the proposed Westminster Bridge in the 1730s, Desaguliers was asked to examine and comment on other matters over a period of two decades. On 10 May 1716, Desaguliers, acting as an expert witness, gave his observations on remedies to stop the breach of the river wall at Dagenham.[180] His knowledge as a hydraulic engineer was also requested in connection with improving London's water supply. Parliament directed him to examine the potential effects of redirecting the rivers at Uxbridge to supply London with fresh water and Desaguliers appeared before the Commons to speak on the proposal. His testimony may not have been wholly un-conflicted. Chandos, his patron, was a probable investor in the scheme and, if not in this, then in other similar schemes.[181] Parliamentary records for 24 April 1721 note that:

> Dr Desaguliers . . . had examined and tried the Quantity of Water, contained in the Cowley Stream . . . one of the Streams that run by or near the said Village of Drayton; and that it was able to afford above Three times as much Water as the New River does; and that he had caused a level to be taken, by Persons very well skilled in that way . . . who found, that some Part of the said Cowley Stream . . . was high enough to have Water brought from thence to Marylebone Fields, and that a large reservoir may be there made; from which Hanover Square and above nine parts in ten of the houses of London and Westminster may be plentifully supplied with Water . . . [182]

Desaguliers testified before Parliament again on 5 March 1724 in connection with the 'intended Canal from Denham Point'. He advised that the canal could be constructed 'with a moderate Cut, Six Inches Cut in a Mile' since 'he had known Water run in a Slough in a Coal-Mine, at Two Inches Fall in above Half a Mile'.[183] And as late as June 1738 he was 'examined upon Oath, as to the Balance engine at Manyfold Ditch, the Use thereof, and as to raising Water in the River Lee'.[184]

Desaguliers' earlier work on the ventilation of the Houses of Parliament was described in chapter two:

> That Mr. Disaguliers do view the Chimney in this House, and consider how the same may be made more useful; and report what is proper to be done therein to the Lords Committees, appointed to review the Repairs of The Parliament Office; whose Lordships are hereby empowered to receive the said Report on Friday next.[185]

Although perhaps not particularly remunerative, such official advisory work reinforced Desaguliers' intellectual credibility and scientific standing, and may thereby have had the side effect of adding to the attraction of Freemasonry. There were few places outside of the learned societies or paid lectures that permitted those interested in the practical application of science to enjoy the benefit of associating with scientists and professionals who advised parliament itself and, at the same time, to obtain access to opportunities to network commercially and socially. Importantly, such benefits and opportunities were provided under the aegis of an organisation that was self-evidently respectable and with the patronage of prominent, politically well-connected, Whig aristocrats. Indeed, the Crown itself was involved: during the winter of 1737–8

> Dr. Desaguliers read lectures on astronomy every day to the [Prince of Wales's] household. His observatory [at Kew] was then described as a large room at the top of the house, where he had all his mathematical and mechanical instruments at one end and a Planetarium at the other.[186]

The significance of science was understood from the Crown down. Although Freemasonry's aristocratic leadership and the political and personal relationships of the magistrates' bench and professional associations were instrumental to Freemasonry's metropolitan and provincial success, its fascination also rested on other foundations and was propagated by other means. Among these, Freemasonry's association with the scientific Enlightenment can be regarded as one of the more important factors.

Desaguliers' association of Freemasonry with Newtonian science, a connection continued by Martin Clare, Charles Labelye, George Gordon and other eminent and self-publicising scientists and lecturers, provided another rationale for many to join in a period when social and intellectual self-improvement and financial gain were viewed as complementary. And it may be this which explains the presence of Tory supporting Freemasons in a largely Whig-dominated organisation, notwithstanding the more widely-publicised rationale that has tended to cite Freemasonry's 'spirit of toleration ... which should unite together in harmony those ... divided by religious and political schisms'.[187] We could go further and extend the analysis to conclude that the spread of scientific Enlightenment ideology in Britain and elsewhere was a partial function of the popularity and influence of Freemasonry.

Conclusions

English Freemasonry was transformed in the second and third decades of the eighteenth century. What previously could have been regarded justifiably as a disparate set of largely moribund local groups was reconfigured to emerge in the 1720s as one of the most dynamic, attractive and structured contemporary organisations. Those at the centre of the newly established Grand Lodge of England were at the vanguard of the conversion process, broadening a jurisdiction that expanded rapidly from its initial base in London and Westminster.

Led by a coterie of pro-Hanoverian establishment figures, Grand Lodge operated under the largely nominal leadership of young Whig aristocrats who provided political protection, acted as beacons to aspirant members and stimulated widespread and positive press coverage. Such aristocratic endorsement and the intellectual imprimatur of leading scientists allowed Desaguliers and his colleagues to create a national – then international – organisation with its roots among the gentry and professional classes who dominated its membership.

Although the 1720s represented a period of fundamental transformation for English Freemasonry, the origins of the Craft can be traced back nearly four centuries to the economic dislocation of the Black Death in 1348. The devastation caused by the plague began a process by which the Masonic guilds' mediaeval religious structure fragmented as they gradually became embryonic collective bargaining units. Statute and legislation sought to reduce labour costs to pre-plague levels as elevated mortality rates and the consequential labour shortage drove an increase in real wages. Although the pattern was reversed in the following centuries,[1] volatile real earnings and increasingly insecure working conditions caused labour discontent which found voice in the *Old Charges*, which referred to a faux golden Masonic age and acted as a justification and schematic for higher wage demands and labour protectionism.

The mutual assistance guilds offered their members became commonplace and local labour monopolies an accepted component of economic activity. Over succeeding decades, the guilds evolved and became increasingly influential and more closely integrated into civic society where they gained financial and political influence. There was also a marked increase in the number of non-working members: since the local Justices' authority extended to setting wage rates, and local politicians and the gentry were responsible for granting guild charters and commissioning municipal and other building works, there were obvious advantages to having such men within the fold.

By the sixteenth and, more particularly, the seventeenth century, the guilds were dominated by the more affluent master builders who – as employers – had begun to achieve a social standing comparable to other local dignitaries with whom they shared similar economic interests. Rather than any 'speculative' or spiritual motive, a combination of networking, dining and drinking formed a primary rationale for lodge membership. York and Chester's guild membership records suggest a majority of non-working members and a pattern of invitations to friends and successive generations of family that maintained the drift away from a working membership. In such a context, such seventeenth-century Masonic lodges can be perceived more as clubs, with dining and socialising their key functions.

The Ancient Lodge at York provides an early eighteenth-century yardstick against which the emergent Grand Lodge of England in London can be measured. York was dominated by provincial Tory leaders located at the opposite end of the political spectrum to London's Whig aristocrats, and lacked connections to the scientific Enlightenment and to its key figures. Instead of providing a vehicle for the display and transmission of a new philosophy under the leadership of those with sufficient drive and dynamism to pursue their objectives, York, in its own words, 'seemed gradually to decline'. The absence of intellectual direction and ineffectual political influence were the fundamental causes of York's relative decline, and are in contrast to London's success in advancing its cause and capturing the heights of eighteenth-century society.

Among those exercising authority at Grand Lodge during its seminal years, Desaguliers can be regarded rightly as *primus inter pares*. His formative influences included his family's flight from persecution in France, childhood poverty within London's émigré Huguenot community, and being admitted a servitor scholar at Oxford, where his teacher and mentor, John Keill, introduced Desaguliers to Newtonianism and Newton himself. The connection led to Desaguliers' appointment as a Fellow, Demonstrator and Curator at the Royal Society, roles that enhanced his scientific status. Desaguliers' entertaining and proselytising demonstrations of Newton's theories led to an introduction to the Hanoverian Court and its Whig attendants, and to commissions from affluent aristocrats and the gentry.

Desaguliers was both an effective proselytiser of Newtonian science and a leading expert on hydraulics and a consulting engineer at a time when understanding the practical application of natural philosophy was fundamental to financial success and social status: the scientific Enlightenment. Public lecturing, private projects and his connections at the Royal Society and within Freemasonry, allowed Desaguliers to develop a network of personal and professional relationships that he did not hesitate to use. And the money he earned supported his family and his scientific, publishing and Masonic interests.

Desaguliers' approach to Freemasonry was bound up with personal, philosophical and political objectives, and Grand Lodge provided a means by which these could be advanced. Largely motivated by self-interest, his pro-Hanoverian political views were shared by the Huguenot community as a whole and, more importantly, by many senior Whigs and entwined with Enlightenment theories and the natural rights of John Locke. The reinvention of Freemasonry as a bulwark of the Hanoverian status quo and enlightened thought led to its embrace by the Whig establishment and many of those at its political core. And the forum it provided for education and entertainment resonated with its aspirant members to the extent that it could be regarded as an outpost of the scientific Enlightenment.

Although Desaguliers exercised considerable influence on Freemasonry, the changes and modifications introduced were a result of cooperation with many others. George Payne, Martin Folkes, William Cowper, Nathaniel Blackerby, Charles Delafaye, and other senior Masons, exploited their influence and connections and effected change and expanded membership through a range of over-lapping political, social and professional networks including the magistracy, the learned and professional societies, the civil service and the military.

The influence of the London and Westminster magistracy on Freemasonry has not previously been studied. The political composition of appointments to the post-Hanoverian bench and the manner in which they emulated local and national politics reflected Whig ascendancy, especially in London.[2] Successive Lord Chancellors appointed dependable political allies and removed potential opposition Tories and Jacobite sympathisers. In the sensitive areas of Westminster, Middlesex and Southwark, the bench was overtly supportive of the government's political, religious and economic objectives. In Landau's words, 'fidelity to the Hanoverian [government was] a touchstone for fitness'.[3] The public influence and authority of the magistracy went beyond law enforcement: it was a bulwark against the mob and any potential upsurge of treason.

It was not a coincidence that the most politically sensitive cases were handled by trusted loyalists such as Charles Delafaye and Thomas de Veil, both ardently pro-Hanoverian and each a prominent Freemason. To extend Munsche's phrase, magistrates 'occupied a pivotal position in eighteenth-century England'[4] and nowhere was this more the case than in London, where appointment generated special scrutiny. With their strong belief in the rights and power of the establishment and clear political loyalties, prominent Freemasons such as Cowper, Streate and Blackerby were proposed Chairmen of the bench. Such men ensured that their fellow Justices would, in Cowper's words:

> be vigilant to detect and produce to Punishment all those who . . . attempt the Subversion of the Great basis upon which stands all that is or can be dear to England and Protestants . . . It is . . . for our Religion, our Liberty and our Property.[5]

Such men dominated the upper ranks of Freemasonry. Although the absence of definitive membership records prevents a precise assessment of the number of Freemasons sitting on the Middlesex and Westminster benches and *vice versa*, there is strong evidence of a substantial overlap among senior figures in both organisations throughout the 1720s and into the 1730s. The data suggests that an influential and important network existed; English Freemasonry and Grand Lodge were politically reliable, and the actions of senior Freemasons would in the government's eyes have demonstrated a laudable vigilance in safeguarding the Hanoverian succession and protecting its administration.

Martin Folkes was a second pivot upon which 'Free and Accepted Masonry' turned. A wealthy, clubbable and well-connected intellectual, Folkes provided a personal bridge to the Duke of Montagu, Duke of Richmond and other aristocratic members of the Royal Society, and to many in the antiquarian community. Folkes' social position and relationships with his peers was complementary to that of Desaguliers. And although prominent within Grand Lodge and at the Bedford Head, it was the Royal Society that offered a stage for his influence.

Peter Clark has estimated that nearly half the Fellows of the Royal Society were Freemasons; Trevor Stewart's more conservative interpretation of the evidence suggested a figure of around 30%. Whichever is correct – and it is likely to be towards the higher end – the Royal Society was permeated by Freemasons, many of whom held senior offices throughout the period and, like Folkes, were active in proposing their friends and fellow Masons for membership. Other learned and professional organisations such as the Society of Antiquaries and Royal College of Physicians also provided a reservoir of initiates to Freemasonry over successive years. It is estimated that around 20% or more of the membership of such bodies were probable or possible Freemasons, with a significantly higher proportion of those resident in London.

However, it was the presence of gossip worthy members of the Whig aristocracy that generated most press coverage. The titular leadership of celebrity aristocrats and the publicity that attended their presence at lodge meetings and other Masonic events spurred Freemasonry's expansion into the gentry, the military, the professional classes and other aspirational groups, and was an effective means of encouraging and sustaining public interest. The presence of members of the Whig aristocracy placed Freemasonry at a social and political centre and underlined the credentials of what was now positioned as a fashionable club of consequence.

Montagu, Richmond and other popular aristocrats catalysed public interest in Freemasonry in a period when the most irrelevant acts of the peerage were recorded and remarked. And with extensive press coverage, Freemasonry's profile changed, creating the foundations of what later became a mass movement. Access to aristocratic patronage was not without risk. Montagu's successor Grand Master, the Duke of Wharton, had Jacobite political sympathies and an immaturity and rebellious nature at odds with that of Desaguliers and many of his colleagues within Grand Lodge. But

Wharton's subsequent expulsion demonstrated the willingness of the organisation to hold to a pro-government stance.

In reality, the majority of Grand Lodge's noble Grand Masters were malleable and loyal figureheads who were willing to be positioned and leave operational management to their non-aristocratic colleagues. Probably more than any Grand Master, Richmond stood out in his willingness to go further. His period in office and, from the 1720s onwards, his hosting of lodges whose principal purpose appears to be the initiation of other aristocrats and friends demonstrated an exceptional Masonic commitment. Later Grand Masters came from a different mould and as Freemasonry grew more influential, it became more political, with closer ties both to Walpole and to the patriotic opposition ranged against him. It would be reasonable to conclude that this was not accidental. Given the prominence of Freemasonry, political involvement probably went beyond government acquiescence and Freemasonry became periodically an instrument through which state influence or opposition was exercised.

Within ten years of its first aristocratic Grand Master, Freemasonry was a facet of London's upper strata and popular among provincial society. And within twenty years of Montagu's installation, Freemasonry had been carried by the military, merchants and colonists to outposts in the Caribbean, North America and India, and to other lodges established across Western Europe.

The presence of aristocratic Grand Masters and a network of relationships within the learned societies, professional associations and the magistracy were central to Freemasonry's metropolitan and provincial success and endowed Freemasonry with the characteristics and connections necessary for national and international recognition. However, these factors alone may have been insufficient, particularly in the non-Whiggist provinces. Freemasonry's appeal to an increasingly broad spectrum of potential members was also a function of other dynamics. These were numerous and often contrasting. Many – particularly those that relate to the spiritual and ritualistic aspects of Freemasonry – are discussed elsewhere. Others, such as fraternal drinking and dining and networking, had been in existence for several centuries. In addition, this book contends that the eighteenth-century's fascination with Freemasonry was strongly underpinned by an association with the scientific Enlightenment and that lodge meetings evolved to include education and entertainment and to combine self-improving lectures and topical discussion.

Freemasonry's connection to the professional and learned societies and its proximity to leading figures such as Desaguliers, Folkes, Stukeley, Clare, Demainbray, Labelye, 'sGravesande, Gordon and other Newtonian natural philosophers and antiquaries attracted self-interested men of all parties, particularly in the newly industrialising areas of South Wales, the Midlands and the North East England. And the attraction of association was not restricted to Britain. It extended elsewhere: to lodges in The Hague, Paris, Madrid, Lisbon and Berlin; and to Savannah, Boston, Philadelphia and elsewhere within the American colonies more generally.

If there is a conclusion, it is this: Freemasonry should not be regarded merely as the most prominent of the many fraternal organisations that flowered in the eighteenth century. It was more: a fluid force that helped to shape the structure and development of the social, economic and political evolution that was then in progress. It was a function of its time and of its leadership.

Appendices

Appendix 1: Grand Lodge of England, Grand Officers, 1717–1740

Appendix 2: The *1723 Constitutions*

Appendix 3: The Military Lodges

Appendix 4: The Masonic Membership of Selected Professional Societies

Appendix 1

GRAND LODGE OF ENGLAND, GRAND OFFICERS, 1717–1740

Grand Masters	Dates	Installed	FRS
Anthony Sayer	1672–1741	GM 1717	
George Payne	16__–1757	GM 1718	
J.T. Desaguliers	1683–1744	GM 1719	FRS 1714
George Payne	16__–1757	GM 1720	
John Montagu, 2nd Duke of Montagu	1690–1749	GM 1721	FRS 1718
Philip Wharton, 1st Duke of Wharton	1698–1731	GM 1722	
Francis Scott, 5th Earl of Dalkeith[1]*	1695–1751	GM 1723	FRS 1724
Charles Lennox, 2nd Duke of Richmond	1701–1750	GM 1724/5	FRS 1724
James Hamilton, Lord Paisley[2]	1686–1744	GM 1726	FRS 1715
William O'Brien, 4th Earl of Inchiquin	1694–1777	GM 1727	
Henry Hare, 3rd Baron Coleraine[3]	1693–1749	GM 1728	FRS 1730
James King, 4th Baron Kingston[4]	1693–1761	GM 1729	
Thomas Howard, 8th Duke of Norfolk	1683–1732	GM 1730	
Thomas Coke, Lord Lovell[5]	1697–1759	GM 1731	FRS 1735
Anthony Browne, 7th Viscount Montagu	1686–1767	GM 1732	
James Strathmore, 7th Earl of Strathmore	1702–1735	GM 1733	FRS 1732
John Lindsay, 20th Earl of Crawford*	1702–1749	GM 1734	FRS 1732
Thomas Thynne, 2nd Viscount Weymouth	1710–1750	GM 1735	
John Campbell, 4th Earl of Loudoun*	1705–1782	GM 1736	FRS 1738
Edward Bligh, 2nd Earl of Darnley	1715–1747	GM 1737	FRS 1738
Henry Brydges, Marquis of Carnarvon[6]	1708–1771	GM 1738	
Robert Raymond, 2nd Lord Raymond	1717–1756	GM 1739	FRS 1740
John Keith, 3rd Earl of Kintore[7]	1699–1758	GM 1740	
James Douglas, 14th Earl of Morton[8]*	1702–1768	GM 1741	FRS 1733

Deputy Grand Masters	Dates	Installed	FRS
John Beale	16__–1724	DGM 1721	FRS 1721
J.T. Desaguliers	1683–1744	DGM 1722/3	FRS 1714
Martin Folkes[9]	1690–1754	DGM 1724	FRS 1714
J.T. Desaguliers	1683–1744	DGM 1725	FRS 1714
William Cowper	16__?–1740	DGM 1726	
Alexander Chocke	16__?–1737	DGM 1727	
Nathaniel Blackerby	16__?–1742	DGM 1728/9	
Thomas Batson		DGM 1730/2	
Sir Cecil Wray	16__–17__	DGM 1733	
John Ward[10]	1704–1774	DGM 1733/7	
William Graeme	1700–1745	DGM 1738/9	FRS 1730
Martin Clare	16__?–1750	DGM 1740	FRS 1735

Grand Wardens	Dates	Installed	FRS
Jacob Lambell		GW 1717	
Joseph Elliot		GW 1717	
John Cordwell		GW 1718	
Thomas Morris		GW 1718	
Anthony Sayer		GW 1719	
Thomas Morris		GW 1719	
Thomas Hobby		GW 1720	
Richard Ware		GW 1720	
Josias Villenau		GW 1721	
Thomas Morris		GW 1721	
Joshua Timson		GW 1722	
William Hawkins/James Anderson		GW 1722	
Francis Sorrel		GW 1723	
John Senex	c. 1678–1740	GW 1723	FRS 1728
Francis Sorrel		GW 1724	
George Payne		GW 1724	
Col. Daniel Houghton		GW 1725	
Sir Thomas Prendergast		GW 1725	
Alexander Chocke		GW 1726	
William Burden		GW 1726	
Nathaniel Blackerby	16__–1742	GW 1727	
Joseph Highmore		GW 1727	
Sir James Thornhill	1675–1734	GW 1728	FRS 1723
Martin O'Connor		GW 1728	
Hon. Col. George Carpenter	1694–1749	GW 1729	FRS 1729
Thomas Batson		GW 1729	
Dr George Douglas	16__–1737	GW 1730	FRS 1733
James Chambers		GW 1730	
George Rooke		GW 1731	
James Smythe		GW 1731	
James Smythe		GW 1732	
John Ward	1679–1758	GW 1732	FRS 1723
John Ward	1679–1758	GW 1733	FRS 1723
Sir Edward Mansel	1686–1754	GW 1733	
Sir Edward Mansel	1686–1754	GW 1734	
Martin Clare	16__–1751	GW 1734	FRS 1735
John Ward	1679–1758	GW 1735	FRS 1723
Sir Robert Lawley		GW 1735	
Sir Robert Lawley		GW 1736	
Dr William Graeme	1700–1745	GW 1736	FRS 1730
Lord George Graham		GW 1737	
Andrew Robertson		GW 1737	
John Harvey Thursby		GW 1738	
Robert Foy		GW 1738	
James Ruck		GW 1739	
William Vaughan		GW 1739	
William Vaughan		GW 1740	
Benjamin Gascoyne		GW 1740	

Grand Secretaries	Dates	Installed	FRS
William Cowper		GS 1723	
William Reid		GS 1727	
William Graeme	1700–1745	GS 1735	FRS 1730
John Revis		GS 1736	

Appendix 2

THE 1723 CONSTITUTIONS

A discussion of the origins of the 'Old Charges' and the substance and implications of the non-historical content at the core of the '1723 Constitutions': the 'Regulations' and 'Charges'.

It is frequently argued that the *Regulations* and *Charges* within the *1723 Constitutions* incorporated and followed on from the mediaeval *Old Charges*. David Harrison's study perpetuated this approach, commenting that 'Freemasonry evolved into a society that combined ancient mysticism with the emerging Natural philosophy of the New Science'.[1] Such an argument may be disingenuous. The configuration of the 1723 'Laws, Charges, Orders, Regulations and Usages' suggests that although superficially important and providing a comforting, if largely false, historic context, maintaining continuity with the fabric of earlier Masonic documents was not a main consideration. Although older manuscript wording was incorporated and a similarity of structure is identifiable, it is important to focus on the newly introduced wording, that which was excluded and the contemporary context.

English Freemasonry had its nominal roots in the mediaeval religious guilds, evidence of which can be found across Europe from the early mediaeval period through to the eighteenth century.[2] The allegorical use of stonemasons' tools can be dated back even further – to Greek and Roman times.[3] But the conventional view of English Freemasonry as part of a seamless evolution from the mediaeval Masonic guilds is not supported by the characteristics apparent in the eighteenth century. With its Grand Lodge at the head of a new federal structure, English Freemasonry in the 1720s and 1730s became a vehicle for the dissemination of political and philosophical beliefs that were not part of any centuries' long process of evolution but rather a reflection of contemporary society and the mores of Freemasonry's new Grand Officers.

THE OLD CHARGES

Payne and Desaguliers' *Regulations* and *Charges*[4] were supposedly derived from mediaeval manuscripts: 'I need not tell your Grace what Pains our learned author has taken in compiling and digesting this Book from the old Records . . . still preserving all that was truly ancient and authentic in the old ones'. This was largely fictional. Andrew Prescott has suggested –

convincingly – that different versions of the *Old Charges* were a product of their contemporary context.[5] They certainly held a mirror to the economic, religious, political and social environment. Since the late fourteenth century, the guilds had functioned as local economic pressure groups to support and increase pay rates by combining collective bargaining with restrictive labour practices. They also provided a social and religious function[6] most particularly in education and through the sponsorship of Mystery Plays and church livings.[7] These aspects of guild life had been taken from and continued the guilds' original religious foundations, and they persisted in seventeenth- and eighteenth-century Freemasonry.[8]

The guilds were also necessarily supportive of Crown and Church. Protestations of faithfulness to God, fealty to the King and his lords, and loyalty to the religious authorities, formed the opening portion of each of the *Old Charges* sworn by the membership, even before the guilds were incorporated officially by charter. Acceptance of the religious, royal and feudal status quo was a *conditio sine qua non* of existence. A formal protestation of loyalty could not offer any legal protection to the guild. However, together with a faux history dating back to St. Athelstan or St. Alban, the *Old Charges* provided parameters and a framework in which technically illegal wage negotiation and collective bargaining could be justified morally (and politically). In this way, the *Old Charges* provided an attenuated form of theistic and political insurance to the guild's membership.

The *Cooke* Manuscript[9] was clear on the point:

> whosoever desires to become a mason, it behoves him before all things to [love] God and the holy Church and all the Saints; and his master and fellows as his own brothers;[10]

The *Watson* manuscript written at York around a century later contained similar obligations:

> The first Charge is that you be [a] true man to God, and the Holy Church, and that you use neither error nor heresy, according to your own understanding, and to discreet and wise-men's teaching ... You shall be [a] true liegemen to the King of England without any treason or falsehood.[11]

The *Halliwell* or *Regius* manuscript is one of the earliest of the *Old Charges*.[12] The manuscript has been dated to between *c.* 1390 and *c.* 1450 and takes the form of a 794 line epic poem written in metric verse.[13] The poem begins with 'constituciones artis gemetriae secundum Eucyldem', that is, a history of the art of geometry according to Euclid, which states that the stone masons' art can be traced back to Euclid,[14] 'the father of geometry':

> Bygan furst the craft of masonry, The clerk Euclyde on thys wyse hyt fonde,
> Thys craft of gemetry yn Egypte londe.[15]

The *Regius* MS dated the arrival of Freemasonry in England to the time of King Athelstan:

thys craft com ynto Englond, as yow say, Yn tyme of good kynge Adelstonus day[16]

and noted that it was held in high esteem by God:

Thys goode lorde loved thys craft ful wel.[17]

The brief history of the craft is followed by 'fyftene artyculus they ther sow[g]ton and fyftene poyntys they wro[g]ton',[18] or fifteen articles and fifteen points, that set out various rules designed to regulate stonemasons. For example, the manuscript detailed how apprentices and fellowcraft masons should be paid:

And pay thy felows after the coste,	And when you pay your workers
As vytaylys goth thenne, wel thou woste;	take into account the cost of food;
And pay them trwly, apon thy fay,	you know that they deserve that you
What that they deserven may;[19]	should pay them fairly;[20]

The manuscript also contained restrictions to prevent unacceptable business conduct, for example:

That the mayster be both wyse and felle;	The master should be wise and true,
That no werke he undurtake,	And not undertake work
But he conne bothe hyt ende and make;	Unless he can complete it,
And that hyt be to the lordes profyt also;[21]	And that it be done so honourably;

And the manuscript similarly contained strictures regarding personal conduct, for example:

No fals mantenans he take hym apon,	He should not lie,
Ny maynteine hys felows yn here synne,	Nor allow his colleagues to act sinfully,
For no good that he my[g]th wynne;	Regardless that this may be of benefit;
Ny no fals sware sofre hem to make,	Nor allow others to act falsely,
For drede of here sowles sake;[22]	For they would suffer in hell;

Moreover, among other constraints:[23]

Thou schal not by thy maysters wyf ly,	Do not sleep with your master's wife,
Ny by the felows, yn no maner wyse,	Nor with that of any colleague,
Lest the craft wolde the despyse;	For you would be scorned by the Craft;
Ny by the felows concubyne,	Nor with a colleague's girlfriend,
No more thou woldest he dede by thyne.	For you would not wish to be treated as such by him.

The *Regius* MS established the principle that all masons were subject to the rules of the lodge and, *inter alia*, enjoined that each mason should attend the annual meeting:

every mayster, that ys a mason,	every master mason wherever they may be
Most ben at the generale congregacyon ...	must be present at a general assembly
[the] asemblé to be y-holde every [g]er,	that is to be held each year
whersever they wolde, to amende the defautes,	to correct any faults if any are to be found
ef any where fonde amonge the craft	among the craftsmen
withynne the londe assemblies.24	so assembled.

The balance of the poem, lines 497–794, is substantially religious in content and largely unrelated to masonry. The manuscript refers to 'ars quatuor coronatorum', the art of the Four Crowned Martyrs, and to the 'syens seven', the seven sciences:

Gramatica ys the furste syens y-wysse,	Know that Grammar is the first science,
Dialetica the secunde, so have y blysse,	Dialect the second,
Rethorica the thrydde, withoute nay,	Rhetoric the third, without doubt,
Musica ys the fowrth, as y [g]ow say,	Music the fourth, as I say,
Astromia ys the v, by my snowte,	Astronomy the fifth, by my nose,
Arsmetica the vi, withoute dowte	Arithmetic the sixth, without doubt,
Gemetria the seventhe maketh an ende25	Geometry the seventh is the last.

The *Regius* MS concludes with a sermon on good behaviour in Church:

In holy churche lef nyse wordes	In holy church leave aside your
Of lewed speche, and fowle bordes,	lewd words and unpleasant jokes,
And putte away alle vanyté,	and put away thoughts about yourself;
And say thy pater noster and thyn ave;	And say 'our Father' and 'hail Mary';
Loke also thou make no bere,	Be certain that you maintain respect
But ay to be yn thy prayere;	and concentrate on prayer,
[G]ef thou wolt not thyselve pray,	and if you are not at prayer yourself,
Latte non other mon by no way.26	Do not disturb others who are.

Although much of the poem's phraseology is religious, a substantial component can be regarded as providing a contextual wrap to a number of principally commercial points and practical instructions. However, as Knoop and Jones noted, it is not clear whether such regulations and instructions were rules to which Masons were expected to aspire, a reflection of existing practice, or a combination of the two.[27]

Similar commercial and operative components appear in other versions of the *Old Charges* written in the fifteenth and sixteenth centuries. Of these, the *Cooke* MS, dated to 1450–90, is one of the more prominent and is regarded as the manuscript most likely to have been used by Payne in his compilation of the *Charges*.[28] The *Cooke* MS expanded the historical antecedents of Freemasonry and justified and substantiated Freemasonry's place in both a contemporary and historical context.

Cooke placed the origins of the Craft 'seven generations' after Adam:

> before Noah's flood, there was a man that was named Lamech . . . he begat two sons . . . The elder son, Jabal, was the first man that ever found geometry and Masonry.[29]

Cooke also advanced the date of introduction of Freemasonry to England to the time of St. Alban,[30] one of the earliest English Christian martyrs, noting that:

> Saint Alban loved well masons, and he gave them first their charges and manners first in England.[31]

Cooke set out in detail an historical context and provided its contemporary readers and listeners with both a sociological and psychological justification for the Craft's existence. Given the contemporary economic circumstances and in particular the statutory constraints that had been enacted, it was significant that *Cooke* argued that there were powerful historical precedents with regard to appropriate wage rates.

Cooke stated that these had been dictated by King Athelstan and, equally importantly, that Athelstan had given his imprimatur to masonic guilds and lodge assemblies:

> and he loved well masonry and masons. And he became a mason himself, and he gave them charges and names as it is now used in England, and in other countries. And he ordained that they should have reasonable pay and purchased a free patent of the king that they should make [an] assembly when they saw a reasonable time.[32]

Cooke's historical perspective validated and justified collective wage bargaining and sanctioned the right to 'reasonable pay', notwithstanding a century of legislative restrictions. The words were not literary embroidery. In common with the *Regius* MS, *Cooke*'s principal role was to sanction the existence of the guild and legitimate its activities. Implicit were the long-standing rights of stonemasons to 'make assembly' and enjoy an appropriate level of pay. Tangentially, the comparably artificial history written by Anderson two hundred and fifty years later had a similar sub-text: to validate the newly created Grand Lodge and its new rulebook, and to place it within the context of a 'tradition of many ages'.

In this analysis, the core components of the *Regius*, *Cooke* and other *Old Charges*, were principally economic and financial. They were a response to the government's continuing attempts to hold down wage rates and frustrate collective bargaining. In *The Mediaeval Mason*, Knoop and Jones noted the petition of the Commons against assemblies of Masons in the 1425 Parliament,[33] one of several petitions that related to Edward III's *Ordnance of Labourers* and *Statute of Labourers*, passed in 1349 and 1351, respectively. The purpose, outlined in the (translated) text below, was clear:

> The commons humbly request: whereas by annual meetings and confederacies held by masons in their general chapters and assemblies, the good intent and effect of the statutes of labourers have been publicly violated and broken, in subversion of the law, and the grievous damage of all the commons . . . Such chapters and assemblies must not be held henceforth; and if any such are held, those who have caused these chapters and assemblies to be convened and held, if they are convicted of this will be adjudged as felons. And that all other masons who attend such chapters and assemblies will be punished by imprisonment of their bodies, and will make fine and ransom, at the king's will.[34]

In 1423, Parliament had confirmed:

> the powers of justices to bring before them those suspected of receiving wages higher than those stipulated in the statute of labourers were . . . confirmed up to the next parliament.[35]

And in 1425, Parliament observed:

> that the said justices of the peace, shall have the power to summon before them by attachment, masons, carpenters . . . and all other labourers, and to examine them, and if they find by examination, or by other means, that any of the said persons has been paid contrary to the laws and ordinances made in the past, that then he who is found receiving thus, should be imprisoned for one month.[36]

Parliament also ordained that the Justices should have the power to arraign any employers suspected of paying wages above those levels enacted by Statute:

> And if it be founden by examination, or in other wise, that the seid maistres yeven more than accordyng to the seid ordinaunce, thanne ther seid maistres that yeven more, and iche of hem, payng to the kyng, for every salarie paied to the servaunte, contrarie to the seid ordinaunce of Leycestre, the excesse; and the seid servauntz so takyng, and ther of atteint, by hir

knoulich, or in other laufull wise, have imprisonement of a moneth, withoute baill or mainpris. And if any sheref, baillif of fraunchise, gaoler, or any other, havyng kepyng of prisons with inne fraunchise, or withoute, or any of here deputes, put any such persone to baill or mainpris, thanne lese to the kyng, for every suche man let to baill or mainpris, XXs.[37]

Translation:

And if it be found by examination or by other means that the said masters pay more than is stipulated by the said ordinance, that then the said masters who pay more . . . shall be fined the excess by the Crown for every salary so paid to the servant contrary to the said ordinance of Leicester; and the said servants thus receiving, and convicted of this . . . shall be imprisoned for a month without bail or mainprise.[38] And if any sheriff, bailiff of a franchise, gaoler, or any other person in charge of prisons within or outside a franchise, or any of their deputies, put any such person on bail or mainprise, then they shall forfeit 20s to the crown for every such man allowed bail or mainprise.

The government was aware of the reaction to their legislation:

because of certain ordinances issued by the mayor and aldermen of London against the excessive wages taken by masons, carpenters, tilers, plasterers, and other labourers for their daily work and approved by the king's advice and that of his council, there were generated many grudges and seditious bills in the name of such labourers, threatening a rising of many thousands, and threatening the estates of the land.[39]

The *Old Charges* represented an element of the guilds' response to the pressures imposed by ordinance and statute. They addressed the issue of pay specifically and were directed at both the workers and those who employed them. As noted above, the first article in *Regius* dealt explicitly with the issue of applying fixed wages at a time of price inflation: 'pay thy felows after the coste as vytaylys goth thenne . . . and pay them trwly, apon thy fay, what that they deserve'.[40] Given the contemporary economic context, it is unsurprising that the *Cooke* MS contained similar wording:

That every master of this art should be wise and true to the lord that he serveth, dispending his goods truly as he would his own were dispensed, and not give more pay to no mason than he wot he may deserve, after the dearth of corn and victual in the country, no favour withstanding, for every man to be rewarded after his travail.[41]

Labour conflict remained a visible thread from the mid-fourteenth century as artisans sought to gain more control over wage rates and unskilled workers to take advantage of the labour shortages that followed the recurrent outbreaks of plague and other economic disruptions.[42] The *Ordnance of Labourers* was followed by others statutes setting wage rates and seeking to contain labour, and was reinforced by Henry VI in 1424:

> whereas by the yearly congregations and confederacies made by the masons in their general chapiters and assemblies, the good course and effect of the statutes of labourers be openly violated and broken, in subversion of the law, and to the great damage of all the commons ; our said lord the King willing in this case to provide remedy by the advice and assent aforesaid, and at the special request of the said commons, hath ordained and established, That such chapiters and congregations shall not be hereafter holden.[43]

Restrictive legislation was only one of several factors that had an impact upon the mediaeval labour market. The principal features of the market were unpredictability and instability, with sporadic growth and decline periodically affecting different economic sectors and regions.[44] Nonetheless, stonemasons, along with other skilled and unskilled labourers generally benefited from market forces as labour shortages improved their bargaining position across both urban and rural areas; the most important losers were the larger employers.[45] And although Acts were passed successively in 1436, 1444, 1495 and 1514, in a sustained attempt to regulate away market forces, the attempt to set daily pay rates and prescribe maximum wages and, conversely, to open the labour markets by proscribing minimum work qualifications, were contentious and largely ineffective.[46] Infractions by employers, labourers and by those officials tasked with policing and prosecuting the legislation were commonplace.[47] During the early 1550s, inflation and the erosion of real wages resulted in strikes and riots in Coventry, London, York, and elsewhere, and made clear to Elizabeth's government that an alternative approach was required.

The Acts of 1495 and 1514 had imposed maximum daily rates of pay across diverse groups of workers but these had not been revised to take into account inflation and by 1550, the stated wage rates were unrealistic and impractical. In York in 1552, building workers went on strike and refused to work for a pay rate of 6*d* per day that had been determined in 1514. Their leaders were jailed but despite this, similar protests occurred in other towns in the North and Midlands, including Chester and Hull. The government was forced to adopt and maintain a more conciliatory approach closer to London and in the Home Counties and south Midlands for fear of popular insurrection.[48] Eventually, Parliament responded and in 1563 passed the *Statute of Artificers* which lay down a new framework for wage regulation and delegated the necessary powers to settle local wage rates to local Justices of the Peace based on local market conditions and prices.[49]

Donald Woodward has demonstrated that for most labourers, employment was discontinuous and insecure and that the cash wage was their primary source of income.[50] That the guilds provided only limited support for wage rates in the mid- and late sixteenth century may reflect that they had begun to represent the more entrepreneurial and successful master masons whose economic interests were not necessarily shared with the masons they employed. In contrast, Prescott has argued compellingly in *The Old Charges Revisited* that it was no coincidence that the York manuscripts, written in the mid-sixteenth century, echoed contemporary labour discontent.[51] He pointed out that the wages demanded by the striking craftsmen in 1552 were virtually identical to those set out in contemporary manuscripts that purported to refer to the rate of pay applicable at the time of St. Alban, namely '2*s*6*d* a week for work and 3*d* a day for food'.[52] Setting aside the religious schematic, it can be argued that the central core of the *Old Charges* was protectionist.

The *Old Charges* provided a justification to establish and maintain the structures necessary or beneficial to the support of local wage rates. They laid out an operational framework to restrict labour supply: limiting the admission of apprentices; setting minimum quality standards; enforcing action against 'unqualified' workers; and controlling and regulating operational issues through the lodge. In order to avoid the charge of sedition in what remained a strictly stratified society, the guilds simultaneously proclaimed their loyalty to the Crown and to the natural hierarchical order. However, the willingness to riot suggests that this may have been considered by some of those concerned as no more than a veneer. At the same time, the guild sought to bind its membership, both to one another and to the lodge, through oath-laden initiation ceremonies, ritual and dining and drinking. And it can be argued that it was this aspect of Freemasonry that was later to attract the respective interest and patronage of scholars and the gentry.

The *Dowland* (c. 1500), *Lansdowne* (c. 1560) and *York* (c. 1600) manuscripts are three of over 120 extant fifteenth, sixteenth and seventeenth century documents held at the British Library, the library of the United Grand Lodge of England, that of the Grand Lodge at York and in private Masonic lodges in England, Scotland and elsewhere.[53] The manuscripts are generally known by the names of their owners, writers, publishers or printers, or similarity to another text. A few are named in honour of a notable Freemason.[54] Despite being written over a period of more than a century, and around 150 years after *Regius* and *Cooke*, each shares common components and follows the same broad pattern: a short prayer to the Trinity; a discourse on the seven liberal arts and sciences; an embroidered history of Masonry; and the kernel of the document, the *Oath* and *Charges*.

Each set of *Charges* contains the same principal obligations: to be true to God and the Church; the King and the 'natural' social order – 'true to the lord, or Master, that you serve . . . that his profit and advantage be promoted';[55] and to other Masons. In this last respect, Masons were enjoined to secrecy: to 'keep truly all the counsel of Lodge and Chamber, and all other counsel, that ought to be kept by way of Masonry'.[56] As before, other individual *Charges* were more mundane.

The texts embody restrictions against name-calling, adulterous and immoral behaviour and dishonesty. Craftsmen were obliged to 'pay truly for your meat and drink where you go to table' and to do nothing 'whereby the Craft may be scandalised, or receive disgrace'. Other *Charges* were concerned with the governance of the lodge and its operations and set out the then current working practices for operative stonemasons. That the *Charges* were un-illuminated documents suggest that they were designed for regular use rather than display.

By the beginning of the seventeenth century, Freemasons' guilds in common with other craft guilds were governed by charters by which the guild was recognised and incorporated. The charter set out the structure, governance and operations of the guild; determined when the lodge would meet, usually up to four times a year, with the main meeting occurring on St. John the Baptist's day; and how the master, wardens and clerk would be chosen by the members, customarily on an annual basis by election. The charter also set out how apprentices were to be admitted and employed, the obligations and responsibilities of members, and operational ordinances, such as fines and stipends. In short, the guild charter combined a warrant or permit with articles of association, providing a constitutional framework and a set of regulations that governed day-to-day business.

Over time, the guilds gradually engaged in a process of becoming more firmly and commercially embedded into provincial and metropolitan society. In Newcastle, for example, a charter of 1 September 1581 constituted the Masons a body incorporated with perpetual succession. In return for their rights, the guild was obliged *inter alia* to meet annually, 'choose two wardens, who might sue and be sued in the courts of Newcastle, make byelaws', and adopt a system of fines:

> every absent brother to forfeit 2s. 6d.; no Scotsman should be taken apprentice, under a penalty of 40s. nor ever be admitted into the company on any account whatever; each brother to be sworn; that apprentices should serve seven years; . . . that one half of their fines should go to the maintenance of the great bridge, and the other half to the said fellowship.[57]

However, by the end of the sixteenth century and into the seventeenth, the local guilds' monopolies were under threat. Their ability to levy fines, operate a right of search, set prices, exclude 'strangers' and restrict apprenticeships, were beginning to be viewed as anachronistic at a time of burgeoning economic development and commercial trade. They were also subject to litigation and dispute as Tudor labour regulations and the new Elizabethan statutes enacted from 1563 fell into abeyance.[58] But the retreat of the guild system was not uniform across the country and pockets of influence survived. In 1713, a reform committee established in York had advised that all craft ordinances should be 'brought in' so that the committee might discover what tended to 'limit and discourage trade and industry'.[59] However, reform was not on the agenda. As a testament to the particularly close relationship between the guilds and city authorities, York went against the recommendations of its own committee and against the general trend and 'free-working masons' were given a new charter in 1726. Other York guilds were similarly favoured by the city. Such a response was conspicuous at a time when guild influence was more often being accepted as harmful and placing unacceptable restrictions on the local economy. Indeed, a few years later, in 1736, York's support for the guilds' restrictive practices was condemned by one of their own, the antiquarian, scholar and York Freemason, Francis Drake[60] (1696–1771). Drake noted the main reason for there being little development and employment opportunities for the poor:

> Our magistrates have been too tenacious of their privileges, and have for many years last past, by virtue of their charters, as it were locked themselves up from the world, and wholly prevented any foreigner from settling any manufacture amongst them.[61]

Within London, the influx of provincial and continental stonemasons during the construction boom that followed the Great Fire[62] combined with rising municipal affluence and the widespread use of brick to break down monopolistic barriers in the building trades. Charles II had granted a petition in November 1677 for a royal charter of incorporation for the Company of Masons:

> to prevent the deceits and abuses . . . lately observed to be too frequently practised by many of the same trade in and about London and Westminster, who refuse all manner of subjection to the good rules and orders made by the said Company.[63]

But the Company of Masons did not prosper. The earlier suspension of the Company's monopoly in 1666 was later made permanent[64] and undermined its regulatory authority and economic purpose. It became one of the smaller London guilds, ranking only thirtieth in order of precedence and with around fifty members in 1677. It has been estimated by the Company itself that at the end of the seventeenth century, the vast majority of London masons fell outside its jurisdiction.

By the beginning of the eighteenth century with their principal commercial functions no longer an important justification for existence and with membership declining, traditional stone masons' guilds were economically irrelevant. In certain cases, their integrity had been compromised to the extent that a number merged with other construction trades.[65] But the re-working of the *Charges* and *Regulations* should be viewed not only within the context of the fragmentation of the mediaeval social and economic structures that had given the guild its consequence. Other factors were also relevant, particularly those linked to the Hanoverian succession.

The New Charges

Each version of the *Old Charges* followed a similar blueprint: the legendary 'history' of Freemasonry legitimised and provided a historical context for Masonic traditions; the *Regulations* dealt with moral issues and, perhaps more importantly, commerce and trade, and covered the operational 'working' of the lodge, including oath taking, the annual assembly, the election of officers, the admission of apprentices and the penalties and fines for any breach of the rules and regulations. Finally, there were the *Charges* themselves.

The *Charges* set out in the *1723 Constitutions* were distinctly different. Grand Lodge sought to make certain that the new version was widely disseminated and uniformly applied: 'all the Tools used in working shall be approved by the Grand Lodge.'[66]

For the first time, a Masonic charge – *Concerning God and Religion* – set out a key statement in favour of morality and religious tolerance, and not a simple obligation to follow the religion of the country or nation 'whatever it was':

> A Mason is obliged ... to obey the Moral Law ... But tho in ancient times Masons were charged in every Country to be of the Religion of that Country or Nation, whatever it was, yet 'tis now thought more expedient only to oblige them to that Religion in which all Men agree, leaving their particular Opinions to themselves; that is, to be good Men and true, or Men of Honour and Honesty, by whatever Denominations or Persuasions they may be distinguished; whereby Masonry become[s] the Centre and Union, and the means of conciliating true Friendship and Persons that must have remained at a perpetual Distance.

This fundamental modification replaced the invocation of the Trinity and the traditional statement of Christian belief with an obligation only to 'that Religion in which all Men agree', albeit that there was an implicit assumption of the Christian faith. In essence, this was an affirmation of an amorphous divine being rather than one in favour of a specific church or religious doctrine. Such a latitudinarian statement of religious tolerance was novel, perhaps dangerous. And it provided the basis for later attacks on Freemasonry, including that of the 1738 Papal encyclical.[67]

In one sense, the Pope had little choice. Religious toleration explicitly undermined Catholic teaching: that the Church of Rome was the sole route to spiritual salvation. The Vatican came to view Freemasonry as seditious and undermining the Church's spiritual – and thus its temporal – authority. In this context, Papal condemnation was political as well as religious. However, latitudinarianism and toleration of other faiths was central to Desaguliers and Folkes' intellectual beliefs, a view shared by many Whigs and a core tenet of Masonic principles:

as Masons we only pursue the universal Religion or the Religion of Nature. This is the Cement which unites Men of the most different Principles in one sacred Band and brings together those who were most distant from one another.[68]

It is possible to see the foundations of this approach in Newton:

the essential part of religion [was] of an immutable nature because [it was] grounded upon immutable reason . . . religion may therefore be called the Moral Law of all nations.[69]

Such a view was central to an intellectual approach that united rational observation of the natural world. Other contemporary texts such as *Long Livers* reflected a similar pantheistic approach; dedicated to the Freemasons and to 'Men excellent in all kinds of Sciences', *Long Livers* proclaimed that 'it is the Law of Nature which is the Law of God, for God is Nature'.[70]

Desaguliers was not the only latitudinarian at Grand Lodge. His views were shared to a larger degree by Folkes. Indeed, Folkes was considered by some to be a Deist – a belief in the divine without the need for any revealed or organized religion : 'we are all citizens of the world, and see different customs and tastes without dislike or prejudice, as we do different names and colours'.[71] As Wigelsworth noted, theology and natural philosophy were closely connected and the 'nature' of God was one of the foundations on which natural philosophy and a rational interpretation of the natural world rested.[72] And in this sense, the inter-play between theology and natural philosophy was integral to contemporary political and theological debate.

The second Masonic charge – *Of the Civil Magistrate Supreme and subordinate* – addressed obliquely the political uncertainties that surrounded the Hanoverian succession and contemporary Jacobite threat:

A Mason is a peaceable Subject to the Civil Powers . . . is never to be concerned in Plots and Conspiracies against the Peace and Welfare of the Nation . . . if a Brother should be a Rebel against the State, he is not to be countenanced in his Rebellion, however he may be pitied as an unhappy Man; and, if convicted of no other Crime, though the loyal Brotherhood must and ought to disown his Rebellion, and give no Umbrage or Ground of political Jealousy to the Government for the time being; they cannot expel him from the Lodge, and his Relation to it remains indefeasible.

It was a new concept that a Mason could be 'a Rebel against the State' and although he might be 'disowned', his rebellion would provide insufficient grounds for expulsion. The logic followed from the first Masonic charge whereby 'Masonry [was] . . . the means of conciliating . . . persons that must have remained at a perpetual distance'. Once again, *Long Livers* reflected the same approach: 'avoid politicks and religion: have nothing to do with these'.[73] Even so, the obligation to pay due obedience to the state was evident[74] and in his formal welcome to the lodge as a newly made 'Entered Apprentice' an initiate was enjoined to:

> behave as a peaceable and dutiful Subject, conforming cheerfully to the Government under which he lives.[75]

Given their substantial number within Freemasonry and Desaguliers' own background, the second Charge may also have been addressed directly to the Huguenot émigré audience which populated many lodges and with an eye to the mollifying effect that such words might have on a nervous government. Although allegiance to the Crown – 'to be a true liege man to the king' – had historically been a specific oath required of operative masons, the *1723 Constitutions* stated only that Freemasons should be 'Subject to the Civil Powers'.

This directly contradicted the English and Scottish Masonic ritual that had gone before which required the immediate reporting of any plot against the Crown.[76] Unlike earlier ritual, the *1723 Constitutions* did not oblige a lodge to take action against a seditious member. However, Desaguliers, Folkes and Payne were not advocates of Bishop George Berkeley's (1685–1753) *Passive Obedience*,[77] and the *Constitutions* were not associated with such theories.[78] They were rather a reflection of contemporary Whig views: insurrection could conceivably be regarded as acceptable, at least in principle, if a King were in breach of his moral contract with those he governed. This was after all the philosophical and intellectual justification of the *Glorious Revolution* of 1688 and the replacement of James II by William and Mary.

The third Masonic charge – *Of Lodges* – reinforced the point that although membership was open, the Society was select:

> The persons admitted Members of a Lodge must be good and true Men, free-born, and of mature and discreet Age, no Bondmen, no Women, no immoral or scandalous men, but of good Report.

This was reinforced by the next Masonic charge – *Of Masters, Wardens, Fellows and Apprentices* – which offered a radical approach to preferment in an age when rank and precedence was fundamental to social order and promotion rarely based on merit:

> All preferment among Masons is grounded upon real Worth and personal Merit only; that so the Lords may be well served, the Brethren not put to Shame, nor the Royal Craft despised . . . no Master or Warden is chosen by Seniority, but for his Merit . . .

The charge continued and emphasized that Freemasonry had its own route to preferment:

No Brother can be a Warden until he has passed the part of a Fellow-Craft; nor a Master until he has acted as a Warden, nor Grand Warden until he has been Master of a Lodge, nor Grand Master unless he has been a Fellow-Craft before his Election, who is also to be nobly born, or a Gentleman of the best Fashion, or some eminent Scholar, or some curious Architect, or other Artist, descended of honest Parents, and who is of similar great Merit in the Opinion of the Lodges. And for the better, and easier, and more honourable Discharge of his Office, the Grand-Master has a Power to choose his own Deputy Grand-Master, who must be then, or must have been formerly, the Master of a particular Lodge, and has the Privilege of acting whatever the Grand Master, his Principal, should act, unless the said Principal be present, or interpose his Authority by a Letter.

The power of the Grand Master to 'choose his own Deputy Grand-Master, who must be then, or must have been formerly, the Master of a particular Lodge' may have been inserted by Desaguliers as a specific reaction to the attempt by the Duke of Wharton to take control of Grand Lodge in 1722. The charge also obliged brethren to obey the rulers and governors of the Craft 'in their respective Stations', and thereby placed Masonic rank nominally in precedence over noble rank within the lodge.

The fifth Masonic charge – *Of the Management of the Craft* – was a continuation of the long-standing practice of substituting allegorical, or 'speculative', uses for operative Masonic tools. It later became a core aspect of post 1723 Freemasonry. In this charge, all tools used in Masonic working were to be 'approved by Grand Lodge' and:

> no Labourer shall be employ'd in the proper Work of Masonry, nor shall Free Masons work with those that are not free, without an urgent necessity, nor shall they teach Labourers and Unaccepted Masons.

The references to 'receiving their Wages justly' and 'receive their Wages without Murmuring or Mutiny' were not used in a literal sense. The references were to 'the Lord's Work' and 'for increasing and continuing . . . Brotherly Love'.

The sixth charge – *Of Behaviour* – dealt with six issues: etiquette within the lodge; conduct once the lodge had concluded; meetings with fellow Masons outside of the lodge; meeting with non-Masons; behaviour at home and at work; and how one 'proved' a genuine brother. Desaguliers and his colleagues wished to ensure that Grand Lodge would become a focal point not only in the governance of the order but also as a means of settling external disputes. This may have been less naivety than an attempt to ensure that Freemasonry would be protected from external interference:

> And if any of them do you Injury, you must apply to your own or his Lodge, and from thence you may appeal to the Grand Lodge, at the Quarterly Communication and from thence to the annual Grand Lodge at the

Quarterly Communication, and from thence to the annual Grand Lodge . . . never taking a legal Course but when the Case cannot be otherwise decided . . . [in order that] all may see the benign Influence of Masonry.

A catechism was later added requiring affirmation from the Master-elect in each instance.[79] The content and structure reinforces the arguments outlined above. The ritual was designed to strengthen the Masonic and moral authority of Grand Lodge and its officers, and to ensure obedience to the established civil order.

You agree to be a good man and true, and strictly to obey the moral law.

You agree to be a peaceable subject, and cheerfully to conform to the laws of the country in which you reside.

You promise not to be concerned in plots and conspiracies against government, but patiently to submit to the decisions of the supreme legislature.

You agree to pay a proper respect to the civil magistrate, to work diligently, live creditably, and act honourably by all men.

You agree to hold in veneration the original rulers and patrons of the Order of Masonry, and their regular successors, supreme and subordinate, according to their stations; and to submit to the awards and resolutions of your brethren when convened, in every case consistent with the constitutions of the Order. You agree to avoid private piques and quarrels, and to guard against intemperance and excess.

You agree to be cautious in carriage and behaviour, courteous to your brethren, and faithful to your Lodge.

You promise to respect genuine brethren, and to discountenance impostors, and all dissenters from the original plan of Masonry.

You agree to promote the general good of society, to cultivate the social virtues, and to propagate the knowledge of the art.

You promise to pay homage to the Grand Master for the time being, and to his officers when duly installed; and strictly to conform to every edict of the Grand Lodge, or general assembly of Masons, that is not subversive of the principles and ground-work of Masonry.

You admit that it is not in the power of any man, or body of men, to make innovations in the body of Masonry.

You promise a regular attendance on the committees and communications of the Grand Lodge, on receiving proper notice, and to pay attention to all the duties of Masonry on convenient occasions.

You admit that no new Lodge shall be formed without permission of the Grand Lodge; and that no countenance be given to any irregular Lodge, or to any person clandestinely initiated therein, being contrary to the ancient charges of the Order.

You admit that no person can be regularly made a Mason in, or admitted a member of, any regular Lodge, without previous notice, and due inquiry into his character.

You agree that no visitors shall be received into your Lodge without due examination, and producing proper vouchers of their having been initiated in a regular Lodge.

Taken as a whole, the *Charges* were designed to complement the revised set of *Regulations* compiled by Payne.

THE REGULATIONS

Payne had been asked by Grand Lodge to 'compile' a set of *Regulations* for the *1723 Constitutions*. However, whereas previous *Regulations* were essentially working documents governing the local trade operations, protecting a local monopoly and providing a framework for running the lodge, Payne's *Regulations* were fundamentally different.

Each focused specifically on the operation of Grand Lodge and its constituent lodges. None dealt with operative issues or matters of trade. Given their significance and level of detail, it is hard to conceive of Payne drafting them alone. They were not – as incorrectly advertised – a reduction of the 'ancient Records and immemorial Usages of the Fraternity',[80] but rather a new set of rules designed for a new organisation with a style and content that suggests a collaboration with Desaguliers.

The new *Regulations* and *Charges* underlined that Freemasonry embedded Whiggish views but not slavishly so. The *Constitutions* incorporated the relatively radical concept of democratic accountability: Article 10 for example stated that a 'majority of every particular Lodge, when congregated, shall have the privilege of giving instructions to their Master and Wardens . . . because the Master and Wardens are their representatives'.[81] And Article 6 required the unanimous consent of members prior to any new entrant to the lodge, notwithstanding that this was often observed in the breach.[82] Similarly, although the Grand Master had the right to nominate his successor, if that nominee were not approved unanimously, Articles 23 and 24 specified that members would be balloted.[83]

The *Charges* and *Regulations* comprised the most important components of the new *Constitutions*. Their primary purpose was to confirm Freemasonry's support for the government and the Hanoverian succession; set out the importance of Grand Lodge and its Rules; and provide the Craft with a moral and social framework.

The schematic of the new *Charges* and *Regulations* represented in only the most limited manner a continuation of the traditions of the mediaeval guilds. Under Desaguliers and his colleagues' aegis, Freemasonry had been reinvented with a new character and dimension with a membership that embraced intellectual self-improvement, religious tolerance, relative egalitarianism and support for elected self-government and constitutional monarchy.

Appendix 3

The Military Lodges

IRELAND

	Lodge Numbers and Warrant Dates
Artillery Regiments	
7th Battalion, Royal Artillery	68 (1813–1834)
	226 (1810–1825)
9th Battalion, Royal Artillery	313 (1823–1828)
Royal Irish Artillery	374 (1761–1818)
	528 (1781–1787)
Corps of Artillery Drivers	241 (1811, but not issued)
Cavalry	
1st King's Dragoon Guards	571 (1923–1985)
2nd The Queen's Bays	960 (1805–1834)
4th Royal Irish Dragoon Guards	295 (1757–1796)
5th (Princess Charlotte of Wales) Dragoon Guards	277 (1757–1818)
	570 (1863–1970)
6th Dragoon Guards, the Carabiniers	577 (1780–1799)
	exchanged for 876, (1799–1858)
7th (Princess Royals) Dragoon Guards – the Black Horse	305 (1758)
	exchanged for 7, (1817–1855)
1st or Blue Irish Horse, later 4th Dragoon Guards	295 (1758 – current)
2nd or Green Irish Horse, later 5th Dragoon Guards	277 (1757–1818)
	570 (1780–1824)
	44 re-issued (1863–1970)
3rd or Irish Horse, later 6th Dragoon Guards	577 (1780)
	876 issued 1799
	in lieu of 577, lost 1794
4th or Black Irish Horse, later 7th Dragoon Guards	305 (1758
	exchanged for No. 7, 1817)
4th Dragoons – Queen's Own Hussars	50 (1815)
	exchanged for No. 4, 1818
	cancelled 1821
5th Dragoons – Queen's Own Hussars	289 (1757–1796)
	297 (1758–1818)
5th Royal Irish Lancers	595 (1914–1922)
8th Dragoons – Kings Royal Irish Hussars	280 (1757–1815)
	646 (1932–1980)
9th Dragoons – Queen's Royal Lancers	158 (1747–1815)
	356 (1760–1818)

Appendix 3

12th Dragoons – Royal Lancers (Prince of Wales)	179 (1804–1717)
	exchanged for 12 (1817–1827)
	179 (1868–1891)
	255 (1755–1815)
13th Dragoons – Hussars	234 (1752–1815)
	400 (1791–1849)
	607 (1782–1789)
14th Dragoons – King's Hussars	273 (1756–1827)
16th Dragoons – Queen's Lancers	929 (1803–1821)
17th Dragoons – Lancers (Duke of Cambridge Own)	218 (1873–1883)
	478 (1769–1801)
18th Lord Drogheda's Light Dragoons – 1st Squadron	388 (1762–1813)
18th Lord Drogheda's Light Dragoons – 2nd Squadron	389 (1762–1821)
20th Jamaica Light Dragoons	759 (1792–1815)
23rd Light Dragoons (1794–1802)	873 (1799–1802)
23rd (26th) Light Dragoons (1802–1817)	164 (1808–1817)

Regiments of the Line

1st Foot Royal Scots 1st Battalion	11 (1732–1847)
	381 (1762–1814)
1st Foot Royal Scots 2nd Battalion	74 (1737–1801)
2nd Foot Queen's Royal Regiment (West Surrey)	2 (1818)
	in lieu of 244 (1754–1825)
	390 (1762–1815)
4th Foot King's Own Royal Regiment (Lancaster)	4 (1818) in lieu of 50
	91 (1857–1876)
	522 (1785–1823)
5th Foot Royal Northumberland Fusiliers	86 (1738–1784)
6th Foot Royal Warwickshire	45 (1735?–1801)
	643 (1785–1800)
	646 (1785–1818)
7th Foot Royal Fusiliers (City of London)	231 (1752–1801)
9th Foot Royal Norfolk	246 (1754–1817)
10th Foot Lincolnshire	177 (1748–1755)
	299 (1858–1818)
	378 (1761–1815
11th Foot Devonshire	604 (1782–1794)
13th Foot Somerset Light Infantry	637 (1784–1818)
	661 (1787–1819)
14th Foot West Yorkshire (Prince of Wales Own)	211 (1750–1815)
15th Foot East Yorkshire	245 (1754–1801)
16th Foot Bedfordshire & Hertfordshire	293 (1758–1817)
	300 (1758–1786)
17th Foot Leicestershire	158 (1743–1771)
	136 (1743–1801)
	921 (1802–1824)
	258 (1824 in lieu of 921, 1847)
18th Foot Royal Irish	168 (1747–1801)
	351 (1760–1818)
19th Foot Green Howards	156 (1747–1779)

Appendix 3

Regiment	Number (dates)
20th Foot Lancashire Fusiliers	63 (1737–1869)
20th Foot Lancashire Fusiliers 2nd Battalion	263 (1860–1907)
21st Foot Royal Scots Fusiliers	33 (1734–1801)
	936 (1803–1817) in exchange for 33 (1817–1864)
22nd Foot Cheshire	251 (1754–1817)
23rd Foot Royal Welsh Fusiliers	252?
	738 (2) (1808–1821)
	revived (1882–1892)
25th Foot King's Own Scottish Borderers	250 (1819–1823)
	exchanged for 25 (1823–1839)
	92 (1738–1815)
26th Foot 1st Battalion, The Cameronians	309 (1758)
	exchanged for 26 1823)
26 (1810–1823 and 1823–1922)	
27th Foot 1st Battalion Royal Inniskilling Fusiliers	23 (1733?–1801),
	205 (1750–1785),
	528 (1787–1790),
	692 (1808–1818)
28th Foot 1st Battalion Gloucestershire	28 (1818 in lieu of 510?); 35 1734–1801)
	510 (1773–1858)
	985 (1808 but not issued)
28th Foot 2nd Battalion Gloucestershire	260 (1809–1815)
29th Foot 1st Battalion Worcestershire	322 (1759– current)
30th Foot 1st Battalion East Lancashire	85 (1738–1793 exchanged for No. 30, 1805–1823),
	535 (1776 exchanged for No. 30 by Seton, 1805–6)
32nd Foot 1st Battalion Duke of Cornwall's Light Infantry	61 (1736–1801)
	524 (1921–1937),
	617 (1783–1815)
33rd Foot 1st Battalion Duke of Wellington's	12 (1732–1817)
35th Foot 1st Battalion Royal Sussex	205 (1785–1790)
38th Foot 1st Battalion South Staffordshire	38 (1734–1801)
	441 (1765–1840)
39th Foot 1st Battalion Dorsetshire	128 (1742–1886)
	290 (1758–1785)
40th Foot 1st Battalion Prince of Wales Volunteers (S. Lancs.)	204 (1810–1813)
	284 (1821–1858)
42nd Foot 1st Battalion Black Watch (Royal Highlanders)	42 (1809–1840)
	195 (1749–1815)
44th Foot 1st Battalion Essex	788 (1793–?)
45th Foot 1st Battalion Sherwood Foresters	445 (1766–1815)
46th Foot 2nd Battalion Duke of Cornwall's Light Infantry	174 (1896–1921)
	227 (1752–1847)
47th Foot 1st Battalion The Loyal Regiment (North Lancs)	147 (1810–1823)
	192 (1749–1823)

48th Foot 1st Battalion Northamptonshire   86 (1738–1784)
                                                     218 (1750–1858)
                                                     631 (May–Aug. 1784)
                                                     reissued (Oct. 1784–1818)
                                                     982 (1806–1815)
49th Foot 1st Battalion Royal Berkshire   354 (1760–1851)
                                                     616 (1783–1817)
50th Foot 1st Battalion Queen's Own Royal West Kent   58 (1857–1876)
                                                     113 (1763–1815)
51st Foot 1st Battalion King's Own Yorkshire Light Infantry   94 (1761–1815)
                                                     690 (1788–1796)
52nd Foot 2nd Battalion Oxford and Bucks. Light Infantry   244 (1832–1845)
                                                     370 (1761–1825)
53rd Foot 1st Battalion King's Shropshire Light Infantry   236 (1773–1815)
                                                     950 (1804–1824)
56th Foot 2nd Battalion Essex   420 (1765–1817)
58th Foot 2nd Battalion Northamptonshire   466 (1769–1816)
                                                     692 (1789–1808)
59th Foot 2nd Battalion East Lancashire
                                                     219 (1810–1819)
                                                     243 (1754–1815)
62nd Foot 1st Battalion Wiltshire (Duke of Edinburgh)   407 (1763–1786)
63rd Foot 1st Battalion Manchester   512 (1774–1814)
64th Foot 1st Battalion North Staffordshire (Prince of Wales)   130 (1817–1858)
686   (1788)
                                                     exchanged for No. 130, 1817)
65th Foot 1st Battalion York and Lancaster   631 (1784–1818)
66th Foot 2nd Battalion Royal Berkshire   392 (1763–1817)
                                                     538 (1777–1811)
                                                     580 (1780–1817)
66th Foot 2nd Battalion Royal Berkshire   656 (1808) not confirmed by GLI
67th Foot 2nd Battalion Royal Berkshire   388 (1762–1813)
68th Foot 1st Battalion Durham Light Infantry   714 (1790–1815)
69th Foot 2nd Battalion The Welsh   174 (1791–1821)
                                                     983 (1807–1836)
70th Foot 2nd Battalion East Surrey   770 (1871–1875)
71st Foot 1st Battalion Highland Light Infantry   895 (1801–1835)
72nd Foot 1st Battalion Seaforth Highlanders   65 (1854–1860)
75th Foot 1st Battalion Gordon Highlanders   292 (1810–1825)
76th Foot 2nd Battalion Gordon Highlanders   359 (1760–1763)
77th Foot Atholl Highlanders   578 (1780–1818)
82nd Foot 2nd Battalion Prince of Wales Volunteers, S. Lancs.   138 (1817–1858)
83rd Foot 1st Battalion Royal Ulster Rifles   435 (1808)
                                                     exchanged for 83, (1817)
83rd Foot 16th Service Battalion Royal Irish Rifles   420 (1915–1921)
83rd Foot (1758 – 1763)   339 (1759–1764)
87th Foot 7th Service Battalion Royal Irish Fusiliers   415 (1915–1924)
88th Foot 1st Battalion Connaught Rangers   19 (1907–1920)
                                                     176 (1821–1871)

Appendix 3

89th Foot 2nd Battalion Royal Irish Fusiliers	538 (1811–1815)
	863 (1802–1818)
92nd Foot Donegal Light Infantry	364 (1761–1763)
96th/97th Foot Queen's Germans	984 (1807–1818 exchanged for 176, (1818–19)
103rd Foot Bombay European Regiment	292 (1834–1856)
112th Foot Lord Donoughmore's	816 (1795–1815)
4th Foot Garrison Battalion	986 (1810–1815)
5th Foot Garrison Battalion	125 (1808–1814)
7th Foot Garrison Battalion	992 (1808–1815)
8th Foot Garrison Battalion	995 (1808–1814)
4th Foot Veteran Battalion	988 (1808–1815)
Commissariat Corps	203 (1809–1815)
West Africa Regiment	157 (1908–1928)
West India Regiment	390 (1905–1927)
Colonel Pool's Regiment	177 (1748–1755)
Colonel Folliott's Regiment	168 (1747–1801)
Hon. Brigadier Guise's Regiment	45 (1801), but no GLI record.
Colonel Hamilton's Regiment	23 (1733–1801)
Colonel Lascelle's Regiment	192 (1749–1823)

Militia Regiments

Antrim	289 (1796–1856)
Armagh	888 (1800–1845)
Carlow	903 (1801–1816)
Cavan	300 (1801–1816)
South Cork	495 (1794–1815)
City of Cork	741 (1806–1817)
Donegal	865 (1798–1821
Downshire	212 (1795–1813)
South Down	214 (1810–1815)
City of Dublin	62 (1810–1821)
Fermanagh	864 (1798–1830)
Kerry	66 (1810–1829)
Kildare	847 (1797–1825)
Kilkenny	855 (1797–1825)
King's County	948 (1804–1816)
Leitrim	854 (1797–1868)
Longford	304 (1807–1826)
Louth	10 (1809–1849)
Mayo South	79 (1810–1830)
	81 (1812–1825)
Meath	50 (not Issued)
	898 (1801–1849)
Monaghan	200 (1801–1816)
	552 (1796–1816)
Queen's County	398 (1805–1810)
	857 (1797–1832)
Roscommon	242 (1808–1817)
Sligo	837 (1796–1835)

Appendix 3 223

South Lincoln	867 (1799–1813)
Tipperary	856 (1797–1825)
Tyrone	225 (1808–1814)
	562 (1797–1817)
	846 (1796–1818)
Waterford	961 (1805–1816)
Westmeath	50, 791 (1793–1826)
Wexford	935 (1803–1824)
Wicklow	848 (1796–1815)
	877 (1800–1818)
1st Volunteer Lodge of Ireland in the Royal Independent Dublin Volunteers	620 (1783– current)

Fencible Regiments

1st Fencible Light Dragoons	384 (1799–1802)
Ulster Provincial Regiment of Foot	612 (1783–1783)
Breadalbane	907 (1801–1813)
Elgin	860 (1798–1813)
Essex	852 (1796–1813)
Fife	861 (1798–1804)

SCOTLAND

Lodge	Regiment	Warrant
Lodge Pittefrand[1]	55th Regiment of Foot	Not known
Duke of Norfolk's Mason Lodge	12th Regiment of Foot	1747
Scots Greys Kilwinning[2]	Royal North British Dragoons	1747
General Husk's Regiment	23rd Regiment of Foot	1751
White's Lodge	32nd Regiment of Foot	1792
Prince of Wales from Edinburgh	71st Regiment of Foot	1759
Hooker St. John	70th Regiment of Foot	1759
Fort George	31st Regiment of Foot	1760
King George III	56th Regiment of Foot	1760
The Duke of York's Mason Lodge	64th Regiment of Foot	1761
St. George	31st Regiment of Foot	1761
Union[3]	94th Regiment of Foot	1764
Moriah	22nd Regiment of Foot	1767
The Masons Lodge[4]	23rd Regiment of Foot	1767
United[5]	4th Regiment of Foot	1769
St. Patrick Royal Arch[6]	43rd Regiment of Foot	1769
St. Andrew Royal Arch[7]	Royal North British Dragoons	1770
Unity[8]	17th Regiment of Foot	1771
The Queen's (7th) Dragoons	Queen's (7th) Dragoons	1776
St. Andrew[9]	80th Regiment of Foot	1780
Imp. Scottish Lodge of St. Petersburg	Scots Greys (possibly)	1784
Royal Arch Union	3rd Regiment of Dragoons	1785
Argyllshire Military St. John	2nd Battalion, Argyllshire Fencibles	1795

Union Royal Arch	3rd Dragoons	1797
Ayr St. Paul	Ayr and Renfrew Militia.	1799
Orange Lodge[10]	51st Regiment of Foot	1801
Aboyne North British Militia	6th North British Militia	1799
Royal Thistle[11]	1st Regiment of Foot	1808
Forfar and Kincardine	Forfar and Kincardine Militia	1808
St. Andrew's[12]	42nd Regiment of Foot	1811
Fifeshire Militia	Fifeshire Militia	1811
St. Cuthbert's[13]	25th Durham Militia	1813
St. John	Berwickshire Militia	1819

ENGLISH AND OTHER REGIMENTAL LODGES

Regiment	Warrant
57th Regiment of Foot	1755
King's Own Regiment of Foot	1755
Capt Bell's Troop, Lord Ancram's 11th Regiment of Dragoons	1755
14th Regiment of Foot	1759
51st Regiment of Foot	1761
37th Regiment of Foot (General Stuart's)	1761
33rd Regiment of Foot	1761
50th Regiment of Foot	1763
6th Regiment of Inniskilling Horse	1763
1st Battalion, Royal Artillery, Fort George	1764
2nd Battalion Royal Artillery, Perth	1767
13th Regiment of Foot	1768
52nd Regiment of Foot	1769
3rd Regiment of Foot	1771
67th Regiment of Foot	1772
1st Regiment Yorkshire Militia	1772
Capt Webdell's Co., Regiment of Royal Artillery	1773
1st Battalion Royal Artillery	1774
65th Regiment of Foot	1774
6th Inniskilling Regiment of Dragoons	1777
4th Battalion Royal Artillery	1779
Regiment of Anholt-Zerbst	1780
1st Regiment of Dragoon Guards	1780
2nd Regiment of Anspach Berauth	1781
4th Battalion Regiment of Royal Artillery	1781
First Regiment of East Devon Militia	1781
6th Regiment	1785
76th Regiment	1788
23rd Regiment of Foot (Royal Welsh Fusiliers)	1788
The Coldstream Guards	1793
Royal Regiment of Cheshire	1794
9th Regiment of Dragoons	1794
17th Regiment Light Dragoons	1794
52nd Regiment of Foot	1797
Warwickshire Regiment of Militia	1797
6th Inniskilling Dragoons	1797

Cambridge Regiment of Militia	1799
Cornwall Regiment of Fencible Light Dragoons	1799
Regiment of Loyal Surrey Rangers	1800
2nd Battalion 52nd Regiment	1801
Staffordshire Regiment of Militia	1801
85th Regiment of Foot	1801
78th Regiment	1801
9th Regiment of Foot	1803
2nd regiment of Royal Lancashire Militia	1803
1st Battalion 96th Regiment	1804
92nd Regiment	1805
2nd Battalion 58th Regiment	1805
3rd Regiment of Dragoons	1806
18th Royal Irish Regiment of Foot	1806
Royal Reg. Of Cumberland Militia	1807
45th Regiment	1807
14th Regiment	1807
7th Regiment Light Dragoons	1807
34th Regiment of Foot	1807
79th Regiment of Foot, later 1st Battalion, 91st Regiment	1813
2nd Battalion 50th Regiment of Foot	1808
Royal Scots Regiment	1808
4th Battalion Royal Artillery	1809
68th Regiment	1810
Officers' Lodge	1810
Royal Cornwall Regiment of Militia	1810
2nd Regiment West York Militia	1811
5th Battalion Royal Artillery	1812
9th Battalion Royal Artillery	1812
10th Battalion Royal Artillery	1813
80th Regiment of Foot	1813
1st Regiment of Bengal Artillery	1814
5th Regiment of Dragoon Guards	1815
51st Regiment of Foot	1816
33rd Regiment of Foot	1816
90th Regiment of Foot	1817
46th Regiment	1817
57th Regiment	1818
91st Regiment	1818
6th Regiment of Foot	1820
8th Regiment of Hussars	1822
7th Regiment Native Infantry	1823
1st Battalion, Rifle Brigade	1826
Oxford Light Infantry (52nd Regiment)	1827
5th Regiment of Foot	1830
37th Regiment	1844
89th Regiment of Foot	1844
14th Regiment of Foot	1846
Honourable Artillery Company	1849
31st Regiment of Foot	1858
3rd Regiment of Foot	1858

2nd Battalion, 12th Regiment of Foot	1860
37th Company Royal Engineers	1863

Sources:
Grand Lodge of Ireland, *Register of Warranted Lodges.*
Grand Lodge of Scotland, *Register of Warranted Lodges.*
United Grand Lodge of England, *Register of Warranted Lodges.*
Lane's *Masonic Records, op. cit.*
R.F. Gould, *Military Lodges 1732–1899, op. cit.*

Appendix 4

THE MASONIC MEMBERSHIP OF SELECTED PROFESSIONAL SOCIETIES

The Royal Society of Apothecaries

Member		Admitted FRSA	Masonic Office	Lodge
John	Aldridge	1726		The Half Moon, Cheapside
Robert	Allen	1719		The Ship Behind the Royal Exchange
George	Armstrong	1711	Steward	Not Known
John	Arnold	1702	Warden	The Black Boy & Sugar Loaf
Benjamin	Ballard	1720	Warden	The Bull's Head, Southwark
Richard	Barker	1702		The Lion, Brewers Street
Thomas	Barker	1721		The Rainbow Coffee House, York Buildings
Robert	Barnard	1722		The Queen's Head Turnstile, Holborn
Edward	Boswell	1735		The King's Arms, Cateton Street
Thomas	Boucher	1737		The Horn Tavern, Westminster
Uppington	Bracey	1725		White Heart without Bishopsgate
Charles	Brown	1739	Master	The Griffin, Newgate Street
John	Brown	1704		The Queen's Head Turnstile, Holborn
John	Browne	1738		The Bell Tavern, Westminster
Isaac	Bushell	1732		The Queen's Arms, Newgate Street
Joseph	Chapman	1710		The Rummer, Henrietta Street
Francis	Clark	1739	Warden	The Queen's Head, Knaves Acre
John	Clarke	1714/19		Ben's Coffee House, New Bond Street
Edward	Clement	1715		The Mason's Arms, Fulham
Matthew	Clerk	1707		The Crown at St Giles
Richard	Cole	1711		The Vine Tavern, Holborn
Henry	Collins	1706		The Fountain Tavern, Strand
John	Cook	1720		The Rainbow Coffee House, York Buildings
James	Cooke	1721		The Swan, Tottenham High Cross
Richard	Cox	1734		The Queen's Head, Hollis Street
William	Crow	1714		The Maid's Head, Norwich
John	Davis	1701		The Crown Behind the Royal Exchange
Richard	Davis	1712		The Vine Tavern, Holborn

228   Appendix 4

Thomas	Davis	1732		The Crown Behind the Royal Exchange
John	Devall	1739		The Ship on Fish Street Hill
Walter	Dobell	1711		The Vine Tavern, Holborn
Edward	Edwards	1710		Not Known
John	Everard	1709	Warden	The Bull's Head, Southwark
John	Field	1710		The Griffin, Newgate Street
William	Fletcher	1717		The Vine Tavern, Holborn
Francis	Freeman	1723		The Rummer, Henrietta Street
John	Gardiner	1739		The King's Arms, St Paul's
Thomas	Goodard	1721		The King's Head, Ivy Lane
Thomas	Hankin	1725		The St Paul's Head, Ludgate Street
George	Harris	1708	Master	The Swan, Chichester
Thomas	Harris	1733		The King's Head, Fleet Street
John	Harrison	1716		Lebecks Head, Maiden Lane
Charles	Hay	1704		The Rummer, Charing Cross
Edward	Heath	1708		The Vine Tavern, Holborn
John	Hill	1710		The Sun, Southside, St Paul's
Thomas	Hill	1700		The Queen's Head Turnstile, Holborn
John	Hoyles	1729		The Oxford Arms, Ludgate Street
Charles	Hughes	1739		The Globe Tavern, Moorgate
Richard	Hull	1724		The Queen's Arms, Newgate Street
Edward	Hyde	1707		Black Boy & Sugar Loaf, Stanhope Street
Charles	Jackson	1711		The King's Arms, St Paul's
George	Jackson	1719		The Ship without Temple Bar
John	Jackson	1734	Warden	The Horn & Feathers, Wood Street
John	James	1712		The Swan, East Street, Greenwich
William	James	1721		The Queen's Head, Hoxton
Thomas	Jephson	1730		The Bedford Head, Covent Garden
Edward	Johnson	1730		The Castle Tavern, St Giles
John	Johnson	1701		The Swan Tavern, Fish Street Hill
David	Jones	1700		The Bell Tavern, Westminster
Thomas	Jones	1700		The Griffin, Newgate Street
Thomas	Jones	1704		The Rainbow Coffee House, York Buildings
William	Jones	1714	Warden	The Vine Tavern, Holborn
Samuel	Keck	1721	Warden	The Griffin, Newgate Street
Thomas	Kentish	1727		The Castle & Legg, Holborn
William	Kindleside	1717		The Dolphin, Tower Street
James	Kittleby	1730	Warden	The Blew Posts, Holborn
William	Lane	1735		The Ship on Fish Street Hill
Thomas	Lewis	1736	Master	The Devil at TempleBar
James	Lucas	1714		The Crown Behind the Royal Exchange
Roger	Manley	1717		The Bedford Head, Covent Garden
Richard	Manningham	1709		The Horn Tavern, Westminster
James	Martin	1707		The King's Head, Fleet Street
John	Martin	1726	Warden	The Golden Lion, Dean Street
John	May	1706		The Black Posts, Great Wild Street
William	Miles	1719		The Crown, Acton

Appendix 4 229

Richard	Mitchell	1728		The Horn, Westminster
John	Moor	1700		The Ship Behind the Royal Exchange
Thomas	Moore	1708		The Rose Tavern without Temple Bar
Thomas	Moore	1735		The University Lodge
Robert	Nichols	1720		King's Head, Pall Mall
Thomas	Nicholson	1707		The Baptist Head, Chancery Lane
John	Parsons	1716		Ben's Coffee House, New Bond Street
John	Payne	1718		The Green Lettuce, Brownlow Street
Henry	Perkins	1723		Tom's Coffee House, Clare Street
Henry	Perkins	1723		Not Known
Daniel	Peters	1712		The Griffin, Newgate Street
George	Pile	1731		The Bedford Head, Covent Garden
James	Pitt	1704		The Bedford Head, Covent Garden
Henry	Prude	1721	Master	The Queen's Head, Queen Street
Benjamin	Radcliffe	1727		The Ship without Temple Bar
John	Rawling	1703	Warden	Freemasons Coffee House, New Belton Street
William	Read	1719	Warden	The Swan, Long Acre
John	Reynolds	1711		The Queen's Head, Great Queen Street
Joseph	Riddle	1717		The Castle Tavern, St Giles
Edward	Roberts	1724		The Crown, St Giles
William	Roberts	1703		The Crown Behind the Royal Exchange
Thomas	Row(e)	1702		The King's Arms, St Paul's
Samuel	Ryley	1721		The Red Lyon, Richmond, Surrey
James	Smith	1706	Warden	The Mitre Tavern, Covent Garden
Richard	Springwell	1713		The Swan Tavern, Fish Street Hill
Poston	Starye	1723		The Three Tuns, Newgate Street
Robert	Taylor	1715		The Crown Behind the Royal Exchange
William	Thomas	1704		The Castle & Legg, Holborn
Richard	Thompson	1702		Mitre Tavern Covent Garden
John	Thorpe	1718		The Bell Tavern, Westminster
William	Tomlinson	1714		The Swan Tavern, Fish Street Hill
John	Turner	1702		The Bell Tavern, Westminster
William	Turner	1723		The Vine Tavern, Holborn
Henry	Vaughan	1701		The Nag's Head & Star, Carmarthen
John	Watson	1713		The Crown, Acton
William	Watson	1738		The Queen's Head, Knaves Acre
Thomas	Weeks	1702		The Bear & Harrow, Butcher Row
Thomas	Wharton	1722		The King's Arms, St Paul's
John	White	1718		The Vine Tavern, Holborn
Robert	Willis	1727		The Blue Posts, Holborn
Abraham	Winterbottom	1712		St Paul's Head, Ludgate Street
John	Wood	1703		St Paul's Head, Ludgate Street

John	Wright	1736		The Ship Behind the Royal Exchange
Richard	Wright	1705		King's Arms, St Paul's

Sources:
Membership Lists of Royal Society of Apothecaries, unpublished.
Grand Lodge Minutes.

Disclaimer:
Given the duplication and misspelling of names, and the absence of corroborative evidence, the above list cannot be regarded as definitive.

The Royal College of Physicians

Member		Masonic Rank	Lodge
John	Arbuthnot		The Bedford's Head, Southampton Row
John	Arnold		The Black Boy & Sugar Loaf, Stanhope Street
John	Beauford		The Goat at the Foot of the Haymarket
John	Birch		The Swan in East Street, Greenwich
Charles	Brown	Master	The Griffin, Newgate Street
William	Chambers		The Crown, St Giles
Benjamin	Chandler		The Buffaloe, Bloomsbury
Samuel	Chapman		The Greyhound, Fleet Street
John	Chapman		The Three Kings in Spitalfield
John	Clarke		Ben's Coffee House, Bond Street
Thomas	Clerk		The Swan, Ludgate Street
Daniel	Cox	Prov. GM NY	Not Known
James	Douglas		The Cross Keys, Henrietta Street
John	Elliott		The Bull's Head, Southwark
James	Figg		The Castle Tavern, St Giles
John	Gorman		Denmark's Head, Cavendish Street
John	Green		The Half Moon, The Strand
Stephen	Hall	Master	The Ship, Bartholomew's Lane
George	Harris	Master	The Swan, Chichester
Thomas	Hodgson	Master	The Anchor & Baptists Head
Edward	Hody	GW, GS	The Cross Keys, Henrietta Street
John	Hunter	Warden	The Swan, Ludgate Street
William	Hunter	Master	The Swan, Ludgate Street
John	Latham	Warden	The Crown, Behind the Royal Exchange
John	Leake	Warden	The Goose & Grid Iron, St Paul's Church Yard
Thomas	Leigh		The Star & Garter, Covent Garden
Thomas	Lewis	Master	The Old Devil at Temple Bar
Thomas	Lovell		The Coach & Horses, Maddocks Street

Richard	Manningham		The Horn, Westminster
William	Martin		The Three Kings in Spitalfield
John	Matthews		The Black Lyon in Jockey Fields
John	Misaubin	GW, GS	Not Known
John	Montagu	GM	The Bear & Harrow, Covent Garden
John	Morgan		The Crown behind the Royal Exchange
John	Parsons		Ben's Coffee House, Bond Street
John	Potter	Dep. GS	Not Known
Richard	Powell	Master	The Three Compasses, Silver Street
John	Pringle		The Ship Behind the Royal Exchange
Samuel	Pye		The Queen's Head, Bath
Charles	Richmond & Lennox	GM, Master	The Horn, Westminster
Robert	Robertson		The Crown without Cripplegate
Richard	Saunders		The Queen's Arms in Newgate Street
Isaac	Schomberg	GS	The Swan & Rummer, Finch lane
Charles	Scott	GS	Not Known
Joseph	Shaw		The Wool Pack, Warwick
John	Squire		The Dolphin, Tower Street
Alexander	Stuart		The Rummer, Charing Cross
Robert	Taylor		The Crown behind the Royal Exchange
John	Turner		The Bell Tavern, Westminster
William	Vaughan		The Rummer, Queen Street, Cheapside
James	Walker		The Queen's Head, Knaves Acre
William	Watson		The Queen's Head, Knaves Acre
George	Wharton		The Swan Tavern, Fish Street Hill
John	Whitehead		The White Bear, King Street, Golden Square
William	Williams		The Griffin, Newgate Street
Robert	Willis		The Blue Posts, Holborn
John	Woodward		The Crown behind the Royal Exchange
John	Wright		The Ship Behind the Royal Exchange

Sources:
William Munk, Lives of the Fellows of the Royal College of Physicians (London, 1861), vol. II.
Grand Lodge Minutes.

Disclaimer:
Given the duplication and misspelling of names, and the absence of corroborative evidenced, the above list cannot be regarded as definitive.

List of Abbreviatons

Add.	Additional
AQC *Transactions*	Ars Quatuor Coronatorum: Transactions of the Quatuor Coronati Lodge, No. 2076
BL	British Library
Bodleian	Bodleian Library, University of Oxford
Burney	The Burney newspaper collection at the British Library
CLSes	City of London Sessions
CMRC	Canonbury Masonic Research Centre, London
CRFF	Centre for Research into Freemasonry and Fraternalism, University of Sheffield
CUL	Cambridge University Library
DGM	Deputy Grand Master
ECCO	Eighteenth Century Collections On-line
EEBO	Early English Books On-line
EHR	English Historical Review
fo./fo.s	Folio/folios
FRCP	Fellow of the College of Physicians
FRS	Fellow of the Royal Society
FSA	Fellow of the Society of Antiquarians
GM	Grand Master, Grand Lodge of England
GMY	Grand Master (or President), York
GO	General Orders of the Court
Grand Lodge	Grand Lodge of England (formerly known as the Grand Lodge of London)
Grand Lodge Minutes	*Minutes of the Grand Lodge of Freemasons of England, 1723–39*, reprinted as *QCA*, vol. X (London, 1913). If qualified '1740–58': *Minutes of the Grand Lodge of Freemasons of England, 1740–58*, reprinted as *QCA*, vol. XII (Margate, 1960)
GS	Grand Secretary
GTr	Grand Treasurer
GW	Grand Warden
IHR	Institute of Historical Research
HS	The Huguenot Society, London
JGW	Junior Grand Warden

List of Abbreviations

JP	Justice of the Peace
JWP	Justices' Working Papers / Documents
KG	Knight of the Garter
KT	Knight of the Thistle
LMA	London Metropolitan Archives
MS(S)	Manuscript(s)
MSes	Middlesex Sessions
NA	National Archives
ODNB	*Oxford Dictionary of National Biography*
OKA	Old King's Arms Lodge, the Strand, No. 28
OKA *Minutes*	The first extant Minute book of the OKA
QC	Quatuor Coronati Lodge, No. 2076
QCA	*Quatuor Coronatorum Antigrapha*
QCCC	Quatuor Coronati Correspondence Circle Limited
RS	The Royal Society, London
SA	The Society of Antiquaries, London
Sackler Archives	The Sackler Archive of the Royal Society containing the Biographies of past Fellows
SP	Sessions Papers
SGW	Senior Grand Warden
VCH	Victoria County History
WM	Worshipful Master
WP	Working Papers
WSes	Westminster Sessions

Dating:
The Gregorian calendar was adopted in England in 1752, after which 1 January became the first day of the legal year rather than 25 March. Where feasible, events have dated using the (modern) Gregorian calendar.

Notes

PREFACE

1   R.A. Berman, *The Architects of Eighteenth Century English Freemasonry, 1720–40* (University of Exeter: PhD Thesis, 2010)

INTRODUCTION

1   John Hamill, *The Craft* (London, 1986), pp. 15–40, quote from pp. 17–18.
2   Jan A.M. Snoek, 'Researching Freemasonry. Where Are We?', *CRFF Working Paper Series*, 2 (2008), 1–28.
3   *Ibid.*, 20.
4   Peter Clark, *British Clubs and Societies 1580–1800* (Oxford, 2000).
5   Jessica Harland-Jacobs, *Builders of Empire Builders of Empire: Freemasonry and British Imperialism, 1717–1927* (Chapel Hill, 2007), pp. 1–20.
6   Jürgen Habermas, transl. Thomas Burger, *The Structural Transformation of the Public Sphere: An Inquiry into a Category of Bourgeois Society* (Cambridge, 1989).
7   Pierre-Yves Beaurepaire, 'The Universal Republic of the Freemasons and the Culture of Mobility in the Enlightenment', *French Historical Studies*, 29.3 (2006), 407–31.
8   Douglas Knoop & G.P. Jones, *Genesis of Freemasonry* (Manchester, 1947); and Knoop & Jones, *The Mediaeval Mason* (Manchester, 1933).
9   David Stevenson, *The Origins of Freemasonry, Scotland's Century, 1590–1710* (Cambridge, 1990); and Stevenson, *The First Freemasons: Scotland's Early Lodges and their Members* (Aberdeen, 1988).
10 The comment was made at the 11th International CMRC conference on 'The Origins of Freemasonry' on 23 October 2009.
11 Margaret Jacob, *Living The Enlightenment: Freemasonry and Politics in Eighteenth-Century Europe* (London, 1991); and Jacob, *The Radical Enlightenment*, 2nd rev. edition (Lafayette, 2006).
12 Margaret Jacob, *The Origins of Freemasonry: Facts and Fictions* (London, 2006).
13 David Stevenson, *Reviews in History*, no. 517 (2006): www.history.ac.uk/reviews/review/517.
14 Andrew Prescott, 'A History of British Freemasonry, 1425–2000', *CRFF Working Paper Series*, No. 1 (2008), 1–29, quote taken from 3.
15 'Charge after Initiation', *Emulation Ritual* (London, 1996), p. 98.
16 James Anderson, *The constitutions of the Freemasons . . .* (London, 1723) (the "1723 Constitutions".)

CHAPTER ONE English Freemasonry before the Formation of Grand Lodge

1. Andrew Prescott, 'The Old Charges Revisited', *Transactions of the Lodge of Research, No. 2429, Leicester* (2006).
2. David Loschky and Ben D. Childers, 'Early English Mortality', *Journal of Interdisciplinary History*, 24.1 (1993), 85–97; also Faye Marie Getz, 'Black Death and the Silver Lining' *Journal of the History of Biology*, 24.2 (1991), 265–89.
3. Gervase Rosser, 'Parochial Conformity and Voluntary Religion in Late-Medieval England', *Transactions of the Royal Historical Society*, 6th series, 1 (1991), 173–89.
4. L.R. Poos, 'The Social Context of Statute of Labourers Enforcement', *Law and History Review*, 1.1 (1983), 27–52; and Chris Given-Wilson, 'The Problem of Labour in the Context of the English Government, c. 1350–1450', in Bothwell, Goldberg and Ormrod (eds.), *The Problem of Labour in Fourteenth-Century England* (York, 2000), pp. 85–100.
5. Chris Given-Wilson, *Service, Serfdom and English Labour Legislation, 1350–1500*, in Anne Curry and Elizabeth Matthew (eds.), *Concepts and Patterns of Service in the later Middle Ages* (Woodbridge, 2000), pp. 21–37, provides a detailed overview of the relevant labour legislation.
6. W.M. Ormrod, 'The Peasants' Revolt and the Government of England', *Journal of British Studies*, 29.1 (1990), 1–30.
7. R.S. Gottfried, 'Population, Plague, and the Sweating Sickness: Demographic Movements in Late Fifteenth-Century England', *Journal of British Studies*, 17.1 (1977), 12–37; also Mark Bailey, 'Demographic Decline in Late Medieval England: Some Thoughts', *Economic History Review*, n.s. 49.1 (1996), 1–19.
8. Henry Phelps Brown and Sheila V. Hopkins, *A Perspective of Wages and Prices* (London, 1981), pp. 3–61. Cf. also, Simon A.C. Penn and Christopher Dyer, 'Wages and Earnings in Late Medieval England: Evidence from the Enforcement of the Labour Laws', *Economic History Review*, n.s. 43.3 (1990), 356–76.
9. Knoop and Jones, *The Mediaeval Mason*, p. 206.
10. John Munro, 'The Monetary Origins of the 'Price Revolution': South German Silver Mining, Merchant-Banking, and Venetian Commerce, 1470–1540', *University of Toronto, Dept. of Economics Working Paper*, 8 June 1999, rev. 21 March 2003.
11. G. Davies, *A History of Money from Ancient Times to the Present Day* (Cardiff, 1996), rev. edn., pp. 187, 197–206.
12. Ernest L. Sabine, 'Butchering in Medieval London', *Speculum*, 8.3 (1933), 335–53, provides a useful review of guild regulation and the butchers' trade in medieval London.
13. Avner Greif, Paul Milgrom, Barry R. Weingast, 'Coordination, Commitment, and Enforcement: The Case of the Merchant Guild', *Journal of Political Economy*, 102.4 (1994), 745–66, reviews the origins of and justification for medieval merchant guilds.
14. Gervase Rosser, 'Crafts, Guilds and the Negotiation of Work in the Medieval Town', *Past & Present*, 154 (1997), 3–31, offers a more complete overview of the shifting arrangements surrounding craft guild structures.
15. J.A. Raftis, *Peasant Economic Development within the English Manorial System* (Montreal, 1996), provides an analysis of early agrarian capitalism,

labour segmentation and mobility. It follows his earlier pioneering work, *Tenure and Mobility* (Toronto, 1964).

16   Knoop and Jones, *The Mediaeval Mason*, pp. 86–9, esp. p. 88, fn. 5.
17   P.M. Tillott (ed.), *A History of the County of York* (London, 1961), pp. 91–7, 166–73 and 173–86.
18   Knoop and Jones, *The Mediaeval Mason*, pp. 223–233.
19   Maurice Dobb, *Studies in the Development of Capitalism* (London, 1946), p. 97.
20   Heather Swanson, 'The Illusion of Economic Structure: Craft Guilds in Late Mediaeval English Towns', *Past & Present*, 121 (1988), 29–48, esp. 30–1.
21   Dobb, *Studies in the Development of Capitalism*, pp. 89–90.
22   W. Preston, *Illustrations of Masonry* (London, 1796), p. 184.
23   With regard to York, cf. R.B. Dobson, 'Admissions to the Freedom of the City of York in the Later Middle Ages', *Economic History Review*, n.s. 26.1 (1973), 1–22, and Swanson, 'The Illusion of Economic Structure', 46–8.
24   Sheilagh Ogilvie, 'Guilds, Efficiency, and Social Capital: Evidence from German Proto-Industry', *Economic History Review*, n.s. 57.2 (2004), 286–333, offers a complementary perspective on the German guilds.
25   Gervase Rosser, 'Going to the Fraternity Feast: Commensality and Social Relations in Late Medieval England', *Journal of British Studies*, 33.4 (1994), 430–46.
26   Ibid., 431.
27   Ibid., esp. 433–438, quote from 438.
28   Peter Kebbell, *The Changing Face of Freemasonry, 1640–1740* (University of Bristol, unpublished PhD Thesis, 2009), pp. 13–15.
29   Cf. Jacob, *Living the Enlightenment* (Oxford, 1991), pp. 38–40. The example of a Dundee operative Masonic guild which provided non-Masons or 'strangers' with the benefit of 'freedom' of the guild upon payment of £10, is a clear (albeit Scottish) instance of the principle of admitting non-Masons to alleviate financial problems.
30   R.F. Gould, *The History of Freemasonry: Its Antiquities, Symbols, Constitutions, Customs, Etc.* (Whitefish, 2003), part 2, pp. 141–2, provides such an analysis of the lodge meeting at Warrington in 1646. This reprint was published by the Kessinger Publishing Co. of Whitefish, Montana. The original was published London, 1885.
31   Neville Barker-Cryer, 'The Restoration Lodge of Chester', November Conference of the Cornerstone Society 2002. Cf. www.cornerstonesociety.com/Insight/ Articles/restoration.pdf.
32   Neville Barker-Cryer, *York Mysteries Revealed* (York, 2006), p. 222
33   C.P. Lewis and A.T. Thacker, *A History of the County of Chester: The City of Chester* (2003), vol. 5, part 1, pp. 102–109.
34   Barker-Cryer, *York Mysteries Revealed*, p. 222.
35   The position is wholly in contrast to the myriad written and artistic references to Freemasonry that followed the appointment of the first noble Grand Master in 1720.
36   Elias Ashmole, *Memoirs of the life of that learned antiquary, Elias Ashmole, Esq; drawn up by himself by way of diary* (London, 1717).
37   Richard Rawlinson, *Preface*, in Elias Ashmole, *The Antiquities of Berkshire* (London, 1719), vol. 1, p. vi.
38   Robert Plot, *The Natural history of Staffordshire* (Oxford, 1686).

39 Randle Holme III, *An Academie of Armorie, or, A storehouse of Armory and Blazon* (Chester, 1688).
40 John Aubrey, *The Natural History of Wiltshire* (Oxford, 1691).
41 Tangentially and in common with Ashmole, Aubrey and Plot, Rawlinson was also an Oxford graduate and FRS, albeit several decades later.
42 Cf. O. Bucholz, 'Herbert, Thomas, eighth earl of Pembroke and fifth earl of Montgomery (1656/7–1733)', *ODNB*. His son, Henry Herbert, the 9th Earl, was later a prominent Freemason.
43 John Locke, *Letter to the Right Hon. Thomas Earl of Pembroke, with an old Manuscript on the subject of Freemasonry*, dated 6 May 1696. The letter and MS are quoted in W. Preston, *Illustrations of Freemasonry* (London, 1812), book III, section I, pp. 79–81. Cf. also, Thomas William Tew, J. Matthewman, *Masonic Miscellanea, Comprising a Collection of Addresses and Speeches* (Whitefish, 2003), p. 229.
44 *State Papers Domestic, Entry Book 68*, pp. 59–60, in F.H. Blackburne Daniell (ed.), *Calendar of State Papers Domestic: Charles II, 4 April 1682* (London, 1932), pp. 148–88.
45 Victor Slater, 'John Grenville, Ist Earl of Bath (1628–1701)', *ODNB*.
46 BL, Egerton MS 2872.
47 Cf. Lois G. Schwoerer, 'The Attempted Impeachment of Sir William Scroggs, Lord Chief Justice of the Court of King's Bench', *Historical Journal*, 38.4 (1995), 843–873.
48 Doreen J. Milne, 'The Results of the Rye House Plot and Their Influence upon the Revolution of 1688', *Transactions of the Royal Historical Society*, 5th series, 1 (1951), 91–108.
49 Rosser, 'Going to the Fraternity Feast', 446.
50 'Mr. Robert Parker to the Trustees, Dec, 1734': *The Egmont (Sir John Perceval) Papers: letters from Georgia, June 1732–June 1735*, p. 158. The original papers are in the BL: Add. MSS. Perceval Family, 46920–47213.
51 Cf. respectively, Ashmole, *Memoirs*; Aubrey, *Natural History of Wiltshire*; and Plot, *The Natural History of Staffordshire*.
52 Tobias Churton, *Freemasonry: The Reality* (Hersham, 2007), p. 210.
53 A. Prescott, 'The Earliest Use of the Word Freemason', *Yearbook of the Grand Lodge of Scotland 2004* (Edinburgh, 2004): www.freemasons-Freemasonry.com/prescott02.html.
54 J.S. Brewer (ed.), *Letters and Papers, Foreign and Domestic* (London, 1875), vol. 4, p. 1129: *Henry VIII: September 1526, 16–30*.
55 Johannis Rastell, *The Statutes Prohemium* (London, 1527).
56 John Foxe, *Actes and Monuments* (London, 1583).
57 Raphael Hollinshead, *The Third Volume of Chronicles, beginning at Duke William* (London, 1586).
58 John Stow, *Survey of London* (London, 1633).
59 Alexander Brome, *The Cunning Lovers* (London, 1654).
60 Thomas Blount, *Glossographia, or, A Dictionary* (London, 1661).
61 James Howell, *Londinopolis* (London, 1657), p. 44.
62 Zachary Babington, *Notice to Grand Jurors in Cases of Blood* (London, 1677).
63 *The Tatler*, 7–9 June 1709 and 29 April – 2 May 1710. The quote is from the latter.
64 Richard Steele, *The Lucubrations of Isaac Bickerstaff Esq.* (London, 1712), vol. 3, p. 258.

65   *Poor Robin's Intelligence*, 10 October 1676.
66   Andrew Marvell, *The Rehearsal Transprosed* (London, 1672).
67   B.E. (compiler, known only by his initials), *A New Dictionary of the Terms Ancient and Modern of the Canting Crew* (London, c. 1699).
68   But cf. Knoop and Jones, *The Scottish mason and the Mason Word* (Manchester, 1939).
69   The lodge at Alnwick, Northumberland, the only English masonic lodge of the pre-1720 period for which relatively comprehensive documentation is extant, was at the time also a working or 'operative' lodge. However, the lodge should not be viewed as a reliable guide as to what was occurring elsewhere in England. Being thirty miles south of the Scottish border, the lodge followed Scottish customs. Cf. William James Hughan, *The Alnwick MS, No. E 10* (Newcastle, 1895).
70   Knoop and Jones, *The Genesis of Freemasonry* (Manchester, 1947). Cf. chap. 7: 'The Era of Accepted Masonry'.
71   Holme, *Academie of Armorie*, p. LXVI.
72   *Ibid.*, Preface.
73   I.H. Jeayes (ed.), *The Academy of Armory, or a Storehouse of Armory and Blazon* (London, 1905). Printed from BL: Harleian MSS. 1920–2180.
74   Holme, *Academie of Armorie*, p. 459. However, Neville Barker-Cryer has argued that at least part of Holme's *Academie* can be regarded as allegorical: cf. 'The Restoration Lodge of Chester', *op. cit.*
75   A.T. Thacker & C.P. Lewis (eds.), *Mayors and sheriffs of Chester, A History of the County of Chester: vol. 5, part 2: The City of Chester: Culture, Buildings, Institutions* (London, 2005), pp. 305–321. Cf. also, Cheshire and Chester Archives: ZA/B/2/63v-64, 64v, 64v-65,65–66v, 66v-67, 67–67v, 68-68v, 82; P1/145, *1532–1867*.
76   His heraldic work for the Garrard family in 1672 is mentioned in the Hertfordshire Archives: DE/Gd/27286.
77   J.P. Earwaker, *The four Randle Holmes of Chester, antiquaries, heraldists and genealogists, c. 1571 to 1707* (Chester, 1892), pp. 113–70.
78   'Parliamentary Ordnance 1 October 1646 removing Holme and others from their offices and assemblies on political grounds': Cheshire and Chester Archives: ZA/B/2/76.
79   Frederick Tupper, Jr., 'The Holme Riddles', *PMLA – Journal of the Modern Language Association of America*, 18.2 (1903), 212.
80   The archival records of the Home family are held at the Cheshire and Chester Archives. See Bibliography for detailed references. Holme worked principally as a heraldic painter but was unlicensed and his work deemed unlawful. The contravention led to his being sued by Dugdale as Norroy King of Arms. Dugdale's suit succeeded, but they were later reconciled and Holme subsequently worked for Dugdale at the College of Arms. Cf. Anthony R.J.S. Adolph, 'Randle Holme, (1627–1700)', *ODNB*.
81   Holme, *An Academie of Armorie*, p. 61.
82   *Ibid.*, p. 393.
83   Cf. Henry Sadler, W.J. Chetwode Crawley, *Masonic Reprints and Historical Revelations* (Whitefish, 2003), Preface, p. iv; Alfred Ingham, *Cheshire: Its Traditions and History* (Whitefish, 2003), p. 289; and Stevenson, *The Origins of Freemasonry: Scotland's Century, 1590–1710*, pp. 224–5.

84 Lewis & Thacker (eds.), *A History of the County of Chester* (London, 2003), vol. 5.1, pp. 137–45.
85 John Lane, *Masonic Records 1717–1894* (Sheffield, 2009).
86 Ingham, *Cheshire*, p. 292. Cf. also, Lewis & Thacker, *A History of the County of Chester*, pp. 137–45.
87 Lewis & Thacker, *op. cit.*; also W.B. Stephens (ed.), *A History of the County of Warwick* (London, 1969), vol. 8, pp. 505–14.
88 Thomas Tryon, *Tryon's letters upon several occasions* (London, 1700), also published as *The merchant, citizen and country-man's Instructor* (London, 1701).
89 Thomas Tryon, *Healths Grand Preservative* (London, 1682), chap. 2, Of Flesh.
90 Thomas Tryon, *Pythagoras; His Mystick Philosophy Reviv'd* (London, 1691).
91 William Stukeley, (W.C. Lukis (ed.)), *Family Memoirs of William Stukeley* (London, 1883), vol. 1, p. 51.
92 R.F. Gould, *The Concise History of Freemasonry* (London, 1951), revised edn., p. 113.
93 Jacob cites R.D. Gray, *Goethe, the Alchemist* (Cambridge, 1952), pp. 49, 177 and *passim*, for evidence of a relationship between eighteenth-century Masonic symbolism and the alchemical tradition: cf. Jacob, *The Radical Enlightenment*, p. 107, fn. 12.
94 Ashmole, *Memoirs*, pp. 15–16.
95 *Ibid.*, p. 66.
96 *Ibid.*, p. 66. In the posthumous publication of the Memoirs in 1717, the word 'by' appears after 'Fellowship of Freemasons'. The word is not in Ashmole's original manuscript and has been omitted as redundant.
97 *Ibid.*, pp. 66–7.
98 *The Masonic Magazine: A Monthly Digest of Freemasonry in All Its Branches*. The magazine was published in London by George Kenning. The relevant article by W.H. Rylands, 'Freemasonry in Seventeenth Century Warrington', appeared in the December 1881 issue. Cf. George M. Martin, *British Masonic Miscellany, Part 2* (Whitefish, 2003), p. 25. The article was also mentioned by Gould in *The History of Freemasonry*, pp. 156, 183–8. Rylands' collection of Masonic MSS was donated to the Bodleian: MSS Rylands, b. 1-11, c. 1-30, c. 32-8, c. 40–69, d. 1-57, e. 1-54, f. 1-9.
99 Churton, *Freemasonry – The Reality*, pp. 172–9, 273.
100 Kebbell, *The Changing Face of Freemasonry*, pp. 23–5.
101 Yasha Beresiner, 'Elias Ashmole – Masonic Icon', *MQ Magazine*, 11 (2004), 3–8.
102 Gould, *The History of Freemasonry*, pp. 183–8.
103 'Entry for 20 March, 1684', *Money Book*, vol. IV, pp. 355–6, in William A Shaw (ed.), *Calendar of Treasury Books* (London, 1916), vol. 7, p. 1077.
104 Prescott, 'The Old Charges Revisited', *Transactions of the Lodge of Research*.
105 George T. Noszlopy and Fiona Waterhouse, *Public Sculpture of Staffordshire and the Black Country* (Liverpool, 2005), illustrated edn., p. 273.
106 *Wren Society* (Oxford, 1924–1943), vol. XVIII, pp. 108–9.
107 *Ibid.*, pp. xxv, 198–9, 235–6, 270, 277, 292–3.
108 Michael Hunter, 'Elias Ashmole (1617–1692)', *ODNB*.
109 'An account by Elias Ashmole, then Windsor Herald, of the Feast of the Exaltation of the Cross, and a transcription of the Greek and Latin inscription

on a medal struck by the Emperor Heraclius': Lambeth Palace Library: MS 929, *1611–1723*, 43, 2 ff.
110 Sir Robert Moray had been initiated into Freemasonry when serving with the Scottish forces besieging Newcastle-upon-Tyne. His admittance into St. Mary's Chapel Lodge of Edinburgh was recorded on 20 May 1641. Cf. David Allan, 'Sir Robert Moray (1608/9?–1673)', *ODNB*.
111 Cf. C.H. Josten (ed.), *Elias Ashmole (1617–1692): His Autobiographical and Historical Notes* (Oxford, 1966). The Royal Society was formed in 1660 and granted a Royal Charter on 15 July 1662; a second Royal Charter extending its rights was granted by Charles II on 22 April 1663.
112 Matthew Scanlan, 'Nicholas Stone and the Mystery of the Acception', *Freemasonry Today*, 12 (2002); and 'The Mystery of the Acception, 1630–1723: A Fatal Flaw', *Heredom*, 11 (2003).
113 Scanlan, 'Nicholas Stone and the Mystery of the Acception'.
114 Daily pay rates as per Babington, *Notice to Grand Jurors*.
115 Adam White, 'Nicholas Stone', *ODNB*.
116 Centre for Kentish Studies: U269/A462/5: 1639.
117 Society of Antiquaries: SAL/MS/263.
118 John Newman, 'Nicholas Stone's Goldsmiths' Hall: Design and Practice in the 1630s', *Architectural History*, 14 (1971), 30–141.
119 *Ibid*.
120 White, 'Nicholas Stone', *ODNB*.
121 Douglas Knoop and G. P. Jones, *The Genesis of Freemasonry* (London, 1978), pp. 146–7.
122 W.J. Songhurst (ed.), *The Minutes of the Grand Lodge of Freemasons of England 1723–1739, Masonic Reprints Volume X* (London, 1913), ('*Grand Lodge Minutes*'), pp. 5, 23.
123 *Grand Lodge Minutes*, p. 158.
124 LMA: CC, MC *9 July 1718*.
125 Michael Hunter, *John Aubrey and the Realm of Learning* (London, 1975), pp. 88–9.
126 Adam Fox, 'John Aubrey (1626–1697)', *ODNB*. Cf. also, Herefordshire Record Office: Records of the Belmont Estate, C38.
127 Robert G. Frank Jr., 'John Aubrey, FRS, John Lydall, and Science at Commonwealth Oxford', *RS Notes and Records*, 27.2 (1973), 193–217.
128 *Ibid*., 85, 194.
129 Staffordshire Record Office: D868/5/12b: *21 November 1657*.
130 Graham Parry, 'Sir William Dugdale (1605–1686)', *ODNB*.
131 *Ibid*.
132 'Entry for 18 April 1677, Docquet Book, p. 126', in William A Shaw (ed.) *Calendar of Treasury Books* (London, 1911), vol. 5, p. 602.
133 Philip Styles (ed.), *A History of the County of Warwick* (London, 1945), vol. 3, pp. 13–14, editorial note; also Michael Hunter, *Elias Ashmole*.
134 Parry, 'Sir William Dugdale', *ODNB*, mentions a visit by Ashmole at Christmas 1656.
135 *Ibid*.
136 A diplomat, soldier and MP, Sir Henry Goodricke was later Lieutenant-General of the Ordnance and stationed at the Tower of London. Cf. J.D. Davies, 'Sir Henry Goodricke, 2nd Baronet (1642–1705)', *ODNB*.
137 Cf., for example, Allan Beaver, 'Sir Christopher Wren and the Origins of

English Freemasonry', *Transactions of the Temple of Athene Lodge*, No. 9149, 15 (2008/2009), 22–38.
138 *ECCO: Eighteenth Century Collections Online*, and *EEBO: Early English Books On-line*, contain digital facsimile page images of books printed in England, Ireland, Scotland, Wales and British North America, and works in English printed elsewhere, from 1473–1800.
139 James Anderson, *The new book of constitutions of the antient and honourable fraternity of free and accepted masons. Containing their history, charges, regulations, etc.* (London, 1738) (the '*1738 Constitutions*').
140 The description was capitalised in the original.
141 Somerset Archive and Record Service: Rough General: Order Books Q/SOr 1613–1887.
142 *1738 Constitutions*, pp. 101–108.
143 Michael Leapman, *Inigo: The Troubled Life of Inigo Jones, Architect of the English Renaissance* (London, 2003), pp. 124–5.
144 *1723 Constitutions*, p. 82.
145 Mark Knights, 'A City Revolution: The Remodelling of the London Livery Companies in the 1680s', *English Historical Review*, 112.449 (1997), 1141–78.
146 Prescott, 'The Old Charges Revisited'.
147 Among many examples are Mackey, *Encyclopedia of Freemasonry*, vol. 3, p. 1390; Knoop and Jones, *The Genesis of Freemasonry*, pp. 144–6; Tobias Churton, 'Elias Ashmole and the Origins of Speculative Freemasonry', *Freemasonry Today*, 1 (1997) 8; and John Yarker, *The Arcane Schools* (New York, 2007), pp. 366–7 (originally published in 1909).
148 C.H. Josten, 'Elias Ashmole, FRS (1617–1692)', *Notes and Records of the Royal Society*, 15 (1960), 228. Cf. also, A.J. Turner, 'Robert Plot', *ODNB*.
149 *Ibid.*; also *Sackler Archives*.
150 Robert Plot, *Natural History of Oxfordshire* (Oxford, 1677). Cf. East Sussex Record Office: PAR513/26/1; also, Society of Antiquaries: SAL/MS/85 ff. iii + 13 *c. 1670*.
151 Cf. 'Commission from the Duke of Norfolk, Earl Marshall, appointing Robert Plot as Register of the Court of Chivalry': Society of Antiquaries: SAL/MS/597, 25 September 1687. Also, *Sackler Archives*.
152 Plot, *Natural History of Staffordshire*, pp. 316–17.
153 Plot, *Natural History of Staffordshire*, chapter VIII, pp. 316–17, paragraphs 85–88. Peter Kebbell in his unpublished PhD thesis suggests that the charitable assistance and mutual support offered by Freemasons to one another was the most significant aspect of the organisation during this period. He also argues that the 'sole purpose' of lodge meetings was to initiate new members. Kebbell, *op. cit.*, pp. 28–34. The social and economic aspects are ignored.
154 Gould, *The History of Freemasonry*, chapter XIV.
155 *Post Man and the Historical Account*, 9 August 1722.
156 The three articles were published in the *Post Man and the Historical Account* on 31 July, 4 August and 9 August 1722, respectively.
157 *The Spectator*, 1 March 1711.
158 Quoted in William Bragg Ewald Jr., *Rogues, Royalty and Reporters, The Age of Queen Anne through its Newspapers* (Boston, 1954), pp. 232–3.
159 Although the BL MSS catalogue contains three references to Fonvive, none are linked to Freemasonry.

160 William and Susan Minet (eds.), *Register of the Church of Hungerford Market* (London, 1928), vol. XXXI.
161 John Dunton, *Life and Errors of John Dunton, Citizen of London* (London, 1818), vol. I, p. 428. Originally published 1705.
162 *Ibid.*, vol. I, p. 438.
163 Itamar Raban, *The Post Man and its Editor, Jean Lespinasse de Fonvive* in Randolph Vine and Charles Littleton (eds.), *From Strangers to Citizens* (Brighton, Portland, Toronto, 2001), pp. 397–403.
164 William Minet & Susan Minet, *The Register of the French Churches of Chapel Royal St James's & Swallow Street* (London, 1924), vol. XXVIII, p. vi; *The Register of the French Churches of Le Carre and Berwick Street* (London, 1921), vol. XXV, p. ix; and *Register of the Church of St Martin Orgars* (London, 1935), vol. XXXVII, p. xli.
165 Rawlinson was ordained a priest in the Nonjuring Church of England in 1716; he was consecrated a bishop in 1728.
166 Bodleian: MSS. Rawlinson, 5122. The Rawlinson collection was donated both during his lifetime and as a bequest after his death.
167 *Grand Lodge Minutes*, pp. 164, 167 and 191.
168 Mary Clapinson, 'Richard Rawlinson', *ODNB*.
169 Cf. Raymond N. MacKenzie, 'Edmund Curll (*d.* 1747)', *ODNB*.
170 Ashmole, *Memoirs*, Preface, p. vi.
171 *1723 Constitutions*, p. 50, the *First Charge*.
172 Cf. Barker-Cryer, *York Mysteries Revealed*, pp. 173–218.
173 L.D. Schwarz, *London in the age of industrialisation: entrepreneurs, labour force and living conditions, 1700–1850* (Cambridge, 1992), p. 2.
174 Gould, *History of Freemasonry*, vol. II, p. 408.
175 The term 'Grand Master' came into being in York in *c.* 1725 following the formation of the Grand Lodge of England. The previously adopted term was 'President'.
176 Despite Marlborough's advice to the contrary, Belasyse was subject to court martial and cashiered over the sacking of Puerto Santa Maria in February 1703: cf. John Childs, 'Sir Henry Belasyse', *ODNB*.
177 Stuart Handley, 'Robert Benson, Baron Bingley', *ODNB*. Benson was an initial director of the South Sea Company and lost heavily when the share price plunged.
178 The Treaty of Seville between Britain, France and Spain, concluded the Anglo-Spanish war and paved the way for Treaty of Vienna the following year.
179 P.M. Tillot, *A History of the County of York, The City of York* (London, 1961), pp. 240–45.
180 Barker-Cryer, *York Mysteries Revealed*, pp. 226–7.
181 Tillot, *A History of the County of York*, pp. 240–5.
182 Barker-Cryer, *York Mysteries Revealed*, p. 226.
183 *1738 Constitutions*, p. 108
184 *Ibid.*, p. 106.
185 *Ibid.*, pp. 106–7.
186 Jacob, *The Radical Enlightenment*, p. 88.

CHAPTER TWO **John Theophilus Desaguliers: *Homo Masonicus***

1 Robert Burton, *Martyrs in Flames: or the history of Popery Displaying the horrid persecutions and cruelties exercised upon Protestants by the Papists, for many hundred years past* (London, 1729), 3rd edn., pp. 75–6.
2 John Harland (ed.), *The house and farm accounts of the Shuttleworths of Gawthorpe Hall, Part 2, Chetham Society Papers,* OS 41 (1856), p. 277; cf. also, Guildhall Library: MS 9535/3, fo. 33.
3 Audrey T. Carpenter, *Ingenious Philosopher* (University of Loughborough, unpublished PhD thesis, 2009), p. 15.
4 Ecclesiastical Court Records, Guernsey: transcribed in the *30th Annual Report of the Societe Guernais* (Guernsey, 1937–45), vol. 13–14, p. 339.
5 *Agnew, French Protestant Exiles,* p. 89, recorded a daughter who had died in 1678.
6 Patricia Fara, 'John Theophilus Desaguliers (1683–1744)', *ODNB;* R. William Weisberger, 'John Theophilus Desaguliers: Promoter of the Enlightenment and of Speculative Freemasonry', *AQC Transactions,* 113 (2000), 65–96; J. Stokes, 'Life of John Theophilus Desaguliers', *AQC Transactions,* 38 (1925), for example, all place Desaguliers' departure after the Revocation of the Edict of Nantes. They also state or assume that Desaguliers left with his father rather than his mother.
7 Robin Gwynn, *Huguenot Heritage* (Brighton, Portland, Toronto, 2001), 2nd edn., pp. 29–30.
8 *Le livre des tesmoinages de l'église de Threadneedle Street, 1669–1789* (London, 1909), vol. XXI, p. xv.
9 Jean Claude, *A Short Account of the Complaints and Cruel Persecutions of the Protestants in France (Les Plaintes des Protestantes cruellement opprimés dans le Royaume de France),* (London, 1708), 3rd English translation, Preface, pp. 9–10.
10 William & Susan Minet, *The Register of the French Churches of Chapel Royal St James's & Swallow Street* (London, 1924), vol. XXVIII, p. vi.
11 His name was recorded variously as 'Desagulier' and 'Desagulliers'.
12 Susan Minet (ed.), *The Register of the French Churches of La Patente de Soho, Wheeler Street, Swan Street & Hoxton* (London, 1956), vol. XLV, pp. xvii, 7, 51; and William & Susan Minet, *The Register of the French Churches of Le Carre and Berwick Street* (London, 1921), vol. XXV, pp. ix, 26.
13 William & Susan Minet, *The Register of the French Churches of Le Carre and Berwick Street,* p. 15.
14 William & Susan Minet, *The Register of the French Churches of St Martin Ongars & Swallow St* (London, 1935), vol. XXXVII, p. xxxiii.
15 *Ibid.,* pp. 15–17.
16 *Ibid.,* p. xxx.
17 *Athenian Gazette or Casuistical Mercury,* 10 October 1693: editorial and review of the first volume of John Dunton's, *The French Book of Martyrs, or the History of the Edict of Nantes* (London, 1693).
18 J.M. Hintermaier, 'The First Modern refugees? Charity, Entitlement and Persuasion in the Huguenot Immigration of the 1680s', *Albion,* 32.3 (2000), 429–49. Cf. also, Jean Francois Bion, *An account of the torments the French Protestants endure aboard the galleys* (London, 1708).
19 Gwynn, *Huguenot Heritage,* pp. 71–3.

20 P. Deane and W.A. Cole, *British Economic Growth, 1688–1959* (Cambridge, 1969), 2nd edn., p. 2.
21 E.g. William & Susan Minet, *The Register of the French Churches of St Martin Ongars and Swallow Street*, pp. xx–xxvii.
22 W. Wilson, *The History and Antiquities of Dissenting Churches and Meeting Houses in London* (London, 1814), vol. IV, pp. 33–4.
23 William & Susan Minet, *The Register of the French Churches of St Martin Ongars and Swallow Street*, p. xxxiv.
24 Cf. F.H.W. Sheppard (gen. ed.), *Survey of London* (London, 1963), vol. 31, pp. 57–67.
25 William A. Shaw (ed.), *Calendar of Treasury Books* (London, 1938), vol. 16, pp. 338; and 433–446, Appendix 1: *Lists of Perpetuities, Pensions, French Pensioners and half pay on the Irish Establishment as from 1 Aug. 1701*; also p. 594.
26 Elie Benoist (English trans.), *The History of the famous Edict of Nantes* (London, 1694), Cooke's *Dedication*.
27 Benoist, Cooke's *Dedication*.
28 William & Susan Minet, *Registres des Quatres Eglises du Petit Charenton de West Street de Pearl Street et de Crispin Street* (London, 1929), vol. XXXII, p. xv.
29 Minet, *Registres des Quatres Eglises du Petit Charenton de West Street de Pearl Street et de Crispin Street*, p. xvi.
30 Robin Gwynn, *The Huguenots of London* (Brighton, Portland, Toronto, 1998) pp. 37–8; also *Proceedings of the Huguenot Society* (London, 1887–8), vol. II, pp. 453–6, and vol. XX (1958–64), p. 76.
31 Jean Desaguliers' burial was recorded in 1699 in the register of the Anglican Church of St Mary, Islington. Cf. also, Agnew, *French Protestant Exiles*; and Mike Chrimes & A.W. Skempton (eds.), *A Biographical Dictionary of Civil Engineers in Great Britain and Ireland: 1500 to 1830* (London, 2002), p. 177.
32 Although many sources refer to Desaguliers being tutored by a 'Mr Sanders' at Sutton Coldfield, he was more probably educated at Bishop Vesey's Free Grammar School, founded in 1527, where an unpublished history of the school referred to Desaguliers being a student. Source: verbal communication from Bishop Vesey's School.
33 Although the witticism has been attributed to Johnson, no source has been identified.
34 Roy Porter (ed.), *The Cambridge History of Science* (Cambridge, 2003), vol. 4, p. 290.
35 John Henry, 'John Keill', *ODNB*.
36 John Keill, *Introductio ad veram physicam* (Oxford, 1702). An English translation of the Latin original was published in 1726 by John Senex.
37 Cf. E.W. Strong, 'Newtonian Explications of Natural Philosophy', *Journal of the History of Ideas*, 18.1 (1957), 49–83.
38 Although he was nominally the Sedleian Professor of Natural Philosophy, Millington was predominantly in London where he was a Fellow and later President of the Royal College of Physicians, and had an extensive and lucrative medical practice: A. J. Turner, 'Sir Thomas Millington', *ODNB*.
39 Henry, 'John Keill', *ODNB*.
40 Keill retained his position as Decipherer until 30 June 1716, when he was replaced by Edward Willes of Oriel College: William A Shaw (ed.), *Calendar*

of Treasury Books: 11 June 1716 (London, 1958), vol. 30, p. 252. The Treasury Warrant Book indicates that Keill received a quarterly payment of £25 for his services: Ibid., 26 November 1716, p. 568. The same data is held in Wiltshire & Swindon Archives: 161/130, 1716–1823.
41 Alan Crossley, C.R. Elrington (eds.), A History of the County of Oxford (London, 1990), vol. 12, pp. 188–194; also, Wilfred R. Hurst, An outline of the career of John Theophilus Desaguliers (London, 1928), p. 2; and Pierre Boutin, Jean-Théophile Desaguliers: un Huguenot, philosophe et juriste, en politique (Paris, 1999), pp. 9–10.
42 Natalie Rothstein, Huguenot master weavers: exemplary Englishmen, 1700– c. 1750 in Randolph Vigne & Charles Littleton (eds.), From Strangers to Citizens (Brighton, Portland, Toronto ,2001), pp. 161–2.
43 Guildhall Library: St Andrew's, Holborn, Register, MS 6667/7.
44 City of Westminster Archives: 'Assessment made on Inhabitants of the Parish of St Margaret's Westminster in the County of Middlesex for and towards the Relief of the Poor', E330–E363. The rates were reduced from £30 7s 6d to £24 9s 0d.
45 Post Man and the Historical Account, 28 February 1716.
46 Walter Thornbury, Old and New London (London, 1878), vol. 3, pp. 376–82.
47 Two sons and all three daughters died in infancy.
48 Marguerite Desaguliers was buried at St Margaret's in March 1722; his mother-in-law was buried there in November 1732. City of Westminster Archives: Registers of St Margaret's Church, Westminster.
49 Lectures were given at a variety of taverns and coffee houses across London including Garraway's in Exchange Alley, the Grecian in the Strand, Child's by St Paul's, and Man's at Charing Cross.
50 Larry Stewart, 'John Harris', ODNB.
51 Stephen Pumfrey, 'Francis Hauksbee', ODNB.
52 Stephen D. Snobelen, 'William Whiston (1667–1752)', ODNB.
53 A second edition was published after Hauksbee's death by John Senex (London, 1719).
54 Larry Stewart, The rise of public science: rhetoric, technology, and natural philosophy in Newtonian Britain, 1660–1750 (Cambridge, 1992), pp. 125–6.
55 RS Journal Books, 8 March 1716.
56 P. Fontes da Costa, 'The Culture of Curiosity at The Royal Society in the First Half of the Eighteenth Century', RS Notes and Records, 56.2 (2002), 147–66; also cf., for example, RS Journal Books, 16 March 1738 and 4 May 1738.
57 Cf. I. Bernard Cohen, 'The Fear and Distrust of Science in Historical Perspective', Science, Technology, & Human Values, 6.36 (1981), 20–4.
58 J.H. Plumb, England in the Eighteenth Century (1714–1815) (London, 1950), pp. 101–4.
59 Jeffrey R. Wigelsworth, 'Competing to Popularize Newtonian Philosophy, John Theophilus Desaguliers and the Preservation of Reputation', Isis, 94.3 (2003), 435–455, esp. 435–6.
60 Cf. Helen Berry, 'Rethinking Politeness in Eighteenth Century England', Transactions of the Royal Historical Society, 6th series, 11 (2001), 65–81, esp. 71–3.
61 Stewart, The rise of public science, esp. chapters 7 and 8.
62 London Journal, 27 January 1728.
63 Larry Stewart, 'A Meaning for Machines: Modernity, Utility, and the

Eighteenth-Century British Public', *Journal of Modern History*, 70.2 (1998) 259–294, esp. 268–9; and Stewart, 'Public Lectures and Private Patronage in Newtonian England', *Isis*, 77.1 (1986), 47–58. Cf. also, Michael Ben-Chaim, 'Social Mobility and Scientific Change: Stephen Gray's Contribution to Electrical Research', *British Journal for the History of Science*, 23.1 (1990), 3–24, with regard to Desaguliers' relationship with Stephen Gray and their experiments with electricity. Many of Desaguliers' experiments at the Royal Society are described in *RS Philosophical Transactions (1683–1775)*, vols 29–41.

64 Hauksbee, *Physico-Mechanical Experiments*, Preface.
65 Stewart, 'A Meaning for Machines', 267–8.
66 *Ibid.*, 269.
67 Stewart, 'Public Lectures and Private Patronage', esp. 52–4.
68 Stephen Pumfrey, 'Who Did the Work? Experimental Philosophers and Public Demonstrators in Augustan England', *British Journal for the History of Science*, 28.2 (1995), 131–56.
69 Richard Sorrenson, 'Towards a History of the Royal Society in the Eighteenth Century', *RS Notes and Records*, 50.1 (1996).
70 J.T. Desaguliers, *Lectures in Mechanical and Experimental Philosophy* (London, 1717), *Foreword*.
71 Although both establishments could be regarded as his local churches, Desaguliers had the choice of several other churches within a relatively short distance. The closest conformist French churches were located, respectively, at the Savoy in the Strand, and at Spring Gardens, Westminster. Each would have been only a few hundred yards from Desaguliers' lodgings.
72 *Guardian*, 5 May 1713. A later lecture course was advertised as being 'at the widow Hawksbee's in Mind Court, Fleet Street': *Daily Courant*, 16 March 1714.
73 Carnarvon became Grand Master in 1738.
74 Thomas Parker, proposed by Newton and elected in 1712, was (possibly) a member of the lodge meeting at the Crown & Harp, St Martin's Lane.
75 Campbell was another Freemason with a keen interest in science. Cf. below.
76 Her son, Edward, 2nd Earl Darnley, became Grand Master in 1737/8.
77 Written 'Count La Lippe' in *Grand Lodge Minutes*, p. 23.
78 The Duke of Richmond was Grand Master in 1725. Before becoming GM, and subsequently, he was WM of the Horn and chaired other lodges in England (e.g., Chichester) and France (e.g., Aubigny and Paris).
79 Also written as 'Hewitt'.
80 *Sackler Archives*; also Montague H. Cox (ed.) *Survey of London* (London, 1926), vol. 10, pt. 1, pp. 73–4.
81 Fara, *Jean Theophilus Desaguliers*, and Fara, *Newton, the Making of Genius* (London, 2002), pp. 91–2.
82 Jacques Ozanam, *A Treatise of Fortification* (Oxford, 1711).
83 Webb was promoted Major General in 1709 and Lieutenant General in 1712. He served as Colonel of the 8th Regiment of Foot (1695–1715), and Governor of the Isle of Wight (1710–15); he also sat as Tory MP for Ludgershall in Wiltshire, the family estate. Cf. John B. Hattendorf, 'John Richmond Webb', *ODNB*.
84 Jacques Ozanam, *Treatise of Gnomonicks or Dialling* (Oxford, 1712).
85 Desaguliers, *Fires Improved* . . . (London, 1715).

86 T.F. Henderson, 'Hugh Cholmondeley, first earl of Cholmondeley (1662?–1725)', rev. Philip Carter, *ODNB*.
87 Cheshire and Chester Archives: ZA/B/3/228v-230, *22nd December 1715*. Cf. also, John Armstrong, *A History of Freemasonry in Cheshire* (London, 1901), pp. 2–8, 17; and DCH/L/62, *1720*, for additional information on the relationship between Cholmondeley and Comberbach.
88 Cf. *Grand Lodge Minutes*, pp. 39, 73–4.
89 Desaguliers, *Fires improv'd, Preface*.
90 John H. Appleby, 'John Rowley', *ODNB*.
91 David Boswell Reid, *Ventilation in American Dwellings* (New York, 1858), p. X.
92 *Journal of the House of Lords*, vol. 21, pp. 35–43, 7 *January 1719*.
93 Reid, *Ventilation in American Dwellings*.
94 *Letters of James Brydges, Earl of Carnarvon and later Duke of Chandos, to John Theophilus Desaguliers* (Huntington Library, Pasadena, CA: Stowe MS Collection), ST 57, vol. 17, p. 11. The references are as per the University College London website which has published a transcription of the correspondence.
95 *Desaguliers, Leçons physico-mechaniques (London, 1717)*.
96 *Desaguliers, The Motion of Water and Other Fluids (London, 1718)*.
97 *Ibid., Preface*.
98 *Robin Briggs, 'The Académie Royale des Sciences and the Pursuit of Utility', Past & Present, 131 (1991), 38–88*.
99 *Desaguliers, Lectures of Experimental Philosophy (London, 1719)*.
100 Desaguliers, *A system of experimental philosophy* (London, 1719).
101 Desaguliers, *An experimental course of astronomy* (London, 1725).
102 William-James's Gravesande, Desaguliers (trans.), *Mathematical elements of natural philosophy confirmed by experiments, or an introduction to Sir Isaac Newton's philosophy* (London, 1720).
103 Fara, *Newton, the Making of Genius*, pp. 94–5.
104 *RS Minutes of the Council*, II, *29 July 1714* (unpublished). Desaguliers subsequently succeeded Hauksbee as Newton's principal demonstrator at the Society.
105 The equivalent of *c*. £500 today (using the National Archives Currency Converter).
106 Cf. William Cheselden, *Anatomy of the Human Body* (London, 1712).
107 Cf. for example, J.A. Lohne, 'Experimentum Crucis', *RS Notes and Records*, 23.2 (1968).
108 Desaguliers was paid £30 per annum 1714–17; £35 in 1718 to January 1719; and £20 for the rest of 1719; he earned £40 in each of 1721 and 1722: *RS Books of Accounts, 1683–1722.*.
109 A multiple of *c*. 200–300 reflects the rise in average earnings over the period: cf. National Archives Currency Converter.
110 *RS Minutes of the Council*, 3 July 1718, vol. II, *1682–1727*.
111 Stephen Mason, 'The Spring-Tide of Experimental Philosophy', *RS Notes and Records*, 46.2 (1992), 313–16, a review of Marie Boas Hall, *Promoting Experimental Learning: Experiment and the Royal Society, 1660–1727* (Cambridge, 1991).
112 Cf. Larry Stewart, 'The Selling of Newton: Science and Technology in Early Eighteenth-Century England', *Journal of British Studies*, 25.2 (1986), 185.

113 Susan Jenkins, *Portrait of a Patron: The Patronage and Collecting of James Brydges, 1st Duke of Chandos (1674–1744)* (Aldershot, 2007), pp. 12, 84, 100–1.
114 Skempton & Chrimes, *A Biographical Dictionary of Civil Engineers*, p. 178.
115 Alan F. Cook, 'Henry Beighton', *ODNB*. Desaguliers proposed Beighton for election as FRS in 1720.
116 Cornwall Record Office: HL/2/189 *16 September 1736*, and HL/2/190 *1736*.
117 J.T. Desaguliers, 'The Phenomenon of the Horizontal Moon appearing bigger that when elevated many degrees above the Horizon': East Riding of Yorkshire Archives and Record Service: DDGR/38/157, undated MS: *eighteenth century*. Also, Shropshire Archives 1536/8/1, *No date [early C18]*: notes regarding Desaguliers' lectures on mechanics, including the eclipse of the moon, gravity, hydraulics and the laws of motion.
118 William A. Shaw (ed.), *Calendar of Treasury Books and Papers: 4 August 1730* (London, 1897), vol. 1, p. 429.
119 Stewart, 'A Meaning for Machines', *op. cit.*
120 Cf. John H. Appleby, 'Human Curiosities and the Royal Society, 1699–1751', *RS Notes and Records*, 50.1 (1996), 13–27. For an example of those who later dissented, cf. 'Letter from John Smeaton (1724–92), civil engineer, to Sir George Savile (1726–84), MP for Yorkshire'. Nottinghamshire Record Office: DD/FJ/11/1/7/234 *31 January 1768*.
121 *Weekly Journal or British Gazetteer*, 14 September 1717.
122 Cf., in particular, the frontispiece to post-1727 edn.s of Desaguliers' *A Course of Mechanical and Experimental Philosophy*. Cf. also *Officeholders of the Household of Prince Frederick, 1729–51* (London, 2009).
123 *Whitehall Evening Post*, 22 June 1738: 'the Rev. Dr Desaguliers is made Chaplain to Brigadier General Bowle's Regiment of Dragoons in Ireland'.
124 Simon Schaffer, 'Machine Philosophy: Demonstration Devices in Georgian Mechanics', *Osiris*, 2nd series, 9 (1994), 157.
125 Stewart, *The Rise of Public Science*, *op. cit.*
126 Desaguliers, *A Course of Experimental Philosophy*, vol. II, p. 416.
127 Desaguliers' consulting services included, for example, drainage improvements at Spalding, the plans for which were submitted to him for approval. Cf. Lincolnshire Archives: Spalding Sewers/451/4, p. 9 *1733–76*.
128 Simon Schaffer, 'The Show That Never Ends: Perpetual Motion in the Early Eighteenth Century', *British Journal for the History of Science*, 28.2 (1995), 157–89.
129 Patricia Fara, 'A Treasure of Hidden Vertues', *British Journal for the History of Science*, 28.1 (1995), 5–35.
130 John Loftis, 'Richard Steele's Censorium', *The Huntington Library Quarterly*, 14.1 (1950), 43–66; also Stewart, 'The Selling of Newton', 181.
131 *Letters of the Duke of Chandos*: Huntington Library: MT 57, vol. 51, p. 131.
132 Stewart, 'Public Lectures and Private Patronage', 47.
133 *Letters of the Duke of Chandos*: Huntington Library: ST 57, vol. 25, p. 69.
134 *Ibid.*, Huntington Library: ST 57, vol. 28, p. 33.
135 Margaret Jacob confuses Chandos with his son when she refers to the former's Masonic interests in *The Radical Enlightenment*, p. 92. A further error is her statement that English and Scottish lodges were 'united': they were and remain separate.
136 M. Yakup Bektas and Maurice Crosland, 'The Copley Medal: The

Establishment of a Reward System in the Royal Society, 1731–1839', *RS Notes and Records*, 46.1 (1992), 43–76, esp. 45–6. The financial prize associated with the Copley Medal was £5. However, awards were also made from the Copley bequest to cover the cost of experiments.

137 Dr John Gaspar Scheuchzer (1702–1729), a Swiss Huguenot, was Sloane's protégé and librarian; elected FRS in 1724, Scheuchzer was a physician, antiquary and natural historian. He died aged 27, and was buried in the churchyard at Sloane's Chelsea estate. Cf. Andrea Rusnock, 'John Scheuchzer', *ODNB*.

138 Stewart, 'Public Lectures and Private Patronage', 58.

139 RS Archives: MS 250, fo. 4.25, *13 December 1743*.

140 Stewart, 'Public Lectures and Private Patronage', 57.

141 Huntington Library: ST 57, vol. 51, p. 137.

142 *Ibid.*, ST 57, vol 54, p. 19; ST, vol. 55, p. 212.

143 The Copley Medal was first awarded in 1731; Stephen Gray, the recipient, had been tutored by Desaguliers. Gray also received the medal the following year. No award was made in 1733 or 1735.

144 *Grub Street Journal*, 13 November 1735.

145 *Daily Journal*, 8 July 1717.

146 *Daily Post*, 14 November 1738.

147 *Old England*, 29 April 1749.

148 Agnew, *French Protestant Exiles*, p. 92.

149 Cécile Révauger, 'Anderson's Freemasonry: The true daughter of the British Enlightenment', Cercles 18 (2008), 1–9.

150 Marie Mulvey-Roberts, 'Hogarth on the Square: Framing the Freemasons', *British Journal for Eighteenth Century Studies*, 26.2 (2003), 251–70.

151 Cf. for example, Ronald Paulson, *Hogarth: His Life, Art and Times* (New Haven, 1971), and Paulson, 'New Light on Hogarth's Graphic Works', *Burlington Magazine*, 109.770 (1967), 280–6; also Peter Tomory, 'Review: Paulson, *Hogarth: His Life, Art and Times*', *Art Bulletin*, 54.4 (1972), 557–9.

152 Cf. correspondence between Chandos and Desaguliers and, in particular, the letters dated 10 May 1732, 11 & 20 March 1733, and 20 & 22 March 1738, at ww.ucl.ac.uk/~ucypanp/desagulierssletters.htm.

153 Plays performed by family members were popular with Richmond and other members of the aristocracy. Cf. West Sussex Record Office: Goodwood/140 1721–1732, verses, prologues and epilogues performed by the Duke's family and friends; and Goodwood 141, 1730–1742, ditto.

154 Although no date has been established for Hogarth's initiation, Mulvey-Roberts noted that 'it is traditionally accepted that he was made a Mason at the Hand and Apple Tree in Little Queen Street, Holborn, between 1725 and 1728'. He joined the Bear & Harrow in 1730: cf. *Grand Lodge Minutes* and 'Hogarth on the Square', *op. cit.*, quote from 251.

155 *Grand Lodge Minutes*, p. 43.

156 *Ibid.*, p. 177.

157 *Ibid.*, p. 240.

158 *Ibid.*, p. 96.

159 Mulvey-Roberts, 'Hogarth on the Square', and Paulson, *Hogarth: His Life, Art and Times*.

160 Ronald Paulson (ed.), *Hogarth's Graphic Works* (New Haven, 1965), p. 55.

161   Alphonse Cerza, *Anti-Masonry: Light on the Past and Present Opponents of Freemasonry* (Fulton, 1962), Appendix A, pp. 193–211.
162   Mulvey-Roberts, 'Hogarth on the Square'.
163   Quoted in R.F. Gould, (revised Frederick Crowe), *The Concise History of Freemasonry* (London, 1951), p. 244.
164   'Mick Broughton to the Duke of Richmond, 1 January 1734.' The letter is published in Charles Richmond, Earl of March (ed.), *A Duke and his Friends: The Life and Letters of the Second Duke of Richmond* (London, 1911), vol. 1, p. 295; it was also quoted in *The Builder Magazine*, XI.5 (1925).
165   Charles Calvert was elected FRS in 1731. The Calverts were the proprietary Governors (and owners) of the colony of Maryland.
166   Count Friedrich August von Harrach-Rohrau (1696–1749), interim governor of the Austrian Netherlands between 1741 and 1744.
167   *Daily Gazetteer*, 19 January 1741.
168   Proved at the Prerogative Court of Canterbury. NA: PROB 11/732, *1 March 1744*.
169   Fara, 'Desaguliers', *ODNB*; and W.J. Williams, 'Notes & Queries', *AQC Transactions* 40 (1927), 170.
170   Richard Striner, 'Political Newtoniansim: The Cosmic Model of Politics in Europe and America', *William and Mary Quarterly*, 3rd series, 52.4 (1995), 583–608.
171   Alexander Pope, *Essay on Man* (London, 1734), Epistle I, final stanza.
172   Jacob, *The Radical Enlightenment*, p. 102.
173   John Gay, 'Letter to Dean Swift, 9 November 1729', in Lewis Melville, *Life and Letters of John Gay (1685–1732)* (London, 1921), p. 121.

CHAPTER THREE   Grand Lodge: *The Inner Workings*

1   John Beale died on 20 June 1724 at his Berkshire home. He had been appointed DGM in 1721 and elected FRS the same year proposed by William Stukeley, whose Masonic initiation he had attended, and Edmund Halley. With Desaguliers, Beale was responsible formally for reviewing the *1723 Constitutions*.
2   James Anderson's name is written as 'Jaques Anderson': *Grand Lodge Minutes*, p. 42.
3   *1738 Constitutions*, p. 115.
4   *Grand Lodge Minutes, 1740–58*, pp. xxi–xxiv.
5   *Grand Lodge Minutes, 1723–39*, p. 196, note (d); see also p. 49, note (a).
6   Knoop and Jones, *The Genesis of Freemasonry*, pp. 180–5.
7   Prescott, 'The Publishers of the 1723 Constitutions', *AQC Transactions*, 121 (2008), 147–62.
8   John Senex (*c.* 1678–1740) was a publisher to many in the scientific community. He was elected FRS in 1728. Senex had previously been a surveyor and geographer to Queen Anne. A recognised engraver and scientific instrument maker, the RS Archives contain a number of his astronomical models. Senex may have been a second or third generation Huguenot émigré: the Royal Society's *Sackler Archives* record an alternative spelling of his name as 'Senez', a Huguenot form.
9   Cf. Walter Wilson, *The History and Antiquities of Dissenting Churches and*

Meeting Houses in London (London, 1814), vol. IV, p. 34; and David Stevenson, 'James Anderson: Man & Mason', *Heredom*, 10 (2002), 93–138.

10 F.H.W. Sheppard (gen. ed.), *Survey of London* (London, 1963), vol. 31, pp. 57–67.

11 James Anderson, *A sermon preached in Swallow street, St. James's . . . on Wednesday January 16th 1711/12* (London, 1712); *No king-killers. A sermon preach'd in Swallow-street, St. James's, on January 30th 1714/15* (London, 1715); *Contend earnestly for the faith. A sermon preach'd to a religious society in Goodman's Fields. On Monday, 1st August, 1720* (London, 1720); and *The happy death. A sermon occasion'd by the death of the Reverend William Lorimer* (London, 1724).

12 Anderson's father was a Scottish Mason and Anderson may have been initiated into a Scottish lodge. Cf. A.L. Miller, 'The Connection of Dr James Anderson of the Constitutions with Aberdeen and Aberdeen University', *AQC*, XXXVI (1923). However, there is no evidence that Scottish ritual was incorporated into the Charges or Regulations.

13 Cf. West Sussex Record Office: Goodwood/42,43 *12 September 1737*, for relevant correspondence. Also, Richmond, *A Duke and His Friends*, pp. 206–7, 323–9.

14 Despite continuing to initiate members as Freemasons, *Philo-Musicae et Architecture* was wound up the following year.

15 John Entick was the editor of the revised 1756 *Constitutions*. He used the identical expression on three occasions in *Pocket Companion* (London, 1759), 2nd ed., pp. 284, 297, 325.

16 Cf. Neville Barker-Cryer, *The Restoration Lodge of Chester* (London, 2002).

17 Cheshire and Chester archives: DBW/M/D/A/2.

18 Cheshire and Chester archives: DBW/L/F/11 and DBW/M/J/39, 42, 43 & 44.

19 Judith Curthoys, Archivist, Christ Church, Oxford: email correspondence with author, January 2011.

20 Joyce M. Horn & Derrick Sherwin Bailey, *Fasti Ecclesiae Anglicanae 1541–1857* (London, 1979), vol. 5, pp. 109–18.

21 'Draft writ of *fieri facias* seeking an appearance before the Barons of the Exchequer to show cause why there should not be execution against Samuel Payne for debts': Cheshire and Chester archives: ZS/D/3/10.

22 William A. Shaw (ed.), *Calendar of Treasury Books – Warrant Book: October 1711* (London, 1952), vol. 25, pp. 472–94.

23 Alongside the Glass Office and Stamp Office etc., the Leather Office was a revenue assessing and collecting arm of the Excise. Cf. William A. Shaw (ed.), *Calendar of Treasury Books, Declared Accounts: Excise 1712* (London, 1954), vol. 26, pp. 351–83. Also, Robert Bucholz & Newton Key, *Early Modern England, 1485–1714* (Oxford, 2004), ill. edn., p. 313.

24 For example, *Guardian* and *Post Boy*, 5 May 1713.

25 Cf. William Morgan, *Morgan's map of the whole of London in 1682* (London, 1682), sheets 9 and 13. Two future noble Grand Masters also had properties nearby: the Duke of Montagu at Montagu House, 1–6 Whitehall Gardens; and Montagu's close friend, the Duke of Richmond, at Richmond House, Richmond Terrace.

26 *London Chronicle*, 24 February 1757.

27 William A. Shaw & F.H. Slingsby (eds.), *Calendar of Treasury Books – 1713*

(London, 1955), vol. 27, pp. 363–72. Payne earned £50 per annum: J. Chamberlayne, *Magnae Britanniae Notitia* (London, 1716), book III, p. 523.

28 J. Chamberlayne, *Magnae Britanniae Notitia* (London, 1718), p. 79.

29 Payne was reported as earning £60 as First Clerk to Sorrel. The role of Secretary was one of the more senior administrative functions at the Excise. Cf. *Court and City Register* (London, 1757), 3rd edn., p. 109; also *Weekly Miscellany*, 19 January 1734.

30 William A. Shaw (ed.), *Calendar of Treasury Books and Papers – Warrants for the Payment of Money: April–June 1735* (London, 1900), vol. 3, pp. 106–22.

31 William A. Shaw (ed.), *Calendar of Treasury Books and Papers* (London, 1903), vol. 5, pp. 260–7; cf. also, *London Evening Post*, 7 April 1743.

32 *London Gazette*, 19 October 1745.

33 *London Evening Post*, 18 March 1736.

34 *Abstract of the Act for building a Bridge cross the River Thames* (London, 1736), p. 14; cf. also, *Daily Gazetteer*, 27 May 1736.

35 *London Evening Post*, 22 March 1743.

36 *Daily Advertiser*, 23 May 1744 and *London Evening Post*, 30 July 1747.

37 *Whitehall Evening Post or London Intelligencer*, 5 March 1748. Compton was MP for Northampton; he succeeded as 6th Earl of Northampton in 1754.

38 *General Advertiser*, 23 November 1749. Also *Account of the Proceedings at the Late Election for the City and Liberty or Westminster* (London, 1749), p. 16.

39 His title changes as between the 1723 and 1725 lists of members of the Horn; cf. also his description in *Grand Lodge Minutes*, p. 58 (1724) and p. 62 (1725).

40 There is a reference to Payne's activities as a magistrate at the LMA: WSes: SP, JWP, *20 April 1715*. Others who were mentioned alongside Payne on that date included Charles Delafaye and George Carpenter.

41 *Read's Weekly Journal or British Gazetteer*, 13 July 1751, confirms that Payne had been made a JP many years earlier. The LMA refer to Payne in WSes, SP, JWP as late as 1 April 1748 and 1 January 1750.

42 C. Mackechnie-Jarvis, *Grand Stewards 1728–1978 – The 1978 Prestonian Lecture* (London, 1988).

43 Although the absence of data is never conclusive evidence, there is no record in the membership lists of Grand Lodge of Thomas Payne having been a Freemason.

44 Cf. *Grand Lodge Minutes 1723–39*, pp. 58, 61–3, 68, 74, 88, 93, 103, 106, 119, 125, 131, 144, 196–7, 204, 210, 213, 217, 219, 225, 241, 259, 264, 273, 281, 286, 291, 295 ad 306; and *Grand Lodge Minutes, 1740–58*, pp 1, 3, 8, 10, 25–6, 29, 33, 35, 38–9, 43–4, 55–7, 61–4, 70–2, 78–81.

45 Cowper was appointed Clerk to the Parliaments in *c.* 1715. Cf. *The Humble Address Of the Right Honourable the Lords Spiritual and Temporal In Parliament Assembled, Presented To His Majesty, On Munday the Twentieth Day of February 1715* (London, 1715), Preface.

46 LMA: MSes, SP, JWP, *1715–1735*.

47 For example, *Public Advertiser*, 24 February 1757; *London Chronicle*, 26 February 1757; and *Gentleman's Magazine*, 26 February 1757.

48 P.B. Munsche, 'Review: The Justice of the Peace, 1679–1760', *Eighteenth Century Studies*, 20.3 (1987), 385–7.

49 Norma Landau, 'Indictment for Fun and Profit', *Law and History Review*,

17.3 (1999), 507–36; and Robert B. Shoemaker, 'The London Mob in the Early Eighteenth Century', *Journal of British Studies*, 26.3 (1987), 273–304.
50   *London Journal*, 19 July 1729.
51   Cf. Simon Targett, 'Government and Ideology during the Age of Whig Supremacy', *Historical Journal*, 37.2 (1994), 289–317. Cf. also Targett, 'James Pitt (fl.1744–55)', *ODNB*.
52   Norma Landau, *Justices of the Peace 1679–1760* (Berkeley, CA, 1984), esp. pp. 69–95, 96–145 and 146–73.
53   Norma Landau, 'Country Matters: The Growth of Political Stability a Quarter Century On', *Albion*, 25.2 (1993), 261–74.
54   Landau, *Justices of the Peace 1679–1760*, p. 88.
55   *Grand Lodge Minutes*, p. 142, fn. (a).
56   Charles Delafaye, *The Fellowcraft's Song*, printed in the *1723 Constitutions*, p. 83.
57   Cf. J.C. Sainty, 'The Secretariat of the Chief Governors of Ireland, 1690–1800', *Proceedings of the Royal Irish Academy*, 77.C (1977), 21, for a short biography; cf. also, 'A Huguenot civil servant . . . ', *Proceedings of the Huguenot Society*, xxiii (1975).
58   For example, a classified advertisement for a theatrical presentation of *Oedipus* preceded by a Delafaye composition, appeared in the *Country Journal or The Craftsman*, 17 November 1733.
59   James Vernon, a Commissioner for Excise (1710 until his death) and a Clerk of the Council in Ordinary (1715 until his death), was a member of Folkes' Bedford Head lodge. Vernon was closely involved with Masonic philanthropy, including the establishment and operation of the Georgia colony, the cost of which was co-funded by Freemasons.
60   Cf. Rae Blanchard, 'Was Sir Richard Steele a Freemason?', *PMLA*, 63.3 (1948), 903–17.
61   Cf. for example, *Post Boy*, 30 April 1717.
62   His name is recorded *inter alia* in the MSes, SP, JWP, for April 1715: LMA: MJ/SP *1715*.
63   Cf. among many reported examples, *Country Journal or The Craftsman*, 17 November 1733.
64   *Original Weekly Journal*, 31 August 1717.
65   *Old Whig or The Consistent Protestant*, 29 July 1736.
66   J.C. Sainty, *Office-Holders in Modern Britain* (London, 1973), vol. 2, pp. 63–85.
67   Cf. for example, *Read's Weekly Journal Or British Gazetteer*, 21 April 1739.
68   'Letters to Lord George Sackville': Derbyshire Record Office: D3155/C1015, *24 June 1749*; D3155/C1568-1571, *15 May 1754* and D3155/C1577–1578, *25 July 1754*.
69   P.N. Furbank & W.R. Owens, *A Political Biography of Daniel Defoe* (London, 2006). Cf. also William P. Trent, *Daniel Defoe, how to know him* (Indianapolis, 1916).
70   William Lee, *Daniel Defoe: His Life, and Recently Discovered Writings* (London, 1869). Also, John Robert Moore, 'Daniel Defoe: King William's Pamphleteer and Intelligence Agent', *Huntington Library Quarterly*, 34.3 (1971), 251–60.
71   Patrick McNally, 'Wood's Halfpence, Carteret and the Government of Ireland,

1723–6', *Irish Historical Studies*, 30.119 (1997), 354–76, esp. 359–60, 365–8 and 373–4.
72 Geoffrey Holmes, 'The Sacheverell Riots', *Past and Present*, 72 (1976), 55–85, esp. 59, 66, 75, 77 and 82.
73 Philip Haffenden, 'Colonial Appointments and Patronage under the Duke of Newcastle, 1724–1739', *English Historical Review*, 78.308 (1963), 417–35, esp. 426 and 430–1.
74 J.A. Downie, 'Swift and Jacobitism', *ELH*, 64.4 (1997), 887–901, esp. 892.
75 A.C. Wood, 'The English Embassy at Constantinople, 1600–1762', *English Historical Review*, 40.160 (1925), 553–61, esp. 551.
76 D.W. Hayton, 'The Stanhope/Sunderland Ministry and the Repudiation of Irish Parliamentary Independence', *English Historical Review*, 113.452 (1998), 610–36, esp. 625 and 631.
77 Jeremy Black, 'Hanover and British Foreign Policy 1714–60', *English Historical Review*, 120.486 (2005), 303–39; 'British Foreign Policy in the Eighteenth Century: A Survey', *Journal of British Studies*, 26.1 (1987), 26–53, esp. 39; 'Fresh Light on the Fall of Townshend', 29.1 (1986), 41–64, esp. 57 and 61–2; 'Interventionism, Structuralism and Contingency in British Foreign Policy in the 1720s', *International History Review*, 26.4 (2004), 734–64, esp. 751, 753 and 755; and 'British Neutrality in the War of the Polish Succession, 1733–1735', *IHR*, 8.3 (1986), 345–66, esp. 355.
78 For example, Raymond Turner, 'The Excise Scheme of 1733', *EHR*, 42.165 (1927), 34–57, esp. 36–7, 40–4. Cf. also Bibliography, below.
79 Paul S. Fritz, 'The Anti-Jacobite Intelligence System of the English Ministers, 1715–1745', *Historical Journal*, 16.2 (1973), 265–89, esp. 276, fn. 78, and 277.
80 *Weekly Journal or British Gazetteer*, 2 November 1717.
81 Cf. for example, *Daily Post*, 9 January 1728 and *London Evening Post*, 16 May 1728.
82 Cf. *London Evening Post*, 18 May 1728.
83 A 'Mr Nicholson' was a member of the Baptist Head lodge in Chancery Lane. It is possible that the two were the same person.
84 *Charles Delafaye to Sir Francis Nicholson, 26 Jan 1721*: Houghton Library: MS Am 1455.
85 Derbyshire Record Office: D3155/C1185: *October 1750*.
86 Delafaye, *Fellowcraft's Song*.
87 BL: MSS Add. 23786, f.130, *20 October 1/32*; quoted in Jacob, *The Radical Enlightenment*, p. 105.
88 12 exclusions were reported alongside the 1719 intake, and 11 alongside that for 1721.
89 *Daily Journal*, 24 October 1727.
90 Interestingly, the new entrants included several Huguenots (Corbiére, Dubois, Floyer and Leroche), who could also be expected to be pro-Hanoverian. Cf. for example, *Weekly Journal or Saturday's Post*, 25 April 1724.
91 Maurice F. Bond, 'Clerks of the Parliaments, 1509–1953', *English Historical Review*, 73 (1958), 78–85. Cf. also, *The laws of honour: a compendious account . . . of all titles* (London, 1714), p. 389.
92 *Daily Gazetteer*, 23 May 1739.
93 William A. Shaw & F.H. Slingsby (eds.), *Calendar of Treasury Books* (London,

1962), vol. 32, pp. 372–3; also Hertfordshire Archives: Chancery Administration, misc. items: DE/P/F165, *1714–1717*.
94 Hertfordshire Archives: re. the office of Clerk of the Parliaments: DE/P/F220, *c. 1723*.
95 Cf. *General Evening Post*, 24 May 1735; *Daily Post*, 16 September 1736; and *Daily Gazetteer*, 15 January 1737. In 1735, Cowper appointed Joseph Wight as one of his assistants at a salary of £400 p.a.; in 1736, he appointed John Wight as Reading Clerk to the House of Lords at a salary of £300 p.a. Coincidentally or otherwise, an Edward Wight was at the time a member of the popular lodge at the Rainbow Coffee House, York Buildings.
96 *London Journal*, 19 January 1723; and *Daily Post*, 25 January 1723.
97 *London Evening Post*, 16 December 1727.
98 *Flying Post or The Weekly Medley*, 8 March 1729.
99 *London Evening Post*, 27 April 1731.
100 *St. James's Evening Post*, 31 March 1733.
101 *Pasquin*, 17 January 1723.
102 William Cowper, *The Charge delivered . . .* (London, 1730), pp. 5–6.
103 Hertfordshire Archives: DE/P/T1220 and 1221; and DE/P/F212–218 *c. 1724–39*.
104 Hertfordshire Archives: Miscellaneous papers: DE/P/F17 *c. **1720–50***.
105 Guy Miège, *The present state of Great-Britain and Ireland* (London, 1718), part 1, p. 366. Cf. also, *The establish'd state of the publick offices, under his Majesty King George II* (London, 1728), p. 46.
106 Lambeth Palace Library: MS 2706, *1716–48*.
107 Lambeth Palace Library: MS 2706, *1716–48*, items 267, 275, 313, 337 and 361.
108 *Country Journal or The Craftsman*, 11 January 1729, is one of several press reports.
109 Lambeth Palace Library: MS 2725, *1721–59*; MS 2726, *1713–42* (ff.87v–88).
110 Lambeth Palace Library: MS 2724, *1711–34*.
111 Hawksmoor (written in *Grand Lodge Minutes* as 'Hawkesmoor') was a member of the Oxford Arms, Ludgate Street, of which lodge Richard Rawlinson was also a member.
112 *Read's Weekly Journal*, 27 March 1736. Elizabeth and Nathaniel Blackerby jointly inherited her father's substantial wealth.
113 *The Historical Register* (London, 1726), p. 27. Cf. also, *The True State of England* (London, 1734), pp. 44–5.
114 CUL: Department of Manuscripts and University Archives, Ch(h), Political Papers, 80, 105 *undated*.
115 The prologue and epilogue are at United Grand Lodge of England: 737 BLA Fo. Cf. *Weekly Journal or British Gazetteer*, 4 January 1729 and 31 January 1730, with respect to the relevant performances held at the Theatre Royal.
116 *Grand Lodge Minutes*, p. 299.
117 *The report of the gentlemen appointed by the General Court of the Charitable Corporation . . .* (London, 1732), p. 9.
118 Richard Walker, 'Freemasonry and Neo-Palladianism', *The Burlington Magazine*, 125.969 (1983), 746.
119 Trustees for establishing the Colony of Georgia, *The General Account* (London, 1733), pp. 7, 17.
120 *London Evening Post*, 16 December 1727.

121   LMA: WSes, SP, JWP *1 February 1725*.
122   John Chamberlayne, *Magnæ Britanniæ notitia* (London, 1708), p. 688; and *Magnæ Britanniæ* (London, 1728), p. 206. Also East Sussex Record Office: SAS-H/362: *12 June 1719*. Streate's position as a barrister may suggest a connection to the jurist, Sir Thomas Street (1625–96); he was, possibly, a son or grandson.
123   *A True and Exact List*... (London, 1725) pp. 48–9; *Weekly Journal or British Gazetteer*, 30 January 1725.William A. Shaw (ed.). Cf. also *Calendar of Treasury Books* (London, 1952), vol. 21, p. 300.
124   *London Journal*, 19 January 1723.
125   East Sussex Record Office: AMS2241: *15 & 16 May 1723*; also Hertfordshire Archives: DE/Ru/74463: *16 May 1723*.
126   For example, *Weekly Journal or British Gazetteer*, 4 December 1725 and 9 April 1726.
127   *Daily Post*, 27 January 1729.
128   Cf. LMA: MSes, WSes and CLSes: JWP and GO, *1720–6*.
129   *Flying Post or The Weekly Medley*, 1 February 1729. Streate was succeeded as Steward of the Borough by an Edward Whitacre: *London Evening Post*, 11 February 1729. Interestingly, Streate continued to be named as 'Steward' in books and almanacs published in 1731, 1733 and thereafter, and this raises a substantial question as to the overall reliability of such sources. Cf. esp., Guy Miège, *The Present State of Great Britain* (London, 1731), p. 78; and John Mottley, *A Survey of the Cities of London & Westminster, Borough of Southwark* (London, 1733–5), vol. 2, p. 94. Mottley's *Survey* retained incorrect information as late as the 1753 edition.
130   Cf. LMA: MSes, WSes and CLSes: JWP and GO, *1720–41*. The last record was in connection with the building of a public bridge at Brentford a few months before Blackerby's death: MSes, GO, 9 April 1741.
131   For example: *Applebee's Original Weekly Journal*, 2 September 1721; *Daily Journal*, 16 October 1721; *Weekly Journal or British Gazetteer*, 6 January 1722; *Daily Post*, 24 February 1722; and *Weekly Journal or Saturday's Post*, 1 September 1722. The majority of the more than 400 references in the *Burney Collection* relate to Blackerby's activities in court.
132   Samuel Blackerby, (rev'd Nathaniel Blackerby), *The Justice of the Peace, his Companion; The reports of cases adjudg'd in the courts at Westminster, &c., which particularly concern the office of justices of the Peace* (London, 1722). An enlarged 2nd edn. was published by Nathaniel Blackerby in 1729.
133   John Chamberlayne, *Magnae Britanniae* (1736), p. 160.
134   *Daily Gazetteer*, 6 April 1738.
135   Nathaniel Blackerby, *The Speech of Nathanial Blackerby* (London, 1738), p. 18.
136   Carpenter was first mentioned (with his father) in 1715: LMA: MSes, SP, JWP, *22 April 1715*; he was last mentioned in MSes, SP, JWP *16 November 1747*.
137   Parliamentary Archives: HL/PO/JO/10/6/351: *22 February – 7 March 1726*; and HL/PO/PB/1/1725/12G1n34: Private Act, 12 George 1, c.9.
138   'Churchwardens' accounts for the Parish Church of St George, Hanover Square'. City of Westminster Archives: C756 1725–62. The records contain his and his father's accounts.
139   *Grand Lodge Minutes*, p. 235.

140 Now known as Solomon's Lodge, No. 1, Savannah. Cf. W.B. Clarke, *Early and Historic Freemasonry of Georgia, 1733/4–1800* (Georgia, 1924).
141 *Flying Post or The Post Master*, 9 April 1719.
142 LMA: ACC/0503/445 1720 and LMA: ACC/85/351 31 July 1741; ACC/85/350 & 377 31 July 1741.
143 Berkshire Record Office: D/EZ 77/3/4.
144 A full list of appointees to the Bench was given in the *Evening Post*, 10 June 1721, *Daily Post*, 12 June 1721 and in other newspapers printed that month.
145 Colonel Watkins was a member of the Rummer in 1723 and 1725.
146 *Daily Journal*, 13 March 1729.
147 Miège, *The Present State of Great Britain, 1718*, p. 365; *The True State of England* (1734), p. 64; *Magnae Britanniae* (1723), part III, p. 505; (1726), part II, p. 112; (1729), part III, p. 57; and (1736), part II, p. 58; also *London Gazette*, 19 June 1722; *London Evening Post*, 22 January 1737; and *Daily Gazetteer*, 24 January 1737.
148 *Grand Lodge Minutes*, p. 61.
149 *Grand Lodge Minutes*, pp. 71–6, 80–5, 88, 90–3, 103, 186, 197 and 204.
150 Cf. LMA: MSes, SP, JWP, 1 September 1725; WSes, SP, JWP, 1 October 1726.
151 John Pine, *The procession and ceremonies observed . . . at the installation . . . of the Knights of the Bath* (London, 1734). The details were widely reported in the press. Cf. for example, *Daily Journal*, 22 June 1725.
152 Cambridgeshire County Record Office: CON/3/1/3/10, 11, 16 & 17 12 May 1731.
153 *Weekly Journal or British Gazetteer*, 14 February 1719; and *London Evening Post*, 25 March 1736.
154 William A. Shaw and F.H. Slingsby (eds.), *Calendar of Treasury Books* (London, 1957), vol. 29, p. 515. The *Treasury Warrant Books* for the period contain over 20 additional references. Cf. also, *London Evening Post*, 3 December 1734; and Joseph Reddington (ed.), *Calendar of Treasury Papers* (London, 1889), vol. 6, p. 350.
155 *Daily Journal*, 30 September 1723; and *Weekly Journal or British Gazetteer*, 5 October 1723.
156 *Evening Post*, 19 February 1726.
157 '[12 February, 1728], Requiring by virtue of general letters of Privy Seal of 1727, June 26, the issue of 3,000l. to John Hedges, Esq., Treasurer or Receiver General to Frederick, Prince of Wales, for the Prince's disposal.': William A. Shaw (ed.), *Calendar of Treasury Books and Papers – King's Warrant Book XXIX* (London, 1897), vol. 1, p. 271; also, *British Journal or The Censor*, 14 December 1728.
158 William A. Shaw (ed.), *Calendar of Treasury Books and Papers* (London, 1897), vol. 1, p. 120.
159 K.G. Davies (ed.), *Calendar of State Papers Colonial, America and West Indies* (London, 1969), vol. 44, pp. 162–177.
160 Shaw, *Calendar of Treasury Books and Papers*, vol. 1, p. 486.
161 William A. Shaw and F.H. Slingsby (eds.), *Calendar of Treasury Books* (London, 1960), vol. 32, p. 402.
162 *Ibid.*, vol. 31, p. 145.
163 LMA: MJ/SP/1722.
164 *Evening Post*, 25 August 1724.
165 *Daily Courant*, 4 April 1724.

166 *Weekly Journal or British Gazetteer*, 27 July 1723.
167 *Grand Lodge Minutes*, p. 13 (Bartholomew Lane); p. 30 (Globe); and p. 70 (GW).
168 *Evening Journal*, 4 December 1727.
169 Written as 'Macdoughell' in the Grand Lodge lists.
170 Written as 'Oakey' in the *Evening Journal, op. cit.*
171 Written as 'Pagett' in the Grand Lodge lists.
172 Possibly the son of Richard Parsons (1642–1711), an ecclesiastical judge and antiquary.
173 Nicholas Rogers, 'Money, Land and Lineage: The Big Bourgeoisie of Hanoverian London', *Social History*, 4.3 (1979), 437–54, esp. 448–9.
174 John Noorthouck, *A New History of London* (London, 1773), pp. 889–93.
175 'Proceeding of the Old Bailey', *16 April 1740*: http//www.oldbaileyonline.org.
176 *Evening Post*, 8 March 1722.
177 Ruth Paley (ed.), *Justice in eighteenth century Hackney: The Justicing notebook of Henry Norris* (London, 1991).
178 *Ibid.*, pp. ix–xxxiii.
179 Richard Gifford was part of the 1721 intake: *Post Boy*, 10 June 1721. However, this may have been a reappointment, cf. LMA: MSes, SP, JWP, *14 March 1715* and *passim*.
180 Valentine Hilder was appointed a magistrate in 1727. Cf. *British Journal*, 9 December 1727; also LMA, MSes & WSes, SP, JWP, *22 November 1727* and *passim*.
181 This was probably Richard Manley of Early Court, Reading, a JP for Middlesex and the City of London. Manley also had estates near Chester and (unsuccessfully) contested the seat for Chester City against the Grosvenor interest.
182 John Mercer, later a Colonel in the militia, was a member of the 1719 intake. Cf. *Weekly Journal or British Gazetteer*, 18 April 1719.
183 Thomas Robe's appointment dated from the June 1721 intake of Commissioners: cf., for example, *Post Boy*, 10 June 1721.
184 Cf. Philip Sugden, 'Sir Thomas de Veil (1684–1746)', *ODNB*.
185 Thomas de Veil, *Observations on the practice of a justice of the peace intended for such gentlemen as design to act for Middlesex and Westminster* (London, 1747).
186 Sugden, 'Sir Thomas de Veil', *ODNB*.
187 *Treasury Board Papers CCCII*, No. 23, *13 February 1740*; quoted in William A. Shaw (ed.), *Calendar of Treasury Books and Papers* (London, 1901), vol. 4, pp. 291–306.
188 For example, £438 6s 6d on 8 May 1744: *King's Warrant Book XXXV* p. 422; quoted in William A. Shaw (ed.), *Calendar of Treasury Books and Papers* (London, 1903), vol. 5, pp. 611–20.
189 'Warrant, dated 14 February 1738' in *Customs Book XIV* pp. 262–3; quoted in William A. Shaw (ed.), *Calendar of Treasury Books and Papers* (London, 1900), vol. 3, pp. 623–34. It was also reported in the press, e.g., *Daily Gazette*, 6 April 1738.
190 *General Evening Post*, 18 May 1751.
191 LMA: MSes, SP, JWP, *27 January 1751*.
192 Taylor was an active member of the Court of Governors of Bridewell Royal Hospital.

193 Also written as 'Alexander Hardine'. LMA: WSes, SP, *1 June 1717*; MSes, SP *6 June 1719, 1 February 1722*; and MSes, GO: *1 March 1722*. Harding temporarily served as WM of the Horn while Richmond was Grand Master.
194 The National Archives Access to Archives database contains over 500 references to different 'Thomas Edwards' for the relevant period. However, by restricting the data to London and to 'gentlemen', it is probable that Thomas Edwards was either a barrister at Lincoln's Inn (LMA: ACC/0891/02/01/0137-0138 *27/28 Jan 1723*) or at the Middle Temple (Lambeth Palace Library: AA/V/H/79/32/1-3 *1721*).
195 The LMA contain a record of a Giles Taylor being briefed to defend an action brought by the Earl of Uxbridge in the Court of Common Pleas: ACC/0539/122 *29 January 1732*. Other LMA records refer to Giles Taylor of Lyons Inn, Middx., Gent.: JER/HBY/53/6 *24 May 1732* and ACC/1045/114 *1750*. The *Daily Courant*, 22 May 1725 and other press reports confirm that Taylor practiced at Lyon's Inn, Inner Temple. That he was a JP is indicated by LMA: MSes, JWP, MS/SP *2 March 1727*. Giles Taylor and Brook Taylor were both Governors of the Bridewell Royal Hospital.
196 Not the scientist and FRS who died in 1687. A William Petty 'of the City of London' was recorded in the Suffolk Record Office: FC88/L1/23 *29 September 1743*. Another Petty was recorded as 'of Brentford, Middlesex, gentleman', cf. Wiltshire and Swindon Archives: 9/19/507 *20 January 1717*. If the name was written incorrectly: possibly William Pate or William Pette.
197 Possibly William Richardson (1698–1775), an antiquary, curate of St Olave's Southwark (1723–6), and a member of the lodge at the Bull's Head, Southwark. Cf. *Grand Lodge Minutes*, p. 28. A William Richardson was also a member of the Carpenters' Company and the same person or a man of the same name a member of the Court of Governors of the Bridewell Royal Hospital.
198 West Sussex Record Office: Goodwood/42-3 and 107/676-716. Prendergast (*b.* 1702–1760), succeeded to his father's title in 1709 and was elected to the Irish Parliament as MP for Clonmel (1727–1760) and, briefly, to the British Parliament as MP for Chichester (1733–1734). Richmond secured him Chichester in 1733 but after Prendergast voted against the Excise Bill later that year, Walpole ensured his defeat in the 1734 election: Paul Hopkins, 'Sir Thomas Prendergast, second baronet', *ODNB*. George II described Prendergast as an 'Irish blockhead': cf. Timothy McCann, *The Correspondence of the Dukes of Richmond & Newcastle 1724–50* (Lewes, 1984), p. 3, fn. 6. Cf. also, R. Sedgwick (ed.), *Sir Thomas Prendergast* in *The History of Parliament: the House of Commons, 1715–1754* (Cambridge & London, 1970).
199 *Sackler Archives*; also Lenore Feigenbaum, 'Brook Taylor', *ODNB*. Taylor was a brilliant mathematician and scientist; his published works arguably provided stronger support for Newton's calculus than that provided by Newton himself. Cf. Brook Taylor, *Methodus incrementorum directa et inversa* (London, 1715).
200 *Sackler Archives*.
201 *Evening Post*, 4 July 1724.
202 An advertisement seeking the return of deserters was published in the *Daily Courant* successively on 4, 5 and 6 August 1720.
203 *Grand Lodge Minutes*, p. 121.
204 *Ibid.*, p. 129.

205 Daily Post, 2 January 1730.
206 'Letter of William Reid to the Anchor and Hope Lodge, Bolton' dated 2 December 1732: United Grand Lodge of England Library: HC/8/F/2.
207 Grand Lodge Minutes, p. 227.
208 Grand Lodge Minutes, pp. 233–5.

CHAPTER FOUR **The Professional Nexus**

1   Kebbell, *The Changing Face of Freemasonry*, p. 19.
2   Clark, *British Clubs and Societies*, p. 9.
3   James Bramston, *The Man of Taste. Occasion'd by an Epistle of Mr Pope's on that Subject* (London, 1733), p. 14. Cf. also Borsay, *The English Urban Renaissance: Culture and Society in the Provincial Town 1660–1770* (Oxford, 1989); Paul Langford, *A Polite and Commercial People: England 1727–1783* (Oxford, 1989).
4   Pumfrey, 'Who Did the Work? Experimental Philosophers and Public Demonstrators', *op. cit.*
5   David Boyd Haycock, 'Martin Folkes', *ODNB*. Tangentially, Boyd Haycock mentions *inter alia* that Folkes's uncle later became Archbishop of Canterbury.
6   *Ibid.*
7   *Sackler Archives.*
8   The quote is attributed to Dr James Jurin, Secretary of the Royal Society (1721–7): Dudley Wright, *England's Masonic Pioneers* (Whitefish, 2003), p. 98. Jurin dedicated the 34th volume of the RS *Transactions* to Folkes. They were close friends. Folkes had originally proposed Jurin FRS in November 1717 and both were Council members: Jurin, 1718, 1720–26; Folkes, 1716, 1718–26.
9   The full name of the tavern was the Duke of Bedford's Head.
10 The Maid's Head tavern was close to Hillington Hall, acquired by the Folkes family in 1678 on the marriage of Folkes' father to the daughter of Sir William Hovell. Norfolk Record Office: MC 50. The lodge later hosted the raising of Francis, Duke of Lorraine, at a meeting at Walpole's Houghton Hall.
11 *Grand Lodge Minutes*, pp. 204, 213; *Grand Lodge Minutes 1740–58*, pp. 3, 10, 17.
12 John Byrom, *The Private Journal and Literary Remains of John Byrom* (Whitefish, 2009). The journals were originally published in parts by the Chetham Society as Chetham Society Papers (Old Series), OS 32, OS 34, OS 40 and OS 44 (Manchester, 1854–7).
13 *Ibid.*
14 Richmond, *A Duke and His Friends*, p. 252.
15 2nd Duke of Richmond, *Letter to Princess Pamphili at Rome*, 13 August 1733.
16 Cf., Richmond, *A Duke and His Friends*, pp. 258–9. Letter to the Countess Celia Borromea, 22 October 1733.
17 *Ibid.*, pp. 254–6, 12 August 1733.
18 *Ibid.*, pp. 259–61. Letter to Martin Folkes, 11 October 1733.
19 'Richmond to Newcastle, 18 October 1747': McCann, *The Correspondence of the Dukes of Richmond & Newcastle 1724–50*, p. 259.
20 Richmond, *A Duke and His Friends*, p. 254. Additional examples of correspondence are located in the Goodwood archives at the West Sussex Record Office and, to a lesser extent, at the Royal Society. Cf., for example,

'Part of a Letter from His Grace the Duke of Richmond, Lennox and Aubigne, FRS to M. Folkes, Esq', RS *Philosophical Transactions*, 42 (1742–3), 510–3.
21   *Grand Lodge Minutes*, pp. 26, 37, 58, 62–3, 68, 74, 197, 204 and 213.
22   *Sackler Archives*.
23   Possibly Richard Cantillon (1680–1734), the banker, investor and economist.
24   The membership list of the Bedford Head was compiled in or shortly before 1725.
25   It is also possible but less likely that 'the Hon. Mr Cornwallis' refers to the Hon. Thomas Cornwallis, a commissioner for the national lottery.
26   *Evening Post*, 23 May 1723.
27   Linda and Marsha Frey, 'Charles Townshend, third Viscount Townshend (1700–1764)', *ODNB*.
28   *London Journal*, 15 September 1722.
29   *Weekly Journal or British Gazetteer*, 15 September 1722.
30   *Weekly Journal or British Gazetteer*, 4 April 1724.
31   *Daily Courant*, 12 January 1731.
32   John Harris, *Lexicon Technicum*, 2 volumes (London, 1704 & 1710).
33   Tangentially, Cox would have known John Keill in connection with the Palatine resettlement.
34   There are two records of a marriage settlement between Sir Charles Cox, Gratiana Cox, one of his daughters, and 'Leonard Streate of St Clemet Danes, Middx.' held at East Sussex Record Office: AMS2241 *15 & 16 May 1723*, and Hertfordshire Archives: DE/Ru/74463 *16 May 1723*, respectively. 'Street' or 'Streate' was a member of the Horn, and a barrister at the Middle Temple (East Sussex Record Office: SAS-H/362 *12 June 1719*); he was also deputy to a commissioner in the Alienation Office (William A. Shaw (ed.) *Calendar of Treasury Books* (London, 1952), vol. 21, pp. 299–300. Cox lost several thousand pounds in a fire at his warehouses in 1714 and petitioned the Lords of the Treasury for relief: Joseph Redington (ed.), *Calendar of Treasury Papers, 1714–19* (London, 1883), vol. 5, p. 20.
35   John Times, *Club Life of London* (London, 1866), p. 197.
36   Alexander Pope, *Imitations of Horace, The First Satire of the Second Book of Horace* (London, 1736).
37   Alexander Pope, *Sober Advice from Horace* (London, 1737).
38   Horace Walpole, *Letter to Sir Thomas Mann, 20 November 1741*: quoted in Reginald Jacobs, *Covent Garden . . .* (London, 1913), p. 174.
39   James Stirling (FRS, 1726, proposed by John Arbuthnot), was from 1725 until 1735 a lecturer, then a partner, at Watt's Academy in Little Tower Street, Covent Garden.
40   J.R. Clarke's analysis of members of Masonic lodges who were FRS omits certain Fellows: Clarke, 'The Royal Society and Early Grand Lodge Freemasonry', *AQC Transactions*, 80, Supplement (1967). Cf. also Bruce Hogg (compiler), *Freemasons and the Royal Society, an Alphabetical List of Fellows of the Royal Society who were Freemasons* (London, 2010).
41   Also written as 'Dieskaw' and/or 'Diescau'. Dieskau was wounded fighting against the British colonial forces in Canada in 1755. He was captured and repatriated, but later died of his wounds.
42   The Duke of Queensberry, who quarrelled with George II in the late 1720s, was among five of the Prince of Wales's Gentlemen of the Bedchamber who

were Freemasons. The others were Carnarvon, Baltimore, Darnley and Inchiquin.
43   Richmond also had a close relationship with several non aristocratic FRS. In addition to Folkes, they included Desaguliers, who later accompanied him to France and Holland, and William Stukeley.
44   Later 2nd Duke of Buccleuch.
45   Later 7th Earl of Abercorn.
46   Grand Master of Grand Lodge of Ireland (1731 & 1735).
47   Later Viscount Coke and 1st Earl of Leicester.
48   Later, 2nd Duke of Chandos.
49   Grand Master of the Grand Lodge of Scotland (1738–9).
50   KT, 1738; Grand Master of Scottish Grand Lodge (1739–40); later, PRS (1764–8) and VPRS (1763–4).
51   Parker studied with both Abraham de Moivre (FRS 1697) and William Jones (FRS 1711). He held the title Viscount Parker from 1721 until 1732, when he succeeded as Earl of Macclesfield. A loyal Hanoverian, he had been appointed Teller of the Exchequer (1719–death), where he would have met Blackerby, Chocke and Payne. He was also MP for Wallingford (1722–7).
52   *Sackler Archives*; cf. also, A.M. Clerke, 'George Parker, George, second earl of Macclesfield', rev. Owen Gingerich, *ODNB*.
53   William Sloane's relationship with Hans Sloane was particularly strong given that Hans Sloane's son had died in infancy. He was married to the daughter of John Fuller, the Whig MP for Sussex, who was also proposed FRS by Hans Sloane. Completing the circle, Fuller's wife was Hans Sloane's stepdaughter.
54   Clarke, *The Royal Society and Early Grand Lodge Freemasonry*, pp. 110–19.
55   *Ibid.*, pp. 111–12.
56   Clark, *British Clubs and Societies*, p. 448.
57   Trevor Stewart, 'English Speculative Freemasonry: Some Possible Origins, Themes and Developments', *AQC Transactions*, 117 (2004), 116–82.
58   *Sackler Archives.* Jones proposed or co-proposed over 30 FRS in total.
59   Stukeley, *Family Memoirs*, vol. 1, p. 100.
60   James E. Force, 'Hume and the Relation of Science to Religion among Certain Members of the Royal Society', *Journal of the History of Ideas*, 45.4 (1984), 517–36, esp. 518.
61   Stukeley, *Family Memoirs*, vol. 1, p. 32.
62   *Ibid.*, vol. 1, p. 51. Cf. also, David Haycock, 'Stukeley and the Mysteries', *Freemasonry Today*, 6 (1998), 15–17.
63   Stukeley, *Family Memoirs*, vol. 1, p. 77.
64   *Ibid.*, vol. 1, pp. 60, 62 and 63, respectively.
65   William Stukeley, *Of the Spleen, its Description and History, Uses and Diseases* (London, 1722).
66   J. Evans, *A history of the Royal Society of Antiquaries* (Oxford, 1956), p. xxxviii, quoted in da Costa, 'The Culture of Curiosity at The Royal Society in the First Half of the Eighteenth Century'.
67   Stukeley, *Family Memoirs*, vol. 1, p. 62 entry for 6 January 1721. Kebbell has suggested that Stukeley 'sought out the first lodge he could find' in order to become a Freemason: Kebbell, *op. cit.*, pp. 62–3.
68   Stukeley, *Family Memoirs*, vol. 1, p. 64.
69   *Ibid.*, vol. 1, pp. 66, 133. The lodge records, if any, have not been preserved and no membership lists are extant.

70 Ibid., vol. 1, p. 123.
71 David Boyd Haycock, 'William Stukeley', *ODNB*.
72 Stukeley, *Family Memoirs*, vol. 1, p. 190.
73 Ibid., vol. 1, pp. 261–2.
74 Hewitt has put forward circumstantial evidence that suggests that Johnson was also a Freemason: A.R. Hewitt, 'A Lincolnshire Notable and the Old Lodge at Spalding', *AQC Transactions*, 83 (1970), 96–101.
75 J. Nichols, *Literary anecdotes of the eighteenth century* (New York, 1966), vol. 6, pp. 6–7. This version is a facsimile; the series was originally published London, 1812–6.
76 Stukeley, *Family Memoirs*, vol. 1, p. 190. Cf. also, William E Burns, *Science in the Enlightenment* (Oxford, 2003), p. 77.
77 Sackler Archives.
78 George W. Lowis et al. (eds.), *Midwifery and the Medicalization of Childbirth: Comparative Perspectives* (Waltham, 2004), p. 103. Cf. also *Sackler Archives*.
79 Clark, *British Clubs and Societies*, op. cit.
80 Stukeley, *Family Memoirs*, vol. 1, p. 326.
81 Cf. Jeremy Black, *The British Abroad: The Grand Tour in the Eighteenth Century* (Stroud, 2003), paperback ed., p. 224. The book was originally published in 1992.
82 FRCPs admitted before 1690 have been excluded from the analysis on age grounds.
83 Worshipful Society of Apothecaries, *Membership Records, 1700–1740*, unpublished.
84 Anstis (also written as 'Antis'), was Garter King of Arms.
85 Possibly Peregrine Bertie (1686–1742), 2nd Duke of Ancaster and Kesteven, or his son of the same name (1714–1778), later the 3rd Duke. There was also a cousin and godson of the Duke with the same name who later married a Miss Payne of Chancery Lane, 'a young Lady of considerable fortune'. Cf. *Daily Journal*, 26 November 1734; *London Evening Post*, 21 December 1736; and *Daily Journal*, 24 December 1736.
86 Charles Hayes (1678–1760), the geographer and mathematician.
87 Col. Daniel Houghton.
88 Probably John Johnson, the barrister.
89 Richard Richardson (1663–1741), botanist and physician. He was elected FRS in 1712.
90 Shelvocke was appointed Secretary to the Post Office.
91 John Ward (c. 1679–1758), Professor of Rhetoric at Gresham College (1720), elected FRS in 1723, and a member of the Spalding Society. Not the John Ward who was later a Grand Steward, GW, DGM and, as Viscount Ward, Grand Master. Cf. chapter 6.
92 John Woodward (1668–1728), the physician and natural historian. He was elected FRS in 1703.
93 The Spalding Society's detailed membership records are contained in Michael Honeybone's *The Spalding Gentlemen's Society: Scientific communication in the East Midlands of England* (Open University, unpublished PhD Thesis, 2002). Cf. also, Honeybone, *Sociability, Utility and Curiosity in the Spalding Gentleman's Society, 1710–60* in David M. Knight and Matthew D. Eddy (eds.), *Science and Beliefs: From Natural Philosophy to Natural Science* (Aldershot, 2005) pp. 64–75. The Society's members comprised active local

members and honorary members, often from London, to whom membership was granted in return for corresponding. Prominent non-Masonic members included Harley, Newton, Sloane, Pope and Gay.
94 The Hon. Colonel (later General) Churchill.
95 Viscount Falkland; *d.* 1732.
96 George Edwards – a 'possible' rather than a certainty.
97 Richard Ellis, MP for Boston.
98 John Grano, Handel's trumpeter and a composer in his own right.
99 John Green, a physician (FRCP) and secretary of the Spalding Society.
100 Probably John King, later 2nd Baron Ockham. Another 'John King' was a physician and classicist.
101 Jacques Leblon, a well known painter.
102 John Lynwood, a London merchant and vintner.
103 Michael Mitchell, a physician; a 'possible' Freemason.
104 John Morton, a cleric; another 'possible'.
105 John Perry, an engineer.
106 John Roberts, a surgeon.
107 Stevens, a London merchant; Vice President of the Spalding Society; a 'possible'.
108 John Tatham, a cleric; a 'possible'.
109 'John Thomas', a 'possible' member of three other lodges.
110 James Weeks, an artist.
111 Colonel Williamson, Deputy Lieutenant at the Tower of London.
112 Wilson, a barrister; another 'possible'.

CHAPTER FIVE **The Rise of the First Noble Grand Masters**
1 A Gentleman, *Love's last shift: or, the mason disappointed* . . . (London, *c.* 1720).
NB. Although 1720 is the generally assumed publication date, the content suggests that it was probably written and published later *c.* 1722.
2 Harcouët de Longeville, *Long livers: a curious history of such persons of both sexes who have liv'd several ages, and grown young again* (London, 1722).
3 Cf. Andrew Pink, *The Musical Culture of Freemasonry in Early Eighteenth-century London* (University College London, unpublished PhD thesis, 2007).
4 *Applebee's Original Weekly Journal*, 9 September 1721.
5 *Ibid.*
6 *Weekly Journal or Saturday's Post*, 1 July 1721.
7 Harry Wildair, *The Sermon Taster: or Church Rambler* (London, 1723).
8 The *1738 Constitutions* mention on page 110 that in 1719/20 'some Noblemen were also made brothers'. This could be taken as an oblique reference to Montagu.
9 W.G. Fisher, 'John Montague, 2nd Duke of Montagu', *AQC Transactions*, 79 (1966), 72.
10 *Universal Spectator and Weekly Journal*, 20 June 1730.
11 K.H. Ledward (ed.), *Journals of the Board of Trade & Plantations – 1 February 1722* (London, 1925), pp. 341–4; Cecil Headlam (ed.), *Calendar of Sate Papers Colonial, America and West Indies* (London, 1934), vol. 33, pp. 5–51, 197–206. Cf. also *New England Courant*, 17 September 1722.
12 Nathaniel Uring, *A Relation of the late Intended Settlement of the Islands of*

St Lucia and St Vincent in America (London, 1725), pp. 4, 95, 112. Also *Calendar of State Papers Colonial, America and West Indies, Volume 33: 1722–1723* (London, 1934), pp. 425–429.
13 *Daily Courant*, 28 July 1722.
14 His role as chief mourner was endorsed by his mother-in-law, Lady Churchill. Cf. *Daily Journal*, 13 August 1722.
15 *Freeholder's Journal*, 13 February 1723.
16 *Universal Spectator and Weekly Journal*, 19 June 1731.
17 *New England Courant*, 17 September 1722.
18 Edward Charles Metzger, 'John Montagu, second Duke of Montagu', *ODNB*.
19 *London Gazette*, 2 July 1715.
20 *London Gazette*, 19 February 1715.
21 *John Montagu, letter to Robert Walpole*, quoted in Jacob, *The Radical Enlightenment*, p. 102. The original is at CUL: Chol. MSS 2008, *5 July 1734*.
22 H.M. Stephens, 'Thomas Desaguliers (1721–1780)', rev. Jonathan Spain, *ODNB*. Cf. also chapter 2, with respect to the disposition of Desaguliers' assets at his death.
23 Tangentially, there is an interestingly ironic Masonic reference to the Excise Bill in *A Candid Answer to A Letter from a Member of Parliament to his Friends in the Country, concerning the Duties on Wine and Tobacco* (London, 1730), p. v. Commenting on prior correspondence, the author noted: 'I should think him a Freemason of the lowest Order . . . he seems to write not so much for Bread as for good Drink'.
24 W.R. Williams, *rev.* Jonathan Spain, *ONDB*.
25 R.F. Gould, *Military Lodges: the Apron and the Sword of Freemasonry under Arms* (London, 1889), pp. 26–52.
26 Cf. H. Lloyd Wilkerson, *History of Military Lodges in Freemasonry* (Blackmer, 2002); R.J. Sutherland, *Military Lodges* (1988); M. Ripley, *Military Lodges* (Alexandria, 2006); and Michael Baigent and Richard Leigh, *The Temple and the Lodge* (New York, 1989).
27 Clark, *British Clubs and Societies*, pp. 139, 310, 332, 340, 348 and 442. The quotation is from p. 127.
28 *Ibid.*, p. 345.
29 For example, J. Harland-Jacobs, 'All in the Family: Freemasonry and the British Empire in the Mid-Nineteenth Century', *Journal of British Studies*, 42.4 (2003), 448–82; and 'Hands across the Sea: The Masonic Network, British Imperialism, and the North Atlantic World', *Geographical Review*, 89.2 (1999), 237–53.
30 Harland-Jacobs, *Builders of Empire*, op. cit.
31 R.A. Berman, 'A Short Note on Politics, Masonry & India in Victorian England', *Transactions of the Temple of Athene Lodge, No. 9149*, 12 (2006), 33–47.
32 Harland-Jacobs, 'Hands across the Sea', 241–3.
33 *1723 Constitutions*, p. 51: *Of Lodges*.
34 William O'Brien, Lord Kingston, was Grand Master England in 1728 and Grand Master Ireland in 1729–30. The cross over between the home nations' jurisdictions was relatively common: Sir Thomas Prendergast was JGW in England and SGW in Ireland; James Douglas, 14th Earl of Morton, was Grand Master Scotland from 1739–40 and Grand Master England 1741–42; and Earl

Crawford (Grand Master England 1734) was a member of both English and Scottish Grand Lodges.

35   Jacob suggests that Walpole 'allowed himself to be painted wearing the insignia of the Master of the Grand Stewards' Lodge': *The Radical Enlightenment*, p. 97. Although Walpole was made a Mason, there is no evidence that he became a Steward; Colin Dyer in his *The Grand Stewards and Their Lodge* (London, 1985), p. 44, suggests that the relevant portrait by J.B. Vanloo was not of Walpole.
36   Cf. William C. Lowe, 'Jeffrey Amherst, first Baron Amherst', *ODNB*.
37   Sir John Fortescue, *A History of the British Army* (Uckfield, 2004), vol. 2, pp. 296, 300, 316, 323, 325 and 361. Cf also, Gould, *History of Freemasonry*, vol. 4, pp. 400–3.
38   The exception was the 44th Foot; the regiment did not have a lodge until 1784 (Lodge No. 467, English, Moderns).
39   Gould, *History of Freemasonry*, vol. 4, p. 255.
40   *The Egmont Papers, op. cit.*
41   Harland-Jacobs, 'Hands across the Sea', pp. 241–2.
42   A duplicate warrant was issued in 1748.
43   The Duke of Brunswick commanded the Allied forces at Minden; he had been initiated into Freemasonry in Berlin in 1740, cf. Gould, *Military Lodges*, p. 130. The Colonel of the 20th Foot, Major General William Kingsley, was also a Freemason: cf. Gould, *Military Lodges*, p. 108.
44   Harland-Jacobs, 'Hands across the Sea', p. 242.
45   *Grand Lodge Minutes*, pp. 38–9.
46   In keeping with pre-eighteenth century practice, at least one member of the lodge, in this case, a Jonathan Hicks, was also an operative mason. The point is substantiated by a classified advertisement seeking the return of an absconded stonemason's apprentice published in the *London Journal*, 22 May 1725.
47   L.R. Harborne and R.L.W. White, *The History of Freemasonry in Berkshire and Buckinghamshire* (Abingdon, 1990), pp. 1–3.
48   *Post Man and the Historical Account*, 31 July 1714.
49   *London Gazette*, 29 March 1718.
50   Jeremy Black, *Culture in eighteenth century England: A Subject for Taste* (London, 2006), p. 24.
51   Sarah Churchill, *Private correspondence of Sarah, Duchess of Marlborough* (London, 1838), vol. II, pp. 195–6.
52   Stukeley, *Family Memoirs*, vol. 1, pp. 100 & 114. Stukeley may have written these comments in around 1751; in the 1720s, his relationship with Folkes was far less antagonistic. Cf. also, David Boyd Haycock, *William Stukeley: Science, Religion and Archaeology in Eighteenth-Century England* (Woodbridge, 2002), chapter 9.
53   William Jones, FRS, a member of the Queens Head. See chapter 4 above.
54   Stukeley, *Family Memoirs*, vol. 1, pp. 99–100.
55   Lotte Mulligan and Glenn Mulligan, 'Reconstructing Restoration Science', *Social Studies of Science*, 11.3 (1981), 327–64, esp. 351, 360 fn. 51, and 363 fn. 109. Cf. also, Dieter Turck, 'Review: Liebniz's Correspondence (1692)', *Journal of the History of Ideas*, 32.4 (1971), 627–30, esp. 629.
56   *Sackler Archives*; also, Boughton House Trust, *Information for Teachers* (2004), p. 11.

57 Bedfordshire and Luton Archives and Record Service: X800, Antonie family of Colworth. (Marc Antonie was Steward to the 1st Duke.)
58 Edward Charles Metzger, 'John Montagu, second Duke of Montagu', *ODNB*.
59 *Emulation Ritual* (Hersham, 2003), pp. 249–50, *Explanation of the First Tracing Board*.
60 *1738 Constitutions*, pp. 112–13, and Stukeley, *Family Memoirs*, vol. 1, p. 64.
61 Lord Herbert inherited as 9th Earl of Pembroke in 1733. Herbert was a noted antiquary and had a particular interest in architecture, working with both Colen Campbell and Roger Morris, Campbell's assistant. He was later responsible with Charles Labelye for overseeing construction of the new Westminster Bridge. Cf. T.P. Connor, 'Henry Herbert', *ODNB*.
62 Richmond's father, the 1st Duke, was also reputed to have been a Freemason; his uncle, the Duke of St Albans, was in 1725 Master of the Queen's Head in Bath.
63 *Grand Lodge Minutes*, pp. 60, 116, 196, 217, 229.
64 Villeneau was certainly a Huguenot; the various spellings of Morris (e.g. 'Morrice') are anglicizations of 'Maurice'.
65 Lawrence B. Smith, 'Philip Wharton, Duke of Wharton and Jacobite Duke of Northumberland', *ODNB*.
66 The Centre for Buckinghamshire Studies: D-LE/A/2/4/j, *29 November 1721*.
67 Lewis Benjamin, *South Sea Bubble* (Manchester, New Hampshire, 1967), p. 49; also, John Noorthouck, *A New History of London*, vol. 1, pp. 306–25.
68 Lewis Melville, *South Sea Bubble* (London, 1921), p. 157.
69 *1738 Constitutions*, p. 114; also discussed in R.F. Gould, *History of Freemasonry*, vol. 2, p. 289.
70 Cf. *Weekly Journal or Saturday's Post*, 22 June 1723; *British Journal*, 29 June 1723; and *London Journal*, 29 June 1723.
71 *Grand Lodge Minutes* were usually signed by the Grand Master (in this case Dalkeith) at the next regular meeting of Grand Lodge. On this occasion they were signed in Dalkeith's absence by Desaguliers.
72 J.T. Desaguliers, *The Newtonian System of the World, the best Model of Government* (Westminster, 1728).
73 Randolph Trumbach, *Sex and the Gender Revolution: Heterosexuality and the Third Gender in Enlightenment London* (Chicago, 1998), p. 83.
74 'Letter to the Countess of Mar, February 1724', in Lady Mary Wortley Montagu, Lord Wharcliffe (ed.), *The Letters and Works of Lady Mary Wortley Montagu* (New York, 1893), vol. 1, p. 477. The correspondence was previously published by Richard Bentley (London, 1837).
75 Tangentially, a letter to a 'Madam Gell' held in the Derbyshire Record Office: D258/38/6/28 1726, recorded intelligence from Rome that Wharton was to be governor to the Pretender's son.
76 James Scott was styled as 'Earl of Doncaster' (1674–85), and 'Earl of Dalkeith' (1685–1705).
77 In addition to his own assets, he also inherited an income of £12,000 per year on the death of his mother in 1724: *Parker's London News or the Impartial Intelligencer*, 13 April 1724.
78 For example, *Weekly Packet*, 19 March 1720.
79 Rosalind K. Marshall, 'Lady Jane Douglas (1698–1753)', *ODNB*, has stated that Dalkeith's wife, Lady Jane Douglas (1701–29) was Lady Mary Kerr's sister-in-law. A review of *The Peerage* does not appear to substantiate this.

None of Lady Mary Kerr's three brothers (Charles Kerr, Lord of Cramond; Sir William Kerr, 2nd Marquess of Lothian; and General Mark Kerr) was related through marriage to Lady Jane Douglas. Similarly, neither Kerr's husband stepbrother nor stepsister (Lady Margaret Douglas and Archibald Douglas, 1st Earl of Forfar) appear to be related to Lady Jane Douglas, although all were members of the extended Douglas clan.

80 Marshall, 'Lady Jane Douglas', *ODNB*.
81 *Evening Post*, 26 March 1720; *Weekly Packet*, 26 March 1720; and *Original Weekly Journal*, 2 April 1720.
82 *Original Weekly Journal*, 9 April 1720.
83 This Lady Jane Douglas was also the sister of the 3rd Duke of Queensbury. Cf. *Post Boy*, 5 April 1720.
84 Dalkeith had five children, the first of which was born the following year: *Weekly Packet*, 18 February 1721. The Duchess of Dalkeith died of smallpox in 1729, aged 28.
85 *Weekly Journal or British Gazetteer*, 29 June 1723.
86 Cf. *Grand Lodge Minutes*, Preface, p. ix.
87 'Richmond to Newcastle, 9 March 1745': McCann, *The Correspondence of the Dukes of Richmond and Newcastle 1724–1750*, p. 209.
88 *Grand Lodge Minutes*, 25 November 1723, p. 54.
89 Cf. *Grand Lodge Minutes*, p. 146; also pp. 91, 102, 105, 128 and 134.
90 At the February 1735 meeting of Grand Lodge, Dalkeith was recorded in the *Minutes* as the Duke of Buccleuch. He donated £27 10s to the General Charity with a recommendation that charitable assistance be given to a member of the Rummer. The payment was later made by Grand Lodge on Desaguliers' proposition.
91 *British Journal*, 28 March 1724; and *Daily Post*, 23 November 1724.
92 'Richmond to Newcastle, 28 November 1742': McCann, *The Correspondence of the Dukes of Richmond and Newcastle*, pp. 91–2.
93 *1738 Constitutions*, pp. 117–19.
94 One of the earliest Masonic songs was Matthew Birkhead's 'The Free Masons's Health' (London, 1720). The vocal score is at United Grand Lodge of England: M/10 BIR.
95 Cf. Dorothy George, *London Life in the Eighteenth Century* (London, 1966), 2nd edn.; Roy Porter, *London: A Social History* (London, 1984); and Schwarz, *London in the Age of Industrialisation*, op. cit. Other sections of society would have been unable to afford the membership and dining fees.
96 The 1st Duke was the illegitimate son of Charles II and his French mistress, Louise Renée de Penancoët de Keroualle, created Duchess of Portsmouth. Cf. M. Wynne, 'Louise Renée de Penancoët de Kéroualle, suo jure duchess of Portsmouth and suo jure duchess of Aubigny in the French nobility (1649–1734)', *ODNB*.
97 Timothy McCann, 'Charles Lennox, second Duke of Richmond, second Duke of Lennox, and Duke of Aubigny in the French nobility', *ODNB*.
98 British Library, Add. MS 32700, fol. 264.
99 'Newcastle to Bishop Bowers, 6 June 1723': McCann, *Correspondence of the Dukes of Richmond and Newcastle*, pp. xxiii, xxvi.
100 *Ibid.*, pp. xxxi.
101 *Ibid.*, p. xxxi.
102 McCann, 'Charles Lennox, second Duke of Richmond', *ODNB*.

103 'Note from Walpole appointing Richmond to vote as his proxy at the General Court of the Royal Academy of Music, 4 December 1727': West Sussex Record Office: Goodwood/142–145, *1727–1735*. Cf. also, 'Letters from Walpole to Richmond regarding the Shoreham election' at West Sussex Record Office: Goodwood/1961.
104 McCann, 'Charles Lennox, second Duke of Richmond', *ODNB*.
105 *Ibid*.
106 *Ibid*.
107 Although extremely cordial, Desaguliers' personal relationship with Richmond also reflected their relative status. Cf. 'Letter in verse to Richmond from 'JTD'': West Sussex Record Office: Goodwood 110 D Correspondents, *November 1721 – December 1749*. Their relationship and relative status was in clear contrast to that of Folkes/Richmond.
108 Cf. Andrew Prescott, 'Freemasonry and the Problem of Britain', *CRFF Working Paper*, http://www.freemasonry.dept.shef.ac.uk/index.php.
109 R. William Weisberger, 'Parisian Masonry, the Lodge of the Nine Sisters & the French Enlightenment', *Heredom*, 10 (2002), 155–62.
110 D. Ligou, *Histoire des francs-maçons en France, 1725–1815* (Paris, 2000).
111 Pope Clement XII. Cf. http://www.papalencyclicals.net/Clem12/c15inemengl.htm.
112 Pierre Chevallier, *Les Ducs Sous L'Acacia* (Paris, 1964), pp. 101–3.
113 Weisberger, *op. cit.*, p. 161.
114 Quoted in R.F. Gould, *History of Freemasonry throughout the World*, vol. III, p. 22. On p. 21, Gould bemoaned the 'total absence of any other [academic or historical] authority' for the statement.
115 Reed Browning, 'Thomas-Pellam-Holles, Duke of Newcastle upon Tyne and first Duke of Newcastle under Lyme (1693–1768)', *ODNB*.
116 The Hon. George Churchill was a member of the Rummer, Charing Cross.
117 Edward Young was the Registrar of the Order of the Bath. Cf. *London Evening Post*, 5 September 1734.
118 *St James's Evening Post*, 7 September 1734.
119 Louis de Brancas de Forcalquier (1672–1750), Marquis de Brancas, was a French aristocrat. He was appointed a Chevalier de la Toison d'Or in 1713, served as French Ambassador to Madrid, and was made a Marshal of France in 1740. He also held office as governor of Provence.
120 Major General Lord Skelton, who died two years later in May 1736, 'followed the fortunes of the later King James II': *Weekly Miscellany*, 29 May 1736. He was buried 'without ceremony' at St Sulpice in Paris: *Daily Gazetteer*, 27 May 1736.
121 *Daily Courant*, 6 September 1734. Montesquieu's son was Jean Baptiste Secondat de Montesquieu. Cf. below.
122 Hill was later appointed Secretary to the Council of Trade and Plantations (the Board of Trade); he held the office from 19 October 1737–20 September 1758. Cf. J.C. Sainty, *Office-Holders in Modern Britain* (London, 1974), vol. 3, pp. 28–37.
123 *Amadis de Gaula* is a sixteenth-century Spanish tale of knight errantry. It was the subject of an opera by Handel in 1715: *Amadigi di Gaula*.
124 'Tyled' – the reference is to a closed and guarded Masonic lodge.
125 Literally the 'Old Gaul', probably 'ancient or historical French'.
126 A copy of the letter is at the United Grand Lodge of England Library: HC/8/F/3.

It provides tangential evidence of Desaguliers' attendance at The Hague in 1734 in connection with the establishment of La Chapelle's lodge. Cf. below. Richmond is also known to have visited The Hague in May and September / October 1734.

127 *Old Whig or The Consistent Protestant*, 25 September 1735. Cf. also, *General Evening Post*, 18 September 1735, and George Kenning and A.F.A. Woodford, *Kenning's Masonic Encyclopedia and Handbook of Masonic Archaeology, History and Biography* (Oxford, 2003), p. 233.
128 *Grand Lodge Minutes*, pp. 6 & 24.
129 Philip Woodfine, 'James, first earl Waldegrave', *ODNB*.
130 George Teissier was physician to George I, George II and to the Chelsea and St George's Hospitals.
131 St. Hyacinthe, a soldier, rake and author, also co-founded the influential *Journal litteraire* with Willem Jacob 'sGravesande in 1713: Sackler Archives.
132 *The British Journal*, 16 May 1730. Cf. also Melvin Richter, *Charles de Secondat Montesquieu, The Political Theory of Montesquieu* (Cambridge, 1977), p. 15.
133 *Whitehall Evening Post*, 5 September 1734.
134 'Montesquieu to Richmond, 2 July 1735' published in R. Shackleton, 'Montesquieu's Correspondence', *French Studies*, XII.4 (1958), 324–45, esp. 328. Original at Goodwood, Box 36, bundle IX.
135 'Montesquieu to Richmond, 20 May 1734': *Ibid.*, 327.
136 Evelyn Pierrepont, 2nd Duke of Kingston (1711–73), succeeded to his grandfather's title in 1726. He opened the batting for Eton against an All England eleven in 1725, which may suggest how he was known to Richmond, who was a cricket fanatic. Kingston spent ten years on the Grand Tour where he was known for what may be politely termed his 'loose living'. He was a loyal Hanoverian and later played an active role in the 1745, raising and becoming Colonel of his own Regiment, 'Kingston's Light Horse', which fought against the Jacobites at Culloden.
137 *Amsterdamse Courant*, 2 October 1731. Quoted in Johan A. van Reijn, 'John Theophilus Desaguliers, 1683–1983', *Thoth*, 5 (1983), 194, and referred to by Carpenter, *op. cit.*, pp. 51–2.
138 NA: SP 84/314, fs. 187–8.
139 Cf. Horace Wapole, *Speeches and Debates in the Fifth Session of the First Parliament of King George II, History & Proceedings of the House of Commons* (London, 1742), vol. 7, pp. 87–133, 13 January 1731.
140 Cf. CUL: Manuscripts and Archives, Ch(H), Correspondence, 1, 1178, 1371 (Horace Walpole), 1454, 1864.
141 Cf. 'Letter from Chesterfield to Richmond (undated)': A Duke and his Friends, pp. 157–8.
142 The Duke and Duchess had friends and family at The Hague and were frequent visitors. Cf. Richmond, *A Duke and his Friends*, pp. 34–5, 46–7, 50–1, 60–2, 64, 75–6, 142, 154, 162, 282.
143 The 'Hague Lodge in Holland for Constitution': *Grand Lodge Minutes*, p. 262. Cf. also, Lane, *Masonic Records*.
144 *Saturdagshe Courant* (Amsterdam), 3 November 1734: quoted by Gould, *History of Freemasonry Throughout the World*, p. 204.
145 *Ibid.*, p. 203.
146 Jacob, *The Radical Enlightenment*, p. 81.

147 Ibid., p. 81.
148 Jane Clark, *Lord Burlington is Here*, in Tony Barnard and Jane Clark (eds.), *Lord Burlington: Architecture, Art and Life* (London, 1995), p. 308.
149 The Earl of Essex, a senior courtier and first Gentleman of the Bedchamber in Prince George's household.
150 Romney Sedgwick (ed.), *Lord Hervey's Memoirs* (London, 1931), vol. III, p. 12.
151 Henry Fielding, *An Enquiry into the Causes of the late increase in Robbers* (London, 1751), 2nd edn., p. 107.
152 McCann, *Correspondence of the Dukes of Richmond and Newcastle*, pp. xxiii–xxx.
153 *Daily Post*, 23 November 1724.
154 *London Daily Post and General Advertiser*, 22 September 1739.
155 *Grand Lodge Minutes*, pp. 30, 36.
156 *Grand Lodge Minutes*, p. 216, 2 March 1732. Questions were put to Hall and, after discussion, it was resolved that he be awarded six guineas 'for his present subsistence'.
157 Grand Lodge Minutes: pp. 54–8 elected and presides at Grand Lodge; p. 60, orders lodges to consider proposals for a General Charity; p. 62, term of office extended by 6 months; p. 63, proposes Paisley as his successor; pp. 64–8, report of committee re General Charity; p. 72, proposes that Past Grand Wardens be admitted members of Grand Lodge; pp. 116, 119, 114, 197, 213, 216, 217, 229, 241, 251, 263, 264, 271, 286, 300: present in Grand Lodge; p. 218, dines at Hampstead.
158 For example, the initiation of the Earl of Sunderland: *London Journal*, 3 January 1730.
159 *Sackler Archives*.
160 *Sackler Archives*.
161 'Letter from Richmond to Folkes, Aubigny, 3 October 1728': *A Duke and his Friends*, pp. 154–6.
162 *Grand Lodge Minutes*, pp. 58–9
163 Ibid., p. 59.
164 Richmond, *A Duke and His Friends*, pp. 120–1. Cf. also, pp. 119–20, 156, 180, 188, 215, 218, 253, 255–6, 258–60, 295–6, 302, 349.
165 Ibid., pp. 119–20. Desaguliers was DGM in 1725.
166 Ibid., pp. 295–6, regarding Webber's initiation.
167 *Grand Lodge Minutes*, pp. 59–60.
168 Ibid., pp. 64–8.
169 Ibid., p. 69.
170 Cf. for example, the *Daily Post*, 28 December 1725; and the *Weekly Journal or British Gazetteer*, 1 January 1726.
171 James Hamilton, *Calculations and Tables on the Attractive Power of Lodestones, that is, Magnetism* (London, 1729). He also translated a work on harmony by the German-born composer and founder of London's Academy of Ancient Music, Johann Christoph Pepusch.
172 *1738 Constitutions*, p. 120.
173 The National Archives Access to Archives database contains over 180 published entries for the Duke of Norfolk for the period 1729–30. None relate specifically to his Freemasonry and no relevant documents have yet been located elsewhere.

174 *London Evening Post*, 6 February 1729.
175 *Daily Post*, 22 January 1730.
176 *Grand Lodge Minutes*, p. 128.
177 *Ibid*.
178 Cf. for example, *Flying Post or The Weekly Medley*, 11 January 1729; and the *Daily Journal*, 19 February 1729. Norfolk featured in over 440 press articles between 1720 and his death in 1732.
179 Cf. for example, a report of his journey to Bath and return *Daily Post*, 24 November 1729.
180 *London Evening Post*, 3 March 1730.
181 *London Evening Post*, 12 March 1730.
182 The *London Evening Post*, 3 March 1730, recorded twelve Masons being admitted to the lodge at the Prince William Tavern in the presence of Norfolk, Lord Kingston, Sir William Saunderson, Sir William Young, Nathaniel Blackerby, Col. Carpenter and others. The same report was carried elsewhere, including the *Daily Post*, 5 March 1730, and the *Weekly Journal or British Gazetteer* and the *British Journal*, both on 7 March 1730.
183 *Grand Lodge Minutes*, p. 140.
184 *London Evening Post*, 21 May 1730.
185 The engraving was undertaken by George Moody, Master of the lodge at the Devil Tavern and Sword Cutler to the royal household. Moody was later appointed Grand Sword Bearer. The sword remains in use today.
186 *1738 Constitutions*, p. 127.
187 *Grand Lodge Minutes*, p. 142.
188 A.A. Hanham, 'Thomas Coke, earl of Leicester (1697–1759)', *ODNB*. Coke's name was pronounced 'Cook', and was often spelled the same way. Cf. Anderson, *1738 Constitutions*, pp. 128, 142. A 'Thomas Cook' was Warden of the lodge at King Henry VIII's Head, Seven Dials. Cf. *Grand Lodge Minutes*, p. 43.
189 *British Journal or The Censor*, 27 April 1728. Also, *London Journal*, 27 April 1728.
190 *London Evening Post*, 7 April 1730; also *Sackler Archives*.
191 *London Gazette*, 17 April 1722.
192 *Weekly Journal or British Gazetteer*, 29 May 1725.
193 Hanham, 'Thomas Coke', *ODNB*.
194 Cf. for example, *London Evening Post*, 15 May 1731; *Daily Post*, 17 May 1731; and *Daily Post*, 14 June 1731.
195 *London Evening Post*, 3 September 1730. An early (and possibly the first) Masonically-linked play post-1720 was Charles Johnson's 'Love in a Forest, a comedy acted at the Theatre Royal in Drury-Lane, by His Majesty's Servants' (London, 1723). Cf. United Grand Lodge of England: BE 737 JOH. The dedication, 'To The Worshipful Society of Freemasons', reflected the image Freemasonry most wished to project: 'encouraging and being instructed in useful Arts . . . [and] all the social Virtues which raise and improve the Mind of Man'.
196 *London Evening Post*, 25 November 1731; and *Grub Street Journal*, 2 December 1731.
197 Alexander Brodie (1679–1754), was a government loyalist; he was rewarded in July 1727 with appointment as Lord Lyon, King of Arms, at an annual salary of £300. The position had previously been known as a 'centre of Jacobite

sympathies' in Scotland. He is discussed below. Cf. Andrew M. Lang, 'Alexander Brodie of Brodie', *ODNB*.
198 This was reported in many newspapers, cf. for example, *General Evening Post*, 17 April 1735.
199 Cf. John Lindsay, Earl of Crawford, *Memoirs of the life of the late Right Honourable John Earl of Craufurd* (London, 1769), for a description of his early life and military campaigns.
200 Cf. also, Richard Rolt (ed.) *Memoirs of the life of the late Right Honourable John Lindesay Earl of Craufurd* (London, 1753); and Joseph G. Rosengarten, 'The Earl of Crawford's Ms. History in the Library of the American Philosophical Society', *Proceedings of the American Philosophical Society*, 42.174 (1903), 397–404.
201 Marianna Birkeland, 'James Murray, second duke of Atholl', *ODNB*.
202 E. Maxtone Graham, 'Margaret Nairne: A Bundle of Jacobite Letters', *Scottish Historical Review*, 4.13 (1906), 11–23, esp. 20.
203 The appointment was reported widely: cf. for example, *Whitehall Evening Post*, 5 October 1727.
204 Cf. Lang, 'Alexander Brodie of Brodie', *ODNB*.
205 *London Gazette*, 12 June 1725.
206 Timothy Mowl, 'Rococo and Later Landscaping at Longleat', *Garden History*, 23.1 (1995), 55–66.
207 Finch's father, the 2nd Earl, a moderate Tory, had been in favour of the Protestant succession and was appointed Secretary of State under William III and Lord President of the Council at George I's accession, serving until his resignation in 1716. Cf. Henry Horwitz, *The Career of Daniel Finch, Second Earl of Nottingham, 1647–1730* (New York, 1968); also Horwitz, 'Daniel Finch, second earl of Nottingham and seventh earl of Winchilsea', *ODNB*.
208 J.G. Simms, 'Dean Swift and County Armagh', *Seanchas Ardmhacha: Journal of the Armagh Diocesan Historical Society*, 6.1 (1971), 131–40.
209 *Ibid.*, 134.
210 *Daily Post*, 2 January 1730.
211 Cf. for example, *British Journal*, 11 June 1726.

CHAPTER SIX **'Through the paths of heavenly science'**
1 The full quotation is from *The Third Degree*: 'To contemplate the intellectual faculty and to trace it from its development, through the paths of heavenly science'. *Emulation Ritual* (London, 1996), p. 175.
2 Lane, *Masonic Records*.
3 For example: *The Mystery of Masonry brought to Light by the Gormogons* (1724); *A Midnight Modern Conversation* (1732); *The Sleeping Congregation* (1736); and *Night – The Four Times of the Day* (1738).
4 *The Weekly-Journal or Saturday's-Post*, 10 January 1719.
5 *Evening Post*, 13 January 1719.
6 'James Brydges to William Mead, 16 June 1718', Huntington Library: Stowe MS, ST 57, XV, 252.
7 Cf. Mary Fissell and Roger Cooter, *Exploring Natural Knowledge – Science and the Popular*, in Roy Porter (ed.), *The Cambridge History of Science, Vol. 4: Eighteenth-century science* (Cambridge, 2003), pp. 129–58, for an introductory overview of the period.

8   Nicholas Hans, *New Trends in Education in the Eighteenth Century* (London, 1966), pp. 138–41.
9   Cf. for example: the *Post Boy*, 10 October 1721; *Post Boy*, 17 October 1721; *Daily Courant*, 20 October 1721; *Daily Courant*, 15 January 1722; *Daily Courant*, 11 April 1722; *Daily Courant*, 13 April 1722; *Daily Courant*, 17 April 1722; and *Post Boy*, 19 April 1722.
10 Cf. for example, the *Daily Courant*, 18 October 1723; *Daily Post*, 4 January 1724; and *Daily Courant*, 9 March 1724.
11 *Post Man and the Historical Account*, 28 February 1716.
12 Alan Q. Morton, 'Concepts of Power: Natural Philosophy and the Uses of Machines in Mid-Eighteenth-Century London', *British Journal for the History of Science*, 28.1 (1995), 63–78. The quote is taken from 63.
13 *British Journal*, 9 May 1724.
14 Simon Schaffer, *Natural Philosophy and Public Spectacle in Eighteenth Century England* in *History of Science* (Cambridge, 1983), vol. XXI, p. 2.
15 Larry Stewart, 'A Meaning for Machines: Modernity, Utility, and the Eighteenth-Century British Public', *Journal of Modern History*, 70.2 (1998), 259–294. The quotation is from 269.
16 Weymouth did not attend Grand Lodge as Grand Master other than at his installation. As DGM, John Ward deputised throughout 1735.
17 Lane, *Masonic Records*. No data is extant other than the list of lodges held at Grand Lodge; the lodge was erased in 1754.
18 Gould, *History of Freemasonry Throughout the World*, vol. 2, p. 94.
19 He was recorded as 'John Ward of Newcastle'.
20 He was granted the title Viscount Dudley and Ward in 1763.
21 Leveson-Gower remained an MP until 1761. As noted in chapter 1, the family was a dominant influence in local Staffordshire politics.
22 *Weekly Journal or British Gazetteer*, 17 February 1728.
23 *Flying Post or The Weekly Medley*, 12 July 1729.
24 *London Gazette*, 20 January 1730.
25 *Annual Register for the Year 1774* (London, 1801), 6th edn., p. 192.
26 Cf. Paul Langford, 'William Pitt and Public Opinion, 1757', *English Historical Review*, 88.346 (1973), 54–80, esp. 63.
27 *Journals of the House of Commons*, Seventh Parliament of Great Britain: 6th session, p. 155, *18 May 1733*.
28 Ward was married twice: in December 1723, to Anna Maria Bourchier, who died in 1725; and in January 1745, to Mary Carver, a Jamaican heiress. Cf. among several reports, *Universal Spectator and Weekly Journal*, 5 January 1745.
29 Cf. for example, *Journals of the House of Lords*, Ninth Parliament of Great Britain: 3rd session, p. 464, *21 March 1744*; 5th session, p. 51, *24 February 1747*; 6th session, p. 93, *3 April 1747*; Tenth Parliament of Great Britain: 1st session, p. 220, *26 April 1748*; and General Index, vols XX–XXXV, p. 855.
30 Unfortunately, the Dudley and Ward archives held at Staffordshire and Stoke-on-Trent contain only limited personal archival records.
31 David Brown, 'John Ward, second Viscount Dudley and Ward (1725–1788)', *ODNB*. Cf. also, T. J. Raybould, 'The Development and Organization of Lord Dudley's Mineral Estates, 1774–1845, *Economic History Review*, n.s. 21.3 (1968), 529–44.

32 T.J. Raybould, *The Economic Emergence of the Black Country* (Newton Abbot, 1973).
33 George J. Barnsby, 'Review', *Economic History Review*, n.s. 27.3 (1974), 475–76.
34 *London Evening Post*, 31 October 1738.
35 John Money, 'The West Midlands, 1760–1793: Politics, Public Opinion and Regional Identity in the English Provinces during the Late Eighteenth Century', *Albion*, 2.2 (1970), 73–93.
36 Gould, *History of Freemasonry*, pp. 94–6.
37 Charles Delafaye, 'The Fellowcraft's Song', *op. cit.*
38 In addition to Campbell, George Preston, Hugh Hathorn, James Nimmo and William Livingston were admitted Freemasons on 25 August, and Sir Duncan Campbell of Lochnell, Robert Wightman, George Drummond, Archibald McAulay and Patrick Lindsay on 28 August. The names are given by Trevor Stewart in *AQC Transactions*, 113 (2000), 81–4, and by Gould in his *History of Freemasonry throughout the World*, vol. II, p. 6. Each was a prominent dignitary in Edinburgh: Preston and Hathorn were Baillies (or Aldermen); Nimmo, Treasurer, and later Receiver-General of Excise for Scotland; Livingston, Dean Convener of Trades; Irving, Clerk to the Dean of the Guild Court; Wightman, Dean of the Guild; Drummond, past Treasurer; and McAulay, an Alderman. Sir Duncan Campbell was a baronet, and Lindsay a prominent merchant.
39 His name was written as 'Harvey' in *Grand Lodge Minutes*, p. 37.
40 J.T. Desaguliers, *A Course of Experimental Philosophy* (London, 1734), vol. 2, contains an account of the wooden railway constructed to bring stone from the quarries. Cf. also, Francis Ring, *Proceedings, Bath Royal Literary and Scientific Institution Proceedings*, 9 (2005): http://www.brlsi.org/proceed05/Astronomy 0904.htm; and G.N. Cantor, *Quakers, Jews, and Science: Religious Responses to Modernity and the Sciences in Britain, 1650–1900* (Oxford, 2005), p. 185. Reports are also contained *inter alia* in the *British Journal*, 9 May 1724 and *Weekly Journal or Saturday's Post*, 9 May 1724.
41 'Letter from Bath dated 11 May 1724' published in *Parker's London News or the Impartial Intelligencer*, 18 May 1724.
42 The lodge had relocated from the Queen's Head in the intervening years. Cf. R. William Weisberger, *AQC Transactions*, 113 (2000), 65–96, esp. 74.
43 *London Evening Post*, 31 October 1738.
44 *Sackler Archives*.
45 *London Evening Post*, 11 February 1738.
46 The Nag's Head popularised its own idiosyncratic versions of the standard Masonic songs. Cf. in particular, *A Curious Collection of the Most Celebrated Songs in Honour of Masonry* (London, 1731), pp. 3–15.
47 *Grand Lodge Minutes*, pp. 45, 199 and 231–2; cf. also, Philip Jenkins, 'Jacobites and Freemasons in eighteenth century Wales', *Welsh History Review*, 9.4 (1979), 391–406.
48 G. Norman, 'Early Freemasonry at Bath, Bristol and Exeter', *AQC Transactions*, XL (1927), 244.
49 Jenkins, 'Jacobites and Freemasons'; cf. also, Jenkins, 'Tory Industrialism and Town Politics: Swansea in the Eighteenth Century', *Historical Journal*, 28.1 (1985), 103–23.

50   Cf. Harland-Jacobs, *Builders of Empire*, pp. 103–11.
51   Jenkins, 'Jacobites and Freemasons', 393.
52   Bertie George Charles, *Philipps family, of Picton, Pembrokeshire*, Welsh Biography On-line, National Library of Wales; also Ian Christie, 'The Tory Party, Jacobitism and the 'Forty-Five: A Note', *Historical Journal*, 30.4 (1987), 921–31.
53   *Monthly Chronicle*, October 1731; and *Weekly Miscellany*, 25 November 1737.
54   Francis Jones, 'Portraits and Pictures in Old Carmarthenshire Houses – Taliaris', *Carmarthenshire Historian*, V (1968), 43–66.
55   *Ibid.*
56   For example, *London Evening Post*, 11 May 1732; 24 April 1735; and 28 April 1737.
57   *London Evening Post*, 11 May 1732.
58   Jenkins, 'Jacobites and Freemasons', 395.
59   Peter D.G. Thomas, The Remaking of Wales in the Eighteenth Century, in Trevor Herbert and Gareth Elwyn Jones (eds.), *The Remaking of Wales in the Eighteenth Century* (Cardiff, 1988), pp. 1–5, Introductory Essay.
60   *Ibid.*
61   Philip Jenkins, 'Tory Industrialism and Town Politics: Swansea in the Eighteenth Century', *Historical Journal*, 28.1 (1985), 103–23.
62   Gwyn A. Williams, *Beginnings of Radicalism*, in Trevor Herbert and Gareth Elwyn Jones (eds.), *The Remaking of Wales in the Eighteenth Century*, pp. 111–47, especially pp. 118–20. Williams refers specifically to Philip Jenkins' study: *The making of a ruling class: the Glamorgan gentry 1640–1790* (Cambridge, 1983).
63   Williams, *Beginnings of Radicalism*, pp. 118–20.
64   In 1734, a Bill was enacted 'to enable Walter Calverley Esq., now called Walter Blackett Esq., and his Issue Male, to take and use the Surname of Blackett only, pursuant to the Will of Sir William Blackett Bt, deceased'. *Journal of the House of Lords*, vol. 24, *21 March 1734*. Calverley had married Sir William Blackett's daughter in 1729.
65   John Money, 'The Masonic Moment; Or, Ritual, Replica, and Credit: John Wilkes, the Macaroni Parson, and the Making of the Middle-Class Mind', *Journal of British Studies*, 32.4 (1993), 358–95, esp. 363.
66   Calverley-Blackett was elected Mayor in 1735, 1748, 1756, 1764 and 1771.
67   E. Mackenzie, *A Descriptive and Historical Account of the Town and County of Newcastle-upon-Tyne* (Newcastle, 1827), vol. 1, pp. 663–70, esp., pp. 669–70.
68   *Weekly Journal* (Newcastle), 6 June 1730.
69   *St James Evening Post*, 28 December 1734.
70   Stewart, 'The Selling of Newton'. The quotation from the *Newcastle Courant* (1741) is on p. 182.
71   *London Evening Post*, 5 November 1737. Cf. also *London Spy Revived*, 9 November 1737.
72   *Daily Gazetteer*, 13 September 1737.
73   *London Evening Post*, 31 October 1738.
74   Quoted in Tanis Hinchcliffe, 'Robert Morris, Architecture, and the Scientific Cast of Mind in Early Eighteenth-Century England', *Architectural History*, 47 (2004), 127–38.

75 Eileen Harris, *British Architectural Books and Writers 1556–1785* (Cambridge, 1994), p. 334.
76 The OKA *Minute* books are held at United Grand Lodge of England. The first volume is one of the oldest extant Minute books of any London lodge and provides a detailed record of meetings from 1734 onwards. The author would like to thank the Master, Secretary and members of the OKA for permission to access its records.
77 OKA *Minutes*, 6 August 1733. The OKA had a second claim to renown: its Tyler was Anthony Sayer, Grand Master in 1717.
78 That is, after its move to the King's Arms tavern in the Strand; the lodge originally met at the Freemasons' Coffee House, near Long Acre (until 1728), and thereafter (from 1731) at the Cross Keys in Henrietta Street. The lodge was established originally in c. 1725. There are no earlier Minutes.
79 George Eccleshall, *A History of the Old King's Arms Lodge No. 28, 1725–2000* (London, 2000), p. 20.
80 *Ibid.*, p. 10, 24–5.
81 Clare served as a Grand Steward in 1734; he was appointed a GW in 1735 and DGM in 1741. He was the author, among other works, of *A Defence of Masonry* (London, 1730), a response to Samuel Prichard's *Masonry Dissected* (London, 1730). It was reprinted in *Read's Weekly Journal*, 24 October 1730. Clare was also a FSA.
82 Graeme served as a Grand Steward in 1734, as GW in 1735, 1736 and 1744, and as DGM in 1738 and 1739.
83 Hody served as a Grand Steward in 1735 and as a GW in 1740.
84 Alexander Stuart (1673–1742), was physician to Westminster Hospital (1719–33), to St George's Hospital (1733–36), and to the Queen. He was elected FRS in 1714, the same year as Desaguliers and Folkes, and elected FRCP in 1728.
85 *Sackler Archives*.
86 A 'John Hellot' was also a member of the Horn, and a 'Mr Helot' a member of the Huguenot lodge meeting at Prince Eugene's Head Coffee House in St Alban's Street: *Grand Lodge Minutes*, pp. 23, 193.
87 OKA *Minutes*, 6 August 1733.
88 The *Discourse* was given by Martin Clare to the Quarterly Communication of Grand Lodge on 11 December 1735.
89 Bernard Burke, *A genealogical and heraldic history of the extinct and dormant baronetcies of England, Ireland and Scotland* (London, 1844), 2nd edn., p. 585.
90 Erased 1760 (Lane, *Masonic Records*). Members of the Old Lodge at Lincoln, considered a 'sister' lodge, were proposed for membership of the OKA, for example, John Beck, on 1 October 1733.
91 For example, *Grub Street Journal*, 1 April 1731; also *Fog's Weekly Journal*, 3 April 1731.
92 *Grand Lodge Minutes*, p. 240. The appointment was unusual in two respects: Wray had not served previously as a Grand Warden and only spent one year as DGM. He was succeeded by John Ward. Wray was reported as having been chosen by Weymouth to act as GW in 1734, but does not appear to have done so. Cf. for example, *Read's Weekly Journal* or *British Gazetteer*, 1 March 1735.
93 In the past, Clare's *Oration* was read annually in certain lodges: OKA *Minutes*. Cf. also, A.G. Mackey *et al.*, *Encyclopedia of Freemasonry* (Whitefish, 2003), pt. 1, p. 209.

94   F.H.W. Sheppard (gen. ed.), *Survey of London – Portland Estate: Nos. 8 and 9 Soho Square: The French Protestant Church* (London, 1966), vols 33–4, pp. 60–3.
95   Martin Clare, *Youth's introduction to trade and business* (London, 1720).
96   OKA *Minutes*, 11 March 1734.
97   The eldest son of Robert Bertie, 1st Duke of Ancaster and Kesteven, and his second wife, Albinia Farington. Peregrine Bertie, the 1st Duke's son from his prior marriage to Jane Brownlow, inherited the title and his father's office of Lord Great Chamberlain.
98   A 'William Todd' was nominated as Sheriff of Cheshire (*London Journal*, 11 November 1732) and appointed Keeper of the King's Wine Cellar at St James's (*London Evening Post*, 8 March 1740). A Mr Todd was also a member of the Rummer, Henrietta Street (*Grand Lodge Minutes*, p. 40).
99   OKA *Minutes*, 1 April 1734.
100 OKA *Minutes*, 5 May 1735. That the OKA rules contradicted Grand Lodge's Regulation VI, which demanded the unanimous consent of 'all the members of that lodge then present', is self-evident.
101 Eccleshall, *A History of the Old King's Arms Lodge*, p. 24.
102 Anonymous, *A Word to the Wise* (London, 1795).
103 He was also a member of the OKA. Cf. Eccleshall, *The Old King's Arms Lodge, 1725–2000*, pp. 27, 153.
104 *Grand Lodge Minutes*, p. 260.
105 Stewart, 'English Speculative Freemasonry', 179, fn. 110.
106 OKA *Minutes*, 2 June 1735.
107 Lane, *Masonic Records*; cf. also *The History of the Province of West Lancashire* (Liverpool, 2009). The Dissenting Academy was established in 1757.
108 Edgar Samuel, 'Meyer Schomberg', *ODNB*.
109 Jacob, *The Radical Enlightenment*, p. 96.
110 Cf. Stephen D. Snobelen, 'William Whiston', *ODNB*.
111 W. Smith, *A Pocket Companion for Freemasons* (London, 1735), p. 45.
112 Charles Labelye, *The Present State of Westminster Bridge* (London, 1743), 2nd edn.
113 Cf. Skempton and Chrimes, pp. 389–92.
114 *Ibid.*, p. 178.
115 *Grand Lodge Minutes*, p. 90, 26 November 1728.
116 *Grand Lodge Minutes*, p. 101.
117 Norman, 'Early Freemasonry at Bath, Bristol and Exeter', 244.
118 Cf. *Grand Lodge Minutes*, p. 228.
119 *The Ancient Constitutions of the Free and Accepted Masons* (London, 1731), 2nd ed., unnumbered pages.
120 *A Curious Collection of the Most Celebrated Songs in Honour of Masonry* (London, 1731).
121 John Gordon, *The Young Mathematician's Guide* (London, 1730).
122 *Daily Journal*, 20 January 1730. The price of his lectures was at a substantial discount to that commanded by Desaguliers.
123 *London Evening Post*, 23 July 1730.
124 *Daily Journal*, 26 December 1730.
125 *Daily Journal*, 9 May 1732.

126 M.J. Charlesworth, 'The Wentworths: Family and Political Rivalry in the English Landscape Garden', *Garden History*, 14.2 (1986), 120–37.
127 *London Evening Post*, 17 October 1732 and *Daily Post*, 19 October 1732.
128 *Daily Journal*, 11 March 1731.
129 George Gordon, *A compleat discovery of a method of observing the longitude at sea* (London, 1724); and *An introduction to geography, astronomy, and dialling* (London, 1726).
130 *London Evening Post*, 18 March 1731 and 23 October 1731. Cf. also, *The Report of the Gentlemen Appointed by the General Courts of the Charitable Corporation* (London, 1732), p. 9.
131 *Grand Lodge Minutes*, p. 254.
132 Cf. http://www.freemasons-Freemasonry.com/arnaldoGeng.html. As an aside, in his *History of Freemasonry throughout the World*, vol. 3, pp. 273–5, Gould suggested that the lodge was a Catholic lodge: the Royal House of Lusitanian Freemasons.[1] This seems unlikely.
133 Lord George Graham was appointed a Grand Steward in 1734 but declined or was unable to attend, possibly because of his naval duties. He was appointed a GW in 1737.
134 Probably the pro-Hanoverian George Forrester, 6th Lord Forrester.
135 *London Evening Post*, 1 June 1736.
136 *Daily Journal*, 18 October 1736.
137 A Swiss Huguenot who had been born in Berne, Coustos was naturalized British in 1716 following his family's resettlement in London.
138 William R. Denslow, *10,000 Famous Freemasons* (Whitefish, 2004), vol. 1, p. 256.
139 James Caulfield, *Portraits, Memoirs and Characters of Remarkable Persons* (London, 1820), vol. 3, pp. 213–14.
140 John Coustos, *The sufferings of John Coustos, for Freemasonry, and for his refusing to turn Roman Catholic* (London, 1746). The quotation is from an advertisement in the *Daily Advertiser*, 15 March 1745.
141 The petition for assistance from Coustos to Newcastle is at BL. MS Add. 33054, f. 313.
142 *General Advertiser*, 24, 27, 29, 30, 31 May 1749.
143 Larry Stewart, 'Public Lectures and Private Patronage in Newtonian England', *Isis*, 77.1 (1986), 47–58.
144 Roy Porter, 'Science, Provincial Culture and Public Opinion in Enlightenment England', *Journal for Eighteenth Century Studies*, 3.1 (2008), 20–46.
145 Benjamin Martin, quoted, *Ibid.*, 28.
146 Stukeley, *Family* Memoirs, vol. 2, p. 378.
147 Paul Elliott and Stephen Daniels, 'The "school of true, useful and universal science?" Freemasonry, natural philosophy and scientific culture in eighteenth century England', *British Journal for the History of Science*, 39 (2006), 207–29.
148 Larry Stewart and Paul Weindling, 'Philosophical Threads: Natural Philosophy and Public Experiment among the Weavers of Spitalfields', *British Journal for the History of Science*, 28.1 (1995), 37–62.
149 Ben-Chaim, 'Social Mobility and Scientific Change'. As noted above, Gray was the first person to be awarded the Copley medal.
150 *Ibid.*, 18.
151 Cf. also, Simon Schaffer, 'Experimenters' Techniques, Dyers' Hands, and the

Electric Planetarium', *Isis*, 88.3 (1997), 456–83, for the skills developed by dyer's used in electrical experimentation.
152 Tony Judt, 'Words', *The New York Review of Books*, 15 July 2010.
153 W.H.G. Armytage, 'Coffee-Houses and Science', *British Medical Journal*, 2.5193 (1960), 213.
154 Armytage, *op. cit*. Cf. also Helen Berry, 'Rethinking Politeness in Eighteenth Century England', 71.
155 Bernard Faÿ, 'Learned Societies in Europe and America in the Eighteenth Century', *American Historical Review*, 37.2 (1932), 255–66.
156 *Ibid.*, 257–8.
157 Ephraim Chambers (1680–1740), a Freemason, originally apprenticed to John Senex, published his *Cyclopaedia, or, An universal dictionary of arts and sciences* in two folio volumes (London, 1728). Chambers was elected FRS in 1729, proposed by William Jones and Hans Sloane.
158 Jacob, *The Radical Enlightenment*, p. 96.
159 Chambers, *Cyclopaedia*, vol. 2, p. 506.
160 Having probably been introduced to Freemasonry while in London in the 1720s, Franklin became a Mason in Philadelphia in 1731; he was elected Grand Master of Pennsylvania in 1734. When later in Paris, he became a member, then Master (1779–80), of Les Neuf Soeurs lodge: part Masonic lodge and part learned society. Les Neuf Soeurs was instrumental in organising support in France for American independence.
161 Jacob, *The Radical Enlightenment, op. cit.*
162 Larry Stewart, 'Newtonians, Revolutionaries and Republicans', *Canadian Journal of History*, 17.2 (1982), 314–21, esp. 320.
163 s'Gravesande had been appointed secretary to a delegation sent to England from the United Provinces to congratulate George I on his accession. He remained in London for almost two years.
164 s'Gravesande was elected FRS in June 1715. He was proposed by William Burnett, a well-connected loyal Whig. Burnett had been born in The Hague, educated at Cambridge and Leiden, and was a godson of William III. Cf. John Collins, 'Perpetual Motion; An Ancient Mystery Solved?', *Lulu.com* (2006), 93–4; and Mary Lou Lustig, 'William Burnet, (1688–1729)', *ODNB*.
165 W.J. s'Gravesande, *Mathematical elements of natural philosophy* (Leiden, 1720). The commercial value of the published translation was such that Desaguliers was subjected to a sustained newspaper attack in 1719 and 1720 by rival publishers, Mears and Woodward.
166 Julia L. Epstein, 'Voltaire's Myth of Newton', *Pacific Coast Philology*, 14 (1979), 27–33.
167 J.J. O'Connor & E.F. Robertson, *Willem Jacob 'sGravesande* (St Andrews, 2006); cf. also *Voltaire to Nicolas Claude Thierot, 24 October 1738* (letter D1635) and letters D1439-D1729 (Geneva, 1969) referred to in Robert McNamee (ed.), *Electronic Enlightenment* (Oxford, 2008).
168 Stewart, 'Newtonians, Revolutionaries and Republicans', 320.
169 Daniel Lysons, *The Environs of London* (London, 1795), vol. 3, pp. 306–19: 'whilst pursuing his studies [at Westminster School] . . . Dr. Desaguliers . . . instructed him in mathematics and natural philosophy'; cf. also, Alan Morton, 'Stephen Demainbray', *ODNB*.
170 Clifford K. Shipton, *New England Life in the 18th Century: Representative*

Notes   281

       Biographies from Sibley's Harvard Graduates (Cambridge, MA, 1963), vol. 6, p. 473.
171 Burns, *Science in the Enlightenment*, p. 77.
172 *Grand Lodge Minutes*, pp. 12, 30. Cf. also, the reference to 'his great-uncle Thomas' in Colin Bonwick, 'Thomas Hollis (1720–1774)', *ODNB*. Greenwood's *A Philosophical Discourse Concerning the Mutability and Changes in the Material World* (Harvard, 1731), was written following Hollis' death.
173 Silvio Bedini, 'The Fate of the Medici-Lorraine Scientific Instruments', *Journal of the History of Collections* 7.2 (1995), 159–70.
174 Fara, *Newton, the Making of Genius*, pp. 95–6.
175 Cf. Margaret Jacob, *Polite Worlds of Enlightenment*, in Martin Fitzpatrick, Peter Jones, Christa Knellwolf (eds.), *The Enlightenment World* (Abingdon, 2004), p. 276.
176 A.G. Mackey *et al.* (eds.), *Encyclopaedia of Freemasonry* (Whitefish, 2003), p. 374. Harrison's contention in *Genesis of Freemasonry* (*op. cit.*, p. 102) that Voltaire was a Mason when he attended Newton's funeral in 1727 is surely in error.
177 Desaguliers, *Course of Experimental Philosophy* (London, 1734), Preface, p. 2.
178 Desaguliers, *The Newtonian System of the World*, Dedication, pp. iii-iv.
179 *Ibid.*, p. 27.
180 *Journals of the House of Commons*, Fifth Parliament of Great Britain: 1st session continued (9 January 1716–26 June 1716), pp. 440–1, *10 May 1716*.
181 Desaguliers, *A Plan of the Design for bringing Water from the Village of Drayton for the better Supplying the Cities of London and Westminster with Water*: NA: State Papers (SP) (Domestic) 35/25, no. 104, 4 March 1720; cf. also, *Journals of the House of Commons*; Fifth Parliament of Great Britain: 6th session, vol. 19, 24 April 1721.
182 *Journals of the House of Commons*, Fifth Parliament of Great Britain: 6th session, p. 526, 8 December 1720 – 29 July 1721.
183 *Journals of the House of Commons*, Sixth Parliament of Great Britain: 1st session (9 October 1722–17 May 1723), p. 285, 5 March 1724.
184 *Journal of the House of Lords*, vol. 25 (1737–41), pp. 405–21, 7 June 1738.
185 *Journal of the House of Lords*, vol. 21 (1718–21), pp. 35–43, 21 January 1721.
186 H.E. Malden, *A History of the County of Surrey* (London, 1911), vol. 3, pp. 482–7.
187 John Ginger (ed.), *Handel's Trumpeter: The Diary of John Grano* (New York, 1998), p. 279.

CONCLUSIONS

1 Philip Arestis and Peter Howells, 'The 1520–1640 "great inflation": an early case of controversy on the nature of money', *Journal of Post-Keynesian Economics*, 24.2 (2001/2), 181–203.
2 Landau, 'Country Matters', *Ibid.*, 261–74.
3 Landau, *Justices of the Peace 1679–1760*, p. 88.
4 Munsche, 'Review', 385–7.
5 Cowper, *Charge to the Middlesex Grand Jury*, 9 January 1723.

APPENDIX 1 **Grand Lodge of England, Grand Officers, 1717–1740**

1 Later 2nd Duke of Buccleuch.
2 Later 7th Earl of Abercorn.
3 Proposed FRS by Hans Sloane, Roger Gale and Desaguliers.
4 Grand Master of Grand Lodge of Ireland (1731 & 1735).
5 Later Viscount Coke and 1st Earl of Leicester.
6 Later 2nd Duke of Chandos.
7 Grand Master of the Grand Lodge of Scotland (1738–9).
8 KT, 1738; Grand Master of Grand Lodge of Scotland (1739–40); later, PRS (1764–8) and VPRS (1763–4).
* = Scottish Representative Peer
9 PRS, 1741.
10 Later Rt. Hon. Viscount Dudley & Ward, Grand Master 1742.

APPENDIX 2 **The *1723 Constitutions***

1 Harrison, *The Genesis of Freemasonry*, p. 43.
2 One of the earliest references to the 'guild' was in Bologna in the thirteenth century. Cf. B.R. Carniello, 'The rise of an administrative élite in medieval Bologna: notaries and popular government, 1282–1292', *Journal of Mediaeval History*, 28.4 (2002), 319–47.
3 David Stephenson, *Circles and Straight Lines: Compasses and Squares*, lecture (CMRC, 25 October 2009).
4 *1723 Constitutions*, p. 58.
5 For example, Prescott, 'The Old Charges Revisited', *op. cit.*, and Prescott, 'The Old Charges and the Origins of Freemasonry', *op. cit.*
6 S.R. Epstein, 'Craft Guilds, Apprenticeship, and Technological Change in Preindustrial Europe', *Journal of Economic History*, 58.3 (1998), 684–713.
7 Seligman, *Two Chapters on the Mediaeval Guilds of England*, *op. cit.*
8 Neville Barker Cryer, *York Mysteries Revealed* (York, 2006).
9 Matthew Cooke (ed.), *Cooke Manuscript* (London, 1861). The original is at BL: Additional MS 23,198.
10 G.W. Speth (trans.), *The Cooke Manuscript* (London, 1890) in *QCA Masonic Reprints*, vol. 2.
11 *William Watson MS* (York, 2005). Online at http://www.rgle.org.uk/RGLE_1535.htm.
12 The *Regius MS* was acquired by the Royal Library, hence '*Regius*', and donated to the British Museum in 1757. The MS was transcribed by James Halliwell in *The Early History of Freemasonry in England* (London, 1840). The original is at BL: Royal MS. 17 A.1.
13 A. Prescott, *Some Literary Contexts of the Regius and Cooke Manuscripts* in Trevor Steward (ed.), *Freemasonry in Music and Literature* (London, 2005), pp. 1–36; cf. also, Alvin J. Schmidt and Nicholas Babchuk, 'The Unbrotherly Brotherhood: Discrimination in Fraternal Orders', *Phylon*, 34.3 (1973), 276.
14 Euclid was born *c.* 300 BC and lived and worked in Alexandria. His *Elements* remained in use as a geometry textbook for nearly two millennia.
15 *Regius*, *op. cit.*, lines 55–6.
16 *Ibid.*, lines 61–2.
17 *Ibid.*, line 67.
18 *Ibid.*, lines 85–6.

19 Ibid., lines 91–4.
20 Author's translation, as are the paragraphs that follow.
21 Ibid., lines 194–7.
22 Ibid., lines 256–8.
23 Ibid., lines 324–8.
24 Ibid., lines 107–18.
25 Ibid., lines 557–63.
26 Ibid., lines 619–26.
27 Douglas Knoop and G.P. Jones, 'Masons and Apprenticeship in Mediaeval England', *Economic History Review*, 3.3 (1932), 346–66.
28 Cf., for example, http://Freemasonry.bcy.ca/aqc/cooke.html.
29 *Cooke, op. cit.*, lines 160–80.
30 St Alban, a Christian convert, was martyred by the Romans at Verulamium (now known as St Albans). The precise date of death is not known.
31 *Cooke, op. cit.*, lines 605–9.
32 Ibid., lines 625–37.
33 Knoop and Jones, *The Mediaeval Mason*, p. 183.
34 Chris Given-Wilson (gen. ed.), *Parliament Rolls of Medieval England: Henry VI: 1422–1461 – April 1425* (London), item 43. This is a transcription of the original scrolls by the Institute of Historical Research. The original is at C 65/86; RP, IV.261-294; SR, II.227-8.
35 Ibid., October 1423. The original is at C 65/85; RP, IV.197-260; SR, II.217-26
36 Ibid., April 1425, item 48. The original is at C 65/86; RP, IV.261-294; SR, II.227-8.
37 Ibid., October 1423, item 56.
38 Mainprise = to release upon finding sureties or 'mainpernors'.
39 Parliament Rolls of Medieval England, Henry VI, February 1426, Appendix 1426: 'The case between Humphrey, Duke of Gloucester and Henry Beaufort, bishop of Winchester'. The original is at C 65/87; RP, IV.295-308; SR, II.229-32.
40 Author's translation.
41 *Cooke*, lines 728–40.
42 Joseph Patrick Byrne, *Daily life during the Black Death* (Santa Barbara, 2006), pp. 250–4.
43 Danby Pickering, *The Statutes at Large* (Cambridge, 1762), vol. II, p. 95.
44 John Hatcher, 'England in the Aftermath of the Black Death', *Past & Present*, 144.1 (1994), 3–35.
45 Christopher Dyer, *Making a Living in the Middle Ages: The People of Britain 850–1520* (New Haven, 2002) pp. 239–40, 278–83, 293–4, 310, 344, 358.
46 Pickering, *The Statutes at Large*, (1763), book V, p. 313–47.
47 Byrne, *Daily life during the Black Death*, p. 252; cf. also, Penn and Dyer, *Wages and Earnings in Late Medieval England, op. cit.*, and Donald Woodward, 'Wage Rates and Living Standards in Pre-Industrial England', *Past & Present*, 91 (1981), 28–46, which summarises the material.
48 Donald Woodward, 'The determination of wage rates in the early modern north of England', *Economic History Review*, n.s. 47.1 (1994), 22–43. Cf. also, Woodward, *Wage Regulation in Mid-Tudor York* (York, 1980) pp. 1–7; and Woodward, *Men at Work: Labourers and Building Craftsmen in the Towns of Northern England, 1450–1750* (Cambridge, 2002), pp. 169–207.

49 Woodward, 'The Background to the Statute of Artificers: The genesis of Labour Policy, 1558–63', *Economic History Review*, n.s. 33.1 (1980), 32–44.
50 Woodward, *Men at Work, op. cit.*
51 Prescott, 'The Old Charges Revisited', *op. cit.*
52 *Ibid.*
53 Martin Cherry, *Champions of the Old Charges*, lecture (CMRC, 25 October, 2009).
54 Wallace McLeod, 'The Old Charges', *Heredom*, 14 (2006), 105–44.
55 G.W. Speth and C.C. Howard, *William Watson MS* in *QCA Antigrapha*, 3.4 (1891). The *William Watson* MS was copied in York in 1687; it is held in London at the United Grand Lodge of England library.
56 *Ibid.*
57 Eneas Mackenzie, *Historical Account of Newcastle-upon-Tyne, Incorporated Companies: The fifteen bye-trades* (London, 1827), pp. 679–98.
58 B.H. Putnam, 'Records of Courts of Common Law, especially of the Sessions of the Justices of the Peace', *Proceedings of the American Philosophical Society*, 91.3 (1947), 258–73; cf. also, R.F. Gould, *The History of Freemasonry, The Statutes relating to the Freemasons* (Philadelphia, 1902), vol. 1, pp. 327–80.
59 Tillott, *A History of the County of York*, pp. 215–29.
60 Drake was elected FRS in June 1736. He was an antiquary and a member of Spalding Society; a historian, writing *Eboracum* or *The History and Antiquities of the City of York from its Original to the Present Time* in 1736; and a surgeon, becoming York City Surgeon in 1727. He joined the Grand Lodge at York in 1725 and the following year as Junior Grand Warden, gave a speech on the history of Freemasonry. This was later printed in York by Thomas Gent (1727) and reprinted in London in 1729. Drake was made Grand Master at York in 1761. In common with other York Masons, Drake was a probable Jacobite sympathiser. Sources: *Sackler Archive*; C. Bernard L. Barr, 'Francis Drake', *ODNB*. Drake attended English Grand Lodge at the installation of the Viscount Montague on 19 April 1732: *Grand Lodge Minutes*, p. 217.
61 Tillott, *A History of the County of York, op. cit.* The civic support for the guilds may also have been in part religious, given that a group of French Protestants was also refused admission to the city.
62 An immediate effect of the fire was to cause an unprecedented demand for builders, masons, carpenters and journeymen of all sorts 'who put up their charges to a fantastic height.' G.H. Gater and Walter H. Godfrey (gen. eds), *Survey of London: All Hallows, Barking-by-the-Tower, Pt II, Custom House Quay and the Old Custom House* (London, 1934), vol. 15, pp. 31–43.
63 F.H. Blackburne Daniell (ed.), *Calendar of State Papers Domestic: Charles II, 1677–8* (London, 1911), pp. 437–85. The Charter was approved on 21 November 1677 and granted formally on 17 December.
64 The relevant section was: 'That all Carpenters Brickelayers Masons Plaisterers Joyners and other Artificers Workemen and Labourers to be imployed in the said Buildings who are not Freemen of the said City shall for the space of seaven yeares next ensueing and for soe long time after as untill the said buildings shall be fully finished have and enjoy such and the same liberty of workeing and being sett to worke in the said building as the Freemen of the Citty of the same Trades and Professions have and ought to enjoy, Any Usage or Custome of the City to the contrary notwithstanding: And that such Artificers as aforesaid which for the space of seaven yeares shall have wrought

in the rebuilding of the Citty in their respective Arts shall from and after the said seaven yeares have and enjoy the same Liberty to worke as Freemen of the said Citty for and dureing their naturall lives'. Source: John Raithby (ed.), *Statutes of the Realm, Charles II, 1666: An Act for rebuilding the City of London* (London, 1819), vol. 5, pp. 603–12.

65 For example, the Stonemasons and Carpenters were recorded as a single company in Lichfield in 1698: M.W. Greenslade (ed.), *A History of the County of Stafford: Lichfield* (London, 1990), vol. 14, pp. 131–4.
66 *1723 Constitutions*, p. 53.
67 Pope Clement XII, Papal Bull, *In Eminenti*, 28 April 1738.
68 William Smith, *A Pocket Companion for Freemasons* (London, 1735), pp. 43–5.
69 H. Peters, 'Sir Isaac Newton and the "Oldest Catholic Religion"', *AQC Transactions* (1987), vol. c, 193–4.
70 Eugenius Philalethes (probably Robert Samber), translated from the French of Harcouët de Longeville, *Long livers: a curious history of such persons of both sexes who have liv'd several ages, and grown young again* (London, 1722), p. xvii.
71 Quoted in David Boyd Haycock, 'Martin Folkes', *ODNB*.
72 Jeffrey Robert Wigelsworth, *'Their Grosser Degrees of Infidelity': Deists, Politics, Natural Philosophy, and the Power or God in Eighteenth Century England* (Saskatoon, 2005), PhD Thesis, pp. 1–19, 147–197, 198–237, 238–74.
73 Philalethes, *Long livers*, p. xvi.
74 Smith, *A Pocket Companion for Freemasons, op. cit.*
75 *Ibid.*, pp. 43–5, *The Charge*. The first (prior) date at which the ritual was first used is not known.
76 Cf. the discussion of Dumfries Lodge No. 4, MS (*c.* 1700/10) in David Stevenson, *The Origins of Freemasonry: Scotland's Century, 1590–1710* (Cambridge, 1990), ill. edn., pp. 137–65.
77 George Berkeley, *Passive Obedience* (London, 1712).
78 Cf. also, Révauger, 'Anderson's Freemasonry: the True Daughter of the British Enlightenment', *op. cit.*
79 The catechism was in use in the latter part of the eighteenth century. Cf. William Preston, *Illustrations of Masonry* (London, 1775), 2nd edn., pp. 114–19. It is not known when it was first introduced.
80 *1723 Constitutions*, p. 58.
81 *Ibid.*, p. 61.
82 Cf. chapter 6; also OKA *Minutes*.
83 *1723 Constitutions*, p. 69.

APPENDIX 3 **The Military Lodges**

1 The Border Regiment, later the Essex.
2 The Scots Greys (Second Dragoons).
3 The Connaught Rangers.
4 Royal Welch Fusiliers.
5 The King's Own Royal Regiment.
6 The Oxfordshire & Buckinghamshire Light Infantry.
7 The Scots Greys.

8 The Leicestershire Regiment.
9 South Staffordshire Regiment.
10 King's Own Yorkshire Light Infantry.
11 4th Battalion, Royal Scots.
12 The Black Watch.
13 Durham Light Infantry.

Electronic Reading and Research

Over the past several years there has been a revolution in the availability and depth of online digitised data sources. The relative ease of access and provision of rapid search facilities has opened up Masonic historical research in a manner that was barely conceivable five years ago and would have been regarded as incomprehensible as recently as twenty five years ago.

One of the most valuable data sources, the *Burney* newspaper collection at the British Library, a digitised collection of seventeenth- and eighteenth-century newspapers, is now generally available via the electronic portals of many academic libraries and represents a comprehensive collection of early English newspapers. Albeit that *Burney* is not exhaustive, the collection contains over one million newspapers from London, elsewhere in Britain and certain British colonies.

Other online digitised resources that have been critical to the research undertaken for this book and which are recommended include the following:

British History Online, a digital collection of primary and secondary sources containing over 450 volumes including the complete *Victoria County History of England* and the *Journals of the House of Commons* and *House of Lords*.

Primary sources include:

British Periodicals Online

The resource is split into two collections: the first consists of the more than 160 journals that comprise the UMI microfilm collection *Early British Periodicals*, and is the equivalent of over 5,200 volumes; the second comprises more than 300 journals from the UMI microfilm collections *English Literary Periodicals* and *British Periodicals in the Creative Arts*, together with additional titles.

Early English Books Online

EEBO makes available more than 125,000 titles published between 1473 and 1700 starting with the earliest printed works in the English language. The collection reproduces the works listed in the Short-Title Catalogue I (Pollard & Redgrave, 1475–1640); the Short-Title Catalogue II (Wing, 1641–1700); the Thomason Tracts, a compendium of broadsides on the English Civil War printed between 1640 and 1661; and the Early English Books Tract Supplements.

Eighteenth Century Collections Online
ECCO consists of the digital images of every page of around 150,000 books published during the eighteenth century. It allows researchers to undertake a full text search of around 33 million pages.

House of Commons Parliamentary Papers
The resource comprises a searchable text of parliamentary papers from the House of Commons from 1688 to 2007.

JSTOR
The scholarly journal archive contains searchable back issues of a comprehensive range of academic journals. There is usually a gap of 2 to 4 years between publication and availability on *JSTOR*.

London Lives, 1690–1800
London Lives was made available online in 2010. It contains c. 240,000 eighteenth-century manuscripts selected from eight different archives including those of the City of London, Middlesex, Southwark and Westminster. It now contains records from the London Magistrates' Court and criminal justice records; and selected guild and hospital records.

National Archives: Access to Archives
A2A is part of the UK archives network and provides a searchable resource for locating archival data held in a range of local and national archives.

National Archives: ARCHON Directory
ARCHON includes contact data for repositories in the UK and elsewhere which contain substantial collections of manuscripts noted under the indices to the National Register of Archives.

Old Bailey Online
Old Bailey Online is a searchable record of proceedings of the Old Bailey – London's central criminal court – from 1674 to 1913.

ODNB – the Oxford Dictionary of National Biography
The *ODNB* is a key reference work containing biographies of people in British history. The online version, first published in 2004, is currently updated three times each year.

Oxford Scholarship Online
Oxford Scholarship Online is an expanding cross-searchable library providing full text access to over 2,250 books.

Select Bibliography

Manuscript Collections

Bedfordshire and Luton Archives and Record Service, Bedford
   X800: Antonie family of Colworth

Berkshire Record Office, Reading
   Vyner family papers: D/EZ 77/3/4

Bodleian Library, Oxford
   MSS Rawlinson
   MSS Carte 79, fo.s 529–541 (Letters of Sir William Dugdale)

British Library, London
      The Egmont (Sir John Percival) Papers: Add. MSS. 46920–7213 and Additional Charters 74863–929
   Harleian MS 2054, fo. 34
   The Matthew Cooke MS: Add. MS 23,198
   The Regius MS: Royal MS. 17 A.1
   Sloane MS 3329

Cambridgeshire County Record Office, Cambridge
   CON/3/1/3/10, 11, 16 & 17: *12 May 1731*
   Cambridge University Library, Cambridge
   Department of Manuscripts and University Archives
   Political Papers: 80, 105 *undated*
   Cholmondeley (Houghton) Papers: Correspondence, 1, 1178, 1371, 1454, 1864

Centre for Buckinghamshire Studies, Aylesbury
   D-LE/A/2/4/j *29 November 1721*
   D-LE/A/2/2k *27 March 1722*
   D-X852/20 *1722*

Cheshire and Chester Archives, Chester
   Cholmondeley family papers: DCH/L/62, 1720
   Comberbach family papers: ZA/B/3/228v-230, *22 December 1715*
   Cowper family papers
   Holme family records: ZA/B/2/76, 82; ZA/B/3/61-63, 76–77, 124–125, 154R;
      ZA/F/47A/24; ZA/F/48D/5, 46a/12, 39a/7; ZS/D/3/19; ZS/F/138; ZM/L/2/307
   Payne family records: DBW/M/D/A/2; DBW/L/F/11; DBW/M/J/39, 42, 43 & 44;
      and ZS/D/3/10;
   ZA/B/2/63v-64, 64v, 64v-65,65–66v, 66v-67, 67-67v, 68-68v;
   ZA/B/2/82; P1/145, 1532–1867

City of London Record Office, London
Lists and Indices of Lord Mayors and Councillors of the City of London

City of Westminster Archives, London
Registers of St Margaret's Church, Westminster
Churchwardens' Accounts for St George, Hanover Square
Subscribers' Rolls – London Hospitals
Poor Relief Records E330–E363

Cornwall Record Office, Truro
HL/2/189 and HL/2/190.

Cumbria Record Office, Carlisle
Buccleuch Manors BD/BUC, BD/HJ 176–183

Derbyshire Record Office, Matlock
Letters to Lord George Sackville
Gell family of Hopton papers: D258/38/6/28 *1726*

East Riding of Yorkshire Archives and Record Service, Beverley
Grimston family of Grimston Garth and Kilnwick papers DDGR/38/157

East Sussex Record Office, Lewes
Cox family papers
Plot family papers: PAR513/26/1.
Richmond & Lennox family papers
AMS2241: 15 & 16 May 1723

Ecclesiastical Court of the Bailiwick of Guernsey, St Peter Port, Guernsey
Court Records: Abjurations, Baptisms, Marriages, Deaths

Grand Lodge of Ireland, Library & Archives, Dublin, Ireland
Minutes of the Grand Lodge of Ireland
Register of Lodges

Guildhall Library, London
St Andrews Church, Holborn: Register

Hampshire Record Office, Winchester
Carpenter family papers

Herefordshire Record Office, Hereford
Records of the Belmont Estate, C38, relating *inter alia* to Aubrey family estate

Hertfordshire Archives, Hertford
Chancery Administration
Clerk of the Parliaments papers
Cowper family papers: DE/P/F165, 1714–1717; DE/P/F220 *c. 1723*;
    DE/P/T1220-1221; DE/P/F212-218 *c. 1724–39*; DE/P/F17 *c. 1720–50*;
    A-K DE/P/F203 *1708–1723*
Cox family papers: DE/Ru/74463, 16 May 1723
Garrard family papers: DE/Gd/27286
Streate family papers

Houghton Library, Harvard, Cambridge, MA, USA
MS Am 1455

Houses of Parliament Archives, London
House of Commons Parliamentary Papers: *1715–1745*
(http://parlipapers.chadwyck.co.uk/search/initSearch.do – accessed 1 March—
    8 April 2010)

George Carpenter: Private Act, 12 George 1, c.9; HL/PO/JO/10/6/351: *22 Feb 1726–7 Mar 1726*; HL/PO/PB/1/1725/12G1n34

Huntington Library (on-line access), Pasadena, CA, USA
Stowe MS. Collection

Lambeth Palace, Library & Archives, London
Commission on Building Fifty Churches
AA/V/H/79/32/1-3: 1721, re Thomas Edward
MS 929, *1611–1723*; MS 2706, *1716–48*; MS 2725, *1721–59*; MS 2726, *1713–42*; MS 2724, *1711–34*

Lincolnshire Archives, Lincoln
Earl Dalkeith family papers: SAYE/2, SAYE/3, SAYE/2/3, 5–7, 13, 15–17, 22–4
Add. MSS 5806
Spalding Sewers/451/4, p. 9

London Metropolitan Archives, London
Carpenter's Company, Minute Books of Courts and Committees
Legal and Property Records
Middlesex Sessions of the Peace:
Justices of the Peace: MJP
Sessions Papers: MJ/SP
Quarter Sessions of the Peace for the City and Liberty of Westminster, *1618–1844*: WJ
Giles Taylor: ACC/0539/122 29: *January 1732*; JER/HBY/53/6 *24 May 1732*; ACC/1045/114 *1750*
Thomas Edward: ACC/0891/02/01/0137-0138: *27/28 Jan 1723*

Norfolk Record Office, Norwich
Folkes family papers: MC 50
North Yorkshire County Record Office, Northallerton
Carpenter family papers: ZBL VIII/2
ZBL VIII/2/1 *29 May 1719*: *Letters Patent creating George Carpenter esq. Baron Carpenter of Killagy, co. Wexford, Ireland*
ZBL VIII/2/2: *Letters Patent creating George 3rd Baron Carpenter, Viscount Carlingford and Earl of Tyrconnel in the Irish Peerage*

Northumberland Collections Service, Morpeth
Calverley-Blackett family papers
NRA 42305 Blackett

Northumberland Record Office, Morpeth
Calverley-Blackett family papers
NRO 324, 672, 712, 2762, 5327

Nottinghamshire Record Office, Nottingham
Foljambe family of Osberton, Nottinghamshire
DD/FJ/11/1/7/234 *31 January 1768*

Shakespeare Centre Library and Archive, Stratford upon Avon
Dugdale correspondence and papers: DR 3, esp DR3/754; DR 10; DR 18/1/660; DR 18/17/7/44; DR 18/1/441a; DR 18/10/39/56-7; DR 18/15/4; DR 422/165; DR 37/1/1 – DR 37/2/Box 97; DR 37/2/Box 98 – DR 37/3/64; ER 1/101/20; ER 12/40/2

292 Select Bibliography

Shropshire Archives, Shrewsbury
  Cholmondely family papers re. Condover Hall and the Condover Estate 1536/8/1

Society of Antiquaries, London
  Membership Records
  SAL/MS/263, Nicholas Stone re. Viscount Dorchester
  SAL/MS/597, *25 September 1687* re. Duke of Norfolk
  SAL/MS/85 ff. iii + 13 *c.* 1670 re. Robert Plot

Somerset Archive and Record Service, Taunton
  Rough General: Order Books Q/SOr *1613–1887*

Staffordshire and Stoke-on-Trent Archive Service, Stafford and Stoke on Trent
  Dudley & Ward archives
  Leveson-Gower family papers
  Dugdale-correspondence and papers: 2/2/00/pp.138–147a; DDKE/acc.7840
    HMC/579 *18 November 1684*; D868/5/3, D868/5/4, D868/5/5, D868/5/6,
    D868/5/7, D868/5/9, D868/5/10, D868/5/12a, D868/5/12b, D868/5/13,
    D868/5/14, D868/5/15

Suffolk Record Office, Ipswich
  FC88/L1/23: *29 September 1743* re. William Petty

The Royal Society Archives, London
  Books of Account
  Journal Books
  Minute of the Council
  Notes and Records
  Philosophical Transactions (1683–1775), volumes 29–41
  The Raymond and Beverley Sackler Archive Resource
  MS 250, fo. 4.25, *13 December 1743*

Thorseby Society, Leeds
  SD.II: William Dugdale, *Pedigrees of the Nobility*

United Grand Lodge of England, Library & Archives, London
  Minutes of the Grand Lodge of England, 1723–31 and 1731–50.
  Historic Correspondence, esp. HC 8/F/3 *23 August 1734*; HC 8/F/4 *3 September 1734*; 3HC 8/F/5 *2 July 1735*
  Letterbooks
  Other Lodge Files, MSS and publications esp. BE 42 BRI; BE 200 CHA; A 795 MYS; M/10 BIR; A 70 SAM; BE 750 FRE; BE 737 JOH; A 795 GRA fo.; A 795 WHO fo.; A 791 FRE; BE 94 COL; B 68 DRA; BE 737 BLA fo.; A 798 PER; M/10 BIC

West Sussex Record Office, Chichester
  Goodwood Papers, Charles Lennox, 2nd Duke of Richmond, Lennox and Aubigny, *1701–50*

West Yorkshire Archive Service, Leeds
  Calverley-Blackett family papers
  WYL 500

Wiltshire and Swindon Archives, Chippenham
  John Keill papers 161/130, *1716–1823*

9/19/507, *20 January 1717* re. William Petty
D/1/14/2/1 *1674–1708*

York City Archives, York
 Robinson family papers: ACC M31

Yorkshire Archaeological Society, Leeds
 Calverley-Blackett family papers
 DD12

British Parliamentary Papers

Letters and Papers, Foreign and Domestic (Henry VIII).
Calendar of State Papers, Domestic (Charles II).
Calendar of State Papers, Domestic (George I and George II).
Calendar of Treasury Books.
House of Commons Parliamentary Papers.
House of Lords, Journal.
House of Commons, Journal.
House of Commons, Debates (Grey)
Parliament Rolls of Mediaeval England
Statutes of the Realm

History of Parliament Trust

Raithby, John. Statutes of the Realm. Volumes 5, 6 and 7. London, 1819–20.

Institute of Historical Research Publications

Blackburne Daniell, F.H. *Calendar of State Papers Domestic: Charles II.* London, 1932.
Brewer, J.S. *Henry VIII, Letters and Papers, Foreign and Domestic.* Volume 4. London, 1875.
Davies, K.G. *Calendar of State Papers Colonial, America and West Indies.* Volume 44. London, 1969.
Given-Wilson, Chris, *et al. Parliament Rolls of Medieval England: Henry VI.* London.
Headlam, Cecil. *Calendar of Sate Papers Colonial, America and West Indies.* Volume 33. London, 1934.
Ledward, K.H. *Journals of the Board of Trade & Plantations.* London, 1925.
Mackenzie, Eneas. *Historical Account of Newcastle-upon-Tyne.* London, 1827.
Reddington, Joseph. *Calendar of Treasury Papers.* Volumes 1 – 6. London, 1868–89.
Sainty, J.C. *Office-Holders in Modern Britain.* Volumes 2 & 3. London, 1973 & 1974.
Shaw, William A. *Calendar of Treasury Books.* Volumes 1 – 26. London, 1897–1954.
Calendar of Treasury Books and Papers. Volumes 1 – 5. (London, 1897–1903).
Shaw, William A., and Slingsby, F.H. *Calendar of Treasury Books.* Volumes 27–32 London, 1955–62.

Masonic Constitutions, Records, Lodge Minutes etc.

Anderson, James. *The Constitutions of the Freemasons.* London: John Senex & John Hooke, 1723.

The Ancient Constitutions of the Free and Accepted Masons. Enlarged Second Edition. London: B. Creake, 1731.

The new book of constitutions of the antient and honourable fraternity of free and accepted masons. London: Caesar Ward and Richard Chandler for Anderson, 1738.

The Constitutions of the Ancient and honourable fraternity of Free and Accepted Masons. Revised and enlarged by John Entick. London: J. Scott, 1756.

Dashwood, J.R. *Early Records of the Grand Lodge of England according to the Old Institutions*, Quatuor Coronatum Antigrapha, Volume XI. London: QC, 1958.

The Minutes of the Grand Lodge of Freemasons of England 1740–58, Masonic Reprints, vol. XII. London: QC, 1960.

Lane, John. *Masonic Records 1717–1894*. Sheffield: CRFF, 2009.

Songhurst, W.J. *The Minutes of the Grand Lodge of Freemasons of England 1723–1739*, Masonic Reprints, vol. X. London: QC, 1913.

Emulation Ritual. Hersham: Lewis Masonic, 2003, revised edition.

Grand Lodge, 1717–1967. Oxford: UGLE, 1967.

William Watson MS. York: Regular Grand Lodge of England, 2005.

Masonic Periodicals/Transactions

MQ Magazine. 2002–7. London: UGLE.
Freemasonry Today. 2007–10. London: UGLE.
The Builder Magazine. 1915–30. London: National Masonic Research Society.
The Masonic Magazine. 1873 – unknown. London: George Kenning.
AQC Transactions. 1886–2009. London: QC/QCCC Limited.
 Cf., in particular, volumes: II, 1889; VI, 1893; VIII, 1895; XXIII, 1910; XXVIII, 1915; XXIX, 1916; XXX, 1917; XXXVI, 1923; XXXVII, 1924; XXXVIII, 1925; XLV, 1932; XLVI, 1933; XLVIII, 1935; L, 1937; LVIII, 1945; LXVI, 1953; 79, 1966; 81, 1968; 83, 1970; 91, 1978; 95, 1982; 100, 1987; 113, 2000; 114, 2001; 115, 2002; 116, 2003; 117, 2004; 118, 2005; 119, 2006; 120, 2007; and 121, 2008.

Masonic Minute Books

The Minutes of the Grand Lodge of Freemasons of England, 1723–1739 and 1740–1758.

Note: The original Minutes of the Grand Lodge of England are at the Library and Archives of the UGLE. Page references herein are to the more accessible QCA Masonic Reprints, vols X and XII, published by QC (1913 and 1960, respectively), both in hard copy and on CD-ROM.

The Minute Book of the Lodge of Antiquity, No. 2. Original at UGLE, London.
The Minute Book of the Old King's Arms, No. 28. Original at UGLE, London.

Survey of London, English Heritage

Gater, G.H. and Godfrey, Walter H. *Survey of London*, volume 15: All Hallows, Barking-by-the-Tower, Pt II, Custom House Quay and the Old Custom House. London, 1934.

—— *Survey of London*, volume 16: St Martin-in-the-Fields I: Charing Cross. London, 1935.

—— *Survey of London*, volume 18: St Martin-in-the-Fields II: The Strand. London, 1937.

Sheppard, F.H.W. *Survey of London*, volume 27: Spitalfields and Mile End New Town. London, 1957.
—— *Survey of London*, volumes 29–30: St James, Westminster, Part 1. London 1960 & 1963.
—— *Survey of London*, volumes 31–32: St James, Westminster, Part 2. London 1960 & 1963.
—— *Survey of London*, volumes 33–34: St Anne, Soho. London, 1966.
Survey of London, volume 35: The Theatre Royal, Drury Lane, and the Royal Opera House, Covent Garden. London, 1970.
—— *Survey of London*, volume 36: Covent Garden. London, 1970.

The Huguenot Society of London

Minet, William & Susan. *Livres des Conversiones et des Reconnoissances faites a L'Eglise Francoise de la Savoye, 1684–1702* (London, 1914).
—— *Register of the Church of Hungerford Market, later Castle Street, London* (London, 1928).
—— *Registers of the Church of Le Carre and Berwick Street* (London, 1921).
—— *Register of the Church of Rider Court, London, 1700–1738* (London, 1927).
—— *Register of the Church of St Martin Orgars with its History and that of Swallow Street* (London, 1935).
—— *Registers of the Churches of The Tabernacle Glasshouse Street and Leicester Fields, London 1688–1783* (London, 1926).
—— *Registres des Eglises de la Chapelle Royale de Saint James, 1700–1756, et de Swallow Street, 1690–1709* (London, 1924).
—— *Registres des Eglises de la Savoye de Spring Gardens et des Grecs 1684–1900* (London, 1922).
—— *Registres des Quatres Eglises du Petit Charenton de West Street de Pearl Street et de Crispin Street* (London, 1929).
Minet, Susan. *Register of the Church of the Artillery, Spitalfields, 1691–1786* (London, 1948).
—— *Registers of the French Churches of La Patente de Soho, Wheeler Street, Swan Street & Hoxton, also The Repetoire General* (London, 1956).
Proceedings of the Huguenot Society vols II (London, 1887–8); XX (1958–64); and XXIII (1975).

Newspapers (1680–1780)

Applebee's Original Weekly Journal
Athenian Gazette or Casuistical Mercury
British Journal
British Journal or The Censor
Caledonian Mercury
Country Journal or The Craftsman
Daily Advertiser
Daily Courant
Daily Gazetteer
Daily Journal
Daily Post
Evening Journal
Evening Post

Flying Post or The Post Master
Flying Post or The Weekly Medley
Fog's Weekly Journal
Freeholder's Journal
General Advertiser
General Evening Post
Gentleman's Magazine
Grub Street Journal
Guardian
London Chronicle
London Evening Post
London Gazette
London Journal
London Spy Revived
Mist's Weekly Journal
Monthly Chronicle
New England Courant
Old Whig or The Consistent Protestant
Original Weekly Journal
Parker's London News or the Impartial Intelligencer
Pasquin
Plain Dealer
Poor Robin's Intelligence
Post Boy
Post Man and the Historical Account
Public Advertiser
Read's Weekly Journal or British Gazetteer
St. James's Evening Post
St. James's Journal
The Censor
The Evening Post
The Spectator
The Tatler
The True Briton.
Universal Spectator and Weekly Journal
Weekly Journal or British Gazetteer
Weekly Journal or Saturday's Post
Weekly Miscellany
Weekly Packet
Whitehall Evening Post or London Intelligencer

Other Primary Sources

A True and Exact List. London, 1725.
The Historical Register. London, 1726.
The True State of England. London, 1734.
Anderson, James. *The Constitutions of the Freemasons*. London: John Senex & John Hooke, 1723.
—— *A sermon preached in Swallow street, St. James's . . . on Wednesday January 16th 1711/12*. London: Anderson, 1712.

—— *A sermon preached in Swallow street, St. James's . . . on Wednesday January 16th 1711/12*. Second edition. London: Anderson, 1715.

—— *No king-killers. A sermon preach'd in Swallow-street, St. James's, on January 30th 1714/15*. London: printed for M. Lawrence, 1715.

—— *Contend earnestly for the faith. A sermon preach'd to a religious society in Goodman's Fields. On Monday, 1st August, 1720*. London: printed for R. Ford, 1720.

—— *The happy death. A sermon occasion'd by the death of the Reverend William Lorimer . . .* London, printed for Richard Ford, 1724.

—— *The Ancient Constitutions of the Free and Accepted Masons* (London: 1731), 2nd edition.

—— *The new book of constitutions of the antient and honourable fraternity of free and accepted masons*. London: Caesar Ward and Richard Chandler for Anderson, 1738.

Anonymous. *A Candid Answer to A Letter from a Member of Parliament to his Friends in the Country, concerning the Duties on Wine and Tobacco*. London: J. Clarke, 1730.

Anonymous. *A Curious Collection of the Most Celebrated Songs in Honour of Masonry*. London: B. Creake, 1731.

Anonymous. *A Grand Mystery of Freemasons Discover'd*. London, 1724.

Anonymous. *A Seasonal Apology for Mr Heidegger*. London, 1724.

Anonymous. *A Word to the Wise*. London, 1795.

Anonymous. *The Freemasons Accusation and Defence*. London: J. Peele, 1726.

Anonymous. *The Grand Mystery of Freemasons Discovered*. London: T. Payne, 1724.

Armstrong, John. *A History of Freemasonry in Cheshire*. London: George Kenning, 1901.

Ashmole, Elias. *Memoirs of the life of that learned antiquary, Elias Ashmole, Esq; drawn up by himself by way of diary. With an appendix of original letters*. London: Charles Burman, 1717.

—— *The Antiquities of Berkshire*. London: 1719. Preface by Rawlinson, Richard.

Aubrey, John. *Natural History of Wiltshire*. Oxford: Bodleian, 1691. MS 1685.

—— *Natural History of Wiltshire*. Whitefish, MT: Kessinger Publishing, 2004 (reprint).

Auld, William. *The Free Masons Pocket Companion*. Edinburgh, 1761.

Babington, Zachary. *Notice to Grand Jurors in Cases of Blood*. London: John Amery, 1677.

Benoist, Elie. *The history of the famous Edict of Nantes*. London: John Dunton, 1694.

Berkeley, George. *Passive Obedience*. London, 1712.

Bion, Jean Francois. *An account of the torments the French Protestants endure aboard the galleys*. London, 1708.

Blackerby, Nathaniel. *The Speech of Nathanial Blackerby . . .* London: 1738.

Blackerby, Samuel (rev'd Blackerby, Nathaniel). *The Justice of the Peace, his Companion; The reports of cases adjudg'd in the courts at Westminster, &c., which particularly concern the office of justices of the Peace*. London: J. Walthoe, 1722.

—— *The Justice of the Peace, his Companion; The reports of cases adjudg'd in the courts at Westminster, &c., which particularly concern the office of justices of the Peace*. London: Nathaniel Blackerby, 1729.

Blount, Thomas. *Glossographia, or, A Dictionary* . . . London: George Sawbridge, 1661.
Boulton, Richard. *Some thoughts concerning the unusual qualities of the air.* London: John Hooke, 1724.
Bramston, James. *The Man of Taste. Occasion'd by an Epistle of Mr Pope's on that Subject.* London: Lawton Gilliver, 1733.
Briscoe, Sam. *Secret History of the Freemasons.* London, 1724.
Brome, Alexander. *The Cunning Lovers.* London: William Sheares, 1654.
Burdon, Capt. William. *The gentleman's pocket-farrier.* London: Burdon, 1730.
Burton, Robert. *Martyrs in Flames: or the history of Popery Displaying the horrid persecutions and cruelties exercised upon Protestants by the Papists, for many hundred years past.* London: A. Bettesworth and J. Batley, 1729, 3rd edition.
Cheselden, William. *Anatomy of the Human Body.* London: William Bowyer, 1712.
Churchill, Sarah. *Private correspondence of Sarah, Duchess of Marlborough, volume II.* London: H. Colburn, 1838.
Claude, Jean. *A Short Account of the Complaints and Cruel Persecutions of the Protestants in France (Les Plaintes des Protestantes cruellement opprimés dans le Royaume de France)* London: W. Redmayne, 1708, 3rd English edition.
Clement XII. Papal Bull, *In Eminenti.* Vatican: 28 April 1738.
Cooke, Matthew (ed.). *Cooke Manuscript.* London: Spencer, 1861.
Cowper, William. *The Humble Address Of the Right Honourable the Lords Spiritual and Temporal In Parliament Assembled, Presented To His Majesty, On Munday the Twentieth Day of February, 1715.* London: House of Commons, Parliamentary Papers, 1715.
—— *The Charge delivered* . . . London, 1730.
Coustos, John. *The sufferings of John Coustos, for Freemasonry, and for his refusing to turn Roman catholic.* London: by subscription, 1746.
de Longeville, Harcouët. *Long livers: a curious history of such persons of both sexes who have liv'd several ages, and grown young again.* London, 1722.
de Veil, Sir Thomas. *Observations on the practice of a justice of the peace intended for such gentlemen as design to act for Middlesex and Westminster.* (London: de Veil, 1747).
Desaguliers, J.T. *Fires Improved.* London: John Senex, 1715.
—— *Lectures in Mechanical and Experimental Philosophy.* London: Desaguliers, 1717.
—— *Leçons physico-mechaniques.* London: Desaguliers, 1717.
—— *The Motion of Water and Other Fluids.* London: John Senex, 1718.
—— *Lectures of Experimental Philosophy.* London: W. Mears, B. Creake and J. Sackfield, 1719.
—— *A system of experimental philosophy.* London: B. Creake and J. Sackfield, 1719.
—— *A Plan of the Design for bringing Water from the Village of Drayton for the better Supplying the Cities of London and Westminster with Water*: State Papers (Domestic) 35/25, no. 104, March 4, 1720.
—— *An experimental course of astronomy.* London: Desaguliers, 1725.
—— *A Course of Experimental Philosophy.* London: Desaguliers, 1727 and 1734.
—— *The Newtonian System of the World, the best Model of Government.* Westminster: J. Roberts, 1728.
Drake, Francis. *A Speech Deliver'd to the Worshipful and Ancient Society of Free and Accepted Masons.* York, 1727.
Eboracum: or The History and Antiquities of the City of York. London, 1736.

Dunton, John. *The French Book of Martyrs, or the History of the Edict of Nantes.* London, 1693.
—— *The Life and Errors of John Dunton, Citizen of London.* London: J. Nichols & Sons, 1818. Originally published 1705, in two volumes.
E. B. (compiler, known only by his initials). *A new dictionary of the terms ancient and modern of the canting crew.* London: W. Hawes, P. Gilbourne and W. Davis, c. 1699.
Entick, John. *The Pocket Companion and History of Freemasons.* London: R. Baldwin et al., 1759.
Farmer, Peter. *A New Model for the Rebuilding Masonry on a Stronger Basis than the former.* London: J. Wilford, 1730.
Fielding, Henry. *An Enquiry into the Causes of the late increase in Robbers.* London: A. Millar, 1751, 2nd edition.
Freemason, A. *The Freemasons; An Hudibrastick Poem.* London: A. Moore, 1723.
Freemason, A. *The Perjured Freemason Detected.* London: T. Warner, 1730.
General Court of the Charitable Corporation. *The report of the gentlemen appointed by the General Court of the Charitable Corporation . . .* London, 1732.
Gentleman, A. *Love's last shift: or, the mason disappointed . . .* London, c. 1720–22.
Gordon, George. *A compleat discovery of a method of observing the longitude at sea.* London, 1724.
—— *An introduction to geography, astronomy, and dialling.* London, 1726.
Grano, John; Ginger, John (ed.). *Handel's Trumpeter: The Diary of John Grano.* New York: Pendragon Press, 1998.
Hamilton, James. *Calculations and Tables on the Attractive Power of Lodestones, that is, Magnetism.* London: Hamilton, 1729.
Harris, John. *Lexicon Technicum.* London, 1704 (vol. 1); and London, 1710 (vol. 2).
Hauksbee, Francis. *Physico-Mechanical Experiments on Various Subjects.* London: Hauksbee, 1709.
—— *Physico-Mechanical Experiments on Various Subjects.* London: John Senex, 1719, 2nd edition.
Hayes, Charles. *Treatise of Fluxions, An Introduction to Mathematical Philosophy.* London: 1704.
Hogg, Bruce (compiler). *Freemasons and the Royal Society, an Alphabetical List of Fellows of the Royal Society who were Freemasons* (London: UGLE, 2010).
Holme III, Randle. *An Academie of Armorie, or, A storehouse of Armory and Blazon.* Chester: Randle Holme, 1688.
Howell, James. *Londinopolis.* London: Henry Twiford et al., 1657.
Hughan, William James. *The Alnwick Manuscript, No. E 10. Reproduction and Transcript.* Newcastle: Privately Printed for Societas Rosicruciana in Anglia, 1895.
Johnson, Charles. *Love in a Forest.* London: W. Chetwood, 1723.
Keill, John. *Introductio ad veram physicam.* Oxford: at the Sheldonian Theatre, 1702.
—— English Translation. London: John Senex, 1726.
Labelye, Charles. *The Present State of Westminster Bridge.* London: J. Millan, 1743.
Langley, Batty. *Ancient masonry, both in the theory and practice.* London: J. Milan; and J. Huggonson, 1736.
Ancient architecture, restored, and improved, by a great variety of grand and useful designs. London: Batty & Thomas Langley, 1742.

McCann, Timothy. *The Correspondence of the Dukes of Richmond & Newcastle 1724–50*. Lewes: Sussex Record Society, 1984.
Macky, John. *Memoirs of the secret services . . . during the reigns of King William, Queen Anne, and King George I*. London: Spring Macky, 1733, 2nd edition.
March, Earl of. *A Duke and his Friends: The Life and Letters of the Second Duke of Richmond*. London, 1911.
Marvell, Andrew. *The Rehearsal Transprosed*. London: John Calvin & Theodore Beza, 1672.
Moore, Francis. *Travels into the inland parts of Africa*. London: J. Knox, 1738.
Morgan, William. *Morgan's map of the whole of London in 1682*. London: Morgan, 1682.
Munk, William. *Lives of the Fellows of the Royal College of Physicians*. London: William Monk, 1861.
Newton, Isaac. *The Chronology of Ancient Kingdoms Amended*. London: J. Tonson, J. Osborn and T. Longman, 1728.
Noorthouck, John. *A New History of London: Including Westminster and Southwark*. London: 1773.
Ozanam, Jacques. *A Treatise of Fortification*. Oxford: J. Nicholson, 1711.
Treatise of Gnomonicks or Dialling. Oxford: J. Nicholson, 1712.
Pemberton, Henry. *A View of Sir Isaac Newton's Philosophy*. London, 1728.
Pine, John. *The procession and ceremonies observed . . . at the installation . . . of the Knights of the Bath*. London, 1734.
Plot, Robert. *The Natural History of Staffordshire*. Oxford, 1686.
—— *Natural History of Oxfordshire*. Oxford, 1677.
Pope, Alexander. *Imitations of Horace, The First Satire of the Second Book of Horace*. London: Pope, 1736.
—— *Sober Advice from Horace*. London: Pope, 1737.
—— *Epistle to Cobham: Of the Knowledge and Characters of Men*. London: Pope 1734.
—— *Essay on Man*. London: Pope, 1734.
Prichard, Samuel. *Masonry Dissected*. London: J. Wilford, 1730.
Quincy, John. *Lexicon physico-medicum*. London: Andrew Bell, William Taylor and others, 1719.
Rastell, Johannis. *The Statutes Prohemium*. London: Johannis Rastell, 1527.
Richmond, Charles. *A Duke and His Friends: The Life and Letters of the Second Duke of Richmond*. London: Hutchinson & Co., 1911. Reprinted Husain Press, 2008.
'sGravesande, William-James (J.T. Desaguliers trans). *Mathematical elements of natural philosophy confirmed by experiments, or an introduction to Sir Isaac Newton's philosophy*. London: J. Senex and W. Taylor, 1720.
Mathematical elements of natural philosophy. Leiden: s'Gravesande, 1720.
Samber, Robert (aka Eugenius Philalethes). (translated from the French of Harcouët de Longeville) *Long livers: a curious history of such persons of both sexes who have liv'd several ages, and grown young again*. London, 1722.
Senex, John. *A New General Atlas*. London: Senex, 1721.
Smith, William. *A Pocket Companion for Freemasons*. London: E. Rider, 1735.
—— *A Pocket Companion for Freemasons*. London: R. Baldwin, P. Dawney and B. Law and J. Scott, 1759.
Stow, John. *Survey of London*. London: Nicholas Bourn, 1633.

Stukeley, William. *The Commentarys, Diary, & Common-Place Book of William Stukeley & Selected Letters*. London: Doppler Press for the Surtees Society, 1980.
—— *Of the Spleen, its Description and History, Uses and Diseases*. London, 1722.
Taylor, Brook. *Methodus incrementorum directa et inversa*. London, 1715.
Trustees for Establishing the Colony of Georgia, *The General Account of All Monies*. London, 1733.
Tryon, Thomas. *Tryon's letters upon several occasions*. London: Thomas Tryon, 1700.
—— *Healths Grand Preservative*. London: Thomas Tryon, 1682.
—— *The Complaints of the Birds and Fowls of Heaven*. London: Thomas Tryon, 1684.
—— *Of Moyst Airs*. London: Thomas Tryon, 1688.
—— *Pythagoras; His Mystick Philosophy Revived*. London: Thomas Tryon, 1691
—— *The Merchant, Citizen and Country-mans Instructor*. London: E. Harris and G.Conyers, 1701.
—— *Some memoirs of the life of Mr Tho. Tryon*. London: Thomas Tryon, 1705.
Uring, Nathaniel. *A Relation of the late Intended Settlement of the Islands of St Lucia and St Vincent in America*. London: J. Peele, 1725.
Walpole, Horace. *Reminiscences*. London: John Sharp, 1819. Originally published London, 1788.
Ward, Edward. *The Dancing Devils*. London: A. Bettesworth, J. Bately and J. Brotherton, 1724.
Wharton, Philip. *The life and writings of Philip, late Duke of Wharton*. London: 1732.
Wildair, Harry. *The Sermon Taster: or Church Rambler*. London: J. Roberts, 1723.
Wynter, John. *Cyclus metasyncriticus: or, an essay on chronical diseases*. Bath & London: Innys and Leake, 1725.
Young, Edward. *The Universal Passion. Satire IV to the Rt Hon Sir Spencer Compton*. London, 1725.

Journal Articles

Allen, James Smith, 'Sisters of Another Sort: Freemason Women in Modern France, 1725–1940', *Journal of Modern History*, 75.4 (2003), 783–835.
Allibone, T.E. 'The Club of the Royal College of Physicians, the Smeatonian Society of Civil Engineers and Their Relationship to the Royal Society Club', *RS Notes and Records*, 22.1/2 (1967), 186–192.
—— 'The Diaries of John Byrom, M.A., F.R.S., and Their Relation to the Pre-History of the Royal Society Club', *RS Notes and Records*, 20.2 (1965), 162–83.
Alsop, J.D. 'New Light on Joseph Addison', *Modern Philology*, 80.1 (1982), 13–34.
Appleby, John H. 'Human Curiosities and the Royal Society, 1699–1751', *RS Notes and Records*, 50.1 (1996), 13–27.
Archer, Ian. 'The London Lobbies in the Later Sixteenth Century', *Historical Journal*, 31.1 (1988), 17–44.
Arestis, Philip and Howells, Peter. 'The 1520–1640 "great inflation": an early case of controversy on the nature of money', *Journal of Post-Keynesian Economics*, 24.2 (2001/2), 181–203.
Armytage, W. H. G. 'Coffee-Houses and Science', *British Medical Journal*, 2.5193 (1960), 213.

Asfour, Amal. Hogarth's Post-Newtonian Universe, *Journal of the History of Ideas*, 60.4 (1999) 693–716.

Bailey, Mark. 'Demographic Decline in Late Medieval England: Some Thoughts', *Economic History Review*, n.s. 49.1 (1996), 1–19.

Barker-Cryer, Neville. 'The Restoration Lodge of Chester', November Conference of the Cornerstone Society 2002: www.cornerstonesociety.com/Insight/Articles/restoration.pdf.

Barnsby, George J. 'Review', *Economic History Review*, n.s. 27.3 (1974), 475–476.

Beattie, J.M. 'The Pattern of Crime in England 1660–1800', *Past & Present*, 62 (1974), 47–95.

Beaurepaire, Pierre-Yves, 'The Universal Republic of the Freemasons and the Culture of Mobility in the Enlightenment', *French Historical Studies*, 29.3 (2006), 407–31.

Beaver, Allen. 'Sir Christopher Wren and the Origins of English Freemasonry', *Transactions of the Temple of Athene Lodge, No. 9149*, 15 (2008/2009), 22–38.

Bedini, Silvio. 'The Fate of the Medici-Lorraine Scientific Instruments', *Journal of the History of Collections*, 7.2 (1995), 159–170.

Bektas, M. Yakup and Crosland, Maurice. 'The Copley Medal: The Establishment of a Reward System in the Royal Society, 1731–1839', *RS Notes and Records*, 46.1 (1992), 43–76.

Ben-Chaim, Michael. 'Social Mobility and Scientific Change: Stephen Gray's Contribution to Electrical Research', *British Journal for the History of Science*, 23.1 (1990), 3–24.

Beresiner, Yasha. 'Elias Ashmole – Masonic Icon', *MQ Magazine*, 11 (2004).

—— '18th Century Masonic Ephemera', A paper delivered to the European Masonic Museums and Libraries Conference, Bayreuth, Germany, July 2009: http://www.freemasons-freemasonry.com/beresiner18.html, accessed 16 July 2010.

Berry, Helen. 'Rethinking Politeness in Eighteenth Century England', *Transactions of the Royal Historical Society*, 6th series, 11 (2001), 65–81.

Black, Jeremy. 'Hanover and British Foreign Policy 1714–60', *English Historical Review*, 120.486 (2005), 303–39.

—— 'British Foreign Policy in the Eighteenth Century: A Survey', *Journal of British Studies*, 26.1 (1987), 26–53.

—— 'Fresh Light on the Fall of Townshend', *Journal of British Studies*, 29.1 (1986), 41–64.

—— 'An Underrated Journalist: Nathaniel Mist and the Opposition Press during the Whig Ascendancy', *Journal of Eighteenth Century Studies*, 10.1 (published on-line 2008), 27–41.

—— 'Interventionism, Structuralism and Contingency in British Foreign Policy in the 1720s' *International History Review*, 26.4 (2004), 734–64.

—— 'The Development of the Provincial Newspaper Press in the Eighteenth Century', *Journal of Eighteenth Century Studies*, 14.2 (published on-line 2008), 159–70.

—— 'British Neutrality in the War of the Polish Succession, 1733–1735', *IHR*, 8.3 (1986), 345–66.

Blanchard, Rae. 'Was Sir Richard Steele a Freemason?', *PMLA*, 63.3 (1948), 903–17.

Blomfield, Reginald. 'English Architecture in the Seventeenth and Eighteenth

Centuries', *Transactions of the Royal Historical Society*, 4th series, 14 (1931), 121–40.

Boas, Marie. 'The Establishment of the Mechanical Philosophy', *Osiris*, 10 (1952), 412–541.

Bond, Maurice F. 'Clerks of the Parliaments, 1509–1953', *English Historical Review*, 73 (1958),

Borsay, Peter. 'The English Urban Renaissance: The Development of Provincial Urban Culture c. 1680–c. 1760', *Social History*, 2.5 (1977), 581–603.

Briggs, Robin. 'The Académie Royale des Sciences and the Pursuit of Utility', *Past & Present*, 131 (1991), 38–88.

Calvert, Albert F. 'George Payne, 2nd Grand Master', *AQC Transactions*, 30 (1917), 258–62.

Carniello, B.R. 'The rise of an administrative élite in medieval Bologna: notaries and popular government, 1282–1292', *Journal of Mediaeval History*, 28.4 (2002), 319–347.

Charlesworth, M. J. 'The Wentworths: Family and Political Rivalry in the English Landscape Garden', *Garden History*, 14.2 (1986) 120–137.

Cherry, Martin. 'Champions of the Old Charges', *CMRC Lecture*, 25 October, 2009.

Chipman, Robert A. 'The Manuscript Letters of Stephen Gray, F.R.S. (1666/7–1736)', *Isis*, 49.4 (1958), 414–33.

Christie, Ian. 'The Tory Party, Jacobitism and the 'Forty-Five: A Note', *Historical Journal*, 30.4 (1987), 921–31.

Clark, Peter. 'Migration in England during the Late Seventeenth and Early Eighteenth Centuries', *Past and Present*, 83 (1979), 57–90.

—— 'The 'Mother Gin' Controversy in the Early Eighteenth Century', *Transactions of the Royal Historical Society*, 5th series, 38 (1988), 63–84.

Clarke, J.R. 'The Royal Society and Early Grand Lodge Freemasonry', *AQC Transactions*, 80, Supplement (1967).

Cohen, Abner. 'The Politics of Ritual Secrecy', *Man*, n.s. 6.3 (1971), 427–48.

Cohen, I. Bernard. 'The Fear and Distrust of Science in Historical Perspective', *Science, Technology, & Human Values*, 6.36 (1981) 20–4.

—— —— 'Neglected Sources for the Life of Stephen Gray (1666 or 1667–1736)', *Isis*, 45.1 (1954), 41–50.

—— 'The Newtonian Scientific Revolution and Its Intellectual Significance', *Bulletin of the American Academy of Arts and Sciences*, 41.3 (1987), 16–42.

Collins, Jeffrey. 'Redeeming the Enlightenment: New Histories of Religious Toleration', *Journal of Modern History*, 81 (2009), 607–636.

Collins, John. 'Perpetual Motion; An Ancient Mystery Solved?', *Lulu.com*, (2006), 93–4.

Collins, H.M. 'Public Experiments and Displays of Virtuosity: The Core-Set Revisited', *Social Studies of Science*, 18.4 (1988), 725–748.

Corfield, P.J. 'Small Towns, Large Implications: Social and Cultural Roles of Small Towns in Eighteenth Century England and Wales', *Journal for Eighteenth Century Studies*, 10.2 (published on-line 2008), 126–38.

Cowan, Brian. 'What Was Masculine about the Public Sphere? Gender and the Coffeehouse Milieu in Post-Restoration England', *History Workshop Journal*, 51 (2001), 127–57.

da Costa, P. Fontes. 'The Culture of Curiosity at The Royal Society in the First Half of the Eighteenth Century', *RS Notes and Records*, 56.2 (2002), 147–66.

Crossland, Maurice. 'Explicit Qualifications as a Criterion for Membership of the

Royal Society: A Historical Review', *RS Notes and Records*, 37.2 (1983), 167 - 187.
Dabhoiwala, Faramerz. 'Summary Justice in Early Modern London', *English Historical Review*, 121 (2006), 796–822.
Dawson, Warren R., 'The First Egyptian Society', *Journal of Egyptian Archaeology*, 23.2 (1937), 259–60.
Desaguliers, J.T. 'Animadversions upon Some Experiments Relating to the Force of Moving Bodies; with Two New Experiments on the Same Subject', *Philosophical Transactions (1683–1775)*, 32 (1722–3), 285–290.
—— 'A Dissertation concerning the Figure of the Earth', *Philosophical Transactions (1683–1775)*, 33 (1724–5), 201–222.
—— 'An Account of Two Experiments of the Friction of Pullies', *Philosophical Transactions (1683–1775)*, 37 (1731–2), 394–396.
—— 'Some Thoughts and Experiments concerning Electricity', *Philosophical Transactions (1683–1775)*, 41 (1739–41), 186–193.
—— 'Experiments Made before the Royal Society', Feb. 2. 1737–8, *Philosophical Transactions (1683–1775)*, 41 (1739–41), 193–199.
—— 'An Account of Some Electrical Experiments Made at His Royal Highness the Prince of Wales's House at Cliefden, on Tuesday the 15th of April 1738. Where the Electricity Was Conveyed 420 Feet in a Direct Line. By the Same', *Philosophical Transactions (1683–1775)*, 41 (1739–41), 209–210.
—— 'Several Electrical Experiments, Made at Various Times, before the Royal Society', *Philosophical Transactions (1683–1775)*, 41 (1739–41), 661–667.
Dickson, P.G.M. and Beckett, J.V. 'The Finances of the Dukes of Chandos: Aristocratic Inheritance, Marriage, and Debt in Eighteenth-Century England', *Huntington Library Quarterly*, 64.3/4 (2001), 309–55.
Dobson, R.B. 'Admissions to the Freedom of the City of York in the Later Middle Ages', *Economic History Review*, n.s. 26.1 (1973), 1–22.
Downie, J.A. 'Swift and Jacobitism', *ELH*, 64.4 (1997), 887–901.
Eiche, Sabine. 'Henry Hare, Lord Coleraine, and his Visits to Italy', *The Pelican Record – the Journal of Corpus Christi College*, 43.1 (2006), 79–84.
Elliott, Paul and Daniels, Stephen. 'The "school of true, useful and universal science?" Freemasonry, natural philosophy and scientific culture in eighteenth century England', *British Journal for the History of Science*, 39 (2006), 207–29.
Epstein, Julia L. 'Voltaire's Myth of Newton', *Pacific Coast Philology*, 14 (1979), 27–33.
Epstein, S. R. 'Craft Guilds, Apprenticeship, and Technological Change in Preindustrial Europe', *Journal of Economic History*, 58.3 (1998), 684–713.
Erwin, Timothy. 'William Hogarth and the Aethetics of Nationalism', *Huntington Library Quarterly*, 64.3/4 (2001), 396.
Fara, Patricia. 'A Treasure of Hidden Vertues', *British Journal for the History of Science*, 28.1 (1995) 5–35.
Faÿ, Bernard. 'Learned Societies in Europe and America in the Eighteenth Century', *American Historical Review*, 37.2 (1932), 255–266.
Fenning, Hugh. 'Dublin Imprints of Catholic Interest.' *Collectanea Hibernica*, 41 (1999), 65–116.
Findlen, Paula. 'Jokes of Nature and Jokes of Knowledge: The Playfulness of Scientific Discourse in Early Modern Europe', *Renaissance Quarterly*, 43.2 (1990), 292–331.

Fisher, W.G. 'John Montague, 2nd Duke of Montagu', *AQC Transactions*, 79 (1966), 72.
Force, James E. 'Hume and the Relation of Science to Religion among Certain Members of the Royal Society', *Journal of the History of Ideas*, 45.4 (1984), 517–36.
Frank Jr., Robert G. 'John Aubrey, FRS, John Lydall, and Science at Commonwealth Oxford', *RS Notes and Records*, 27.2 (1973), 193–217.
Frankl, Paul. 'The Secret of the Medieval Masons', *Art Bulletin*, 27.1 (1945), 46–60.
Franklin, James. 'Catholics versus Masons', *Journal of the Australian Catholic Historical Society*, 20 (1999), 4–6.
Fritz, Paul S. 'The Anti-Jacobite Intelligence System of the English Ministers, 1715–1745', *Historical Journal*, 16.2 (1973), 276, fn. 78.
Fry, Carole. 'Spanning the Political Divide: Neo-Palladianism and the Early Eighteenth-Century Landscape', *Garden History*, 31.2 (2003), 180–92.
Furbank, P.N. and Owens, W.R. 'The Myth of Defoe as 'Applebee's Man'", *Review of English Studies*, n.s. 48.190 (1997), 198–204.
Gascoigne, John. 'Politics, Patronage and Newtonianism: The Cambridge Example', *Historical Journal*, 27.1 (1984), 1–24.
Getz, Faye Marie. 'Black Death and the Silver Lining' *Journal of the History of Biology*, 24.2 (1991), 265–89.
Gibbs, G.C. 'Parliament and Foreign Policy in the Age of Stanhope and Walpole', *EHR*, 77.302 (1962), 18–37.
Gobson-Wood, Carol. 'The Political Background to Thornhill's Paintings in St Paul's Cathedral', *Journal of the Warburg and Courtauld Institutes*, 56 (1993), 229–37.
Gottfried, R. S. 'Population, Plague, and the Sweating Sickness: Demographic Movements in Late Fifteenth-Century England', 16H*Journal of British Studies*, 17.1 (1977), 12–37.
Graham, E. Maxtone. 'Margaret Nairne: A Bundle of Jacobite Letters' *Scottish Historical Review*, 4.13 (1906), 11–23.
Granziera, Patrrizia. 'Freemasonic Symbolism and Georgian Gardens', *Esoterica*, 5 (2003), 41–72.
Greene, D.J. 'Smart, Berkeley, the Scientists and the Poets: A Note on Eighteenth-Century Anti- Newtonianism', *Journal of the History of Ideas*, 14.3 (1953), 327–352.
Greif, Avner, *et al.* 'Coordination, Commitment, and Enforcement: The Case of the Merchant Guild', *Journal of Political Economy*, 102.4 (1994), 745–66.
Haffenden, Philip. 'Colonial Appointments and Patronage under the Duke of Newcastle, 1724–1739', *English Historical Review*, 78.308 (1963), 417–35.
Harland, John (ed.). 'The house and farm accounts of the Shuttleworths of Gawthorpe Hall, part 2, *Chetham Society*, OS 41 (1856).
Harland-Jacobs, Jessica. 'All in the Family: Freemasonry and the British Empire in the Mid-Nineteenth Century', *Journal of British Studies*, 42.4 (2003), 448–82.
—— 'Hands across the Sea: The Masonic Network, British Imperialism, and the North Atlantic World', *Geographical Review*, 89.2 (1999), 237–53.
Harris, Eileen. 'Batty Langley: A Tutor to Freemasons (1696–1751)', *Burlington Magazine*, 119.890 (1977), 327–35.
Harris, John. 'Freemasonry and Neo-Palladianism', *Burlington Magazine*, 124.951 (1982), 366.
Hatcher, John. 'England in the Aftermath of the Black Death', *Past & Present*, 144.1 (1994), 3–35.

Hayton, D.W. 'The Stanhope/Sunderland Ministry and the Repudiation of Irish Parliamentary Independence', *English Historical Review*, 113.452 (1998), 610–36.

Hinchcliffe, Tanis. 'Robert Morris, Architecture, and the Scientific Cast of Mind in Early Eighteenth-Century England', *Architectural History*, 47 (2004), 127–38.

Hintermaier, John M. 'The First Modern refugees? Charity, Entitlement and Persuasion in the Huguenot Immigration of the 1680s', *Albion*, 32.3 (2000), 429–49.

Hoffbrand, Barry. 'John Misaubin, Hogarth's quack: a case for rehabilitation', *Journal of the Royal Society of Medicine*, 94 (2001), 143–7.

Hoffmann, Stefan-Ludwig. 'Democracy and Associations in the Long Nineteenth Century: Toward a Transnational Perspective', *Journal of Modern History*, 75.2 (2003), 269–99.

Holmes, Geoffrey. 'The Sacheverell Riots', *Past and Present*, 72 (1976), 55–85.

Hoock, Holger. 'From Beefsteak to Turtle: Artists' Dinner Culture in Eighteenth-Century London', *Huntington Library Quarterly*, 66.1/2 (2003), 27–54.

Hoppit, Julian. 'Financial Crises in Eighteenth-Century England', *Economic History Review*, n.s. 39.1 (1986), 39–58.

—— 'Myths of the South Sea Bubble', *Transactions of the Royal Historical Society*, 6th series, 12 (2002), 141–65.

Hume, Robert D. 'Theatre as Property in Eighteenth century London', *Journal for Eighteenth Century Studies*, 31.1 (2008) 17–46.

Iltis, Carolyn. 'The Leibnizian-Newtonian Debates: Natural Philosophy and Social Psychology', *British Journal for the History of Science*, 6.4 (1973), 343–77.

Jacob, James R. and Jacob, Margaret C. 'The Anglican Origins of Modern Science: The Metaphysical Foundations of the Whig Constitution', *Isis*, 71.2 (1980), 251–67.

Jacob, Margaret Candee. 'John Toland and the Newtonian Ideology', *Journal of the Warburg and Courtauld Institutes*, 32 (1969), 307–331.

—— Review (of William Stukeley. Science, Religion and Archaeology in Eighteenth-Century England by David Boyd Haycock), *Albion*, 35.3 (2003), 493–494.

—— 'Newtonianism and the Origins of the Enlightenment: A Reassessment', *Eighteenth-Century Studies*, 11.1 (1977), 1–25.

—— 'The Mental Landscape of the Public Sphere: A European Perspective', *Eighteenth-Century Studies*, 28.1 (1994), 95–113.

—— 'Review of Science, Technology, and Society: A Historical Perspective by Martin Fichman', *Isis*, 86.2 (1995), 303–4.

—— 'Enlightenment Redefined: The Formation of Modern Civil Society', *Social Research*, 58.2 (1991), 475–95.

James, F.G. 'The Active Irish Peers in the Early Eighteenth Century', *Journal of British Studies*, 18.2 (1979), 67.

Janowitz, Anne. '"What a Rich Fund of Images Is Treasured up Here": Poetic Commonplaces of the Sublime Universe', *Studies in Romanticism*, 44.4 (2005) 469–92.

Jenkins, Philip. 'Jacobites and Freemasons in eighteenth century Wales', *Welsh History Review*, 9.4 (1979) 391–406.

—— 'Tory Industrialism and Town Politics: Swansea in the Eighteenth Century', *Historical Journal*, 28.1 (1985), 103–123.

—— 'Anti-Popery on the Welsh Marches in the Seventeenth Century', *Historical Journal*, 23.2 (1980), 275–93.

—— 'Party Conflict and Political Stability in Monmouthshire, 1690–1740', *Historical Journal*, 29.3 (1986), 557–75.
Jones, Francis. 'Portraits and Pictures in Old Carmarthenshire Houses – Taliaris', *Carmarthenshire Historian*, V (1968), 43–66.
Jones, R.V. Physical Science in the eighteenth century', *Journal for Eighteenth Century Studies*, 1.2 (published on-line 2008), 73–88.
Josten, C.H. 'Elias Ashmole, FRS (1617–1692)', *RS Notes and Records*, 15 (1960), 228.
Kelsall, Malcom. Vitruvian man and the Iconography of Opposition . . . ', *Journal for Eighteenth Century Studies*, 18.1 (published on-line 2008), 1–17.
Kerrish, William. 'Practical Aspects of Mediæval Guilds', *Irish Monthly*, 63.746 (1935) 504–12.
Kliger, Samuel. 'Whig Aesthetics: A Phase of Eighteenth-Century Taste', *ELH*, 16.2 (1949), 135–50.
Knights, Mark. 'A City Revolution: The Remodelling of the London Livery Companies in the 1680s', *English Historical Review*, 112.449 (1997), 1141–1178.
Knoop, Douglas & Jones, G. P. 'Masons and Apprenticeship in Mediaeval England', *Economic History Review*, 3.3 (1932), 346–66.
Kwaadgras, Evert. 'Masonry with a Message and a Mission', *Address to Internet Lodge, Kingston-Upon-Hull*, 8 August 2002.
Landau, Norma. 'Indictment for Fun and Profit: A Prosecutor's Reward at Eighteenth-Century Quarter Sessions', *Law and History Review*, 17.3 (1999) 507–36.
—— 'Country Matters: The Growth of Political Stability a Quarter Century On', *Albion*, 25.2 (1993) 261–74.
—— 'The Regulation of Immigration, Economic Structures and Definitions of the Poor in Eighteenth-Century England', *Historical Journal*, 33.3 (1990), 541–71.
—— 'Eighteenth-Century England: Tales Historians Tell', *Eighteenth-Century Studies*, 22. 2 (1988/9), 208–18.
—— 'Independence, Deference, and Voter Participation: The Behaviour of the Electorate in Early-Eighteenth-Century Kent', *Historical Journal*, 22.3 (1979), 561–83.
Langford, Paul. 'William Pitt and Public Opinion, 1757', *English Historical Review*, 88.346 (1973) 54–80.
Layton, David. 'Diction and Dictionaries in the Diffusion of Scientific Knowledge: An Aspect of the History of the Popularization of Science in Great Britain', *British Journal for the History of Science*, 2.3 (1965), 221–234.
Loftis, John. 'Richard Steele's Censorium', *Huntington Library Quarterly*, 14.1 (1950), 43–66.
—— 'The London Theaters in Early Eighteenth-Century Politics', *Huntington Library Quarterly*, 18.4 (1955), 367–8.
Lohne, J. A. 'Experimentum Crucis', *RS Notes and Records*, 23.2 (1968).
Lord, John. 'J M Rysbrack and a Group of East Midlands Commissions', *Burlington Magazine*, 132.1053 (1990) 866–70.
Loschky, David, and Childers, Ben D. 'Early English Mortality', *Journal of Interdisciplinary History*, 24.1 (1993), 85–97.
Lyons, H.G. 'The Officers of the Society (1662–1860)', *RS Notes and Records*, 3 (1940/1), 116–40.
Lyttle, Charles H. 'Historical Bases of Rome's Conflict with Freemasonry', *Church History*, 9.1 (1940), 3–23.

McCahill, Michael W. 'Peerage Creations and the Changing Character of the British Nobility, 1750–1830', *English Historical Review*, 96.379 (1981), 259–84.
McLeod, Wallace. 'The Old Charges', *Heredom*, 14 (2006), 105–44.
McNally, Patrick. 'Wood's Halfpence, Carteret and the Government of Ireland, 1723–6', *Irish Historical Studies*, 30.119 (1997), 354–76.
Maddison, R.E.W. 'A Note on the Correspondence of Martin Folkes, P.R.S.', *RS Notes and Records,*, 11.1 (1954), 100–9.
Manuel, Frank E. 'Newton as Autocrat of Science', *Daedalus*, 97.3 (1968), 969–1001.
Mason, Stephen. 'The Spring-Tide of Experimental Philosophy', *RS Notes and Records*, 46.2 (1992), 313–16.
Merton, Robert K. 'Science, Technology and Society in Seventeenth Century England', *Osiris*, 4 (1938), 360–632.
Milburn, John R. 'Benjamin Martin and the Development of the Orrery', *British Journal for the History of Science*, 6.4 (1973), 378–399.
—— 'Benjamin Martin and the Royal Society', RS Notes and Records, 28.1 (1973), 15– 23.
Miller, David Philip. 'The Usefulness of Natural Philosophy: The Royal Society and the Culture of Practical Utility in the Later Eighteenth Century', *British Journal for the History of Science*, 32.2 (1999), 185–201.
Milne, Doreen J. 'The Results of the Rye House Plot and Their Influence upon the Revolution of 1688', *Transactions of the Royal Historical Society*, 5th Series, 1 (1951), 91–108.
Mitchell, Trent A. 'The Politics of Experiment in the Eighteenth Century: The Pursuit of Audience and the Manipulation of Consensus in the Debate over Lightning Rods', *Eighteenth-Century Studies*, 31.3 (1998), 307–31.
Money, John. 'The West Midlands, 1760–1793: Politics, Public Opinion and Regional Identity in the English Provinces during the Late Eighteenth Century', *Albion*, 2.2 (1970), 73–93.
—— 'The Masonic Moment; Or, Ritual, Replica, and Credit: John Wilkes, the Macaroni Parson, and the Making of the Middle-Class Mind', *Journal of British Studies*, 32.4 (1993), 358–395.
Moore, John Robert. 'Daniel Defoe: King William's Pamphleteer and Intelligence Agent', *Huntington Library Quarterly*, 34.3 (1971), 251–60.
Morton, Alan Q. 'Concepts of Power: Natural Philosophy and the Uses of Machines in Mid-Eighteenth-Century London', *British Journal for the History of Science*, 28.1 (1995), 63–78.
—— 'Lectures on Natural Philosophy in London, 1750–1765: S. C. T. Demainbray (1710–1782) and the 'Inattention' of His Countrymen', *British Journal for the History of Science*, 23.4 (1990), 411–34.
—— Review (of *The Rise of Public Science: Rhetoric, Technology and Natural Philosophy in Newtonian Britain, 1660–1750* by Larry Stewart), RS Notes and Records, 48.1 (1994), 157–9.
Mowl, Timothy. 'Rococo and Later Landscaping at Longleat', *Garden History*, 23.1 (1995), 55–66.
Mulligan, Lotte and Glenn. 'Reconstructing Restoration Science', *Social Studies of Science*, 11.3 (1981), 327–364.
Multhauf, Robert P. 'The Scientist and the "Improver" of Technology', *Technology and Culture*, 1.1 (1959), 38–47.

Mulvey-Roberts, Marie. 'Hogarth on the Square: Framing the Freemasons', *British Journal for 18th Century Studies*, 26.2 (2003), 251–70.

Munro, John. 'The Monetary Origins of the 'Price Revolution': South German Silver Mining, Merchant-Banking, and Venetian Commerce, 1470–1540', *University of Toronto, Dept. of Economics Working Paper*, 8 June 1999, rev. 21 March 2003.

Munsche, P.B. 'Review: The Justice of the Peace, 1679–1760', *Eighteenth Century Studies*, 20.3 (1987) 385–7.

Murphy, Seán. 'Irish Jacobitism and Freemasonry', *Eighteenth-Century Ireland*, 9 (1994), 75–82.

Newman, John. 'Nicholas Stone's Goldsmiths' Hall: Design and Practice in the 1630s', *Architectural History*, 14 (1971), 30–141.

Norman, G. 'Early Freemasonry at Bath, Bristol and Exeter', *AQC Transactions*, XL (1927), 244.

Ogilvie, Sheilagh. 'Guilds, Efficiency, and Social Capital: Evidence from German Proto-Industry', *Economic History Review*, n.s. 57.2 (2004), 286–333.

Oldham, James. 'Truth-Telling in the Eighteenth-Century English Courtroom', *Law and History Review*, 12.1 (1994), 95–121.

Ormrod, W. M. 'The Peasants' Revolt and the Government of England', *Journal of British Studies*, 29.1 (1990), 1–30.

Owens, W.R. and Furbank, P.N. 'Defoe and the dutch Alliance: Some Attributions Examined', *Journal for Eighteenth Century Studies*, 9.2 (published on-line 2008), 169–82.

—— 'Defoe, the De la Faye letters and *Mercurius politicus*', *Journal for Eighteenth Century Studies*, 23.1 (published on-line 2008), 13–19.

Paulson, Ronald. 'New Light on Hogarth's Graphic Works', *Burlington Magazine*, 109.770 (1967), 280–6.

Penn, Simon A. C., and Dyer, Christopher. 'Wages and Earnings in Late Medieval England: Evidence from the Enforcement of the Labour Laws', *Economic History Review*, n.s. 43.3 (1990), 356–76.

Peters, H. 'Sir Isaac Newton and the "Oldest Catholic Religion"', *AQC Transactions*, vol. c (1987), 193–4.

Piggot, S. 'William Stukeley: Doctor, Divine, And Antiquary', *British Medical Journal*, 3.5933 (1974), 725–27.

Poos, L.R. 'The Social Context of Statute of Labourers Enforcement', *Law and History Review*, 1.1 (1983), 27–52.

Porter, Roy. 'Science, Provincial Culture and Public Opinion in Enlightenment England', *Journal for Eighteenth Century Studies*, 3.1 (published on-line 2008), 20–46.

Prescott, Andrew. 'A History of British Freemasonry 1425–2000', *CRFF Working Paper Series 1* (2008).

—— 'Freemasonry and the Problem of Britain', Inaugural lecture, CRFF, 5 March 2001, subsequently published as a *CRFF Working Paper*.

—— 'Freemasonry and its Inheritance', lecture to the Masonic Museums and Libraries Group Freemasons' Hall, Great Queen Street, London, 30 September 2000, subsequently published as a *CRFF Working Paper*.

—— 'Druidic Myths and Freemasonry', a lecture presented at the Masonic Weekend, Kirkcaldy Masonic Hall, 4–6 May 2000, subsequently published as a *CRFF Working Paper No. 1*.

—— 'The Old Charges Revisited', *Transactions of the Lodge of Research, No. 2429, Leicester* (2006).

—— 'The Old Charges and the Origins of Freemasonry', *lecture transcript*, EXESESO Conference, University of Exeter, 31 January 2010.

—— 'The publishers of the 1723 Constitutions', *AQC Transactions*, 121 (2008), 147–62.

Prest, Wilfred. 'Judicial Corruption in Early Modern England', *Past & Present*, 133 (1991), 67–95.

Pumfrey, Stephen. 'Who Did the Work? Experimental Philosophers and Public Demonstrators in Augustan England', *British Journal for the History of Science*, 28.2 (1995), 131–56.

Putnam, B. H. 'Records of Courts of Common Law, Especially of the Sessions of the Justices of the Peace', *Proceedings of the American Philosophical Society*, 91.3 (1947), 258–73.

Ratton, J.J.L. 'Origin and Progress of Freemasonry', *Irish Monthly*, 41.478 (1905), 175–82.

—— 'Origin and Progress of Freemasonry II', *Irish Monthly*, 41.479 (1913), 257–62.

Raybould, T.J. 'The Development and Organization of Lord Dudley's Mineral Estates, 1774–1845', *Economic History Review*, n.s. 21.3 (1968), 529–44.

Révauger, Cécile. 'Anderson's Freemasonry: The true daughter of the British Enlightenment', *Cercles* 18 (2008), 1–9.

Roberts, John M. 'Freemasonry: Possibilities of a Neglected Topic', *English Historical Review*, 84.331 (1969), 323–35.

Robertson, J. 'Concerning the Fall of Water Under Bridges', *Philosophical Transactions (1683–1775)*, 50 (1757–8), 492–9.

Rogers, G.A.J. 'Locke's Essay and Newton's Principia', *Journal of the History of Ideas*, 39.2 (1978), 217–232.

Rogers, Nicholas. 'Popular Protest in Early Hanoverian London', *Past & Present*, 79 (1978), 70–100.

—— 'Money, Land and Lineage: The Big Bourgeoisie of Hanoverian London', *Social History*, 4.3 (1979), 437–454.

Rogers, Pat. 'The Conduct of the Earl of Nottingham: Curll, Oldmixon and the Finch Family', *Review of English Studies*, n.s. 21.82 (1970), 175–81.

Rosengarten, Joseph G. 'The Earl of Crawford's Ms. History in the Library of the American Philosophical Society', *Proceedings of the American Philosophical Society*, 42.174 (1903), 397–404.

Rosser, Gervase. 'Crafts, Guilds and the Negotiation of Work in the Mediaeval Town', *Past & Present*, 154 (1997), 3–31.

—— 'Going to the Fraternity Feast: Commensality and Social Relations in Late Mediaeval England, *Journal of British Studies*, 33.4 (1994), 430–46.

—— 'Parochial Conformity and Voluntary Religion in Late Mediaeval England', *Transaction of the Royal Historical Society*, 6th series, 1 (1991), 173–89.

Sabine, Ernest L. 'Butchering in Medieval London', *Speculum*, 8.3 (1933), 335–53.

Sainty, J.C. 'The Secretariat of the Chief Governors of Ireland, 1690–1800', *Proceedings of the Royal Irish Academy*, 77.C (1977), 21.

—— 'A Huguenot civil servant . . . ', *Proceedings of the Huguenot Society*, xxiii (1975).

Sasche, Julius F. 'The Masonic Chronology of Benjamin Franklin', *Pennsylvania Magazine of History and Biography*, 30.2 (1906), 238–40.

Scanlan, Matthew. 'Nicholas Stone and the Mystery of the Acception', *Freemasonry Today*, 12 (2002).

—— 'The Mystery of the Acception, 1630–1723: A Fatal Flaw', *Heredom*, 11 (2003).
Schaffer, Simon. 'Machine Philosophy: Demonstration Devices in Georgian Mechanics', *Osiris*, 2nd series, 9 (1994), 157.
—— 'The Show That Never Ends: Perpetual Motion in the Early Eighteenth Century', *British Journal for the History of Science*, 28.2 (1995), 157–189.
—— 'Experimenters' Techniques, Dyers' Hands, and the Electric Planetarium', *Isis*, 88.3 (1997), 456–483.
—— 'Self Evidence', *Critical Inquiry*, 18.2 (1992), 327–362.
—— 'Halleys's Atheism and the End of the World', *RS Notes and Records*, 32.1 (1977) 17–40.
Schmidt, Alvin J., and Babchuk, Nicholas. 'The Unbrotherly Brotherhood: Discrimination in Fraternal Orders', *Phylon*, 34.3 (1973), 276.
Schwoerer, Lois G. 'The Attempted Impeachment of Sir William Scroggs, Lord Chief Justice of the Court of King's Bench', *Historical Journal*, 38.4 (1995), 843–873.
Seligman, Edwin R.A. 'Two Chapters on the Mediaeval Guilds of England', *American Economic Association*, 2.5 (1887), 9–113.
Shackleton, Robert. 'Montesquieu's Correspondence', *French Studies*, XII.4 (1958), 324–45.
Shelby, Lon R. 'The Geometrical Knowledge of Mediaeval Master Masons', *Speculum*, 47.3 (1972), 395–421.
Shoemaker, Robert B. 'The London Mob in the Early Eighteenth Century', *Journal of British Studies*, 26.3 (1987) 273–304.
—— 'The Decline of Public Insult in London 1660–1800', *Past & Present*, 169 (2000), 97–131.
Sicca, Cinzia Maria. 'Lord Burlington at Chiswick: Architecture and Landscape', *Garden History*, 10.1 (1982), 36–69.
Simms, J.G. 'Dean Swift and County Armagh', *Seanchas Ardmhacha: Journal of the Armagh Diocesan Historical Society*, 6.1 (1971), 131–40.
Smith, Bruce P. 'Did the Presumption of Innocence Exist in Summary Proceedings?', *Law and History Review*, 23.1 (2005), 191–9.
Smith, Douglas. 'Freemasonry and the Public in Eighteenth-Century Russia', *Eighteenth-Century Studies*, 29.1 (1995), 25–44.
Snoek, Jan A.M. 'Researching Freemasonry: Where Are We?', *CRFF Working Paper Series*, 2 (2008).
Sorrenson, Richard. 'Towards a History of the Royal Society in the Eighteenth Century', *RS Notes and Records*, 50.1 (1996), 29–46.
Stevenson, David. 'James Anderson: Man & Mason', *Heredom*, 10 (2002), 93–138.
—— 'Circles and Straight Lines: Compasses and Squares', *CMRC Lecture* (25 October 2009).
—— Review of 'The Origins of Freemasonry. Facts and Fictions', *Reviews in History*, IHR (2006), http://www.history.ac.uk/reviews/review/517, accessed 21 June 2010.
Stewart, J. Douglas. 'Some Portrait Drawings by Michael Dahl and Sir James Thornhill', *Master Drawings*, 11.1 (1973), 34–102.
Stewart, Larry. 'A Meaning for Machines: Modernity, Utility, and the Eighteenth-Century British Public', *Journal of Modern History*, 70.2 (1998) 259–294.
—— 'Public Lectures and Private Patronage in Newtonian England', *Isis*, 77.1 (1986), 47–58.
—— 'The Selling of Newton: Science and Technology in Early Eighteenth-Century England', *Journal of British Studies*, 25.2 (1986), 185.

—— 'Other Centres of Calculation, or, Where the Royal Society Didn't Count: Commerce, Coffee-Houses and Natural Philosophy in Early Modern London', *British Journal for the History of Science*, 32.2 (1999), 133–53.

—— 'Samuel Clarke, Newtonianism, and the Factions of Post-Revolutionary England', *Journal of the History of Ideas*, 42.1 (1981), 53–72.

—— 'Newtonians, Revolutionaries and Republicans', *Canadian Journal of History*, 17.2 (1982), 314–321.

Stewart, Larry and Weindling, Paul. 'Philosophical Threads: Natural Philosophy and Public Experiment among the Weavers of Spitalfields', British Journal for the History of Science, 28.1 (1995), 37–62.

Stewart, Trevor. 'English Speculative Freemasonry: Some Possible Origins, Themes and Developments', *AQC Transactions*, 117 (2004), 116–82.

Stokes, J. 'Life of John Theophilus Desaguliers', *AQC Transactions*, 38 (1925).

Striner, Richard. 'Political Newtonianism: The Cosmic Model of Politics in Europe and America', William and Mary Quarterly, 3rd series, 52.4 (1995), 583–608.

Strong, E.W. 'Newtonian Explications of Natural Philosophy', *Journal of the History of Ideas*, 18.1 (1957), 49–83.

Sutherland, James. 'James Sutherland to My Lord', *South Carolina Historical Magazine*, 68.2 (1967), 79–84.

Swanson, Heather. 'The Illusion of Economic Structure: Craft Guilds in late Mediaeval English Towns, *Past & Present*, 121 (1988), 29–48.

Sweet, Rosemary. 'Antiquaries and Antiquities in Eighteenth-Century England', *Eighteenth-Century Studies*, 34.2 (2001), 181–206.

Targett, Simon. 'Government and Ideology during the Age of Whig Supremacy', *Historical Journal*, 37.2 (1994), 289–317.

Temperley, Harold W.V. 'The Causes of the War of Jenkins' Ear, 1739'. *Transactions of the Royal Historical Society*, 3rd series, 3 (1909) 197–236.

Thomas, Peter D.G. 'Party Politics in Eighteenth century Britain: Some Myths and a Touch of Reality', *Journal for Eighteenth Century Studies*, 10.2 (published on-line 2008), 201–10.

Thompson, E.P. 'Patrician Society, Plebeian Culture', *Journal of Social History*, 7.4 (1974), 382–405.

Thompson, F.H. 'The Society of Antiquaries of London: Its History and Activities', *Proceedings of the Massachusetts Historical Society*, 3rd series, 93 (1981), 1–16.

Tomory, Peter. 'Review of Ronald Paulson's "Hogarth: His Life, Art and Times"', *Art Bulletin*, 54.4 (1972), 557–9.

Treadwell, J.M. 'Swift, William Wood, and the Factual Basis of Satire', *Journal of British Studies*, 15.2 (1976), 76–91.

Tupper, Jr., Frederick. 'The Holme Riddles', *PMLA – Journal of the Modern Language Association of America*, 18.2 (1903), 212.

Turck, Dieter. 'Review: Leibniz's Correspondence (1692)', *Journal of the History of Ideas*, 32.4 (1971) 627–30.

Turner, Raymond. 'The Excise Scheme of 1733', *EHR*, 42.165 (1927), 34–57.

Von Buttlar, Adrian. 'Neo-Palladianism and Freemasonry', *Burlington Magazine*, 124.957 (1982), 762.

Wahrmann, Dror. 'National Society, Communal Culture: An Argument about the Recent Historiography of Eighteenth-Century Britain', *Social History*, 17.1 (1992), 43–72.

Walker, Richard. 'Freemasonry and Neo-Palladianism', *Burlington Magazine*, 125.969 (1983), 746.

Warner, Jessica and Ivis, Frank. '"Damn You, You Informing Bitch." Vox Populi and the Unmaking of the Gin Act of 1736', *Journal of Social History*, 33.2 (1999), 299–330.

Warner, Jessica, Ivis, Frank and Demers, Andree. 'A Predatory Social Structure: Informers in Westminster, 1737–1741', *Journal of Interdisciplinary History*, 30.4 (2000), 617–34.

Wasserman, Earl R. 'Nature Moralized: The Divine Analogy in the Eighteenth Century', *ELH*, 20.1 (1953), 39–76.

Weisberger, R. William. 'John Theophilus Desaguliers: Promoter of the Enlightenment and of Speculative Freemasonry', *AQC Transactions*, 113 (2000).

—— 'Parisian Masonry, the Lodge of the Nine Sisters & the French Enlightenment', *Heredom*, 10 (2002), 155–162.

—— 'Review' (of *Living the Enlightenment: Freemasonry and Politics in Eighteenth-Century Europe* by Margaret C. Jacob), *Journal of Social History*, 28.1 (1994), 209–211.

Wess, Jane. 'Lecture Demonstrations and the Real World: The Case of Cart-Wheels', *British Journal for the History of Science*, 28.1 (1995), 79–90.

Whipple, Robert S. 'Some Scientific Instrument Makers of the Eighteenth Century', *Science*, n.s. 72.1861 (1930), 208–13.

White, Jonathan. 'The "Slow but Sure Poyson": The Representation of Gin and Its Drinkers, 1736–1751', *Journal of British Studies*, 42.1 (2003), 35–64.

Wigelsworth, Jeffrey R. 'Competing to Popularize Newtonian Philosophy John Theophilus Desaguliers and the Preservation of Reputation', *Isis*, 94.3 (2003), 435–455.

Williams, W.J. 'Notes & Queries', *AQC Transactions*, 40 (1927), 170.

Winter, H.J.J. 'Scientific Notes from the Early Minutes of the Peterborough Society 1730–1745', *Isis*, 31.1 (1939), 51–9.

Wood, A.C. 'The English Embassy at Constantinople, 1600–1762', *English Historical Review*, 40.160 (1925), 551.

—— 'The Duke of Kingston's regiment of light horse', *Transactions of the Thoroton Society of Nottinghamshire*, 49 (1946), 73–83.

Woodward, Donald. 'Wage Rates and Living Standards in Pre-Industrial England', *Past & Present*, 91 (1981), 28–46.

—— 'The Determination of Wage Rates in the Early Modern North of England', *Economic History Review*, n.s. 47.1 (1994), 22–43.

—— 'The Background to the Statute of Artificers: The Genesis of Labour Policy, 1558–63', *Economic History Review*, n.s. 33.1 (1980), 32–44.

Worsley, Giles. 'Nicholas Hawksmoor: A Pioneer Neo-Palladian?', *Architectural History*, 33 (1990), 60–74.

Wright, C.E. 'Four Stukeley Notebooks', *British Museum Quarterly*, 27.3/4 (1963–4), 61–5.

Biographies: Oxford Dictionary of National Biography, OUP, Oxford

Note: All biographies are taken from the hard copy edition published 2004, or on-line edition published January 2008, unless indicated otherwise. All on-line references were sourced between June 2009 and August 2010 and re-verified 10–11 August 2010.

Allan, David. 'Sir Robert Moray (1608/9?–1673)'. Online edition October 2007.

Appleby, John H. 'John Rowley'. Online edition.

Select Bibliography

Baker, J.H. 'William Hawkins (1681/2–1750)'. Online edition.
Barr, C. Bernard L. 'Francis Drake'.
Barry, Helen. 'John Dunton'.
Birkeland, Marianna. 'James Murray, second duke of Atholl'.
Bonwick, Colin. 'Thomas Hollis (1720–1774)'. Online edition.
Brown, David. 'John Ward, second Viscount Dudley and Ward (1725–1788)'. Online edition.
Browning, Reed. 'Thomas-Pellam-Holles, Duke of Newcastle upon Tyne and first Duke of Newcastle under Lyme (1693–1768)'. Online edition October 2009.
Bucholz, O. 'Herbert, Thomas, eighth earl of Pembroke and fifth earl of Montgomery (1656/7–1733)'. Online edition, May 2009.
Childs, John. 'Sir Henry Belasyse'. Online edition May 2006.
Clerke, A.M., rev. Gingerich, Owen. 'George Parker, George, second Earl of Macclesfield (c. 1697–1764)'.
Cook, Alan F. 'Henry Beighton'.
Connor, T.P. 'Herbert, 9th Earl of Pembroke and 6th Earl of Montgomery (c. 1689–1750)'. Online edition, May 2009.
Davies, J. D. 'Sir Henry Goodricke, 2nd Baronet (1642–1705)'. Online edition.
Fara, Patricia. 'John Theophilus Desaguliers (1683–1744)'. Online edition.
Feigenbaum, Lenore. 'Brook Taylor'. Online edition.

Frey, Linda and Marsha. 'Charles Townshend, third Viscount Townshend (1700–1764)'.
Handley, Stuart. 'Robert Benson, Baron Bingley'. Online edition.
Hanham, A. A. 'Thomas Coke, Earl of Leicester'. Online edition May 2008.
Hattendorf, John B. 'John Richmond Webb'. Online edition.
Haycock, David Boyd. 'Martin Folkes (1690–1754)'. Online edition May 2008.
Henderson, T. F., rev. Carter, 'Philip. Hugh Cholmondeley, first Earl of Cholmondeley (1662?–1725)'.
—— rev. Spain, Jonathan. 'George Cholmondeley, second Earl of Cholmondeley'.
Henry, John. 'John Keill'.
Hopkins, Paul. 'Sir Thomas Prendergast, second baronet'. Online edition.
Hunter, Michael. 'Elias Ashmole (1617–1692)'. Online edition May 2006.
Lang, Andrew M. 'Alexander Brodie of Brodie (1697–1754)'. Online edition October 2009.
Lowe, William C. 'Jeffrey Amherst, first Baron Amherst'. Online edition.
MacKenzie, Raymond N. 'Edmund Curll (d. 1747)'. Online edition.
McCann, Timothy J. 'Charles Lennox, second Duke of Richmond, second Duke of Lennox, and Duke of Aubigny in the French nobility (1701–1750)'.
Marshall, Rosalind K. 'Lady Jane Douglas (1698–1753)'.
Melton, Frank. 'Sir Robert Clayton (1629–1707)'. Online edition, October 2007.
Metzger, Edward Charles. 'John Montagu, second Duke of Montagu'.
Milhous, Judith. 'Johann Jakob Heidegger'.
Midgley, Graham. 'John Henley (1692–1756)'. Online edition.
Morton, Alan. 'Stephen Demainbray'. Online edition.
Pumfrey, Stephen. 'Francis Hauksbee'.
Riding, Jacqueline. 'Joseph Highmore'. Online edition.
Rusnock, Andrea. 'John Scheuchzer'. Online edition, Sept. 2004.
Samuel, Edgar. 'Meyer Schomberg'.
Slater, Victor. 'John Grenville, Ist Earl of Bath (1628–1701)'. Online edition.

Smith, Lawrence B. 'Philip Wharton, Duke of Wharton and Jacobite Duke of Northumberland'. Online edition.
Snobelen, Stephen D. 'William Whiston'. Online edition, Oct. 2009.
Stephens, H.M., rev. Place, Timothy Harrison. 'George Carpenter, first Baron Carpenter of Killaghy (1657–1732)'. Online edition May 2008.
—— rev. Spain, Jonathan. 'Thomas Desaguliers (1721–1780)'.
Stewart, Larry. 'John Harris'. Online edition.
Sugden, Philip. 'Sir Thomas de Veil (1684–1746)'.
Targett, Simon. 'James Pitt (fl.1744–55)'. Online edition January 2010.
Turner, A. J. 'Robert Plot'.
'Sir Thomas Millington'.
Wallis, Ruth. 'William Jones (c.1675–1749)'. Online edition May 2009.
Wauchope, Piers. 'Robert King, second Baron Kingston (c. 1660–1693)'.
White, Adam. 'Nicholas Stone'.
Woodfine, Philip. 'James, first Earl Waldegrave'.
Wynne, M. 'Louise Renée de Penancoët de Kéroualle, suo jure duchess of Portsmouth and suo jure duchess of Aubigny in the French nobility (1649–1734)'. Online edition.

Other Secondary Sources

Agnew, Rev. David C. A. *French Protestant Exiles*. London: Reeves & Turner, 1871.
Baigent, Michael, and Leigh, Richard. *The Temple and the Lodge*. New York, NY: Arcade Publishing, 1989.
Barker-Cryer, Neville. *The Restoration Lodge of Chester*. London: Cornerstone Society, 2002.
—— *York Mysteries Revealed*. York: Barker-Cryer, 2006.
Bauer, Alain. *Isaac Newton's Freemasonry*. Rochester, VT: Inner Traditions, 2003.
Benjamin, Lewis. *South Sea Bubble*. Manchester, NH: Ayer Publishing, 1967.
Besterman, Theodore (ed.), *The Complete Works of Voltaire v. 89: Correspondence and Related Documents, February – December 1738, letters D1439-D1729*. Geneva: Voltaire Foundation, 1969.
Black, Jeremy. *Culture in eighteenth century England: A Subject for Taste*. London: Continuum, 2006.
—— *The British Abroad: The Grand Tour in the Eighteenth Century*. Stroud: Sutton Publishing, 2003.
—— *Walpole in Power*. Stroud: Sutton Publishing, 2001.
Boas Hall, Marie. *Promoting Experimental Learning: Experiment and the Royal Society, 1660–1727*. Cambridge: CUP, 1991.
Borsay, Peter. *The English Urban Renaissance: Culture and Society in the Provincial Town 1660–1770*. Oxford: OUP, 1989.
Bothwell, James, Goldberg, P.J.P., Ormrod, W.M. (eds). *The Problem of Labour in Fourteenth-Century England*. York: York Mediaeval Press (Boydell & Brewer imprint), 2000.
Boughton House Trust, *Information for Teachers*. Kettering: The Living Landscape Trust, 2004.
Boutin, Pierre. *Jean-Théophile Desaguliers: un Huguenot, philosophe et juriste, en politique*. Paris: Honoré Champion Éditeur, 1999.
Bucholz, Robert and Key, Newton. *Early Modern England, 1485–1714, illustrated edition*. Oxford: Wiley Blackwell, 2004.

Bull, Stephen. *A General Plague of Madness: The Civil Wars in Lancashire 1640–1660*. Lancaster: Carnegie Publishing, 2009.

Burke, Bernard. *A genealogical and heraldic history of the extinct and dormant baronetcies of England, Ireland and Scotland*. London: John Russell Smith, 1844. 2nd edition.

Burns, William E. *Science in the Enlightenment*. Oxford: ABC-CLIO, 2003.

Byrne, Joseph Patrick. *Daily life during the Black Death*. Santa Barbara: Greenwood, 2006.

Byrom, John. *The Private Journal and Literary Remains of John Byrom*. Whitefish, MT: Kessinger Publishing, 2009 (reprint). Originally published Manchester: the Chetham Society, 1854-7.

Cantor, G. N. *Quakers, Jews, and Science: Religious Responses to Modernity and the Sciences in Britain, 1650–1900*. Oxford: OUP, 2005.

Carpenter, Audrey. *Ingenious Philosopher: John Theophilus Desaguliers (1683–1744), Popularizer of Newtonianism and Promoter of Freemasonry*. University of Loughborough: unpublished PhD Thesis, 2009.

Carr, Harry (ed.). *The Collected Prestonian Lectures 1925–1960*. London: Lewis Masonic, 1984.

—— *The Early French Exposures*. London: QC, 1971.t5

Caulfield, James. *Portraits, Memoirs and Characters of Remarkable Persons, from the revolution in 1688 to the end of the reign of George II*. London: T.H. Whiteley, 1820. Volume 3 of 4 volumes.

Cerza, Alphonse. *Anti-Masonry: Light on the Past and Present Opponents of Freemasonry*. Fulton: Ovid Bell, 1962.

Chamberlayne, John. *Magnae Britanniae Notitia*. London: various editions published in 1708, 1716, 1718, 1723, 1728 and 1736.

Chambers, Ephraim. *Cyclopædia: or, an universal dictionary of arts and sciences*. London, 1728.

Chevallier, Pierre. *Les Ducs Sous L'Acacia*. Vrin, Paris, 1964.

Chrimes, Mike, and Skempton, A.W. (eds) *A Biographical Dictionary of Civil Engineers in Great Britain and Ireland: 1500 to 1830*. London: Thomas Telford, 2002.

Churton, Tobias. *Freemasonry: The Reality*. Hersham: Lewis Masonic, 2007.

Clare, Martin. *Youth's introduction to trade and business*. London: Clare, 1720.

—— *A Defense of Masonry*. London: Clare, 1730.

Clark, Jane. *Lord Burlington is Here*, in Barnard, Tony and Clark, Jane (eds), *Lord Burlington: Architecture, Art and Life*. London: Hambledon Press, 1995.

Clark, Peter. *British Clubs and Societies 1580–1800*. Oxford: OUP, 2000.

Clarke, W.B. *Early and Historic Freemasonry of Georgia, 1733/4–1800*. Georgia: privately published, 1924.

Collins, John. *Perpetual Motion; An Ancient Mystery Solved?*, Raleigh, N.C.: Lulu.com, 2006) .

Curry, Anne, and Matthew, Elizabeth (eds). *Concepts and Patterns of Service in the Later Middle Ages*. Woodbridge: The Boydell Press, 2000.

Davies, Glyn. *A History of Money from Ancient Times to the Present Day*. Cardiff: University of Wales Press, 1996, rev. edition.

Deane, Phyllis, and Cole, W.A. *British Economic Growth, 1688–1959*. Cambridge: CUP, 1999, 2nd edition.

Denslow, William R. *10,000 Famous Freemasons*. Whitefish, MT: Kessinger. 2004. 2 vols.

Dickson, Paul. *Toasts*. New York: Dell Publishing, 1981.
Dobb, Maurice. *Studies in the Development of Capitalism*. London: Routledge & Kegan Paul Limited, 1946. Revised edition, 1963.
Dyer, Christopher. *Making a Living in the Middle Ages: The People of Britain 850–1520*. New Haven: Yale University Press, 2002.
Dyer, Colin. *The Grand Stewards and Their Lodge*. London: Grand Steward's Lodge, 1985.
Earwaker, J. P. *The four Randle Holmes of Chester, antiquaries, heraldists and genealogists, c. 1571 to 1707*. Chester: Chester Antiquarian Society, 1892.
Eccleshall, George. *The Old King's Arms Lodge, 1725–2000*. London: published privately, 2001.
Ewald Jr., William Bragg. *Rogues, Royalty and Reporters, The Age of Queen Anne through its Newspapers*. Boston, MA: Houghton Mifflin Company, 1954.
Fara, Patricia. *Newton, the Making of Genius*. London: Macmillan, 2002.
Finlayson, J. Finlay and Tice, Paul. *Symbols and Legends of Freemasonry*. San Diego: The Book Tree, 2003. Revised edition. Originally published London: George Kenning & Son, 1910.
Fortescue, John. *A History of the British Army*. Uckfield: Naval & Military Press, 2004 (reprint).
Furbank, P.N. and Owens, W.R. *A Political Biography of Daniel Defoe*. London: Pickering & Chatto, 2006.
George, M. Dorothy. London Life in the Eighteenth Century. London: Routledge, 1996. Reprint of 3rd edition, 1951. Originally published London: Kegan Paul *et al.*, 1925.
Gould, Robert Freke. *The History of Freemasonry: Its Antiquities, Symbols, Constitutions, Customs, Etc.* London: J. Beacham, 1885.
—— *The History of Freemasonry, The Statutes relating to the Freemasons*. Philadelphia: John C. Yorston Publishing Co., 1902.
—— *The Concise History of Freemasonry*. London: Gale & Polden, 1951. (rev. Crowe, Frederick.)
—— *Military Lodges: the Apron and the Sword, or Freemasonry under Arms*. London: Gale and Polden, 1899.
—— *Military Lodges: the Apron and the Sword, or Freemasonry under Arms*. Whitefish, MT: Kessinger Publishing, 2003 (reprint).
—— *A History of Freemasonry throughout the World*. London: Thomas Jack, 1884.
—— *Gould's History of Freemasonry throughout the World, Volume's I, II and III*. New York: Charles Scribener's Sons, 1936 (reprint).
—— *The Four Old Lodges*. London: Spencer's Masonic, 1879.
Gould, Robert Freke, *et al. A Library of Freemasonry, Volume's 1 – 4*. New York: The John C. Yorston Publishing Company, 1906.
Gwynn, Robin. *Huguenot Heritage*. Brighton, Portland, Toronto: Sussex Academic Press, 2001, 2nd revised edition.
—— *The Huguenots of London*. Brighton, Portland, Toronto: Sussex Academic Press, 1998.
Habermas, Jürgen. *The Structural Transformation of the Public Sphere: An Inquiry into a Category of Bourgeois Society*, transl. Thomas Burger. Cambridge, Mass.: MIT Press, 1989.
Halliwell, James. *The Early History of Freemasonry in England*. London, 1840.
Hamill, John. *The Craft. A History of English Freemasonry*. London: Crucible, 1986.

Hans, Nicholas. *New Trends in Education in the Eighteenth Century*. London: Routledge and Kegan Paul, 1966.

Harborne, L.R. and White, R.L.W. *The History of Freemasonry in Berkshire and Buckinghamshire*. Abingdon: Abbey Press, 1990.

Harland-Jacobs, Jessica. *All in the Family: Freemasonry and the British Empire in the Mid-Nineteenth Century*. Chicago, Ill.: University of Chicago Press, 2003.

—— *Builders of Empire: Freemasonry and British Imperialism, 1717–1927*. Chapel Hill, NC: University of North Carolina Press, 2007.

Harris, Eileen. *British Architectural Books and Writers 1556–1785*. Cambridge: CUP, 1994.

Harrison, David. *The Genesis of Freemasonry*. Hersham: Lewis Masonic, 2009.

Haycock, David Boyd. *William Stukeley: Science, Religion and Archaeology in Eighteenth-Century England*. Woodbridge: Boydell Press, 2002.

Hollinshead, Raphael. *The Third Volume of Chronicles, beginning at Duke William*. London: Henry Denham, 1586.

Honeybone, Michael. *The Spalding Gentlemen's Society: Scientific communication in the East Midlands of England* (The Open University: PhD Thesis, unpublished, 2002).

—— *Sociability, Utility and Curiosity in the Spalding Gentleman's Society, 1710–60* in Knight, David M. and Eddy, Matthew D. (eds). *Science and Beliefs: From Natural Philosophy to Natural Science*. Aldershot: Ashgate Publishing, 2005.

Horn, Joyce M., & Bailey, Derrick Sherwin. *Fasti Ecclesiae Anglicanae 1541–1857*. Vol. 5: *Bath and Wells diocese*. London: IHR, 1979.

Horwitz, Henry. *The Career of Daniel Finch, Second Earl of Nottingham, 1647–1730*. New York: CUP, 1968.

Hunter, Michael. *John Aubrey and the Realm of Learning*. London: Duckworth & Co., 1975.

Hurst, Wilfred R. *An outline of the career of John Theophilus Desaguliers*. London: Edson, 1928.

Ingham, Alfred. *Cheshire: Its Traditions and History*. Whitefish, MT: Kessinger Publishing, 2003 (reprint).

Jacob, Margaret C. *Living the Enlightenment*. Oxford: OUP, 1991.

—— *The Radical Enlightenment*. Lafayette, Louisiana: Cornerstone, 2006, 2nd rev. edition

—— *Polite Worlds of Enlightenment*, in Fitzpatrick, Martin *et al.*, *The Enlightenment World*. Abingdon, Oxon.: Routledge, 2004.

—— *The Origins of Freemasonry. Facts and Fictions*. Philadelphia: University of Pennsylvania Press, 2006.

Jacobs, Reginald. *Covent Garden*. London: Simpkin, Marshall, Hamilton, Kent & Co., 1913.

Jenkins, Philip. *The making of a ruling class: the Glamorgan gentry 1640–1790*. Cambridge: CUP, 1983.

Jenkins, Susan. *Portrait of a Patron: The Patronage and Collecting of James Brydges, 1st Duke of Chandos (1674–1744)*. Aldershot: Ashgate Publishing, 2007.

Josten, C. H. (ed.). *Elias Ashmole (1617–1692): His Autobiographical and Historical Notes*, 5 Volumes. Oxford: OUP, 1966.

Kaemper, Engelbert. *A History of Japan*. London, 1728.

Kebbell, Peter. *The Changing Face of Freemasonry, 1640–1740*. University of Bristol: unpublished PhD Thesis, 2009.

Kenning, George, and Woodford, A.F.A. *Kenning's Masonic Encyclopedia and*

    Handbook of Masonic Archaeology, History and Biography. Oxford: Kenning, 2003 (reprint).
Knight, Christopher, and Lomas, Robert. *The Hiram Key.* London: Century Books, 1996.
Knoop, Douglas, *The Genesis of Speculative Masonry.* Whitefish, MT: Kessinger, 1997. Originally published London, 1941.
Knoop, Douglas, & Jones, G. P. *Genesis of Freemasonry.* London: QCCC, 1978. First published Manchester: Manchester University Press, 1947.
—— *Early Masonic Pamphlets.* Manchester: Manchester University Press, 1945.
—— *The Mediaeval Mason.* Manchester: Manchester University Press, 1933.
Landau, Norma. *Justices of the Peace 1679–1760.* Berkeley, CA: University of California Press, 1984.
Langford, Paul. *Englishness Identified: Manners and Character, 1650–1850.* Oxford: OUP, 2000.
Langford, Paul. *A Polite and Commercial People: England 1727–1783.* Oxford: OUP, 1989.
Leapman, Michael. *Inigo: The Troubled Life of Inigo Jones, Architect of the English Renaissance.* London: Review Books, 2003.
Lee, William. *Daniel Defoe: His Life, and Recently Discovered Writings.* London, 1869.
Ligou, D. *Histoire des francs-maçons en France, 1725–1815.* Paris: privately published, 2000.
Lindsay, John, Earl of Crawford. *Memoirs of the life of the late Right Honourable John Earl of Craufurd.* London: T. Beckett, 1769.
Lowis, George W. et al., *Midwifery and the Medicalization of Childbirth: Comparative Perspectives.* Waltham: Nova Biomedical, 2004.
Lukis, W.C. (ed.) *Family Memoirs of William Stukeley.* Durham: Surtees Society, 3 vols, 1882–7.
Lysons, Daniel. *The Environs of London.* Volume 3. London: Institute of Historical Research, 1795.
McNamee, Robert (ed.). *Electronic Enlightenment.* Oxford: OUP, 2008.
Mackechnie-Jarvis, C. *Grand Stewards 1728–1978* in *The Collected Prestonian Lectures 1975–1987.* London: QC, 1988.
Mackenzie, Eneas. *Historical Account of Newcastle-upon-Tyne, Incorporated Companies: The fifteen bye-trades.* London: IHR, 1827.
—— *A Descriptive and Historical Account of the Town and County of Newcastle-upon-Tyne.* Newcastle: Mackenzie and Dent, 1827. Volume 1.
Mackey, Albert Gallatin et al. *Encyclopedia of Freemasonry.* Whitefish, MT: Kessinger Publishing, 2003 (reprint).
Martin, George M. *British Masonic Miscellany.* Whitefish, MT: Kessinger Publishing, 2003 (reprint).
Melville, Lewis. *South Sea Bubble.* London: Daniel O'Connor, 1921.
—— *Life and Letters of John Gay (1685–1732).* London: Daniel O'Connor, 1921.
Member of the Ancient Society of Freemasons, A. *A Vindication of the Reverend Dr Snape and Dr Sherlock . . .* London: A. Dod, 1722.
Miège, Guy. *The present state of Great-Britain and Ireland.* London: 1718.
—— *The establish'd state of the publick offices, under his Majesty King George II.* London, 1728.
Montagu, Lady Mary Wortley (Lord Wharcliffe (ed.)). *The Letters and Works of*

Lady Mary Wortley Montagu. New York, NY: Swan Sonnenschein & Co., 1893. Originally published London: Richard Bentley, 1837.

Newman, P.R. *Atlas of the English Civil War*. London: Taylor & Francis, 1985.

Newton, Joseph. *The Builders*. Cedar Rapids, Iowa: Torch Press, 1916.

Nichols, J. *Literary anecdotes of the eighteenth century*, 9 Volumes, facsimile reproduction. New York: Centaur Press, 1966. Originally published London, 1812–16.

Noble, Mark, and Granger, James. *A Biographical History of England*. London: W. Richardson, 1806.

Noszlopy, George T., and Waterhouse, Fiona. *Public Sculpture of Staffordshire and the Black Country*, Illustrated Edition. Liverpool: Liverpool University Press, 2005.

Paulson, Ronald. *Hogarth: His Life, Art and Times*. New Haven: Yale University Press, 1971.

—— *Hogarth's Graphic Works*. New Haven: Yale University Press, 1965.

Paley, Ruth (ed.). *Justice in 18th century Hackney. The Justicing notebook of Henry Norris*. London: London Record Society, 1991.

Phelps Brown, Henry, and Hopkins, Sheila V. *A Perspective of Wages and Prices*. London: Methuen, 1981.

Pickering, Danby. *The Statutes at Large*. Cambridge: Joseph Bentham, 1762.

Pickrill, D.A. *Ministers of the Crown*. London: Routledge & Kegan Paul, 1981.

Pink, Andrew. *The Musical Culture of Freemasonry in Early Eighteenth-century London*. University College London, unpublished PhD thesis, 2007.

Plumb, J. H. *England in the Eighteenth Century* (1714–1815). London: Penguin, 1950.

Porter, Roy (ed.) *The Cambridge History of Science, Volume 4, Eighteenth-Century Science*. Cambridge: CUP, 2003.

—— *Enlightenment*. London: Penguin Books, 2001.

—— *London: a Social History*. London: Penguin Books, 1994.

Prescott, Andrew. *Some Literary Contexts of the Regius and Cooke Manuscripts* in Stewart, Trevor (ed.), *Freemasonry in Music and Literature*. London: CMRC, 2005.

—— 'The Earliest Use of the Word Freemason', in *Year Book of the Grand Lodge of Scotland, 2004*. Edinburgh: Grand Lodge of Scotland, 2004.

Preston, William. *Illustrations of Freemasonry*. London: J Wilkie, 1775, 2nd edition.

—— *Illustrations of Freemasonry*. London: G & T Wilkie, 1796.

—— *Illustrations of Freemasonry*. London: G. Wilkie, 1812.

—— *Illustrations of Freemasonry*. New York: Masonic Publishing and Manufacturing Co., 1867.

Raban, Itamar. *The Post Man and its Editor, Jean Lespinasse de Fonvive* in Vigne, Randolph and Littleton, Charles (eds). *From Strangers to Citizens*. Brighton, Portland, Toronto: Sussex Academic Press, 2001.

Raftis, J.A. *Peasant Economic Development within the English Manorial System*. Montreal: McGill-Queen's University Press, 1996.

—— *Tenure and Mobility*. Toronto: Pontifical Institute of Mediaeval Studies, 1964.

Raybould, T.J. *The Economic Emergence of the Black Country: A Study of the Dudley Estate*. Newton Abbot: David & Charles, 1973.

Reid, David Boswell. *Ventilation in American Dwellings*. New York: Wiley & Halsted, 1858.

Richter, Melvin. *The Political Theory of Montesquieu*. Cambridge: CUP, 1977.

Ripley, Col. Richard M. *Military Lodges*. Alexandria, VA: National Sojourners Inc., 2006.
Roberts, J.M. *The Mythology of the Secret Societies*. London: Watkins Publishing, 2008. Originally published London, 1972.
Rolt, Richard. *Memoirs of the life of the late Rt Hon John Lindesay, Earl of Crauford and Lindesay*. London: Henry Köpp, 1753.
Rothstein, Natalie. *Huguenot master weavers: exemplary Englishmen, 1700–c. 1750* in Vigne, Randolph and Littleton, Charles (eds). *From Strangers to Citizens*. Brighton, Portland, Toronto: Sussex Academic Press, 2001.
Sadler, Henry, and Chetwode Crawley, W. J. *Masonic Reprints and Historical Revelations*. Whitefish, MT: Kessinger Publishing, 2003 (reprint).
Schaffer, Simon. *Natural Philosophy and Public Spectacle in Eighteenth Century England, Volume XXI*. Cambridge: History of Science, 1983.
Schwarz, L.D. *London in the age of industrialisation: entrepreneurs, labour force and living conditions, 1750–1850*. Cambridge: CUP, 1992.
Sedgwick, R. (ed.) *The History of Parliament: the House of Commons, 1715–1754*. Cambridge: CUP, 1970.
—— *Lord Hervey's Memoirs*. London: B.T. Batsford, 1931.
Shipton, Clifford K. *New England Life in the 18th Century: Representative Biographies from Sibley's Harvard Graduates*. Cambridge, MA: Harvard University Press, 1963.
Smith, George. *The Use and Abuse of Freemasonry*. London, 1783.
Speth, G. W., and Howard, C. C. *William Watson MS*. London: QC, 1891.
Steele, Richard. *The Lucubrations of Isaac Bickerstaff, Esq*. London: H. Lintot, J. and P. Knapton, *et al.*, 1710–1712. Published in 3 Volumes.
Stephenson, David. *The Origins of Freemasonry, Scotland's Century, 1590–1710*. Cambridge: CUP, 1990.
—— *The First Freemasons: Scotland's Early Lodges and their Members*. Aberdeen: Aberdeen University Press, 1988.
Stewart, Larry. *The rise of public science: rhetoric, technology, and natural philosophy in Newtonian Britain, 1660–1750*. Cambridge: CUP, 1992.
Stewart, Trevor (ed.), *Freemasonry in Music and Literature*. London: CMRC, 2005.
Tew, Thomas William, and Matthewman, J. *Masonic Miscellanea, Comprising a Collection of Addresses and Speeches*. Whitefish, MT: Kessinger Publishing, 2003 (reprint).
Thomas, Peter D.G. *The Remaking of Wales in the Eighteenth Century*, in Herbert, Trevor and Jones, Gareth Elwyn (eds), *The Remaking of Wales in the Eighteenth Century*. Cardiff: University of Wales Press, 1988.
Thomson, Mark A. *The Secretaries of State 1681–1782*. Oxford: Clarendon Press, 1932.
Thornbury, Walter. *Old and New London, Volume 3*. London: Centre for Metropolitan History, 1878.
Times, John. *Club Life of London*. London: Bentley, 1866.
Trent, William P. *Daniel Defoe, How to Know him*. Indianapolis, 1916.
Trumbach, Randolph. *Sex and the Gender Revolution: Heterosexuality and the Third Gender in Enlightenment London*. Chicago: University of Chicago Press, 1998.
Uglow, Jenny. *Hogarth – A Life and World*. London: Faber & Faber, 1997.
Vigne, Randolph, and Littleton, Charles (eds). *From Strangers to Citizens*. Brighton, Portland, Toronto: Sussex Academic Press, 2001.

Watson, William. *An historical account of the ancient town and port of Wisbech*. Wisbech: H. and J. Leach, 1827.

White, Michael. *The Last Sorcerer*. London: Fourth Estate, 1997.

Wigelsworth, Jeffrey Robert. *'Their Grosser Degrees of Infidelity': Deists, Politics, Natural Philosophy, and the Power or God in Eighteenth Century England*. Saskatoon: University of Saskatchewan, 2005. PhD Thesis.

Wilkerson, H. Lloyd. *History of Military Lodges in Freemasonry*. Blackmer, NC: Blackmer Lodge No. 127, 2002.

Williams, Gwyn A. *Beginnings of Radicalism* in Herbert, Trevor and Jones, Gareth Elwyn (eds), *The Remaking of Wales in the Eighteenth Century*. Cardiff: University of Wales Press, 1988.

Wilson, Walter. *The History and Antiquities of Dissenting Churches and Meeting Houses in London*. London: Walter Wilson, 1814.

Woodward, Donald. *Wage Regulation in Mid-Tudor York*. York: The York Historian, 1980.

Men at Work: Labourers and Building Craftsmen in the Towns of Northern England, 1450–1750. Cambridge: CUP, 2002.

Wren Society. *Wren Society Papers*. Oxford: privately published by subscription, 1924–1943.

Wright, Dudley. *England's Masonic Pioneers*. Whitefish, MT: Kessinger Publishing, 2003 (reprint).

Yarker, John. *The Arcane Schools*. New York: Cosimo Inc, 2007 (reprint). Originally published 1909.

Victoria County History Publications

Crossley, Alan, et al. *A History of the County of Oxford*. Volume 12. London, 1990.

Farrer, William, and Brownbill, J. *A History of the County of Lancashire*. Volume 3. London, 1907.

Greenslade, M.W. *A History of the County of Stafford*. Volume 14. London, 1990.

Lewis, C.P., and Thacker. A.T. *A History of the County of Chester*. Volume 5, part 1. London, 2003.

Malden, H.E. *A History of the County of Surrey*. Volume 3. London, 1911.

Stephens, W.B. *A History of the County of Warwick*. Volume 8. London, 1969.

Styles, Philip. *A History of the County of Warwick*. Volume 3. London, 1945.

Thacker, A.T., and Lewis, C.P. *A History of the County of Chester*. Volume 5, part 2. London, 2005.

Tillott, P.M. *A History of the County of York: the City of York*. London, 1961.

Cited Website Sources

Note: All website sources were verified correct as of 3–8 August 2010.

http://freepages.history.rootsweb.ancestry.com/~frpayments/Der.htm.
http://freepages.history.rootsweb.ancestry.com/~frpayments/F.htm.
http://www.themasonictrowel.com/masonic_talk/stb/stbs/36-05.htm; and
http://www.prismeshebdo.com/prismeshebdo/article.php3?id_article=576.
http://www.ucl.ac.uk/~ucypanp/desaguliersletters.htm
19Hhttp://www.history.ac.uk/resources/office/fred#chap.
http://www.boughtonhouse.org.uk/htm/trust/information_pack_for_teachers_web.pdf.
http://www.thefreemason.com/cnm/templates/article.asp?articleid=105&zoneid=3.

http://www.rgle.org.uk/RGLE_1535.htm.
http://www.westlancsfreemasons.org.uk/pages/pgl/provhistory.htm

Selected Mediaeval Guild-Related Source Material

Journal Articles

Epstein, S. R., 'Craft Guilds, Apprenticeships, and Technological Change in Pre-Industrial Europe', *Journal of Economic History*, 58 (1998), 684–713.

Gustafsson, Bo, 'The Rise and Economic Behavior of Medieval Craft Guilds: An Economic-Theoretical Interpretation', *Scandinavian Journal of Economics*, 35.1 (1987), 1–40.

Richardson, Gary, 'A Tale of Two Theories: Monopolies and Craft Guilds in Medieval England and Modern Imagination', *Journal of the History of Economic Thought* (2001).

'Guilds, Laws, and Markets for Manufactured Merchandise in Late-Medieval England', *Explorations in Economic History*, 41 (2004), 1–25.

'Christianity and Craft Guilds in Late Medieval England: A Rational Choice Analysis', *Rationality and Society* 17 (2005): 139–189.

Other Secondary Sources

Basing, Patricia. *Trades and Crafts in Medieval Manuscripts*. London: British Library, 1990,

Epstein, Steven. *Wage and Labor Guilds in Medieval Europe*. Chapel Hill, NC: University of North Carolina Press, 1991.

Hatcher, John and Edward Miller. *Medieval England: Towns, Commerce and Crafts, 1086–1348*. London: Longman, 1995.

Thrupp, Sylvia. *The Merchant Class of Medieval London 1300–1500*. Chicago: University of Chicago Press, 1989.

Unwin, George. *The Guilds and Companies of London*. London: Methuen & Company, 1904.

Ward, Joseph. *Metropolitan Communities: Trade Guilds, Identity, and Change in Early Modern London*. Palo Alto: Stanford University Press, 1997.

Index

Acception, London Company of Masons
　as an inner circle, 13, 22, 23, 24, 25
　and Ashmole, 22, 23, 24
　ceases to exist, 29
　and Locke, 14
　relations with Freemasonry, 25, 28
　social dimension, 24–5
　and Wren, 28
Acheson, Sir Arthur, 159, 162
Addison, Joseph, 185
Agnew, David, 39
Aislabie, John, 35
Aislabie, Mary, 35
Aitchison, Sir Arthur, 159, 162
Alban, St., 201, 204, 208, 283n
Alberoni, Giulio, 43
Alnwick Lodge, 238n
American Philosophical Society, 186
Amherst, Jeffrey, 130
Anchor & Baptist's Head lodge, 112
Ancients Grand Lodge, 6, 66, 119, 168
Anderson, James, plate 2
　1723 Constitutions, 65–8, 145, 204–5
　1738 Constitutions, 27, 28, 37, 65, 68, 120, 133, 146, 151
　Dalkeith's installation as Grand Master, 133–4
　Gale as a Freemason, 110
　influence on English Freemasonry, 64, 65, 71
　Montagu's installation as Grand Master, 133
　Prince of Wales's initiation, 175
　prominence within Grand Lodge, 65, 67–8
　relations with Desaguliers, 65
　speculative lodges in London, 36
　Swallow Street church, 42
　Wharton's installation as Grand Master, 136, 139, 140
　Wren as a Freemason, 27, 28
Andrews, Grantham, 86, 89
Andrews, Sir Jonathan, 89
Anne, Queen of Great Britain, 35, 136
antiquarianism, 183–4
Apple Tree lodge, Charles Street, 102, 120, 154
Applebee, John, 121
Applebee's Original Weekly Journal, 122, 136

apprenticeships, 9, 10, 202, 209
AQC Transactions, 67, 71, 107
Arabin, John, 165
Arbuthnot, John, 101, 103
Argyll, Archibald Campbell, 3rd Duke of, 48, 144, 160, 161, 246n
Armytage, Harry, 185
Ashmole, Elias, 21–5
　Antiquities of Berkshire, 13–14, 33
　College of Arms, 13
　connections to Plot, 29–30
　Dugdale's son-in-law, 13
　esoteric aspects of lodge traditions, 12
　initiation in Warrington (1646), 21
　London Company of Masons, 21–3, 24, 25
　Masonic activity in Staffordshire, 16
　Memoirs, 13, 21–3, 33
　relations with Dugdale, 26
　roles and positions, 23–4
　Royal Society, 13, 24
Ashmolean Museum, 21, 24, 29
Athelstan, King, 201, 202, 204
Atholl, James Murray, 2nd Duke of, 159, 160, 177
Atterbury, Francis, 140, 141, 142
Aubigny lodge, 147, 149, 155
Aubrey, John, 13, 14, 16, 25–7, 33
Augusta of Saxe-Gotha, Princess of Wales, 57, 111, 169–70
Augustus III of Poland, 60
Aylesford, Heneage Finch, 1st Earl of, 35

Babington, Zachary, 17
Balcarres, Alexander Lindsay, 4th Earl of, 159, 160, 161
Baldwin, Richard, 32
Ball, Papillon, 71
Baltimore, Charles Calvert, 5th Lord, 61, 130, 158, 174–5, 250n
Bank of Charity see General Bank of Charity
Baptist's Head lodge, Chancery Lane, 86
Barker-Cryer, Neville, 12, 13, 36
Barlow, George, 171
Barnsby, George, 168
Barry, Robert, 88
Bateman, Sir Henry, 101
Bath, John Granville, 1st Earl of, 15
Bathurst, Charles, 35–6

Batson, Edward, 74
Batson, James, 74
Batson, Thomas, 75, 85, 97, 157, 158
Beal, Dr., 110, 121
Beale, John, 64, 67, 105, 109, 136, 250*n*
  1723 Constitutions, 67, 250*n*
  influence on English Freemasonry, 64
  prominence within Grand Lodge, 105, 250*n*
  Royal Society, 105, 109, 250*n*
  Wharton's installation as Grand Master, 136, 139
Bear and Harrow lodge, Butcher Row
  consecration of new lodge, 158
  Desaguliers' membership, 39, 58
  Hogarth's membership, 59, 249*n*
  Montagu's membership, 58, 135
  Ward's membership, 166
Bear Tavern lodge, Bath, 168, 169–70, 174, 180
Beaufort Hinkes, T.R., *plate 1*, *plate 4*
Beaurepaire, Pierre-Yves, 2
Beckett, William, 109
Bedford Coffee House lodge, 56, 102
Bedford Head lodge, Covent Garden, 4, 64
  Buttons' post box, 185
  Carpenter's membership, 84
  Cox's membership, 84
  culinary reputation, 102
  Folkes' membership, 76, 95, 99, 101, 102, 176, 193
  Manley's membership, 92
  Pellet's membership, 103, 112, 176
  Pitt's membership, 76
  and Royal Society, 99, 101, 102–3, 104
  Rutty's membership, 103, 112
  Taylor's membership, 95, 102
Beighton, Henry, 52
Belasyse, Sir Henry, 35, 242*n*
Bell and Raven lodge, Wolverhampton, 166
Bell Tavern lodge, Westminster, 94, 95, 113
Ben-Chaim, Michael, 184
Benson, Robert, 1st Baron Bingley, 35, 242*n*
Bereseiner, Yasha, 22
Berkeley, George, 213
Berkeley, James, Lord Dursley, 149
Bertie, Lord Vere, 177, 278*n*
Billers, Sir William, 90, 91
Bingley, Robert Benson, 1st Baron, 35, 242*n*
Black Death, 8, 9, 190
Black, Jeremy, 78
Blackerby, Nathaniel
  career, 81–2, 106
  General Bank of Charity, 96, 181
  Georgia Society, 83, 85
  influence on English Freemasonry, 64, 82, 192
  introduction to Freemasonry, 74
  municipal rates inquiry, 89
  prominence within Grand Lodge, 70, 82–3, 88, 157

  senior magistrate, 75, 77, 79, 81, 83, 84, 93, 101, 106, 192
  sued by Westminster turnpike collectors, 87
  Westminster Bridge project, 179
Blackerby, Samuel, 84
Blackett, Sir Walter, 173, 276*n*
Blackwell, Elizabeth, 162
Blackwell, Sir Lambert, 162
Blaney, Lord, 162
Bligh, Edward *see* Darnley, Edward Bligh, 2nd Earl of
Bligh, John, 1st Earl of Darnley, 48
Bligh, Theodosia, 10th Baroness Clifton, 48
Blount, Thomas, 17
Booth, Barton, 60
Booth, William, 86
Borthwick, Richard, 22
Botelcy (Bedford Head member), 101
Boulton, Richard, 126
Bowen, Emanuel, 171
Bowen, Thomas, 171
Boyde, George, 165
Boyle, Richard, 3rd Earl of Burlington, 152
Bradshawe, Lucretia, 98
Bramston, James, 98
Brancas de Forcalquier, Louis de, Marquis, 148, 269*n*
Brewer, Hugh, 21
Bridewell Royal Hospital, 95, 103, 258*n*, 259*n*
Briscoe, Samuel, 123
British Journal, 27, 84, 142
Brodie, Alexander, 159, 161, 272–3*n*
Brome, Alexander, 17
Broughton, Mick, 60–1
Brown, David, 168
Brown, Lancelot "Capability", 168
Browne, John, 106
Brudenel, George, 126
Brydges, Henry, Marquis of Carnarvon, 48, 54, 61, 175, 246*n*
Brydges, James, 1st Duke of Chandos, 39, 48, 51, 52, 54–7, 165, 188
bubonic plague, 8, 9, 190
Bull's Head lodge, Southwark, 136
Burdon, William, 88
Burlington, Richard Boyle, Lord, 152
Burney collection, 27, 72, 121, 138, 153, 173
Bury's Coffee House lodge, Bridges Street, 102
Bussy-Aumont lodge, 148
Buttons coffee house, Russell Street, 185

Cadogan, Lady Sarah, Duchess of Richmond, 48, 59
Calcutta lodge, 70
Calverley, Sir Walter, 173, 276*n*
Calvert, Albert, 71

326 Index

Calvert, Charles, 5th Lord Baltimore, 61, 130, 158, 174–5, 250*n*
Campbell, Archibald, 3rd Duke of Argyll, 48, 144, 160, 161, 246*n*
Campbell, Sir Duncan, 275*n*
Campbell, John, 4th Earl of Loudoun, 104, 129, 131, 134, *plate 22*
Campbell, John (Edinburgh's Provost), 52, 169
Cantillon, Richard, 101, 261*n*
Capell, William, 152
Carnarvon, Henry Brydges, Marquis of, 48, 54, 61, 175, 246*n*
Carnarvon, James Brydges, 1st Marquis of, 39, 48, 51, 52, 54–7, 165, 188
Carpenter, Audrey, 43, 62
Carpenter, George, 1st Baron Carpenter of Killaghy, 85
Carpenter, George, 2nd Baron Carpenter of Killaghy
  1st Foot Guards, 85, 95
  Georgia Society, 85
  Horn membership, 84, 104
  influence on English Freemasonry, 64
  introduction to Freemasonry, 74
  political positions, 161
  prominence within Grand Lodge, 157
  Royal Society, 105
  senior magistrate, 75, 79, 84–5
  Weymouth as Grand Master, 159
Carpenters' Company, 20, 25
Carteret, John, 2nd Earl Granville, 161, 162
Carteret, Lady Louisa, 161
Cartwright, Thomas, 37
Castle lodge, Highgate, 87
Castle Tavern, Fleet Street, 142, 143
Castle Tavern lodge, St Giles, 92
Caswell, John, 44
Caulfield, James, 182
Cavendish, James, 108
Cawthorn, James, 62
Chaloner, Thomas, 12, 13
Chamberlain, John, 72
Chambers, Ephraim, 108, 185–6, 280*n*
Chandos, Cassandra Willoughby, Duchess of, 48
Chandos, Henry Brydges, 2nd Duke of, 48, 54, 61, 175, 246*n*
Chandos, James Brydges, 1st Duke of, 39, 48, 51, 52, 54–7, 165, 188
Charges, 64, 65, 66–7, 97, 124–5, 211–17
  Concerning God and Religion, 211–12
  Desaguliers, 58, 66, 73, 135, 200, 214, 216
  Fonvive's editorials, 32
  Of Behaviour, 214–16
  Of the Civil Magistrate Supreme and subordinate, 212–13
  Of Lodges, 213
  Of the Management of the Craft, 214
  Of Masters, Wardens, Fellows and Apprentices, 213–14
  and *Old Charges*, 200
  Payne, 66, 73, 81, 200, 204, 216
  Post Man articles, 31, 32
Charitable Corporation, 83, 153, 181
Charity Committee *see* General Bank of Charity
Charles II, King of England
  beheaded, 144
  French interests at court, 149
  illegitimate children, 147, 162
  James II's succession to the throne, 15
  London Company of Masons, 29, 210
  Rye House Plot, 16
  State Papers, 14–15
  statue at Lichfield cathedral, 23
Charles VI, Holy Roman Emperor, 60
Charles VII, King of France, 147
Chaworth, William, 131
Chelsea Hospital, 23
Cheselden, William, 51
Cheshire Cheese lodge, Arundel Street, 121
Chester
  formation of new guilds, 20
  Freemasons prominent within Grand Lodge, 50
  guild civic influence, 10, 20
  Holme family, 19
  lodge numbers, 20
  non-operative masons' membership, 12–13, 20, 22, 191
  Sun Inn lodge, 50, 131
Chesterfield, Philip Dormer Stanhope *see* Stanhope, Philip Dormer, 4th Earl of Chesterfield
Chewton, James Waldegrave, Lord, 150, 151
Chocke, Alexander. *plate 15*
  career, 81, 87, 106
  godparent to Desaguliers child, 49
  Horn membership, 82, 87
  influence on English Freemasonry, 64
  introduction to Freemasonry, 74, 87
  prominence within Grand Lodge, 70, 81, 87–8
  senior magistrate, 73, 75, 77, 81, 86, 87, 106
  sued by Westminster turnpike collectors, 87
  Swan lodge membership, 82, 87
Cholmondeley, George, 49–50
Cholmondeley, Hugh, 1st Earl of Cholmondeley, 49
Churchill, George, 148, 152
Churchill, John, 1st Duke of Marlborough, 126, 127
Churchill, Mary, 127
Churchill, Sarah, 132
Churton, Tobias, 16, 22
Cibber, Colley, 60, 143
Cibber, Theobald, 76

Clare, Martin
  Discourse, 175, 176, 178, 277*n*
  King's Arms lodge membership, 93
  prominence within Grand Lodge, 93, 277*n*
  Royal Society, 105, 176
  scientific Enlightenment, 34, 165, 175, 176, 177, 178, 189
  senior magistrate, 93
  Soho Academy, 93, 177
Clarendon , Edward Hyde, 3rd Earl of, 48
Clark, Peter, 2, 107, 111, 128, 193
Clarke, J.R., 107
Clayton, Sir Robert, 37
Clement XII, Pope, 60, 148, 211
Clifton, Theodosia Bligh, 10th Baroness, 48
Cobham, Richard Temple, 1st Viscount, 130
coffee houses, 47, 102, 185
Coke, Thomas, Lord Lovel, 54, 104, 158–9, 177
Cole, Alfred Benjamin, *plate 8*
Cole, Christian, 86, 89
Cole, W.A., 41
Coleraine, Henry Hare, 3rd Baron, 88, 104, 113, 115, *plate 20*
Colles, John, 24
Collier, James, 21
Collins, John, 86
Columbine, Francis, 50, 88, 131
Colville, John, 6th Lord Colville and Culross, 159, 161
Colyear, Charles, 2nd Earl of Portmore, 158
Comberbach, Roger, 50
Compton, George, 6th Earl of Northampton, 73
Compton, Henry, 39, 42, 45
Conduitt, Catherine, 59
Conduitt, John, 59
Constitutions (1723), 64, 120, 123, 125, *plate 7*
  advertisements for, 28
  Anderson, 65–8, 145, 204–5
  Beale, 67, 250*n*
  Dalkeith as Master of the Rummer, 145
  democratic accountability, 216
  Desaguliers, 66–7, 73
  Dutch translator and publisher, 152
  gentlemen Freemasons, 27
  Grand Lodge formal acceptance, 141
  lodge definition, 129
  London Company of Masons, 29
  Montagu, 66–7
  and *Old Charges*, 65, 66, 200
  Payne, 70, 73
  Wharton's installation as Grand Master, 136
  see also Charges ; *Regulations*
Constitutions (1738)
  Anderson, 27, 28, 37, 65, 68, 120, 133, 146, 151
  Charges and *Regulations*, 66
  dedicated to Prince of Wales, 174
  Lorraine's initiation, 151
  Montagu's installation as Grand Master, 133
  Richmond's installation as Grand Master, 146
  Wren as a Freemason, 27, 28
Constitutions (1754), 70
Cook, Sir George, 90, 91
Cook, James, 90
Cook, Thomas, 86
Cooke manuscript, 201, 204–5, 206
Copley bequest, 52, 56, 248–9*n*
Copley Medal, 57, 106, 155, 184
Coram, Thomas, 88, 158
Corneille, John, 165
Corner, Andrew, 131
Cornwall, Robert, 131
Cornwallis, Charles, 5th Baron, 101
Cornwallis, Thomas, 261*n*
Cotton, Charles, 71
Country Journal or Craftsman, 143
Courteville, Raphael, 76
Coustos, John, 182, 279*n*
Coustos-Villeroy lodge, 148
Cowper, Ashley, 80
Cowper, John, 77
Cowper, Spencer, 79, 81
Cowper, William, 1st Earl Cowper, 49, 77, 80, 81
Cowper, William
  Blackerby's appointment, 82
  career, 79–80
  Charges, 80–1, 84
  chimney work at Houses of Parliament, 51
  Dalkeith's installation as Grand Master, 140
  General Bank of Charity, 94, 95, 96
  godparent to Desaguliers child, 49
  Horn membership, 51, 74, 77, 81, 82, 95
  influence on English Freemasonry, 64, 81, 192
  municipal rates inquiry, 89
  networks and relationships, 74
  prominence within Grand Lodge, 34, 50, 68, 70, 74, 76, 77, 81, 88, 141
  relations with Payne, 74
  Richmond's installation as Grand Master, 146
  scientific Enlightenment, 141
  senior magistrate, 73, 75, 77, 79–81, 83, 93, 95, 101, 192
  Society of Antiquaries, 113
Cox, Sir Charles, 83–4, 101–2, 261*n*
Cox, Gratiana, 83, 261*n*
Craftsman journal, 92
Crawford, 20th Earl of *see* Lindsay, John, 20th Earl of Crawford
Cress, John, 90
Crosby, Charles, 131
Cross Keys lodge, Henrietta Street, 102, 162, 168, 177, 277*n*

328 Index

Crown & Anchor lodge, St. Clement's Church, 67
Crown lodge, Parker's Lane, 120, 154
Crown lodge, Royal Exchange, 112, 113, 187
Cumberland, Prince Henry, Duke of, 162
Cumberland, Prince William, Duke of, 59
Curll, Edmund, 14, 33

Daily Advertiser, 134
Daily Courant, 32, 76
Daily Gazetteer, 76, 87
Daily Journal, 84, 124, 143, 170, 181
Daily Post, 46, 142
Dalkeith, Earl of *see* Scott, Francis, 5th Earl of Dalkeith
Dalkeith, Francis Scott, Earl of, 145
Dalkeith, James Scott, Earl of, 144
Danby, Earl of, 24
Daniels, Stephen, 183, 184
Darnley, Edward Bligh, 2nd Earl of
 installation as Grand Master, 134–5
 Prince of Wales's initiation, 175
 Prince of Wales's visit to Bath, 169–70, 174
 prominence within Grand Lodge, 61, 132
 Royal Society, 104
Darnley, John Bligh, 1st Earl of, 48
Darnley, Sir John Stewart, 147
Dartmouth, William Legge, 1st Earl of, 77
Davis, David, 171
de Beer, Esmond Samuel, 14
de Massue, Henri, 132
de Massue, Rachel, 125–6, 133
de Ruvigny, 1st Earl of Galway, 42, 43, 132–3
de Veil, Thomas, 7, 16, 75, 92–3, 192
Deane, Phyllis, 41
Defoe, Daniel, 78
Delafaye, Charles
 career, 77–9, 142
 Horn membership, 73, 77, 82, 104, 142, 148
 influence on English Freemasonry, 64, 79, 82, 142, 192
 introduction to Freemasonry, 74
 municipal rates inquiry, 89
 Payne's appointment to the magistracy, 73
 relations with Richmond, 18
 Royal Society, 79
 scientific Enlightenment, 141
 senior magistrate, 75, 76, 78, 93, 192
Delorraine, Henry Scott, 1st Earl of, 59, 88, 128, 154, 160, 162
Delorraine, Mary, Duchess of, 59
Demainbray, Stephen, 187
Dennis, John, 143
Denslow, William, 182
Des Grecs church, Hog Lane, 41
Desaguliers, Jean, 39–41, 42, 43, 244*n*
Desaguliers, Joanna, 45, 62

Desaguliers, John, 62
Desaguliers, John Theophilus, *plate 1*
 1723 Constitutions, 66–7, 73
 academic qualifications, 45
 attraction to Freemasonry, 66
 Bedford Coffee House, 56, 102
 Berkeley's *Passive Obedience*, 213
 birth, 39
 Charges and *Regulations*, 58, 66, 73, 135, 200, 214, 216
 childhood, 40, 41
 children, 48–9, 161
 chimney work at Houses of Parliament, 50–1, 188
 Chocke's support, 88
 church duties, 55
 collaboration with Payne, 70, 71, 73–4
 connections to Fonvive, 32
 Copley Medal awards, 57
 Dalkeith's installation as Grand Master, 140, 141, 144, 145
 death of, 62, 168
 Duke of Chandos' patronage, 39, 48, 51, 52, 54–7, 165, 188
 Duke of Lorraine's initiation, 151
 Edinburgh visit (1721), 52, 169
 education, 43–4, 244*n*
 Experimental Philosophy, 44, 180, *plate 18*, *plate 19*
 financial insecurity, 56
 as a firework impresario, 57
 Folkes' support, 101
 French Academy of Science, 154
 French Freemasonry, 149–50
 friendship with Folkes, 132
 friendship with Newton, 132
 General Bank of Charity, 94, 96, 156
 Gregorian calendar, 105–6
 Hogarth's *Indian Emperor*, 59
 Horn membership, 39, 65, 82, 95, 104, 154, 176
 Huguenot community, 32, 39, 41, 58, 62
 hydraulic projects, 53, 54, 168, 181, 188
 influence on English Freemasonry, 4, 12, 25, 38–9, 58, 60, 61–2, 63, 64, 71, 119, 120, 175, 191–2, 217
 introduction to Freemasonry, 57–8, 73
 introduction to Payne, 73
 lecturer at Hart Hall, 44
 lectures and displays, 39, 45–7, 52, 53, 54, 57, 102, 120, 165–6, 169, 173–4, 179, 181, 182, 183
 lodge meetings format, 66
 lodge memberships, 39
 Montagu as Grand Master, 120, 125, 126, 132, 133
 networks and relationships, 74
 'The Newtonian System of the World', 63, 141
 Newtonianism, 39, 44, 46–7, 48, 51, 52, 53, 62–3, 179, 184, 186, 187, 189, 191

Index 329

perception of, 58–9
Prince of Wales's initiation, 174
Prince of Wales's visit to Bath, 168, 169–70, 174
project commissions, 50–1, 52–3
prominence within Grand Lodge, 4, 34, 38, 58, 61–2, 70, 190, 191
publications, 49–52
relations with Anderson, 65
relations with Dalkeith, 95, 145, 146
relations with Labelye, 83, 143, 165, 179–80, 186–7
relations with Montesquieu, 150–1
relations with Richmond, 119, 147, 155–6, 269n
relationship with s'Gravesande, 186
religious tolerance, 211, 212
return to London (1713), 45–9
Rily's initiation, 153
Royal Society, 95, 98, 102, 105, 107, 119, 132, 156, 176, 191
Royal Society Curator and Operator, 39, 51–2, 191
Royal Society experiments and demonstrations, 45, 46, 47, 49, 52, 57, 186
Royal Society FRS, 39, 48, 51–2, 104
Rummer & Grapes membership, 58, 72
scientific Enlightenment, 34, 141, 165, 169, 186–8, 191
scientific expertise, 52–3, 54, 167–8, 188–9, 191
Solomon's Temple lodge, 39, 65, 180
Spalding Society, 95, 115
The Hague lodge, 151, 152, 165
Westminster Bridge project, 83, 188
Wharton's departure from Grand Lodge, 140, 141
as Wharton's Deputy, 135
Wharton's installation as Grand Master, 136, 139
Wren as a Freemason, 27, 28
Desaguliers, Thomas, 48–9, 57, 62, 127
Desaiguillers, Sara, 41
Desaiguillers, Marguerite, 41
Desbrostes (Bedford Head member), 101
Devlin, Lord, 157
Dickens, Ambrose, 90
Dieskau, Jean Erdman, Baron, 104, 261n
Dobb, Maurice, 10–11
Dolphin lodge, Tower Street, 58, 95, 106, 113
Dorchester, Viscount, 24
Douglas, Archibald, 1st Duke of Douglas, 144
Douglas, Charles, 3rd Duke of Queensberry, 104, 154, 261–2n
Douglas, Dr. George, 105
Douglas, James, 106, 176
Douglas, James, 2nd Duke of Queensberry, 144

Douglas, James, 14th Earl of Morton, 61, 99, 160, 265n
Douglas, Lady Jane, 144
Douglas, Lady Jane, Duchess of Dalkeith, 144
Douglas, Sholto, 15th Earl of Morton, 104
Dowland manuscript, 208
Downie, James, 78
Dragonnades, 40
Drake, Francis, 210, 284n
Drummond, George, 275n
Dryden, John, 59
Du Bois, Charles, 104
Du Fay, Charles, 104
Dubois, Raphael, 86
Dugdale, Elizabeth, 26
Dugdale, Sir William, 13, 26, 29–30, 33, 238n
Dundee, non-operative masons' membership, 236n
Dunning, Thomas, 131
Dunton, John, 32
Dursley, James Berkeley, Lord, 149
Duvernett, John, 131

ECCO (Eighteenth Century Collections Online), 27
Edgeley, Hewer, 103
Edict of Nantes, Revocation of, 40
Edinburgh council, 52, 169
Edward III, King of England, 8, 205
Edwards, Samuel, 86, 89
Edwards, Thomas, 94, 95, 259n
EEBO (Early English Books On-line), 27
Egerton Manuscript, 15
Egyptian Society, 112
Ellam, John, 21
Ellam, Richard, 21
Elliott, Paul, 183, 184
English Freemasonry
  constitution, 119–20
  environmental influences, 1–2, 38
  gradualist theory, 1, 13, 29
  lack of contemporary records, 4
  meetings, 24, 58, 66, 120
  military lodges, 222–6
  military membership, 127–31
  non-operative (speculative) membership, 11–18, 20, 21–5, 36–7, 191
  press comments, 31–2, 88, 118, 121–4
Enlightenment *see* scientific Enlightenment
Entick, John, 71, 251n
Entwistle, Edward, 97
Erdman, Jean, Baron Dieskau, 104, 261n
Erskine, John, Duke of Mar, 136
Euclid, 136, 201, 282n
Eugene of Savoy, Prince, 160
Evening Journal, 84
Evening Post, 53
Excise Bill, 127, 259n, 265n
Exclusion Bill crisis (1679-81), 16

Faber Jr., John, *plate 11*, *plate 15*
Fairfax, Charles, 35
Faÿ, Bernard, 185, 186
Fermor, Thomas, Earl of Pomfret, 59
Ferrers, Washington Shirley, 5th Earl of, 104
Ferrier, Henry, 41
Ferrier, Marguerite, 41
Fielding, Henry, 152
Finch, Daniel, 2nd Earl of Nottingham, 273*n*
Finch, Daniel, 8th Earl of Winchelsea, 159, 161–2
Finch, Heneage, 1st Earl of Aylesford, 35
The Flying Post, 123–4
Fog's Weekly Journal, 88
Folkes, Martin
  antiquarianism, 183
  Bedford Head lodge, 76, 95, 99, 101, 102, 176, 193
  Berkeley's *Passive Obedience*, 213
  Buttons' post box, 185
  Desaguliers' book purchase request, 56
  education, 98
  Egyptian Society membership, 112
  failing heath, 168
  Freemasonry dissension and division, 168
  friendship with Desaguliers, 132
  friendship with Montagu, 132, 193
  friendship with Richmond, 99, 100–1, 119, 132, 146, 155, 193
  General Bank of Charity, 94, 96, 99
  Hewer as FRS, 103
  Hogarth's portrait, 102, *plate 5*
  Hogarth's patron, 59
  Horn membership, 95
  Infidel Club, 109, 132
  influence on English Freemasonry, 64, 99–101, 119, 192, 193
  marriage, 98
  Montagu as Grand Master, 120, 126, 132
  Morgan's investiture, 88
  networks and relationships, 74, 104
  Newtonianism, 186
  Newton's *Chronology of Ancient Kingdoms*, 103
  Philo-Musicae, 71
  prominence within Grand Lodge, 34, 70, 99, 193
  relations with Montesquieu, 150
  relations with Stukeley, 111, 132, 266*n*
  relationship with Newton, 99
  religious tolerance, 211, 212
  Richmond's installation as Grand Master, 146
  Royal Society, 95, 99, 101, 105, 106, 107, 119, 156, 176, 182, 193
  scientific Enlightenment, 34, 141
  Society of Antiquaries, 99, 155
  Spalding Society, 99, 111, 115
  Wren as a Freemason, 27
Folkes, Snr., Martin, 98

Fonvive, Jean Lespinasse de, 32
Force, James, 109
Forrester, George, 6th Lord Forrester, 181, 279*n*
Foundling Hospital, 88, 158
Fountain lodge, Strand, 110, 112, 145
Fox, Henry, 161
Foxe, John, 17
Foy, Thomas, 171
France
  Aubigny lodge, 147, 149, 155
  Freemasonry, 2, 147–51, 165, 187
  see also French Academy of Science
Francklin, Richard, 92
Franco, Francisco, 143
Franklin, Benjamin, 186, 187, 280*n*
Frazier, Robert, 131
Frederick the Great, 61
Frederick I, King of Sweden, 60
Frederick, Prince of Wales, 89, 104, 135, 160, *plate 17*
  Desaguliers as chaplain, 53
  initiation as Freemason, 125, 127, 130, 174–5
  patriotic opposition, 53, 61, 170, 174
  Royal Society, 184
  visit to Bath (1738), 168, 169–70, 174
  visit to Bristol (1738), 57
freemason
  early uses of the term, 16–18
  origin of term, 10
freemasons guilds *see* guilds
French Academy of Science, 99, 104, 150, 154
Fritz, Paul, 78
Furbank, P.N., 78

Gale, Elizabeth, 111
Gale, Roger, 110–11
Gale, Samuel, 110, 111
Galway, Lord, Marquis de Ruvigny, 42, 43, 132–3
Garraway's Coffee House, Change Alley, 185
Garrick, David, 59
Gascoigne, Joseph, 89
Gascoyne, Crisp, 55
Gascoyne, John, 55
Gascoyne, Susannah, 55
Gauger, Nicolas, 49
Gay, John, 63
General Bank of Charity, 70, 87, 94–7, 135, 146, 156, 157, 158, 181, *plate 10*
General Evening Post, 71
Gentleman's Magazine, 14, 62
George I, King of Great Britain, 48, 50, 104, 147
  coronation (1714), 126
  Desaguliers' experiments and demonstrations, 53
  Jacobite threat, 42

Jones' loyal address, 101
Montagu's loyal address, 126
George II, King of Great Britain, 48, 92, 127, 147
  coronation (1727), 126
  Cowper's address, 80
  Desaguliers' experiments and demonstrations, 53
  Prince's annual allowance petition, 161
  proclamation as King, 57
George lodge, Charing Cross, 76
George, Prince of Wales, 162
Georges, John, 103
Georgia Society, 83, 85–6, 164–5
Germany, Freemasonry, 2
Gifford, Richard, 86, 92, 258n
Gin Act (1736), 84, 93
Globe lodge, Moorgate, 90, 112
Gloucester, Duke of, 162
Godolphin, William, 131
Goldsmiths Company, 24
Goodricke, Sir Henry, 27, 28, 240n
Goose & Gridiron lodge, St. Paul's, 120, 124, 136, 154
Gordon, Charles, 131
Gordon, George, 165, 181–2, 185, 187, 189
Gordon-Lennox, Charles Henry, Earl of March, 155
Gormogons, 88, 142–3
Goston, William, 167
Gould, Robert Freke
  Bell and Raven lodge, Wolverhampton, 166
  Freemasonry in Lancashire, 21
  Grand Lodge authority, 168
  initiation of Wren into Freemasonry, 27
  Military Lodges, 128
  Plot's comments, 30
  The Hague lodge, 152
Gower, Sir Thomas, 15
Graeme, William, 105, 176, 277n
Graham, Lord George, 181, 279n
Graham, Maxtone, 160
Grand Charity *see* General Bank of Charity
Grand Feasts, 96, 110, 124, 159–62
Grand Lodge of England
  1738 Constitutions, 65, 68
  Anderson's membership, 65, 67–8
  Beale's membership, 105, 250n
  Blackerby's membership, 70, 82–3, 88, 157
  categorisation as 'Moderns', 66
  Chocke's membership, 70, 81, 87–8
  Clare's membership, 93, 277n
  Constitutions (1723) formal acceptance, 141
  Cowper's membership, 34, 50, 68, 70, 74, 76, 77, 81, 88, 141
  Dalkeith's membership, 87–8, 104, 118, 123, 132, 133–4, 135, 140–1, 144–6, 162

  Darnley's membership, 61, 132
  Desaguliers' membership, 4, 34, 38, 58, 61–2, 70, 190, 191
  Folkes' membership, 34, 70, 99, 193
  founding of (1717), 2, 31, 68–9, 120
  Grand Officers, 197–9
  granting of warrants, 129
  Inchiquin's membership, 88, 156, 159
  Lindsay's membership, 129, 159, 160, 177, 265–6n
  lodge meetings format, 66
  military membership, 130
  Montagu's membership, 49, 74, 88, 104, 110, 118, 120, 121–2, 125–6, 132–3, 135, 193
  Noble Grand Masters, 34, 36, *105*, 118–63, 193–4
  Officers (1720-30), *69*
  Old Charges, 65
  Paisley's membership, 104, 119, 156–7
  Payne's membership, 34, 50, 70, 74
  philanthropy, 94, 97, 120, 164–5
  Philo-Musicae, 71
  presence in Whig camps, 36, 38, 53–4, 64, 118
  press comments, 118, 120, 134–5
  pro-Hanoverian stance, 36, 64, 76–7, 93–4, 118, 120, 132, 190
  regulation and control role, 64
  Richmond's membership, 99, 104, 118–19, 129, 132, 135, 144, 146, 153–4, 155–6, 162, 193, 194
  Westminster and Middlesex magistrates' benches, 75–7
  Weymouth's membership, 70, 159, 161, 168, 177, 274n
  Wharton's membership, 118, 119, 132, 135, 136, 138–40, 193–4, 214
  see also General Bank of Charity
Grand Lodge of Ireland, 129, 130, 131, 165
Grand Lodge Minutes
  absence of (pre-1723), 68
  Anderson's role as a Grand Warden, 65
  Blackerby's resignation, 83
  Clare's influence, 93
  control of Grand Lodge, 97
  Cowper's visit to London, 50
  Desaguliers' authority, 145–6
  Desaguliers and Dalkeith relationship, 95
  Desaguliers' death, 62
  Freemasonry dissension and division, 168
  General Bank of Charity, 95–6, 156
  military in Grand Lodge, 130
  Payne's commitment to Freemasonry, 70
  Sorrel's attendance at Grand Charity meetings, 87
'Grand Master', origin of term, 242n
Grand Orient of Spain, 143
Granville, Lady Jane, 15
Granville, John, 1st Earl of Bath, 15
Granville, John Carteret, 2nd Earl, 161, 162

Gray, Robert, 103, 108
Gray, Stephen, 183, 184–5, 187
Grecian Coffee House, Devereux Court, 185
Green, John, 167
Greenwood, Isaac, 187
Gregory, David, 43–4
Grey, William, 22, 23
Griffin lodge, Newgate Street, 112, 113
Griffiths, William, 171
Grub Street Journal, 142–3
Guardian, 185
guilds
  apprenticeships, 9, 10, 202, 209
  charters, 209
  English Freemasonry, 200
  Holme's definition, 19–20
  members' progression, 9–10
  municipal authorities' ties, 10–11, 209–10
  principal functions, 9, 201
  threats to the system, 209–10
  traditional ritual, 10, 11
  transformation of, 8, 9, 190–1
  wage rates, 8, 9, 205, 206, 207–8
  see also London Company of Masons; Old Charges
Gun Tavern lodge, Jermyn Street, 170
Gustavus Adolphus, King of Sweden, 158
Gwynn, Robin, 43
Gwynne, Richard, 171

Haffenden, Philip, 78
Halifax, George Montagu, 1st Earl of, 87, 88
Hall, Edward, 153
Hall, Stephen, 90, 112
Halley, Edmund, 53, 108, 109, 185, 250n
Halliwell manuscript *see Regius* manuscript
Hamill, John, 1
Hamilton, James *see* Paisley, James Hamilton, Lord
Hamon, William, 23
Hand and Apple Tree lodge, Holborn, 59, 249n
Handel, George Frideric, 57, 269n
Hans, Nicholas, 165
Harding, Alexander, 94, 95, 259n
Hardwick, Richard, 27
Hardwicke, Philip Yorke, 1st Earl of, 108
Hare, Henry, 3rd Baron Coleraine, 88, 104, 113, 115, *plate 20*
Harland-Jacobs, Jessica, 2, 3, 128, 129, 130–1, 170
Harley, Robert, 1st Earl of Oxford, 35, 44, 78
Harrington, William Stanhope, 1st Earl of, 182
Harris, John, 46, 101, 108, 179, 185
Harrison, David, 66, 200
Harrison, Edward, 90
Hathorn, Hugh, 275n
Hatton, Sir Christopher, 24

Hauksbee, Francis, 46, 47, 48, 102, 179, 183
Hauksbee, Mary, 48
Hawkins, William, 65, 136
Hawksmoor, Elizabeth, 82
Hawksmoor, Nicholas, 82, 255n
Hawksworth, Sir Walter, 35
Hawley, William, 175
Hayes, Charles, 90, 91
Haynes, Joseph, 89
Hayton, David, 78
Hedges, John, 86, 89
Heidegger, John, 60
Hell Fire Club, 138
Hellot, Jean (John), 176, 277n
Henry III, King of England, 33
Henry of Navarre, 150
Henry, Prince, Duke of Cumberland, 162
Henry VI, King of England, 207
Henry VIII, King of England, 17
Hérault, Rene, 148
Herbert, Henry, 9th Earl of Pembroke, 83, 103, 125, 135, 179, 267n
Herbert, Thomas, 8th Earl of Pembroke, 14
Hervey, John, Lord, 76, 152, 169
Hewer, Hewer E., 103
Hewer, William, 103
Hewet, Lady, 48
Hewet, Sir Thomas, 48
Hickman, Nathan, 104
Hicks, John, 90
Hicks, Jonathan, 266n
Highmore, Joseph, 87, 88, *plate 4*, *plate 15*
Highmore, Thomas, 88
Hilder, Valentine, 92, 258n
Hill, Thomas, 59, 88, 149, 269n
Hillsborough, Trevor Hill, 1st Viscount, 143
Hinchingbrook, Edward Montagu, Lord, 135
Hodgson, James, 53
Hodgson, Thomas, 112
Hody, Edward, 176, 277n
Hogarth, William
  Bear and Harrow lodge, 59, 249n
  Cunicularii, 111
  engravings featuring Freemasonry, 164
  Folkes' patronage, 59
  Freemasonry, 59, 164, 249n
  The Indian Emperor, 59
  mezzotint of John Pine, *plate 16*
  The Mystery of Masonry Brought to Light by the Gormogons, 59, 60, 142, *plate 2*
  Night, 16, 60, 92–3
  portrait of Folkes, 102, *plate 5*
  Rake's Progress, 59
  St. Martin's Lane Art Academy, 88, 176
  Sleeping Congregation, 58–9
Holland *see* Netherlands
Hollinshead, Raphael, 17
Hollis, Thomas, 187
Holloway, Benjamin, 103

Holme I, Randle, 12, 13, 19
Holme II, Randle, 12, 13, 19
Holme III, Randle, 12, 13, 18–20, 21, 238*n*
Holmes, Geoffrey, 78
Holtzendorf, John, 151
Hooke, John, *plate 7*
Hooke, Robert, 67, 185
Hopetoun, John Hope, 2nd Earl of, 108
Hopkins, Sheila, 9
Horace, 102
Horn Tavern lodge, Westminster
 Anderson's membership, 65
 Batson's membership, 75
 Blackerby's membership, 82
 Carpenter's membership, 84, 104
 Chocke's membership, 82, 87
 Count La Lippe's membership, 48
 Cowper's membership, 51, 74, 77, 81, 82, 95
 Dalkeith's membership, 95
 Delafaye's membership, 73, 77, 82, 104, 142, 148
 Desaguliers's membership, 39, 65, 82, 95, 104, 154, 176
 Folkes' membership, 95
 Justices of the Peace, 73
 Manningham's membership, 104, 111, 112, 176
 Montagu's membership, 95, 104
 Montesquieu's membership, 150
 non-operative masons' membership, 31
 Norfolk's membership, 157
 Paisley's membership, 95, 104, 154, 156
 Payne's membership, 73, 82, 154
 political and government connections, 34
 prominence of, 4, 64, 154
 reinstatement, 71
 Richmond's membership, 54, 104, 153, 155
 and Royal Society, 104, 107
 Rummer & Grapes transfer, 45, 58
 Streate's membership, 74, 261*n*
 temporary erasure of, 71
 Waldegrave's membership, 150
 Woodman's membership, 25, 31
Horsey, Samuel, 86, 89
Hotham, Sir Charles, 95
Houghton, Daniel, 88, 89, 94, 95
Houghton Hall, 76, 151, 152, 260*n*
Howard, Thomas, 8th Duke of Norfolk, 119, 129, 134, 156, 157–8
Howell, James, 17
Howell, Joshua, 53
Hudibrastick Poem, 122–3
Huguenot community
 attempts to ease religious persecution, 120
 Channel Islands presence, 40
 conformist and non-conformist communities, 42
 Desaguliers, 32, 39, 41, 58, 62
 Dragonnades period, 40
 financial support, 41
 Fonvive's editorials, 32
 Grand Lodge of Ireland, 165
 Jacobite threat, 42–3
 London refugees, 32, 39, 41–3, 120, 165
 Montagu's connections with, 132–3
 poverty, 41
 Prince Eugene's Head Coffee House, 152, 182
 role in Freemasonry, 165, 213
Hume, Alexander, 2nd Earl of Hume, 160
Hungerford Market French Anglican church, 40
Huntbach, Margery, 26
Hutton, Richard, 157
Hyde, Edward, 3rd Earl of Clarendon, 48
Hyde, Theodosia Bligh, 10th Baroness, 48
Hysing, Hans, *plate 1*

Inchiquin, 4th Earl of *see* O'Brien, William, 4th Earl of Inchiquin
'Infidel Club', 109, 132
inflation, 9, 206, 207
Ingham, Alfred, 20
Ireland
 Freemasonry, 2
 military lodges, 218–23
 see also Grand Lodge of Ireland
Islay, Archibald Campbell, Earl of, 48, 144, 160, 161, 246*n*

Jackson, Robert, 89
Jackson, Thomas, 90
Jacob, Margaret, 2, 3, 248*n*
 Chambers' *Cyclopaedia*, 185
 'mentality of official masonry', 63
 scientific Enlightenment, 179, 186
 speculative London lodges, 37
 The Hague lodge, 152
Jacobite Rising (1715), 42–3
Jacobite Rising (1745), 43
Jacobites, 35, 141–2
James II, King of England
 assassination attempts, 16
 beheading of Charles, II 144
 City livery companies' restrictions, 29
 Glorious Revolution (1688), 213
 Knights of the Thistle, 160
 opposition of Thomas Wharton, 136
 support for succession, 15
James, John, 82, 88
Jenkins, Leoline, 14–15, 16
Jenkins, Philip, 170, 171, 172, 173
Jewin Street French Anglican church, 40
Joe's Coffee House, Mitre Court, 185
Johnson, Charles, 272*n*
Johnson, Maurice, 111, 115
Johnson, Samuel, 43
Jones, Francis, 171
Jones, G.P.
 assemblies of Masons, 205

Early Masonic Pamphlets, 17
economic aspects of Freemasonry, 2
The Mediaeval Mason, 9
Old Charges, 203–4
origin of the term 'freemason', 10
social dimension to the Acception, 24–5
Jones, Inigo, 28
Jones, Noble, 86
Jones, Sir Thomas, 101
Jones, William
   Infidel Club, 109, 132
   Philo-Musicae, 71
   Queen's Head lodge, Hollis Street, 33, 77
   Royal Society, 103, 105, 106, 107–9
   senior magistrate, 90
   Society of Antiquaries, 33
Journal Littéraire, 186
Joy, William, 53
Judt, Tony, 185
Jurin, James, 99, 106, 182, 183, 260*n*
Justel, Henri, 133
Justices of the Peace, 8, 75
   see also Westminster and Middlesex magistrates' benches

Kaemper, Engelbert, 133
Kebbell, Peter, 12, 22, 98, 241*n*
Keill, John
   correspondence with s'Gravesande, 186
   Desaguliers' mentor, 43–4, 48, 95, 191
   roles and positions, 43–4, 244–5*n*
   Royal Society, 44, 102
Keith, John, 3rd Earl of Kintore, 99
Kendrick, Frances, 71
Kéroualle, Louise de, 148–9
Kerr, Lady Mary, 144
Kerr, William, 3rd Marquess of Lothian, 159, 160–1
King, James, 4th Baron Kingston, 129, 134, 156, 157, 159, 265*n*
King, John, 2nd Baron of Ockham, 77
King, Peter, 1st Baron King of Ockham, 77
King's Arms lodge, New Bond Street, 25
King's Arms lodge, St. Paul's
   Georges' membership, 103
   Mackworth's membership, 153
   Montagu's installation as Grand Master, 133
   prominence of, 113
   Wharton's initiation, 122, 136
   Wharton's installation as Grand Master, 139
King's Arms lodge, Strand
   Clare's membership, 93, 176
   Payne's membership, 70, 71
   prominence of, 64
   scientific Enlightenment, 176, 177–8
   Wray's membership, 85, 162, 176
King's Head lodge, Ivy lane, 113, 145
King's Head lodge, Seven Dials, 86

Kingston, Evelyn Pierrepont, 2nd Duke of, 150, 151, 270*n*
Kingston, James King, 4th Baron, 129, 134, 156, 157, 159, 265*n*
Kinsale, Lord, 157
Kinsman, Edmund, 24
Kintore, John Keith, 3rd Earl of, 99
Kirby, John, 90
Kneller, Sir Godfrey, *plate 6*, *plate 11*
Knight, John, 131
Knoop, Douglas
   assemblies of Masons, 205
   Early Masonic Pamphlets, 17
   economic aspects of Freemasonry, 2
   Old Charges, 203–4
   origin of the term 'freemason', 10
   social dimension to the Acception, 24–5
   The Mediaeval Mason, 9
Kuenen, Jean, 152
Kwaadgras, Evert, 151

la Chapelle, Marguerite Thomas, 40
La Chapelle, Vincent, 151–2
La Patente church, Soho, 40
Labelye, Charles
   Desaguliers' protégé, 83, 143, 165, 179–80, 186–7
   hydraulic projects, 181
   Madrid lodge, 143, 180
   Newtonianism, 189
   Westminster Bridge project, 179
labour guilds *see* guilds
labour wages, 8, 9, 205, 206, 207–8
Lalande, Jérôme, 148
Lambert, Samuel, 90
Landau, Norma, 76–7, 192
Lansdell, John, 86
Lansdowne manuscript, 208
Laurence, Herbert, 131
Lawley, Sir Robert, 159, 162, 168, 175, 178
Lawley, Robert, 168
Lawley, Sir Thomas, 168
Le Carré church, Berwick Street, 40
Le Vassor, Michael, 133
Leapman, Michael, 28
Lebeck's Head lodge, Maiden Lane, 102
Lee, John, 131
Lee, William, 78
Leeds Mercury, 36
Legge, William, 1st Earl of Dartmouth, 77
Leibnitz, Gottfried, 95, 102, 103
Lennox, Charles, 1st Duke of Richmond, 153
Lennox, Charles, 2nd Duke of Richmond & Lennox, *plate 14*
   connections to Walpole, 118, 147
   contemporaries' views on, 152
   Egyptian Society membership, 112
   family background, 147
   French Freemasonry, 147–51
   friendship with Dalkeith, 145

friendship with Folkes, 99, 100–1, 119, 132, 146, 155, 193
friendship with Montagu, 125
General Bank of Charity, 94, 156
Hogarth's *Indian Emperor*, 59
Horn membership, 54, 104, 153, 155
influence on English Freemasonry, vii–viii, 4
installation as Grand Master, 146
marriage, 147
military career, 147
Morgan's investiture, 88
Norfolk's initiation, 157
Parker's initiation, 106
patronage of Payne, 146
patronage of Prendergast, 95
Philo-Musicae, 71
Prendergast's appointment, 70
press comments, 153
prominence within Grand Lodge, 99, 104, 118–19, 129, 132, 135, 144, 146, 153–4, 155–6, 162, 193, 194
relations with Coke, 158
relations with Desaguliers, 119, 147, 155–6, 269n
relations with Montesquieu, 150
relations with Newcastle, 118, 145, 146, 147, 148, 155
Richmond House rebuilding, 103
roles and positions, 147
Royal College of Physicians, 112, 155
Royal Society, 101, 104, 118–19, 154, 176
scientific and antiquarian interests, 154–5
senior magistrate, 90
Society of Antiquaries, 113, 155
The Hague lodge, 152
Webber's initiation, 60–1
Weymouth as Grand Master, 159
Lennox, Charles Gordon, 8th Duke of Richmond, 100
Leveson, Frances, 15
Leveson, Sir Richard, 15
Leveson-Gower, Baptist, 167
Leveson-Gower family, 15, 26
Leveson-Gower, Frances, 15
Leveson-Gower, George Granville, 2nd Duke of Sutherland, 15
Leveson-Gower, William, 4th Baronet, 14–15, 16
Lewis, C.P., 12–13, 20
Lewis, John, 171
Lichfield cathedral, 23
Lichfield, Earl of, 162
Ligonier, Sir John, 130
Ligou, Daniel, 148
Lily, Mr. (Rainbow Coffee House), 157
Lindsay, Alexander, 4th Earl of Balcarres, 159, 160, 161
Lindsay, John, 20th Earl of Crawford, *plate 21*
    installation as Grand Master, 134
    military lodges, 131
    prominence within Grand Lodge, 129, 159, 160, 177, 265–6n
    roles and positions, 160
    Royal Society, 104
Lindsay, Patrick, 275n
Lippe, Count and Countess de la, 48
Lisbon lodge, 181–2
Littler, Henry, 21
Livingston, William, 275n
Lloyd, William, 86
Lock, William, 90
Locke, John, 14, 192
lodge, origin of term, 10
Lodge of Felicity, No. 58., 170
Lodge of Lights, Warrington, 178
Loge des Neuf Soeurs, 187
Lomaria, Marquis de, 149
London
    Freemasonry membership, 146, 164
    Great Fire, 210, 284n
    guild civic influence, 10
    Huguenot community, 32, 39, 41–3, 120, 165
London Company of Masons
    1723 Constitutions, 29
    Ashmole's attendance, 21–3, 24, 25
    decline of, 210
    formal incorporation of (1677), 29, 210
    'speculative' inner circle, 25
    see also Acception, London Company of Masons
London Evening Post, 71, 84, 134, 170
London Freemasonry, late seventeenth century, 36–7
London Gazette, 32, 77–8, 80
London Journal, 76, 122, 139, 142
Long Livers, 119, 212
Lorraine, Francis, Duke of, 76, 151, 152, 159, 187
Lothian, William Kerr, 3rd Marquess of, 159, 160–1
Loudoun, John Campbell, 4th Earl of, 104, 129, 131, 134, *plate 22*
Louis d'Argent lodge, 148
Louis XIV, King of France, 40, 42, 120, 126, 149
Louis XV, King of France, 148, 151
Louisa, Princess, 59
Lovel, Thomas Coke, Lord, 54, 104, 158–9, 177
Love's last shift, 119
Lumley, James, 175
Lyn, Charles Townshend, Lord, 101, 142

McAulay, Archibald, 275n
McCann, Timothy, 147
Macclesfield, George Parker, 2nd Earl of, 77, 103, 105–6, 108, 262n

336 Index

Macclesfield, Thomas Parker, 1st Earl of, 48, 77, 108, 246*n*
Machin, John, 103, 106
Mackechnie-Jarvis, C., 73
Mackey, Albert G., 71
Mackworth, Sir Thomas, 4th Baronet, 153, 161
Macky, John, 126
McNally, Patrick, 78
Madden, Major, 175
Madrid lodge, 143, 180
magistrates *see* Westminster and Middlesex magistrates' benches
Maid's Head lodge, Norwich, 99, 260*n*
Mainwaring, Henry, 21, 22
Mainwaring, Peter, 22
Majou, Jérémie, 40
Makdowal, Richard, 91
Malpas, Lord, 88
Malton, Thomas Watson-Wentworth, Lord, 181
Manchester, William Montagu, 2nd Duke of, 126
Manley, Richard, 92, 258*n*
Mann, Sir Horace, 60
Manningham, Sir Richard
 career, 111
 Horn Membership, 104, 111, 112, 176
 Royal College of Physicians, 111, 112
 Royal Society, 104, 105, 111, 176
 Spalding Society, 111, 115
Manningham, Thomas, 18
Mansel, Sir Edward, 169–70, 171, 174
Mar, John Erskine, Duke of, 136
March, Charles Henry Gordon-Lennox, Earl of, 155
Marine Coffee House, Birchin Lane, 46, 101, 185
Markham, Sir George, 86, 88–9, 106
Marlborough, John Churchill, 1st Duke of, 126, 127
Marriotte, Edme, 51
Marvell, Andrew, 17–18
Mary II, Queen of England, 136, 213
Mary, Princess, 59
Mason, Daniel, 167
Mason, Samuel, 167
Mason, Stephen, 52
Mason, Thomas, 167
Mason, William, 167
'Mason Word', 18
Masonic Magazine, 22
'Masonic Tools', 17, 20, 214
masons' guilds *see* guilds
La Matritense lodge, 143
Medlicott, Charles, 74
Medlicott, Thomas, 74, 91–2
Mercer, John, 92, 258*n*
Middlesex, Countess of, 24
Middlesex magistrates' benches *see* Westminster and Middlesex magistrates' benches
Millington, Sir Thomas, 44, 244*n*
Millis, William, 24
Minden Lodge, No. 63, 130–1
Minet, Susan, 87
Mirmand, Henri de, 42
Misaubin, John, 151
Mist's Weekly Journal, 88
Mitchel, Simon, 90
Mitre lodge, Reading, 128, 131
Monmouth, James Scott, 1st Duke of, 144, 154
Montagu, Edward, Lord Hinchingbrook, 135
Montagu, George, 1st Earl of Halifax, 87, 88
Montagu, John, 2nd Duke of Montagu, plate 11, plate 12
 1723 *Constitutions*, 66–7
 association with royal household, 126–7
 association with Stukeley, 109
 Bear and Harrow membership, 58, 135
 Colonel 1st Life Guards, 85, 127
 connections to Desaguliers, 49, 132
 Egyptian Society membership, 112
 family background, 125–6
 friendship with Folkes, 132, 193
 friendship with Newton, 132
 friendship with Richmond, 125
 General Bank of Charity, 94–5, 135
 head of the Ordnance at Woolwich, 49, 62
 Hogarth's *Indian Emperor*, 59
 Horn membership, 95, 104
 Huguenot connections, 132–3
 influence on English Freemasonry, 124–5
 installation as Grand Master, 124, 125, 132, 133, 135
 military lodges, 131
 military positions, 127
 Morgan's investiture, 88
 press reports, 126
 prominence within Grand Lodge, 49, 74, 88, 104, 110, 118, 120, 121–2, 125–6, 132–3, 135, 193
 relations with Coke, 158
 roles and positions, 126–7, 132
 Royal College of Physicians, 112
 Royal Society, 104, 132
 Society of Antiquaries, 113
 Wharton's installation as Grand Master, 136, 139, 140
Montagu, John, 4th Earl of Sandwich, 112
Montagu, Mary, 126
Montagu, Ralph, 1st Duke of Montagu, 125–6, 132–3
Montagu, William, 2nd Duke of Manchester, 126
Montesquieu, Charles Louis de Secondat, 148, 149, 150–1

Montesquieu, Jean Baptiste de Secondat, 148, 150
Moody, George, 272*n*
Moor, Thomas, 86
Moore, Francis, 126
Moore, Thomas, 140
Moray, Sir Robert, 24, 240*n*
Morgan, Sir William, 88
Morley, George, 39
Morrice, Thomas, 96
Morris, Thomas, 136
Morton, Alan, 166
Morton, James Douglas, 14th Earl of, 61, 99, 160, 265*n*
Morton, Sholto Douglas, 15th Earl of, 104
MQ Magazine, 22
Mulvey-Roberts, Marie, 60
municipal authorities', ties with guilds, 10–11, 209–10
Munk, William, 112
Munsche, P.B., 75, 192
Murray, James, 2nd Duke of Atholl, 159, 160, 177

Nag's Head and Star lodge, Carmarthenshire, 86, 170, 171, 172
Naish, James, 91
Nangle, John, 131
Nantes, Edict of, Revocation of, 40
Netherlands
 Freemasonry, 2, 179, 187
 The Hague lodge, 151, 152, 165
Newcastle, Freemasonry, 173–4
Newcastle, Thomas Pellam-Holles, 1st Duke of
 Coustos' arrest, 182
 Freemasonry, 76, 130, 151
 raising of the Duke of Lorraine, 152
 recommendation of Cook, 91
 relations with Richmond, 118, 145, 146, 147, 148, 155
 Secretary of State, 78
Newsham, Richard, 179
Newton, Sir Isaac
 calculus committee, 95, 102, 103, 108
 Chambers' *Cyclopaedia*, 185
 Chronology of Ancient Kingdoms, 103
 coffee house lectures, 185
 Desaguliers as FRS, 51, 52
 Desaguliers' promotion of, 39, 44, 46–7, 48, 51, 52, 53, 62–3, 179, 184, 186, 187, 189, 191
 exploitation of Hauksbee, 46
 friendship with Desaguliers, 132
 friendship with Montagu, 132
 godparent to Desaguliers child, 48
 lecturers' popularisation of, 54
 Master of the Mint, 59
 popular interest in, 45
 relations with Folkes, 99
 relations with s'Gravesande, 186
 relations with Stukeley, 109
 religious tolerance, 212
 Royal Society presidency, 46, 48, 106
 support for Keill, 44
Niblet, Daniel, 52, 55
Nichol, John, 90
Nicholson, Sir Francis, 79
Nimmo, James, 275*n*
Nine Muses lodge, 148
Norfolk, Thomas Howard, 8th Duke of, 119, 129, 134, 156, 157–8
Norris, Henry, 91, 92
Northampton, George Compton, 6th Earl of, 73
Northumberland, Freemasonry, 173–4
Nottingham, Daniel Finch, 2nd Earl of, 273*n*
Nottingham, Daniel Finch, 3rd Earl of, 159, 161–2

Oakley, Edward, 172–3, 176
Oakley, John, 91
O'Brien, William, 4th Earl of Inchiquin
 Norfolk's initiation, 157
 Prince of Wales's initiation, 175
 prominence within Grand Lodge, 88, 156, 159
 Walpole supporter, 54
 Warburton's appointment, 131
Ockham, John King, 2nd Baron of, 77
Ockham, Peter King, 1st Baron King of, 77
Official Gazette, 87
Oglethorpe, James, 85
Old Charges, 9, 11, 13, 200–10
 Anderson's comments, 65
 attraction to antiquaries, 37
 blueprint of versions, 211
 Constitutions (1723), 65, 66, 200
 Constitutions (1738), 65
 Cooke manuscript, 201, 204–5, 206
 Dowland manuscript, 208
 Egerton Manuscript, 15
 labour protectionism, 190, 201, 205, 207–8
 Lansdowne manuscript, 208
 Plot's access to, 30
 Post Man précis, 30, 31
 Regius manuscript, 201–3, 205, 206
 Sloane's ownership of, 106
 Watson manuscript, 201
 York manuscript, 208
Old King's Arms (OKA) *see* King's Arms lodge, Strand
Ordinance of Labourers, 8, 205
Osborn, Andrew, 91
Oughton, Sir Adolphus, 127
Owens, W.R., 78
Oxford Arms lodge, Ludgate Street, 33
Oxford, Robert Harley, 1st Earl of, 35, 44, 78
Ozanam, Jacques, 49

338 Index

Paget, Thomas, 91
Pagitt, James, 24
Paisley, James Hamilton, Lord
   General Bank of Charity, 94–5, 156
   Horn membership, 95, 104, 154, 156
   installation as Grand Master, 156
   prominence within Grand Lodge, 104, 119, 156–7
   Royal Society, 104, 156
   senior magistrate, 79
Paley, Ruth, 92
Palladio, Andrea, 176
Parker, George, 2nd Earl of Macclesfield, 77, 103, 105–6, 108, 262*n*
Parker, Thomas, 1st Earl of Macclesfield, 48, 77, 108, 246*n*
Parsons, Richard, 91
Payne, Amelia, 74
Payne, Anne, 74
Payne, Catherine, 73, 74
Payne, Elizabeth, 71
Payne, Frances, 73
Payne, George, 70–5
   1723 *Constitutions*, 70, 73
   Berkeley's *Passive Obedience*, 213
   Charges and *Regulations*, 66, 73, 81, 200, 204, 216
   Chocke's support, 88
   collaboration with Desaguliers, 70, 71, 73–4
   death of, 74–5
   Desaguliers' introduction to London Freemasonry, 57–8, 73
   earnings, 72, 252*n*
   family, 71–2
   Folkes' support, 101
   General Bank of Charity, 70, 87, 94, 96
   Grand Feast (1721), 110
   Horn membership, 73, 82, 154
   influence on English Freemasonry, 64, 87, 192
   introduction to Desaguliers, 73
   King's Arms lodge, Strand, 70, 71
   Montagu's installation as Grand Master, 133, 135
   networks and relationships, 74
   Philo-Musicae, 70–1
   prominence within Grand Lodge, 34, 50, 70, 74
   relations with Cowper, 74
   Richmond's installation as Grand Master, 146
   Richmond's patronage, 146
   roles and positions, 72–3
   Rummer & Grapes membership, 72
   senior magistrate, 70, 73, 95, 101
   Westminster Bridge project, 72, 83, 179
   Wren as a Freemason, 27
Payne, Joseph, 74
Payne, Mary (George Payne's aunt), 71
Payne, Mary (George Payne's niece), 74
Payne, Samuel, 71
Payne, Thomas (George Payne's brother), 72, 73, 74
Payne, Thomas (George Payne's nephew), 74
Peasants' Revolt (1381), 8
Pelham, Peter, *plate 1*
Pellam-Holles, Thomas *see* Newcastle, Thomas Pellam-Holles, 1st Duke of
Pellet, Thomas, 103, 108, 112, 176
Pembroke, Henry Herbert, 9th Earl of, 83, 103, 125, 135, 179, 267*n*
Pembroke, Thomas Herbert, 8th Earl of, 14
Penkett, Richard, 21
Pepys, Samuel, 103
Persehouse, Jonah, 167
Petty, William, 94, 95, 259*n*
Phelps Brown, Henry, 9
Phélypeaux, Louis, Comte de Saint-Florentin, 150, 151
Philip V, King of Spain, 60
Philips, Charles, *plate 17*
Philips, Clifford William, 92
Phillips, Sir John, 170, 171, 172
Philo-Musicae et Architecture Societas-Apollini, 70–1
Philosophical Transactions, 29, 44, 46
Pierrepont, Evelyn, 2nd Duke of Kingston, 150, 151, 270*n*
Pile, Sir Seymour, 171
Pine, John, *plate 9*, *plate 10*, *plate 16*
Pitt, James, 76
Pitt, William, 167
plague, 8, 9, 190
Plain Dealer, 142
Plot, Robert, 13, 16, 29–30, 31
Plumb, Sir John, 46
Poll Tax, 8
Pomfret, Thomas Fermor, Earl of, 59
Poor Robin's Intelligence, 17
Pope, Alexander, 59, 63, 101, 102, 111, 139, 141
Porter, Roy, 183
Portmore, Charles Colyear, 2nd Earl of, 158
Portugal, Freemasonry, 181–2
Post Boy, 27, 28, 32, 125
Post Man and the Historical Account, 30–2, 124
Powell family of Nanteos, 170
Prendergast, Sir Thomas, 70, 90, 94, 95, 259*n*, 265*n*
Prescott, Andrew, 2
   1723 *Constitutions*, 67
   economic factors, 3
   English Freemasonry origins, 8
   Grand Lodge formation, 29
   Locke's letter, 14
   London Company of Masons, 23
   Old Charges, 200–1, 208
   religious factors, 3
   'syndicalist phase', 9
   wage rates, 208

Index   339

Preston, George, 275n
Preston, William, 11
Price, Sir John, 171
Price, Richard, 171
Prichard, Samuel, 123
Prince Eugene's Head Coffee House, 152, 182
Prince William Tavern lodge, Charing Cross, 158
Pryse family of Glamorgan, 170
Pudsey, Jane, 23
Pudsey, Joanna, 45, 62
Pulteney, William, 111
Pumfrey, Stephen, 47, 98
Pythagoras, 21

Queen's Arms, Newgate Street, 25
Queen's Head lodge, Bath, 130, 169, 170
Queen's Head lodge, Holborn, 113, 154
Queen's Head lodge, Hollis Street, 33, 71, 77, 108
Queen's Head lodge, Knave's Acre, 154, 181
Queensberry, Charles Douglas, 3rd Duke of, 104, 154, 261–2n
Queensberry, James Douglas, 2nd Duke of, 144
Quincy, John, 126

Raban, Itamar, 32
Radcliff, Ralph, 90
Rademacher, Jacob Cornelis, 152
Rankine, Anthony, 131
Raphael, 176
Rawlinson, Richard, 13–14, 33–4, 108, 242n
Rayboud, T.J., 168
Raymond, Robert, 2nd Lord Raymond, 104, plate 23
Red Lyon lodge, Surrey, 153
Regius manuscript, 201–3, 205, 206
Regulations, 64, 65, 66–7, 97, 124–5, 211, 216–17
  1738 Constitutions, 68
  Desaguliers, 58, 66, 73, 135, 200, 214, 216
  Fonvive's editorials, 32
  and *Old Charges*, 200
  Payne, 66, 73, 81, 200, 204, 216
Reid, William, 97
Reynolds, Francis, 90
Rich, James, 128
Rich, Sir Robert, 89, 127–8, 130
Richardson, Jonathan, plate 14
Richardson, William, 94, 95, 113, 259n
Richmond, 2nd Duke of see Lennox, Charles, 2nd Duke of Richmond & Lennox
Richmond, Charles Gordon Lennox, 8th Duke of, 100
Richmond, Lady Sarah Cadogan, Duchess of, 48, 59

Ridley, Edward, 74, 90
Ridley, Matthew, 173
Rily, John, 153
Robe, Thomas, 92, 258n
Robinson, George, 83
Robinson, Sir Thomas, 35
Robinson, Sir William, 35
Rogers, Nicholas, 91
Rose Tavern lodge, Cheapside, 33
Rosser, Gervase, 12, 16
Rotheram, John, 86
Roubillac, Louis-François, 59
Rouse, Joseph, 86
Rowley, John, 50, 51
Roxburghe Club, 19
Royal African Company, 91
Royal College of Physicians
  Freemasonry, 98, 109, 112, 113, 193, 230–1
  Manningham's membership, 111, 112
  Montagu's membership, 112
  Pellet's membership, 103, 112
  Richmond's membership, 112, 155
  Rutty's membership, 103, 112
  Stukeley, s membership, 111, 112
Royal Society of London
  Ashmole's membership, 13, 24
  Aubrey's membership, 13, 25–6
  Aubrey's *Natural History of Wiltshire*, 25
  Beale's membership, 105, 109, 250n
  and Bedford Head lodge, 99, 101, 102–3, 104
  Carpenter's membership, 105
  Cholmondeley's membership, 49
  Clare's membership, 105, 176
  Dalkeith's membership, 104, 145
  Darnley's membership, 104
  Delafaye's membership, 79
  Desaguliers' experiments and demonstrations, 45, 46, 47, 49, 52, 57, 186
  Desaguliers as FRS, 39, 48, 51–2, 104
  Desaguliers' membership, 95, 98, 102, 105, 107, 119, 132, 156, 176, 191
  Douglas' membership, 176
  Folkes' membership, 95, 99, 101, 105, 106, 107, 119, 156, 176, 182, 193
  Freemasonry membership, 168, 193
  Freemasons proposing Freemasons, 108
  Gray's electrical experiments, 184
  Hauksbee as FRS, 46
  and Horn Tavern, 104, 107
  Jones' membership, 103, 105, 106, 107–9
  Keill's membership, 44, 102
  Lindsay's membership, 104
  Manningham's membership, 104, 105, 111, 176
  Masonic proselytising, 109
  Montagu's membership, 104, 132
  Montesquieu's membership, 150
  Newton's presidency, 46, 48, 106

Paisley's membership, 104, 156
Pellet's membership, 103, 108
Pembroke's Presidency, 14
Philosophical Transactions, 29, 44, 46
Plot's membership, 13, 29
Rawlinson's breach with colleagues, 33
Richmond's membership, 101, 104, 118–19, 154, 176
Royal Charters, 240*n*
Rutty's membership, 103, 106, 109
scientific Enlightenment, 173, 182–3
Sloane's membership, 51, 99, 104, 105, 106, 107, 150, 154
Stukeley's membership, 103, 106, 109–10, 250*n*
support for Grand Lodge of England, 36
Taylor's membership, 95, 102, 105, 106, 108
Rue Bussy lodge, 149–50, 151
Rummer & Grapes lodge, Channel Row
 Desaguliers' lectures, 166
 Desaguliers' membership, 58, 72
 founding lodge, 120
 Payne's membership, 72
 Richmond's membership, 153
 transfer to Horn, 45, 58
Rummer lodge, Charing Cross
 Bateman's membership, 101
 Dalkeith's membership, 95, 145
 Godolphin's membership, 131
 Houghton's membership, 95
 military membership, 131
 political and government connections, 34
 prominence of, 4, 64
 Strahan's membership, 86
 Stuart's membership, 176
 Vyner's membership, 86
 Watkins' membership, 89
Rummer lodge, Queen Street, 89
Rummer Tavern lodge, Bristol, 169
Russia, Freemasonry, 2
Rutty, William, 103, 106, 109
Rye House Plot, 16
Rylands, W.H., 22

St Albans, Charles Beauclerk, 1st Duke of, 162, 169, 267*n*
St. Andrew' church, Holborn, 45, 48, 246*n*
St. George's and Corner Stone Lodge No. 5, 84
St. Hyacinthe, Paul de, 150, 270*n*
St. James' French Anglican church, 40
St. James's Evening Post, 149–50
St. John the Baptist lodge, Exeter, 180
St. Margaret's church, Westminster, 48, 246*n*
St. Paul's Head lodge, Ludgate Street, 33, 113
St. Thomas's Hospital, 37
Saint-Evremond, Charles, 133
Saint-Florentin, Louis Phélypeaux, Comte de, 150, 151

Salutation lodge, Tavistock Street, 110, 112
Samuell, William, 171
Sandwich, John Montagu, 4th Earl of, 112
Sankey, Richard, 21
Saracen's Head lodge, Lincoln, 176, 178
Savage, John, 91
Savill, Samuel, 91
Savoy church, 42, 246*n*
Sayer, Anthony, 94, 96, 156, *plate 4*
Scanlan, Matthew, 24
Schaffer, Simon, 54, 166
Schaw, William, 3, 4
Schemers society, 143
Scheuchzer, John, 56, 249*n*
Schomberg, Meyer, 178–9
Schwartz, L.D., 34
scientific Enlightenment, 2, 6, 175–89, 194
 Anglican Church, 44
 Chandos, 55
 Clare, 34, 165, 175, 176, 177, 178, 189
 Desaguliers, 34, 141, 165, 169, 186–8, 191
 Folkes, 34, 141
 Freemasonry in France, 148
 King's Arms lodge, Strand, 176, 177–8
 Royal Society, 173, 182–3
Scotland
 Freemasonry, 2–3, 4, 18
 military lodges, 223–4
Scott, Francis, 5th Earl of Dalkeith
 family background, 144
 friendship with Richmond, 145
 General Bank of Charity, 94–5, 146, 156
 initiation as a Freemason, 144–5
 installation as Grand Master, 133–4, 140, 141, 144, 145
 as Knight of the Thistle, 160
 marriage, 144
 prominence within Grand Lodge, 87–8, 104, 118, 123, 132, 133–4, 135, 140–1, 144–6, 162
 relations with Desaguliers, 95, 145, 146
 Rily's initiation, 153
 Royal Society, 104, 145
 Rummer membership, 95, 145
 Spalding Society, 95, 115
Scott, Francis, Earl of Dalkeith, 145
Scott, Henry, 1st Earl of Deloraine, 59, 88, 128, 154, 160, 162
Scott, J., *plate 20*
Scott, James, 1st Duke of Monmouth, 144, 154
Scott, James, Earl of Dalkeith, 144
Sea Serjeants Society, 170, 171–2, 173
Senex, John
 background, 250*n*
 Constitutions (1723), 67, *plate 7*
 Dalkeith's installation as Grand Master, 140, 145
 Desaguliers' works, 49, 51, 67, 105
 friendship with Desaguliers, 67

Gordon's works, 181
New General Atlas, 133
Royal Society, 105, 250*n*
s'Gravesande's works, 186
Seville, Treaty of, 35, 242*n*
Seymour, Francis, 73, 74
s'Gravesande, Willem-Jacob, 185, 186, 187, 280*n*
Shackleton, Robert, 150
Shadbolt, Thomas, 23
Shakespeare's Head lodge, Little Marlborough Street, 102, 178
Shaw, Peter, 182–3
Ship lodge, Bartholomew Lane, 90, 112
Ship lodge, Royal Exchange, 55, 112, 113
Ship lodge, without Temple Bar, 89
Shirley, Washington, 5th Earl Ferrers, 104
Shorthose, John, 23
Shorthose, Thomas, 23
Shrewsbury, Charles Talbot, Lord, 78, 136
Simon, John, *plate 13*
Skelton, Charles, 148, 269*n*
Slaughter, Thomas, 59
Sloane, Hans
  coffee house lectures, 185
  Desaguliers's fees, 56
  Gray's Charterhouse pension, 184
  Horn membership, 104
  introduced to Stukeley, 111
  relationship with Hans Sloane, 106, 262*n*
  Royal Society, 51, 99, 104, 105, 106, 107, 150, 154
  Spalding Society, 111
Sloane, Sarah, 104
Sloane, William, 106, 109, 262*n*
Smith, Barwell, 91
Smith, John (Griffin, Newgate Street), 91
Smith, John (London Company of Masons), 24
Smith, John (printmaker), *plate 6*
Smith, John (Queen's Head, Knaves Acre), 90
Smith, Laurence, 139
Snoek, Jan, 1, 4
Society of Antient Britons, 101
Society of Antiquaries
  Coleraine's membership, 113
  Cowper's membership, 113
  Folkes' membership, 99, 155
  Freemasonry, 109, 113–15, 193
  Gale brothers, 110
  Montagu's membership, 113
  Rawlinson's membership, 33
  Richardson's membership, 95
  Richmond's membership, 113, 155
  scientific Enlightenment, 183
  Stukeley's membership, 109–10, 113
  Taylor's membership, 95
Society of Apothecaries, 98, 113, 227–30
Society of Dilettanti, 112
Society of Sea Serjeants, 170, 171–2, 173

Soho Academy, 93, 177
Soho Square French Anglican church, 40
Solomon's Temple lodge
  Anderson's membership, 65
  Desaguliers' membership, 39, 65, 180
  Labelye's membership, 180
Sommers, Lord, 46
Song on Freemasons, 119
Songhurst, William John, 65
Sorrel, Francis
  career, 72
  Dalkeith's installation as Grand Master, 140, 145
  General Bank of Charity, 87, 94, 96
  godparent to Desaguliers child, 49
  introduction to Freemasonry, 74, 87
  municipal rates inquiry, 89
  prominence within Grand Lodge, 87
  Richmond's installation as Grand Master, 146
  senior magistrate, 73, 87
South Sea Company, 68, 138, 242*n*
Spain, Madrid lodge, 143, 180
Spalding Society
  Coleraine's membership, 115
  Dalkeith's membership, 95, 115
  Desaguliers' membership, 95, 115
  Folkes' membership, 99, 111, 115
  Freemasonry, 113, 115–16
  Gale brothers' membership, 110, 111
  Manningham's membership, 111, 115
  Sloane's membership, 111
  Stukeley's membership, 111, 115
Spencer, Charles, 3rd Earl of Sunderland, 77, 78
Spencer, Charles, 5th Earl of Sunderland, 158
Spring Gardens church, Westminster, 246*n*
Staffordshire, Masonic activity, 15–16, 30
Stanhope, James, 1st Earl Stanhope, 78, 85
Stanhope, John, 151
Stanhope, Philip Dormer, 4th Earl of Chesterfield, 101
  ambassador at The Hague, 150, 151, 152
  friendship with Richmond, 125
  Gregorian calendar, 105–6
  Montagu's installation as Grand Master, 125, 133, 135
Stanhope, William, 1st Earl of Harrington, 182
Stanley, George, 104
Stanton, William, 23, 25
Statute of Labourers, 8, 205
Steele, Richard, 17, 54, 77–8
Stephenson, David, 65, 66
Stevenson, David, 2–3, 139
Steward's Lodge, 178
Stewart, John,, Lord Darnley, 147
Stewart, Larry
  correspondence between Chandos and Desaguliers, 56–7

Desaguliers's fees, 56
Desaguliers's lectures, 166
industrial development, 54
scientific Enlightenment, 182–3, 184, 186
world of mechanics, 47
Stewart, Trevor, 107, 193
Stirling, James, 102
Stone, Nicholas, 24, 28
stonemasons' guilds *see* guilds
Stow, John, 17
Strahan, Alexander, 86
Strathmore, James, 7th Earl of Strathmore, 104
Streate, Leonard
  Horn membership, 74, 261*n*
  relations with Cox, 102
  senior magistrate, 74, 75, 83–4, 89, 192, 256*n*
Street, Sir Thomas, 256*n*
Strickland, Walter, 148
Strong Jr., Edward, 82
Strype, John, 45
Stuart, Alexander, 105, 106, 176, 277*n*
Stuart, James (Old Pretender), 137
Stukeley, Elizabeth, 111
Stukeley, Frances, 111
Stukeley, William, *plate 6*
  antiquarianism, 183
  career, 111
  Dalkeith's lodge attendance, 145
  education, 109, 111
  Egyptian Society membership, 112
  Folkes' inheritance, 98
  Freemasonry, 109, 110
  gentlemen members of operative lodges, 21
  Infidel Club, 109, 132
  relations with Folkes, 111, 132, 266*n*
  Royal College of Physicians, 111, 112
  Royal Society, 103, 106, 109–10, 250*n*
  Society of Antiquaries, 109–10, 113
  Spalding Society, 111, 115
  spread of scientific lectures, 183
Suffolk, Earl of, 88
Sugen, Philip, 93
Sun Fire insurance company, 54–5
Sun Inn lodge, Chester, 50, 131
Sun lodge, by St. Paul's, 89
Sun lodge, Fleet Street, 112
Sunderland, Charles Spencer, 3rd Earl of, 77, 78
Sunderland, Charles Spencer, 5th Earl of, 158
Swallow Street French Anglican church, 40–2, 68
Swan lodge, Chichester, 77, 106, 153, 155
Swan lodge, Greenwich, 59, 82, 87
Swan lodge, Long Acre, 58, 187
Swan lodge, Ludgate Street, 112
Swan and Rummer lodge, Finch Lane, 178
Swanson, Heather, 10–11
Sweden, Freemasonry, 2

Swift, Jonathan, 162
Swynfen, Elizabeth, 26
Sylvestre, Pierre, 133

Talbot, Charles, Lord Shrewsbury, 78, 136
Tatler, 17
Taylor, Brook
  Bedford Head lodge, Covent Garden, 95, 102
  General Bank of Charity, 94
  Royal Bridewell Hospital governor, 103, 258*n*, 259*n*
  Royal Society, 95, 102, 105, 106, 108
Taylor, Giles, 94, 95, 259*n*
Taylour, Samuel, 22, 23
Teissier, George, 150, 270*n*
Tempest, Sir George, 35
Temple, Richard, 1st Viscount Cobham, 130
Tench, William, 131
Thacker, A.T., 12–13, 20
The Hague lodge, 151, 152, 165
Theatre Coffee House lodge, Bridges Street, 102
Thomas, Peter, 172
Thomason, John, 83
Thompson, Edward, 36
Thompson, John, 23
Thompson, William, 91
Thornhill, Sir James, 59, 82, 87, 88, 105, 108, *plate 3*
Threadneedle Street church, 42
Three Compasses lodge, Silver Street, 172
Three Kings lodge, Spitalfields, 33
Thynne, Thomas *see* Weymouth, Thomas Thynne, 2nd Viscount
Timson, George, 151
Timson, Joshua, 96, 136, 139
Tindall, John, 171
Todd, William, 177, 278*n*
Toft, Mary, 111
Tong, William, 131
Townsend, William, 131
Townshend, Charles, 2nd Viscount Townshend, 78, 101, 142
Townshend, Charles, 3rd Viscount Townshend, 101, 142
Townshend, Elizabeth, 101
Treasury Papers, 72
Trelawney, Edward, 53
Trembley, Abraham, 155
Trevor, John, 2nd Lord, 103
Truchsess von Waldburg, Count, 61
The True Briton, 142
Tryon, Thomas, 18, 20–1
Turner, Henry, 87
Two Black Posts lodge, Maiden Lane, 102
Tyrconnel, Viscount, 88
Tyssen, Samuel, 92

Utrecht, Treaty of (1713), 42, 120

van Eiest, Johannes, *plate 12*
van Ruytenburgh, Albert, 49
Vanberg, John, 131
Vanbrugh, Sir John, 82
Varenne (Bedford Head member), 101
Vaughan, Gwin, 89
Vaughan, William, 89
Vayringe, Philippe, 187
Vernon, Bowater, 90
Vernon Jnr., James, 77, 103
Vernon Snr., James, 77, 103, 253*n*
Vertue, George, *plate 23*
Villeneau, Josias, 136
Vincent, Henry, 91
Vine Tavern lodge, Holborn, 113
Voltaire, 186, 187
Vream, William, 52
Vyner, Robert, 86
Vyner, Thomas, 86

Waindsfford, Mr., 23
Waldegrave, James, 1st Earl Waldegrave, 148, 149, 150, 151, 154
Waldegrave, James, Lord Chewton, 150, 151
Wales, Freemasonry, 170–3
Wallis, Ruth, 54
Walpole, Horace, 60, 102, 112, 171
Walpole, Horatio, 76
Walpole, Sir Robert
  Benson's opposition, 35
  Coke's support of, 159
  connections to Oughton, 127
  connections to Rich, 127
  connections to Richmond, 118, 147
  continental European spy network, 143, 152
  Darnley's opposition, 61
  doctorate of law from Cambridge University, 79
  Freemasonry, 130, 158, 194, 266*n*
  Gordon's publications, 181
  Houghton Hall, 76, 151, 152, 260*n*
  initiation as Freemason, 76, 159
  Phélypeaux's initiation, 151
  political opposition within Freemasonry, 53–4, 174
  Stukeley's invitation, 110
  Yorkshire Masonry opposition, 34
Warburton, Hugh, 131
Warburton, Walter, 131
Ward, John, 1st Viscount Dudley and Ward, 61, 99, 166–8, 169–70, 174, 274*n*
Ward, John, 2nd Viscount Dudley and Ward, 167, 168
Ward, William, 167
Ware, Isaac, 176
Warrington
  Lodge of Lights, Warrington, 178
  non-operative masons' membership, 12
Watkins, George, 87, 89
Watson, Hugh, 74

Watson manuscript, 201
Watts, Thomas, 54–5
Way, Lewis, 74
Way, Sarah, 74
Webb, John Richmond, 49, 246*n*
Webber, Robert, 60–1, 155–6
Weekly Journal or British Gazetteer, 103, 122, 123, 125
Wendling, Paul, 184
West, Robert, 176
Westminster Bridge, 45, 72, 83, 179, 188
Westminster and Middlesex magistrates' benches, 64, 70, 75–7, 192–3
  April 1719 intake, 79–86
  June 1721 intake, 86–9
  September 1722 intake, 101
  August 1724 intake, 89–90
  November 1727 intake, 90–4
Weymouth, Thomas Thynne, 2nd Viscount
  installation as Grand Master, 132
  Lisbon lodge, 181–2
  prominence within Grand Lodge, 70, 159, 161, 168, 177, 274*n*
  roles and positions, 161
Wharton, Philip, 1st Duke of, *plate 13*
  appointment of Anderson, 65
  background, 136–7
  death of, 143
  departure from Grand Lodge, 140–1, 142
  Gormogons, 88, 142–3
  initiation as Freemason, 122, 136
  installation as Grand Master, 136, 139, 140, 141
  Madrid lodge, 143
  Montagu's installation as Grand Master, 135
  prominence within Grand Lodge, 118, 119, 132, 135, 136, 138–40, 193–4, 214
  roles and positions, 137–8
  Schemers society, 143
Wharton, Thomas, 1st Marquess of Wharton, 136
Whig aristocrats, Grand Lodge leadership, 36, 38, 53–4, 64, 118
Whig governments
  acceptance of Freemasonry, 76
  Huguenot loyalty, 43
  Westminster and Middlesex benches, 76, 93
Whig political establishment
  Duke of York's accession, 15
  patriotic opposition, 53–4
  Post Man bias, 31–2
  Rye House Plot, 16
Whiston, William, 46, 179, 183
Whitacre, Edward, 256*n*
White Bear lodge, King Street, 180
Whitehouse, Benjamin, 167
Wigelsworth, Jeffrey, 46–7, 212
Wight, Edward, 255*n*

Wight, John, 255n
Wight, Joseph, 255n
Wightman, Robert, 275n
Wilkins, John, 43
Wilks, Robert, 60
William III, King of England, 37, 136, 213
William, Prince, Duke of Cumberland, 59
Williams, Gwyn, 173
Williamson, Sir Joseph, 77
Willoughby, Cassandra, Duchess of Chandos, 48
Wilson, Edward, 87
Wilson, Sir William, 22, 23
Winchelsea, Daniel Finch, 8th Earl of, 159, 161–2
Wise, Thomas (King's Arms, New Bond Street member), 25
Wise, Thomas (Master of the Masons Company), 23
Wise, William, 22, 23
Wood, A.C., 78
Woodman, William, 22, 23, 25, 31
Woodward, Donald, 207

Wool Pack lodge, Warwick, 131
workers' guilds *see* guilds
Wray, Sir Cecil, 11th Baronet, 61, 85, 159, 162, 176–7, 277n
Wray, Sir Christopher, 10th Baronet, 162
Wren, Sir Christopher, 23, 26–8, 29, 37
Wren Society, 23
Wright, Thomas, 184
Wriothesley, Elizabeth, 125
Wynter, John, 126

York
  guild civic influence, 10, 209–10
  non-operative masons' membership, 12, 13, 191
York Buildings Company, 89
York Grand Lodge, relative decline, 34–6, 191
York manuscript, 208
Yorke, Philip, 1st Earl of Hardwicke, 108
Young, Nicholas, 23
Young (Yonge), Edward, 148, 269n